RESEARCH BIBLIOGRAPHIES AND CHECKLISTS

NEW SERIES, 3

CHRÉTIEN DE TROYES

RESEARCH BIBLIOGRAPHIES AND CHECKLISTS

NEW SERIES

ISSN 1476–9700

General Editors

Alan Deyermond
Abigail Lee Six

CHRÉTIEN DE TROYES

AN ANALYTIC BIBLIOGRAPHY
SUPPLEMENT 1

Douglas Kelly

with

Maciej Abramowicz, Katalin Halász,
Ceridwen Lloyd-Morgan, Mihaela Voicu
Kôji Watanabe

TAMESIS

First published 2002 by Tamesis, London

ISBN 1 85566 083 0

T

1002965426

Tamesis is an imprint of Boydell & Brewer Ltd
PO Box 9, Woodbridge, Suffolk IP12 3DF, UK
and of Boydell & Brewer Inc.
PO Box 41026, Rochester, NY 14604–4126, USA
website: www.boydell.co.uk

A catalogue record for this book is available
from the British Library

Library of Congress Cataloging-in-Publication Data
applied for

This publication is printed on acid-free paper

Printed in Great Britain by

IBT Global, London

CONTENTS

PREFACE

'Il est bien des manières d'aborder aujourd'hui une œuvre littéraire' (Ja37 p. 15). Jacques Ribard's observation rings especially true in the ears of Chrétien scholars contemplating the ways their author is read today. This is not entirely new. Thus, the outline of the diverse and multifarious topics in the 1976 Bibliography (Cb9) is still correct by and large, although there has been a proliferation of approaches beyond what was then apparent. To be sure, adjustments and additions have been necessary, but there is no need to revise or rethink it radically. Specific local changes are commented on in the introductions to the sections in which they appear.

Chrétien de Troyes's name and works appear everywhere today. His influence is still recognized as immense. His romances are a standard reference – indeed, they seem to fix a norm – not only for studies on French romances, but on romances in other medieval languages as well. The norm is only now beginning to be questioned as study of epigonal romances grows in importance (Cb27). Much of Chrétien scholarship in the coming years will doubtless probe the place, influence, and originality of his achievements in the broad, intertextual contexts of twelfth- and thirteenth-century romance. Students will assess Chrétien's writing in the context not only of the Matter of Britain but also of other works familiar to his publics (see Fe30(C), Lc4). Shall we not better understand medieval reception when we can say, like the author of the *Roman du Hem*, 'Oï avés des Troiiens / Et du remant que Crestiiens / Trova si bel de Perceval [...]' (Pa65 v. 474–76)? How many assiduous readers of Chrétien's Round Table and Grail romances can claim to be equally familiar with the *Roman de Troie*, a work not infrequently bound in medieval manuscripts with his and other Arthurian romances (Ld2) and which, indeed, survives in more twelfth- and thirteenth-century copies than any of his works?[1] Yet it is certainly a major intertextual

---

[1] See especially Marc-René Jung, *La légende de Troie en France au Moyen Âge: analyse des versions françaises et bibliographie raisonnée des manuscrits*, Romanica Helvetica, 114 (Basel: Francke, 1996); this study is useful for its descriptions of manuscripts that include Chrétien's romances and other, non-Arthurian romances like the *Roman de Troie*. It can be usefully consulted together with Ba22.

reference for Chrétien's medieval audiences. The same is true for many other works outside the usual Arthurian canon. Much remains to be done.

Chrétien scholarship is, as always, international. It is now extending, in some cases rapidly, beyond the Western European and North American spheres into Eastern Europe, Asia, Central and South America, and Africa. This will continue. Yet even bibliographers never know enough languages. To remedy this defect in my case, I have had the assistance of colleagues all over the world. The five scholars named on the title page have made invaluable contributions: Maciej Abramowicz deals with Polish scholarship, Katalin Halász with Hungarian, Ceridwen Lloyd-Morgan with Welsh, Mihaela Voicu with Rumanian, and Kôji Watanabe with Japanese – including in all these instances publications by scholars writing in other languages, but publishing in their countries. I regret that my efforts to obtain the assistance of a Russian scholar failed. However, I have identified and included a few items published in Russian and other Eastern European languages.

The numbering system used to identify each entry in the 1976 bibliography has often been referred to (see, for example, Cb6). To avoid confusion, the numbering here begins where that in the 1976 volume leaves off. The standards for inclusion and cross-listing used in the earlier bibliography still obtain for the most part. The principal changes include full first name and the publisher as well as the place of publication; cross-reference to *BBSIA* occurs only when that publication contains a resumé, as there is no need to consult it if there is none. Moreover, cross-references are no longer numbered, but are expanded to include the author's name and an abbreviated title from the full entry. Additions and corrections to items in the 1976 Bibliography are inserted here after their section and number in that volume; these include reprints and *BBSIA* references not available when it appeared. An asterisk before an entry indicates a work that we have not directly examined.

The index gives the fullest name for each author (with cross-references for major changes), whereas the bibliographical entry gives the name only as it appears in the work cited. Alphabetizing surnames is a special problem. In general, I have endeavoured to follow common usage in the author's native language. Surnames with 'de,' 'du,' 'de la,' 'van,' and 'von' are generally alphabetized by the following name (e.g., Combarieu du Grès, Micheline de), but exceptions are made for some names that capitalize 'De' (e.g., De Paepe, Norbert) and 'Di' (e.g., Di Girolamo, Costanzo). Some anglicized names are, however, alphabetized as, for example, Van Emden, Wolfgang. Surnames in Italian and Spanish are alphabetized by the full surname (e.g., Colombo Timelli, Maria, and Carmona Fernández, Fernando), whilst those in English and Portuguese by the final surname (e.g., Grimbert, Joan Tasker, and Buescu, Maria Gabriela Carvalhão). Icelandic names are alphabetized by approximate Icelandic usage (e.g., Ásdís R. Magnúsdóttir), but with a cross-reference (e.g., Magnúsdóttir: See Ásdís R. Magnúsdóttir).

By and large, this supplement corresponds to the format for the 1976 volume. Most changes will be obvious and will not interfere with consultation. I should note that several abbreviations have been altered to conform to more common usage today (e.g., *Med.Aev* has become *MAe*). There are more abbreviations, especially for Festschriften, proceedings, and other collections when they contain more than one article; complete information on them is found under the short title in the Abbreviations.

A regrettable development has been the decline in research library purchasing during the past thirty years. With this retreat from progress, interlibrary communication becomes ever more important. Preparation of this Supplement has been greatly aided by the Interlibrary Loan Department of the University of Wisconsin Memorial Library; its staff has cooperated generously and resourcefully in obtaining material from North American and European libraries; I am especially grateful for the efforts of Tanner Wray. In addition, while I was a Fellow at the Netherlands Institute for Advanced Study in 1997–98, the Institute's librarian, Dinny Young, tirelessly obtained for me much material from the rich holdings of Dutch libraries. To these libraries and persons I offer sincere thanks.

Finally – last but not least – invaluable assistance has been forthcoming not only from those mentioned on the title page, but also, on numerous occasions for great and small, but always important, matters, from Frank Brandsma, Keith Busby, Maria Colombo-Timelli, Barbara Ferrari, Jean-Guy Gouttebroze, David F. Hult, Jonna Kjær, Claude Lachet, Jan Miernowski, Francesca Nicholson, Peter Noble, Marie-Louise Ollier, and Colette-Anne van Coolput-Storms. Alan Deyermond has made sure that most of my blunders will not reach the users of this bibliography. I thank all these scholars for their contributions. At Boydell & Brewer, Raymond Howard provided a very careful reading of the Bibliography; he was especially helpful with the Russian entries. Elspeth Ferguson readily responded to my various queries during proof reading with friendly efficiency and competence. However, it goes without saying that the ultimate responsibility for the accuracy, scope, and pertinence of the bibliography rests with me.

ABBREVIATIONS

Periodicals and books are in italics, series in roman type.

AA	Ausgaben und Abhandlungen aus dem Gebiete der Romanischen Philologie
ABäG	*Amsterdamer Beiträge zur älteren Germanistik*
ABK	*Academic Bulletin Kyoto University of Foreign Studies*
ABLs	*Analele Universităţii din Bucureşti, Limbi şi Literaturi Străine*
ACLin	*Analele Universităţii 'Al. I. Cuza' Iaşi, Secţiunea Lingvistică*
ACLit	*Analele Universităţii 'Al. I. Cuza' Iaşi, Secţia Literatură*
Acme	*Acme: Annali della Facoltà di Filosofia e Lettere dell'Università di Milano*
ACT	Arthurian Characters and Themes
ActaUpsa	Acta Universitatis Upsaliensis: Studia Romanica Upsaliensia
Actas Almagro	*Actas del II Coloquio sobre los Estudios de Filología Francesa en la Universidad Española (Almagro, 3–5 de mayo de 1993)*, ed. Juan Bravo Castillo, Estudios, 22 ([Cuenca]: Servicio de Publicaciones de la Universidad de Castilla-La Mancha, 1994)
Actas Granada	*Medioevo y literatura: Actas del V Congreso de la Asociación Hispánica de Literatura Medieval (Granada, 27 septiembre–1 octubre 1993)*, ed. Juan Paredes, 4 vols (Granada: Universidad de Granada, 1995)
Actas Santiago	*Actas do XIX Congreso Internacional de Lingüística e Filoloxía Románicas, Universidade de Santiago de Compostela, 1989*, ed. Ramón Lorenzo (Corunna:

Fundación Pedro Barrié de la Maza. Conde de
Fenosa, 1994)

Actas Zaragoza   *Actas del IX Simposio de la Sociedad Española de
Literatura General y Comparada. I: La mujer: elogio
y vituperio; II: La parodia; el viaje imaginario.
Zaragoza, 18 al 21 de noviembre de 1992*, ed. Túa
Blesa [et alii] (Saragossa: Universidad de Zaragoza,
1994)

Actes Laval   *Actes du XIIIᵉ Congrès International de Linguistique
et de Philologie Romanes tenu à l'Université de
Laval (Québec, Canada) du 29 août au 5 septembre
1971)*, 2 vols (Québec: Presses de l'Université de
Laval, 1976)

*Actes Moyen
Français*   *Actes du IVᵉ Colloque International sur le Moyen
Français*, ed. Anthonij Dees, Faux Titre, 16
(Amsterdam: Rodopi, 1985)

Actes Odense   *Actes du VIIIᵉ Congrès des Romanistes Scandinaves
(Odense, 17–21 août 1981)*, ed. Palle Spore [et alii],
Études Romanes de l'Université d'Odense, 13
(Odense: Odense University Press, 1983)

Actes Poitiers   *Moyen Âge et littérature comparée: Société
Française de Littérature Comparée: Actes du
Septième Congrès National, Poitiers 27–29 mai
1965*, Études de Littérature Étrangère et Comparée
(Paris: Didier, 1967)

Actes Rennes   *Actes du XIVᵉ Congrès International Arthurien,
Rennes, 16–21 août*, 2 vols (Rennes: Presses
Universitaires de Rennes 2, 1984)

Actes Trèves   *Actes du XVIIIᵉ Congrès International de
Linguistique et de Philologie Romanes*, Université de
Trèves (Trier) (Tübingen: Niemeyer, 1988)

Actes Turku   *Actes du 5ᵉᵐᵉ Congrès des Romanistes Scandinaves,
Turku (Åbo), du 6 au 10 août 1972*, Turun Yliopiston
Julkaisuja – Annales Universitatis Turkuensis, B 127
(Turku: Turun Yliopisto, 1973)

Actes Zurich   *Actes du XXᵉ Congrès International de Linguistique
et Philologie Romanes, Université de Zurich (6–11
avril 1992)*, ed. Gerold Hilty, 5 vols (Tübingen:

	Francke, 1993), vol. 5: section 8: *L'art narratif aux XIIe et XIIIe siècles*
AIBL	*Académie des Inscriptions et Belles-Lettres: Comptes-rendus*
AInt	*Arthurian Interpretations*
AION	*Annali dell'Istituto Universitario Orientale di Napoli, Sezione Romanza*
AJP	*American Journal of Philology*
AL	*Arthurian Literature*
ALC	*Annales de Littérature Comparée (Institut de Littérature Comparée, Université Waseda)*
ALFA	*ALFA: Actes de Langue Française et de Linguistique – Symposium on French Language and Linguistics*
ALib	*Artes Liberales (Bulletin of the College of Humanities and Social Sciences, Iwate University)*
AMainz	Akademie der Wissenschaften und der Literatur Mainz: Abhandlungen der Geistes- und Sozialwissenschaftlichen Klasse
Amour mariage	*Amour, mariage et transgressions au Moyen Âge: Actes du Colloque des 24, 25, 26 et 27 mars 1983*, ed. Danielle Buschinger and André Crépin, GAG, 420 (Göppingen: Kümmerle, 1984)
Amour Troyes	*Amour et chevalerie dans les romans de Chrétien de Troyes: Actes du Colloque de Troyes (27–29 mars 1992)*, ed. Danielle Quéruel, Annales de l'Université de Besançon, 581: série 'Littéraires,' 5 (Paris: Belles Lettres, 1995)
AN&Q	*American Notes and Queries*
ANF	*Arkiv för Nordisk Filologi*
AnFil	*Anuari di Filologia: Filologia Romanza*
Annales	*Annales: Économies, Sociétés, Civilisations*
AnnBud	*Annales Universitatis Scientiarum Budapestinensis de Rolando Eötvös Nominatae: Sectio Philologica Moderna*
AnNice	Annales de la Faculté des Lettres et Sciences Humaines de l'Université de Nice
AnP	*Annales de l'Université de Paris*

AnR	Analecta Romanica
Antichità	*L'Antichità nella cultura europea del Medioevo – L'Antiquité dans la culture européenne du Moyen Âge: Ergebnisse der Internationalen Tagung in Padua, 27.09–01.10.1997*, ed. Rosanna Brusegan, Alessandro Zironi, Anne Berthelot, and Danielle Buschinger (Greifswald: Reineke, 1998)
ANTS	Anglo-Norman Text Society: Occasional Publications
APSL	Amsterdamer Publikationen zur Sprache und Literatur
ARCA	ARCA: Classical and Medieval Texts, Papers and Monographs
ArR	*Archivum Romanicum*
Arturistiek	*Arturistiek in artikelen: een bundel fotomechanisch herdrukte studien over Middelnederlandse Arturromans*, ed. F. P. van Oostrom (Utrecht: H&S, 1978)
Arturus rex	*Arturus rex: Acta Conventus Lovaniensis 1987*, ed. Willy Van Hoecke, Gilbert Tournoy, and Werner Verbeke, MedL, ser. I: Studia, 17 (Leuven: Leuven University Press, 1991), vol. 2
Artusliteratur	*Spätmittelalterliche Artusliteratur: Ein Symposion der neusprachlichen Philologien auf der Generalversammlung der Görres-Gesellschaft Bonn, 25.–29. September 1982*, ed. Karl Heinz Göller, Beiträge zur englischen und amerikanischen Literatur, 3 (Paderborn: Schöningh, 1984)
Artusrittertum	*Artusrittertum im späten Mittelalter: Ethos und Ideologie. Vorträge des Symposiums der deutschen Sektion der Artusgesellschaft vom 10. bis 13. November 1983, Gießen*, ed. Friedrich Wolfzettel, BdP, 57 (Giessen: Schmitz, 1984)
Artusroman	*Artusroman und Intertextualität: Beiträge der Deutschen Sektionstagung der Internationalen Artusgesellschaft vom 16. bis 19. November 1989 an der Johann Wolfgang Goethe Universität Frankfurt a. M.*, ed. Friedrich Wolfzettel (Giessen: Schmitz, 1990)
AS	Arthurian Studies

Asahi	*Asahi / Encyclopédie Hebdomadaire : Littérature du Monde (Journal Asahi)*
AStnSpr	*Archiv für das Studium der neueren Sprachen und Literaturen*
Auctor	*'Auctor' et 'auctoritas': invention et conformisme dans l'écriture médiévale: Actes du Colloque tenu à l'Université de Versailles-Saint-Quentin-en-Yvelines (14–16 juin 1999)*, ed. Michel Zimmermann, Mémoires et Documents de l'École des Chartes, 59 (Paris: École des Chartes, 2001)
Aufführung	*'Aufführung' und 'Schrift' in Mittelalter und Früher Neuzeit*, ed. Jan-Dirk Müller, Germanistische Symposien: Berichtsbände, 17 (Stuttgart, Weimar: Metzler, 1996)
AUMLA	*Journal of Australian Universities Modern Language and Literature Association*
AUS:CL	American University Studies, ser. 3: Comparative Literature
AUS:RL	American University Studies, ser. 2: Romance Languages and Literatures
Autor	*Autor und Autorschaft im Mittelalter*, Kolloquium Meißen 1995, ed. Elizabeth Andersen [et alii] (Tübingen: Niemeyer, 1998)
AY	*Arthurian Yearbook*
BArR	Biblioteca dell'*Archivum Romanicum*. Ser. 1: Storia – Letteratura – Paleografia
BBSIA	*Bulletin Bibliographique de la Société Internationale Arthurienne – Bibliographical Bulletin of the International Arthurian Society*
BdNL	Bibliothek der gesammten deutschen National-Literatur
BdP	Beiträge zur deutschen Philologie
Beau et laid	*Le Beau et le laid au Moyen Âge*, Senefiance, 43 (Aix-en-Provence: CUER-MA, 2000)
BEFC	*Bulletin d'Études Françaises de l'Université Chuo*
Beiträge ZrP	*Beiträge zum romanischen Mittelalter*, ed. Kurt Baldinger, *ZrP: Sonderband zum 100jährigen Bestehen* (Tübingen: Niemeyer, 1977)

BEng	*Bulletin of the Department of English (Teikyo University)*
BF	*Les Bonnes Feuilles*
BFPLUL	Bibliothèque de la Faculté de Philosophie et Lettres de l'Université de Liège
BFR	Bibliothèque Française et Romane
BHR	*Bibliothèque d'Humanisme et Renaissance*
BibSP	Bibliothèque Scientifique Payot
Bien dire	*Bien Dire et Bien Aprandre*
BJRL	*Bulletin of the John Rylands Library*
BLAN	*Bulletin of the Faculty of Liberal Arts (Nagasaki University, Humanities)*
BLFC	*Bulletin Annuel de la Société de Langue et Littérature Françaises du Chûbu*
BM:S	Biblioteca Medievale: Saggi
BNF	Bibliothèque Nationale de France
BNFS	*Bulletin of the Nagoya University of Foreign Studies*
Bonheur	*L'Idée de bonheur au Moyen Âge: Actes du Colloque d'Amiens de mars 1984*, ed. Danielle Buschinger, GAG, 414 (Göppingen: Kümmerle, 1990)
BRABL	*Boletín de la Real Academia de Buenas Letras de Barcelona*
BRPMA	Beiträge zur romanischen Philologie des Mittelalters
BulJR	*Bulletin des Jeunes Romanistes*
BulLSMP	*Académie Royale de Belgique: Bulletins de la Classe des Lettres et des Sciences Morales et Politiques – Koninklijke Belgische Akademie: Mededelingen van de Afdeeling Letteren en Staat- en Zedekundige Wetenschappen*
BWAS	*Bulletin de l'École des Hautes Études (École des Hautes Études, Université de Tokyo-Waseda)*
Cahiers	*Cahiers de la Nouvelle Littérature (Tokyo: Tôjusha)*
CAIEF	*Cahiers de l'Association Internationale des Études Françaises*
Cantar	*O cantar dos trobadores: Actas do Congreso celebrado en Santiago de Compostela entre os días*

	26 e 29 de abril de 1993, Colección de Difusión Cultural, 2 (Santiago de Compostela: Xunta de Galicia, 1993)
Casopis	*Casopis pro Moderni Filologii a Literatury*
CCM	*Cahiers de Civilisation Médiévale*
CCMed	Cultures et Civilisations Médiévales
C&M	*Classica et Medievalia*
CEMN	*Cahiers d'Études Médiévales (Nagoya: Centre d'Études Médiévales et Romanes)*
CENSJF	Collection de l'École Normale Supérieure de Jeunes Filles
CERMEIL	Centre d'Études et de Recherches sur le Merveilleux, l'Étrange et l'Irréel en Littérature
CFMA	Classiques Français du Moyen Âge
CGFT	Critical Guides to French Texts
ChauR	*Chaucer Review*
Cheval	*Le Cheval dans le monde médiéval*, Senefiance, 32 (Aix-en-Provence: CUER-MA, 1992)
Chevalier au lion	*Le Chevalier au lion de Chrétien de Troyes: approches d'un chef-d'œuvre*, ed. Jean Dufournet, Unichamp, 20 (Paris: Champion, 1988)
Chivalry	*The Study of Chivalry: Resources and Approaches*, ed. Howell Chickering and Thomas H. Seiler (Kalamazoo: Medieval Institute Publications, Western Michigan University, 1988)
Chloe	Chloe: Beiträge zum Daphnis
Chrétien Bruges	*Chrétien de Troyes et le Graal: Colloque Arthurien Belge de Bruges* (Paris: Nizet, 1984)
CI	*Critical Inquiry*
CIF	*Cuadernos de Investigación Filológica*
CL	*Comparative Literature*
CLS	*Comparative Literature Studies*
CMCS	*Cambridge Medieval Celtic Studies*
CML	*Classical and Modern Literature*
CN	*Cultura Neolatina*
ComH	*Computers and the Humanities*

Conformité	*Conformité et déviances au Moyen Âge: Actes du Deuxième Colloque International de Montpellier, Université Paul-Valéry (25–27 novembre 1993)*, Les Cahiers du CRISIMA., 2 (Montpellier: Université Paul-Valéry, Montpellier III, 1995)
Congresso Napoli	*XIV Congresso Internazionale di Linguistica e Filologia Romanza, Napoli, 15–20 aprile 1975: Atti*, ed. Alberto Vàrvaro, 5 vols (Naples: Macchiaroli; Amsterdam: Benjamins, 1978–81)
Conjointure	*Conjointure arthurienne: Actes de la 'Classe d'Excellence' de la Chaire Franqui 1998, Liège, 20 février 1998*, ed. Juliette Dor, Université Catholique de Louvain – Publications de l'Institut d'Études Médiévales: Textes, Études, Congrès, 20 (Louvain-la-Neuve: Institut d'Études Médiévales de l'Université Catholique de Louvain, 2000)
Constante	*Constante în literatura franceză medievală*, Hegagon, 4 (Iaşi: Editura Demiurg, 1997)
Couleurs	*Les Couleurs au Moyen Âge*, Senefiance, 24 (Aix-en-Provence: CUER-MA, 1988)
Courtly Romance	*Courtly Romance: A Collection of Essays*, ed. Guy R. Mermier, Medieval and Renaissance Monograph Series, 6 (Detroit: Fifteenth-Century Symposium, 1984)
CPT	*Collected Papers on Foreign Language and Literature at Teikyo University*
Craft	*The Craft of Fiction: Essays in Medieval Poetics*, ed. Leigh A. Arrathoon (Rochester, MI: Solaris, 1984)
CRCL	*Canadian Review of Comparative Literature*
CRR	*Cincinnati Romance Review*
CSF	Cambridge Studies in French
CSML	Cambridge Studies in Medieval Literature
CUCJ	*Chiba University of Commerce Journal*
Cuer	*Le 'Cuer' au Moyen Âge (réalité et sénéfiance)*, Senefiance, 30 (Aix-en-Provence: CUER-MA, 1991)
DB	*Doitsu Bungaku Ronshu (Matsue, Zweigstelle Chugoku-Shikoku der japanischen Gesellschaft für Germanistik)*

DFS	*Dalhousie French Studies*
Diable	*Le Diable au moyen âge (doctrine, problèmes moraux, représentations)*, Senefiance, 6 (Aix-en-Provence: CUER-MA; Paris: Champion, 1979)
Diesseits	*Diesseits- und Jenseitsreisen im Mittelalter/Voyages dans l'ici-bas et dans l'au-delà au moyen âge*, ed. Wolf-Dieter Lange, Studium Universale: Studienreihe der Universität Bonn, 14 (Bonn: Bouvier, 1992)
DR	*Dalhousie Review*
DVj	*Deutsche Vierteljahrsschrift für Literaturwissenschaft und Geistesgeschichte*
ECAM	The Edward C. Armstrong Monographs on Medieval Literature
Ecriture	*Ecriture et modes de pensée au Moyen Age (VIIIe-XVe siècles)*, ed. Dominique Boutet and Laurence Harf-Lancner (Paris: Presses de l'Ecole Normale Supérieure, 1993)
Education	*Education, apprentissages, initiation au moyen âge: Actes du Premier Colloque International de Montpellier, Université Paul-Valéry, Novembre 1991*, Les Cahiers du CRISIMA., 1, 2 vols (Montpellier: d'Arceaux, 1993)
EF	*Études Françaises (Université Sophia, Daïgakuïn)*
EFrH	*Études de Langue et Littérature Françaises de l'Université de Hiroshima*
EH:D	Europäische Hochschulschriften – Publications Universitaires Européennes – European University Studies. Ser. 1: Deutsche Sprache und Literatur – Langue et Littérature Allemandes – German Language and Literature
EH:F	Europäische Hochschulschriften – Publications Universitaires Européennes – European University Studies. Ser. 13: Französische Sprache und Literatur – Langue et Littérature Françaises – French Language and Literature
EIn	*Études Indo-Européennes*

Eleanor	*Eleanor of Aquitaine: Patron and Politician*, ed. William W. Kibler, University of Texas Symposia in the Arts and Humanities, 3 (Austin, TX: University of Texas Press, 1976)
ELE	*Études de Littératures Européennes (Université Waseda, Faculté des Lettres)*
ELF	*ELF (Showa Women's University)*
ELH	*ELH: Journal of English Literary History*
ELLF	*Études de Langue et Littérature Françaises (Société Japonaise de Langue et Littérature Françaises)*
Enfant	*L'Enfant au Moyen-Âge (Littérature et civilisation)*, Senefiance, 9 (Aix-en-Provence: CUER-MA; Paris: Champion, 1980)
Epica arturiana	*Studi di epica arturiana/Studien zur Artusepik*, ed. Michael Dallapiazza and Paola Schulze-Belli, Studi Tergestini sul Medioevo, 2 (Trieste: Associazione di Cultura Medievale, 1993)
Erec	*Erec, ou l'ouverture du monde arthurien: Actes du Colloque du Centre d'Études Médiévales de l'Université de Picardie-Jules Verne, Amiens 16–17 janvier 1993*, ed. Danielle Buschinger and Wolfgang Spiewok, WODAN 18: EG–TS, 6 (Greifswald: Reineke, 1993)
Erzählstrukturen	*Erzählstrukturen der Artusliteratur: Forschungsgeschichte und neue Ansätze*, ed. Friedrich Wolfzettel and Peter Ihring (Tübingen: Niemeyer, 1999)
ESC	*English Studies in Canada*
EsFL	*Essays in French Literature*
ES-G	*Études de Langue et Littérature Françaises de l'Université Seinan-Gakuin*
EsL	*Essays in Literature*
Esp	*L'Esprit Créateur*
Essays Grigsby	*Continuations: Essays on Medieval French Literature and Language in Honor of John L. Grigsby*, ed. Norris J. Lacy and Gloria Torrini-Roblin (Birmingham, AL: Summa, 1989)

Essays Lacy	*'Por la soie amisté': Essays in Honor of Norris J. Lacy*, ed. Keith Busby and Catherine M. Jones, Faux Titre, 183 (Amsterdam: Rodopi, 2000)
Essays Lagorio	*Culture and the King: The Social Implications of the Arthurian Legend. Essays in Honor of Valerie M. Lagorio*, ed. Martin B. Shichtman and James P. Carley, SUNY Series on Medieval Studies (Albany: State University of New York Press,1994)
Essays Pickford	*The Changing Face of Arthurian Romance: Essays on Arthurian Prose Romances in Memory of Cedric E. Pickford: A Tribute by the Members of the British Branch of the International Arthurian Society*, AS, 16 (Cambridge: Brewer; Wolfeboro, NH: Boydell, 1986)
Essays Powell-Hodgins	*Voices of Conscience: Essays on Medieval and Modern French Literature in Memory of James D. Powell and Rosemary Hodgins*, ed. Raymond J. Cormier (Philadelphia: Temple University Press, 1977)
Essays Thorpe	*An Arthurian Tapestry: Essays in Memory of Lewis Thorpe*, ed. Kenneth Varty (Glasgow: French Department of the University of Glasgow, 1981)
Essays Topsfield	*Chrétien de Troyes and the Troubadours: Essays in Memory of the Late Leslie Topsfield*, ed. Peter S. Noble and Linda M. Paterson (Cambridge: St Catharine's College, 1984)
Essays Uitti	*Translatio Studii: Essays Karl D. Uitti*, ed. Renate Blumenfeld-Kosinski [et alii], Faux Titre, 179 (Amsterdam: Rodopi, 2000)
EstRom	*Estudios Románicos*
EtAngl	*Études Anglaises*
EtCelt	*Études Celtiques*
EtCin	*Études Cinématographiques*
EtGerm	*Études Germaniques*
Études Horrent	*Études de philologie romane et d'histoire littéraire offertes à Jules Horrent à l'occasion de son soixantième anniversaire*, ed. Jean-Marie D'Heur and Nicoletta Cherubini (Liège: [n.p.], 1980)

Études Lanly	*Études de langue et de littérature françaises offertes à André Lanly* (Nancy: Université de Nancy II, 1980)
Études Matoré	*Études de lexicologie, lexicographie et stylistique offertes à Georges Matoré par ses collègues et ses élèves*, ed. Irène Tumba (Paris: Bibliothèque de *l'InfGram*, 1987)
Études Poirion	*L'Hostellerie de pensée: Études sur l'art littéraire au Moyen Âge offertes à Daniel Poirion par ses anciens élèves*, CCMed, 12 (Paris: Presses de l'Université de Paris-Sorbonne, 1995)
Euph	*Euphorion*
Eureka	*Eureka (Tokyo: Seïdosha)*
Evolución	*Evolución narrativa e ideológica de la literatura caballeresca*, ed. María Eugenia Lacarra (Bilbao: Universidad del País Vasco, 1991)
Exclus	*Exclus et systèmes d'exclusion dans la littérature et la civilisation médiévales*, Senefiance, 5 (Aix-en-Provence: CUER-MA; Paris: Champion, 1978)
F-b	*Furansu-bungeï [Littérature Française]*
FBGK	*Furansu Bungaku Gogaku Kenkyû (Université de Tokyo-Waseda)*
FBR	*Furansu Bungaku Ronshû (Société de Langue et Littérature Françaises de Kyûshû)*
FCS	*Fifteenth-Century Studies*
FdSD	Forschungen zur deutschen Sprache und Dichtung
FeS	*Le Forme e la Storia*
F&MS	*Folklore and Mythology Studies*
Festschrift Asher	*Interpretation und Edition deutscher Texte des Mittelalters: Festschrift für John Asher zum 60. Geburtstag* (Berlin: Schmidt, 1981)
Festschrift Henzen	*Philologia deutsch: Festschrift Walter Henzen*, ed. Werner Kohlschmidt and Paul Zinsli (Bern: Francke, 1965)

Festschrift Hoffmann	*Uf der mâze pfat: Festschrift für Werner Hoffmann zum 60. Geburtstag*, ed. Waltraud Fritsch-Rößler and Liselotte Homering, GAG, 555 (Göppingen: Kümmerle, 1991)
Festschrift Johnson	*Blütezeit: Festschrift L. Peter Johnson*, ed. Marc Chinca, Joachim Heinzle, and Christopher Young (Tübingen: Niemeyer, 2000)
Festschrift Kennedy	*Shifts and Transpositions in Medieval Narrative: A Festschrift for Dr Elspeth Kennedy*, ed. Karen Pratt [et aliae] (Cambridge: Brewer, 1994)
Festschrift Klein	*Lebendige Romania: Festschrift für Hans-Wilhelm Klein überreicht von seinen Freunden und Schülern*, GAB, 88 (Göppingen: Kümmerle, 1976)
Festschrift Mölk	*Literatur: Geschichte und Verstehen. Festschrift für Ulrich Mölk zum 60. Geburtstag*, ed. Hinrich Hudde, Udo Schöning, and Friedrich Wolfzettel, StR, 87 (Heidelberg: Winter, 1997)
Festschrift Nellmann	*'bickelwort' und 'wildiu mære': Festschrift für Eberhard Nellmann zum 65. Geburtstag*, ed. Dorothea Lindemann, Berndt Volkmann, and Klaus-Peter Wegera, GAG, 618 (Göppingen: Kümmerle, 1995)
Festschrift Ruh	*Medium Aevum deutsch: Beiträge zur deutschen Literatur des hohen und späten Mittelalters. Festschrift Kurt Ruh* (Tübingen: Niemeyer, 1979)
Festschrift Rupp	*Gotes und der werlde hulde: Literatur in Mittelalter und Neuzeit. Festschrift für Heinz Rupp zum 70. Geburtstag* (Bern: Francke, 1989)
Festschrift Schepp	*'ze hove und an der strâzen': die deutsche Literatur des Mittelalters und ihr 'Sitz im Leben'. Festschrift für Volker Schepp*, ed. Anna Keck and Theodor Nolte (Stuttgart: Hirzel, 1999)
Festschrift Schon	*Studia Neolatina: Festschrift für Peter M. Schon*, ed. Johannes Thomas (Aachen: Mayer, 1978)
Festskrift Swaton	*Résonances de la recherche: Festskrift till Sigbrit Swaton*, ed. Kerstin Jonasson [et alii], ActaUpsa, 59 (Uppsala: Uppsala University Library, 1999)
Feu	*Feu et lumière au Moyen Âge I*, Collection Moyen Âge (Toulouse: Editions Universitaires du Sud, 1998)

FF	*French Forum*
FFM	French Forum Monographs
FFRSH	*Futsugo-Futsubungaku-Ronshû [Études de Langue et Littérature Françaises] (Université Sophia, Tokyo)*
FGädL	Forschungen zur Geschichte der älteren deutschen Literatur
Fiktionalität	*Fiktionalität im Artusroman: Dritte Tagung der Deutschen Sektion der Internationalen Artusgesellschaft in Berlin vom 13.–15. Februar 1992*, ed. Volker Mertens and Friedrich Wolfzettel with Matthias Meyer and Hans-Jochen Schiewer (Tübingen: Niemeyer, 1993)
Filologia Verona	*Filologia romanza, filologia germanica: intersezioni e diffrazioni. Convegno Internazionale, Verona, 3–5 aprile 1995: Atti*, ed. Anna Maria Babbi and Adele Cipolla, Medioevi: Studi, 1 (Verona: Fiorini, 1997)
FiR	*Filologia Romanza*
FK	*Filológiai Közlöny*
FMLS	*Forum for Modern Language Studies*
FMSt	*Frühmittelalterliche Studien*
ForL	*Forum der Letteren*
FR	*French Review*
France	*La France (Tokyo: Hakusuisha)*
FRLH	*Fukuoka University Review of Literature & Humanities*
FS	*French Studies*
FSB	*French Studies Bulletin*
GAB	Göppinger Akademische Beiträge
GAG	Göppinger Arbeiten zur Germanistik
Gastenboek van Es	*Taal- en letterkundig gastenboek voor Prof. Dr G. A. van Es: Opstellen, de 70–jahrige aangeboden ter gelegenheid van zijn afscheid als hoogleraar aan de Rijksuniversiteit te Groningen* (Groningen: Archief voor de Nederlandse Syntaxis, 1975)
Gedenkband Ringger	*Vom Mittelalter zur Moderne: Beiträge zur französischen und italienischen Literatur. Gedenkband*, ed. Erich Loos (Tübingen: Narr, 1991)

Gengo	*Gengo-Bunka (Université Meiji-Gakuin)*
Gensô	*Gensô-bungaku [Littérature fantastique] (Tokyo)*
Geste	*Le Geste et les gestes au Moyen Âge*, Senefiance, 41 (Aix-en-Provence: CUER-MA, 1998)
GIF	*Giornale Italiano di Filologia*
G-k	*The Geibun-kenkyû [Journal of Arts and Letters] (The Keio Society of Arts and Letters)*
GLL	*German Life and Letters*
GLML	Garland Library of Medieval Literature
GMC	Garland Medieval Casebooks
GR	*Germanic Review*
Graph	*The Graph of Sex and the German Text: Gendered Culture in Early Modern Germany 1500–1700*, ed. Lynne Tatlock, Chloe, 19 (Amsterdam: Rodopi, 1994)
Grenzen	*An den Grenzen höfischer Kultur: Anfechtungen der Lebensordnung in der deutschen Erzähldichtung des hohen Mittelalters*, ed. Gert Kaiser, FGädL, 12 (Munich: Fink, 1991)
GRLH	Garland Reference Library of the Humanities
GRLMA	*Grundriß der romanischen Literaturen des Mittelalters*
GRM	*Germanisch-romanische Monatsschrift*
Grote Lijnen	*Grote Lijnen: Syntheses over Middelnederlandse Letterkunde*, Nederlandse Literatuur en Cultuur in de Middeleeuwen, 11 (Amsterdam: Prometheus, 1995)
GS	*Gendai Shisô [Revue de la Pensée d'Aujourd'hui] (Tokyo: Shichôsha)*
GSML	Garland Studies in Medieval Literature
Heli	*Helikon (Budapest)*
HICL	Histoire des Idées et Critique Littéraire
HLF	*Histoire Littéraire de la France*
Hof und Kloster	*Mittelalterliche Literatur und Kunst im Spannungsfeld von Hof und Kloster: Ergebnisse der Berliner-Tagung, 9.–11. Oktober 1997*, ed. Nigel F. Palmer and Hans-Jochen Schiewer (Tübingen: Niemeyer, 1999)

Hommage Dufournet	*'Et c'est la fin pour quoy sommes ensemble':* *hommage Jean Dufournet: littérature, histoire et langue du Moyen Âge*, NBMA, 25, 3 vols (Paris: Champion; Geneva: Slatkine, 1993)
Hommage Onimus	*Hommage à Jean Onimus*, AnNice, 38 (Paris: Belles-Lettres, 1979)
Hommage Payen	*'Farai chansoneta novele': hommage à Jean-Charles Payen: essais sur la liberté créatrice au Moyen Âge* (Caen: Centre de Publications de l'Université de Caen, 1989)
Hommage Richer	*Hommage à Jean Richer*, AnNice, 51 (Paris: Belles Lettres, 1985)
Hommage Zumthor	*Le nombre du temps: en hommage à Paul Zumthor*, NBMA, 12 (Paris: Champion, 1988)
HR	*Hispanic Review*
Hum	*The Humanities (Department of Liberal Arts, Kyoto University)*
ICLS Athens	*The Expansion and Transformations of Courtly Literature: Selected Papers from the Second Triennial Congress of the International Courtly Literature Society*, ed. Nathaniel B. Smith and Joseph T. Snow (Athens: University of Georgia Press, 1980)
ICLS Belfast	*The Court and Cultural Diversity: Selected Papers from the Eighth Triennial Congress of the International Courtly Literature Society, The Queen's University of Belfast, 26 July–1 August 1995*, ed. Evelyn Mullally and John Thompson (Cambridge: Brewer, 1997)
ICLS Dalfsen	*Courtly Literature: Culture and Context, Selected Papers from the 5th Triennial Congress of the International Courtly Literature Society, Dalfsen, The Netherlands, 9–16 August, 1986*, ed. Keith Busby and Erik Kooper, UPGC, 25 (Amsterdam: Benjamins, 1990)
ICLS Liverpool	*Court and Poet: Selected Proceedings of the Third Congress of the International Courtly Literature Society (Liverpool 1980)*, ed. Glyn S. Burgess [et alii], ARCA, 5 (Liverpool: Cairns, 1981)

ICLS Salerno	*L'Imaginaire courtois et son double: Actes du VIème Congrès Triennal de la Société Internationale de Littérature Courtoise (ICLS), Fisciano (Salerno), 24–28 juillet 1989*, ed. Giovanna Angeli and Luciano Formisano, Pubblicazioni dell'Università degli Studi di Salerno: Sezione Atti, Convegni, Miscellanee, 35 (Naples: Edizioni Scientifiche Italiane, 1992)
ICLS Toronto	*The Spirit of the Court: Selected Proceedings of the Fourth Congress of the International Courtly Literature Society (Toronto 1983)*, ed. Glyn S. Burgess and Robert A. Taylor (Cambridge: Brewer, 1985)
Image	*L'Image au Moyen Âge: Actes du Colloque, Amiens 19–23 mars 1986*, ed. D. Buschinger and W. Spiewok, WODAN: Recherches en Littérature Médiévale, 15 – Tagungsbände und Sammelschriften, 5 (Amiens: Publications du Centre d'Études Médiévales, Université de Picardie, 1992)
ImRif	*L'Immagine Riflessa*
InfGram	*L'Information Grammaticale*
InfLitt	*L'Information Littéraire*
Interregionalität	*Interregionalität der deutschen Literatur im europäischen Mittelalter*, ed. Hartmut Kugler (Berlin: de Gruyter, 1995)
Iris	*Iris (Centre de Recherche sur l'Imaginaire, Université Grenoble 3)*
ItC	*Italian Culture*
JA	*Journal (Literature Department of Aoyama Gakuin University, Tokyo)*
JAF	*Journal of American Folklore*
JCIS	*Journal of College of International Studies (Chûbu University)*
JCSC	*Journal of the Institute of Cultural Science (Chuo University)*
JDLA	*The Journal of the Department of Liberal Arts (University of Tokyo)*
JEGP	*Journal of English and Germanic Philology*

JFLN	*The Journal of the Faculty of Letters (Nagoya University)*
JG	*Jimbun Gakuhô (The Journal of Social Sciences and Humanities, The Faculty of Social Sciences and Humanities of Tokyo Metropolitan University)*
JGIS	*The Journal of Global and Inter-Cultural Studies (The Faculty of Global and Inter-Cultural Studies of Ferris University)*
JHI	*Journal of the History of Ideas*
JHum	*Journal of the Graduate School of Humanities (Seikei University)*
JIES	*Journal of Indo-European Studies*
JK	*Jinbun Kenkyû, Studies in the Humanities (The Journal of the Literary Association of Osaka City University)*
JMEMS	*Journal of Medieval and Early Modern Studies*
JMRS	*Journal of Medieval and Renaissance Studies*
JRMMRA	*Journal of the Rocky Mountain Medieval and Renaissance Association*
JS	*Journal des Savants*
JSFLN	*Journal of School of Foreign Languages (Nagoya University of Foreign Studies)*
K-f	*Kiso-furansugo [Français Elémentaire] (Tokyo: Sanshûsha)*
KFLQ	*Kentucky Foreign Language Quarterly*
KJFRP	*Kritischer Jahresbericht über die Fortschritte der romanischen Philologie*
KN	*Kwartalnik Neofilologiczny*
Knighthood IV	*Medieval Knighthood IV: Papers from the Fifth Strawberry Hill Conference 1990*, ed. Christopher Harper-Bill and Ruth Harvey (Woodbridge: Boydell, 1992)
König Artus	*König Artus und der heilige Graal: Studien zum spätarturischen Roman und zum Graals-Roman im europäischen Mittelalter*, ed. Danielle Buschinger and Wolfgang Spiewok, WODAN: EG, 32–TS, 17 (Greifswald: Reineke, 1994)

KRQ	*Kentucky Romance Quarterly*
Kuhn Gedenken	*Deutsche Literatur im Mittelalter: Kontakte und Perspektiven. Hugo Kuhn zum Gedenken* (Stuttgart: Metzler, 1979)
Lancelot Mythique	*Lancelot*, ed. Mireille Séguy, Figures Mythiques (Paris: Autrement, 1996)
Lancelot Picardie	*Lancelot: Actes du Colloque des 14 et 15 janvier, Université de Picardie, Centre d'Études Médiévales*, ed. Danielle Buschinger, GAG, 415 (Göppingen: Kümmerle, 1984)
Lancelot Wégimont	*Lancelot, Yvain et Gauvain: Colloque Arthurien Belge de Wégimont*, Lettres Médiévales, 2 (Paris: Nizet, 1984)
Lecture	*La Lecture sociocritique du texte romanesque*, ed. Graham Falconer and Henri Mitterand (Toronto: Hakkert, 1975)
Legacy	*The Legacy of Chrétien de Troyes*, ed. Norris J. Lacy, Douglas Kelly, and Keith Busby, 2 vols, Faux Titre, 31, 37 (Amsterdam: Rodopi, 1987–88)
LE:L	Librairie Européenne: Collection Littératures
LF	*Langue Française*
LiC	*Lilia candida (Université Shirayuri, Tokyo)*
Liebe Gießen	*Liebe-Ehe-Ehebruch: Vorträge des Symposiums vom 13. bis 16. Juni 1983 am Institut für deutsche Sprache und Literatur, Gießen*, ed. Xenja von Ertzdorff and Marianne Wynn, BdP, 58 (Giessen: Schmitz, 1984)
Liebe Triest	*Liebe und Aventiure im Artusroman des Mittelalters: Beiträge der Triester Tagung 1988*, ed. Paola Schulze-Belli and Michael Dallapiazza, GAG, 532 (Göppingen: Kümmerle, 1990)
LingI	*Lingvisticæ Investigationes*
Literatur in der Gesellschaft	*Literatur in der Gesellschaft des Spätmittelalters*, ed. Hans Ulrich Gumbrecht, Begleitreihe zum *GRLMA*, 1 (Heidelberg: Winter, 1980)
LJG	*Literaturwissenschaftliches Jahrbuch im Auftrage der Görres-Gesellschaft*
LlC	*Llên Cymru*

LLF	*La Langue et la Littérature Françaises (Société de Littérature Française à l'Université du Kansai, Osaka)*
LMS	*Limbile Moderne în Şcoală*
Love Leuven	*Love and Marriage in the Twelfth Century*, ed. Willy Van Hoecke and Andries Welkenhuysen, MedL: Studia, 8 (Leuven: Leuven University Press, 1981)
LR	*Les Lettres Romanes*
MA	*Le Moyen Âge*
MAe	*Medium Aevum*
Magie	*Magie et illusion au Moyen Âge*, Senefiance, 42 (Aix-en-Provence: CUER-MA, 1999)
Matériaux	*Matériaux pour l'histoire des cadres de vie dans l'Europe Occidentale (1050–1250)* (Nice: Centre d'Études Médiévales, Faculté des Lettres et Sciences Humaines, Université de Nice, 1984)
MDKR	*Meiji-Daigaku Kyôyô-Ronshû (Université de Meiji, Tokyo)*
Mediaeval World	*The Mediaeval World*, ed. David Daiches and Anthony Thorlby, Literature and Western Civilization, 2 (London: Aldus, 1973)
Medieval West	*The Medieval West Meets the Rest of the World*, ed. Nancy van Deusen, Claremont Cultural Studies: Wissenschaftliche Abhandlungen –Musicological Studies, 62:2 (Ottawa: Institute of Mediaeval Music, 1995)
Medioneerland- istiek	*Medioneerlandistiek: een inleiding tot de Middelnederlandse letterkunde*, ed. Ria Jansen-Sieben, Jozef Janssens, and Frank Willaert (Hilversum: Verloren, 2000)
MedL	Mediaevalia Lovaniensia
MedPer	*Medieval Perspectives*
MedR	*Medioevo Romanzo*
MedS	*Medieval Scandinavia*
Mélanges Bezzola	*Orbis mediaevalis: mélanges de langue et de littérature médiévales offerts à Reto Raduolf Bezzola à l'occasion de son quatre-vingtième anniversaire* (Bern: Francke, 1978)

Mélanges Camproux	*Mélanges de philologie romane offerts à Charles Camproux*, 2 vols (Montpellier: Centre d'Estudis Occitans, 1978)
Mélanges Delbouille	*Mélanges de linguistique romane et de philologie médiévale offerts à M. Maurice Delbouille*, 2 vols (Gembloux: Duculot, 1964)
Mélanges de Mandach	*De l'aventure épique à l'aventure romanesque: mélanges offerts à André de Mandach*, ed. Jacques Chocheyras (Bern: P. Lang, 1997)
Mélanges Demarolle	*Mélanges de langue et de littérature françaises du Moyen Âge offerts à Pierre Demarolle*, ed. Charles Brucker, Champion-Varia, 31 (Paris: Champion; Geneva: Slatkine, 1998)
Mélanges Faucon	*Guerres, voyages et quêtes au moyen âge: mélanges Claude Faucon*, ed. Alain Labbé, Daniel W. Lacroix, and Danielle Quéruel, Colloques, Congrès et Conférences sur le Moyen Âge, 2 (Paris: Champion, 2000)
Mélanges Foulon	*Mélanges de langue et littérature françaises du Moyen Âge et de la Renaissance offerts à Monsieur Charles Foulon par ses collègues, ses élèves et ses amis*, vol. 1 (Rennes: Institut de Français, Université de Haute Bretagne), vol. 2 (Liège: Marche Romane, 1980)
Mélanges Frappier	*Mélanges de langue et de littérature du Moyen Age et de la Renaissance offerts à Jean Frappier, Professeur à la Sorbonne, par ses collègues, ses élèves et ses amis*, PRF, 112, 2 vols (Geneva: Droz, 1970)
Mélanges Jonin	*Mélanges de langue et littérature françaises du Moyen Âge offerts à Pierre Jonin*, Senefiance, 7 (Aix-en-Provence: CUER-MA; Paris: Champion, 1979)
Mélanges Jung	*'Ensi firent li ancessor': mélanges de philologie médiévale offerts à Marc-René Jung*, ed. Luciano Rossi [et alii], 2 vols (Alessandria: dell'Orso, 1996)
Mélanges Larmat	*Mélanges Jean Larmat: regards sur le Moyen Age et la Renaissance: histoire, langue et littérature*, AnNice, 39 (Paris: Belles-Lettres, 1982)

Mélanges Le Gentil	*Mélanges de langue et de littérature médiévales offerts à Pierre Le Gentil par ses collègues, ses élèves et ses amis* (Paris: SEDES-CDU, 1973)
Mélanges Lods	*Mélanges de littérature du Moyen Age au XXe siècle offerts à Mademoiselle Jeanne Lods par ses collègues, ses élèves et ses amis*, CENSJF, 10, 2 vols (Paris: Ecole Normale Supérieure de Jeunes Filles, 1978)
Mélanges Ménard	*Miscellanea mediaevalia: mélanges offerts à Philippe Ménard*, ed. J. Claude Faucon, Alain Labbé, and Danielle Quéruel, NBMA, 46, 2 vols (Paris: Champion, 1998)
Mélanges Planche	*Mélanges de langue et de littérature médiévales offerts à Alice Planche*, AnNice, 48 (Nice: Belles Lettres, 1984)
Mélanges Rostaing	*Mélanges d'histoire littéraire, de linguistique et de philologie romanes offerts à Charles Rostaing par ses collègues, ses élèves et ses amis*, 2 vols (Liège: Association Intercommunale de Mécanographie, 1974)
Mélanges Rychner	*Mélanges d'études romanes du Moyen Âge et de la Renaissance offerts à Jean Rychner*, in *TLL*, 16:1 (1978)
Mélanges Suard	*'Plaist vos oïr bone cançon vallant?' Mélanges François Suard*, ed. Dominique Boutet, Marie-Madeleine Castellani, Françoise Ferrand, and Aimé Petit, 2 vols (Lille: Conseil Scientifique de l'Université Charles-de-Gaulle–Lille III, Centre d'Études Médiévales et Dialectales de Lille 3; Paris: Université de Paris X–Nanterre, 1999)
Mélanges Subrenat	*'Si a parlé par moult ruiste vertu': mélanges Jean Subrenat*, ed. Jean Dufournet, Colloques, Congrès et Conférences sur le moyen âge, 1 (Paris: Champion, 2000)
Mélanges Wathelet-Willem	*Mélanges de philologie et de littérature romanes offerts à Jeanne Wathelet-Willem* (Liège: Marche Romane, 1978)

Meraviglioso	*Il Meraviglioso e il verosimile tra antichità e medioevo*, ed. Diego Lanza and Oddone Longo, BArR, 221 (Florence: Olschki, 1989)
M&H	*Medievalia et Humanistica*
MF	*Le Moyen Français*
MFN	*Medieval Feminist Newsletter*
MGRS	*The Meiji Gakuin Ronso (Meiji Gakuin University)*
MGS	*Michigan Germanic Studies*
MHRATD	Modern Humanities Research Association Texts and Dissertations
MichA	*Michigan Academician*
Mid-H	*Mid-Hudson Language Studies*
Miscellanea Gasca Queirazza	*Miscellanea di studi romanzi offerta a Giuliano Gasca Queirazza per il suo 65° compleanno*, ed. Anna Cornagliotti [et alii], 2 vols Alessandria: dell'Orso, 1988)
Misrahi Volume	*Jean Misrahi Memorial Volume: Studies in Medieval Literature*, ed. Hans R. Runte, Henri Niedzielski, and William L. Hendrickson (Columbia, SC: French Literature Publications Company, 1977)
Mittelalter-studien Köhler	*Mittelalterstudien: Erich Köhler zum Gedenken*, StR, 55 (Heidelberg: Winter, 1984)
MLN	*Modern Language Notes*
MLQ	*Modern Language Quarterly*
MLR	*Modern Language Review*
MMS	Münsterische Mittelalter-Schriften
MP	*Modern Philology*
MrR	*Marche Romane*
MRS	Michigan Romance Studies
MRTS	Medieval & Renaissance Texts & Studies
MS	*Medieval Studies*
MSB	Middeleeuwse Studies en Bronnen
MSFM	Mindere Skrifter udgivet af Laboratorium for Folkesproglige Middelalderstudier
N&Q	*Notes and Queries*

Nature	*The Nature of Medieval Narrative*, ed. Minnette Grunmann-Gaudet and Robin F. Jones, FFM, 22 (Lexington, KY: French Forum, 1980)
NBMA	Nouvelle Bibliothèque du Moyen Age
Neophil	*Neophilologus*
NFS	*Nottingham French Studies*
NI	*Nyelvpedagógiai Irások (Budapest)*
NLH	*New Literary History*
NM	*Neuphilologische Mitteilungen*
NMS	*Nottingham Medieval Studies*
Normandie	*Les Romans de la Table Ronde: la Normandie et au-delà…*, ed. R. Bonsard [et alii] (Condé-sur-Noireau: Corlet, 1987)
NSH	*Nagoya Studies in Humanities*
NTg	*De Nieuwe Taalgids*
NZJFS	*New Zealand Journal of French Studies*
OetC	*Œuvres et Critiques*
Omaggio Folena	*Omaggio a Gianfranco Folena*, 2 vols(Padua: Editoriale Programma, 1993)
Opstellen Gerritsen	*Hoort wonder! Opstellen voor W. P. Gerritsen*, ed. Bart Besamusca, Frank Brandsma, and Dieuwke van der Poel, MSB, 70 (Hilversum: Verloren, 2000)
Opstellen Schenkeveld	*'In onse scole': Opstellen over middeleeuwse letterkunde voor Margaretha H. Schenkeveld* (Amsterdam: Stichting Neerlandistiek VU, 1989)
OrL	*Orbis Litterarum*
Papers Kittredge	*Anniversary Papers by Colleagues and Pupils of George Lyman Kittredge Presented on the Completion of his Twenty-Fifth Year of Teaching in Harvard University June 1913* (Boston: Ginn, 1913)
PapR	*Papers in Romance*
Paroles	*Paroles Gelées: UCLA French Studies*
PBB	*Pauls und Braunes Beiträge zur Geschichte der deutschen Sprache und Literatur*
PerM	*Perspectives Médiévales*

PFLT	*The Proceedings of the Department of Foreign Languages and Literatures (College of Arts and Sciences, University of Tokyo)*
PG	Philologica Germanica
PH	Poetik und Hermeneutik
Philologica Lommatzsch	*Philologica Romanica Erhard Lommatzsch gewidmet* (Munich: Fink, 1975)
PLC	*Princeton University Library Chronicle*
PLL	*Papers on Language and Literature*
Plume	*Plume: Etudes de Langue et Littérature Françaises (Nagoya)*
PMLA	*Publications of the Modern Language Association of America*
Positionen	*Positionen des Romans im späten Mittelalter*, ed. Walter Haug and Burghart Wachinger, Fortuna Vitrea, 1 (Tübingen: Niemeyer, 1991)
PQ	*Philological Quarterly*
PRF	Publications Romanes et Françaises
Proteus	*The Binding of Proteus: Perspectives on Myth and the Literary Process: Selected Papers of the Bucknell University Program on Myth and Literature and the Bucknell-Susquehanna Colloquium on Myth and Literature Held at Bucknell and Susquehanna Universities, 21 and 22 March 1974*, ed. Marjorie W. McCune, Tucker Orbison, and Philip M. Withim (Lewisburg, PA: Bucknell University Press; London: Associated University Presses, 1980)
Provinces	*Provinces, régions, terroirs au moyen âge, de la réalité à l'imaginaire: Actes du Colloque International des 'Rencontres Européennes de Strasbourg', Strasbourg, 19–21 septembre 1991*, ed. Bernard Guidot (Nancy: Presses Universitaires de Nancy, 1993)
PSQ	Philologische Studien und Quellen
PUR	Publications de l'Université de Rouen
Purdue Film	*Purdue University Fifth Annual Conference on Film: Proceedings Oct. 30–Nov. 1, 1980*, ed. Maud S.

	Walther (West Lafayette, IN: Department of Foreign Languages, Purdue University-West Lafayette, [1980])
QBologna	*Quaderni di Filologia Romanza della Facoltà di Lettere e Filosofia dell'Università di Bologna*
QCatania	*Quaderni di Filologia Medievale, Istituto Universitario di Magistero – Catania*
QetF	*Quondam et Futurus*
QMacerata	*Quaderni di Filologia e Lingue Romanze dell'Università di Macerata*
Quatre Éléments	*Les Quatre Éléments dans la culture médiévale: Actes du Colloque des 25, 26 et 27 mars 1982*, ed. Danielle Buschinger and André Crépin, GAG, 386 (Göppingen: Kümmerle, 1983)
Rapports	*Rapports – Het Franse Boek*
RBC	Research Bibliographies and Checklists
RBM	*Research Bulletin of Meisei University, Humanities and Social Sciences*
RBN	*Research Bulletin (Foreign Languages and Literatures, The Department of General Education, Nagoya University)*
RBPH	*Revue Belge de Philologie et d'Histoire*
Réception	*Réception et identification du conte depuis le moyen âge: Actes du Colloque de Toulouse, janvier 1986*, ed. Michel Zink et Xavier Ravier (Toulouse: Université de Toulouse-Le Mirail, 1987)
Recueil Fourquet	*Perceval–Parzival hier et aujourd'hui et autres essais sur la littérature allemande du Moyen Age et de la Renaissance pour fêter les 95 ans de Jean Fourquet: recueil d'articles*, ed. Danielle Buschinger and Wolfgang Spiewok, WODAN: EG, 48–TS, 28 (Greifswald: Reineke, 1994)
Recueil Micha	*Lancelot-Lanzelet hier et aujourd'hui: recueil d'articles assemblés pour fêter les 90 ans de Alexandre Micha*, ed. Danielle Buschinger et Michel Zink, WODAN: EG, 51–TS, 29 (Greifswald: Reineke, 1995)

Relations	*Les Relations de parenté dans le monde médiéval*, Senefiance, 26 (Aix-en-Provence: CUER-MA, 1989)
RES	*Review of English Studies*
ResPL	*Res Publica Litterarum*
RevLA	*The Review of Liberal Arts (The Society of Liberal Arts, Otaru University of Commerce)*
RevR	*Revue Romane*
RF	*Romanische Forschungen*
RFE	*Revista de Filología Española*
RG	*Romanica Gandensia*
RH	*Revue de Hiyoshi Langue et Littérature Françaises (Université Keio, Tokyo)*
Rhetoric	*Rhetoric Revalued: Papers from the International Society for the History of Rhetoric*, MRTS, 19; International Society for the History of Rhetoric Monograph, 1 (Binghamton, NY: Center for Medieval and Early Renaissance Studies, 1982)
RHL	*Revue d'Histoire Littéraire de la France*
RITL	*Revista de Istorie şi Teorie Literară*
Ritter mit dem Löwen	*Die Romane von dem Ritter mit dem Löwen*, ed. Xenja von Ertzdorff and Rudolf Schulz, Chloe, 20 (Amsterdam: Rodopi, 1994)
RJ	*Romanistisches Jahrbuch*
RLA	*RLA: Romance Languages Annual*
RLingR	*Revue de Linguistique Romane*
RLLF	*Revue de Langue et Littérature Françaises (Société de Langue et Littérature Françaises de l'Université de Tokyo)*
RLM	*Revista de Literatura Medieval*
RLR	*Revue des Langues Romanes*
RMAL	*Revue du Moyen Age Latin*
RMS	*Reading Medieval Studies*
Rom	*Romania*
RomN	*Romance Notes*
RomQ	*Romance Quarterly*

Ronshû	*Ronshû: Aoyama Journal of General Education (Aoyama Gakuin University)*
RPh	*Romance Philology*
RR	*Romanic Review*
RRG	Recherches et Rencontres: Publications de la Faculté de Lettres de Genève
RRL	*Revue Roumaine de Linguistique*
RSCL	*The Review of Studies in Christianity and Literature (The Japanese Society for Literature and Religion. Yokohama : Ferris Women's University)*
RSH	*Revue des Sciences Humaines*
RT	*Recherches et Travaux (Grenoble)*
RTr	*Rapports sur les Travaux: Etudes Générales*
Ruse	*Ecriture de la ruse*, ed. Elzbieta Grodek, Faux Titre, 190 (Amsterdam: Rodopi, 2000)
RZLG	*Romanistische Zeitschrift für Literaturgeschichte – Cahiers d'Histoire de la Littérature Romane*
SandS	*Sight and Sound*
Sang	*Le Sang au moyen âge: Actes du quatrième Colloque International de Montpellier, Université Paul-Valéry (27–29 novembre 1997)*, Cahiers du CRISIMA, 4 (Montpellier: Université Paul-Valéry, 1999)
Schwierige Frauen	*Schwierige Frauen – schwierige Männer in der Literatur des Mittelalters*, ed. Alois M. Haas and Ingrid Kasten (Bern: P. Lang, 1999)
SdLS	*Studien zur deutschen Literatur und Sprache (Zweigstelle Tôkai der Japanischen Gesellschaft für Germanistik)*
SF	*Studi Francesi*
SFL	Studies in French Literature
SFR	*Stanford French Review*
SGAK	Studien zur Germanistik, Anglistik und Komparatistik
SGS	*Seinan Gakuin University Graduate School, Graduate Studies in Literature*
Shisô	*Shisô (Tokyo: Iwanami-shoten)*

Shunjû	*Shunjû (Tokyo: Shunjûsha)*
SiG	*Siculorum Gymnasium*
Sign	*Sign, Sentence, Discourse: Language in Medieval Thought and Literature*, ed. Julian N. Wasserman and Lois Roney (Syracuse, NY: Syracuse University Press, 1989)
SLCN	*Studies in Language and Culture (Faculty of Language and Culture, Nagoya University)*
SLCO	*Studies in Language and Culture (Faculty of Language and Culture, Graduate School of Language and Culture, Osaka University)*
SM	*Studi Medievali*
SMC (also *SMC*)	Studies in Medieval Culture
SML	Studies in Medieval Literature
SMV	*Studi Mediolatini e Volgari*
SN	*Studia Neophilologica*
Sophia	*Sophia (Université Sophia, Tokyo)*
Souffrance	*La Souffrance au moyen âge (France, XIIe-XVe s.): Actes du Colloque organisé par l'Institut d'Etudes Romanes et le Centre d'Etudes Françaises de Varsovie (Varsovie, octobre 1984)*, Les Cahiers de Varsovie, 14 (Warsaw: Editions de l'Université de Varsovie, 1988)
Sower	*The Sower and His Seed*, ed. Rupert T. Pickens, FFM, 44 (Lexington, KY: French Forum, 1983)
SP	*Studies in Philology*
Spannungen	*Spannungen und Konflikte menschlichen Zusammenlebens in der deutschen Literatur des Mittelalters, Bristoler Colloquium 1993*, ed. Kurt Gärtner, Ingrid Kasten, and Frank Shaw (Tübingen: Niemeyer, 1996)
Spec	*Speculum*
SpecMA	*Speculum Medii Aevi: Zeitschrift für Geschichte und Literatur des Mittelalters – Revue d'Histoire et de Littérature Médiévales*
SpL	*Spiegel der Letteren*

Sprk	*Sprachkunst*
SRD	Studia Romanica Debreceniensis de Ludovico Kossuth Nominatae: Series Litteraria
SS	*Scandinavian Studies*
StC	*Studia Celtica*
StCJ	*Studia Celtica Japonica (The Celtic Society of Japan)*
StMed	*Studies in Medievalism*
StR	Studia Romanica
Stranger	*The Stranger in Medieval Society*, ed. F. R. P. Akehurst and Stephanie Cain Van D'Elden, Medieval Cultures, 12 (Minneapolis: University of Minnesota Press, 1997)
Studi D'Arco Silvio Avalle	*Studi di filologia medievale offerti a D'Arco Silvio Avalle* (Milan: Ricciardi, 1996)
Studi Melli	*Filologia romanza e cultura medievale: studi in onore di Elio Melli*, ed. Andrea Fassò, Luciano Formisano, and Mario Mancini, 2 vols (Alessandria: dell'Orso, 1998)
Studia de Riquer	*Studia in honorem prof. M. de Riquer*, 4 vols (Barcelona: Quaderns Crema, 1986–91)
Studia Remy	*Studia Occitanica Paul Remy*, ed. Hans-Erich Keller [et alii], 2 vols (Kalamazoo: Medieval Institute Publications, Western Michigan University, 1986)
Studies Brault	*Echoes of the Epic: Studies in Honor of Gerard J. Brault*, ed. David P. Schenck and Mary Jane Schenck (Birmingham, AL: Summa, 1998)
Studies Diverres	*The Legend of Arthur in the Middle Ages: Studies Presented to A. H. Diverres by Colleagues, Pupils and Friends*, ed. P. B. Grout [et alii], AS, 7 (Cambridge: Brewer; Totowa, NJ: Biblio, 1983)
Studies Ewert	*Studies in Medieval French Presented to Alfred Ewert in Honour of his Seventieth Birthday* (Oxford: Clarendon Press, 1961)
Studies Gerritsen	*Tussentijds: Bundel Studies aangegeben aan W. P. Gerritsen ter gelegenheid van zijn vijftigste verjaardag* (Utrecht: H&S, 1985)

Studies Kaske	*Magister regis: Studies in Honor of Robert Earl Kaske*, ed. Arthur Groos [et alii] (New York: Fordham University Press, 1986)
Studies Kastner	*A Miscellany of Studies in Romance Languages and Literatures Presented to Leon E. Kastner* (Cambridge: Heffer, 1932)
Studies Keller	*Studies in Honor of Hans-Erich Keller: Medieval French and Occitan Literature and Romance Linguistics*, ed. Rupert T. Pickens (Kalamazoo: Western Michigan University, Medieval Institute Publications, 1993)
Studies Kelly	*Conjunctures: Medieval Studies in Honor of Douglas Kelly*, ed. Keith Busby and Norris J. Lacy, Faux Titre, 83 (Amsterdam: Rodopi, 1994)
Studies Reid	*Medieval French Textual Studies in Memory of T. B. W. Reid*, ANTS, 1 (London: Birkbeck College, 1984)
Studies Sinclair	*Medieval Codicology, Iconography, Literature, and Translation: Studies for Keith Val Sinclair*, ed. Peter Rolfe Monks and D. D. R. Owen, Litterae Textuales (Leiden: Brill, 1994)
Studies Woledge	*Studies in Medieval French Language and Literature Presented to Brian Woledge in Honour of his 80th Birthday*, PRF, 180 (Geneva: Droz, 1988)
Symp	*Symposium*
Symposium Antwerpen	*De Studie van de Middelnederlandse Letterkunde: Stand en Toekomst: Symposium Antwerpen 22–24 september 1988*, ed. F. P. van Oostrom and Frank Willaert, MSB, 14 (Hilversum: Verloren, 1989)
Symposium Odense	*Medieval Narrative: A Symposium: Proceedings of the Third International Symposium Organized by the Centre for the Study of Vernacular Literature in the Middle Ages, Held at Odense University on 20–21 November 1978*, ed. Hans Bekker-Nielsen, Peter Foote, Andreas Haarder, and Preben Meulengracht Sørensen (Odense: Odense University Press, 1979)
TAPS	Transactions of the American Philosophical Society
TATE	*Tategoto (Tokyo)*

TCE	*Thought Currents in English Literature (English Literary Society of Aoyama Gakuin University, Tokyo)*
Telling Tales	*Telling Tales: Medieval Narratives and the Folk Tradition*, ed. Francesca Canadé Sautman, Diana Conchado, and Giuseppe Carlo Di Scipio (New York: St Martin's, 1998)
Temps Reims	*Le Temps et la durée dans la littérature au moyen âge et à la Renaissance: Actes du Colloque organisé par le Centre de Recherche sur la Littérature du Moyen Age et de la Renaissance de l'Université de Reims (novembre 1984)* (Paris: Nizet, 1986)
TgA	Tübinger germanistische Arbeiten
Théories	*Théories et pratiques de l'écriture au moyen âge*, Actes du Colloque Palais du Luxembourg-Sénat, 5 et 6 mars 1987, ed. Emmanuèle Baumgartner and Christiane Marchello-Nizia, Littérales, 4 (Paris: Centre de Recherches du Département de Français de Paris X-Nanterre, Fontenay/St Cloud: Centre Espace-Temps-Histoire de l'E. N. S. de Fontenay/Saint-Cloud, 1988)
TLF	Textes Littéraires Français
TLL	*Travaux de Linguistique et de Littérature (Strasbourg)*
TMA	Typologie des Sources du Moyen Age Occidental
TNTL	*Tijdschrift voor Nederlandse Taal- en Letterkunde*
To-s	*Tosho-shinbun [The Book Review Press] (Tokyo)*
TR	*Translation Review*
Trad	*Traditio*
Translation	*Translation Theory and Practice in the Middle Ages*, ed. Jeanette Beer, SMC, 38 (Kalamazoo: Medieval Institute Publications, Western Michigan University, 1997)
Tris	*Tristania*
TrL	*Travaux de Littérature*
TSLL	*Texas Studies in Language and Literature*
Turnier	*Das ritterliche Turnier im Mittelalter: Beiträge zu einer vergleichenden Formen- und*

	Verhaltensgeschichte des Rittertums, ed. Josef Fleckenstein, VMPG, 80 (Göttingen: Vandenhoeck und Ruprecht, 1985)
TWAS	Twayne's World Authors Series
Twelfth Century	*The Twelfth Century*, ed. Bernard Levy and Sandro Sticca, Acta, 2 (Binghamton: The Center for Medieval and Early Renaissance Studies, State University of New York at Binghamton, 1975)
UBM	Utrechtse Bijdragen tot de Mediëvistiek
UCPMPh	University of California Publications in Modern Philology
UNCSRL	University of North Carolina Studies in the Romance Languages and Literatures
UPGC	Utrecht Publications in General and Comparative Literature
USFLQ	*The USF Language Quarterly*
UTQ	*University of Toronto Quarterly*
Verba	*Verba: Anuario Galego de Filoloxía*
Verbum	*Revista Catolică Verbum*
VerKA	Verhandelingen der Koninklijke Nederlandse Akademie van Wetenschappen: Afdeeling Letterkunde
Vernacular Poetics	*Vernacular Poetics in the Middle Ages*, ed. Lois Ebin, SMC, 16 (Kalamazoo: Medieval Institute, Western Michigan University, 1984)
Vieillesse	*Vieillesse et vieillissement au moyen âge*, Senefiance, 19 (Aix-en-Provence: CUER-MA, 1987)
Violence	*La Violence dans le monde médiéval*, Senefiance, 36 (Aix-en-Provence: CUER-MA, 1994)
Vitality	*The Vitality of the Arthurian Legend: A Symposium: Proceedings of the Twelfth International Symposium Organized by the Centre for the Study of Vernacular Literature in the Middle Ages Held at Odense University on 16–17 November, 1987* (Odense: Odense University Press, 1988)
VMPG	Veröffentlichungen des Max-Planck-Instituts für Geschichte

Voyage	*Voyage, quête, pèlerinage dans la littérature et la civilisation médiévales*, Senefiance, 2 (Aix-en-Provence: CUER-MA; Paris: Champion, 1976)
VR	*Vox Romanica*
Welt	*Weltliteratur (Die Gesellschaft der Weltliteratur)*
WF	Wege der Forschung
WFS	*Women in French Studies*
What Is Literature?	*What Is Literature? France 1100–1600*, ed. François Cornilliat, Ullrich Langer, and Douglas Kelly, ECAM, 7 (Lexington, KY: French Forum, 1993)
WODAN: EG-TS	WODAN: Greifswalder Beiträge zum Mittelalter-Études Médiévales de Greifswald – ser. 3: Tagungsbände und Sammelschriften-Actes de Colloques et Ouvrages Collectifs
WomS	*Women's Studies*
Word and Image	*Word and Image in Arthurian Literature*, ed. Keith Busby (New York: Garland, 1996)
W-S	*Wolfram-Studien*
WW	*Wirkendes Wort*
YB	*Ysgrifau Beirniadol*
YBK	*Yôroppa Bungaku Kenkû (Université de Tokyo-Waseda)*
YFS	*Yale French Studies*
YIS	*Yearbook of Italian Studies*
ZcP	*Zeitschrift für celtische Philologie*
ZdP	*Zeitschrift für deutsche Philologie*
ZfdA	*Zeitschrift für deutsches Altertum*
ZfG	*Zeitschrift für Germanistik*
ZfSL	*Zeitschrift für französische Sprache und Literatur*
ZLiLi	*Zeitschrift für Literaturwissenschaft und Linguistik*
ZrP	*Zeitschrift für romanische Philologie*
ZvL	*Zeitschrift für vergleichende Litteraturgeschichte*

A: EDITIONS

Several new series of editions of Chrétien's works have appeared since 1975. Only one, the 'Vinaver Chrétien' (Ai), so called because of support from the Eugène Vinaver Foundation, relies on collation of all known manuscripts; but progress has been slow since the two volumes that have appeared. On this project, see the annual reports of the Foundation in *BBSIA*. Ac16 and Ag use BNF fr 794 as base manuscript; Ah is more eclectic. Each provides only selected variants. The special place of BNF fr 794 is still in dispute, especially regarding corrections (see, for example, Ba22(D), Bb28, and Pa209), as it is judged defective, although the best manuscript today. Af includes not only new manuscripts reported since 1975, but also earlier identifications that are missing in the 1976 Bibliography.

a: Foerster's Editions

3   Important reviews of Foerster's editions (IV) *Yvain*. Add E. S. Sheldon, *RR*, 12 (1921), 297–317.

5   **Yvain, nach W. Foerster letzter Aufgabe in Auswahl bearbeitet und mit Einleitung and Glossar versehen von Rudolf Baehr*, 3d rev. ed. (Tübingen: Niemeyer, 1976).

See Ad7 Klüppelholz.

6   *Perceval ou Le Conte du Graal*, ed. Alfons Hilka, trans. Jean Dufournet (Paris: GF Flammarion, 1997). (L.166)

b: Roques's CFMA Editions

5   *Le Conte du Graal (Perceval)*, ed. Félix Lecoy, 2 vols, CFMA, 100, 103 (Paris: Champion, 1972–75). (XXVI.108, XXVII.231)

c: Separate Editions

See Eb2 Auguis.

Contains: 'Préambule du roman d'*Erec et Enide*,' p. 450; 'Description de l'ouïe, tirée du roman intitulé: *Le Chevalier au lion*,' p. 451; 'Autre morceau tiré du roman intitulé: *Le Chevalier au lion* [on 'cortois mort' and 'vilain vis'],' p. 452.

2 Keller, Adelbert, ed., *Li romans dou Chevalier au Leon: Bruckstücke aus einer vaticanischen Handschrift* (Tübingen: Fues, 1841); repr. in *Romvart: Beitræge zur Kunde mittelalterlicher Dichtung aus italiænischen Bibliotheken* (Mannheim: Bassermann; Paris: Renouart, 1844), pp. 512–75.

The 1841 edition is from Vatican Christina 1725. *Romvart* also contains a *chanson* from Vatican Christina 1490 (pp. 306–8), and a passage from the *Charrette*, Christina 1725 (pp. 453–512).

3 Tarbé, P., ed., *Le Roman du Chevalier de la charrette par Chrétien de Troyes et Godefroy de Laigny* (Rheims: Regnier, 1849).

Based on BNF fr. 794 (former Cangé 73).

4 Jonckbloet, W. J. A., ed., *Le Roman de la charrette d'après Gauthier Map et Chrestien de Troies* (The Hague: Belinfante, 1850).

5 Tarbé, P., ed., *Yvain* as far as 'Qu'il croit veoir la fontaine', pp. 114–33 in his edition of *Le Tornoiement de l'Antechrist* by Huon de Mery (Rheims: Regnier, 1851).

Based on BNF fr. 12560 (here Ms. 210).

6 Bekker, Immanuel, 'Des Chrestien von Troyes Erec und Enide,' *ZfdA*, 10 (1856), 373–550.

7 *Holland, Wilhelm L., ed., *Li romans dou Chevalier au lyon* (Hannover: Rumpler, 1862; 2nd ed., 1880; 3rd ed., Braunschweig, 1886; 4th ed., Berlin: Mayer und Müller, 1902, with glossary by Albert Schulze).

8 Potvin, Charles, ed., *Perceval le Gallois ou le Conte du Graal, publié d'après les manuscrits originaux*, 6 vols (Mons: Dequesne-Masquillier, 1866–71; repr. 3 vols, Geneva: Slatkine, 1977). (XXX.261)

Chrétien's *Perceval* in vol. 1.

9 Baist, [G.], ed., *Crestien's von Troyes Contes del Graal (Percevaus li Galois): Abdruck der Handschrift Paris, français 794* (Nicht in Buchhandel, [1909]; Freiburg/Br.: Ragoczy (K. Nick) [1912]).

10   Nolting-Hauff, Ilse, ed. and trans., *Yvain*, Klassische Texte des romanischen Mittelalters in zweisprachigen Ausgaben, 2 (Munich: Fink, 1983).

11   Riquer, Martín de, ed., *Li Contes del Graal / El Cuento del Grial*, Biblioteca Filológica (Barcelona: Festín de Esopo, 1985). (XLI.223)

12   *Gier, Albert, ed. and trans., *Erec et Enide – Erec und Enide*, Universal-Bibliothek, 8360 (Stuttgart: Reclam, 1987).

13   Pickens, Rupert T., 'Towards an Edition of Chrétien's *Li Contes del Graal*: Hilka vv. 1869–2024,' *Esp*, 27:1 (1987), 53–66. (XL.252)

14   Foulet, Alfred, and Karl D. Uitti, ed. and trans., *Le Chevalier de la charrette (Lancelot)*, Classiques Garnier (Paris: Bordas, 1989).

15   Atkinson, J. Keith, ed., *The 'Perceval' of Chrétien de Troyes According to Guiot* (Mont Nebo, Queensland: Boombana, 1991).

16   Poirion, Daniel, general ed., *Chrétien de Troyes: Œuvres complètes*, Bibliothèque de la Pléiade: Littérature Française du Moyen Age (Paris: Gallimard, 1994). (XLVII.243)
   A.   *Erec et Enide*, ed. and trans. Peter F. Dembowski.
   B.   *Cligès*, ed. and trans. Philippe Walter.
   C.   *Yvain ou Le Chevalier au lion*, ed. Karl D. Uitti and trans. Philippe Walter.
   D.   *Lancelot ou Le Chevalier de la charrette*, ed. and trans. Daniel Poirion.
   E.   *Perceval ou Le Conte du Graal*, ed. and trans. Daniel Poirion.
   F.   'Œuvres diverses': *Philomena, Guillaume d'Angleterre*, and two *chansons* attributed to Chrétien, ed. and trans. Anne Berthelot.

17   *Rousse, Michel, ed. and trans., *Erec et Enide: texte original et français moderne* (Paris: GF Flammarion, 1994).

18   Meyer, Kajsa, ed., *La copie de Guiot: fol. 79v–105r du manuscrit f. fr. 794 de la Bibliothèque Nationale: 'li chevaliers au lyeon' de Crestien de Troyes*, Faux Titre, 104 (Amsterdam: Rodopi, 1995). (XLVIII.606)
Diplomatic edition with a facsimile.

19   *Demaules, Mireille, ed., Daniel Poirion, trans., *Lancelot, ou, Le Chevalier de la charrette*, Folio Classique (Paris: Gallimard, 1996).

See Ec9 Carroll.

d: Editions of Disputed Attribution (see W)

6   *Three Ovidian Tales of Love ('Piramus et Tisbé', 'Narcisus et Dané', and 'Philomena et Procné')*, ed. and trans. Raymond J. Cormier, GLML, A26 (New York: Garland, 1986). (XLI.327)

7   **Guillaume d'Angleterre: der altfranzösische Text nach Bd. IV/2 der Sämtlichen Werke herausgegeben von W. Foerster*, ed. and trans. with an Introduction by Heinz Klüppelholz, Klassische Texte des romanischen Mittelalters in zweisprachigen Ausgaben, 24 (Munich: Fink, 1987). (XL.512)

8   *Guillaume d'Angleterre*, ed. A. J. Holden, TLF, 360 (Geneva: Droz, 1988).

See Ac16(F) Poirion.

9   *Pyrame et Thisbé, Narcisse, Philomena: trois contes du XIIᵉ siècle français imités d'Ovide*, ed. Emmanuèle Baumgartner, Folio Classique, 3448 (Paris: Gallimard, 2000).

e: The *Chansons*

5   Roquefort-Flaméricourt, B. de, *De l'état de la poésie françoise dans les XIIᵉ et XIIIᵉ siècles* (Paris: Fournier, 1815).
'Joie ne guerredons d'amours,' pp. 72–73.

See Eb2 Auguis.
First two stanzas of 'Joie ne guerredon d'amours,' p. 453.

6   Hasselt, André van, *Essai sur l'histoire de la poésie française en Belgique*, Mémoires Couronnés par l'Académie Royale de Belgique, 13 (Brussels: Hayez, 1838).
'Joie ne guerredon d'amors,' pp. 71–72.

7   Dinaux, Arthur, *Les trouvères de la Flandre et du Tournaisis*, Trouvères, Jongleurs et Ménestrés du Nord de la France et du Midi de la Belgique, 2 (Paris: Téchener, 1839; repr. Geneva: Slatkine, 1969).
'Joie ne guerredon d'amors,' pp. 349–50. Questions attribution.

See Ac2 Keller.

8   Wackernagel, Wilhelm, ed., *Altfranzœzische Lieder und Leiche aus Handschriften zu Bern und Neuenburg* (Basel: Schweighauserische Buchhandlung, 1846).
'Amors tenson,' pp. 15–16; 'De iolit cuer,' pp. 16–17; 'Damors ki mait,' pp. 17–19.

9   Tarbé, Prosper, ed., *Les chansonniers de Champagne aux XIIe et XIIIe siècles*, Collection des Poètes de Champagne Antérieurs au XVIe siècle, 9 (Rheims: [Regnier], 1850; repr. Geneva: Slatkine, 1980).
See pp. xxviii–xxix and 38–39.

10   Mätzner, Eduard, ed., *Altfranzösische Lieder berichtigt und erläutert mit Bezugnahme auf die provenzalische, altitalienische und mittelhochdeutsche Liederdichtung nebst einem altfranzösischen Glossar* (Berlin: Dümmler, 1853; repr. Wiesbaden: Sändig, 1969).
Pp. 63–65, 258–62: 'Damour ki ma tolu a moi'.

11   Cremonesi, Carla, ed., *Lirica francese del medio evo* (Milan: Istituto Editoriale Cisalpino, 1955), pp. 75–81.

12   Zai, Marie-Claire, ed., *Les chansons courtoises de Chrétien de Troyes: édition critique avec introduction, notes et commentaire*, EH:F, 27 (Bern: H. Lang; Frankfurt/M.: P. Lang, 1974).
Contains: 'Amors, tençon et bataille', 'D'Amors, qui m'a tolu a moi', 'De joli cuer chanterai', 'Quant li dous estez decline', 'Joie ne guerredons d'Amors', and 'Soufrés, maris et si ne vous anuit'.

See Ac16(F) Poirion.

See Ah2 *Cligés* and Ah6.

f: New or Newly Analysed Manuscripts

14   Potvin, Ch., 'Le Perceval de Chrestien de Troyes: un manuscrit inconnu. – Fragment unique de ce manuscript,' *Jahrbuch für romanische und englische Sprache und Literatur*, 5 (1864), 25–50.
The fragment edited contains the *Bliocadran* and the first twelve lines of *Perceval*.

15   Stengel, Edm., 'Sul codice riccardiano 2943 contenente un nuovo testo del *Percheval* di Chrétien de Troyes,' *Rivista di Filologia Romanza*, 1 (1872), 192–93.

16   Kelle, Johann, 'Perceval le Gallois,' *ZfdA*, 18 (1875), 314–17.
Prague Univ. Bibl. I.E.35 (*Perceval* fragments).

See Ba4 Rahilly.

See Ba8 Rahilly.

17 Gregory, Stewart, 'Fragment inédit du *Cligés* de Chrétien de Troyes: le manuscrit de l'Institut de France,' *Rom*, 106 (1985), 254–69. (XL.25)
Bibl. de l'Institut de France 6138.

See Ba11 Nixon.
On Amsterdam Univ. 446 and Brussels BR IV.837.

18 Gregory, Stewart, and Claude Luttrell, 'Les fragments d'Oxford du *Cligés* de Chrétien de Troyes,' *Rom*, 113 (1992–95), 320–48. (XLVIII.301)

See Bb70 Meyer.

g: Garland Editions

1 *Erec and Enide*, ed. and trans. Carleton W. Carroll, Introduction by William W. Kibler, GLML, A25 (New York: Garland, 1987). (XL.249)

2 *Lancelot, or, The Knight of the Cart (Le Chevalier de la charrete)*, ed. and trans. William W. Kibler, GLML, A1 (New York: Garland, 1981). (XXXIV.101)

3 *The Knight of the Lion, or Yvain (Le Chevalier au lion)*, ed. and trans. William W. Kibler, GLML, A48 (New York: Garland, 1985). (XXXIX.209)

4 *Li Contes del Graal (Perceval)*, ed. Rupert T. Pickens, trans. William W. Kibler, GLML, A62 (New York: Garland, 1989). (XLII.267)

See Ad6 Cormier.

h: 'Lettres Gothiques' Editions

1 *Erec et Enide: édition critique d'après le manuscrit B. N. fr. 1376*, ed. and trans. Jean-Marie Fritz (Paris: Livre de Poche, 1992). (XLV.155)

2 *Cligès: édition critique du manuscrit B. N. fr. 12560*, ed. and trans. Charles Méla and Olivier Collet, *Suivi des 'chansons courtoises' de Chrétien de Troyes*, ed. and trans. Marie-Claire Gérard-Zai (Paris: Livre de Poche, 1994).

3 *Le Chevalier de la charrette: édition critique d'après les manuscrits existants*, ed. and trans. Charles Méla (Paris: Livre de Poche, 1992). (XLV.154).

4 *Le Chevalier au lion ou le Roman d'Yvain: édition critique d'après le manuscrit B. N. fr. 1433*, ed. and trans. David F. Hult (Paris: Livre de Poche, 1994).

5 *Le Conte du Graal ou le Roman de Perceval: édition du manuscrit 354 de Berne*, ed. and trans. Charles Méla (Paris: Livre de Poche, 1990). (XLIII.155).

6 *Romans suivis des Chansons avec en appendice, Philomena*, Classiques Modernes (Paris: La Pochothèque (Le Livre de Poche), 1994). (XLVII.244)
Collects Ah1–5 in one volume.

i: The 'Vinaver Chrétien' Editions

1 *Cligés*, ed. Stewart Gregory and Claude Luttrell, AS, 28 (Cambridge: Brewer; Rochester, NY: Boydell & Brewer, 1993). (XLVI.403)

2 *Le Roman de Perceval ou Le Conte du Graal: édition critique d'après tous les manuscrits*, ed. Keith Busby (Tübingen: Niemeyer, 1993). (XLVI.32)

B: PROBLEMS OF EDITING

For a variety of reasons considerable controversy has arisen during the last quarter-century regarding textual editing, selection and interpretation of manuscripts, and the significance of variant manuscripts vis-à-vis the 'best' manuscript or that deemed closest to what the author wrote. Debate turns on the traditional conflict between Lachmanian and Bédiériste editing, or consultation of all manuscripts in order to recover as nearly as possible the original author's version over against reliance on a single manuscript (with perhaps variants from a few other 'good' manuscripts). The differences between a standard edition, critical or not, and manuscript layout and illustrations have received attention (see also Ld and X). Moreover, the reason or reasons for which a specific manuscript was copied is important in evaluating reception.

a: The Manuscript Tradition

4   Rahilly, Leonard J., 'La tradition manuscrite [...]'. (XXVII.255)

5   Holland, Wilhelm Ludwig, 'Über eine Handschrift: Crestiens Gedichte Li Contes del Graal,' *Germania*, 2 (1857), 426–27.
Mons ms. 4568.

See Pb95 Heller.

6   Ketrick, Paul J., *The Relation of Golagros and Gawane to the Old French Perceval* (Washington, DC: The Catholic University of America, 1931).
See Chap. 4.

See Pb103 Rachbauer.

See Pe1 Fuehrer.

See Pb114 Frank.

7 François, Charles, 'Perrot de Neele, Jehan Madot et le ms. BN fr. 375,' *RBPH*, 41 (1963), 761–79.

8 Rahilly, Leonard J., 'La tradition manuscrite du *Chevalier au lion* et le manuscrit Garrett 125,' *Rom*, 99 (1978), 1–30. (XXXI.300)

9 Tekaat, Manfred, *Konsonantengrapheme und ihre Phonie in der handschriftlichen Überlieferung des 'Erec' Chrétiens de Troyes*, diss. Cologne (Aachen: Mainz, 1978). (XXXIII.73)

See Bb38 Woledge.

See Cb15 Woledge.

10 Rickard, Peter, 'Système ou arbitraire? Quelques réflexions sur la soudure des mots dans les manuscrits français du Moyen Age,' *Rom*, 103 (1982), 470–512.
Includes BNF fr. 12576 (*Perceval*) and BNF fr. 794 (*Erec et Enide*).

See Ld3 Huot.

11 Nixon, Terry, '*Amadas et Ydoine* and *Erec et Enide*: Reuniting *membra disjecta* from Early Old French Manuscripts,' *Viator*, 18 (1987), 227–51. (XL.306)
Amsterdam Univ. 446 and Brussels BR IV. 837.

12 Petit, Aimé, '*Miaus vaut lor ris et lor baisiers / Que ne fait Londres ne Poitiers*: tradition manuscrite et critique littéraire: note sur le *Roman de Thèbes* et *Cligès*,' *Bien dire*, 5 (1987), 123–28. (XL.55)

13 Dees, Anthonij, 'Analyse par l'ordinateur de la tradition manuscrite du *Cligès* de Chrétien de Troyes,' in *Actes Trèves*, vol. 6, pp. 62–75. (XLI.588)

14 Mancarella, P. Giovan Battista, 'Li Romanz de Perceval: note al ms. 354 di Berna,' *Quaderni del Dipartimento di Lingue e Letterature Straniere dell'Università di Lecce*, 10 (1998), 193–212. (XLVI.563)

15 Short, Ian, 'L'avènement du texte vernaculaire: la mise en recueil,' in *Théories*, pp. 11–24.

See Pa209 Gallais, vol. 1, pp. 113–433.

16 Cerquiglini, Bernard, 'Szerzői variánsok és másolói variancia,' *Heli*, 3–4 (1989), 363–77. (XLIII.329)

17 Mulken, Margot van, 'Het Raadsel der "scriptoria": hun rol in de tekstgeschiedenis,' *Rapports*, 60 (1990), 64–69. (XLIII.430)
Treats *Perceval*.

18 Carroll, Carleton W., 'A Reappraisal of the Relationship between Two Manuscripts of *Erec et Enide*,' *NFS*, 30:2 (1991), 34–42. (XLIV.95)
The two mss. are BNF fr. 375 and BNF fr. 1376.

See Jb42 Helm.

19 Walters, Lori, 'The Creation of a "Super Romance": Paris, Bibliothèque Nationale, fonds français, MS 1433,' *AY*, 1 (1991), 3–25 + 13 plates. (XLIV.338)

20 Carroll, Carleton W., 'Un fragment inédit d'*Erec et Enide* et sa place dans la tradition manuscrite,' *Scriptorium*, 46 (1992), 242–50 + 1 plate. (XLVI.2)
Cf. Af2.

21 Busby, Keith, 'The Text of Chrétien's *Perceval* in MS London, College of Arms, Arundel XIV,' in *Anglo-Norman Anniversary Essays*, ed. Ian Short, ANTS, 2 (London: Anglo-Norman Text Society, 1993), pp. 75–85.

22 *Les Manuscrits de Chrétien de Troyes: The Manuscripts of Chrétien de Troyes*, ed. Keith Busby, Terry Nixon, Alison Stones, and Lori Walters, Faux Titre, 71–72, 2 vols (Amsterdam: Rodopi, 1993). (XLVI.623)
    Vol. I:
    A.   Alison Stones, 'General Introduction,' pp. 1–8.
    B.   Terry Nixon, 'List of Manuscripts,' pp. 9–15.
        Listed by current shelf order, by date of attribution, and by romance text.
    C.   Terry Nixon, 'Romance Collections and the Manuscripts of Chrétien de Troyes,' pp. 17–25. (XLVI.638)
    D.   Tony Hunt, 'Chrestien de Troyes: The Textual Problem,' pp. 27–40. Slightly revised Bb33 Hunt.
    E.   Margot van Mulken, '*Perceval* and Stemmata,' pp. 41–48. (XLVI.637)
    F.   Keith Busby, 'The Scribe of MSS *T* and *V* of Chrétien's *Perceval* and its *Continuations*,' pp. 49–65. (XLVI.621)
    G.   Stewart Gregory and Claude Luttrell, 'The Manuscripts of *Cligés*,' pp. 67–95. (XLVI.631)
    H.   Françoise Gasparri, Geneviève Hasenohr, and Christine Ruby, 'De l'écriture à la lecture: réflexion sur les manuscrits d'*Erec et Enide*,' pp. 97–148. (XLVI.628)

I. Roger Middleton, 'Coloured Capitals in the Manuscripts of *Erec et Enide*,' pp. 149–93. (XLVI.635)

J. Patricia Stirnemann, 'Some Champenois Vernacular Manuscripts and the Manerius Style of Illumination,' pp. 195–226. (XLVI.648)

K. Alison Stones, 'The Illustrated Chrétien Manuscripts and their Artistic Context,' pp. 227–322. (XLVI.649)

L. Elizabeth Burin, 'Pierre Sala's Manuscript of *Le Chevalier au lion*,' pp. 323–30. (XLVI.620)

M. Lori Walters, 'The Use of Multi-Compartment Opening Miniatures in the Illustrated Manuscripts of Chrétien de Troyes,' pp. 331–50. (XLVI.650)

N. Keith Busby, 'The Illustrated Manuscripts of Chrétien's *Perceval*,' pp. 351–63.
Slightly revised Xa8 Busby.

O. Keith Busby, 'Text, Miniature, and Rubric in the *Continuations* of Chrétien's *Perceval*,' pp. 365–76. (XLVI.622)

P. Angelica Rieger, 'Le programme iconographique du *Perceval* montpelliérain, BI, Sect. Méd. H 249 (*M*), avec la description détaillée du manuscrit,' pp. 377–435. (XLVI.643)

Q. Lori Walters, 'The Image of Blanchefleur in Montpellier, BI, Sect. Méd. H 249,' pp. 437–55. (XLVI.651)

R. Laurence Harf-Lancner, 'L'image et le fantastique dans les manuscrits des romans de Chrétien de Troyes,' pp. 457–88. (XLVI.632)

S. Emmanuèle Baumgartner, 'Les scènes du Graal et leur illustration dans les manuscrits du *Conte du Graal* et des *Continuations*,' pp. 489–503. (XLVI.618)

Vol. II:

T. Terry Nixon, 'Catalogue of Manuscripts,' pp. 1–85.

U. Roger Middleton, 'Index of Former Owners,' pp. 87–176.

V. Roger Middleton, 'Additional Notes on the History of Selected Manuscripts,' pp. 177–243.

W. Michel Pastoureau, 'Les armoiries arthuriennes,' pp. 245–47. (XLVI.641)

X. Keith Busby, Laurence Harf-Lancner, Terry Nixon, Alison Stones, and Lori Walters, 'Appendices: I. Other Contents of the Manuscripts of Chrétien de Troyes; II. Modern Copies of Medieval Manuscripts Containing the Romances of Chrétien de Troyes; III. Manuscripts Containing Texts Attributed to Chrétien de Troyes; IV. Rubrics and Subjects of Illuminations in the Romances,' pp. 249–303.

Y. Keith Busby, Terry Nixon, Alison Stones, and Françoise Vielliard, 'Bibliography: A. List of Romances of Chrétien de Troyes in Modern Editions; B. Works Cited,' pp. 305–41.

Z. Alison Stones, 'List of Colour Plates,' pp. 343–49, and 'List of Illustrations,' pp. 350–541.

ZZ. Terry Nixon, 'Index of Manuscripts Cited,' pp. 543–53.

23   Gehrke, Pamela, *Saints and Scribes: Medieval Hagiography in its Manuscript Context*, UCPMPh, 126 (Berkeley: University of California Press, 1993).
On BNF fr. 1374, containing *Cligés*, see chap. 3: '"Literature in the True Sense": Aristocratic Virtues and Textual Travels.'

24   Besamusca, Bart, 'De vele gezichten van Chrétien de Troyes: naar aanleiding van "Les manuscrits de Chrétien de Troyes",' *Madoc*, 8 (1994), 233–41. (XLVII.528)

See Xa18–19 Hindman.

See Fe25 Mattiacci.

25   Mulken, Margot van, 'La tradition manuscrite du *Perceval*,' in *Actas Santiago*, vol. 7, pp. 43–56.

26   Trachsler, Richard, 'Le recueil Paris, BN fr. 12603,' *CN*, 54 (1994), 189–211.

See Pa269 Walters.
On Chantilly ms. 472.

27   Wolfgang, Lenora D., 'Chrétien's *Lancelot*: The Fragments of Manuscript 6138 of the Institut de France,' in *Studies Kelly*, pp. 559–74. (XLVII.606)

See Gb125(F) Gouttebroze.

28   Klein, Jan Willem, '(Middelnederlandse) handschriften: produktieomstandigheiden, soorten, functies,' *Queeste*, 2 (1995), 1–30. (XLVIII.629).
For their relation to Chrétien mss, see pp. 29–30.

See Pa291 Servet.

29   Charpentier, Hélène, 'Notes sur le(s) texte(s) du *Conte du Graal* dans quelques éditions de référence,' *Op. cit.*, 11 (1998), 5–13. (LII.219)

See Db71 Hult.

30   Dees, Anthonij, 'La tradition manuscrite du *Perceval* de Chrétien de Troyes,' *RLingR*, 62 (1998), 417–42 (LI.233); and 'Epilogue,' *RLingR*, 63 (1999), 503–08. (LII.226)

See La47 Pickens.

31 Vielliard, Françoise, 'Le manuscrit avant l'auteur: diffusion et conservation de la littérature médiévale en ancien français (XIIe-XIIIe siècles),' *TrL*, 11 (1998), 39–53.

32 Wolfgang, Lenora D., 'The Manuscripts of the *Chevalier de la Charrette* (*Lancelot*) of Chrétien de Troyes: Preliminary Remarks to a New Edition: The Care of MS. *E*,' in *Mélanges Ménard*, vol. 2, pp. 1477–88. (LI.319)

33 Carroll, Carleton W., 'The Knights of the Round Table in the Manuscripts of *Erec et Enide*,' in *Essays Lacy*, pp. 117–27.

34 Varvaro, Alberto, trans. Stéphanie Bertrand, 'Élaboration des textes et modalités du récit dans la littérature française médiévale,' *Rom*, 119 (2001), 1–75.
See esp. pp. 31–35.

b: Textual Editing

9 Bar, Francis, 'Sur un passage [...]'; repr. in his *Etudes littéraires et linguistiques* (Caen: Université de Caen, UER des Sciences de l'Homme, 1985), pp. 47–50. (XXXVIII.179)

16 Mussafia, Adolf, 'Zum französischen Erec,' *Germania*, 8 (1863), 51–54.

17 Huet, G., '*Ogre* dans le *Conte du Graal* de Chrétien de Troyes,' *Rom*, 37 (1908), 301–05.

See Wa14 Gay.

18 Huck, F., 'Zum Yvain (ed. Foerster) V. 385–6,' *ZrP*, 38 (1914), 352–54.

19 Schulze, Alfred, 'Textkritisches zum Percevalroman hrg. von A. Hilka,' *ZfSL*, 59 (1935), 75–90.

20 Fourquet, Jean, 'Fautes communes ou innovations communes?,' *Rom*, 70 (1948), 85–95. (I.93)

21 Castellani, Arrigo, *Bédier avait-il raison? La méthode de Lachmann dans les éditions de textes du Moyen Age*, Discours Universitaires, n. s. 20 (Fribourg: Éditions Universitaires, 1957).

22   Marichal, Robert, 'La critique des textes,' in *L'Histoire et ses méthodes*, ed. Charles Samaran, Encyclopédie de la Pléiade, 11 (Paris: Gallimard, 1961), pp. 1247–1366.

23   Dufournet, J., 'Chrétien de Troyes: *Le Chevalier de la charrette* (à propos d'un livre récent),' *MA*, 70 (1964), 505–23. (XVIII.131)
On Jean Frappier's translation of the *Charrette* (see *BBSIA* XV.101 and Bb26).

24   Galliot, Marcel, *Etudes d'ancien français: Moyen Age et XVIe siècle. Licence–CAPES–Agrégation* (Paris: Didier, 1967).
See pp. 126–39 on Chrétien's *Yvain*, v. 2852–80 (ed. Roques).

25   Cocito, Luciana, 'Per un'edizione critica del *Cligès*,' *Omaggio a Camillo Guerrieri-Crocetti* (Genoa: Bozzi, 1971), pp. 123–33.
Preference for ms. *S* = BNF fr. 1374; cf. Bb10.

26   Frappier, Jean, 'Remarques sur le texte du *Chevalier de la charrette*,' in *Mélanges Rostaing*, 2 vols (Liège: Association Inter-communale de Mécanographie, 1974), vol. 1, pp. 317–31. (XXVII.97)
On Ab3 v. 209–11, 360–61, 1546, 1837–39, 1888, 2164, 3124–29, 4232, 4275–76, 5070, 6554, 6894, 6918–19.

27   Delbouille, Maurice, 'La philologie médiévale et la critique textuelle,' in *Actes Laval*, vol. 1, pp. 57–73.

28   Reid, T. B. W., 'Chrétien de Troyes and the Scribe Guiot,' *MAe*, 45 (1976), 1–19. (XXIX.311)

29   Foulet, Alfred, 'Guinevere's Enigmatic Words: Chrétien's *Lancelot*, vv. 211–213,' in *Misrahi Volume*, pp. 175–80. (XXXII.175)

30   Marchello-Nizia, Christiane, 'Ponctuation et "unités de lecture" dans les manuscrits médiévaux ou: je ponctue, tu lis, il théorise,' *LF*, 40 (1978), 32–44.

31   Rahilly, Leonard J., 'Mario Roques avait-il raison? Une question d'amour courtois dans le *Chevalier de la charrette*, de Chrétien de Troyes,' *Rom*, 99 (1978), 400–4. (XXXI.301)
With Princeton Garrett 125 as control, discusses vv. 30 and 32, 209–11, 240, 972, 1128, 1225, 1536–37, 2324–27, 2336–39, 2961, 2964, 3700, 3718 in Roques's edition.

32   Foulet, Alfred, and Mary Blakely Speer, *On Editing Old French Texts*, ECAM, 1 (Lawrence: Regents Press of Kansas, 1979). (XXXII.176)

Extensive bibliography with critical history; includes commentary on Chrétien manuscripts. See also: Franca Brambilla Ageno, *L'edizione critica dei testi volgari*, Medioevo e Umanesimo, 22 (Padua: Antenore, 1975; 2nd ed., 1984).

33 Hunt, Tony, 'Chrestien de Troyes: The Textual Problem,' *FS*, 33 (1979), 257–71. (XXXII.420)
On BNF fr. 794 and editions based on it. Rev. version in Ba 22(D) Hunt.

34 Ménard, Philippe, 'Note sur le texte du *Conte du graal*,' *Mélanges Jonin*, pp. 447–57; repr. in Dc29. (XXXII. 357 *bis*)

35 Woledge, Brian, 'Traits assurés par la rime ou par la mesure: l'exemple de Guiot copiste de Chrétien,' *Mélanges Jonin*, pp. 717–27. (XXXII.369)

36 *Bettini Biagini, Giuliana, *'Le Chevalier de la charrette' di Chrétien de Troyes: problemi di edizione* (Messina: La Grafica, 1980).

37 Speer, Mary B., 'Wrestling with Change: Old French Textual Criticism and *Mouvance*,' *Olifant*, 7 (1980), 311–26. (XXXVI.190)

38 Woledge, Brian, 'Les couples *com/con* et *dom/don* chez le copiste Guiot,' in *Mélanges Foulon*, vol. 1, pp. 403–08. (XXXIII.381)

39 Dembowski, Peter, 'Intertextualité et critique des textes,' *Littérature*, 41 (1981), 17–29. (XXXV.315)

See Hf45 Shirt.

40 Hicks, Eric, 'Éloge de la machine: transcription, édition, génération de textes,' *Rom*, 103 (1982), 88–107. (XXXV.323)

41 Amazawa, Taijirô, 'On Certain Variants in Chrétien de Troyes's *Conte del Graal*,' *MGRS*, 341 (1983), 1–21. (XXXVI.545)
In Japanese.

42 Cerquiglini, Bernard, 'Éloge de la variante,' *Langages*, 69 (1983), 25–35.

43 Speer, Mary B., 'Textual Criticism Redivivus,' *Esp*, 23:1 (1983), 38–48. (XXXVII.465)
Treats Guiot pp. 46–48.

44 Foulet, Alfred, and Karl D. Uitti, 'Chrétien's "Laudine": *Yvain*, vv. 2148–55,' *RPh*, 37 (1983–84), 293–302. (XXXVII.372)

45 Kibler, William W., '*Le Chevalier de la charrete* de Mario Roques: corrections,' *Rom*, 105 (1984), 558–64. (XXXIX.647)
Also treats Foerster's edition.

46 Reid, T. B. W., 'The Right to Emend,' in *Studies Reid*, pp. 1–32. (XXXVII.183)
On *Erec* 15–17, 2084–87 (pp. 20–23).

47 Uitti, Karl D., 'Autant en emporte *li funs*: remarques sur le prologue du *Chevalier de la charrette* de Chrétien de Troyes,' *Rom*, 105 (1984), 270–91. (XXXVIII.273)

48 Woledge, Brian, 'The Problem of Editing *Yvain*,' in *Studies Reid*, pp. 254–67. (XXXVII.192)

See Na.f26 Woledge.

49 Amazawa, Taijirô, 'On Verse 6501 in the *Conte del Graal*,' *Gengo*, 3 (1985), 36–46. (XXXIX.183).
In Japanese.

See Ea37(G) Foulet.

50 *Critique et édition de textes: Actes du XVIIe Congrès International de Linguistique et de Philologie Romanes (Aix-en-Provence, 29 août–3 septembre 1983)*, vol. 9 (Aix-en-Provence: Université de Provence, 1986).
    A.   Anthony J. Holden, 'L'édition des textes médiévaux,' pp. 375–82.
    B.   Jacques Monfrin, 'Problèmes d'éditions de textes,' pp. 351–64.

51 Hult, David F., 'Lancelot's Two Steps: A Problem in Textual Criticism,' *Spec*, 61 (1986), 836–58. (XXXIX.279)
Cf. Bb55 Uitti and Bb56 Hult.

52 Woledge, Brian, *Commentaire sur 'Yvain' ('Le chevalier au lion')* de Chrétien de Troyes. I: vv. 1–3411, II: vv. 3412–6808*, PRF, 170 and 186 (Geneva: Droz, 1986–88). (XL.508, XLI.321)

53 Uitti, Karl D., ed., *The Poetics of Textual Criticism: The Old French Example*, in *Esp*, 27:1 (1987).
    A.   Karl D. Uitti, 'Preface', pp. 5–14. (XL.326)
    B.   Alfred Foulet, 'On Grid-Editing Chrétien de Troyes,' pp. 15–23. (XL.276)
    C.   Lionel J. Friedman, 'Embedded Format and Extra-Text,' pp. 101–10.
    See also Ac13 Pickens, Db35 Richards.

54 Dembowski, Peter F., 'Quelques considérations sur les titres littéraires en France au Moyen Age,' in *Miscellanea Gasca Queirazza*, vol. 1, pp. 251–69.
See pp. 261–65, 269.

55 Uitti, Karl D., with Alfred Foulet, 'On Editing Chrétien de Troyes: Lancelot's Two Steps and Their Context,' *Spec*, 63 (1988), 271–92. (XL.325)

See Ba16 Cerquiglini.

56 Hult, David F., 'Steps Forward and Steps Backward: More on Chrétien's *Lancelot*,' *Spec*, 64 (1989), 307–16. (XLII.316)

See Kd110 Gregory.

57 Hult, David F., 'Reading It Right: The Ideology of Text Editing,' in Dd4, pp. 113–30.

58 Masters, Bernadette A., 'The Distribution, Destruction and Dislocation of Authority in Medieval Literature and its Modern Derivatives,' *RR*, 82 (1991), 270–85.

59 Wolfgang, Lenora D., 'Chrétien's *Lancelot*: Love and Philology,' *RMS*, 17 (1991), 3–17. (XLIV.136)

See Ba21 Busby.

60 Cocito, Luciana, 'Un'ipotesi per uno "stemma codicum",' *Letterature*, 16 (1993), 7–13.
Based on *Cligés*.

61 Dembowski, Peter F., 'Critique textuelle, critique littéraire et l'art narratif en ancien français,' in *Actes Zurich*, pp. 225–49.

62 Dembowski, Peter F., 'De nouveau: *Erec et Enide*, Chrétien et Guiot,' in *Hommage Dufournet*, vol. 1, pp. 409–17. (XLVI.320)

63 Dembowski, Peter F., 'The "French" Tradition of Textual Philology and its Relevance to the Editing of Medieval Texts,' *MP*, 90 (1993), 512–32.

64 Frank, Roberta, ed., *The Politics of Editing Medieval Texts: Papers Given at the Twenty-Seventh Annual Conference on Editorial Problems, University of Toronto 1–2 November 1991* (New York: AMS, 1993).
See Ross G. Arthur, 'On Editing Sexually Offensive Old French Texts,' pp. 19–64.

65 Mulken, Margot van, *The Manuscript Tradition of the 'Perceval' of Chrétien de Troyes: A Stemmatological and Dialectological Approach*, diss. Amsterdam (Amsterdam: M. J. P. van Mulken, 1993). (XLVI.636)

66 Perugi, Maurizio, 'Patologia testuale e fattori dinamici seriali nella tradizione dell'*Yvain* di Chrétien de Troyes,' *SM*, ser. 3, 34 (1993), 841–60. (XLVII.467)

67 Uitti, Karl D., 'Poetico-Literary Dimensions and the Critical Editing of Medieval Texts: The Example of Old French,' in *What Is Literature?*, pp. 143–79.

68 Dembowski, Peter F., 'Textual and Other Problems of the Epilogue of *Erec et Enide*,' in *Studies Kelly*, pp. 113–27. (XLVII.544)

69 Uitti, Karl D., and Gina Greco, 'Computerization, Canonicity and the Old French Scribe: The Twelfth and Thirteenth Centuries,' *Text*, 6 (1994), 133–52. (L.576)

70 *Meyer, Kajsa, *De Guiot à Crestien de Troyes: la critique textuelle d'un manuscrit d'Yvain*, Noter og Kommentarer, 108 (Odense: Odense Universitet, 1995).

71 Speer, Mary B., 'Old French Literature,' in *Scholarly Editing: A Guide to Research*, ed. D. C. Greetham (New York: Modern Language Association of America, 1995), pp. 382–416.

72 Uitti, Karl D., 'A la recherche du texte perdu: réflexions sur la textualité en ancien français,' in *Etudes Poirion*, pp. 476–86.

73 Luttrell, Claude, 'Southampton dans le *Cligés* de Chrétien de Troyes,' *Rom*, 114 (1996), 231–34. (XLIX.168)

74 Salemans, Ben J. P., 'Cladistics or the Resurrection of the Method of Lachmann: On Building the Stemma of *Yvain*,' in *Studies in Stemmatology*, ed. Pieter van Reenan and Margot van Mulken, with Janet Dyk (Amsterdam: Benjamins, 1996), pp. 3–70.

75 Greco, Gina L., Toby Paff, and Peter W. Shoemaker, 'The *Charrette* Project: Manipulating Text and Image in an Electronic Archive of a Medieval Manuscript Tradition,' *ComH*, 30 (1997), 407–15.

76 Beltrami, Pietro G., 'Chrétien de Troyes, la rima leonina e qualche osservazione sui critici metrici nelle scelte testuali,' in *Filologia classica e filologia romanza: esperienze ecdotiche a confronto: Atti del*

Convegno Roma 25–27 maggio 1995, Incontri di studio, 2 (Spoleto: Centro Italiano di Studi sull'Alto Medioevo, 1998), pp. 193–218.

77 *Bianchini, Simonetta, 'Chrétien de Troyes: dieci anni di edizioni recenti,' *Critica del Testo*, 1:3 (1998), 1035–51. (LI.551)

See Hg109 Blons-Pierre, pp. 167–86: 'Du château de Gornemant au château du roi Pêcheur dans la copie de Guiot et les autres manuscrits du *Conte du Graal*: texte et iconographie.'

78 Lepage, Yvan G., 'La tradition éditoriale d'œuvres majeures: de la *Chanson de Roland* au *Testament* de Villon,' in *Mélanges Demarolle*, pp. 39–51.
See pp. 44–48.

See Pa321 Colombo Timelli.

79 Mulken, M. van, 'Les changements de parenté dans le *Cligès* de Chrétien de Troyes,' in *I nuovi orizzonti della filologia: ecdotica, critica testuale, editoria scientifica e mezzi informatici elettronici, Accademia Nazionale dei Lincei in Collaborazione con l'Associazione Internazionale per gli Studi di Lingua e Letteratura Italiana (Roma, 27–29 maggio 1998)*, Atti dei Convegni Lincei, 151 (Rome: Accademia Nazionale dei Lincei, 1999), pp. 103–14.

C: BIBLIOGRAPHY

Most annual bibliographies listed in the 1976 Bibliography continue to appear, although their coverage can be uneven. Interest in Chrétien de Troyes, notably in Eastern Europe, Central and South America, and parts of Africa, has not always been recognized or identified. The contributions from Japan have grown remarkably, although much of it has gone unnoticed or unread in Western Europe and North America.

a: Annual and Other Serials

9 *International Medieval Bibliography 400–1500* (Leeds: University of Leeds; Turnhout: Brepols).
Since 1967.

10 *Encomia: Bibliographical Bulletin of the International Courtly Literature Society.*
Since 1976.

b: General Bibliographies (see also Vb)

6 Bossuat, Robert, *Manuel bibliographique* [...] Supplément III:1, *Les origines. Les Légendes épiques, Le roman courtois*, prepared by Françoise Vielliard and Jacques Monfrin (Paris: Editions du CNRS, 1986). (XXXIX.679)
§§3202–3896 include material within the scope of Chrétien bibliography.

See Sa60 Baron and Davis.

8 Mieder, Wolfgang, 'The Proverb and Romance Literature,' *RomN*, 15 (1973–74), 610–21.
See p. 617.

See Qa36 Erickson.

9   Kelly, Douglas, *Chrétien de Troyes: An Analytic Bibliography*, RBC, 17 (London: Grant & Cutler, 1976). (XXX.347)

10   Zotter, Hans, *Bibliographie faksimilierter Handschriften* (Graz: Akademische Druck- u. Verlagsanstalt, 1976). (XXXI.51)
See § 9 (Annonay ms.).

11   Buridant, Claude, 'Sélection bibliographique: études sur les proverbes,' *RSH*, 163 (1976–77), 431–36.

12   Neubuhr, Elfriede, *Bibliographie zu Hartmann von Aue*, Bibliographien zur deutschen Literatur des Mittelalters, 6 (Berlin: Schmidt, 1977). (XXX.55)
See §§1082–1149. Supplement by Petra Hörner, 'Bibliographie 1976–1997,' in *Hartmann von Aue: mit einer Bibliographie 1976–1997*, ed. Petra Hörner, Information und Interpretation, 8 (Frankfurt/M.: P. Lang, 1998), pp. 167–283.

13   Shirt, David J., *The Old French Tristan Poems: A Bibliographical Guide*, RBC, 28 (London: Grant & Cutler, 1980). (XXXIV.376)
See pp. 135–38 and index s. v. 'Chrétien de Troyes' and titles of his romances.

14   Pickford, Cedric E., Rex Last, comp., and Christine R. Barker, assistant ed., *The Arthurian Bibliography: I. Author Listing. II. Subject Index*, AS, 3 and 6 (Cambridge: Brewer, 1981–83); Caroline Palmer, comp., *Arthurian Bibliography III: 1978–1992. Author Listing and Subject Index*, AS, 31 (Cambridge: Brewer, 1998). (XXXIV.364, XXXVI.451, LI.398; cf. LII.217)

15   Woledge, Brian, and Ian Short, 'Liste provisoire de manuscrits du XIIe siècle contenant des textes en langue française,' *Rom*, 102 (1981), 1–17. (XXXIV.258)

16   Bourlet, Caroline, Charles Doutrelepont, and Serge Lusignan, *Ordinateur et études médiévales: Bibliographie I* (Montréal: Institut d'Etudes Médiévales, 1982).

See Ra14 Han.

17   Alford, John A., and Dennis P. Seniff, *Literature and Law in the Middle Ages: A Bibliography of Scholarship*, GRLH, 378 (New York: Garland, 1984). (XXXVIII.458)
Annotated bibliography; see §§26, 275, 360, 451, 636–46.

18   Reiss, Edmund, Louise Horner Reiss, and Beverly Taylor, *Arthurian Legend and Literature: An Annotated Bibliography*, vol. 1:

The Middle Ages, GRLH, 415 (New York: Garland, 1984). (XXXVII.446)

19   Krueger, Roberta L., and E. Jane Burns, 'A Selective Bibliography of Criticism: Women in Medieval French Literature,' *RomN*, 25 (1984–85), 375–90. (XXXVIII.476)

20   Bassan, Fernande, Donald C. Spinelli, and Howard A. Sullivan, *French Language and Literature: An Annotated Bibliography*, GRLH, 954 (New York: Garland, 1989). (XLII.274)
See §§ 562–96.

21   Cigni, Fabrizio, *Bibliografia degli studi italiani di materia arturiana (1940–1990), con una 'lettura' di Valeria Bertolucci Pizzorusso*, Biblioteca della Ricerca: Medio Evo di Francia, 2 (Fasano: Schena, 1992). (XLV.324)

22   *Francesistica: bibliografia delle opere e degli studi di letteratura francese e francofona in Italia 1980–1989*, ed. Giovanni Bogliolo, Paolo Carile, and Mario Matucci (Fasano: Schena; Paris: Slatkine, 1992).

See Ba22 *Manuscrits* vol. 2.
Includes complete listings of manuscripts and editions.

23   Haubrichs, Wolfgang, 'Kleine Bibliographie zu "Anfang" und "Ende" in narrativen Texten (seit 1965),' *ZLiLi*, 99 (1995), 36–50.
See §§ 1.4.1 and 2.4.1.

24   Bromwich, Rachel, *Medieval Welsh Literature to c. 1400, Including Arthurian Studies: A Personal Guide to University of Wales Press Publications* (Cardiff: University of Wales Press, 1996). (XLIX.238)
Annotated.

25   *Francesistica: bibliografia delle opere e degli studi di letteratura francese e francofona in Italia 1990–94*, ed. Giovanni Bogliolo, Paolo Carile, and Mario Matucci (Fasano: Schena; Paris: Slatkine, 1996).

26   Lacy, Norris J., ed., *Medieval Arthurian Literature: A Guide to Recent Research*, GRLH, 1955 (New York: Garland, 1996). (XLIX.515)
See Keith Busby and Karen A. Grossweiner, 'France,' pp. 121–209.

27   Trachsler, Richard, *Les Romans arthuriens en vers après Chrétien de Troyes*, Bibliographica: Bibliographie des Écrivains Français, 11 (Paris: Memini, 1997). (L.233)

28   Fritz, Jean-Marie, 'Chrétien de Troyes: *Le Conte du Graal (Perceval)*,' *InfLitt*, 50:4 (Sept.-Oct. 1998), 40–41.
'Bibliographie sélective.'

29   Sasaki, Shigemi, 'L'Arthuriana au Japon,' in *Mélanges Takeshi Shimmura* (Tokyo: France Tosho, 1998), pp. 325–44. (LI.671)

See Qb82 Takamiya.

30   Watanabe, Kôji, 'Aperçu général des recherches sur Chrétien de Troyes – contribution à l'"ironologie" et à l'approche mythologique,' in *Mélanges Takeshi Shimmura* (Tokyo: France Tosho, 1998), pp. 315–24 (LI.674).
In Japanese.

31   Watanabe, Kôji, 'Bibliographie générale des études sur Chrétien de Troyes au Japon,' *BEFC*, 31 (1999), 1–21. (LII.659)

32   *Francesistica: Bibliografia delle opere e degli studi di letteratura francese e francofona in Italia 1995–1999*, ed. Graziano Benelli [et alii] (Turin: L'Harmattan Italia; Paris: L'Harmattan, 2001).

D: CRITICAL REVIEWS OF SCHOLARSHIP

Two additions to this section reflect recent innovations in critical scholarship that have some bearing on our current understanding of philology, although neither can be said to have had a great impact on Chrétien scholarship. Dc reveals a marked increase in the publication of selected articles by prominent scholars. They bring to a potentially larger public articles sometimes out of print or in publications that are not available everywhere, and that the author him- or herself or the editor of the volume deems significant. Those including more than one or two Chrétien articles are listed here; others are identified under their first date and place of publication. These publications also provide an overview of a given scholar's career, allowing the reader to assess its impact on and contribution to understanding our author. The student can also consult the colloquia some of these scholars have organized by referring to the Abbreviations and the Name Index.

The publication of Dd2 in 1990 proclaims a 'new' philology. Although its authors do not constitute a school or movement or propose a unified programme, and although publications deriving from it in this section do not emphasize Chrétien de Troyes – those that do are noted in the appropriate sub-sections elsewhere – the aggressively critical gauntlet thrown down by the Dd2 authors to traditional scholarship as they describe it has not gone unanswered. It therefore seems appropriate to record here the major publications elicited by or parallel to Dd2 so that the student can evaluate the diverse, sometimes emotional reactions for and against the 'new' philology, and assess their relevance to study of Chrétien's romances and other writings. It is not yet possible to gauge how well received the 'new' views will have been, or what effect, if any, they will have on critical paradigms used to read and interpret Chrétien's romances.

a: General

7   Freymond, E., 'Altfranzösisches Kunstepos und Romane: Crestien de Troyes,' *KJFRP*, 3 (1891–94), 173–77; 8:2 (1904), 239–57; and 'Gralsage und Graltexte,' 3 (1891–94), 177–85; 8:2 (1904), 263–71.

8   Wechssler, Eduard, 'Einflüsse der altftanzösischen Literatur auf die altdeutsche: 3. Bretonisches,' *KJFRP*, 4:2 (1895–96), 390–402; 'Höfisches Epos,' 5:2 (1897–98), 400–09.

9   Hilka, A., 'Altfranzösisches Kunstepos: Kristian von Troyes,' *KJFRP*, 8:2 (1904), 306–14; 10:2 (1906), 77–84.

10   Rohr, Rupprecht, *Matière, sens, conjointure: methodologische Einführung in die französische und provenzalische Literatur des Mittelalters*, Die Romanistik (Darmstadt: Wissenschaftliche Buch-gesellschaft, 1978).

11   *Epische Stoffe des Mittelalters*, ed. Volker Mertens and Ulrich Müller, Kröners Taschenausgabe, 483 (Stuttgart: Kröner, 1984).
See Volker Mertens, 'Artus,' pp. 290–340; Dieter Welz, 'Gralromane,' pp. 341–64; Peter K. Stein, 'Tristan,' pp. 365–94; and Ursula Peters, 'Geschichte der Interpretation,' pp. 475–90.

12   *Le Roman jusqu'à la fin du XIIIᵉ siècle: partie historique*, ed. Jean Frappier and Reinhold R. Grimm, in *Grundriß der romanischen Literaturen des Mittelalters*, vol. 4:1 (Heidelberg: Winter, 1978). (XXXVII.611)
See pp. 231–64, by Alexandre Micha, and pp. 332-54 by Jean Frappier.

13   Busby, Keith, 'Medieval French Arthurian Literature: Recent Progress and Critical Trends,' in *Vitality*, pp. 45–70.

14   Gottzmann, Carola L., *Artusdichtung*, Sammlung Metzler, 249 (Stuttgart: Metzler, 1989). (XLII.526)
See pp. 43–56.

15   *King Arthur through the Ages*, ed. Valerie M. Lagorio and Mildred Leake Day, GRLH, 1269, 1301, 2 vols (New York: Garland, 1990) (XLIII.569).
See He61 Arden; Me29 Nightingale; Pk52 Goebel; and Qa92 Moorman.

16   Brewer, Derek, 'Some Current Trends in Arthurian Scholarship and Criticism 1987,' in *Arturus rex*, pp. 3–18. (XL, pp. 315–17)

17   Berlioz, Jacques [et alii], *Identifier sources et citations*, L'Atelier des Médiévistes, 1 ([Turnhout]: Brepols, 1994).
Information related to sections F, G, M, N, R, and X. See Chap. 2: 'Identifier un auteur ou une œuvre du Moyen Age latin et français', Chap. 14: 'Contes et motifs, croyances et "superstitions",' Chap. 16: 'Images littéraires, comparaisons et lieux communs,' and Chap. 17: 'Les sources iconographiques.'

18   Zink, Michel, 'Trente ans avec la littérature médiévale: note brève sur de longues années,' *CCM*, 39 (1996), 27–40.

19   *Literature of the French and Occitan Middle Ages: Eleventh to Fifteenth Centuries*, ed. Deborah Sinnreich-Levi and Ian S. Laurie, Dictionary of Literary Biography, 208 (Detroit: Gale, 1999).
    A.   Norris J. Lacy, 'French Arthurian Literature,' pp. 296–306. (LII.790)
    B.   Gerald Seaman, 'Chrétien de Troyes (circa 1140–circa 1190)', pp. 72–85.

b: Special Problems

4   Minis, Cola, 'Französisch-deutsche Literaturbeziehungen [...]'; repr. in her *Zur Vergegenwärtigung vergangener philologischer Nächte*, APSL, 96 (Amsterdam: Rodopi, 1981), pp. 88–156.

10   Wilmotte, Maurice, 'Les origines du roman breton,' *MA*, 4 (1891), 186–91.

11   Wilmotte, Maurice, 'L'état actuel des études sur la légende du Gral,' *BulLSMP*, ser. 5, 15 (1929), 100–22.

12   Wilmotte, Maurice, 'Travaux récents sur les premiers poèmes relatifs à la légende du Graal,' *MA*, 49 (1939), 161–85. (I.110)

13   Adolf, Helen, 'Studien zur Gralssage (eine Zusammenfassung),' *AStnSpr*, 188 (1951), 66–72.

14   Payen, Jean-Charles, 'Les études médiévales et la rénovation pédagogique,' *MrR*, 20:4 (1970), 9–14.

15   Dakyns, Janine R., *The Middle Ages in French Literature 1851–1900* (London: Oxford University Press, 1973).
See Chap. 4 II B: 'Medieval Literature.'

16   Altman, Charles, 'Medieval Narrative vs. Modern Assumptions: Revising Inadequate Typology,' *Diacritics*, 4:2 (1974), 12–19.

17   Lohse, Gerhart, 'Die Darstellung der romanisch-deutschen Literaturbeziehungen des Mittelalters in Meyers Konversations-Lexikon,' in *Festschrift Klein*, pp. 215–30.

See Sa72 Boase.

18   Grigsby, John L., 'Symbolism and Source-Hunting vs. the Creative Spirit,' *RPh*, 31 (1977–78), 321–43. (XXXII.182)

19   Cormier, Raymond J., 'Toward Some Definitions of Courtly Literature,' *Encomia*, 2:1 (1978), 5–23.

20   Shirt, David J., 'Chrétien's *Charrette* and its Critics, 1964–74,' *MLR*, 73 (1978), 38–50. (XXXI.389)

21   Zumthor, Paul, 'Le Moyen Age et nous: questions de méthode,' *RR*, 70 (1979), 205–18.

22   Payen, Jean-Charles, 'Le romaniste et l'idéologie,' *MrR*, 29:3–4 (1979), 15–23. (XXXIV.526)

See Ec6 Ménage.

23   Ollier, Marie-Louise, 'Modernité de Chrétien de Troyes,' *RR*, 71 (1980), 413–44. (XXXIII.161)

See Qe12 Poirion.

24   *Réception critique de l'œuvre de Chrétien de Troyes*, ed. Raymond Cormier, special issue of *OetC*, 5:2 (1980–81).
   A.   Karl D. Uitti, 'Nouvelle critique et Chrétien de Troyes: quelques perspectives,' pp. 5–13. (XXXIV.256)
   B.   Rosemarie Jones, 'Chrétien devant la critique anglaise contemporaine: questions de structure,' pp. 15–22. (XXXIV.227)
   C.   Claude Luttrell, 'The Arthurian Traditionalist's Approach to the Composer of Romance: R. S. Loomis on Chrétien de Troyes,' pp. 23–30. (XXXIV.234)
   D.   Douglas Kelly, 'Psychologie/pathologie et parole dans Chrétien de Troyes,' pp. 31–37. (XXXIV.228)
   E.   Jean-Charles Payen, 'Une approche classiciste du roman médiéval: Jean Frappier, lecteur de Chrétien de Troyes,' pp. 45–52. (XXXIV.242)
   F.   Faith Lyons, 'Interprétations critiques au XXe siècle du Prologue de *Cligès*: la *translatio studii* selon les historiens, les philosophes et les philologues,' pp. 39–44. (XXXIV.235)
   G.   Amelia A. Rutledge, 'Perceval's Sin: Critical Perspectives,' pp. 53–60. (XXXIV.245)
   H.   Sara Sturm-Maddox, 'Hortus non conclusus: Critics and the *Joie de la cort*,' pp. 61–71. (XXXIV.253)
   I.   Donald Maddox, 'Trois sur deux: théories de bipartition et de tripartition des œuvres de Chrétien,' pp. 91–102. (XXXIV.236)
   J.   David P. Schenck, 'Vues sur le temps et l'espace chez Chrétien de Troyes,' pp. 111–17. (XXXIV.247)
   K.   Harry F. Williams, '*Le Conte du graal* de Chrétien de Troyes: positions critiques et nouvelles perspectives,' pp. 119–23, 127–28. (XXXIV.257)

See also Hf42 Thorpe; Hg52 Freeman; Jd23 Ribard; Pa120 Sweetser; Pa121 Wolfgang.

25 Stuip, René E. V., '"kar il n'avoit mie apris a planchoier!" Quelques remarques sur la traduction des textes d'ancien français en néerlandais moderne,' *PerM*, 7 (1981), 89–100. (XXXIV.252)

See Ra14 Han.

26 Hrubý, Antonín, 'Das Dichterbild Hartmanns und Chrétiens in der Literaturkritik,' *PapR*, 4 (1982), 1–26. (XXXV.163)

27 Lecco, Margherita, 'Metodi e romanzo cortese (note su Chrétien de Troyes e uno studio recente),' *Im Rif*, 5 (1982), 161–72. (XXXVI.521)

28 Ollier, Marie-Louise, 'Chrétien de Troyes aujourd'hui,' *Europe*, 642 (Oct. 1982), 5–16. Repr. in Dc32. (XXXV.336)

29 Williams, Harry F., 'Interpretations of the *Conte del graal* and their Critical Reactions,' in *Sower*, pp. 146–54. (XXXV.196)

30 Marotta, Joseph, 'Teaching Medieval Narrative,' in *1983 NEH Institute Resource Book for the Teaching of Medieval Civilization*, ed. Howell Chickering (Amherst, MA: Five Colleges, 1984), pp. 13–35.

31 Grigsby, John L., 'Truth and Method in Arthurian Criticism,' *RPh*, 38 (1984–85), 53–64. (XXXVII.380)

See Ub27 Wolfzettel.

32 Grimbert, Joan Tasker, 'Chrétien in Translation: The Inexpressible Effervescence of the Champagne Poet,' *TR*, 19 (1986), 16–22. (XXXIX.268)

See He55 Bruckner.

33 Keller, Joseph, 'Paradigm Shifts in the Grail Scholarship of Jessie Weston and R. S. Loomis: A View from Linguistics,' *AInt*, 1:2 (1987), 10–22. (XLI.403)

See Wb42 Nerlich.

34 Pleij, H., 'Met een boekje in een hoekje? Over literatuur en lezen in de middeleeuwen,' in *Het woord aan de lezer: zeven literatuurhistorische verkenningen*, ed. W. van den Berg and J. Stouten (Groningen: Wolters-Noordhoff, 1987), pp. 16–48.

35 Richards, Earl Jeffrey, 'Finding the "Authentic" Text: Editing and Translating Medieval and Modern Works as Comparable Interpretive Exercises (Chrétien's *Charrette*, Christine de Pizan's *Cité des dames*, and Diderot's *Neveu de Rameau*),' *Esp*, 27:1 (1987), 111–21. (XL.308)

36 Zumthor, Paul, 'Critical Paradoxes,' *MLN*, 102 (1987), 799–810. (XL.335)

37 Gilbert, Dorothy, 'But Why Are You Doing It in *Verse*? Further Thoughts on Translating the Poet of Champagne,' *TR*, 27 (1988), 9–16.

See Pb316 Haase.
Critical review of scholarship on the relation between Chrétien's and Hartmann von Aue's *Erec*.

See Pb336 Buschinger.

38 Wolfzettel, Friedrich, 'Zum Stand und Problem der Intertextualitätsforschung im Mittelalter (aus romanistischer Sicht),' in *Artusroman*, pp. 1–17. (XLIII.74)

39 Haidu, Peter, Alexandre Leupin, and Eugene Vance, 'Medievalism: Testing Ground for Historicism(s)? Round Table Discussion,' *Paroles*, 9 (1991), 1–32.

40 Lacy, Norris J., 'Medieval French Arthurian Literature in English,' *QetF*, 1:3 (1991), 55–74. (XLV.491)

41 Rider, Jeffrey, 'A Report on the Chrétien de Troyes Industry,' *Envoi*, 3 (1991), 24–32.
On recent editions and translations.

See Xa13 Stones.

42 Bumke, Joachim, 'Höfische Kultur: Versuch einer kritischen Bestandsaufnahme,' *PBB*, 114 (1992), 414–92. (XLV.22)

43 Delcorno Branca, Daniela, 'Sette anni di studi sulla letteratura arturiana in Italia: rassegna (1985–1992),' *Lettere Italiane*, 44 (1992), 465–97. (XLV.327)

44 Fries, Maureen, and Jeanie Watson, ed., *Approaches to Teaching the Arthurian Tradition*, Approaches to Teaching World Literature, 40 (New York: Modern Language Association of America, 1992). (XLVI.715)
    A. Burton Raffel, 'Translating *Yvain* and *Sir Gawain and the Green Knight* for Classroom Use,' pp. 88–93.

B.   Maureen Fries, 'Women in Arthurian Literature,' pp. 155–58.

45   Hardman, Philippa, 'Scholars Retelling Romances,' *RMS*, 18 (1992), 81–101. (XLV.253)

See Bb63 Dembowski.

46   Glencross, Michael, 'La littérature française du Moyen Age dans la critique littéraire sous la Monarchie de Juillet,' *ZfSL*, 103 (1993), 244–55.

47   Glencross, M. J., 'La littérature française du Moyen Age vue par quelques historiens de l'époque romantique,' *RHL*, 93 (1993), 191–206.

48   Greco, Gina L., and Peter Shoemaker, 'Intertextuality and Large Corpora: A Medievalist Approach,' *ComH*, 27 (1993), 349–55.

49   Masters, Bernadette A., '*Yvain* in Translation: Medieval Myth or Twentieth-Century Novel?' *Parergon*, 11:1 (1993), 107–30.

50   Pensom, Roger, 'Zumthor and After: A Survey of Some Current Trends in the Reading of Old French Literature,' *MAe*, 62 (1993), 294–306.

51   Sturges, Robert S., 'Chrétien de Troyes in English Translation: A Guide to the Issues,' *Arthuriana*, 4 (1994), 205–23. (XLVII.793)

52   *Cyclification: The Development of Narrative Cycles in the 'Chansons de geste' and the Arthurian Romances: Proceedings of the Colloquium, Amsterdam, 17–18 December, 1992*, ed. Bart Besamusca, Willem P. Gerritsen, Corry Hogetoorn, and Orlanda S. H. Lie, VerKA, n.s., 159 (Amsterdam: North Holland, 1994). (XLVII.525)
Position papers on cyclification, many of which treat Chrétien's romances, their place in manuscripts, and his influence (see index for references).

53   Glencross, Michael, 'Débat des origines et origines d'un débat: l'étude des sources de la matière de Bretagne à l'époque romantique,' *RZLG*, 18 (1994), 93–107. (XLVII.89)

54   Biesterfeldt, Corinna, 'Werkschlüsse in der höfischen Epik des Mittelalters: ein Forschungsbericht,' *ZLiLi*, 99 (1995), 51–68. (XLVIII.57)

55   Haidu, Peter, 'Althusser Anonymous in the Middle Ages,' *Exemplaria*, 7 (1995), 55–74. (XLVIII.695)

56 Ruiz Domènec, José Enrique, 'Interpretaciones de la caballería medieval,' *Ínsula*, no. 584–85 (Aug.-Sept. 1995), pp. 3–5.

57 Sasaki, Shigemi. 'Découverte du Moyen Age français au Japon,' in *Recueil Micha*, pp. 321–28. (XLVIII.147)

58 Walter, Philippe, 'La mémoire et le grimoire des textes: réflexions sur une lecture mythologique de la littérature médiévale,' in *Etudes Poirion*, pp. 487–98. (XLVIII.348)

59 Dubost, Francis, 'Merveilleux et fantastique au Moyen Age: positions et propositions,' *RLR*, 100:2 (1996), 1–35. (XLIX.145)

60 Lacy, Norris J., 'König Artus: Mythos und Entmythologisierung,' in *Herrscher, Helden, Heilige*, ed. Ulrich Müller, Werner Wunderlich, and Lotte Grabel, Mittelalter-Mythen, 1 (St Gallen: UVK, 1996), pp. 47–63. (XLVIII.118)

61 Ridoux, Charles, 'L'élaboration du mythe du Graal au Moyen Age,' in Pk72 *Graal*, pp. 31–51.

62 Gingras, Francis, 'L'anneau merveilleux et les deux versants du désir: présentation du *Thesaurus* informatisé des motifs merveilleux de la littérature médiévale,' *RLR*, 101:2 (1997), 163–83.

63 Greco, Gina L., Toby Paff, and Peter W. Shoemaker, 'The *Charrette* Project: Manipulating Text and Image in an Electronic Archive of a Medieval Manuscript Tradition,' *ComH*, 30 (1997), 407–15. (L.474)
On Princeton *Charrette* Archive.

64 Kibler, William W., 'Translating Chrétien de Troyes: How Faithful?' in *Translation*, pp. 255–69. (L.502)

65 Markale, Jean, *Petite Encyclopédie du Graal* (Paris: Pygmalion/ Gérard Watelet, 1997).

See Ja37 Ribard.

66 Staines, David, 'On Translating Chrétien de Troyes,' in *Translation*, pp. 271–82. (L.561)

67 Zambon, Francesco, 'Il ciclo romanzesco del Graal,' *Minas Tirith*, 2 (1997), 7–30. (LI.575)

68 Armstrong, Grace M., 'Recent Gender Benders,' *WFS*, 6 (1998), 114–26.

69 Beltrami, Pietro G., 'Appunti di lavoro da una tradizione poetica del *Chevalier de la charrete*,' in *Studi Melli*, vol. 1, pp. 69–86. (LI.536)

See Hg112 Döffinger-Lange.
See Part IA: 'Die Diskussion über die Einheit des *Conte du Graal*,' pp. 31–71; and B: 'Beiträge zur Deutung der Gauvain-Handlung,' pp. 73–120.

70 Gracia, Paloma, 'El mito del Graal,' in *Literatura de caballerías y orígenes de la novela*, ed. Rafael Beltrán (Valencia: Universitat de València, 1998), pp. 63–75. (LI.631)

71 Hult, David F., *Manuscript Transmission, Reception and Canon Formation: The Case of Chrétien de Troyes*, Morrison Library Inaugural Address Series, 13 (Berkeley: The Doe Library, University of California, 1998).

72 Zambon, Francesco, 'Il catarismo e i miti del Graal,' in *Tradizione letteraria, iniziazione, genealogia*, BM:S, 2 (Milan: Luni, 1998), pp. 82–112.

73 Calin, William, 'Making a Canon,' *Philosophy and Literature*, 23 (1999), 1–16. (LII.739)

74 Riquer, Isabel de, 'Interpretación de la indumentaria en las traducciones de las novelas de Chrétien de Troyes,' in *Traducir la Edad Media: la traducción de la literatura medieval románica*, ed. Juan Paredes and Eva Muñoz Raya (Granada: Universidad de Granada, 1999), pp. 103–34. (LII.184)

75 Schmid, Elisabeth, 'Weg mit dem Doppelweg: wider eine Selbstverständlichkeit der germanistischen Artusforschung,' in *Erzählstrukturen*, pp. 69–85. (LII.107)

76 Wood, Juliette, 'The Holy Grail: From Romance Motif to Modern Genre,' *Folklore*, 111 (2000), 169–90. (LIII.572)

c: Collected Papers by Single Authors

1 Frappier, Jean, *Du Moyen Age à la Renaissance: études d'histoire et de critique littéraires*, NBMA, 3 (Paris: Champion, 1976). (XXVIII.253)
Includes Fc4, 5; Kd3.

2 Frappier, Jean, *Histoire, mythes et symboles: études de littérature française*, PRF, 137 (Geneva: Droz, 1976). (XXVIII.252)
Includes Gd9, 17; Ha62; Hc13; Ja24.

3   Micha, Alexandre, *De la chanson de geste au roman: études de littérature médiévale*, PRF, 139 (Geneva: Droz, 1976). (XXIX.245, 411)
Includes Fa46; Gb6; Gd14; Gf11; Ma12; Md7, 8; Qc6; Sc5; Ta6; Tb6.

4   Raynaud de Lage, Guy, *Les Premiers Romans français et autres études littéraires et linguistiques*, PRF, 138 (Geneva: Droz, 1976). (XXVIII.261, XXIX.250)
Includes Fb12; Fb16; Pa34.

5   Frappier, Jean, *Autour du Graal*, PRF, 147 (Geneva: Droz, 1977). (XXX. 274, XXXI.484)
Includes Hg7, 9, 16; Jd13; Mb3; Pa75; Qc9; Ta2, 3, 8, 10, 14; Tb5.

6   Guiette, Robert, *Forme et senefiance: études médiévales*, ed. J. Dufournet, M. De Grève, and H. Braet, PRF, 148 (Geneva: Droz, 1978). (XXXI.487)
Includes Fa43; Hb3; Jf6.

7   Schröder, Walter Johannes, *'rede' und 'meine': Aufsätze und Vorträge zur deutschen Literatur des Mittelalters* (Cologne: Böhlau, 1978). (XXXI.42)
Includes Pb28, 115, 119, 130, 182.

8   Fourquet, Jean, *Recueil d'études: linguistique allemande et philologie germanique, littérature médiévale*, 2 vols (Amiens: Centre d'Etudes Médiévales, 1979).
Includes La7, 19, 25; Pb18, 23, 44, 127, 169, 200.

9   Hatto, A. T., *Essays on Medieval German and Other Poetry* (Cambridge: Cambridge University Press, 1980). (XXXIII.445)
Includes Pb24, 107, 111, 146.

10   Robertson, D. W., Jr., *Essays in Medieval Culture* (Princeton: Princeton University Press, 1980).
Includes Fb6; Jc2, 7, 10.

11   Cremonesi, Carla, *Studi romanzi di filologia e letteratura* (Brescia: Paideia, 1984). (XXXVII.274)
Includes Qb16; Pa113; Wb30.

12   Jackson, W. T. H., *The Challenge of the Medieval Text: Studies in Genre and Interpretation*, ed. Joan M. Ferrante and Robert W. Hanning (New York: Columbia University Press, 1985). (XXXVIII.507)
Includes Ha49(IV); Hb7; Sa14.

13 Rychner, Jean, *Du Saint-Alexis à François Villon: études de littérature médiévale*, PRF, 169 (Geneva: Droz, 1985).
Includes Fb 17, 26; Jb5, 6.

14 Lecoy, Félix, *Mélanges de philologie et de littérature romanes*, PRF, 181 (Geneva: Droz, 1988). (XLI.67, 319)
Includes Kd46, 52, 60.

15 Haug, Walter, *Strukturen als Schlüssel zur Welt: kleine Schriften zur Erzählliteratur des Mittelalters* (Tübingen: Niemeyer, 1989). (XLII.533–540, 542–548)
Includes: Fa91; Gb81; Ha30, 42, 92, 107; Ja18; Pb174.

16 Benton, John F., *Culture, Power and Personality in Medieval France*, ed. Thomas N. Bisson (London: Hambledon, 1991).
Includes Ha103; Qa15; Sa30(II).

17 Roberts, Brynley F., *Studies on Middle Welsh Literature*, Welsh Studies, 5 (Lewiston, NY: Mellen, 1992). (XLV.266)
Includes Na.a22; Na.b26, 29; Na.c100.

18 Zink, Michel, *Les voix de la conscience: parole du poète et parole de Dieu dans la littérature médiévale*, Varia, 1 (Caen: Paradigme, 1992).
Includes Gc13(A); Gf31; Pa208.

19 Méla, Charles, *'Le beau trouvé': études de théorie et de critique littéraires sur l'art des 'trouveurs' au Moyen Age*, Varia, 7 (Caen: Paradigme, 1993).
Includes Fa145; Gd.a27; Ge56; Ha117; Hg32, 43(A-B); Jd27; Me34; Sa118.

20 Baumgartner, Emmanuèle, *De l'histoire de Troie au livre du Graal: le temps, le récit (XIIe-XIIIe siècles)*, Varia, 18 (Orléans: Paradigme, 1994).
Includes Fc14; Ga41; Gb79; Ge40; Ha117, 137; Me34; Na.b32; Pa177, 187, 218, 223.

21 Poirion, Daniel, *Écriture poétique et composition romanesque*, Medievalia, 11 (Orléans: Paradigme, 1994).
Includes Fa137; Gd.a6; La29.

22 Saly, Antoinette, *Image, structure et sens: études arthuriennes*, Senefiance, 34 (Aix-en-Provence: CUER-MA, 1994). (XLVI.363, XLVII.295)
Includes Gd.b14; He27, 49; Hf70; Hg42, 57, 101; Nb17; Pa175; Pi21.

23 Buschinger, Danielle, *Studien zur deutschen Literatur des Mittelalters*, WODAN: EG, 53, ser. 2: Studien zur mittelalterlichen Literatur, 6 (Greifswald: Reineke, 1995). (XLVIII.72)
Includes Pb253(A), 336; Pk36, 46(A); Ub24(A).

24 Haug, Walter, *Brechungen auf dem Weg zur Individualität: kleine Schriften zur Literatur des Mittelalters* (Tübingen: Niemeyer, 1995). (XLVIII.103)
Includes Ge59(B); Ha148–49; Pb337, 346–47; Sc28.

25 Ribard, Jacques, *Du mythique au mystique: la littérature médiévale et ses symboles*, NBMA, 31 (Paris: Champion, 1995). (XLVIII.333)
Includes Ga45; Gd.c9; Hf69; Jb26, 31, 34; Jd18, 23.

26 Knapp, Fritz Peter, *Historie und Fiktion in der mittelalterlichen Gattungspoetik: sieben Studien und ein Nachwort*, Beiträge zur älteren Literaturgeschichte (Heidelberg: Winter, 1997). (L.93)
Includes Fa105; Pb363, 413.

27 Huchet, Jean-Charles, *Essais de clinique littéraire du texte médiéval*, Medievalia, 24 (Orléans: Paradigme, 1998).
Includes Gb83; He73; Pa197; Ub37 Chap. 1.

28 Planche, Alice, *Des plantes, des bêtes et des couleurs*, Medievalia, 23 (Orléans: Paradigme, 1998).
Includes Ga20; Gc25; Gd.a4, 20.

29 Ménard, Philippe, *De Chrétien de Troyes au 'Tristan en prose': études sur les romans de la Table Ronde*, PRF, 224 (Geneva: Droz, 1999). (LI.273, LII.715)
Includes Bb34; Eg16, 17(L); Gb12; Gf21, 29; Hb4; Hg99; Rb22.

30 Saly, Antoinette, *Mythe et dogmes: roman arthurien, épopée romane*, Medievalia, 29 (Orléans: Paradigme, 1999).
Includes Gb77, 123; Hg102; Jd43; Lc3; Na.c112.

31 Wolf, Alois, *Erzählkunst des Mittelalters: komparatistische Arbeiten zur französischen und deutschen Literatur*, ed. Martina Backes, Francis G. Gentry, and Eckart Conrad Lutz (Tübingen: Niemeyer, 1999).
Includes Ga22; Gf37; Hf89; Jb10; Pb154, 204, 299.

32 Ollier, Marie-Louise, *La forme du sens: textes narratifs des XIIe et XIIIe siècles. Études littéraires et linguistiques*, Medievalia, 33 (Orléans: Paradigme, 2000). (LIII.269)

Includes Db28; Fa96; Fb31 (in French), 42; Ha50, 51 and 88 (with different titles); Hb32; Hf20; Kc86, 89, 112.

d: The 'New' Philology

1   *Modernité au Moyen Age: le défi du passé*, ed. Brigitte Cazelles and Charles Méla, RRG: Littérature, 1 (Geneva: Droz, 1990). (XLIII.450)

2   *The New Philology*, ed. Stephen G. Nichols, = *Spec*, 65:1 (January 1990). (XLII.337)

3   *On Philology: Proceedings from the Conference 'What Is Philology?' Sponsored by the Center for Literary and Cultural Studies, Harvard University, March 1988*, ed. Jan Ziolkowski, *CLS*, 27:1 (1990); repr. University Park: Pennsylvania State University Press, 1990.

4   *The New Medievalism*, ed. Marina S. Brownlee, Kevin Brownlee, and Stephen G. Nichols (Baltimore: Johns Hopkins University Press, 1991).

5   Atkinson, Keith, 'Old (French) Wine, New Bottles?' in *In the Place of French: Essays on and around French Studies Michael Spenser* ([St Lucia]: University of Queensland; Mount Nebo, Queensland: Boombana, 1992), pp. 235–55.

6   Mok, Q. I. M., 'Néophilologie (?)' *Neophil*, 76 (1992), 508–18.

7   *Towards a Synthesis? Essays on the New Philology*, ed. Keith Busby, Faux Titre, 68 (Amsterdam: Rodopi, 1993).

8   Janssens, Jozef, *De middeleeuwen zijn anders: cultuur en literatuur van de 12de tot de 15de eeuw* (Leuven: Davidsfonds, 1993).

9   *The Future of the Middle Ages: Medieval Literature in the 1990s*, ed. William D. Paden (Gainesville: University Press of Florida, 1994).

10   *Medievalism and the Modernist Temper*, ed. R. Howard Bloch and Stephen G. Nichols (Baltimore: Johns Hopkins University Press, 1996).

11   *Alte und neue Philologie*, ed. Martin-Dietrich Gleßgen and Franz Lebsanft, Beihefte zu Editio, 8 (Tübingen: Niemeyer, 1997).

12   *Medieval Studies*, ed. Michael Uebel and D. Vance Smith, = *NLH*, 28:2 (1997).

13   *Philologie als Textwissenschaft: alte und neue Horizonte*, ed. Helmut Tervooren and Horst Wenzel, in *ZdP*, 116 Sonderheft (1997).

14   *The Practice of Medieval Literature*, ed. Simon Gaunt and Sarah Kay, *FMLS*, 33 (1997).
See pp. 193–203.

15   Glejzer, Richard R., 'The New Medievalism and the (Im)Possibility of the Middle Ages,' *StMed*, 10 (1998), 104–19.

16   Dembowski, Peter F., 'Les débats américains sur la philologie textuelle de l'ancien français,' in *Mélanges Ménard*, vol. 1, pp. 395–405.

E: GENERAL STUDIES ON CHRETIEN

Inclusion in this section conforms to the guidelines set out in the 1976 Bibliography: 'introductory, survey, and synthetic works embracing all or most traditional fields of Chrétien scholarship and general Arthurian' and romance 'studies that reserve a large place for Chrétien.' Included in this Supplement are important recent articles in encyclopedias, dictionaries, and other such compendia that can be useful to the student or the non-specialist scholar seeking a general or broad orientation or introduction to Chrétien and his works. Forthcoming, but still in press at the time this Supplement went to press, is *The Arthur of the French*, which is to appear at the University of Wales Press and will contain a chapter on Chrétien as well as other romances influenced by or related to his *œuvre*; this volume is appearing with a number of others that are meant to supplement *ALMA* (Da3).

a: Surveys of All Romances

4   Cohen, Gustave, *Un Grand Romancier* [...]
Add Gustave Cohen, 'Un grand romancier au XIIe siècle: Crestien de Troies, sa vie et son œuvre,' *Revue bimensuelle des cours et conférences*, 27:1 (1926), 289–310, 495–509, 602–14; 27:2 (1926), 27–39, 164–77, 301–22, 577–96; 28:1 (1926), 75–94, 158–68, (1927), 458–76, 707–23, 28:2 (1927), 193–209, 444–67, 617–38, 735–48; 29:1 (1927), 81–94, (1928), 364–84, 634–56; 29:2 (1928), 67–79, 241–56, 449–66, 536–54; 30:1 (1929), 254–76, 468–80, 657–72; 30:2 (1929), 269–88, 590–68.
See also A. Micha, 'Le Chrétien de Troyes de G. Cohen,' *Revue de l'Université de Lyon* (Feb. 1931), pp. 60–62; and Paul F. Schurmann, 'Leyendo *Chrétien de Troyes et son œuvre* del Doctor Gustave Cohen,' *Boletin de Filología*, 1 (1936–37), 281–303.

11   Frappier, Jean, *Chrétien de Troyes* [...]

English translation, Jean Frappier, *Chrétien de Troyes: The Man and his Work*, trans. Raymond J. Cormier (Athens: Ohio University Press, 1982). (XXXV.156)
With up-dated bibliography.

18   Correct and complete as Katô, Kyôko, *Chrétien de Troyes: peintre de l'amour* (Amherst, MA: Hamilton Newell, 1971). (XXV.100)
Cf. his 'Chrétien de Troyes en tant qu'écrivain d'amour,' Doctoral Dissertation, Department of French, Waseda University, 1967.

20   G. [= Pierre-Louis Guinguené], 'Chrestien de Troyes,' *HLF*, 15 (1823, 1869), 193–264.

21   Holland, Wilhelm Ludwig, *Über Crestiens de Troies und zwei seiner Werke* (Tübingen: Fues, 1847).
Part II on *Perceval* and *Cligés*.

22   Paris, Gaston, 'Romans en vers du cycle de la Table Ronde,' in *HLF*, 30 (1888), 1–270, 600.
See 'Chrétien de Troyes et son œuvre,' pp. 22–29.

23   Emecke, Heinrich, *Chrestien von Troyes als Persönlichkeit und als Dichter*, diss. Straßburg (Würzburg: Etlinger, 1892).

24   Baker, Ernest A., *The History of the English Novel: The Age of Romance; from the Beginnings to the Renaissance* (London: Witherby, 1924; repr. 1934, and New York: Barnes and Noble, 1950, 1961, 1967).
See Chap. 5: 'Chrétien de Troyes.'

25   Siciliano, Italo, 'Chrétien de Troyes e il romanzo cortese,' *La Rassegna*, ser. 4, 40 (1932), 1–27.

26   Bruel, Andrée, *Romans français du Moyen Age: essais* (Paris: Droz, 1934).
See pp. 9–140.

27   Guerrieri Crocetti, Camillo, 'Nel mondo di Chrétien de Troyes: I. *Erec, Cligés, Lancelot, Yvain*,' *GIF*, 1 (1948), 296–322; 'II. "Perceval",' 2 (1949), 1–21.

See Eg10 Riquer, pp. 9–34.

28   Cocito, Luciana, *Le origini della narrativa francese* (Genoa: Tilgher, 1973).
See pp. 29–38.

29 Pandelescu, Silvia, 'Chrétien de Troyes,' in *Scriitori francezi*, ed. Angela Ion (Bucarest: Editura Ştiinţifică şi Enciclopedică, 1978), pp. 68–72.

30 *Le roman jusqu'à la fin du XIIIe siècle*, ed. Jean Frappier and Reinhold R. Grimm, vol. 4.1–2 of the *GRLMA* (Heidelberg: Winter, 1978–84). (XXXII.31, XXXVII. 611)
See vol. 1, pp. 231–64 by Alexandre Micha, 332–54 by Jean Frappier; vol. 2, pp. 94–107.

31 Köhler, Erich, 'Der Roman in der Romania,' in *Neues Handbuch der Literaturwissenschaft*, vol. 7: *Europäisches Hochmittelalter*, ed. Henning Krauss (Wiesbaden: Athenaion, 1981), pp. 243–82. (XXXV.41)

32 Topsfield, L. T., *Chrétien de Troyes: A Study of the Arthurian Romances* (Cambridge: Cambridge University Press, 1981). (XXXIV.385)

33 Voicu, Mihaela, 'Formes narratives au XIIe et au XIIIe siècles: Chrétien de Troyes,' in *Histoire de la littérature française*, ed. Angela Ion (Bucarest: Presses de l'Université de Bucarest, 1981), vol. 1, pp. 106–19.

34 Gyurcsik, Margareta, 'Le discours romanesque: les romans de Chrétien de Troyes,' in *La Littérature française du Moyen Age et de la Renaissance* (Timişoara: Tipografia Universităţii din Timişoara, 1982), pp. 60–89.

35 García Gual, Carlos, *Historia del rey Arturo y de los nobles y errantes caballeros de la Tabla Redonda: análisis de un mito literario* (Madrid: Alianza Editorial, 1983). (XXXVII.265)
See Chap. 2 and 3.

36 Meguro, Simon, 'Birth of the Humanist – Introduction to the Study of Chrétien de Troyes,' *ALib*, 32 (1983), 91–103.
In Japanese.

37 *The Romances of Chrétien de Troyes: A Symposium*, ed. Douglas Kelly, ECAM, 3 (Lexington, KY: French Forum, 1985). (XXXVIII.513)
    A. Douglas Kelly, 'Chrétien de Troyes: The Narrator and His Art,' pp. 13–47, 311–18.
    B. Edward J. Buckbee, '*Erec et Enide*,' pp. 48–88, 318–20.
    C. Michelle A. Freeman, '*Cligés*,' pp. 89–131, 320–23.
    D. Matilda Tomaryn Bruckner, '*Le Chevalier de la charrette (Lancelot)*,' pp. 132–81, 323–31.
    E. Karl D. Uitti, '*Le Chevalier au lion (Yvain)*,' pp. 182–231, 331–35.

F.   Rupert T. Pickens, '*Le Conte du Graal (Perceval)*,' pp. 232–86, 335–39.

G.   Alfred Foulet, 'On Editing Chrétien's *Lancelot*,' pp. 287–304, 340.

H.   Alfred Foulet, 'Chrétien's Indebtedness to the *Alexandre décasyllabique*,' pp. 305–09, 340–41.

38 Köhler, Erich, *Vorlesungen zur Geschichte der französischen Literatur: Mittelalter I–II*, ed. Henning Krauß and Dietmar Rieger, 2 vols (Stuttgart: Kohlhammer, 1985). (XXXVIII.35)
See vol. 1, pp. 117–70 and 182–213.

39 Cirlot, Victoria, *La novela artúrica: orígenes de la ficción en la cultura europea*, Biblioteca de Divulgación Temática, 45 (Barcelona: Montesinos, 1987). (XLI.238)
See Chap. 4: 'Chrétien de Troyes: la creación de la ficción novelesca.'

40 Lacy, Norris J., and Geoffrey Ashe, *The Arthurian Handbook* (New York: Garland, 1988), pp. 80–84; 2nd ed. with Deborah Mancoff (1997), pp. 68–72. (XL.296)

41 Amazawa, Taijirô, Eizô Kamizawa, and Shun'ichi Niikura, *Poets and Romancers of the Middle Ages*, 2 (Tokyo: Hakusuisha, 1991). (XLIV.234)
In Japanese. See *Le Chevalier de la Charrette* (*Lancelot*), trans. E. Kamizawa, pp. 7–140 ; *Le Roman de Perceval ou le Conte du Graal*, trans. T. Amazawa, pp. 141–323 ; and Postface (commentary) by T. Amazawa, pp. 397–410: the third chapter is devoted to Chrétien de Troyes.

42 Uitti, Karl D., with Michelle A. Freeman, *Chrétien de Troyes Revisited*, TWAS, 855 (New York: Twayne, 1995).

43 Nykrog, Per, *Chrétien de Troyes: romancier discutable*, PRF, 213 (Geneva: Droz, 1996). (XLIX.438)

44 Mancini, Mario, 'Chrétien de Troyes e il romanzo,' in *La letteratura francese medievale*, ed. Mario Mancini, Strumenti: Linguistica e Critica Letteraria (Bologna: Il Mulino, 1997), pp. 159–212. (LI.564)

45 Sasu, Maria-Voichiţa, 'Le roman courtois et d'aventure,' in *Littérature et civilisation françaises – Moyen Age* (Cluj-Napoca: Presa Universitară, 1997), pp. 35–79.

46 Walter, Philippe, *Chrétien de Troyes*, Que sais-je? 3241 (Paris: Presses Universitaires de France, 1997). (L.237)

47 Pânzaru, Ioan, 'Le roman courtois: Chrétien de Troyes,' in *Introduction à l'étude de la littérature médiévale française (IXe–XIVe*

siècles) (Bucarest: Presses de l'Université de Bucarest, 1999), pp. 139–57.

See Ha206 Delcourt, Chap. 2: 'Chrétien de Troyes.'

48   Watanabe, Kôji, 'Chrétien de Troyes: The Blade and Love,' *Asahi*, 56 (2000), 164–68.
In Japanese.

49   Duggan, Joseph J., *The Romances of Chrétien de Troyes* (New Haven: Yale University Press, 2001).

b: Appreciation

2   Auguis, P. R., *Les Poètes françois depuis le XIIe siècle jusqu'à Malherbe avec une notice historique et littéraire sur chaque poète* (Paris: Crapelet, 1824), vol. 1, pp. 448–49.

3   *Clédat, L., '*Erec et Enide* par Chrétien de Troyes: extraits traduits et analyse,' *Revue de Philologie Française et Provençale*, 10 (1896), 177–213, 275–88; 11 (1897), 223–35; 12 (1898), 81–104, 161–81.

4   Clédat, L., 'Traductions archaïques et rythmées: 2. Début du *Perceval* de Chrétien de Troyes,' *Revue de Philologie Française et Provençale*, 11 (1897), 3–21.

5   Cohen, Gustave, 'Le fondateur du roman français: Chrétien de Troyes,' *AnP*, 6 (1931), 128–39.

6   Aury, Dominique, 'Les enchantements de Bretagne,' in her *Lecture pour tous* (Paris: Gallimard, 1958), pp. 31–37; English trans.: 'Chrétien de Troyes: The Magic of Brittany,' in *Literary Landfalls* (London: Chatto & Windus, 1960), pp. 25–30.

7   Cohn, Robert Greer, *The Writer's Way in France* (Philadelphia: University of Pennsylvania Press; London: Oxford University Press, 1960).
See pp. 260–66.

8   Paxson, Diana, 'The Holy Grail,' *Mythlore*, 3:1 (1973), 10–11, 31.

9   Gallais, Pierre, 'Chrétien de Troyes et Mozart (ou l'initiation à la vie),' in *Mélanges Foulon*, vol. 1, pp. 127–39. (XXXIII.330)

10 Han, Françoise, 'Matière de Bretagne,' *Europe*, 625 (May 1981), 183–90.

11 Han, Françoise, 'Le premier romancier français,' *Europe*, 642 (Oct. 1982), 3–4. (XXXV.321)

12 Held, Jacqueline and Claude, 'Chrétien de Troyes et les jeunes d'aujourd'hui,' *Europe*, 642 (Oct. 1982), 125–32. (XXXV.322)

13 Montrozier, Yves Jocteur, 'Qui lit Chrétien de Troyes à Troyes?' *Europe*, 642 (Oct. 1982), 132–34. (XXXV.335)

14 Janssens, J. D., 'Middeleeuwse Arturvisies voor divers gebruik,' *Bzzlletin*, 124 (March 1985), 7–19. (XXXVIII.689)

15 *Payen, Jean-Charles, 'Actualité de l'initiation: quelques réflexions d'un médiéviste,' *Graal*, 6 (1986), 1–6; repr. as 'Actualité de l'initiation,' in *Normandie*, pp. 43–47.

16 Calin, William, *In Defense of French Poetry: An Essay in Revaluation* (University Park: Pennsylvania State University Press, 1987).

17 Busby, Keith, 'Arthur en Tristan,' in *Franse literatuur van de middeleeuwen*, ed. R. E. V. Stuip (Muiderberg: Coutinho, 1988), pp. 102–20. (XLII.181)
Cf. C. Hogetoorn, 'Arthur en Tristan,' in *Franse teksten uit de Middeleeuwen*, ed. R. E. V. Stuip (Muiderberg: Coutinho, 1991), pp. 113–33. (XLIV.240)

18 *Chrétien de Troyes*, special issue of *La Vie en Champagne*, 428 (Feb. 1992).
A. Philippe Ménard, 'Modernité de Chrétien de Troyes,' pp. 1–2.
B. Danielle Quéruel, 'Chrétien de Troyes, premier romancier français,' pp. 3–9.
C. Danielle Quéruel, 'Les œuvres de Chrétien de Troyes,' pp. 10–21.
D. Monique Santucci and Danielle Quéruel, 'Mythes et légendes,' pp. 23–30.
E. Christine Ferlampin-Acher and Danielle Quéruel, 'Amour et chevalerie,' pp. 31–38.
F. Danielle Quéruel, 'Bibliographie,' pp. 39–40.

19 Matthews, John, *King Arthur and the Grail Quest: Myth and Vision from Celtic Times to the Present* (London: Blandford, 1994, repr. 1995; Brockhampton, 1998). (XLVII.371)
See pp. 82–90.

20   Bonnin, Paule, and Jacqueline Casalis, *Les Expressions littéraires françaises du Moyen Age, des origines à la fin du XIIe siècle* (Paris: Ellipses-Marketing, 1995).
See pp. 44–55.

See He72 Ferlampin-Acher.

21   Day, David, *The Quest for King Arthur* (London: De Agostini Editions, 1995; O'Mara Books, 1999). (LII.372)
See pp. 112–17.

22   Berthelot, Anne, *Arthur et la Table Ronde: la force d'une légende*, Découvertes Gallimard: Littérature (Paris: Gallimard, 1996).
See Chap. 4 and 5.
English trans.: *King Arthur: History and Legend* (London: Thames and Hudson, 1997) (L.253); Japanese trans. by Nobuko Murakami, with Takeshi Matsumara (Tokyo: Sôgensha, 1997).

23   Stanesco, Michel, *Lire le Moyen Age*, Lettres Sup: Lire (Montrouge: Dunod, 1998).
See Chap. 4: 'La "Matière de Bretagne".'

24   *Modernité du Moyen Âge, = Magazine Littéraire*, 382 (Dec. 1999), 18–64.
   A.   Michel Zink, 'Le succès de la littérature médiévale,' pp. 38–42.
   B.   Charles Méla, 'Translatio,' pp. 44–47.
   C.   Jean-Marie Fritz, 'Modernité de Chrétien de Troyes,' p. 47.

c: *Erec et Enide*

3   Zenker, Rudolf, 'Erekiana,' *RF*, 40 (1927), 458–82.

4   Kamizawa, Eizô, 'In Quest of the "Couple Both Courtly and Royal" – The World of *Erec et Enide*,' *JFLN*, 70 (1977), 153–76. (XXX.470).
In Japanese.

5   Meguro, Simon, 'Commentary on *Erec et Enide* by Chrétien de Troyes (I),' *RevLA*, 54 (1977), 89–106.
In Japanese.

6   Ménage, René, '*Erec et Enide*: quelques pièces du dossier,' *Mélanges Foulon*, vol. 2, pp. 203–21. (XXXIII.359)

7 Katô, Kyôko, 'Various Problems in *Erec et Enide* by Chrétien de Troyes (I)(II),' *FFRSH*, 16 (1981), 75–93; 17 (1982), 17–36. (XXXV. 530; XXXVI.546).
In Japanese.

8 Burgess, Glyn S., *Chrétien de Troyes: Erec et Enide*, CGFT, 32 (London: Grant & Cutler, 1984). (XXXVII.161)

9 Carroll, Carleton W., and Maria Colombo Timelli, 'L'*Extrait du Roman d'Erec et Enide* de La Curne de Sainte-Palaye,' *AL*, 18 (2001), 89–123.

d: *Cligés*

3 *Nastasi, Johann, Monographie sur Cligés de Chrestien de Troyes (Linz: [n.p.], 1893).

4 *Müller, Albin, *Li Contes de Cliges: Studie* (Iglau: Verlag der Landesoberschule, 1904–05).

5 Polak, Lucie, *Chrétien de Troyes: Cligés*, CGFT, 23 (London: Grant & Cutler, 1982). (XXXVI.452)

6 Katô, Kyôko, 'A propos *Cligès* by Chrétien de Troyes (I)(II),' *FFRSH*, 18 (1983), 1–17; 19 (1984), 55–72. (XXXVII.319; XXXVIII.445)
In Japanese.

7 Panvini, Bruno, *Il 'Cligès' di Chrétien de Troyes*, Università di Catania: Quaderni del *SiG*, 17 (Catania: Università di Catania, Facoltà di Lettere e Filologia, 1989).

e: *Le Chevalier de la Charrette (Lancelot)*

2 Meguro, Simon, 'Episodes in the *Chevalier de la charrette* (I),' *ALib*, 33 (1983), 53–64.
In Japanese.

3 Katô, Kyôko, 'Various Problems in *Lancelot ou Le Chevalier de la Charrette*,' *FFRSH*, 20 (1985), 1–19. (XL.220).
In Japanese.

4 Baumgartner, Emmanuèle, *Chrétien de Troyes: Yvain, Lancelot, la charrette et le lion*, Etudes Littéraires, 38 (Paris: Presses Universitaires de France, 1992). (XLV.166)

5 Suzuki, Tetsuya, 'Illumination for Chrétien de Troyes – On "Lancelot" in *Le Chevalier de la charrette*,' *CPT*, 2 (1995), 29–53. (XLIX.372).
In Japanese.

6 *Analyses et réflexions sur Chrétien de Troyes: 'Lancelot, le Chevalier de la Charrette'* (Paris: Ellipses Marketing, 1996).
   A.   Christophe Carlier, 'Préface,' p. 5.
   B.   Irène Moillo, 'Moyen Age et civilisation occidentale,' pp. 6–14.
   C.   Sylvie Lenormand-Petit, 'Vie et œuvre de Chrétien de Troyes,' pp. 15–16.
   D.   Sylvie Lenormand-Petit, 'Généalogie des principaux personnages,' p. 17.
   E.   Sylvie Lenormand-Petit, 'Le schéma narratif de l'œuvre,' pp. 18–21.
   F.   Emmanuèle Baumgartner, 'Sur quelques structures du *Chevalier de la Charrette*,' pp. 22–24.
   G.   Didier Lamaison, 'La courtoisie et l'amour,' pp. 25–35.
   H.   Nicole Riffault, 'Le chemin de honte,' pp. 36–40.
   I.   Catherine Blons-Pierre, 'Espaces et lieux,' pp. 41–45.
   J.   Dominique Odier, 'Lancelot, Gauvain, Méléagant "chevaliers inexistants",' pp. 46–52.
   K.   Claudine Dubois, 'Les personnages féminins,' pp. 53–59.
   L.   Emmanuèle Baumgartner, 'Lancelot et les "demoiselles",' pp. 60–64.
   M.   Marie-Françoise Minaud, 'Le merveilleux: "Mervoilles li sont avenues",' pp. 65–70.
   N.   Claudine Dubois, 'L'humour,' pp. 71–76.
   O.   Serge Mainguy, 'Silence, babil et secret,' pp. 77–82.
   P.   Jean-Michel Mondoloni, 'Chrétien de Troyes et l'artifice,' pp. 83–93.
   Q.   Agnès Baril, 'Retour au texte,' pp. 94–97.
   R.   Mario Bastide, 'Un incipit en guise de prologue,' pp. 98–100.
   S.   Claire-Marie Duplessis, 'Le pont-de-l'épée (v. 3003–3141),' pp. 101–06.
   T.   Agnès Baril, 'Réalités médiévales,' pp. 107–13.
   U.   Irène Moillo, 'Du *Chevalier de la Charrette* au cycle du Corpus-Lancelot,' pp. 114–19.
   V.   Christophe Carlier, 'Anthologie,' pp. 120–24.

7 Gaucher, Elisabeth, and Laurence Mathey-Maille, *Le Chevalier de la Charrette (XIIe siècle) — Chrétien de Troyes: résumé, personnages, thèmes*, Projet Littérature: Profil d'une Œuvre, 205–06 (Paris: Hatier, 1996).

8 *'Lancelot ou Le Chevalier de la Charrette' de Chrétien de Troyes*, ed. Claude Lachet, in *L'Ecole des Lettres*, 88:10 (March 1, 1997).
   A.   Claude Lachet, 'Préface,' pp. 3–4.
   B.   Corinne Pierreville, 'Schéma narratif,' pp. 5–8.

C. Corinne Pierreville, 'La "conjointure" du *Chevalier de la Charrette*,' pp. 9–19.
D. Valérie Méot-Bourquin and Jean-Claude Vallecalle, 'La chevalerie dans le *Lancelot* de Chrétien,' pp. 21–30.
E. Claude Lachet, 'L'amour,' pp. 31–45.
F. Claude Lachet, 'L'épisode de la charrette: étude littéraire des vers 314 à 397,' pp. 47–55.
G. Marc Le Person, 'La mort,' pp. 57–66.
H. Marc Le Person, 'La tombe de marbre ou le cimetière futur,' pp. 67–75.
I. Jacques Ribard, '*Le Chevalier de la Charrette*, une allégorie du salut?' pp. 77–84.
J. Didier Verney, 'Le pont de l'épée: étude littéraire des vers 3003 à 3141,' pp. 85–91.
K. Jean-René Valette, 'Les fenêtres: architecture et écriture romanesque,' pp. 93–107.
L. Didier Verney, 'Premier combat contre Méléagant: étude littéraire des vers 3489 à 3757,' pp. 109–14.
M. Lydie Louison, 'Les présences féminines,' pp. 115–27.
N. Alban Georges, 'Pères et fils,' pp. 129–39.
O. Pierre Servet, 'Le merveilleux,' pp. 141–52.
P. Carine Bouillot, 'Traitement narratif et rôle social de l'accueil,' pp. 153–60.
Q. Marie-Luce Chênerie, 'Le *Lancelot en prose* et l'évolution du roman arthurien au XIIIe siècle,' pp. 161–72.
R. Guy Lavorel, '*Lancelot* et la littérature française du XXe siècle,' pp. 173–82.
S. 'Notes de lecture" by Jean-Pierre Tusseau, pp. 128 and 140, and Michel Marbeau, p. 183.
T. Claude Lachet, 'Bibliographie sélective,' pp. 191–92.

f: *Yvain (Le Chevalier au lion)*

4 Brand, Wolfgang, 'Chrétien de Troyes: *Yvain*,' in *Der französische Roman: vom Mittelalter bis zur Gegenwart*, ed. Klaus Heitmann, 2 vols (Düsseldorf: Bagel, 1975), vol. 1, pp. 37–62 and 360–62. (XXVIII.15)

5 Kamizawa, Eizô, 'Comment on the "sen" of the *Chevalier au lion* (*Yvain*),' *JFLN*, 64 (1975), 85–100. (XXVIII.459)
In Japanese.

6 Hunt, Tony, 'Chrétien de Troyes' Arthurian Romance, *Yvain*,' in *The New Pelican Guide to English Literature*, vol. 1:2: *Medieval Literature: The European Inheritance*, ed. Boris Ford (Harmondsworth: Penguin, 1983), pp. 126–41. (XXXVI.388, 421)

7   Hunt, Tony, *Chrétien de Troyes: Yvain (Le Chevalier au lion)*, CGFT, 55 (London: Grant & Cutler, 1986). (XXXIX.62)

8   Katô, Kyôko, 'Various Problems in *Le Chevalier au lion* (*Yvain*),' *FFRSH*, 21 (1986), 15–29. (XL.221).
In Japanese.

9   Ogura, Hiroshi, 'Study of *Yvain ou le Chevalier au Lion* (1),' *ABK*, 27 (1986), 169–91.
In Japanese.

See Bb52 Woledge.

See Ee4 Baumgartner.

10   *'Le Chevalier au Lion', de Chrétien de Troyes*, ed. Claude Lachet, in *L'Ecole des lettres*, 84:12 (May 15, 1993).
A.   Claude Lachet, 'Préface,' pp. 5–6
B.   Didier Verney, 'Le XIIᵉ siècle: repères chronologiques, pp. 7–9.
C.   Corinne Pierreville, 'Chrétien de Troyes et son œuvre,' pp. 11–17.
D.   Claude Lachet, 'La naissance du roman,' pp. 19–24.
E.   Jean-Pierre Tusseau, 'Édition Foerster ou édition Roques?' pp. 25–28.
F.   Elisabeth Kraft and Monique Lagarde, 'Lecture suivie du *Chevalier au lion*,' pp. 29–57.
G.   Didier Verney, 'Le temps dans *Le Chevalier au lion*,' pp. 59–71.
H.   Fabienne Decorsaire, 'L'espace dans *Le Chevalier au lion*,' pp. 73–83.
I.   Corinne Pierreville, 'La composition du *Chevalier au lion*,' pp. 85–94.
J.   Jean-Marie Privat, '*Le Chevalier au lion*, un conte de fees?' pp. 95–98.
K.   Claude Lachet, '*Le Chevalier au lion*, roman d'aventures,' pp. 99–112.
L.   Marie-Pierre Chaumeny and Béatrice Graillat, 'Les personnages féminins dans *Le Chevalier au lion*,' pp. 113–20.
M.   Marie-Dominique Dany, 'L'amour dans *Le Chevalier au lion*,' pp. 121–30.
N.   Claude Lachet, 'La chevalerie dans *Le Chevalier au lion*,' pp. 131–46.
O.   Marie-Odette Schmitt-Ardizio, 'L'art de Chrétien, les figures de style dans *Le Chevalier au lion*,' pp. 147–54.
P.   Pierre Servet, 'Le lion dans *Le Chevalier au lion* et dans la littérature du Moyen Age,' pp. 155–78.
Q.   Josèphe-Henriette Abry, '*Le lion d'Androclus*, étude de texte [d'Aulu-Gelle],' pp. 179–94.

R.   Guy Lavorel, 'Le lion dans la littérature française postmédiévale,' pp. 195–206.
S.   Marc Le Person, 'A la rencontre du texte d'ancien français [v. 815–81 de l'éd. Roques],' pp. 207–23.
T.   Claude Lachet, 'Bibliographie sélective sur *Le Chevalier au lion* de Chrétien de Troyes,' pp. 225–29.

11   Meyer, Kajsa, 'Crestien de Troyes – hans baggrund og kilder herunder specielt deres udmøntning i *Le Chevalier au lion*,' in *Om Arthur- og Gralsromanen*, ed. Reinhold Schröder, Mindere Skrifter udgivet af Laboratorium for Folkesproglige Middelalderstudier, 12 (Odense: Odense Universitet, 1994), pp. 23–41.

g: *Perceval (Le Conte du graal)*

4   Frappier, Jean, *Chrétien de Troyes et le mythe* [...]; 2nd rev. and corrected ed. (Paris: SEDES/CDU, 1979).

5   Paris, Gaston, 'Perceval et la légende du Saint Graal,' *Bulletin de la Société Historique et Cercle Saint-Simon* (1883–2), pp. 98–102.

6   Newell, William Wells, *The Legend of the Holy Grail and the Perceval of Crestien de Troyes* (Cambridge, MA: Sever, 1902).
See Chap. 1: 'The Perceval of Crestien,' pp. 1–18.

7   Baist, Gottfried, 'Parzival und der Gral,' Part II of *Reden Gehalten am 15. Mai 1909 bei der Feier der Übergabe des Prorektorats der Universität Freiburg i. Br.* (Freiburg/B.: Poppen, 1909), pp. 27–44.

8   Jaffray, Robert, *King Arthur and the Holy Grail: An Examination of the Early Literature Pertaining to the Legends of King Arthur and of The Holy Grail, together with a Brief Review of the Theories Relating to the Latter – Intended to Serve as an Introduction to Further Reading and More Extended Research* (New York: Putnam's, 1928).
See Chap. 3: 'Chrétien's Perceval.'

9   Sandkühler, C., 'Le *Perceval* de Chrestien de Troyes,' *Cahiers d'Etudes Cathares*, 9 (1958–59), 80–95.

10   Riquer, Martín de, *La leyenda del Graal y temas épicos medievales*, El Soto, 6 (Madrid: Prensa Española, 1968). (XXII.132)
See pp. 35–171.

11   Satomi, Sadayo, 'Le monde de Chrétien de Troyes dans *Perceval*,' *EF*, 3 (1971), 29–44.

12 Ribard, Jacques, *Le Conte du Graal (Perceval): anthologie thématique* (Paris: Hatier, 1976). (XXVIII.232)

13 Katô, Kyôko, 'Various Problems in *Le Roman de Perceval ou Le Conte du Graal,' FFRSH*, 22 (1987), 47–61. (XLI.306)
In Japanese.

14 Shitanda, Sô, '*Le Conte du Graal (Perceval)* by Chrétien de Troyes – Japanese Translation and Commentary (1),' *BLAN*, 29:2 (1989), 35–51.
In Japanese.

15 Busby, Keith, *Chrétien de Troyes: Perceval (Le Conte du graal)*, CGFT, 98 (London: Grant & Cutler, 1993) (XLVI.420).

16 Ménard, Philippe, 'Énigmes et mystères dans le *Conte du Graal* de Chrétien de Troyes,' *EFrH*, 12 (1993), 1–25; repr. in Dc29. (XLVIII.593).

17 '*Le Conte du Graal' de Chrétien de Troyes*, ed. Claude Lachet, in *L'Ecole des Lettres*, 87:6 (January 15, 1996).
    A.   Claude Lachet, 'Préface,' p. 3.
    B.   Virgine Souvignet, 'Schéma narratif,' pp. 5–9.
    C.   Lydie Louison, 'La rencontre de Perceval et des chevaliers: étude littéraire des vers 67 à 334,' pp. 11–18.
    D.   Mireille Broyer, 'Le portrait de Blanchefleur: explication linéaire des vers 1746–1787,' pp. 19–26.
    E.   Corinne Pierreville, 'Le cortège du Graal: explication linéaire des vers 3128–3191,' pp. 27–36.
    F.   Marie-Dominique Dany, 'L'interrogatoire de Perceval par sa cousine: commentaire composé des vers 3485–3533,' pp. 37–44.
    G.   Didier Verney, 'Les trois gouttes de sang sur la neige: lecture méthodique des vers 4105–4149,' pp. 45–54.
    H.   Alban Georges, 'La malédiction de la Demoiselle Hideuse: explication linéaire des vers 4540–4613,' pp. 55–62.
    I.   Fabienne Decorsaire, 'Gauvain à Escavalon: étude littéraire des vers 5731–6124,' pp. 63–73.
    J.   Jacques Ribard, 'L'écriture romanesque du *Conte du Graal*: "conjointure" et "senefiance",' pp. 75–84.
    K.   Jean Dufournet, '*Le Conte du Graal*, roman d'éducation,' pp. 85–92.
    L.   Philippe Ménard, 'Le rire et le sourire dans le *Conte du Graal*,' pp. 93–106; repr. in Dc29.
    M.   Marc Le Person, 'Réécritures bibliques dans le *Conte du Graal*,' pp. 107–14.
    N.   Pierre Servet, 'Le roi Pêcheur,' pp. 115–28.
    O.   Marie-Pierre Chaumeny, 'Blanchefleur et l'Orgueilleuse de Logres: les paradoxes de l'*alter ego*,' pp. 129–36.

P.   Jean-Marie Privat, 'Le chevalier "salvaige",' pp. 137–41.
Q.   Claude Lachet, 'Le Graal chez Chrétien de Troyes et ses épigones,' pp. 143–60.
R.   Nicole Gonthier, 'Le culte des reliques au XIIe siècle,' pp. 161–68.
S.   Alain Marc Plasman, '*Saint Graal*, poème de Verlaine,' pp. 169–74.
T.   Jean-Yves Debreuille, 'La quête inachevée: Chrétien de Troyes et Julien Gracq,' pp. 175–83.
U.   Béatrice Graillat, 'Quelques réflexions sur *Perceval le Gallois*, d'Éric Rohmer,' pp. 185–96.
V.   Claude Lachet,' Bibliographie sélective,' pp. 197–98.

18   *Chrétien de Troyes: Le Conte du graal*, ed. Danielle Quéruel (Paris: Ellipses, 1998). (LI.228, LII.224)
A.   Danielle Quéruel, 'Avant-propos,' pp. 7–9.
B.   Roger Bellon, 'Partir, s'arrêter, revenir... Sur les pas des chevaliers errants dans *Le Conte du graal*,' pp. 12–25. (LI.208, LII.200)
C.   Laurence Hélix, 'Perceval ou l'apprentissage du temps,' pp. 28–42. (LI.250, LII.241)
D.   Micheline Combarieu du Grès, 'Les enjeux de la langue dans *Le Conte du graal*,' pp. 43–61. (LI.231, LII.223)
E.   Claude Lachet, 'La confession de Perceval chez l'ermite: étude littéraire des vers 6136 à 6217,' pp. 62–71. (LI.259, LII.247)
F.   Frédérique Le Nan, 'La *male pucelle* aux bornes de Galvoie,' pp. 74–88. (LI.266, LII.250)
G.   Corinne Pierreville, 'Figures féminines dans *Le Conte du graal*,' pp. 89–101. (LI.286, LII.269)
H.   Romaine Wolf-Bonvin, 'Gauvain et la Demoiselle aux Petites Manches: l'enfance de l'aventure,' pp. 102–16. (LI.317, LII.293)
I.   Jean-René Valette, 'Merveille et merveilleux dans *Le Conte du graal*: éléments de poétique,' pp. 118–35. (LI.311, LII.289)
J.   Cristina Noacco, 'Le château entre réalité et *merveille* dans *Le Conte du graal*,' pp. 136–46. (LI.280, LII.257)
K.   Danielle Quéruel, 'Le roi qui "fet les chevaliers": du mythe celtique au roman arthurien,' pp. 147–63. (LI.291, LII.273)
L.   Jean-Pierre Perrot, '*Le Conte du graal* et les figures de l'individuation, ou la difficile quête de soi,' pp. 166–79. (LI.285, LII.267)

19   *Polyphonie du Graal*, ed. Denis Hüe, Medievalia, 26 (Orléans: Paradigme, 1998). (LI.287)
Contains (all in French): Hg83 Aronstein, Hg28 Baumgartner, Hg30 Gallais (LI.242), Hg59 Ménard, Uc7 Poirion, Gd.a6 Poirion, Jb24 Ribard (LI.294), Jd22 Ribard (LI.295), Hg42 Saly, Hg57 Saly, Hg78 Sargent-Baur, and Richard O'Gorman, 'Deux siècles de recherches sur le Graal,' pp. 181–88.

20   Szkilnik, Michelle, '*Perceval*' ou '*le Roman du graal*' de Chrétien de Troyes, Foliothèque, 74 (Paris: Gallimard, 1998). (LI.306)

21 Baumgartner, Emmanuèle, *Chrétien de Troyes: Le Conte du Graal*, Etudes Littéraires, 62 (Paris: Presses Universitaires de France, 1999). (LII.199)

22 Lucía Megías, José Manuel, 'Introducción' to his translation *Chrétien de Troyes: El libro de Perceval (o El cuento del Grial)*, Clásicos Medievales, 20 (Madrid: Gredos, 2000), pp. 7–72. Useful notes.

23 Yokoyama, Ayumi, 'Chrétien de Troyes: the Origin of the Grail and its Quest,' *Asahi*, 56 (2000), 178–81. In Japanese.

h: Selected Recent Entries in Dictionaries, Encyclopedias, and Other Compendia

1 *Dictionary of the Middle Ages*, ed. Joseph R. Strayer, 13 vols (New York: Scribner's for the American Council of Learned Societies, 1982–89).
See Michelle A. Freeman, 'Chrétien de Troyes,' vol. 3, pp. 308–11.

2 *European Writers: The Middle Ages and the Renaissance*, 2 vols (New York: Scribner's, 1983).
See D. D. R. Owen, 'Chrétien de Troyes,' in vol. 1, pp. 185–209.

3 *Dictionnaire des littératures de langue française*, ed. J.-P. de Beaumarchais, Daniel Couty, and Alain Rey, 3 vols (Paris: Bordas, 1984).
See J.-Ch. Payen, 'Chrétien de Troyes,' vol. 1, pp. 453–60.

4 *The Arthurian Encyclopedia*, ed. Norris J. Lacy [et alii], GRLH, 585 (New York: Garland, 1986) (XL.296); rev. ed. *The New Arthurian Encyclopedia*, ed. Norris J. Lacy [et alii], GRLH, 931 (New York: Garland, 1991).
See Norris J. Lacy, 'Chrétien de Troyes,' pp. 104–9 (1986 ed.), pp. 88–91 (1991 ed.)

5 *A New History of French Literature*, ed. Denis Hollier (Cambridge, MA: Harvard University Press, 1989, 1994); French trans.: *De la littérature française* (Paris: Bordas, 1992). (XLII.314)
See Eugene Vance, '*Erec et Enide*,' pp. 41–46.

6 Alvar, Carlos, *El rey Arturo y su mundo: diccionario de mitología artúrica* (Madrid: Alianza Editorial, 1991). (XLVI.223)

7   *Dictionnaire des lettres françaises: Le Moyen Age*, ed. Robert Bossuat, Louis Pichard, and Guy Raynaud de Lage, rev. and updated by Geneviève Hasenohr and Michel Zink (Paris: Fayard, 1992).
See Jean-Marie Fritz, 'Chrétien de Troyes,' pp. 266–80.

8   *Patrimoine littéraire européen: anthologie en langue française,* vol. 4b: *Le Moyen Age, de l'Oural à l'Atlantique: littératures d'Europe Occidentale*, ed. Jean-Claude Polet (Brussels: De Boeck Université, 1993), pp. 477–88.

9   *Medieval France: An Encyclopedia*, ed. William W. Kibler, Grover A. Zinn [et alii], Garland Encyclopedias of the Middle Ages, 2 – GRLH, 932 (New York: Garland, 1995).
See Douglas Kelly, 'Chrétien de Troyes,' pp. 219–22.

10   Bruce, Christopher W., *The Arthurian Name Dictionary*, GRLH, 2063 (New York: Garland, 1999). (LI.733)

11   Lindahl, Carl, John McNamara, and John Lindow, ed., *Medieval Folklore: An Encyclopedia of Myths, Legends, Tales, Beliefs, and Customs*, 2 vols (Santa Barbara, CA: ABC-CLIO, 2000). (LIII.962)
    A.   Norris J. Lacy, 'Chrétien de Troyes (fl. 1165–1191),' vol. 1, pp. 177–80.
    B.   Francesca Canadé Sautman, 'French Tradition: The Folklore Culture of France,' vol. 1, pp. 379–89.
    C.   Nancy Mason Bradbury, 'Romance,' vol. 2, pp. 838–46.

F: RHETORIC, POETICS, AND STYLISTICS

The most striking development in the area of this topic has been the growing interest in orality. Rhetoric has traditionally been an oral art, although scholarship has focused on it as a written art. Since Chrétien's voice has fallen silent, scholars have examined manuscripts for clues as to how his poems were performed and how spoken word and even gesture may have featured in such performances. Corollary to the interest in orality has been the awareness that performances could be quite diverse, and that different kinds of evidence illustrate that diversity. Study of versification in particular has benefited from these approaches since verse can reveal features of oral performance. Indeed, the common medieval practice of reading aloud requires attention to some features of the Old French language; see sections Kc and Kd. More recently it has been proposed that we distinguish radically between scholastic rhetoric and jongleur or minstrel performances. Some have relocated Chrétien among the latter, thereby depriving him of his clerical status and the education that went with that status, including rhetoric.

For recent work on the medieval arts of poetry, see Paul Klopsch, *Einführung in die Dichtungslehren des lateinischen Mittelalters*, Das lateinische Mittelalter (Darmstadt: Wissenschaftliche Buchgesellschaft, 1980); Douglas Kelly, *The Arts of Poetry and Prose*, TMA, 59 (Turnhout: Brepols, 1991); and Jean-Yves Tilliette, *Des mots à la Parole: une lecture de la 'Poetria nova' de Geoffroy de Vinsauf*, RRG, 16 (Geneva: Droz, 2000).

a: General Studies

43   Guiette, Robert, 'Observations [...]' Repr. in Dc6.

46   Micha, Alexandre, 'Le Discours [...]' Repr. in Dc3.

See Kd31 Kadler.

57 Schepp, Fritz, *Altfranzösische Sprichwörter und Sentenzen aus den höfischen Kunstepen über antike Sagenstoffe und aus einigen didaktischen Dichtungen nebst einer Untersuchung über Sprichwörtervarianten*, diss. Greifswald (Borna-Leipzig: Noske, 1905).

58 Stevenson, William M., *Der Einfluss des Gautier d'Arras auf die altfranzösische Kunstepik, insbesondere auf den Abenteuerroman*, diss. Göttingen (Göttingen: Dieterich, 1910).
See 'III. Hauptteil: Das Verhältnis Gautiers zu anderen Dichtern, in Bezug auf den Stil, im Besonderen zu Chrétien de Troies,' pp. 70–101.

59 Wilmotte, M., 'Observations sur le roman de Troie,' *MA*, 18 (1914), 93–119.
Comparison with Chrétien's *Cligés*.

See Kc23 Biller.

60 Schultz-Gora, Oskar, 'Das Adynaton in der altfranzösischen und provenzalischen Dichtung nebst Dazugehörigem,' *AStnSpr*, 161 (1932), 196–209.

61 Schaar, Claes, *The Golden Mirror: Studies in Chaucer's Descriptive Technique and its Literary Background*, Skrifter utgavna av kungl. Humanistiska Vetenskapssamfundet i Lund, 54 (Lund: Gleerup, 1955).
See pp. 141–43.

62 Elwert, W. Theodor, 'Zur Synonymendoppelung als Interpretationshilfe,' *AStnSpr*, 195 (1959), 24–26.
Includes *Cligés* v. 584–91 (ed. Foerster).

See Qc28 Russo.

63 Sutherland, D. R., 'The Love Meditation in Courtly Literature (A Study of the Terminology and its Development in Old Provençal and Old French),' in *Studies Ewert*, pp. 165–93.

64 Bernhard, Erwin, *Les Pinceaux des trouvères: essai sur la technique descriptive des épopées et des romans français du XIIe siècle*, diss. Zürich (Bologna: Palmaverde, 1962). (XV.200)
Cf. his 'Abstractions médiévales ou critique abstraite,' *SMV*, 9 (1961), 19–70.

See Ge19 Rohr.

65 Renzi, Lorenzo, *Tradizione cortese e realismo in Gautier d'Arras*, Università di Padova: Pubblicazioni della Facoltà di Lettere e Filosofia, 42 (Padua: CEDAM, 1964). (XVII.158)

See Part II, Chap. 1: 'Le battaglie: abbozzo di paragone tra Gautier d'Arras e Chrétien de Troyes' (pp. 79–96), Chap. 2: ' "Descriptiones personarum": l'arte del ritratto in Gautier d'Arras e Chrétien de Troyes' (pp. 97–120), and Chap. 3: 'Astrazione e realtà' (pp. 121–44).

66 Brinkmann, Hennig, 'Der Prolog im Mittelalter als literarische Erscheinung: Bau und Aussage,' *WW*, 14 (1964), 1–21; repr. in his *Studien zur Geschichte der deutschen Sprache und Literatur*, 2 vols (Düsseldorf: Schwann, 1965–66), vol. 2, pp. 79–105.

On Middle High German prologues, applicable to French romance, but see Fa126.

See Pa81 Lyons.

See Ge21 Worstbrock.

67 Zumthor, Paul, 'Topique et tradition,' *Poétique*, 7 (1971), 354–65.

68 Stempel, Wolf-Dieter, 'Perspektivische Rede in der französischen Literatur des Mittelalters,' in *Interpretation und Vergleich: Festschrift für Walter Pabst* (Berlin: Schmidt, 1972), pp. 310–30.

Treats narrative point of view and the unreliable narrator.

69 Bertau, Karl, *Deutsche Literatur im europäischen Mittelalter*, 2 vols Munich: Beck, 1972–73).
  A. 'Tristan und Erec,' vol. 1, pp. 437–49.
  B. 'Roman als Romanparodie,' vol. 1, pp. 498–509.
  C. 'Deutscher und französischer Artusroman gegen 1180,' vol. 1, pp. 562–69.
  D. 'Jenseits der Artus-Thematik: Perceval und Gregorius,' vol. 1, pp. 601–35.
  E. 'Neue Strukturen im *Perceval*,' vol. 2, pp. 601–12.
  F. '*Perceval*-Prolog und *Perceval*-Fragment,' vol. 2, pp. 612–21.

70 Dronke, Peter, 'Mediaeval Rhetoric,' in *Mediaeval World*, pp. 315–45.

See Pg9 Durán.

71 Niemeyer, Karina H., 'Latin *Arts poétiques* and Medieval French Literature,' in *SMC*, 4:1 (1973), 147–51.

See Gd.b7 Pearsall and Salter.

72 Zumthor, Paul, 'Autobiography in the Middle Ages,' *Genre*, 6 (1973), 29–48.

73 Badel, Pierre-Yves, 'Pourquoi une poétique médiévale?' *Poétique*, 18 (1974), 246–64.
On Fa49 Zumthor.

74 Ray, Roger D., 'Medieval Historiography through the Twelfth Century: Problems and Progress of Research,' *Viator*, 5 (1974), 33–59.
Useful critical evaluation of narrative in historical writing, applicable to romance as an emergent genre in 12th century.

75 Aragón Fernández, Mª Aurora, 'Paralelismos léxicos en el lenguaje poético del *roman courtois*,' *Archivum*, 25 (1975), 65–79.

76 Badel, Pierre-Yves, 'Rhétorique et polémique dans les prologues de romans au Moyen Age,' *Littérature*, 20 (1975), 81–94.

77 Green, Dennis H., 'Alieniloquium: zur Begriffsbestimmung der mittelalterlichen Ironie,' in *Verbum et signum*, vol. 2: *Beiträge zur mediävistischen Bedeutungsforschung. Studien zur Semantik und Sinntradition im Mittelalter*, ed. Hans Fromm, Wolfgang Harms, and Uwe Ruberg (Munich: Fink, 1975), pp. 119–59. (XXVIII.30)

78 Green, D. H., 'On Damning with Faint Praise in Medieval Literature,' *Viator*, 6 (1975), 117–69.

79 Rossman, Vladimir R., *Perspectives of Irony in Medieval French Literature*, De Proprietatibus Litterarum: Series Maior, 35 (The Hague: Mouton, 1975).
See Chap. 3:2 on *Cligés* and 4:2 on *Yvain*.

See Gb37 Wisbey.

80 Aragón Fernández, María Aurora, 'Campos semánticos y recurrencia léxica en la narrativa francesa del siglo XII,' *MedR*, 3 (1976), 66–84.

81 Bornscheuer, Lothar, *Topik: zur Struktur der gesellschaftlichen Einbildungskraft* (Frankfurt/M.: Suhrkamp, 1976).
On theory of topoi in antiquity and Middle Ages.

82 Hardison, O. B., Jr., 'Toward a History of Medieval Literary Criticism,' *M&H*, 7 (1976), 1–12.

83   Payen, Jean-Charles, 'Le clos et l'ouvert dans la littérature française médiévale et les problèmes de la communication (éléments d'une problématique),' *PerM*, 2 (1976), 61–72. (XXX.287)

84   Vance, Eugene, 'La théorie du signe et les genres littéraires au moyen-âge,' *Actes Laval*, vol. 2, pp. 935–43 (discussion pp. 944–46).

85   Zumthor, Paul, 'L'épiphonème proverbial,' *RSH*, 163 (1976), 313–28.

86   Cherchi, Paolo A., 'Tradition and Topoi in Medieval Literature,' *CI*, 3 (1976–77), 281–94; repr. in his *Andrea Cappellano, i trovatori e altri temi romanzi*, Biblioteca di Cultura, 128 (Rome: Bulzoni, 1979), pp. 1–18.

87   Freeman, Michelle A., 'Problems of Romance Composition: Ovid, Chrétien de Troyes, and the *Romance of the Rose*', *RPh*, 30 (1976–77), 158–68.

88   Ballet Lynn, Thérèse, *Recherches sur l'ambiguïté et la satire au Moyen Age (art et littérature)* (Paris: Nizet, 1977).
See pp. 58–76 and 103–21.

89   Beer, Jeanette M. A., 'Style and Styles in Medieval French Literature,' *Parergon*, 17 (April 1977), 11–15.
On archaisms.

90   Haidu, Peter, 'Repetition: Modern Reflections on Medieval Aesthetics,' *MLN*, 92 (1977), 875–87.

91   Haug, Walter, 'Gebet und Hieroglyphe: zur Bild- und Architektur-beschreibung in der mittelalterlichen Dichtung,' *ZfdA*, 106 (1977), 163–83; repr. in Dc15. (XXX.28)
Includes discussion of Enide's horse in Hartmann von Aue.

92   Pastré, J.-M., 'La notion d'*ornement difficile* dans les arts poétiques et dans la littérature française et allemande des XIIe et XIIIe siècles,' in *Histoire et littérature: les écrivains et la politique*, Centre d'Etude et de Recherche d'Histoire des Idées et de la Sensibilité: PUR, 42 (Paris: Presses Universitaires de France, 1977), pp. 185–204.

See Gb45 Schmolke-Hasselmann.

See Va11 Allen.

93 Kaiser, Gert, 'Zum Literaturbegriff des Hohen Mittelalters,' *RZLG*, 2 (1978), 275–97.

See La27 Kelly.

See Sa81 Kelly.

94 Kelly, Douglas, 'Rhetoric in French Literature: Topical Invention in Medieval French Literature,' in *Medieval Eloquence: Studies in the Theory and Practice of Medieval Rhetoric*, ed. James J. Murphy (Berkeley: University of California Press, 1978), pp. 231–51. (XXXI.105)

95 Liborio, Mariantonia, 'Problèmes théoriques de la description,' *AION: Sezione Germanica, Studi Nederlandesi-Studi Nordici*, 21 (1978), 315–33. (XXXIII.532, XXXVI.522)
See pp. 325–29 on *Erec*.

See Gd.b12 Notz.

96 Ollier, Marie-Louise, 'Le présent du récit: temporalité et roman en vers,' *LF*, 40 (1978), 99–112. Repr. in Dc32.

See Da10 Rohr.

See Ha85 Sklute.

97 Zumthor, Paul, 'Le texte-fragment,' *LF*, 40 (1978), 75–82.
Considers the text fragmented by transmission, deliberate failure to complete, and *mouvance*. Refers to the *Charrette* and *Perceval*.

98 Green, D. H., *Irony in the Medieval Romance* (Cambridge: Cambridge University Press, 1979). (XXXII.417)
See 'Index of Passages Discussed,' s. n. Chrétien de Troyes, pp. 419–20.

99 Hunt, Tony, '*Prodesse et delectare*: Metaphors of Pleasure and Instruction in Old French,' *NM*, 80 (1979), 17–35.

100 Kamizawa, Eizô, 'Portraits in Medieval French Literature – The Evolution of the Description of Personal Portraits,' *JFLN*, Special Thirtieth Anniversary Number (1979), pp. 385–97. (XXXIII.574)
In Japanese.

101 Lacy, Norris J., 'Typology and Analogy,' in *Authors and Philosophers*, University of South Carolina French Literature Series, 6 (Columbia: University of South Carolina, 1979), pp. 126–30. (XXXIV.137)

See Pb230–31 Pastré.

102 Pickens, Rupert T., 'Historical Consciousness in Old French Narrative,' *FF*, 4 (1979), 168–84. (XXXII.212)

103 Schulze-Busacker, Elisabeth, 'Eléments de culture populaire dans la littérature courtoise,' in *La Culture populaire au Moyen Age: Etudes présentées au Quatrième Colloque de l'Institut d'Etudes Médiévales de l'Université de Montréal, 2–3 avril 1977*, ed. Pierre Boglioni (Montréal: L'Aurore, 1979), pp. 81–101. (XXXVII.458)
On use of proverbs.

See Ja29 Brinkmann.
Sequel to Fa7.

See Gd.c18 Bruckner.

104 Buridant, Claude, 'Les binômes synonymiques: esquisse d'une histoire des couples de synonymes du Moyen Age au XVIIe siècle,' *Bulletin du Centre d'Analyse du Discours*, 4 (1980), 5–79.

105 Knapp, Fritz Peter, 'Historische Wahrheit und poetische Lüge: die Gattungen weltlicher Epik und ihre theoretische Rechtfertigung im Hochmittelalter,' *DVj*, 54 (1980), 581–635; repr. in Dc26. (XXXV.39)
See pp. 624–28.

106 Limentani, Alberto, 'Effetti di specularità nella narrativa medievale,' *RZLG*, 4 (1980), 307–21. (XXXIII.47)

See Gd.c19 Peron.

107 Sinclair, K. V., 'The Proverbial Question in French Literature,' *NZJFS*, 1:2 (1980), 5–25.

108 Uitti, Karl D., 'The Myth of Poetry in Twelfth- and Thirteenth-Century France,' in *Proteus*, pp. 142–56. (XXXIV.153)

109 Zumthor, Paul, 'D'une poésie littérale,' *RSH*, 179 (1980), 7–21.

See Kc66 Cerquiglini.

110 Hunt, Tony, 'Irony and the Rise of Courtly Romance,' *GLL*, 35 (1981–82), 98–104. (XXXIV.327)
On Fa98 Green.

111 Lebsanft, Franz, 'Perspektivische Rededarstellung (erlebte Rede) in Texten des französischen und spanischen Mittelalters,' *ZrP*, 97 (1981), 65–85. (XXXV.44)

112 Reiss, Edmund, 'Medieval Irony,' *JHI*, 42 (1981), 209–26.

113 Schnell, Rüdiger, 'Grenzen literarischer Freiheit im Mittelalter: I. Höfischer Roman und Minnerede,' *AStnSpr*, 218 (1981), 241–70.

See Gf20 Schulze-Busacker.

See Ha110 Zink.

114 Hult, David F., 'Vers la société de l'écriture: *Le Roman de la Rose*', *Poétique*, 50 (1982), 155–72.
Includes discussion of orality and Chrétien.

115 Hunt, Tony, 'Rhetoric and Poetics in Twelfth-Century France,' in *Rhetoric*, pp. 165–71. (XXXVII.397)

116 Nordahl, Helge, 'Figure rhétorique, rhétorisabilité et rhétorisation: quelques réflexions sur les tautologies binaires en ancien français,' *ZfSL*, 92 (1982), 124–31.

117 Perret, Michèle, 'De l'espace romanesque à la matérialité du livre: l'espace énonciatif des premiers romans en prose,' *Poétique*, 50 (1982), 173–82. (XXXV.342)
See p. 178.

See Pb268 Ranawake, pp. 79–92.

118 Willaert, Frank, '*Matière* et *sens* chez Chrétien de Troyes et Hadewijch (d'Anvers?),' *MA*, 88 (1982), 421–34. (XXXV.259)

119 Busby, K. R., 'Ironisering en ridiculisering van de hoofsheid,' in *Hoofse Cultuur: Studies over een aspect van de middeleeuwse cultuur*, ed. R. E. V. Stuip and C. Vellekoop (Utrecht: H&S, 1983), pp. 139–53. (XXXVIII.678)
On irony, parody, and burlesque.

See Gb72 Ginsberg, Chap. 3: 'Literary Typology and the Medieval Idea of Character.'

See Ke9 Härmä.

120 Kelly, Douglas, 'La spécialité dans l'invention des topiques,' in *Archéologie du signe*, ed. Lucie Brind'Amour and Eugene Vance,

Recueil d'Etudes Médiévales, 3 (Toronto: Pontifical Institute of Medieval Studies, 1983), pp. 101–25. (XXXV.167)

121 Payen, Jean Charles, 'Le statut de l'écrivain dans les fabliaux de Jean Bodel,' in *Comique, satire et parodie dans la tradition renardienne et les fabliaux: Actes du Colloque des 15 et 16 janvier 1983*, ed. Danielle Buschinger and André Crépin, GAG, 391 (Göppingen: Kümmerle, 1983), pp. 47–58.
Compares with *Cligés* Prologue.

122 Saly, Antoinette, 'Métaphore et invention littéraire au Moyen Age,' *TLL*, 21:2 (1983), 239–46. (XXXVI.367)
Includes motif of comb found by fountain (*Charrette*).

123 Szabics, Imre, *Epika és költőiség, A XII. Századi francia elbeszélő költészet stíluseszközei* (Budapest: Akadémiai Kiadó, 1983). (XL.203)

124 Kelly, Douglas, 'Obscurity and Memory: Sources for Invention in Medieval French Literature,' in *Vernacular Poetics*, pp. 33–56. (XXXVII.408)

See Ha123 Kelly.

125 Kennedy, Elspeth, 'Etudes sur le *Lancelot* en prose: I. Les allusions au *Conte Lancelot* et à d'autres contes dans le *Lancelot* en prose,' *Rom*, 105 (1984), 34–46. (XXXVIII.232)
Comparisons with Chrétien.

See Pg15 Paredes Núñez.

126 Schultz, James A., 'Classical Rhetoric, Medieval Poetics, and the Medieval Vernacular Prologue,' *Spec*, 59 (1984), 1–15. (XXXVII. 456)

127 Schulze-Busacker, Elisabeth, 'Proverbe ou sentence: essai de définition,' *MF*, 14–15 (1984), 134–67.

128 Specht, Henrik, 'The Beautiful, the Handsome, and the Ugly: Some Aspects of the Art of Character Portrayal in Medieval Literature,' *SN*, 56 (1984), 129–46.
The Giant Herdsman in *Yvain*.

129 Ziolkowski, Jan, 'Avatars of Ugliness in Medieval Literature,' *MLR*, 79 (1984), 1–20. (XXXVII.194)
Treats the Giant Herdsman in *Yvain* and the Loathly Damsel in *Perceval*.

See Gb80 Brandt.

130 Haug, Walter, *Literaturtheorie im deutschen Mittelalter: von den Anfängen bis zum Ende des 13. Jahrhunderts. Eine Einführung*, Germanistische Einführungen (Darmstadt: Wissenschaftliche Buchgesellschaft, 1985; 2nd ed. revised and enlarged, 1992). (XXXVIII.30)

See Chap. 5: 'Chrétiens de Troyes "Erec"-Prolog und das arthurische Strukturmodell,' and Chap. 6: 'Inspiration und dichterisches Selbstverständnis in Chrétiens "Lancelot" und "Cligés".'

English trans.: *Vernacular Literary Theory in the Middle Ages: The German Tradition, 800–1300, in its European Context*, trans. Joanna M. Catling, CSML, 29 (Cambridge: Cambridge University Press, 1997). (L.265)

131 Haupt, Barbara, ed., *Zum mittelalterlichen Literaturbegriff*, WF, 557 (Darmstadt: Wissenschaftliche Buchgesellschaft, 1985). (XXXVIII.65)

Includes Fa24 Köhler, Fa52 Zumthor and Fa93 Kaiser.

132 Liborio, Mariantonia, 'L'*Effictio ad vituperium*: le funzioni del "brutto",' *AION*, 27 (1985), 39–48.

133 Ruhe, Ernstpeter, '*Inventio* devenue *troevemens*: la recherche de la matière au Moyen Age,' in *ICLS Toronto*, pp. 289–97. (XXXVIII.343)

See Ha133 Sasu.

134 Schulze-Busacker, Elisabeth, *Proverbes et expressions proverbiales dans la littérature narrative du Moyen Age français: recueil et analyse*, NBMA, 9 (Paris: Champion, 1985). (XXXVIII.265)

On Chrétien see pp. 46–64; the appendix is a 'Relevé des occurrences proverbiales.'

135 Trimborn, Karin, *Syntaktisch-stilistische Untersuchungen zu Chrétiens 'Yvain' und Hartmanns 'Iwein': ein textlinguistischer Vergleich*, PSQ, 103 (Berlin: Schmidt, 1985). (XXXVIII.61)

See La37 Worstbrock.

136 Maddox, Donald, 'Roman et manipulation au 12e siècle,' *Poétique*, 66 (1986), 179–90. (XXXIX.657)

137 Poirion, Daniel, 'Théorie et pratique du style au Moyen Age: le sublime et la merveille,' *RHL*, 86 (1986), 15–32; repr. in Dc21.

138 Serper, Arié, 'Le concept de l'ironie, de Platon au Moyen Age,' *CAIEF*, 38 (1986), 7–25. (XXXIX.673).

Treats the *Charrette* and *Yvain*, pp. 18–25.

See Gb89 Aercke.

139 Amazawa, Taijirô, *Dream Essays* (Tokyo: Shichôsha, 1987). (XL.215)

In Japanese. See esp. pp.11–61 (a series of articles collected under the title 'Who Speaks of the Dream?' and first published in *Gendaishi-Techo*, March-September 1983). (XXXVII.318)

See Kd103 Brucker.

140 Hanning, Robert W., '"I Shal Finde It in a Maner Glose": Versions of Textual Harassment in Medieval Literature,' in *Medieval Texts and Contemporary Readers*, ed. Laurie A. Finke and Martin B. Shichtman (Ithaca, NY: Cornell University Press, 1987), pp. 27–50. (XL.283)

See Qa85(A) Martineau-Genieys.

141 Kelly, Douglas, 'The Art of Description,', in *Legacy*, vol. 1, pp. 191–221. (XLII.213)

See Pa198 Krueger.

See Pa201 Pickens.

See Gf26 Cerquiglini.

See Bb54 Dembowski, pp. 262–65 and 269

142 Dragonetti, Roger, 'Rhétoriques du silence,' in *Théories*, pp. 235–49.

See Qb54 Kelly.

143 Marchello-Nizia, Christiane, 'L'invention du dialogue amoureux: le masque d'une différence,' in *Masques et déguisements dans la littérature médiévale*, ed. Marie-Louise Ollier, Etudes Médiévales (Montreal: Presses de l'Université de Montréal; Paris: Vrin, 1988), pp. 223–31. (XLI.413)

144 Rohr, Rupprecht, 'Die Schönheit des Menschen in der mittelalterlichen Dichtung Frankreichs,' in *Schöne Frauen – schöne Männer: literarische Schönheitsbeschreibungen: 2. Kolloquium der Forschungsstelle für europäische Literatur des Mittelalters* (Mannheim: Forschungsstelle für europäische Lyrik des Mittelalters an der Universität Mannheim; Tübingen: Narr, 1988), pp. 89–107.

See Kc87 Rychner.

See Hf82 Edwards.

See Pb327 Haupt.

145 Méla, Charles, '*Poetria nova* et *homo novus*,' *Littérature*, 74 (1989), 4–26; repr. in Dc19.

See Ha151 Peron.

146 Rychner, Jean, 'Le monologue de discours indirect dans quelques récits français des XIIe et XIIIe siècles,' in *Miscellanea di studi in onore di Aurelio Roncaglia a cinquant'anni dalla sua laurea*, 4 vols (Modena: Mucchi, 1989), vol. 4, pp. 1187–97. (XLII.127)

147 Stanesco, Michel, '"D'armes et d'amour": la fortune d'une *devise* médiévale,' *TrL*, 2 (1989), 37–54. (XLII.78)

148 Dornbush, Jean M., *Pygmalion's Figure: Reading Old French Romance*, ECAM, 5 (Lexington, KY: French Forum, 1990). (XLIII.524)

See Pa224 Berthelot.

149 De Looze, Laurence, 'Signing Off in the Middle Ages: Medieval Textuality and Strategies of Authorial Self-Naming,' in *Vox intexta: Orality and Textuality in the Middle Ages*, ed. A. N. Doane and Carol Braun Pasternack (Madison: University of Wisconsin Press, 1991), pp. 162–78.

150 Köhler, Gisela Ruth, *Das literarische Porträt: eine Untersuchung zur geschlossenen Personendarstellung in der französischen Erzählliteratur vom Mittelalter bis zum Ende des 19. Jahrhunderts*, Abhandlungen zur Sprache und Literatur, 38 (Bonn: Romanistischer Verlag, 1991).
Treats descriptions in *Erec*, the *Charrette*, and *Yvain*.

151 Clemente, Linda M., *Literary 'objets d'art': 'Ekphrasis' in Medieval French Romance 1150–1210*, AUS:RL, 166 (New York: P. Lang, 1992).

152 Fein, David A., 'Que vous en mentiroie? The Problem of Authorial Reliability in the Twelfth-Century French Narrative,' *PQ*, 71 (1992), 1–14.

See Gb111 Fritz.

153 Graevenitz, Gerhart von, '*Contextio* und *conjointure*, Gewebe und Arabeske: über Zusammenhänge mittelalterlicher und romantischer

Literaturtheorie,' in *Literatur, Artes und Philosophie*, ed. Walter Haug and Burghart Wachinger, Fortuna Vitrea, 7 (Tübingen: Niemeyer, 1992), pp. 229–57.

See Pb355 Kellermann.

154 Kelly, Douglas, *The Art of Medieval French Romance* (Madison: University of Wisconsin Press), 1992. (XLIV.319)

155 Melkersson, Anders, *L'Itération lexicale: étude sur l'usage d'une figure stylistique dans onze romans français des XIIe et XIIIe siècles*, Romanica Gothoburgensia, 41 (Göteborg: Acta Universitatis Gothoburgensis, 1992).
Includes all Chrétien's romances.

156 Zumthor, Paul, 'L'imaginaire de la cité dans l'imaginaire médiéval,' in *50 rue de Varenne*, Supplemento Italo-Francese di Nuovi Argomenti, 43 (Paris: Istituto Italiano di Cultura di Parigi, 1992), pp. 17–26. (XLV.204)

157 Dubost, Francis, 'La pensée de l'impensable dans la fiction médiévale,' in *Ecriture*, pp. 47–68. (XLVI.322)

158 Fein, David A., '*Le latin sivrai*: Problematic Aspects of Narrative Authority in Twelfth-Century French Literature,' *FR*, 66 (1993), 572–83.

See La44 Florence.

159 Grünkorn, Gertrud, 'Zum Verständnis von fiktionaler Rede im Hochmittelalter: das Verhältnis von lateinischer Kommentartradition und höfischem Roman,' in *Fiktionalität*, pp. 29–44. (XLVI.69)

See Me34 Méla.

See Pb366 Pastré.

160 Poirion, Daniel, 'Qu'est-ce que la littérature? France 1100–1600,' in *What Is Literature?*, pp. 11–29.

See Pb376 Strasser.

161 Stanesco, Michel, 'Le texte primitif et la parole poétique médiévale,' in *Ecriture*, pp. 151–55. (XLVI.367)

162 Yokoyama, Ayumi, '*Estoire* and the Authority of Romances in the Vernacular – Chrétien de Troyes and Robert de Boron,' *RLLF*, 9 (1993), 3–23. (XLIX.383)
In Japanese.

163 Troyan, Scott D., *Textual Decorum: A Rhetoric of Attitudes in Medieval Literature*, GSML, 12 / GRLH, 1814 (New York: Garland, 1994).
See Chap. 5.

See Gb130 Morales.

See Pe49 Sonnemans.

See Gd.b51 Gally.

164 Gertz, SunHee Kim, *Poetic Prologues: Medieval Conversations with the Literary Past*, AnR, 56 (Frankfurt/M.: Klostermann, 1996).

See Me36 Lutz.

165 Suard, François, 'Littérature sérieuse, littérature de divertissement: le jeu sur les mots au Moyen Age,' in *Sprachspiele und Sprachkomik – Jeux de mots et comique verbal: Akten des Kolloquiums im Rahmen des Erasmus-Netzes der Universitäten Paris X-Nanterre, Duisberg und Trier, 12. bis 13. Mai 1995, Trier*, ed. Michael Herrmann and Karl Hölz, Trierer Studien zur Literatur, 29 (Frankfurt/M.: P. Lang, 1996), pp. 13–33.
See pp. 15–17 and 29–31.

166 Bennett, Philip E., 'Des jongleurs et des rois: réflexions sur le "Prologue" du *Couronnement de Louis*,' *MedR*, 21 (1997), 296–312.

167 Carreto, Carlos F. C., 'Au seuil d'une poétique du pouvoir: manipulation du nom et (en)jeux de la nomination dans le roman arthurien en vers,' in *The Propagation of Power in the Medieval West: Selected Proceedings of the International Conference, Groningen 20–23 November 1996*, ed. Martin Gosman, Arjo Vanderjagt, and Jan Veenstra, Mediaevalia Groningana, 23 (Groningen: Forsten, 1997), pp. 249–63.

168 Crécy, Marie-Claude de, *Vocabulaire de la littérature du moyen-âge* (Paris: Minerve, 1997).

169 James-Raoul, Danièle, *La parole empêchée dans la littérature arthurienne*, NBMA, 40 (Paris: Champion, 1997). (L.204)

170 Villa, Claudia, 'I commenti ai classici fra XII e XV secolo,' in *Medieval and Renaissance Scholarship: Proceedings of the Second European Science Foundation Workshop on the Classical Tradition in the Middle Ages and the Renaissance (London, The Warburg Institute,*

27–28 November 1992), ed. Nicholas Mann and Birger Munk Olsen, Mittellateinische Studien und Texte, 21 (Leiden: Brill, 1997), pp. 19–32. See pp. 29–32.

See Sa148 Camille.
Gradus amoris as topos.

171 Halász, Katalin, *Egy műfaj születése: A középkori francia regény* (Debrecen: Kossuth Egyetemi Kïadó, 1998). (LI.532)

172 Kelly, Douglas, 'The Scope of Medieval Instruction in the Art of Poetry and Prose: Recent Developments in Documentation and Interpretation,' *Studies in Medieval and Renaissance Teaching*, 6:2 (1998), 49–68.

173 Laurent, Françoise, *Plaire et édifier: les récits hagiographiques composés en Angleterre aux XIIe et XIIIe siècles*, NBMA, 45 (Paris: Champion, 1998). (LI.265)
Useful comparisons with Chrétien's romances.

174 Marnette, Sophie, *Narrateur et points de vue dans la littérature française médiévale: une approche linguistique* (Bern: P. Lang, 1998). (LI.717)

See Ha203 Perret.

175 Rohr, Rupprecht, *Lesen und Verstehen französischer und provenzalischer mittelalterlicher Dichtung*, Mannheimer Studien zur Linguistik, Mediävistik und Balkanologie, 10 (Frankfurt/M.: Haag + Herchen, 1998).
Sequel to Da10.

176 Wolf-Bonvin, Romaine, *Textus: de la tradition latine à l'esthétique du roman médiéval: 'Le Bel Inconnu', 'Amadas et Ydoine'*, NBMA, 41 (Paris: Champion, 1998). (LI.318)

177 Baumgartner, Emmanuèle, 'Fins du récit et roman arthurien,' in *Il Tempo, i tempi: omaggio a Lorenzo Renzi*, ed. Rosanna Brusegan and Michele A. Cortelazzo (Padua: Esedra, 1999), pp. 25–36. (LIII.717)

178 Bloch, R. Howard, 'Medieval French Literature and its Devises,' *YFS*, 95 (1999), 237–59.

179 Enders, Jody, 'Memory, Allegory, and the Romance of Rhetoric,' *YFS*, 95 (1999), 49–64.

180 Kelly, Douglas, 'Forlorn Hope: Mutability *Topoi* in Some Medieval Narratives,' in *The World and its Rival: Essays on Literary Imagination in Honor of Per Nykrog*, ed. Kathryn Karczewska and Tom Conley, Faux Titre, 172 (Amsterdam: Rodopi, 1999), pp. 59–77. (LII.683)

181 Kelly, Douglas, 'La rhétorique de la citation dans le roman médiéval,' *RLA*, 10 (1999), 69–74.

See Me41 Kelly.

182 Wolf, Alois, 'Mittelalterliche volksprachliche Dichter über ihr Tun,' in *Festschrift Schepp*, pp. 160–76. (LII.124)

183 Galderisi, Claudio, *Une Poétique des 'enfances': fonctions de l''incongru' dans la littérature française médiévale*, Medievalia, 34 (Orléans: Paradigme, 2000).

See Ha213 Trachsler.

184 Baumgartner, Emmanuèle, 'Sur quelques constantes et variations de l'image de l'écrivain (XIIe-XIIIe siècle),' in *Auctor*, pp. 391–400.

See Qe26 Le Rider.

b: Studies Stressing Chrétien

2   Hilka, Alfons, *Die direkte Rede* […] Repr. Geneva: Slatkine, 1979.

6   Robertson, D. W., Jr., 'Some Medieval Literary Terminology […]' Repr. in Dc10.

12   Raynaud de Lage, Guy, 'Le Procédé […]' Repr. in Dc4.

16   Raynaud de Lage, Guy, 'Insultes […]' Repr. in Dc4.

17   Rychner, Jean, 'Le Prologue […]' Repr. in Dc13.

26   Rychner, Jean, 'Encore le prologue […]' Repr. in Dc13.

29   Duplat, André, 'Etude stylistique […]' (XXVII.243)

30   Mahler, A. E., 'The Representation […]' (XXVII.23)

31   Ollier, Marie-Louise, 'The Author […]' Repr. in French in Dc32. (XXVIII.143)

32 Huckel, Marie-Louise, 'A propos de formules stéréotypées en ancien français,' *BulJR*, 10 (1964), 31–35.
In *Erec.*

33 Stolz, Walter, *Zum Gebrauch der Anrede bei Chrestien de Troyes*, diss. Berlin, Freie Universität (Berlin: Dissertationsdruckstelle, 1970).

34 Laugesen, Anker Teilgård, 'Quelques observations sur l'emploi des allocutifs libres dans le style courtois,' in *Actes Turku*, pp. 93–99.

35 Vance, Eugene, 'Signs of the City: Medieval Poetry as Detour,' *NLH*, 4 (1973), 557–74.

See He24 Borsari.

36 Duplat, André, 'Etude stylistique des apostrophes *chevaliers* et *vassal* dans les romans de Chrétien de Troyes,' *BulJR*, 20 (1974), 83–96.

37 Wiehl, Peter, *Die Redeszene als episches Strukturelement in den Erec- und Iwein-Dichtungen Hartmanns von Aue und Chrestiens de Troyes*, Bochumer Arbeiten zur Sprach- und Literaturwissenschaft, 10 (Munich: Fink, 1974). (XXVII.186)
On numerical composition.

38 Duplat, André, 'Etude stylistique des formules de salutation chez Chrétien de Troyes,' *TLL*, 13:1 (1975), 107–43.

See Pb174 Haug.

39 Hilty, Gerold, 'Zum *Erec*-Prolog von Chrétien de Troyes,' in *Philologica Lommatzsch*, pp. 245–56. (XXIX.25)

40 Altieri, Marcelle, *Les romans de Chrétien de Troyes: leur perspective proverbiale et gnomique* (Paris: Nizet, 1976). (XXIX.222)

41 Freeman, Michelle A., 'Chrétien's *Cligés*: A Close Reading of the Prologue,' *RR*, 67 (1976), 89–101. (XXIX.112)

42 Ollier, Marie-Louise, 'Proverbe et sentence: le discours d'autorité chez Chrétien de Troyes,' *RSH*, 163 (1976), 329–57. Repr. in Dc32.
Examples from *Yvain.*

43 Pagani, Walter, 'Ancora sul prologo dell'*Erec et Enide*,' *SMV*, 24 (1976), 141–52. (XXIX.365)

See Kd76 Gier.

44 Maddox, Donald L., 'The Prologue to Chrétien's *Erec* and the Problem of Meaning,' in *Misrahi Volume*, pp. 159–74. (XXXI.114)

See Ga19 Jacobs.

45 Gallais, Pierre, 'Métonymie et métaphore dans le *Conte du graal*,' in *Mélanges Lods*, vol. 1, pp. 213–48. (XXXI.274)

46 Haidu, Peter, 'Au début du roman, l'ironie,' *Poétique*, 36 (1978), 443–66. (XXXI.274 *bis*)
On *Cligés*; see Fb18.

See Hf32 Noble.

See Hb22 Grisgby.

47 Decrevel, Josiane, 'Irony in Chrétien de Troyes' Uses of the "Merveilleux",' *Parergon*, 25 (1979), 19–24.

See Hd10 Freeman.

See Ha97 Warning.

See Hg49 Dragonetti.

48 Halász, Katalin, 'Conjointure, Chrétien de Troyes regényszerkesztési elvei,' *FK*, 26:1 (1980), 1–19.

49 Ollier, Marie-Louise, 'Le roman au douzième siècle: vers et narrativité,' in *Nature*, pp. 123–44. (XXXIII.162)

See Db24(D) Kelly.

50 Lindvall, Lars, 'Structures syntaxiques et structures stylistiques dans l'œuvre de Chrestien de Troyes,' *Rom*, 102 (1981), 456–500. (XXXIV.233 *bis* [p. 99])

51 Schulze-Busacker, Elisabeth, 'Proverbes et expressions proverbiales chez Chrétien de Troyes, Gautier d'Arras et Hue de Rotelande,' *Incidences*, 5 (1981), 7–16. (XXXV.185)

52 Haidu, Peter, 'Le sens historique du phénomène stylistique: la sémiose dissociative chez Chrétien de Troyes,' *Europe*, 642 (Oct. 1982), 36–47. (XXXV.319)

53 Liborio, Mariantonia, 'Rhetorical *Topoi* as "Clues" in Chrétien de Troyes,' in *Rhetoric*, pp. 173–78. (XXXV.467, XXXVII.417)

See Hb29 Voicu.

54 Kelly, Douglas, 'The Logic of the Imagination in Chrétien de Troyes,' in *Sower*, pp. 9–30. (XXXV.168)

55 Luttrell, Claude, 'The Prologue of Crestien's *Li Contes del graal*,' *AL*, 3 (1983), 1–25. (XXXVI.445)

See Jb32 Varty.

See Hf54 Grimbert.

See Hf55 Hunt.

56 Kelly, Douglas, 'Les fées et les arts dans la représentation du *Chevalier de la charrette*,' in *Lancelot Picardie*, pp. 85–97.
On topical invention and intertextuality.

See Md36 Lloyd.

57 Schulze-Busacker, Elisabeth, 'Proverbes et expressions proverbiales dans les romans de Chrétien de Troyes,' in *Chrétien Bruges*, pp. 107–19. (XXXVII.117)

58 Sturm-Maddox, Sara, and Donald Maddox, 'Description in Medieval Narrative: Vestimentary Coherence in Chrétien's *Erec et Enide*,' *MedR*, 9 (1984), 51–64. (XXXVII.278)

59 Takatô, Mako, 'The Birth of Romance (the History of its Genesis),' *BWAS*, Special Number 11 (1984), 51–61. (XXXVII.323)
In Japanese.

See Hg61Voicu.

60 Chaurand, Jacques, 'Le litote chez Chrétien de Troyes,' *Mélanges de langue et de littérature françaises offerts à Pierre Larthomas*, CENSJF, 26 (Paris: Ecole Normale Supérieure de Jeunes Filles, 1985), pp. 99–111.

See He53 Janssens.

See Hf62 Szabics.

61 D'Alessandro, Domenico, 'La descrizione in Chrétien de Troyes: i segni di demarcazione,' *AION*, 28 (1986), 553–66. (XLI.265)

See Kd101 Janssens.

62 Sasaki, Shigemi, 'Quatre, signe ou signal pour une lecture (remarque sur les scènes du château du Roi Pêcheur dans les romans du Graal (1181–début 1200)),' *BWAS*, 32 (1986) 85–103. (XL.228)

See Wa26 Schulze-Busacker.
On use of proverbs.

63 Takatô, Mako, '"Tautology" in Chrétien's Texts,' *FBGK*, 5 (1986), 1–21. (XXXVIII.449).
In Japanese.

See Wb39 D'Alessandro.

64 Ferroul, Yves, 'Propédeutique à une lecture du prologue du *Cligès*,' *Bien dire*, 5 (1987), 57–71.

65 Liborio, Mariantonia, 'I luoghi privilegiati della descrizione,' *AION*, 29 (1987), 5–12. (XLI.27)

66 Monson, Don A., 'La "surenchère" chez Chrétien de Troyes,' *Poétique*, 70 (1987), 231–46.

67 Press, A. R., 'Death and Lamentation in Chrétien de Troyes's Romances: The Dialectic of Rhetoric and Reason,' *FMLS*, 23 (1987), 11–20. (XL.132)

68 Sargent-Baur, Barbara Nelson, 'The Missing Prologue of Chrétien's *Chevalier au lion*,' *FS*, 41 (1987), 385–94. (XL.135)

69 Vance, Eugene, *From Topic to Tale: Logic and Narrativity in the Middle Ages*, Theory and History of Literature, 47 (Minneapolis: University of Minnesota Press, 1987). (XL.327)

See Sb44 Citton.

70 Gertz, SunHee Kim, 'Rhetoric and the Prologue to Chrétien de Troyes's *Erec et Enide*,' *EsFL*, 25 (1988), 1–8.

71 Hult, David F., 'La double autorité du *Chevalier de la charrete*,' in *Théories*, pp. 41–56.

72 Kelly, Douglas, 'Le jeu de la vérité,' in *Chevalier au lion*, pp. 105–17. (XLI. 64).

73 Kelly, Douglas, 'Le lieu du temps, le temps du lieu,' in *Hommage Zumthor*, pp. 123–26.
Topical inventions using the topos Time.

74 Sakari, Ellen, 'Actes de discours et stratégie argumentative dans le dialogue entre Laudine et Lunete, vers 1593–1880 d'*Yvain* ou *le Chevalier au lion* de Chrétien de Troyes,' in *Miscellanea Gasca Queirazza*, vol. 2, pp. 949–75.

75 Takatô, Mako, '"Romance" in the Making in Chrétien de Troyes,' *YBK*, 35 (1988), 140–54. (XLI.312).
In Japanese.

76 Voicu, Mihaela, 'De la représentation dans la littérature médiévale ou "la quête du sens",' *AnB*, 37 (1988), 7–10.

See He60 Janssens.

77 Katô, Kyôko, 'Chrétien de Troyes's Literary Technique,' *FFRSH*, 24 (1989), 1–14. (XLIII.405).
In Japanese.

78 *La descrizione*, ed. Mariantonia Liborio (Naples: Istituto Universitario Orientale, 1991).
  A. Domenico D'Alessandro, 'Per un'analisi formale del descrittivo nel Medioevo: il caso del romanzo,' pp. 29–48. (XLV.325)
  B. Antonio Saccone, 'Descrizione e azione: la singolar tenzone nei romanzi di Chrétien de Troyes,' pp. 71–81. (XLV.342)

See Gb101 Legros.

79 Castellani, Marie-Madeleine, 'Mythe et représentation du monde: la robe d'Erec, dans *Erec et Enide*, de Chrétien de Troyes,' *Uranie*, 1: 'Mythes et création' (1992), pp. 101–19.

See Hd17 Enders.

80 Watanabe, Kôji, 'Alis, Victim of Chrétien de Troyes's Irony: Interpretive Essay on *Cligès* (Supplement),' *NSH*, 21 (1992), 77–102.
In Japanese.

81 Watanabe, Kôji, 'Irony in Chrétien de Troyes's *Cligès*,' *BLFC*, 16 (1992), 2–15.
In Japanese.

See Hf91 Álvares and Diogo.

82 Amtower, Laurel, 'Courtly Code and *conjointure*: The Rhetoric of Identity in *Erec et Enide*,' *Neophil*, 77 (1993), 179–89. (XLVI.616)

83 *La Description au Moyen Age: Actes du Colloque du Centre d'Études Médiévales et Dialectales de Lille III, Université Charles-de-Gaulle – Lille III, 25 et 26 septembre 1992*, ed. Aimé Petit, = *Bien dire*, 11 (1993).

The following include study of description in Chrétien's romances:
A. Cristina Álvares and Américo Diogo, 'Laudine: entre fin amors et misogyne,' pp. 9–24.
B. Robert Baudry, 'Le sang des oies sur la neige de Chrétien de Troyes à Jean Giono,' pp. 25–40.
C. Catherine Blons-Pierre, 'L'esthétique de la description des personnages chez Chrétien de Troyes,' pp. 55–68.
D. Marie-Madeleine Castellani, 'La description du héros masculin dans *Erec et Enide* de Chrétien de Troyes,' pp. 105–17.
E. Françoise Chambefort, 'Le topos de l'indescriptible dans les portraits romanesques au XIIe siècle,' pp. 119–29.
F. Françoise Fery-Hue, 'La description de la "pierre précieuse" au Moyen Age: encyclopédies, lapidaires et textes littéraires,' pp. 147–76.
G. Yves Ferroul, 'La description du désir dans les romans: l'exemple de *Sone de Nansay*,' pp. 177–90.
See pp. 182–84.

See Ga77 Dottori.

84 Voicu, Mihaela, 'La description chez Chrétien de Troyes: lecture des signes, "effet de reel" ou "effet de texte"?' in *Actes Zurich*, pp. 427–42. (XLVII.662)

85 Bertau, Karl, 'Der Ritter auf dem halben Pferd oder die Wahrheit des Hyperbel,' *PBB*, 116 (1994), 285–301. (XLVII.51)

See Hf93 Chicote.

86 D'Alessandro, Domenico, 'Il "doppio descrittivo": strutture binarie nelle descrizioni di Chrétien,' *AION*, 36 (1994), 151–59. (XLVIII.542)

87 Hunt, Tony, 'Chrétien's Prologues Reconsidered,' in *Studies Kelly*, pp. 153–68. (XLVII.559)

See Hg95 Kelly.

See Hf95 Munson.

88 Watanabe, Kôji, 'Prolegomena to Ironic *imaginaire* in the Works of Chrétien de Troyes,' in *Mélanges Eizô Kamizawa*, *Variété* (Special Number), Published by the Section de la Littérature Française de la

Faculté des Lettres de l'Université de Nagoya, 1994, pp. 1–18 (XLIX.379)
In Japanese.

See Gb125(D) Blons-Pierre.

See Hd18 Blons-Pierre.

89 Chênerie, Marie-Luce, 'Le dialogue de la dame et du chevalier dans les romans de Chrétien de Troyes,' in *Amour Troyes*, pp. 107–19. (XLIX.139)

See Gf39 Dottori.

90 Gouttebroze, Jean-Guy, 'Chrétien de Troyes prédicateur: structure et sens du prologue du *Conte du graal*,' in *Amour Troyes*, pp. 29–45. (XLIX.155)

See Hb47 Voicu.

91 Watanabe, Kôji, '"Paroemia" comme enjeu mythologique – A propos des études parémiologiques chez Chrétien de Troyes,' *NSH*, 24 (1995), 1–16. (XLIX.380)

92 Marchiori, Marina, 'Piano letterale e metafora umoristica nel *Lancelot* di Chrétien de Troyes,' *Letterature*, 19 (1996), 7–13.

93 Pavel, Maria, *Poétique du roman médiéval français: la 'forme-sens' chez Chrétien de Troyes* (Iaşi: Editura Chemarea, 1996).

94 Villa, Claudia, 'Per *Erec*, 14: "une molt bele conjointure",' in *Studi D'Arco Silvio Avalle*, pp. 453–72. (L.341)

95 Watanabe, Kôji, 'L'ironie dans l'œuvre de Chrétien de Troyes: de l'approche rhétorique à l'approche mythologique (présentation de thèse),' *PerM*, 22 (1996), 80–84.

See Hd22 Álvares and Diogo.

96 Corbyn, Nick, 'Irony and Gender Performance in *Le Chevalier de la charrete*,' AL, 15 (1997), 37–54. (L.261)

97 Haupt, Barbara, 'Literarische Memoria im Hochmittelalter, Chrétien de Troyes und der *Discours de la méthode*,' *ZLiLi*, 27 (1997), 39–61. (L.82)

See Ha201 Voicu.

See Ma35 Bianchini.

98 James-Raoul, Danièle, 'La rhétorique du silence dans le *Conte du Graal*,' in *Faits de langue et sens des textes*, ed. Franck Neveu (Paris: SEDES, 1998), pp. 9–32. (LII.246)

See Gd.a40 Kowalski.

99 Laranjinha, Ana Sofia, 'L'ironie comme principe structurant chez Chrétien de Troyes,' *CCM*, 41 (1998), 175–82. (LI.263)

100 Guidot, Bernard, '*Perceval ou le Conte du Graal*: quelques délicates attentions de l'écriture de Chrétien de Troyes,' in *Mélanges Suard*, vol. 1, pp. 361–72. (LII.237)

101 Haupt, Barbara, 'Literarische Bildbeschreibung im Artusroman – Tradition und Aktualisierung: zu Chrestiens Beschreibung von Erecs Krönungsmantel und Zepter,' *ZfG*, 9 (1999), 557–85. (LII.85)

See Kd133 Lemaire.

102 Noacco, Cristina, 'Le "sens" de la lumière dans les portraits de Chrétien de Troyes,' in *Feu et lumière au Moyen Age II*, Travaux du Groupe de Recherches 'Lectures Médiévales', Université de Toulouse II, Collection Moyen Age (Toulouse: Editions Universitaires du Sud; Paris: Champion, [1999], pp. 129–45. (LII.259)

103 Watanabe, Kôji, 'Rhetoric of Ugliness in the *Conte du graal*,' *Plume*, 4 (1999), 12–23.
In Japanese.

104 Benoît, Louis, 'L'autorité de l'auteur: études des prologues des romans de Chrétien de Troyes,' *SLCO*, 26 (2000), 27–53.

105 Heyworth, G. G., 'Perceval and the Seeds of Culture: Work, Project and Leisure in the Prologue of *Perceval*,' *Neophil*, 84 (2000), 19–35.

c: Versification

4 Frappier, Jean, 'Sur la versification […]' Repr. in Dc1.

5 Frappier, Jean, 'La Brisure […]' Repr. in Dc1.

7 Rickard, P., 'Semantic Implications of Old French Identical Rhyme,' *NM*, 66 (1965), 355–401.

8 Aspland, C. W., *A Syntactical Study of Epic Formulas and Formulaic Expressions Containing the '-ant' Forms in Twelfth Century French Verse* (St Lucia, Queensland: University of Queensland Press, 1970).

See Mb12 Legge.

9 Johnston, R. C., 'Sound-Related Couplets in Old French,' *FMLS*, 12 (1976), 194–205. (XXIX.300)

10 Marchello-Nizia, Christiane, 'La forme-vers et la forme-prose: leurs langues spécifiques, leurs contraintes propres,' *PerM*, 3 (1977), 35–42. (XXX.282)

See Ra13 Shirt.

See Pi14 Tecchio.

See Bb35 Woledge.

11 Aragón Fernández, María Aurora, 'El encabalgamiento en las novelas de Chrétien de Troyes,' *Thélème*, 1 (1980), 109–31.

12 Aragón Fernández, Mª Aurora, 'La versificación de Chrétien de Troyes: coincidencia verso/frase y grupos de versos,' *Verba*, 7 (1980), 283–300.

13 Aragón Fernández, Mª Aurora, 'La ruptura del pareado en las novelas de Chrétien de Troyes,' *Verba*, 8 (1981), 289–305.

14 Baumgartner, Emmanuèle, 'Jeu de rimes et roman arthurien,' *Rom*, 103 (1982), 550–60; repr. in Dc20. (XXXVI.331)

See Hc44 Laidlaw.

15 Woledge, Brian, 'Notes on Rhythm in Chrétien's *Yvain*,' in *Studies Diverres*, pp. 213–26, 253. (XXXVI.475)

See Bb44 Foulet and Uitii.

See Kf3 Ollier.

See Ra20 Janssens.

See Pa209 Gallais, vol. 1, pp. 435–634.

See Wc8 Gallais.

See Pi27 Bartoli.

See Ha178 Baumgartner.

See Pe47 Winkelman.

16 Cocito, Luciana, 'Ritmo e discorso nel *Cligès* di Chrétien de Troyes,' *Letterature*, 18 (1995), 9–13. (XLIX.327)

See Bb76 Beltrami.

17 Comes, Annalisa, 'Troia, Elena e Paride: un mito per le rime,' *SMV*, 44 (1998), 195–212. (LIII.722)
See pp. 197–98.

See Hc79 Houdeville.

d: Logic

1 Hunt, Tony, 'The Dialectic of *Yvain*,' *MLR*, 72 (1977), 285–99. (XXX.342)

2 Hunt, Tony, 'Aristotle, Dialectic, and Courtly Literature,' *Viator*, 10 (1979), 95–129. (XXXII.188)
Treats *Cligés* on pp. 109–20.

3 Bradley-Cromey, Nancy, 'Dialectic and Chrétien de Troyes: Exploration of Interrelationships between Romance Literature and the Schools,' in *1983 NEH Institute Resource Book for the Teaching of Medieval Civilization*, ed. Howell Chickering (Amherst, MA: Five Colleges, 1984), pp. 44–54.

4 Maddox, Donald, 'Opérations cognitives et scandales romanesques: Méléagant et le roi Marc,' in *Hommage Payen*, pp. 239–51. (XLII.64)

5 Ciccone, Nancy, 'Practical Reason and Medieval Romance,' *Comitatus*, 25 (1994), 43–58.

6 Discenza, Nicole Guenther, 'Dialectical Structure in Chrétien de Troyes's *Cligés*,' *RLA*, 8 (1996), 21–25.

e: Orality, Reading, and Performance

See Na.c39(A) Wechssler, pp. 159–64.

1   Titchener, Frances H., 'The Romances of Chrétien de Troyes,' *RR*, 16 (1925), 165–73.

2   Roques, Mario, 'Le scribe Guiot et le manuscrit français 794 de la Bibliothèque Nationale,' *AIBL* (1952), pp. 21–22.

3   Legge, M. Dominica, 'The Influence of Patronage on Form in Medieval French Literature,' in *Stil- und Formprobleme in der Literatur: Vorträge des VII. Kongresses der Internationalen Vereinigung für moderne Sprachen und Literaturen in Heidelberg*, ed. Paul Böckmann (Heidelberg: Winter, 1959), pp. 136–41.

See Qb30 Burrow.

4   Jauss, Hans Robert, 'Levels of Identification of Hero and Audience,' *NLH*, 5 (1974), 283–317.
See pp. 303–07.

See Kc51 Hilty.

5   Lough, John, *Writer and Public in France from the Middle Ages to the Present Day* (Oxford: Clarendon Press; New York: Oxford University Press, 1978).
Chap. 1, 'The Middle Ages,' places Chrétien in the medieval context of patronage, the audience, and the manuscript book.

6   Scholz, Manfred Günter, *Hören und Lesen: Studien zur primären Rezeption der Literatur im 12. und 13. Jahrhundert* (Wiesbaden: Steiner, 1980).

See Ha106 Hanning.

See Fa111 Lebsanft.

See Fa114 Hult.

7   Lebsanft, Franz, 'Hören und Lesen im Mittelalter,' *ZfSL*, 92 (1982), 52–64.

8   Paden, William D., Jr., 'Europe from Latin to Vernacular in Epic, Lyric, Romance,' in *Performance of Literature in Historical Perspectives*, ed. David W. Thompson [et alii] (Lanham, MD: University Press of America, 1983), pp. 67–105.

9   Salmen, Walter, *Der Spielmann im Mittelalter*, Innsbrucker Beiträge zur Musikwissenschaft, 8 (Innsbruck: Helbling, 1983).

See Fc15 Woledge.

10   Green, D. H., 'On the Primary Reception of Narrative Literature in Medieval Germany,' *FMLS*, 20 (1984), 289–308. (XXXVII.167)

11   Trindade, W. Ann, 'The Interaction of Oral and Written Traditions in Twelfth-Century Old French Verse Romances,' *Parergon*, 2 (1984), 97–109.

12   Zumthor, Paul, 'L'écriture et la voix: le *Roman d'Eracle*,' in *Craft*, pp. 161–209. (XXXVII.475)
Compares Gautier's *oralité* with Chrétien's, especially in the *Cligés*.

13   Zumthor, Paul, *La poésie et la voix dans la civilisation médiévale*, Collège de France: Essais et Conférences (Paris: Presses Universitaires de France, 1984).

14   Zumthor, Paul, '*Litteratus/illitteratus*: remarques sur le contexte vocal de l'écriture,' *Rom*, 106 (1985), 1–18.

15   Vitz, Evelyn Birge, 'Rethinking Old French Literature: The Orality of the Octosyllabic Couplet,' *RR*, 77 (1986), 309–21. (XL.331)

16   Zumthor, Paul, 'Poésie et théâtralité: l'exemple du Moyen Age,' *AION*, 28 (1986), 509–39. (XLVII.474)

17   Kittay, Jeffrey, 'On Octo (Response to "Rethinking Old French Literature: The Orality of the Octosyllabic Couplet," by Evelyn Birge Vitz, *Romanic Review*, November 1986),' *RR*, 78 (1987), 291–98. (XL.292)

See Fa140 Hanning.

See Db34 Pleij.

18   Zumthor, Paul, *La Lettre et la voix: de la 'littérature' médiévale* (Paris: Seuil, 1987).

19   Zumthor, Paul, 'Pour une conception anthropologique du "style" médiéval,' *MedR*, 12 (1987), 229–40.

20   Duggan, Joseph J., 'Oral Performance of Romance in Medieval France,' in *Essays Grigsby*, pp. 51–61. (XLII.294)

See Ha157 Fleischman.

See Qa93 Schmitt.

See Rb30 Vitz.

See Nc3 Gilet.

21 Fein, David A., '"Vos qui les biaus mos entendez": Audience Collusion in Twelfth-Century French Narrative,' *Neophil*, 77 (1993), 531–39. (XLVI.627)

22 Stempel, Wolf-Dieter, 'La "modernité" des débuts: la rhétorique de l'oralité chez Chrétien de Troyes,' in *Le passage à l'écrit des langues romanes*, ed. Maria Selig, Barbara Frank, and Jörg Hartmann, ScriptOralia, 46 (Tübingen: Narr, 1993), pp. 275–98.

23 Stuip, R. E. V., 'Het chanson de geste en het boek,' in *Oraliteit en schriftcultuur*, ed. R. E. V. Stuip and C. Vellekoop, UBM, 12 (Hilversum: Verloren, 1993), pp. 155–69.

24 Green, D. H., *Medieval Listening and Reading: The Primary Reception of German Literature 800–1300* (Cambridge: Cambridge University Press, 1994). (XLVIII.415)

See Xa18 Hindman.

25 Mattiacci, Angela, 'L'absence d'une vocalité fictive dans le *Chevalier au lion* du manuscrit du Vatican 1725,' *Tropos*, 20 (1994), 5–15.

See Pb392 Butzer.

26 Gerritsen, W. P., 'Een avond in Ardres: over middeleeuwse verhaalkunst,' in *Grote Lijnen*, pp. 157–72 and 220–23. (XLVIII.620)

27 Brandsma, Frank, 'Dialogue and Direct Discourse,' in *The Search for a New Alphabet: Literary Studies in a Changing World in Honor of Douwe Fokkema*, ed. Harald Hendrix [et alii] (Amsterdam: Benjamins, 1996), pp. 34–38. (XLIX.391)

See La45(E) Brandsma.

28 Haug, Walter, 'Die Verwandlungen des Körpers zwischen "Aufführung" und "Schrift",' in *Aufführung*, pp. 190–204.

29 Brandsma, Frank, 'Medieval Equivalents of "Quote-unquote": The Presentation of Spoken Words in Courtly Romance,' in *ICLS Belfast*, pp. 287–96.

30 *Gattungen mittelalterlicher Schriftlichkeit*, ed. Barbara Frank, Thomas Haye, and Doris Tophinke, ScriptOralia, 99 (Tübingen: Narr, 1997).

    A.   Barbara Frank, '"Innensicht" und "Außensicht": zur Analyse mittelalterlicher volkssprachlicher Gattungsbezeichnungen,' pp. 117–36.

    B.   Maria Selig, 'Das Buch im Mittelalter – Überlegungen zu Kommunikationstypik und Medialität,' pp. 137–60.

    C.   Richard Trachsler, '"Genres" et "matières": Überlegungen zum Erbe Jean Bodels,' pp. 201–19.

31 Baumgartner, Emmanuèle, 'Paul Zumthor et le roman médiéval,' in *Paul Zumthor ou l'invention permanente: critique, histoire, poésie*, ed. Jacqueline Cerquiglini-Toulet and Christopher Lucken, RRG, 9 (Geneva: Droz, 1998), pp. 63–72.

32 Brandsma, Frank, 'Knights' Talk: Direct Discourse in Arthurian Romance,' *Neophil*, 82 (1998), 513–25. (LI.686)

See Fa171 Halász.

33 Vitz, Evelyn Birge, 'Remembering Paul Zumthor: Zumthor and Romance,' *DFS*, 44 (1998), 3–11.

See Ke16 Edeline.

34 Vitz, Evelyn Birge, *Orality and Performance in Early French Romance* (Cambridge: Brewer, 1999). (LII.467)

35 Brandsma, Frank, 'Spiegelpersonages,' in *Opstellen Gerritsen*, pp. 37–42. (LIII.856)

See Ha214(B) Bertin.

See Ba34 Varvaro.

G: TOPOS, MOTIF, AND IMAGE

This Section lists studies of the same kinds of sources for original elaboration and amplification as the 1976 Bibliography. However, the great increase in the number of items in section d: 'Objects, Places, and Actions', has required a breakdown into three sub-sections covering, respectively, 'Objects and Plants', 'Places', and 'Actions and Activities'. The new section Gg includes indexes of motifs and themes, all of which potentially function as topoi.

a: Individuals and Individual Types

8   Strucks, Carsten, *Der junge Parzival in Wolframs von Eschenbach 'Parzival', Crestiens von Troyes 'conte del graal', im englischen 'Syr Percyvelle' und italienischen 'Carduino'*, diss. Münster (Borna-Leipzig: Noske, 1910).

9   Jones, W. Lewis, *King Arthur in History and Legend*, The Cambridge Manuals of Science and Literature (Cambridge: Cambridge University Press, 1911; 2nd ed. 1914).

See Pd16 Ven-Ten Bensel, Chap. 4.

10   Königer, Hertha, *Die Darstellung der Personen bei Chrétien de Troyes*, diss. Munich (Munich: Mößl, 1936).

See Na.c64 Marx.

11   Shimizu, Aya, 'King Arthur and Avalon,' *Bulletin of Tokyo Gakugei University*, 20:2 (1969), 33–43.
In Japanese.

See Pa92 Bogdanow.

12   Imbs, Paul, 'La Reine Guenièvre dans le *Conte du Graal* de Chrétien de Troyes,' in *Mélanges Teruo Satô, CEMN* numéro spécial (Nagoya: Centre d'Etudes Médiévales et romanes, 1973), pp. 41–60. (XXVII.385).
See also Ga 4, 6–7 Imbs.

13   Amazawa, Taijirô, 'On the Fisher King's Father in the *Conte del Graal*,' *MGRS*, 229 (1975), 17–39. (XXX.469)
In Japanese.

14   Barnett, D. J., 'Whatever Happened to Gawain?' *English Studies in Africa*, 18 (1975), 1–16.

15   Noble, Peter, 'Kay the Seneschal in Chrétien de Troyes and His Predecessors,' *RMS*, 1 (1975), 55–70. (XXVIII.326)

16   Wells, D. A., *The Wild Man from the 'Epic of Gilgamesh' to Hartmann von Aue's 'Iwein': Reflections on the Development of a Theme in World Literature. Inaugural Lecture, The Queen's University of Belfast on 16 October 1974*, New Lecture Series, 78 (Belfast: The Queen's University, 1975). (XXVIII.334)

17   Huby, Michel, 'Le sénéchal du roi Arthur,' *EtGerm*, 31 (1976), 433–37. (XXIX.238)
On Qe2.

See Hc26 Mandel.

See Pb197 Wynn.

18   Hanning, Robert W., *The Individual in Twelfth-Century Romance* (New Haven, CT: Yale University Press, 1977). (XXXI.97)

See Pb203 Schusky.

19   Jacobs, Madeleine, 'L'espace et la lumière en fonction du développement du protagoniste dans *Perceval* de Chrétien de Troyes et *Saint Julien l'Hospitalier* de Flaubert,' *RomN*, 18 (1977–78), 256–62.

See Pb208 Gnädinger.

See Hg39 Lods.

20   Planche, Alice, 'La dame au sycamore,' in *Mélanges Lods*, vol. 1, pp. 495–516; repr. in Dc28. (XXXI.298)

See Hc32 Coghlan.

See Me16 Fiedler.

21 Nykrog, Per, 'Trajectory of the Hero: Gauvain Paragon of Chivalry 1130–1230,' in *Symposium Odense*, pp. 82–93 (discussion pp. 133–34).

22 Wolf, Alois, '*Ja por les fers ne remanra* (Chrétiens "Karrenritter" V. 4600): Minnebann, ritterliches Selbstbewußtsein und concordia voluntatum,' *LJG*, 20 (1979), 31–69; repr. in Dc31. (XXXII.82)

23 Busby, Keith, *Gauvain in Old French Literature*, Degré Second, 2 (Amsterdam: Rodopi, 1980). (XXXIII.580)

24 Larmat, Jean, 'Le personnage de Gauvain dans quelques romans arthuriens du XIIᵉ et du XIIIᵉ siècle,' in *Etudes Lanly*, pp. 185–202. (XXXIII.341)

See Hc37 Nelson.

25 Wolfgang, Lenora, 'Perceval's Father: Problems in Medieval Narrative Art,' *RPh*, 34 (1980–81), 28–47. (XXXIII.180)

26 Busby, Keith, 'The Enigma of Loholt,' in *Essays Thorpe*, pp. 28–36. (XXXIV.301)
On *Erec* v. 1731 Foerster, v. 1700 Roques.

27 Dugan, Mary, 'Le rôle de la femme dans *Le Chevalier au lion*,' *Chimères*, 15:1 (1981), 29–38.

28 Jennings, Margaret, '"Heavens Defend Me from that Welsh Fairy" (*Merry Wives of Windsor*, V, v, 85): The Metamorphosis of Morgain la Fee in the Romances,' in *ICLS Liverpool*, pp. 197–205. (XXXIV.332)

29 Nelson, Deborah, 'The Public and Private Images of *Cligès'* Fénice,' *RMS*, 7 (1981), 81–88. (XXIV.352)

30 Kosenko, Peter, 'De Troyes's *Yvain*,' *Explicator*, 41:1 (1982), 4–5. (XXXVI.177)

31 Markale, Jean, 'L'étrange rôle de la reine Guenièvre,' *Europe*, 642 (Oct. 1982), 96–105. (XXXV.333)

32 Ménage, René, 'Erec et les intermittences du cœur,' *MrR*, 32:2–4 (1982), 5–14. (XXXVIII.143)

33 Morris, Rosemary, *The Character of King Arthur in Medieval Literature*, AS, 4 (Cambridge: Brewer; Totowa, NJ: Rowman and Littlefield, 1982). (XXXV.406)

34 Ruh, Kurt, *Lancelot: Wandlungen einer ritterlichen Idealgestalt. Festvortrag anläßlich der Überreichung des Brüder-Grimm Preises am 30. Oktober 1981*, Marburger Universitätsreden, 2 (Marburg: Pressestelle der Philipps-Universität, 1982). (XXXV.64)

See He42 Borsari.

35 Brewer, Derek, 'The Presentation of the Character of Lancelot: Chrétien to Malory,' *AL*, 3 (1983), 26–52; repr. in Ga91. (XXXVI.403)

36 Bullock-Davies, Constance, 'The Visual Image of Arthur,' *RMS*, 9 (1983), 98–116. (XXXVI.406)

37 De Looze, Laurence N., 'Chivalry Qualified: The Character of Gauvain in Chrétien de Troyes' *Le Chevalier de la charrette*,' *RR*, 74 (1983), 253–59. (XXXVI.180)

See Na.d54 Foulon.

See Hg56 Lacy.

38 Pastoureau, Michel, 'Formes et couleurs du désordre: le jaune avec le vert,' *Médiévales*, 4 (1983), 62–72. (XXXVI.360)
Includes Sagremor le desreé.

39 Press, A. R., 'Chrétien de Troyes's Laudine: A *Belle dame sans mercy*?' *FMLS*, 19 (1983), 158–71. (XXXVI.454)

See Hc45 Sullivan.

40 Zak, Nancy C., *The Portrayal of the Heroine in Chrétien de Troyes's 'Erec et Enide', Gottfried von Strassburg's 'Tristan', and 'Flamenca'*, GAG, 347 (Göppingen: Kümmerle, 1983). (XXXVI.88)

See Pa142 Atanassov.

41 Baumgartner, Emmanuèle, 'Arthur et les chevaliers *envoisiez*,' *Rom*, 105 (1984), 312–25; repr. in Dc20. (XXXVIII.181)

42 Brewer, Derek S., 'The Image of Lancelot: Chrétien and Malory,' in *Artusliteratur*, pp. 105–17. (XXXVII.582)

See Pa143 Busby.

See He46 Gallais.

See Nb29 Harf-Lancner.

See Qa66 Holzermayr.

43 Korrel, Peter, *An Arthurian Triangle: A Study of the Origin, Development and Characterization of Arthur, Guinevere and Modred* (Leiden: Brill, 1984).

44 Noble, Peter, 'Chrétien's Arthur,' in *Essays Topsfield*, pp. 220–37. (XXXVII.176)

45 Ribard, Jacques, 'Un personnage paradoxal: le Gauvain du *Conte du Graal,*' in *Lancelot Wégimont*, pp. 5–18; repr. in Dc25. (XXXVIII.254)

46 Santoni-Rozier, Claire, 'Keu est-il un "anti-Lancelot" dans l'épisode de la *Charrette?* A propos des différentes versions du *"Chevalier de la charrette"* de la poésie (dans le poème de Chrétien de Troyes) et de la prose (française, dans le *Lancelot,* et allemande, dans le *Prosa-Lancelot*),' in *Lancelot Picardie*, pp. 199–211.

47 Sargent-Baur, Barbara Nelson, '*Dux bellorum / rex militum /* roi fainéant: la transformation d'Arthur au XIIe siècle,' *MA*, 90 (1984), 357–73; repr. in Ga90. (XXXVII.11)

See Pa156 Schmolke-Hasselmann.

48 Schopf, Alfred, 'Die Gestalt Gawains bei Chrétien, Wolfram von Eschenbach und in *Sir Gawain and the Green Knight*,' in *Artusliteratur*, pp. 85–104. (XXXVII.673)

49 Subrenat, Jean, 'Chrétien de Troyes et Guenièvre: un romancier et son personnage,' in *Chrétien Bruges*, pp. 45–59. (XXXVII.122)

50 Boutet, Dominique, 'Carrefours idéologiques de la royauté arthurienne,' *CCM*, 28 (1985), 3–17. (XXXVIII.193)

51 Chauveau, Hervé, 'Perceval le chétif,' in *Littérature et psychanalyse: une clinique de l'écriture*, Atelier d'Éécritures, 1 (Nantes: Département de Psychologie, Université de Nantes, 1985), pp. 69–77.

See Pa158 Chênerie.

52 Lie, Orlanda S. H., 'Guinevere,' in *Middeleeuwers over vrouwen*, ed. R. E. V. Stuip and C. Vellekoop, 2 vols (Utrecht: HES, 1985), vol. 1, pp. 27–39, 180–82. (XXXIX.199)

See Na.c84 Markale.

See Qa76 Stanesco.

53   Sullivan, Penny, 'The Education of the Heroine in Chrétien's *Erec et Enide*,' *Neophil*, 69 (1985), 321–31. (XXXVIII.703)

54   Barber, Richard, *King Arthur: Hero and Legend* (New York: St Martin's Press, 1986). (XXXIX.41).

55   Boyd, Beverly, 'The Continental Mystic of Fiction,' in *Mysticism: Medieval and Modern*, ed. Valerie M. Lagorio (Salzburg: Institut für Anglistik und Amerikanistik, Universität Salzburg, 1986), pp. 72–77.

See Pi19 Busby.

See Sc23 Deist.

See Pa170 Kennedy.

See Pa174 Roussel.

See Pa175 Saly.

56   Armstrong, Grace M., 'Enide and Fenice: Chrétien de Troyes's Clerkly Heroines,' in *Papers on Romance Literary Relations: The Creation of Female Voices by Male Writers in Romance Literatures. Presented at the Romance Literary Relations Group, Modern Language Association of America Convention New York, 27 December 1986*, ed. Martha O'Nan (Brockport: State University of New York College, 1987), pp. 1–8.

See Qc53 Lecouteux.

57   Busby, Keith, 'The Characters and the Setting,' in *Legacy*, vol. 1, pp. 57–89. (XLII.182)

See Pa190 Busby.

See Fa141 Kelly.

58   Armstrong, Grace M., 'Women of Power: Chrétien de Troyes's Female Clerks,' in *Women in French Literature: A Collection of Essays*, ed. Michel Guggenheim, Stanford French and Italian Studies, 58 (Saratoga, CA: ANMA, 1988), pp. 29–46. (XLIII.494)
Treats Enide and Laudine.

See Hc56 Brumlik.

59 Gowans, Linda, *Cei and the Arthurian Legend*, AS, 18 (Cambridge: Brewer, 1988). (XLI.133)

60 Haidu, Peter, 'Temps, histoire, subjectivité aux XIe et XIIe siècles,' in *Hommage Zumthor*, pp. 105–22.

61 Lazard, Madeleine, 'Perceval et Gargantua: deux apprentissages,' in *Prose et prosateurs de la Renaissance: mélanges offerts à Robert Aulotte* (Paris: CDU et SEDES, 1988), pp. 77–83; repr. *Bulletin: Association des Amis de Rabelais et de La Devinière*, 5 (1995), 207–12.

See Jb39 Ribard.

62 Zaddy, Z. P., 'Yvain as the Ideal Courtly Lover,' *Studies Woledge*, pp. 253–75.

See Pa208 Zink.

63 Armstrong, Grace M., 'Enide and Solomon's Wife: Figures of Romance *Sapientia*,' *FF*, 14, Supplement 1 (1989), 401–18. (XLII.273)
See pp. 402–09.

64 Herman, Harold J., 'Sir Kay, Seneschal of King Arthur's Court,' *AInt*, 4:1 (1989), 1–31.

See Fd4 Maddox.

65 Samples, Susann, 'Guinevere: A Re-Appraisal,' *AInt*, 3:2 (1989), 106–18.

66 Bossy, Michel-André, 'The Elaboration of Female Narrative Functions in *Erec et Enide*,' in *ICLS Dalfsen*, pp. 23–38. (XLIII.411)

67 Faivre-Duboz, Brigitte, 'Lunete et le nouvel amour,' *Initiales*, 10–11 (1990–91), 11–15.

See Pa221 Macdonald.

See Ud3 Stanbury.

68 Amazawa, Taijirô, 'The Grail and the Death of King Arthur – King Arthur in French Literature,' *Eureka*, 23:10 (1991), 148–57.
In Japanese.

69 Brugger-Hackett, Silvia, *Merlin in der europäischen Literatur des Mittelalters*, Helfant Studien, S 8 (Stuttgart: Helfant, 1991). (XLV.21)
See pp. 169–71.

See Pa227 Chase.

70 Germain, Ellen, 'Lunete, Women, and Power in Chrétien's *Yvain*,' *RomQ*, 38 (1991), 15–25.

71 Lepri, Alessandra, 'I personaggi minori nei romanzi di Chrétien de Troyes,' *QBologna*, 8 (1991), 7–94. (XLV.335)

72 Matsubara, Hideichi, 'King Arthur and a Fatalistic Vision,' *Eureka*, 23:10 (1991), 200–08.
In Japanese.

73 Yllera, Alicia, 'Gauvain/Gawain: las múltiples transposiciones de un héroe,' *RLM*, 3 (1991), 199–221. (XLVI.288)

74 Álvares, Cristina, 'Gauvain, les femmes et le cheval,' in *Cheval*, pp. 29–41. (XLV.163)

75 Wheeler, Bonnie, 'The Masculinity of King Arthur: From Gildas to the Nuclear Age,' *QetF*, 2:4 (1992), 1–26. (XLVI.790)
Includes *Yvain*.

See Pa243–44 Berthelot.

See Fb83 *Description*.

76 Combarieu du Grès, Micheline de, 'Les "apprentissages" de Perceval dans *Le Conte du graal* et de Lancelot dans le *Lancelot en prose*,' in *Education*, pp. 129–53. (LII.220)

77 Dottori, Daniela, 'L'aspetto fisico nel *Cligès* di Chrétien de Troyes,' *QMacerata*, ser. 3, 8 (1993), 79–100. (XLVI.557)

78 Fulton, Helen, 'A Woman's Place: Guinevere in the Welsh and French Romances,' *QetF*, 3:2 (1993), 1–25. (XLVII.709)

79 Gerritsen, W. P., and A. G. van Melle, ed., *Van Aiol tot de Zwaanridder: Personages uit de middeleeuwse verhaalkunst en hun voortleven in literatuur, theater en beeldende kunst* (Nijmegen: SUN, 1993). (XLVI.629).
Contains articles on Arthur (pp. 39–53, by Frank Brandsma), Cligès (pp. 88–90, by C. Hogetoorn), Erec and Enide (pp. 113–17, by C. Hogetoorn), Gauvain (pp. 340–50, by Bart Besamusca), Kay (pp. 197–99, by Bart Besamusca), Lancelot (pp. 203–17, by Frank Brandsma), Perceval (pp. 245–57, by R. M. T. Zemel), Yder (pp. 365–68, by Ada Postma), and Yvain (pp. 372–75, by C. Hogetoorn).
English trans: *A Dictionary of Medieval Heroes: Characters in Medieval Narrative Traditions and their Afterlife in Literature, Theatre and the Visual*

Arts, trans. Tanis Guest (Woodbridge: Boydell, 1998) (LI.369); Italian trans.: *Miti e personaggi del Medioevo: dizionario di storia, letteratura, arte, musica*, trans. Gabriella Agrati and Maria Letizia Magiri (Milan: Mondadori, 1999). (LII.595)

See Pb364 Mertens.

80 Suard, François, 'Les figures du couple dans le *Chevalier au lion*,' in *Lorraine vivante: hommage à Jean Lanher*, ed. Roger Marchal and Bernard Guidot (Nancy: Presses Universitaires de Nancy, 1993), pp. 455–60. (XLVI.369)

See Hg92 Vincensini.
Gauvain and Perceval.

See Pe42 Zemel, pp. 184–88.

81 Aguiriano, Begoña, Francisca Aramburu, Javier Benito, and Catherine Despres, 'Deux faces de la femme merveilleuse au Moyen Âge: la magicienne et la fée,' *Bien dire*, 12 (1994), 7–22. (XLVII.249)
Morgane as fay.

82 Álvares, Cristina, 'O herói-usurpador em *Cligés* de Chrétien de Troyes,' in *Actas Santiago*, vol. 7, pp. 403–10.

See Pa256 Berthelot.

See Pa257 Bouché.

83 Diverres, Armel, 'Arthur in *Culhwch and Olwen* and in the Romances of Chrétien de Troyes,' in *Essays Lagorio*, pp. 54–69. (XLVII.698)

See Ub43(B) Firestone.

84 Hernández Álvarez, Vicenta, 'El Senescal Keu: necesidad funcional del personaje en las novelas de Chrétien de Troyes,' in *Actas Almagro*, pp. 211–18.

See Hg95 Kelly.

See Ke15 Mendoza Ramos.

See Pa261 Klüppelholz.

85 Pontfarcy, Yolande de, 'Le sénéchal Keu ou la fonction cosmique du rire,' *EtCelt*, 30 (1994), 263–83. (XLVII.291, XLVIII.331)

See Lc3 Saly.

86 Spivack, Charlotte, and Roberta Lynne Staples, *The Company of Camelot: Arthurian Characters in Romance and Fantasy*, Contributions to the Study of Science Fiction and Fantasy, 61 (Westport, CT: Greenwood, 1994). (XLVIII.728)

See Xb13 Bruckner.

See Gb125(E) Ihring.

See Qb69 Kullmann.

See Hg98 Maninchedda.

See Hc74 Nightingale.

87 Paupert, Anne, 'L'amour au féminin dans les romans de Chrétien de Troyes,' in *Amour Troyes*, pp. 95–106. (XLIX.180)

88 Santucci, Monique, 'La femme et le chevalier dans le *Conte du graal*,' in *Amour Troyes*, pp. 121–34. (XLIX.188)

89 Sargent-Baur, Barbara N., 'Perceval's Acculturation in the *Conte du graal*,' *BBSIA*, 47 (1995), 320–36. (XLIX.547)

See Qa117 Duby, vol. 1, pp. 151–67 (trans. pp. 90–100), 'Dorée d'amour et le Phénix.'

See Hf100 Grinnell.
On Lunete.

90 *King Arthur: A Casebook*, ed. Edward Donald Kennedy, ACT, 1/GRLH, 1915 (New York: Garland, 1996).
Reprint of Ga47 Sargent-Baur; includes Pb416 McDonald.

See Db60 Lacy.

See Na.c110 Lacy.

91 *Lancelot and Guinevere: A Casebook*, ed. with an Introduction by Lori J. Walters, ACT, 4 / GRLH, 1513 (New York: Garland, 1996).
Reprints of Ga35 Brewer and He55 Bruckner.
See also Pa287 Kennedy, Pe50 Besamusca, and Xa23 Stones.

92 Murray, Erin, 'The Masculinization of Enide's Voice: An Ambiguous Portrayal of the Heroine,' *RLA*, 8 (1996), 79–83.

See Uf2(D) Sears.

93 *Williamson, Joan B., 'Arthur and the Other in Chrétien de Troyes' Romances,' *SpecMA*, 2:4 (1996), 101–9.

94 Benoît, Louis, 'Le Vieux Roi dans *Le Conte du Graal* de Chrétien de Troyes,' *SLCO*, 23 (1997), 21–48.

See Fb96 Corbyn.

95 Hostetler, Margaret M., 'Enclosed and Invisible? Chrétien's Spatial Discourse and the Problem of Laudine,' *RomN*, 37 (1997), 119–27. (L.490)

96 Zink, Michel, 'Renouart et Perceval: le tinel et le javelot,' in *Festschrift Mölk*, pp. 277–86. (L.116)

97 Luttrell, Claude, 'The Upbringing of Perceval Heroes,' *AL*, 16 (1998), 131–69. (LI.389)

See Hg116 Maninchedda.

98 Merceron, Jacques E., 'De la "mauvaise humeur" du sénéchal Keu: Chrétien de Troyes, littérature et physiologie,' *CCM*, 41 (1998), 17–34. (LI.274)

99 Tolhurst, Fiona, 'The Once and Future Queen: The Development of Guenevere from Geoffrey of Monmouth to Malory,' *BBSIA*, 50 (1998), 272–308.
See pp. 282–84.

100 Toury, Marie-Noëlle, 'Gauvain le magnifique,' *Op. cit.*, 11 (1998), 29–34. (LII.287)

See Hf104 Álvares.

See Ma36 Bertolucci Pizzorusso.

101 Feistner, Edith, 'Bewußtlosigkeit und Bewußtsein: zur Identitäts-konstitution des Helden bei Chrétien und Hartmann,' *AStnSpr*, 236 (1999), 241–64. (LII.74)

102 Markale, Jean, *Les dames du Graal* (Paris: Pygmalion/Gérard Watelet, 1999).

103 Whetter, K. S., 'Reassessing Kay and the Romance Seneschal,' *BBSIA*, 51 (1999), 343–63.

104 Deschepper, Catherine, 'Keu l'ambigu,' in *Conjointure*, pp. 35–51.

105 Gouttebroze, Jean-Guy, 'La Laide Demoiselle du *Conte du graal*: le chant de deuil de la terre,' in *Beau et laid*, pp. 177–84. (LIII.236)

106 Kibler, William W., 'Sagremor in the Arthurian Verse Romances,' *Essays Lacy*, pp. 283–92.

See Jb58 Ribard.

See Nb52 Saly.

See Na.d63 Walter.

107 Watanabe, Kôji, 'Traces of Zoological Mythology in Arthurian Romance – On Arthur and the Mythology of the Bear,' *Gengo*, 29:12 (2000), 63–73.
In Japanese.

See Pa331 Watanabe.

108 *On Arthurian Women: Essays Maureen Fries*, ed. Bonnie Wheeler and Fiona Tolhurst (Dallas: Scriptorium, 2001).
    A. Anne Berthelot, 'From Niniane to Nimüe: Demonizing the Lady of the Lake,' pp. 89–101.
    B. Margaret Jewett Burland, 'Chrétien's Enide: Heroine or Female Hero?' pp. 167–86.
    C. Ellen Lorraine Friedrich, 'The Beaten Path: Lancelot's Amorous Adventure at the Fountain in *Le Chevalier de la Charrete*,' pp. 199–212.
    D. Melanie McGarrahan Gibson, 'Lyonet, Lunete, and Laudine: Carnivalesque Arthurian Women,' pp. 213–27.

b: Figures, Non-Individual Types, and Personifications

6   Micha, Alexandre, 'Le Mari jaloux […]' Repr. in Dc3.

12   Ménard, Philippe, 'Le Thème comique […]' Repr. in Dc29.

22   Kennedy, Angus J., 'The Hermit's Role […]' (XXVII.248)

24   Ferrante, Joan M., *Woman as Image* […] (XXVIII.123)

25   Meyer, Fritz, *Die Stände, ihr Leben und Treiben, dargestellt nach den altfr. Artus- und Abenteuerromanen*, AA, 89 (Marburg: Elwert, 1892).

26 Knowlton, E. C., 'Nature in Old French,' *MP*, 20 (1922–23), 309–29.

27 Woelker, Eva-Maria, *Menschengestaltung in vorhöfischen Epen des 12. Jahrhunderts: Chanson de Roland/Rolandslied des Pfaffen Konrad, König Rother*, Germanische Studien, 221 (Berlin: Ebering, 1940).
See Part III: 'Ausblick: Menschengestaltung im höfischen Roman. Chrestiens *Yvain* und Hartmanns *Iwein*.'

28 Peters, Edward, *The Shadow King: 'Rex Inutilis' in Medieval Law and Literature, 751–1327* (New Haven, CT: Yale University Press, 1970).
See '*Rex inutilis* in the Arthurian Romances,' pp. 170–209.

29 Economou, George D., *The Goddess Natura in Medieval Literature* (Cambridge, MA: Harvard University Press, 1972).
Useful reference on the commonplace Nature topic, but does not treat Chrétien specifically.

30 Holmes, Urban Tigner, 'The Monster in Mediaeval Literature,' in *Studies Alfred G. Engstrom*, UNCSRL, 124 (Chapel Hill: University of North Carolina Press, 1972), pp. 53–62.

See Pd27 Pearcy.

31 Wolfzettel, Friedrich, 'Zur Stellung und Bedeutung der *enfances* in der altfranzösischen Epik I,' *ZfSL*, 83 (1973), 317–48, 'II,' 84 (1974), 1–32. (XXVII.189)

32 Bond, Gerald A., 'The Medieval Conception of the Renaissance Man,' *Paideia* (1975), pp. 45–55.

33 Combridge, Rosemary N., 'Ladies, Queens and Decorum,' *RMS*, 1 (1975), 71–83. (XXVIII.303)

See Ge25 *Concepts*.

See Hc23 Huppé.

34 McMunn, Meradith Tilbury, 'Children and Literature in Medieval France,' *Children's Literature*, 4 (1975), 51–58.

35 Uitti, Karl D., 'The Clerkly Narrator Figure in Old French Hagiography and Romance,' *MedR*, 2 (1975), 394–408.

36 Vitz, Evelyn Birge, 'Type et individu dans l'"autobiographie" médiévale: étude d'*Historia calamitatum*,' *Poétique*, 24 (1975), 426–45.
Some useful comparisons with romance representation of character.

37   Wisbey, Roy A., 'Die Darstellung des Häßlichen im Hoch- und Spätmittelalter,' in *Deutsche Literatur des späten Mittelalters: Hamburger Colloquium 1973*, Publications of the Institute of German Studies, University of London, 22 (Berlin: Schmidt, 1975), pp. 9–34. (XXVIII.84)

38   Bender, Karl-Heinz, 'L'essor des motifs du plus beau chevalier et de la plus belle dame dans le premier roman courtois,' in *Festschrift Klein*, pp. 35–46.

39   Chênerie, Marie-Luce, '"Ces curieux chevaliers tournoyeurs..." des fabliaux aux romans,' *Rom*, 97 (1976), 327–68. (XXIX.230)

40   Colliot, Régine, 'Perspective sur la condition familiale de l'enfant dans la littérature médiévale,' in *Morale pratique et vie quotidienne dans la littérature française du Moyen Age*, Senefiance, 1 (Aix-en-Provence: CUER-MA; Paris: Champion, 1976), pp. 17–33.
Includes Perceval.

41   Green, D. H., 'The King and the Knight in the Medieval Romance,' in *Language and Literature in the Formation of National and Cultural Communities: Proceedings of the XIII Congress of the Fédération Internationale des Langues et Littératures Modernes and the XVII Congress of the Australasian Universities Language and Literature Association Held at Sydney University, 25 to 29 August 1975* (Adelaide: Griffin, 1976), pp. 96–97.

42   Ménard, Philippe, 'Le chevalier errant dans la littérature arthurienne: recherches sur les raisons du départ et de l'errance,' in *Voyage*, pp. 289–310 (discussion p. 311). (XXIX.244)

See Qa43 *Femme*.
On the woman in literature; see especially Qa43(C) Lejeune.

See Qa44 Green.

See Gd.c12 Halász.

43   Ménard, Philippe, 'Les fous dans la société médiévale: le témoignage de la littérature au XIIe et au XIIIe siècle,' *Rom*, 98 (1977), 433–59. (XXX.286 *bis*)

44   Mermier, Guy, 'The Grotesque in French Medieval Literature: A Study in Forms and Meanings,' in *Versions of Medieval Comedy*, ed. Paul D. Ruggiers (Norman: University of Oklahoma Press, 1977), pp. 101–34.
See pp. 114–18.

45   Schmolke-Hasselmann, Beate, '"Camuse chose": das Häßliche als ästhetisches und menschliches Problem in der altfranzösischen Literatur,' in *Die Mächte des Guten und Bösen: Vorstellungen im XII. und XIII. Jahrhundert über ihr Wirken in der Heilsgeschichte*, ed. Albert Zimmermann and Gudrun Vuillemin-Diem, Miscellanea mediaevalia, 11 (Berlin: de Gruyter, 1977), pp. 442–52. (XXX.68)

46   Batany, Jean, 'Normes, types et individus: la présentation des modèles sociaux au XIIe siècle,' in *Littérature et société au Moyen Age: Actes du Colloque des 5 et 6 mai 1978, Université de Picardie*, ed. Danielle Buschinger (Paris: Champion, 1978), pp. 177–200; repr. in his *Approches langagières de la société médiévale*, Varia, 2 (Caen: Paradigme, 1992), pp. 209–28.

47   Brend, Barbara, 'Le développement de "l'Observateur à la Tour" comme motif littéraire dans l'œuvre de Chrétien de Troyes,' *MA*, 84 (1978), 443–77. (XXXII.292)

48   Combarieu, Micheline de, 'Image et représentation du *vilain* dans les chansons de geste (et dans quelques autres textes médiévaux),' in *Exclus*, pp. 9–26. (XXX.268)
Includes *Yvain*.

49   Dubost, Francis, 'L'emploi du mot "géant" dans les chansons de geste,' in *Mélanges Camproux*, vol. 1, pp. 299–313.
References to Chrétien's use of *géant* show that the word refers not to a person of disproportionate size but to a virtual personification of evil.

See He31 Fullman.

50   Norden, Ernest E., 'The Figure of the Father in the Romances of Chrétien de Troyes,' *South Central Bulletin*, 38 (1978), 155–57. (XXXII.210)

51   Stevens, Martin, 'The Performing Self in Twelfth-Century Culture,' *Viator*, 9 (1978), 193–212 + 12 plates.
See pp. 203–05 on Chrétien as subject of his own work.

52   Vadin, Béatrix, 'L'absence de représentation de l'enfant et/ou du sentiment de l'enfance dans la littérature médiévale,' in *Exclus*, pp. 363–82.

53   Verchère, Chantal, 'Périphérie et croisement: aspect du nain dans la littérature médiévale,' in *Exclus*, pp. 251–79. (XXX.295)

54 Brucker, Charles, 'Mentions et représentation du diable dans la littérature française épique et romanesque du XIIe et du début du XIIIe siècle: quelques jalons pour une étude évolutive,' in *Diable*, pp. 37–69. (XXXI.262)
See pp. 48–50.

See Nc1 Carpenter.

55 Ferrante, Joan M., 'Artist Figures in the Tristan Stories,' *Tristania*, 4:2 (1979), 25–35. (XXXII.171)
Pp. 33–34 on *Cligés*.

56 Hartman, Richard, 'The Disinherited Damsel – the Transformation of a Convention in Chrétien's *Yvain* and the *Queste del saint graal*,' in *MichA*, 12 (1979), 61–67. (XXXII.186)

57 Payen, Jean-Charles, 'Pour en finir avec le diable médiéval ou pourquoi poètes et théologiens du moyen-âge ont-ils scrupule à croire au démon?' in *Diable*, pp. 401–25. (XXXI.296)

58 Payen, Jean-Charles, and Huguette Legros, 'La femme et la nuit, ou recherches sur le thème de l'échange amoureux dans la littérature courtoise,' in *Mélanges Jonin*, pp. 515–25. (XXXII.361)

59 Christensen, Lena, 'En analyse af middelalderens bondemyte og dens funktion,' *(Pre)publications*, 57 (1980), 32–46.
On the *Yvain* herdsman, pp. 38–40.

60 Lecouteux, Claude, 'Les Panotéens: sources, diffusion, emploi,' *EtGerm*, 35 (1980), 253–66. (XXXIII.344)
See p. 261.

61 Payen, Jean-Charles, 'L'enfance occultée: note sur un problème de typologie littéraire au moyen-âge,' in *Enfant*, pp. 176–98 (discussion pp. 199–200). (XXXII.360)

See Wb31 Plouzeau.

62 Vinaver, Eugène, 'The Questing Knight,' in *Proteus*, pp. 126–40. (XXXIV.156)

See Ub14 Braet.

63 Braet, Herman, 'Tyolet/Perceval: l'invention du père,' *Incidences*, 5 (1981), 71–77. (XXXV.147)

64 Ferran, Marie-Hélène, 'Deux évocations du peuple dans *Le Chevalier au lion* de Chrétien de Troyes,' in *Peuple et littérature*, ed. R. Mathé, TRAMES: Travaux et Mémoires de l'Université de Limoges, U. E. R. des Lettres et Sciences Humaines, Coll. Français, 3 (Limoges: U. E. R. des Lettres et Sciences Humaines, Université de Limoges, 1981), pp. 31–41.

See Qa54 Foulon.

65 Kennedy, Angus J., 'The Portrayal of the Hermit-Saint in French Arthurian Romance: The Remoulding of a Stock-Character,' in *Essays Thorpe*, pp. 69–82. (XXXIV.335)

See Qe14 Melli.

66 Callay, Brigitte L., 'Noblemen in the Marketplace: Aristocratic versus Bourgeois Values in Old French Literature,' *MichA*, 14 (1981–82), 313–23.

67 Colas, Louise, 'Chrétien de Troyes: le corps et le geste,' *Europe*, 642 (Oct. 1982), 105–13. (XXXV.313)

68 Jonin, Pierre, 'La révision d'un topos ou la noblesse du vilain,' *Mélanges Larmat*, pp. 177–94.
The villein in *Yvain*.

See Pa130 Lecouteux.

69 Payen, Jean-Charles, 'Le peuple dans les romans de Chrétien de Troyes (sur l'idéologie de la littérature chevaleresque),' *Europe*, 642 (Oct. 1982), 61–76. (XXXV.341)

70 Santucci, Monique, 'Le fou dans les lettres françaises médiévales,' *LR*, 36 (1982), 195–211. (XXXV.252)

71 Bornstein, Diane, *The Lady in the Tower: Medieval Courtesy Literature for Women* (Hamden, CN: Archon, 1983). (XXXVII.346)
Comparative examples from Chrétien.

72 Ginsberg, Warren, *The Cast of Character: The Representation of Personality in Ancient and Medieval Literature* (Toronto: University of Toronto Press, 1983). (XXXVII.378)
On *Yvain*, see pp. 90–96.

73 Bender, Karl-Heinz, 'Beauté et mariage selon Chrétien de Troyes: un défi lancé à la tradition,' in *Mittelalterstudien Köhler*, pp. 31–42. (XXXVII.575)
Emphasizes *Erec*.

74 Harf-Lancner, Laurence, *Les Fées au Moyen Age: Morgane et Mélusine – la naissance des fées*, NBMA, 8 (Paris: Champion, 1984). (XXXVII.87)

75 Harf-Lancner, Laurence, 'Le géant et la fée: l'utilisation d'un schéma folklorique dans le *Tristan* en prose,' in *Actes Rennes*, pp. 302–13. (XXXVIII.221)

See Md35 Huchet.
The woman in romance plots.

76 Jezewski, Mary Ann, 'Traits of the Female Hero: The Application of Raglan's Concept of Hero Trait Patterning,' *New York Folklore*, 10:1–2 (1984), 55–73. (XL.287)
Includes Guenevere and Eleanor of Aquitaine (pp. 63–64).

77 Saly, Antoinette, 'La demoiselle "esforciée" dans le roman arthurien,' in *Amour mariage*, pp. 215–24; repr. in Dc30. (XXXVII.664)
Includes examples from the *Charrette* and *Perceval*.

See Fa129 Ziolkowski.

78 Krueger, Roberta L., 'Love, Honor, and the Exchange of Women in *Yvain*: Some Remarks on the Female Reader,' *RomN*, 25 (1984–85), 302–17. (XXXVIII.518)

79 Baumgartner, Emmanuèle, 'Géants et chevaliers,' in *ICLS Toronto*, pp. 9–22; repr. in Dc20. (XXXVIII.302)

80 Brandt, Wolfgang, 'Die Beschreibung häßlicher Menschen in höfischen Romanen: zur narrativen Integrierung eines Topos,' *GRM*, 35 (1985), 257–78. (XXXVIII.10)

See Qa72 Gold.

81 Haug, Walter, 'Der Teufel und das Böse im mittelalterlichen Roman,' *Seminar*, 21 (1985), 165–91; repr. in Dc15. (XXXVIII.502, XXXIX.493)

82   Houstin, Françoise, 'La fonction "chevalier" à travers l'imaginaire des 500 premiers vers du *Perceval* de Chrétien de Troyes,' *PRIS-MA*, 1 (1985), 22–28.

83   Huchet, Jean-Charles, 'Les déserts du roman médiéval: le personnage de l'ermite dans les romans des XIIᵉ et XIIIᵉ siècles,' *Littérature*, 60 (1985), 89–108; repr. in Dc27. (XXXVIII.227)

84   Rousse, Michel, 'Chrétien de Troyes, les femmes et la politique,' *Actes Rennes*, vol. 2, pp. 739–52. (XXXVIII.258)

85   Stanesco, Michel, 'Le héraut d'armes et la tradition littéraire chevaleresque,' *Rom*, 106 (1985), 233–53. (XL.59)

See Ha134 Stanesco.

86   Westoby, Kathryn S., 'A New Look at the Role of the Fée in Medieval French Arthurian Romance,' in *ICLS Toronto*, pp. 373–85. (XXXVIII.348)

87   Chênerie, Marie-Luce, *Le Chevalier errant dans les romans arthuriens en vers des XIIᵉ et XIIIᵉ siècles*, PRF, 172 (Geneva: Droz, 1986). (XL.37 *bis*, 500)

See Pb300 Dick.

88   Gallais, Pierre, 'Les fées seraient-elles nées au XIIᵉ siècle (à propos d'un ouvrage récent),' *CCM*, 29 (1986), 355–71. (XXXIX.643)
On Gb74 Harf-Lancner.

89   Aercke, Kristiaan P., 'Loathly Ladies' Evil Tongues: "Les yeux et les oreilles sont les avenues de l'âme",' *NM*, 88 (1987), 48–54.

90   Ribémont, Bernard, 'Quelques aspects de la relation vieillesse/sagesse au Moyen Age: l'exemple du *Chevalier au barisel*,' in *Vieillesse*, pp. 299–315. (XXXIX.667)
See pp. 306–7.

See Ha140 Urbina.

91   Cavendish, Richard, 'The Knight Errant: the Quest for Integrity,' in *Vitality*, pp. 111–22.

See Gd.c35 Halász.

92   Morris, Rosemary, 'The Knight and the Superfluous Lady: A Problem of Disposal,' *RMS*, 14 (1988), 111–24. (XLII.669)

See Kc87 Rychner.

The messenger.

See Ub36 Álvares.

93 Colliot, Régine, 'Un rapport dramatique Mère-Enfant dans le récit médiéval: la Mère Dénonciatrice du crime,' in *Relations*, pp. 161–76. (XLII.52)

In *Perceval.*

See Qc59(C) Fassò.

See Pa213 Gravdal.

94 Grigsby, John L., 'Les diables d'aventures dans Manessier et *La Queste del saint Graal*,' in *Contemporary Readings of Medieval Literature*, ed. Guy Mermier, MRS, 8 (Ann Arbor: Department of Romance Languages, University of Michigan, 1989), pp. 1–20. (XLIII.541)

On the Male Pucelle in *Perceval* as devil.

See Qa90 Ménard.

See Ue4 Sasaki.

95 Uitti, Karl D., '*Copula sacra*,' *FF*, 14, Supplement No. 1 on 'The Philology of the Couple,' ed. Lionel J. Friedman (1989), 391–99. (XLII.353)

96 Uitti, Karl D., 'Understanding Guillaume de Lorris: The Truth of the Couple in Guillaume's *Romance of the Rose*,' in *Contemporary Readings of Medieval Literature*, ed. Guy Mermier, MRS, 8 (Ann Arbor: Department of Romance Languages, University of Michigan, 1989), pp. 51–70. (XLIII.603)

97 Bonheim, Helmut, 'The Acromegalic in Chrétien's *Yvain*,' *FS*, 44 (1990), 1–9. (XLIII.240)

98 Vilella Morató, Eduard, 'Individuo e doppio nel *roman* medievale: Chrétien de Troyes,' in *QBologna*, 11 (1990), 7–30. (XLIX.334)

99 Alvar, Carlos, 'Mujeres y hadas en la literatura medieval,' in *Evolución*, pp. 21–33. (XLVI.224)

100 Burrell, Margaret, 'The Participation of Chrétien's Heroines in Love's "Covant",' *NFS*, 30:2 (1991), 24–33. (XLIV.93)

See Ga70 Germain.

101 Legros, Huguette, 'De la revendication au magique,' in *Figures de l'écrivain au Moyen Age: Actes du Colloque du Centre d'Etudes Médiévales de l'Université de Picardie, Amiens 18–20 mars 1988*, ed. Danielle Buschinger, GAG, 510 (Göppingen: Kümmerle, 1991), pp. 181–92. (XLIV.450)

See Ga71 Lepri.

See Gd.b43 Morales.

102 Stanesco, Michel, 'Figures de l'auteur dans le roman médiéval,' *TrL*, 4 (1991), 7–19. (XLVI.52)

103 Ueda, Hiroshi, 'The Hermit in the Grail Romances,' *JFLN*, 109 (1991), 123–34.
In Japanese.

104 Zumthor, Paul, 'De Perceval à Don Quichotte: l'espace du chevalier errant,' *Poétique*, 87 (1991), 259–69. (XLV.203)

105 Arden, Heather M., 'Grief, Widowhood, and Women's Sexuality in Medieval French Literature,' in *Upon My Husband's Death: Widows in the Literature and Histories of Medieval Europe*, ed. Louise Mirrer, Studies in Medieval and Early Modern Civilization (Ann Arbor: University of Michigan Press, 1992), pp. 305–19.
Includes *Yvain*.

106 Baumgartner, Emmanuèle, 'Les brodeuses et la ville,' in *50 rue de Varenne*, Supplemento Italo-Francese di Nuovi Argomenti, 43 (Paris: Istituto Italiano di Cultura, 1992), pp. 89–95. (XLV.165)

107 Boutet, Dominique, *Charlemagne et Arthur ou le roi imaginaire*, NBMA, 20 (Paris: Champion-Slatkine, 1992).

See Hc64 Brumlik.

108 Burgess, Glyn S., and Gillian P. Gaughan, 'The Role of the *borgois* in Early Old French Literature,' *ZrP*, 108 (1992), 228–53. (XLV.23)

109 Cohen, Jeffrey J., 'The Use of Monsters and the Middle Ages,' *SELIM, Journal of the Spanish Society for Mediaeval English Language and Literature/Revista de la Sociedad Española de Lengua y Literatura Inglesa Medieval*, 2 (1992), 47–69.
Examples from *Yvain*.

110 Fries, Maureen, 'Female Heroes, Heroines and Counter-Heroes: Images of Women in Arthurian Tradition,' in *Popular Arthurian Traditions*, ed. Sally K. Slocum (Bowling Green, OH: Bowling Green State University Popular Press, 1992), pp. 5–17. (XLVI.716)

111 Fritz, Jean-Marie, *Le discours du fou au Moyen Age: XIIe–XIIIe siècles. Etude comparée des discours littéraire, médical, juridique et théologique de la folie*, Perspectives littéraires (Paris: Presses Universitaires de France, 1992). (XLV.178)

112 Gallais, Pierre, *La fée à la fontaine et à l'arbre: un archétype du conte merveilleux et du récit courtois*, CERMEIL, 1 (Amsterdam: Rodopi, 1992). (XLV.179, 409)

113 Rothschild, Judith Rice, 'Empowered Women and Manipulative Behaviors in Chrétien's *Le Chevalier au lion* and *Le Chevalier de la charrete*,' *MedPer*, 7 (1992), 171–85.

114 Salinero Cascante, Mª Jesús, 'El código vestimentario caballeresco de Lanzarote del Lago de Chrétien de Troyes,' *CIF*, 18 (1992), 149–58. (XLVI.283)

115 Stanesco, Michel, 'Le chevalier dans la ville: le modèle romanesque et ses métamorphoses bourgeoises,' in *ICLS Salerno*, pp. 469–87.

116 Uitti, Karl D., 'The Lady and Her Place in Twelfth-Century France,' in *Literary Generations: Festschrift in Honor of Edward D. Sullivan by His Friends, Colleagues an*

117 *d Former Students*, ed. Alain Toumayan, FFM, 78 (Lexington, KY: French Forum, 1992), pp. 79–97.
On the couple.

117 Baumgartner, Emmanuèle, 'Figures du destinateur: Salomon, Arthur, le roi Henri d'Angleterre,' in *Anglo-Norman Anniversary Essays*, ed. Ian Short, ANTS, 2 (London: Anglo-Norman Text Society, 1993), pp. 1–10.

See Qc69 Coss.

118 McCracken, Peggy, 'Women and Medicine in Medieval French Narrative,' *Exemplaria*, 5 (1993), 239–62. (XLVI.752)

119 Nichols, Stephen G., 'Picture, Image, and Subjectivity in Medieval Culture,' *MLN*, 108 (1993), 617–37. (XLVI.759)

See Ud10 Ramey.

120 Sprunger, David A., 'Wild Folk and Lunatics in Medieval Romance,' in *The Medieval World of Nature: A Book of Essays*, ed. Joyce E. Salisbury, GMC, 5 (New York: Garland, 1993), pp. 145–63.

121 Yamamoto, Jun'ichi, 'Cities and the "bourgeois" in Some Romances of the Middle Ages,' *Hum*, 39 (1993), 51–92.
In Japanese.

See Ha181 Kay.

See Qe24 Larmat.

122 Monson, Don A., 'Les *lauzengiers*,' *MedR*, 19 (1994), 219–35.
On *Yvain*, pp. 227–28.

123 Saly, Antoinette, 'La Demoisele Hideuse dans le roman arthurien,' *TrL*, 7 (1994), 27–51; repr. in Dc30. (XLVII.294)

See Uc38 Vierne.

124 Zanoner, Angela, 'Funzione cavalleresca nel *Conte del Graal* di Chrétien de Troyes e nel *Parzival* di Wolfram von Eschenbach,' *Quaderni di lingue e letterature* (Verona), 19 (1994), 243–51.

125 *Arthurian Romance and Gender – Masculin/Féminin dans le roman arthurien médiéval – Geschlechterrollen im mittelalterlichen Artus-roman (Selected Proceedings of the XVIIth International Arthurian Congress/Actes choisis du XVIIe Congrès International Arthurien/Ausgewählte Akten des XVII. Internationalen Artuskongresses)*, ed. Friedrich Wolfzettel, Internationale Forschungen zur Allgemeinen und Vergleichenden Literaturwissenschaft, 10 (Amsterdam: Rodopi, 1995). (XLVIII. 649)
   A.   Danielle Régnier-Bohler, 'La fonction symbolique du féminin: le savoir des mères, le secret des sœurs et le devenir du héros,' pp. 4–25. (XLVI, p. 465, XLVIII.639 [sic: 638])
   B.   Ad Putter, 'Arthurian Literature and the Rhetoric of "Effeminacy",' pp. 34–49. (XLVI, p. 444, XLVIII.637)
   C.   Angelica Rieger, 'Balade des demoiselles du temps jadis: essai sur l'entrée en scène des personnages féminins dans les romans arthuriens de Chrétien de Troyes,' pp. 79–103. (XLVI, pp. 446–47, XLVIII.641)
   D.   Catherine Blons-Pierre, 'Discours féminin et discours masculin dans les romans de Chrétien de Troyes,' pp. 104–18. (XLVI, pp. 420–21, XLVIII.610)
   E.   Peter Ihring, 'Die überlistete Laudine: Korrektur eines antihöfischen Weiblichkeitskonzepts in Chrétiens *Yvain*,' pp. 147–59. (XLVI, p. 434, XLVIII.626)

F.   Jean-Guy Gouttebroze, 'Un phénomène d'intertextualité biblique dans le *Conte du graal*: "Qu'il soient une char andui" (éd. W. Roach, v. 9064),' pp. 165–75. (XLVI, pp. 385–86, XLVIII.622)
See also Hc74 Nightingale, Hf97 Deist, Hg102 Saly, Qb69 Kullmann.

126 Braet, Herman, '"A thing most brutish": The Image of the Rustic in Old French Literature,' in *Agriculture in the Middle Ages: Technology, Practice, and Representation*, ed. Del Sweeney, Middle Ages Series (Philadelphia: University of Pennsylvania Press, 1995), pp. 191–204.

127 Bretel, Paul, *Les ermites et les moines dans la littérature française du Moyen Age (1150–1250)*, NBMA, 32 (Paris: Champion; Geneva: Slatkine, 1995). (XLIX.134)

See Qc76 Guerreau-Jalabert.

128 Laharie, Muriel, 'Les fous de cour dans l'Occident médiéval (XIe-XVe siècles): de la déviance psychopathologique à la déviance allégorique,' in *Conformité*, pp. 207–21. (LII.248)

129 Mikhaïlova, Miléna, 'Le clerc: personnage de la fiction/personnage-fiction: le clerc écrivant dans la littérature arthurienne,' in *Le clerc au Moyen Age*, Senefiance, 37 (Aix-en-Provence: CUER MA, 1995), pp. 417–33. (XLVIII.324)

130 Morales, Ana María, '"El más hermoso caballero del mundo": un acercamiento al héroe artúrico,' in *Palabra e imagen en la Edad Media (Actas de las IV Jornadas Medievales)*, ed. Aurelio González, Lillian von der Walde, and Concepción Company, Publicaciones Medievalia, 10 (Mexico City: Universidad Nacional Autónoma de México, 1995), pp. 407–17.

131 Brandsma, Frank, 'The Eyewitness Narrator in Vernacular Prose Chronicles and Prose Romances,' in La46 *Text*, pp. 57–69.
Treats Calogrenant.

132 Cereceda, Miguel, *El origen de la mujer sujeto*, Colección Metropolis (Madrid: Tecnos, 1996).

See La45(D) Bruckner.

See Hc77 Burrell.

See Pb425 Dallapiazza.

133 Faaborg, Jens N., *Les Enfants dans la littérature française du Moyen Age*, Etudes Romanes, 39 (Copenhagen: Museum Tusculanum, 1997).

134 James-Raoul, Danièle, 'Le Chevalier démuni ou la non-déclaration amoureuse,' *Bien dire*, 15 (1997), 131–44. (L.203)

135 MacBain, William, 'The Outsider at Court, or What Is So Strange about the Stranger?' in *ICLS Belfast*, pp. 357–65. (L.270)
Includes Perceval.

136 Martineau, Anne, 'La félonie des nains dans les romans arthuriens,' in *Félonie, trahison, reniements au Moyen Age: Actes du Troisième Colloque International de Montpellier, Université Paul-Valéry (24–26 novembre 1995)*, Les Cahiers du CRISIMA, 3 (Montpellier: Publications de l'Université Paul-Valéry Montpellier III, 1997), pp. 281–89. (L.213)

137 Pioletti, Antonio, 'Lo strano e lo straniero nelle letterature romanze: alcuni sondaggi,' in *Lo Straniero: Atti del Convegno di Studi, Cagliari, 16–19 novembre 1994*, ed. Mario Domenichelli and Pino Fasano, Università degli Studi di Cagliari: Dipartimento di Filologie e Letterature Moderne, 14, 2 vols (Rome: Bulzoni, 1997), vol. 2, pp. 339–52. (LIII.737)
Includes Perceval and the Giant Herdsman.

138 Pratt, Karen, 'The Image of the Queen in Old French Literature,' in *Queens and Queenship in Medieval Europe: Proceedings of a Conference Held at King's College London, April 1995*, ed. Anne J. Duggan (Woodbridge: Boydell, 1997), pp. 235–59. (LIII.509)

139 Susong, Gilles, 'L'invention du *Nice*,' *MF*, 39–41 (1997), 569–75.

140 White, Catherine L., 'Women and their Fathers in Three French Medieval Literary Works,' *MFN*, 24 (Fall 1997), 42–45.

141 Arendt, Birgit, *Jetzt reden wir! Das Kommunikationsverhalten der Frauen im französischen Artusroman des Mittelalters*, EH:F, 225 (Frankfurt/M.: P. Lang, 1998).

142 Bretel, Paul, 'Perfection et sainteté: le "saint hermite" dans la littérature des XIIe et XIIIe siècles,' *RSH*, 251 (1998), 169–86. (LI.219)
See p. 177 on *Perceval*.

See Qa122 Coss.

143 Fries, Maureen, 'Gender and the Grail,' *Arthuriana*, 8:1 (1998), 67–79. (LI.750)

See Qc84 Guyon.
On the 'champion du droit.'

144 Jonin, Pierre, 'Vieillesse et vieillards dans *Perceval* de Chrétien de Troyes' in *Mélanges Takeshi Shimmura* (Tokyo: France Tosho, 1998), pp. 69–78. (LI.655)

145 McCracken, Peggy, 'Mothers in the Grail Quest: Desire, Pleasure, and Conception,' *Arthuriana*, 8:1 (1998), 35–98. (LI.786)

146 *La mère au Moyen Age*, = *Bien dire*, 16 (1998).
The following articles include discussion of the mother in Chrétien's romances:
  A. Robert Baudry, '"Pourquoi tant de veuves, tant de fils de veuves?"…,' pp. 19–28. (LI.205)
  B. Danièle James-Raoul, 'Les discours des mères: aperçus dans les romans et lais du [sic] XIIe et XIIIe siècles,' pp. 145–57. (LI.254)
  C. Ana María Holzbacher, 'La mère dans les romans de Chrétien de Troyes,' pp. 159–69. (LI.252)

147 Pioletti, Antonio, 'L'altro d'Oriente nella letteratura arturiana,' in *Studi Melli*, vol. 2, pp. 671–78. (LI.569)
Includes *Cligés*.

148 Taylor, Karen J., 'Desexualizing the Stereotypes: Techniques of Gender Reversal in Chrétien's *Chevalier au lion* and *Chevalier a la charrete*,' in *Gender Transgressions: Crossing the Normative Barrier in Old French Literature*, ed. Karen J. Taylor, GRLH, 2064 (New York: Garland, 1998), pp. 181–203.

149 Wolfzettel, Friedrich, 'Die Frau im Turm: zu einem märchenhaften Motiv in der altfranzösischen Literatur,' in *Ir sult sprechen willekomen: grenzenlose Mediävistik. Festschrift für Helmut Birkhan zum 60. Geburtstag*, ed. Christa Tuczay, Ulrike Hirhager, and Karin Lichtblau (Bern: P. Lang, 1998), pp. 330–59.

150 Allen, Renée, 'The Roles of Women and their Homosocial Context in the *Chevalier au lion*,' *RomQ*, 46 (1999), 141–54.

See Pb450 Baisch.

See Na.c125 Baudry.

151 Bucher, Anne-Laure, 'Féminité et purification du héros dans les romans de Chrétien de Troyes,' *PRIS-MA*, 15 (1999), 215–38. (LII.209)

152 Burns, E. Jane, 'Speculum of the Courtly Lady: Women, Love, and Clothes,' in *JMEMS*, 29 (1999), 253–92. (LI.736)

See Ub50 Cohen.

153 *Constructions of Widowhood and Virginity in the Middle Ages*, ed. Cindy L. Carlson and Angela Jane Weisl, The New Middle Ages (New York: St Martin's, 1999).
  A. Rebecca Hayward, 'Between the Living and the Dead: Widows as Heroines of Medieval Romances,' pp. 221–43.
  B. Leslie Abend Callahan, 'The Widow's Tears: The Pedagogy of Grief in Medieval France and the Image of the Grieving Widow,' pp. 245–63.

See Gf46 Ferroul.

See Pb455 Heckel.

154 Krueger, Roberta L., 'Transforming Maidens: Singlewomen's Stories in Marie de France's *Lais* and Later French Courtly Narratives,' in *Singlewomen in the European Past, 1250–1800*, ed. Judith M. Bennett and Amy M. Froide (Philadelphia: University of Pennsylvania Press, 1999), pp. 146–91.

155 Mandel, Jerome, '"Polymorphous Sexualities" in Chrétien de Troyes and Sir Thomas Malory,' in *The Body and the Soul in Medieval Literature: The J. A. W. Bennett Memorial Lectures, Tenth Series, Perugia, 1998*, ed. Piero Boitani and Anna Torti (Cambridge: Brewer, 1999), pp. 63–78. (LII.424)

156 Milland-Bove, Bénédicte, 'Les Orgueilleux dans le *Conte du Graal*,' in *Mélanges Suard*, vol. 2, pp. 617–27. (LII.256)

157 Nelson, Deborah Hubbard, 'Silent Women,' *RomN*, 40 (1999), 13–24.

158 Nelson, Deborah, 'A Woman Is Like…,' *RomQ*, 46 (1999), 67–73.

See Ga103 Whetter.

159 White, Catherine L., 'Not So Dutiful Daughters: Women and their Fathers in Three French Medieval Works: *Le Roman de Silence, Erec et Enide* and *Le Livre de la Cité des dames*,' *CRR*, 18 (1999), 189–99.

160 Yokoyama, Ayumi, 'The "Stranger" in Medieval European Literature,' *JGIS*, 1 (1999), 65–88.
In Japanese.

See Fe35 Brandsma.

161 Foehr-Janssens, Yasmina, *La Veuve en majesté: deuil et savoir au féminin dans la littérature médiévale*, PRF, 226 (Geneva: Droz, 2000).

162 Hamilton, Janet, 'Ruses du destin: blessures et guérisons dans l'univers chevaleresque,' in *Ruse*, pp. 261–69.
On the wounded knight.

163 Ménard, Philippe, 'Les lutins dans la littérature médiévale,' in *Mélanges Subrenat*, pp. 379–92.
See pp. 385–86 on the *netuns* in *Yvain*.

164 Michel, Alain, 'Du héros antique au héros moderne: l'homme, Dieu et le courage,' *PRIS-MA*, 16 (2000), 157–72. (LIII.262)
See pp. 170–71.

165 Schwartz, Debora B., '*Par bel mentir*: Chrétien's Hermits and Clerkly Responsibility,' in *Essays Uitti*, pp. 287–309.

166 Dessaint, Micheline, *La Femme médiatrice dans de grandes œuvres romanesques du XIIe siècle*, Essais sur le moyen âge, 24 (Paris: Champion, 2001).

c: Animals

2 Thiébaux, M., *The Stag of Love* […] (XXIX.315)

3 Goerke, Georg, *Über Tierverwandlungen in französischer Dichtung und Sage*, diss. Königsberg (Königsberg: Hartung, 1904).

4 Lewis, Gertrud Jaron, *Das Tier und seine dichterische Funktion in Erec, Iwein, Parzival und Tristan*, Kanadische Studien zur deutschen Sprache und Literatur, 11 (Bern: H. Lang, 1974). (XXVII.419)

5 Bichon, Jean, *L'Animal dans la littérature française au XIIe et au XIIIe siècles*, 2 vols (Lille: Service de Reproduction des Thèses, Université de Lille III, 1976).

6 Katô, Kyôko, 'Knights' Horses in Chrétien de Troyes's Works (I)(II)(III) (IV)(V),' *TATE*, 1 (1977), 3–11; 2 (1978), 52–56; 3 (1978),

79–84; 4 (1979), 96–102; 5 (1979), 68–71; 6 (1980), 107–09. (XXX.471, XXXI.463, 463 *bis*, XXXII.507, 508, XXXIII.575)
In Japanese.

7   Dufournet, Jean, 'L'animal dans la littérature française au XIIe siècle et au XIIIe siècle (à propos d'un ouvrage récent),' *RLR*, 83 (1978), 327–44. (XXXII.341)
On Gc5 Bichon.

8   Katô, Kyôko, 'King Arthur, Knight and Horse in Chrétien de Troyes's Works,' *To-s*, 87 (1978), 6.
In Japanese.

9   Châtillon, François, 'La reconnaissance du lion: contribution à l'étude d'un thème littéraire acclimaté dans l'Occident latin,' *RMAL*, 36 (1979), 5–13.
Does not include Chrétien, but useful for background.

See Nb21 Bretèque.

See Pa113 Cremonesi.

10   De Caluwé-Dor, Juliette, 'Yvain's Lion Again: A Comparative Analysis of its Personality and Function in the Welsh, French and English Versions,' in *Essays Thorpe*, pp. 229–38. (XXXIV.305)

See Sa100 Schmolke-Hasselmann.

See Me23 Hunt.

11   Ringger, Kurt, 'La biche blanche et le chevalier ou les avatars d'Eros et d'Agapé,' *Corps Écrit*, 6 (1983), 149–58; repr. in his *Gedenkband Ringger*, pp. 1–7.

See Jb32 Varty.

12   Williams, Harry F., 'A Note on Chrétien's Virtuosity,' *USFLQ*, 22:3–4 (1984), 49–50. (XXXVII.474)

13   *Le Monde animal et ses représentations au Moyen Age (XIe–XVe siècles): Actes du XVème Congrès de la Société des Historiens Médiévistes de l'Enseignement Supérieur Public, Toulouse, 25–26 mai 1984*, Travaux de l'Université de Toulouse-Le Mirail, ser. A, 31 (Toulouse: Université de Toulouse-Le Mirail, 1985).
    A. Michel Zink, 'Le monde animal et ses représentations dans la littérature française au moyen âge,' pp. 47–71; repr. in Dc18. (XXXVIII.279)

B. François de la Bretèque, 'Image d'un animal: le lion: sa définition et ses "limites" dans les textes et l'iconographie (XIe–XVe siècles),' pp. 143–54.

See Wa24 Pfeffer.

14 Knapp-Tepperberg, Eva-Maria, 'Problematische Interaktionen zwischen Mensch und Pferd in den romanischen Literaturen vom Mittelalter bis zum 17. Jahrhundert (Auswahl),' *RZLG*, 10 (1986), 287–326.
On *Yvain* see pp. 289–92.

15 McGrady, Donald, 'The Hunter Loses his Falcon: Notes on a Motif from *Cligés* to *La Celestina* and Lope de Vega,' *Rom*, 107 (1986), 145–82. (XLI.70)
See pp. 145–51.

See Gd.c33 Ors.

See Mf10 Laurie.

See Rb29 Bayer.
The phoenix.

16 Dufournet, Jean, 'Le lion d'Yvain,' in *Chevalier au lion*, pp. 77–104. (XLI.57)

See Hc58 Nelson.

17 Stanesco, Michel, 'Le lion du chevalier: de la stratégie romanesque à l'emblème poétique,' *Littératures*, 19 (1988), 13–35, and 20 (1989), 7–13.

18 Weiss, Gerlinde, 'Der Löwen-Drachen-Kampf in der mittelalterlichen Iwein-Tradition,' in *Festschrift für Ingo Reiffenstein zum 60. Geburtstag*, ed. Peter K. Stein [et alii], GAG, 478 (Göppingen: Kümmerle, 1988), pp. 599–620. (XLII.587)

19 Burgess, Glyn S., and John L. Curry, '"Si ont berbïoletes non" (*Erec et Enide*, l. 6739),' *FS*, 43 (1989), 129–39. (XLII.655)

20 Abeele, Baudouin van den, *La Fauconnerie dans les lettres françaises du XIIe au XIVe siècle*, MedL: Studia, 18 (Leuven: Leuven University Press, 1990). (XLIV.534)

21 Salinero Cascante, María Jesús, 'El caballo, símbolo de transmutación de un destino en *Le Chevalier de la charrette* de Chrétien de Troyes,' *Berceo*, 118–19 (1990), 117–29. (XLVI.282)

22 Burgess, Glyn S., and John L. Curry, '*Berbiolete* and *dindialos*: Animal Magic in Some Twelfth-Century Garments,' *MAe*, 60 (1991), 84–92. (XLIV.92)

23 Zaddy, S. [*sic!* = Z.] P., 'Les castors ichthyophages de Chrétien de Troyes,' *MA*, 97 (1991), 41–45. (XLIV.572)

24 Aguiriano, Begoña, 'Le cheval et le départ en aventure dans les romans de Chrétien de Troyes,' in *Cheval*, pp. 9–27. (XLV.162)

25 Planche, Alice, 'De quelques couleurs de robe (le cheval au Moyen Age),' in *Cheval*, pp. 401–14; repr. in Dc28. (XLV.194)

26 Abeele, Baudouin van den, 'L'aigle d'or sur le pommeau: un motif des romans et des chansons de geste,' *Reinardus*, 6 (1993), 153–69. (XLVII.518)
In *Perceval*.

27 Bretèque, François Amy de la, 'Des animaux machines au Moyen Age? Quelques formes de la confrontation d'un chevalier et de fauves dans la matière arthurienne,' *RLR*, 98 (1994), 321–39. (XLVII.250)
Includes episode at the Château des Reines in *Perceval*.

28 Dubost, Francis, 'Les merveilles du cerf: miracles, métamorphoses, médiations,' *RLR*, 98 (1994), 287–310. (XLVII.263)

29 Ménard, Philippe, 'Le dragon, animal fantastique de la littérature française,' *RLR*, 98 (1994), 247–68. (XLVII.281)

30 Pastré, Jean-Marc, 'Perceval, Parzival et le faucon ou l'image thériomorphe d'un héros,' in *Recueil Fourquet*, pp. 195–202. (XLVIII.143)

31 Prévot, Brigitte, and Bernard Ribémont, *Le cheval en France au Moyen Age – sa place dans le monde médiéval; sa médecine: l'exemple d'un traité vétérinaire du XIVe siècle, la 'Cirurgie des chevaux'*, Medievalia (Caen: Paradigme, 1994).
See Chap. 2: 'Le cheval "écrit": quelques regards.'

32 Trachsler, Richard, '*Si le gita / sor son dos, et si l'en porta* (*Yvain*, vv. 3445–46) ou: comment porter un cerf si vous êtes un lion,' *Reinardus*, 7 (1994), 183–93. (XLVIII.648)

33 Sasu, Maria-Vochiţa, 'Cerbul alb,' in her *Constante*, pp. 85–95. (LI.712)

See Jb54 Le Rider.

34 Hüe, Denis, 'De quelques transformations animales,' in *Magie*, pp. 233–53.

See Gb158 Nelson.

See Pe62 Hogenbirk.

d: Objects, Places, and Actions

3 Minis, Cola, 'Die Bitte der Königin [...]'; repr. in her *Zur Vergegenwärtigung vergangener philologischer Nächte*, APSL, 96 (Amsterdam: Rodopi, 1981), pp. 370–78. (XXXV.50)

9 Frappier, Jean, 'Variations [...]' Repr. in Dc2.

14 Micha, Alexandre, 'Le pays inconnu [...]' Repr. in Dc3.

17 Frappier, Jean, 'Le thème [...]' Repr. in Dc2.

24 Correction: Katô, Kyôko, '*Ecu, Targe* in Chrétien de Troyes's Works,' *ELLF*, 23 (1973), 1–18. (XXVII.387).
In Japanese.

d.a: Objects and Plants

See Pb113 Springer.

1 Lyons, Faith, '"Vin herbé" et "gingembras" dans le roman breton,' in *Mélanges Frappier*, vol. 2, pp. 689–96.

2 Cline, Ruth H., 'Heart and Eyes,' *RPh*, 25 (1971–72), 263–97.

See Me12 Gewehr.
Treats Chrétien pp. 641–45.

3 Dinzelbacher, Peter, *Die Jenseitsbrücke im Mittelalter*, Dissertationen der Universität Wien, 104 (Vienna: Verband der Wissenschaftlichen Gesellschaften Österreichs, 1973). (XXIX.15)

4   Planche, Alice, 'Comme le pin est plus beau que le charme...,' *MA*, 80 (1974), 51–70; repr. in Dc28. (XXVIII.191)
See pp. 63–64.

5   Katô, Kyôko, 'The Lance in Chrétien de Troyes's Works,' *ELLF*, 25–26 (1975), 174–75.
In Japanese.

See Ub7 Chandès.

6   Poirion, Daniel, 'Du sang sur la neige: nature et fonction de l'image dans le *Conte du graal*,' in *Essays Powell-Hodgins*, pp. 143–65; repr. in Dc21. (XXIX.249 *bis*, XXXII.213)

See Jd19 Potters.

See Qa46 Antoine.

7   Mellen, Philip, 'Blood-on-the-Snow: The Development of a Motif,' *CLS*, 15 (1978), 363–71.

8   Schmidt, Margot, 'Identität und Distanz: der Spiegel als Chiffre in der höfischen Dichtung des Mittelalters,' *LJG*, 19 (1978), 233–55. (XXXI.40).
Treats *Cligés* v. 709 on pp. 234–40.

9   Eberlein-Westhues, Hildegard, 'König Arthurs "Table Ronde": Studien zur Geschichte eines literarischen Herrschaftszeichens,' in *Der altfranzösische Prosaroman: Funktion, Funktionswandel und Ideologie am Beispiel des 'Roman de Tristan en prose': Kolloquium Würzburg 1977*, ed. Ernstpeter Ruhe and Richard Schwaderer, BRPMA, 12 (Munich: Fink, 1979), pp. 184–263. (XXXII.24)

10   Miguet, Thierry, 'L'escarboucle médiévale, pierre de lumière,' *MrR*, 29:3–4 (1979), 37–60. (XXXIV.525)

11   Connochie-Bourgne, Chantal, 'La fontaine de Barenton dans l'*Image du monde* de Gossuin de Metz: réflexion sur le statut encyclopédique du merveilleux,' *Mélanges Foulon*, vol. 1, pp. 37–48. (XXXIII.323)
Examines Chrétien's representation of the fountain.

12   Katô, Kyôko, 'The Sword in Chrétien de Troyes's Works,' *FFRSH*, 14 (1980), 39–49. (XXXII.509).
In Japanese.

13 Katô, Kyôko, '"Haubert" in Chrétien de Troyes's Works,' *FFRSH*, 15 (1981), 1–13. (XXXIV.484).
In Japanese.

14 Sleeman, Margaret, 'Medieval Hair Tokens,' *FMLS*, 17 (1981), 322–36. (XXXIV.377)
Treats Soredamors pp. 330–31.

15 Schmolke-Hasselmann, Beate, 'The Round Table: Ideal, Fiction, Reality,' *AL*, 2 (1982), 41–75. (XXXV.410)

16 Colliot, Régine, 'Soleil, lune, étoiles à l'horizon littéraire médiéval, ou les signes de la lumière (textes du XIIIe siècle),' in *Le Soleil, la lune et les étoiles au Moyen Age*, Senefiance, 13 (Aix-en-Provence: CUER-MA; Marseille: Laffitte, 1983), pp. 39–52. (XXXVI.333)
Includes *Cligés*.

See Jf11 Régnier-Bohler.

17 Sasaki, Shigemi, 'Sign of "mémoire" – for Giglio Rosso,' *TATE*, 13 (1983), 18–21.
In Japanese.

18 Hanning, Robert W., 'Poetic Emblems in Medieval Narrative Texts,' in *Vernacular Poetics*, pp. 1–32. (XXXVII.388)
Treats Jehan's tower in *Cligés* as emblem (pp. 13–17).

19 Müller, Irmgard, 'Liebestränke, Liebeszauber und Schlafmittel in der mittelalterlichen Literatur,' in *Liebe Gießen*, pp. 71–87. (XXXVII.645)

20 Planche, Alice, 'Aspects du monde végétal dans la vie quotidienne aux XIIe et XIIIe siècles: le témoignage de quelques œuvres littéraires,' in *Matériaux*, pp. 149–62; repr. in Dc28. (XXXVII.110)

21 Sasaki, Shigemi, 'Observations on an Object in the Arthurian Legend: The Round Table,' *TATE*, 15 (1984), 99–118. (XXXVII.322).
In Japanese.

22 Van Emden, Wolfgang, 'The Castle in Some Works of Medieval French Literature,' in *The Medieval Castle: Romance and Reality*, Medieval Studies at Minnesota, 1 (Dubuque, IA: Kendall/Hunt, 1984), pp. 1–26. (XXXVIII.561)

23 Schleusener-Eichholz, Gudrun, *Das Auge im Mittelalter*, MMS, 35.I–II, 2 vols Munich: Fink, 1985).

24   Hammerstein, Reinhold, *Macht und Klang: tönende Automaten als Realität und Fiktion in der alten und mittelalterlichen Welt* (Bern: Francke, 1986). (XLI.600).
See pp. 165–67 on the 'Lit de la merveille' in *Perceval*.

25   Gallais, Pierre, 'Lexique statistique (comptage) et raisonné des *realia* chez quelques "romanciers" des XIIe et XIIIe siècles,' *PRIS-MA*, 4 (1988), 117–49. (XLIII.177)

26   Gallais, Pierre, 'Travaux du séminaire: les *realia* dans la poésie narrative (comptage et signification),' *PRIS-MA*, 4 (1988), 99–115. (XLII.57)

27   Méla, Charles, 'Elucidation d'une semblance: la fontaine d'Yvain,' *PRIS-MA*, 4 (1988), 1–8; repr. in Dc19. (XLI.73)

See Jd36 Vauthier.

See Gd.c41 Benedetti.
The tree and the color green in *Cligés* and *Yvain*.

28   Colliot, Régine, 'Triple visage de l'arbre: arbre piège, arbre refuge, arbre ennemi,' *PRIS-MA*, 5 (1989), 5–16. (XLII.53, XLIII.172)

29   Colliot, Régine, 'Messages d'amour et de mort dans la légende de Tristan: anneaux et lais,' *PRIS-MA*, 7 (1991), 43–56. (XLIV.26)
On the ring Laudine gives Yvain.

30   Gros, Gérard, 'La *semblance* de la *verrine*: description et interprétation d'une image mariale,' *MA*, 97 (1991), 217–57. (XLIV.530)

31   Paoli, Guy, 'La relation œil-cœur: recherches sur la mystique amoureuse de Chrétien de Troyes dans *Cligès*,' in *Cuer*, pp. 233–44. (XLIV.45)

32   Rosenstein, Roy, '"Celi que del cuer voit": le don du cœur, d'*Yvain* à la chanson de croisade,' in *Cuer*, pp. 363–74. (XLIV.49)

33   Suzuki, Tetsuya, 'On "trois goutes de sanc sor le blanche noif"' in Chrétien de Troyes's *Perceval*,' *BEng*, 22 (1991), 389–412.
In Japanese.

34   Gallais, Pierre, 'Les "images matérielles" dans le roman et le lai au XIIIe siècle,' in *Image*, pp. 105–13.

35 Guerreau-Jalabert, Anita, 'Aliments symboliques et symbolique de la table dans les romans arthuriens (XIIe-XIIIe siècles),' *Annales*, 47 (1992), 561–94. (XLV.181)

See Mc47 Legros.

36 Lerchner, Karin, *Lectulus floridus: zur Bedeutung des Bettes in Literatur und Handschriftenillustration des Mittelalters*, Pictura et Poesis, 6 (Cologne: Böhlaus, 1993).

See Qa109 Abbott.

37 Yokoyama, Ayumi, 'The "Wheel of Fortune" Metaphor in Arthurian Romances,' *Gengo*, 11 (1994), 18–31. (XLIX.384).
In Japanese.

38 Benoît, Louis, 'Le *Conte du Graal*: l'arme du "vallet salvaige",' *SLCO*, 21 (1995), 255–74.

39 Sturm-Maddox, Sara, 'Food for Heroes: The Intertextual Legacy of the *Conte du Graal*,' in La46 *Text*, pp. 117–31.

See Gd.c63 Ménard.

40 *Kowalski, Jacek, 'Architektoniczne Fantazje Krystiana z Troyes: Trzy Zamki "Powiesci o Graalu",' *Rocznik Historii Sztuki*, 23 (1998), 5–57.
Includes French resumé.

See Jb55 Noacco.

See Jb56 Vié.

d.b: Places

See Qa28 Doerks.

1 Krämer, Philipp, *Das Meer in der altfranzösischen Literatur*, diss. Gießen (Giessen: Christ & Herr, 1919).

See Pb99 Lichtenberg.

2 Baker, Imogene, *King's Household in the Arthurian Court from Geoffrey of Monmouth to Malory*, diss. Catholic University of America (Washington, DC: Catholic University of America, 1937).
See pp. 60–70.

See Jc10 Robertson.

See Pg8 Stegagno Picchio.

3   Pickering, F. P., *Augustinus oder Boethius? Geschichtsschreibung und epische Dichtung im Mittelalter – und in der Neuzeit. I. Einführender Teil, II. Darstellender Teil*, 2 vols, PSQ, 39 and 80 (Berlin: Schmidt, 1967–76).
See vol. 2, pp. 212–13, on Greece in *Cligés*.

4   Stavenhagen, Lee, 'The Arena in the Early Court Novel,' in *Studies in German Andrew Lewis*, in *Rice University Studies*, 55:3 (1969), 237–40.
Treats the setting for the villein's herd.

5   Pfeiffer, Ruth, *En route vers l'au-delà arthurien: étude sur les châteaux enchantés et leurs enchantements*, diss. Zürich (Zürich: Juris, 1970).

6   Bauer, Gerhard, *Claustrum animae: Untersuchungen zur Geschichte der Metapher vom Herzen als Kloster: I. Entstehungsgeschichte* (Munich: Fink, 1973).
On the heart as a house, but without reference to *Yvain*.

7   Pearsall, Derek, and Elizabeth Salter, *Landscapes and Seasons of the Medieval World* (London: Elek Books; Toronto: University of Toronto Press, 1973). (XXVIII.327)

8   Pickford, Cedric E., 'Camelot,' *Mélanges Le Gentil*, pp. 633–40. (XXVI.139)

See Fb35 Vance.

9   Pickering, F. P., 'The Western Image of Byzantium in the Middle Ages,' in *GLL*, 28 (1974–75), 326–40.
See pp. 338–39.

10   Elizalde, Ignacio, 'Navarra en "les romans courtois",' *Letras de Deusto*, 5 (July–Dec. 1975), 5–43. (XXIX.212)
Includes Estella, Pamplona, Roncesvalles, Tudela, and Navarre.

See Na.c71 Lozachmeur.

See Qb34 Batany.

11   Seidel, Ilse, *Byzanz im Spiegel der literarischen Entwicklung Frankreichs im 12. Jahrhundert*, EH:F, 49 (Frankfurt/M.: P. Lang, 1977).
See Chap. 6:1 on *Cligés* (pp. 95–99).

12   Notz, Marie-Françoise, '*Hortus conclusus*: réflexions sur le rôle symbolique de la clôture dans la description romanesque du jardin,' in *Mélanges Lods*, vol. 1, pp. 459–72.

13   Gouttebroze, J.-G., 'L'image de la ville dans l'œuvre romanesque de Chrétien de Troyes,' in *L'Image de la ville dans la littérature et l'histoire médiévales* (Nice: Université, Centre d'Etudes Médiévales, 1979), pp. 38–46.

14   Saly, Antoinette, 'Li fluns au deable,' in *Diable*, pp. 493–506; repr. in Dc22. (XXXI.302)

15   Zajadacz, Franziska, *Motivgeschichtliche Untersuchungen zur Artusepik: Szenen an und auf dem Meer*, GAG, 269 (Göppingen: Kümmerle, 1979). (XXXII.85)

16   Chênerie, Marie-Luce, 'Le motif de la *fontaine* dans les romans arthuriens en vers des XIIᵉ et XIIIᵉ siècles,' in *Mélanges Foulon*, vol. 1, pp. 99–104. (XXXIII.320)

17   Galler, Dieter A., 'Topical Description of Nature in Chrestien de Troyes' "Li Contes del Graal",' *USFLQ*, 19:1–2 (1980), 6.

18   Mölk, Ulrich, 'Die literarische Entdeckung der Stadt im französischen Mittelalter,' in *Über Bürger, Stadt und städtische Literatur im Spätmittelalter: Bericht über Kolloquien der Kommission zur Erforschung der Kultur des Spätmittelalters 1975–77*, ed. Josef Fleckenstein and Karl Stackmann, Abhandlungen der Akademie der Wissenschaften in Göttingen: philologisch-historische Klasse, 3rd ser., 121 (Göttingen: Vandenhoeck & Ruprecht, 1980), pp. 203–15. (XXXIV.31)

19   Notz, Marie-Françoise, 'Le verger merveilleux: un mode original de la description?' in *Etudes Horrent*, pp. 317–24.

20   Tattersall, Jill, 'The Island and its Significance in Old French Texts of the Twelfth and Thirteenth Centuries,' *FS*, 34 (1980), 1–11. (XXXIII.457)
Treats *Perceval* pp. 4–5.

21   Bloch, R. Howard, 'Wasteland and Round Table: The Historical Significance of Myths of Dearth and Plenty in Old French Romance,' *NLH*, 11 (1980–81), 255–76. (XXXIV.108)

22   Ajam, Laurent, 'La forêt dans l'œuvre de Chrétien de Troyes,' *Europe*, 642 (Oct. 1982), 120–25. (XXXV.302)

23   Caldarini, Ernesta, 'Un lieu du roman médiéval: le verger,' *CAIEF*, 34 (1982), 7–23. (XXXV.312)

24   Sasaki, Shigemi, 'Departure for "Illusion" and Bluebeard's Invitation (The Enigma of Positive-Negative Signs of the Doorway and its Partially Open Logic),' *TATE*, 11 (1982), 38–42.
In Japanese.

See Qg4 Pickford.

See Qa64 Blaess.

25   Caldarini, Ernesta, 'Le città ideali nel Medio Evo: realtà, retorica, immaginazione,' in *Studi di Letteratura Francese*, 11 (1985), 7–25 (= BArR, 192).

26   Santoni-Rozier, Claire, 'Le pont perdu et le pont de l'épée dans le *Prosa-Lancelot*,' in *L'Eau au Moyen Age*, Senefiance, 15 (Aix-en-Provence: CUER-MA, 1985), pp. 319–34. (XXXVII.115)

27   Sasaki, Shigemi, 'The Oak and the Lime Tree,' *TATE*, 16 (1985), 30–33.
In Japanese.

28   Bouyer, Louis, *Les Lieux magiques de la légende du graal: de Brocéliande en Avalon*, L'Imaginaire Médiéval (Paris: OEIL, 1986).

See Xa5 Dinzelbacher.

29   Ferrante, Joan, 'The Court in Medieval Literature – The Center of the Problem,' in Qa81 *Medieval Court*, pp. 1–25. (XXXIX.256)

30   Giloy-Hirtz, Petra, 'Der imaginierte Hof,' in *Höfische Literatur, Hofgesellschaft, höfische Lebensformen um 1200: Kolloquium am Zentrum für Interdisziplinäre Forschung der Universität Bielefeld (3. bis 5. November 1985)*, ed. Gert Kaiser and Jan-Dirk Müller, Studia Humaniora, 6 (Düsseldorf: Droste, 1986), pp. 253–75. (XXXIX.482)

31   Jackson, W. T. H., 'The Court of the Poet and the Court of the King,' in Qa81 *Medieval Court*, pp. 26–40. (XXXIX. 281)

32   Ringger, Kurt, 'Der Garten in der höfischen Literatur Frankreichs,' *RF*, 98 (1986), 17–35.

33   Colliot, Régine, 'Demeures et châteaux dans *Yvain*, ou les prisons du rêve,' *PRIS-MA*, 3 (1987), 23–31. (XLI.53)

34   Vermette, Rosalie, 'Terrae incantatae: The Symbolic Geography of Twefth-Century Arthurian Romance,' in *Geography and Literature: A Meeting of the Disciplines*, ed. William E. Mallory and Paul Simpson-Housley (Syracuse, NY: Syracuse University Press, 1987), pp. 145–60. (XLII.355)

See Ga57 Busby.

35   Baumgartner, Emmanuèle, 'La fontaine au pin,' in *Chevalier au lion*, pp. 31–46. (XLI.44)

36   Botterill, Steven, 'Re-reading Lancelot: Dante, Chaucer, and *Le Chevalier de la charrette*,' *PQ*, 67 (1988), 279–89. (XLI.351)
On incarceration in a tower.

37   Notz, Marie-Françoise, 'L'arbre aux oiseaux et le lieu du partage,' *PRIS-MA*, 5 (1989), 63–70. (XLIII.192)

38   Studer, Eduard, 'Gralsburgen,' in *Festschrift Rupp* (Bern: Francke, 1989), pp. 118–22. (XLII.478, 580)

39   Gallais, Pierre, 'L'arbre et la forêt dans l'*Eneide* et l'*Eneas*: de la psyché antique à la psyché médiévale, I–II,' *PRIS-MA*, 5 (1989), 17–46, 157–83, and 6 (1990), 209–36.
Includes examples from *Cligés*.

40   Cormier, Raymond J., 'Eilhart's Seminal Tower of Pleasure,' *FCS*, 17 (1990), 57–66. (XLIII.513)
Treats *Erec* and *Cligés*.

41   Ménard, Philippe, 'Le château en forêt dans le roman médiéval,' in *Le Château, la chasse et la forêt*, ed. André Chastel, Les Cahiers de Commarque (Bordeaux: Sud-Ouest, 1990), pp. 190–95. (XLIII.188)

42   *Vergers et jardins dans l'univers médiéval*, Senefiance, 28 (Aix-en-Provence: CUER-MA, 1990).
    A.   Jean-Claude Bibolet, 'Jardins et vergers dans l'œuvre de Chrétien de Troyes,' pp. 31–40. (XLIII.166)
    B.   Huguette Legros, 'Du verger royal au jardin d'amour: mort et transfiguration du *locus amoenus* (d'après *Tristan* de Béroul et *Cligès*),' pp. 215–33. (XLIII.186)

See Gd.c41 Benedetti.

43   Morales, Ana María, 'Los habitantes de Brocelandia,' *Medievalia*, 9 (Dec. 1991), 8–17. (XLVI.266)

44 Villena, Juanita, 'Harmonizing Spatial and Sentimental Aspects of Four Romances of Chrétien de Troyes: *Erec et Enide, Yvain, Cligès* and *Lancelot*,' *Tropos* [Michigan State University], 17 (1991), 71–80.

See Jb44 Hogetoorn.

See Kd115 Ménard.

See Md44 Mora.

45 Van D'Elden, Stephanie Cain, 'The Salerno Effect: The Image of Salerno in Courtly Literature,' in *ICLS Salerno*, pp. 503–15.

46 Wolfzettel, Friedrich, 'Rom und die Anfänge des altfranzösischen Romans: Liebe, Religion und Politik bei Gautier d'Arras,' in *Rom im hohen Mittelalter: Studien zu den Romvorstellungen und zur Rompolitik vom 10. bis zum 12. Jahrhundert. Reinhard Elze zur Vollendung seines siebzigsten Lebensjahres gewidmet*, ed. Bernhard Schimmelpfennig and Ludwig Schmugge (Sigmaringen: Thorbecke, 1992), pp. 139–63.
See pp. 140–45.

See Fa156 Zumthor.

47 Blons-Pierre, Catherine, 'L'utopie dans sa définition originelle chez Chrétien de Troyes,' in *Provinces*, pp. 263–74. (XLVI.312)

48 Marmo, Vittorio, 'La città immaginaria nel romanzo cortese del XII secolo,' *L'Asino d'Oro*, 7 (1993), 19–30. (XLVII.465)

See Pb368 Pastré.

49 Saunders, Corinne J., *The Forest of Medieval Romance: Avernus, Broceliande, Arden* (Cambridge: Brewer, 1993). (LII.454)
See pp. 58–80.

See Gb121 Yamamoto.

See He70 Brusegan.

50 Baumgartner, Emmanuèle, 'Sur quelques "marines" médiévales,' in *L'Eau au Moyen Age: symboles et usages: Actes du Colloque Orléans– mai 1994*, ed. Bernard Ribémont (Orléans: Paradigme, 1996), pp. 11–22. In *Cligés*.

51 Gally, Michèle, 'Variations sur le *locus amoenus*: accords des sens et esthétique poétique,' *Poétique*, 106 (1996), 161–77. (XLIX.153)

52 Курьякова, А., 'Некоторые особенности обозначения понятия "лес" во французских средневековых текстах,' 'Вестник Санкт-Петербургского Университета, Серия 2: История, Языкознание, Литературоведение,' 3:16 (1996), 53–64.

See Pb419 Pastré.

53 Sasu, Maria-Voichiţa, 'Grădina – Lumea cealaltă,' in her *Destinul ideilor literare* (Bucarest: Editura Didactică şi Pedagogică, 1996), pp. 43–58.

See Pa299(I) Le Person.

54 Milin, Gaël, 'L'imaginaire de la fontaine: esquisse d'inventaire,' *KREIZ*, 9 (1997), 131–77. (LI.276)

See Na.c119 Milin.

55 Queille, Anaïg, 'Fontaines sur la lande: l'imaginaire de la fontaine dans quelques textes en vers de la Matière de Bretagne aux XIIe et XIIIe siècles,' *KREIZ*, 9 (1997), 179–96. (LI.289)

56 Sasu, Maria-Voichiţa, 'Loc de trecere periculos,' in her *Constante*, pp. 20–35. (LI.712)

57 *Château et société castrale au Moyen Age, Actes du Colloque des 7–8–9 mars 1997*, ed. Jean-Marc Pastré, PUR, 239 (Rouen: Publications de l'Université de Rouen, 1998).
- A. Catherine Blons-Pierre, 'Fonction dramatique du château, de la maison forte, du manoir et de la tour dans les romans de Chrétien de Troyes,' pp. 179–93.
- B. Hatem Akkari, '"Par desuz et par desoz li degréz": fonctions et symboles de l'escalier dans le château au Moyen Age,' pp. 221–27.
- C. Robert Baudry, 'Châteaux-frères et châteaux-fées de l'autre monde dans *Le Conte du Graal*,' pp. 261–70.
- D. Anton H. Touber, 'Le château dans *Le Chevalier au lion* de Chrétien de Troyes et dans l'*Iwein* de Hartmann von Aue,' pp. 343–55.

58 James-Raoul, Danièle, 'D'une météorologie l'autre: le temps qu'il fait du *Conte du Graal* de Chrétien de Troyes au *Parzival* de Wolfram von Eschenbach,' in *Le Temps qu'il fait au Moyen Age: phénomènes atmosphériques dans la littérature, la pensée scientifique et religieuse*, ed. Claude Thomasset and Joëlle Ducos, CCMed, 15 (Paris: Presses de l'Université de Paris-Sorbonne, 1998), pp. 209–30.

59 Sasaki, Shigemi, 'The Man Who Resembles the Tree...– a Weeping Woman beneath a Tree,' *Plume*, 3 (1999), 13–21.
In Japanese.

60 Stanesco, Michel, 'Une architecture féerique: le palais aux cent/mille fenêtres,' *TrL*, 12 (1999), 237–54. (LII.282)

61 Szkilnik, Michelle, 'Gauvain [à la] fenêtre: l'épisode du château des reines dans le *Conte du Graal*,' *BBSIA*, 51 (1999), 327–42.

62 *Noble, Peter, 'The Flawed Utopias of Chrétien de Troyes,' in *Utopias*, ed. Françoise Le Saux and Neil Thomas, Durham Modern Language Series, GM9 (Durham: University of Durham, 2000), pp. 55–75. (LIII.499)

See Ha209(H) Rider.

See Pb470 Schulz-Grobert.

See Jb59 Thomasset.

d.c: Actions and Activities

1 Mentz, Richard, *Die Träume in den altfranzösischen Karls- und Artus-Epen*, AA, 73 (Marburg: Elwert, 1888).

See Qa29 Oschinsky.

2 Foerster, Wendelin, 'Der Feuertod als Strafe in der altfrz. erzählenden Dichtung,' in *Festschrift für Lorenz Morsbach dargebracht von Freunden und Schülern*, ed. F. Holthausen and F. Spies (Halle/S.: Niemeyer, 1913; repr. Walluf bei Wiesbaden: Sändig, 1973), pp. 180–89.

See Qc25 Webster.

3 Mölk, Ulrich, 'Das Motiv des Wiedererkennens an der Stimme im Epos und höfischen Roman des französischen Mittelalters,' *RJ*, 15 (1964), 107–15.
See pp. 112–14.

4 Dronke, Peter, 'Tradition and Innovation in Medieval Western Colour-Imagery,' *Eranos Jahrbuch*, 41 (1972), 51–107.
Pp. 88–97 on blood-drops-on-snow scene in the *Conte du graal*.

5 Schmitt-von Mühlenfels, Franz, *Pyramus und Thisbe: Rezeptionstypen eines Ovidischen Stoffes in Literatur, Kunst und Musik*, Studien zum Fortwirken der Antike, 6 (Heidelberg: Winter, 1972).
Pp. 34–36 on suicide.

See Pb156 Cometta, pp. 340 and 343–45.

6 Lyons, Faith, 'The Chivalric Bath in the *Roman d'Alexandre* and in Chrétien's *Cligés*,' in *Mélanges Teruo Sato*, Part I, *Cahiers d'Études Médiévales*, Special Number (Nagoya: Kurita, 1973), vol. 1, pp. 85–90. (XXVII.385)

See Pd31 Hexter.

7 Peil, Dietmar, *Die Gebärde bei Chrétien, Hartmann und Wolfram: Erec – Iwein – Parzival*, Medium Aevum, 28 (Munich: Fink, 1975). (XXVIII.60)

8 Cooper, Helen, 'Magic That Does Not Work,' *M&H*, 7 (1976), 131–46.
In *Charrette* and *Yvain*.

9 Ribard, Jacques, 'De Chrétien de Troyes à Guillaume de Lorris: ces quêtes qu'on dit inachevées,' in *Voyage*, pp. 313–21; repr. in Dc25. (XXIX.251)

10 Subrenat, Jean, 'L'attitude des hommes en face du voyage d'après quelques textes littéraires,' in *Voyage*, pp. 395–412.

11 Bruckner, Matilda Tomaryn, '*Florimont*: Extravagant Host, Extravagant Guest,' *SMC*, 11 (1977), 57–63.
Includes comparison with Chrétien's hospitality scenes.

12 Halász, Katalin, 'Éjszakai szállás és vendéglátás Chrétien de Troyes regényeiben,' *FK*, 23 (1977), 1–23.

13 Larmat, Jean, 'Le motif de l'hospitalité dans le *Conte du graal*,' in *Hommage à Pierre Nardin: philologie et littérature françaises*, AnNice, 29 (Monaco: Belles Lettres, 1977), pp. 57–66.

See Qd14 Barron.

14 Caldarini, Ernesta, 'Il bacio del re,' *BHR*, 40 (1978), 143–47.
On *baisiers* in *Erec*.

15 Ruberg, Uwe, *Beredtes Schweigen in lehrhafter und erzählender deutscher Literatur des Mittelalters: mit kommentierter Erstedition spät-mittelalterlicher Lehrtexte über das Schweigen*, MMS, 32 (Munich: Fink, 1978). (XXXI.39)

16 Knapp, Fritz Peter, *Der Selbstmord in der abendländischen Epik des Hochmittelalters*, Germanische Bibliothek, 3. Reihe: Untersuchungen und Einzeldarstellungen (Heidelberg: Winter, 1979). (XXXII. 39)

See pp. 170–84.

See Ge28 Lefay-Toury.

17   Brault, Gerard J., 'Exploration and Discovery in French Literature from the Middle Ages to Rabelais,' *FR*, 53 (1979–80), 550–56.

See Qc41 Benson.

18   Bruckner, Matilda Tomaryn, *Narrative Invention in Twelfth-Century French Romance: The Convention of Hospitality (1160–1200)*, FFM, 17 (Lexington, KY: French Forum, 1980). (XXXIII.134)

See Hb25 Halász.

19   Peron, G., 'Aspects rhétoriques et aspects techniques de la chasse dans les romans français du moyen-âge,' in *La Chasse au Moyen Age: Actes du Colloque de Nice (22–24 juin 1979)*, Publications de la Faculté des Lettres et des Sciences Humaines de Nice, 20 (Centre d'Etudes Médiévales de Nice) (Nice: Belles Lettres, 1980). (XXXIII.364)

20   Delcourt-Angélique, Janine, 'Le motif du tournoi de trois jours avec changement de couleur destiné à préserver l'incognito,' in *Essays Thorpe*, pp. 160–86. (XXXIV.306)

21   Patterson, Lee W., '"Rapt with Pleasaunce": Vision and Narration in the Epic,' *ELH*, 48 (1981), 455–75. (XXXV.182)
Pp. 459–63 treat the blood-drops-in-snow episode in *Perceval* as a vision.

22   Williamson, Joan B., 'Exercise in Power: Suicide for Love in French Romance of the 12th and 13th Centuries,' in *From Linguistics to Literature: Romance Studies Offered to Francis M. Rogers*, ed. Bernard H. Bichakjian (Amsterdam: Benjamins, 1981), pp. 138–54.

23   Esposito, Edoardo, 'Les formes d'hospitalité dans le roman courtois (du *Roman de Thèbes* à Chrétien de Troyes),' *Rom*, 103 (1982), 197–234. (XXXVI.340)

24   Halász, Katalin, 'A la recherche d'un modèle narratif,' *Europe*, 642 (Oct. 1982), 48–52. (XXXV.320)
On court, hospitality, and combat.

25   Halász, Katalin, 'Kommunikációs viszonyok ábrázolása a XII. és XIII. századi francia irodalomban,' *NI*, 5 (1983), 322–36. (XL.200)

See Ke9 Härmä.

26 Maddox, Donald, 'The Awakening: A Key Motif in Chrétien's Romances,' in *Sower*, pp. 31–51. (XXXV.178)

See Ha121 Bozóky.

See Qa67 Matthias.

27 Molle, Jose Vincenzo, 'Le réalisme des cérémonies et des conventions sociales dans le *Lancelot* de Chrétien de Troyes,' in *Lancelot Picardie*, pp. 117–34.

See Nb30 Andersson.

28 Grigsby, John L., 'Le *gab* dans le roman arthurien français,' *Actes Rennes*, vol. 1, pp. 257–72. (XXXVIII.215)
On Keu especially.

29 Hoffmann, Richard C., 'Fishing for Sport in Medieval Europe: New Evidence,' *Spec*, 60 (1985), 877–902. (XXXVIII.504)

30 Owen, D. D. R., 'Theme and Variations: Sexual Aggression in Chrétien de Troyes,' *FMLS*, 21 (1985), 376–86. (XXXVIII.339)

31 Krueger, Roberta L., 'Contracts and Constraints: Courtly Performance in *Yvain* and the *Charrete*,' in Qa81 *Medieval Court*, pp. 92–104. (XXXIX.292)

32 Varty, Kenneth, 'The Giving and Withholding of Consent in Late Twelfth-Century French Literature,' *RMS*, 12 (1986), 27–49. (XXXIX.84)
On rape and adultery especially.

33 Ors, Joan, 'De l'encalç del cérvol blanc al creuer de la balena sollerica: la funció narrativa del motiu de l'animal guia,' in *Studia de Riquer*, vol. 1, pp. 565–77.

34 Brook, Leslie C., 'Some Old French Nose-Bleeds,' *FSB*, 27 (1988), 3–4. (XLI.127)
Includes Guenevere's in the *Charrette*.

35 Halász, Katalin, *A Párviadal: Elbeszélés és szerkezet Chrétien de Troyes regényeiben* (Budapest: Akadémiai Kaidó, 1988). (XLI.253)

See Qa86–87 Rieger.

36   Smith, Kathleen White, 'The Ambiguous Oath in Twelfth-Century Romance: Béroul's *Roman de Tristan* and *Le Chevalier au lion* of Chrétien de Troyes,' *Ball State University Forum*, 29:3 (1988), 37–44.

See Qc58 Chandès.

37   Bartosz, Antoni, 'Fonction du geste dans un texte romanesque médiéval: remarques sur la gestualité dans la première partie d'*Erec*,' *Rom*, 111 (1990), 346–60. (XLVI.306)

38   Gracia, Paloma, 'La prehistoria del *Tristan en prose* y el incesto,' *Rom*, 111 (1990), 385–98.

39   Itô, Yasuharu, '"Turnier", "Buhurt" and "Tjost" – Poetry and Truth,' *SdLS*, 22 (1990), 1–15.
In Japanese.

40   Urbina, Eduardo, 'La aventura guardada: Don Quijote como caballero desventurado,' *RomQ*, 37 (1990), 431–40; rev. version in *Actas del X Congreso de la Asociación Internacional de Hispanistas, Barcelona, 21–26 de agosto de 1989*, ed. Antonio Vilanova, 4 vols (Barcelona: Promociones y Publicaciones Universitarias, 1992), vol. 1, pp. 723–32.

41   Benedetti, Roberto, 'Uno spazio esclusivo: il pino e la donna negli antichi testi francesi,' *Mediaevistik*, 4 (1991), 7–19. (XLVI.41)
The tree as symbolic arena of masculine deeds.

42   *Feste und Feiern im Mittelalter: Paderborner Symposion des Mediävistenverbandes*, ed. Detlef Altenburg, Jörg Jarnut, and Hans-Hugo Steinhoff (Sigmaringen: Thorbecke, 1991).
   The following contributions treat Chrétien:
   A.   Claude Thomasset, 'La chevalerie et l'ostentation dans l'évocation de la fête,' pp. 181–91.
   B.   Joerg O. Fichte, 'Das Fest als Testsituation in der mittelenglischen Artusromanze,' pp. 449–59.

43   Haupt, Barbara, 'Heilung von Wunden,' in *Grenzen*, pp. 77–113.

See Fb78(B) Saccone.

44   Bendinelli Predelli, Maria, 'Il motivo del torneo in incognito e la genealogia dei primi poemi cortesi,' in *ICLS Salerno*, pp. 225–34. (XLV.319)

45 Carré, Yannick, *Le Baiser sur la bouche au Moyen Age: rites, symboles, mentalités à travers les textes et les images, XIe–XVe siècles* (Paris: Léopard d'Or, 1992).

46 Stanesco, Michel, 'Le chevalier médiéval en voyage: du pèlerinage romanesque à l'errance dans l'autre monde,' in *Diesseits*, pp. 189–203.

47 Bonafin, Massimo, 'Millanterie dissimulate: Chrétien de Troyes e Walter Map,' *MedR*, 18 (1993), 83–89. (XLVI.551)

48 Bruña Cuevas, Manuel, 'La reproduction des messages écrits dans les romans français en vers et en prose des XIIe et XIIIe siècles,' in *Actes Zurich*, pp. 211–24. (XLVII.654)
Includes *Charrette*.

49 Drzewicka, Anna, 'L'admonestation fraternelle du Vendredi Saint,' in *Hommage Dufournet,* vol. 1, pp. 441–48.

50 Bromiley, Geoffrey, 'The Creation of New Arthurian Worlds,' in *Nouveaux mondes: From the Twelfth to the Twentieth Century*, ed. Richard Maber, Durham French Colloquies, 4 (Durham: University of Durham Modern Language Series, 1994), pp. 1–17. (XLVIII.394)

51 Bruña Cuevas, Manuel, 'Los saludos de Galván en la obra de Chrétien de Troyes,' in *Actas Almagro*, pp. 203–10.

See Qd20 Sodigné-Coste.

52 Ueda, Hiroshi, 'The Description of Single Combat in Medieval Romance,' *JFLN*, 118 (1994), 161–79.
In Japanese.

53 Vincensini, Jean-Jacques, 'Viol de la fée, violence du féerique: remarques sur la vocation anthropologique de la littérature médiévale,' in *Violence*, pp. 543–59.

54 Ferlampin-Acher, Christine, 'Les tournois chez Chrétien de Troyes: l'art de l'esquive,' in *Amour Troyes*, pp. 161–89. (XLIX.149)

55 Flores Arroyuelo, Francisco J., 'El torneo caballeresco: de la preparación militar a la fiesta y representación teatral,' in *Actas Granada*, vol. 2, pp. 257–78.

56 Kasper, Christine, *Von miesen Rittern und sündhaften Frauen und solchen, die besser waren: Tugend- und Keuschheitsproben in der mittelalterlichen Literatur vornehmlich des deutschen Sprachraums*, GAG, 547 (Göppingen: Kümmerle, 1995).

57   Nickel, Helmut, 'Arthurian Armings for War and for Love,' *Arthuriana*, 5:4 (1995), 3–21. (XLVIII.719)

See Ud14 Steele.

See He71 Williamson.

58   Brunner, Horst, 'Das Bild des Krieges bei Chrestien de Troyes und bei Hartmann von Aue,' in *Spannungen*, pp. 113–22.

See Pa285 Combarieu.

59   Maddox, Donald, 'Generic Intertextuality in Arthurian Literature: The Specular Encounter,' in La46 *Text*, pp. 3–24.

60   Mühlethaler, Jean-Claude, 'Mourir à table: contextualisation et enjeux d'une séquence narrative au XIIe siècle (de la *Chanson de Guillaume* à *Erec et Enide*),' in Tb22 *Banquets*, pp. 215–34.

61   Salinero Cascante, Mª Jesús, 'La "seducción" de la narrativa francesa del siglo XII,' *RLM*, 8 (1996), 201–22.

62   Vitz, Evelyn Birge, 'Reading Rape in Medieval Literature,' *Partisan Review*, 63 (1996), 280–91.

See Hb49 Wieczorkiewicz.

See Fa169 James-Raoul.

63   Ménard, Philippe, 'Tombeaux et gisants dans la littérature française des XIIe et XIIIe siècles,' in *Festschrift Mölk*, pp. 297–310. (L.96)
Discusses burial.

64   Vitz, Evelyn Birge, 'Rereading Rape in Medieval Literature: Literary, Historical, and Theoretical Reflections,' *RR*, 88 (1997), 1–26.

65   Affholder, Anne-Marie, 'Le Chevalier de la onzième heure: l'inaction, révélateur de la société et de l'individu dans les récits du XIIème siècle,' *Cahiers du 'CERF XX'*, 10 (1998), 15–28.

See Gf42 Akkari.

66   Angeli, Giovanna, 'Le dialogue nocturne conjugal: entre "cadre" et *topos*,' in *Mélanges Ménard*, vol. 1, pp. 51–63. (LI.203)
See pp. 60–61, 62–63.

67   Ásdís R. Magnúsdóttir, *La Voix du cor: la relique de Rencevaux et l'origine d'un motif dans la littérature du Moyen Age (XIIe-XIVe siècles)*,

Internationale Forschungen zur allgemeinen und vergleichenden Literaturwissenschaft, 31 (Amsterdam: Rodopi, 1998). (LI.694)

68 Bein, Thomas, '*Hie slac, dâ stich*! Zur Ästhetik des Tötens in europäischen "Iwein"-Dichtungen,' *ZLiLi*, 109 (1998), 38–58. (L.64, LI.53)
See pp. 43–44.

69 Feinstein, Sandy, 'Losing Your Head in Chrétien's *Knight of the Cart*,' *Arthuriana*, 9:4 (1999), 45–62. (LII.759)

See Qc86 Santina.

70 Bouillot, Carine, 'Aux antipodes du beau geste: le geste laid et inconvenant dans la littérature des XIIème et XIIIème siècles,' in *Beau et laid*, pp. 45–56.

71 Grigsby, John L., *The 'Gab' as a Latent Genre in Medieval French Literature: Drinking and Boasting in the Middle Ages*, Medieval Academy Books, 103 (Cambridge, MA: Medieval Academy of America, 2000). (LIII.941)

See Hg120 Guézennec.

73 Mottershead, Kathleen, 'Le scénario de l'épreuve chez Marie de France et Chrétien de Troyes: une ruse du destin?,' in *Ruse*, pp. 271–81.
Based on *Perceval*.

See Hc80 Noacco.

See Ha212 Sweeney.

e: Concepts and Thinking

17 Fisher, Lizette Andrews, *The Mystic Vision in the Grail Legend and in the Divine Comedy*, Columbia University Studies in English and Comparative Literature (New York: Columbia University Press, 1917).

See Me9 Gelzer.

18 Conigliani, Camilla, 'L'amore e l'avventura nei "Lais" di Maria di Francia,' *ArR*, 2 (1918), 281–95.
Marie's use of *aventure* compared with Chrétien's.

19 Rohr, Rupprecht, 'Zur Skala der ritterlichen Tugenden in der altprovenzalischen und altfranzösischen höfischen Dichtung,' *ZrP*, 78 (1962), 292–325.
On *Cligés*, pp. 320–24.

20 Yamada, Jaku, 'Erec's Adventures,' *France*, 37:6 (1962), 68–72.
In Japanese.

21 Worstbrock, Franz Josef, '*Translatio artium*: über die Herkunft und Entwicklung einer kulturhistorischen Theorie,' *Archiv für Kultur- geschichte*, 47 (1965), 1–22.
On *Cligés*, pp. 19–22.

See Qb29 Jongkees.

22 Kamizawa, Eizô, 'The Idea of "Adventure" – The Case of Chrétien de Troyes's *Erec et Enide*,' *MDKR*, 56 (1970), 1–15.
In Japanese.

23 Köhler, Erich, *Der literarische Zufall, das Mögliche und die Notwendigkeit* (Munich: Fink, 1973); French trans. Eliane Kaufholz, *Le Hasard en littérature, le possible et la nécessité*, Collection d'Esthétique, 48 (Paris: Klincksieck, 1986).

24 Gössmann, Elisabeth, *Antiqui und moderni im Mittelalter: eine geschichtliche Standortbestimmung*, Münchener Universitätsschriften: Katholisch-theologische Fakultät: Veröffentlichungen des Grabmann- Institutes zur Erforschung der mittelalterlichen Theologie und Philosophie, n. s. 23 (Munich: Schöningh, 1974).

25 *Concepts of the Hero in the Middle Ages and the Renaissance*, ed. Norman T. Burns and Christopher J. Reagan (Albany: State University of New York Press, 1975). (XXXI.357)
  A. Morton W. Bloomfield, 'The Problem of the Hero in the Later Medieval Period,' pp. 27–48.
  B. R. R. Bolgar, 'Hero or Anti-Hero? The Genesis and Development of the *Miles Christianus*,' pp. 120–46.

See Fb40 Altieri.

26 Chênerie, Marie-Luce, 'Le motif de la *merci* dans les romans arthuriens des XIIe et XIIIe siècles,' *MA*, 83 (1977), 5–52. (XXX.210)

27 Collins, Frank, 'The Terms *cortois*, *cortoise* and *corteisie* in the Works of Chrétien de Troyes,' *VR*, 36 (1977), 84–92.
On representation of character.

See Ha88 Ollier.
On *translatio studii*.

28 Lefay-Toury, Marie-Noëlle, *La Tentation du suicide dans le roman du XIIe siècle*, Essais sur le Moyen Age, 4 (Paris: Champion, 1979). (XXXII.354 *bis*)
See Chap. 2: 'Chrétien de Troyes ou le suicide inachevé' (pp. 92–140).

29 Merino, Jane, 'The Gift in Chrétien de Troyes: *Largesse* or Obligation?' *Chimères*, 13 (1979), 5–15.

30 Todd, Margaret W., 'Time as a Theme in Chrétien's Later Romances,' *Mid-H*, 2 (1979), 9–25.

31 Topsfield, L. T., 'Malvestatz versus Proeza and Leautatz in Troubadour Poetry and the *Lancelot* of Chrétien de Troyes,' *Esp*, 19 (1979), 37–53. (XXXII.227)

See Jd22 Ribard.
On the name and nomination.

See Fa108 Uitti.
On *translatio studii*.

32 Lecouteux, Claude, 'Introduction à l'étude du merveilleux médiéval,' *EtGerm*, 36 (1981), 273–90. (XXXIV.230)

33 Ménard, Philippe, 'Le don en blanc qui lie le donateur: réflexions sur un motif de conte,' in *Essays Thorpe*, pp. 37–53. (XXXIV.350)

See Ge8 Köhler, Ge13 Frappier.

See Qb47 Lecouteux.

34 Pavel, Maria, '"Amors" et "avanture" dans *Yvain*,' *ACLit*, 28 (1982), 312–20.

See Ha114 Poirion.

35 Boutet, Dominique, 'Sur l'origine et le sens de la largesse arthurienne,' *MA*, 89 (1983), 397–411. (XXXVI.287)

36 Martineau, Christine, 'Autour de la folie au Moyen Age,' *Razo*, 4 (1984), 59–63. (XXXVII.97)

See Hc49 Mussetter.

37 Niessen-Poutet, Dominique, 'Royauté et féodalité à travers quelques romans arthuriens français des XIIème et XIIIème siècles,' *Rapports*, 54 (1984), 109–17. (XXXVIII.697)

38 Solterer, Helen, 'Le bel semblant, faus semblant, semblants romanesques,' *Médiévales*, 6 (1984), 26–36. (XXXVII.118)

39 Bozóky, Edina, 'De la parole au monument: marquer la mémoire dans la littérature arthurienne,' in *Jeux de mémoire: aspects de la mnémotechnie médiévale*, Etudes Médiévales (Montréal: Presses Universitaires de Montréal; Paris: Vrin, 1985), pp. 73–82. (XXXIX.219)
Examines the *Conte du graal*.

See Hf61 Lock.

40 Baumgartner, Emmanuèle, 'Temps linéaire, temps circulaire et écriture romanesque (XIIe–XIIIe siècles),' in *Temps Reims*, pp. 7–21; repr. in Dc20. (XXXIX.632)

41 Colliot, Régine, 'De quelques langages de la magie médiévale,' *PRIS-MA*, 2 (1986), 55–66.
Examples from *Cligés*.

42 Colliot, Régine, 'Durée, moments, temps romanesques, d'après quelques intrigues des XIIe et XIIIe siècles,' in *Temps Reims*, pp. 41–54. (XXXIX.639)
Includes the *Charrette*.

See He54 Maddox.

43 Schmid, Elisabeth, *Familiengeschichten und Heilsmythologie: die Verwandschaftsstrukturen in den französischen und deutschen Gralromanen des 12. und 13. Jahrhunderts*, Beihefte zur *ZrP*, 211 (Tübingen: Niemeyer, 1986). (XXXIX.537)
See Chap. 2–3.

See Hc54 Owen.

44 Sasu, Voichița, 'Romanul medieval – În căutarea aventurii,' *RITL*, 35:3–4 (1987), 200–4; repr. in her *Constante*, pp. 77–85. (LI.712)

45 Carmona Fernández, Fernando, 'El motivo del "don contraignant" en la narrativa en verso de los siglos XII y XIII,' in *Actes Trèves*, vol. 6, pp. 427–36. (XLI.585)

46 Dragonetti, Roger, 'Le nombre sans égal,' in *Hommage Zumthor*, pp. 49–61.
Reflections on music and astronomy, including *Erec* and *Perceval* (p. 55).

See Ga60 Haidu.
On *Yvain*, pp. 117–22.

See Fb73 Kelly.

See Hf76 Maddox.

47 Marache, Bernard, 'Le mot et la notion d'aventure dans la "conjointure" et le "sen" du *Chevalier au lion*,' in *Chevalier au lion*, pp. 119–38. (XLI.71)

48 Meneghetti, Maria Luisa, 'Meraviglioso e straniamento,' in *Meraviglioso*, pp. 227–35. (XLII.122)
Includes *Yvain*.

49 Mölk, Ulrich, 'A proposito del senso di *cortois(ie)* nella letteratura del XII secolo,' *ImRif*, 12 (1989), 41–54. (XLV.338)

50 Stuip, R. E. V., 'Oudfranse lichtbeelden,' in *Licht en donker in de middeleeuwen*, ed. R. E. V. Stuip and C. Vellekoop, UBM, 9 (Utrecht: HES, 1989), pp. 90–106. (XLIII.433)

51 Callay, Brigitte L., 'The Concept of Destiny in Chrétien's *Perceval*,' in *Arturus rex*, pp. 134–44. (XL, pp. 318–19).

52 Kennedy, Elspeth, 'Failure in Arthurian Romance,' *MAe*, 60 (1991), 16–32. (XLIV.108)

See Hb38 Maddox.

53 Ménard, Philippe, 'Problématique de l'aventure dans les romans de la Table Ronde,' in *Arturus rex*, pp. 89–119.

54 Voicu, Mihaela, 'Trei spaţii de nicăieri: curtea regelui Arthur, Sala de cleştar şi Thélème sau între ficţiune şi utopie,' *Verbum*, 1 (1991), 63–76.

See Ub39 Holzbacher.

55 Gallais, Pierre, 'Panorama statistique des nombres et étude des premiers nombres chez quelques "romanciers" des XIIe et XIIIe siècles,' *PRIS-MA*, 8 (1992), 95–127, 247–69. (XLVI.332)

56 Méla, Charles, 'Œdipe, Judas, Osiris,' in *ICLS Salerno*, pp. 17–38; repr. in Dc19.

57 Steele, Stephan, 'Qu'est-ce qu'un Chrétien de Troyes?' *Florilegium*, 12 (1993), 99–106.
On *translatio*.

58 Zumthor, Paul, *La Mesure du monde: représentations de l'espace au Moyen Age* (Paris: Seuil, 1993).

See Ha181 Kay.

59 *Fortuna*, ed. Walter Haug and Burghart Wachinger, Fortuna Vitrea, 15 (Tübingen: Niemeyer, 1995).
    A. Walter Haug, 'O Fortuna: eine historisch-semantische Skizze zur Einführung,' pp. 1–22. (XLVIII.104)
    B. Walter Haug, 'Eros und Fortuna: der höfische Roman als Spiel von Liebe und Zufall,' pp. 52–75, esp. 62–66; repr. in Dc24. (XLVIII.105)

60 Marache, Bernard, 'Arthur entre coutume et aventure,' *PRIS-MA*, 11:2 (1995), 165–73. (XLVIII.317)

61 Pastré, Jean-Marc, 'L'oubli des armes, l'oubli de la femme et l'oubli de Dieu: le péché du guerrier dans trois romans médiévaux,' in *Conformité*, pp. 287–301. (XLVIII.329, XLIX.179, LII.265)

62 Schwartz, Debora B., '"Those Were the Days": The *Ubi Sunt Topos* in *La Vie de Saint Alexis*, *Yvain*, and *Le Bel Inconnu*,' *Rocky Mountain Review of Language and Literature*, 49 (1995), 27–51.

See Qb74 Krämer.
See Chap. 5:1: '"Qui or en France est venue": die Translationstheorie des Chrétien de Troyes.'

63 Stierle, Karlheinz, '*Translatio studii* and Renaissance: From Vertical to Horizontal Translation,' in *The Translatability of Cultures: Figurations of the Space Between*, ed. Sanford Budick and Wolfgang Iser, Irvine Studies in the Humanities (Stanford, CA: Stanford University Press, 1996), pp. 55–67.

64 Hausmann, Frank-Rutger, 'Translatio militiae sive retranslatio – Chrétien de Troyes's *Cligés* im Lichte eines altbekannten Topos,' in *Kunst und Kommunikation: Betrachtungen zum Medium Sprache in der Romania. Festschrift zum 60. Geburtstag von Richard Baum*, ed. Maria Lieber and Willi Hirdt (Tübingen: Stauffenburg, 1997), pp. 417–26.

65 Lacy, Norris J., 'Coutumes, merveilles, aventures,' in *Chant et enchantement au Moyen Age: travaux du Groupe de Recherches 'Lectures Médiévales', Université de Toulouse II*, Collection Moyen Age (Toulouse: Editions Universitaires du Sud, 1997), pp. 157–69. (L.208)

66 Nerlich, Michael, *Abenteuer oder das verlorene Selbstverständnis der Moderne: von der Unaufhebbarkeit experimentalen Handelns* (Munich: Gerling Akademie, 1997). (L.102)
See Chap. 8–11.

67 Baumgartner, Emmanuèle, 'La musique pervertit les mœurs,' in *Mélanges Ménard*, vol. 1, pp. 75–89. (LI.207)

See La47 Pickens.
On *translatio*.

See Na.c126 Gouttebroze.

68 Maninchedda, Paolo, '"Non duce tempus eget": tempo e spazio in Chrétien de Troyes,' *FeS*, 12 (1999), 1–52.

69 Noacco, Cristina, '*Par nigromance* et *par enchantement*: niveaux et nuances du magique dans les romans de Chrétien de Troyes,' in *Magie*, pp. 383–406. (LII.258)

70 Ménard, Philippe, 'Réflexions sur les coutumes dans les romans arthuriens,' *Essays Lacy*, pp. 357–70.

f: Sentiments and Emotions

11 Micha, Alexandre, 'Temps et conscience […]' Repr. in Dc3.

13 Lommatzsch, Erhard, 'Darstellung von Trauer und Schmerz in der altfranzösischen Literatur,' *ZrP*, 43 (1923), 20–67.

See Kd53 Simon.

See Sa51 Hill.

See Gd.b6 Bauer.

14 Braet, Herman, 'Le rêve d'amour dans le roman courtois,' in *Essays Powell-Hodgins*, pp. 107–18. (XXXIII.132)

15 Neaman, Judith S., 'Eros and the Literati: Arthurian Transformations of Love Madness,' *Mid-H*, 1 (1978), 17–34. (XXXII.209)

16 Sckommodau, Hans, 'Attraktion zwischen corps und coeur,' in *Festschrift Schon*, pp. 229–37.

See Gb52 Vadin.

17 Braet, Herman, 'Lancelot et Guilhem de Peitieus,' *RLR*, 83 (1979), 65–71. (XXXII.334)
On *pensers*.

18 Morrissey, Robert, 'Vers un topos littéraire: la préhistoire de la rêverie,' *MP*, 77 (1979–80), 261–90.
Pp. 262–72 treat the *Charrette*, *Perceval*, and *Guillaume d'Angleterre*.

19 Payen, Jean-Charles, 'Le bonheur dans la littérature française aux XIIᵉ et XIIIᵉ siècles,' *RZLG*, 4 (1980), 1–18. (XXXIII.56)

20 Schulze-Busacker, Elisabeth, 'Etude typologique de la complainte des morts dans le roman arthurien en vers du 12ᵉ au 14ᵉ siècle,' in *Essays Thorpe*, pp. 54–68. (XXXIV.373)

21 Ménard, Philippe, 'Chrétien de Troyes et le merveilleux,' *Europe*, 642 (Oct. 1982), 53–60; repr. in Dc29. (XXXV.334)

See Gd.c25 Halász.

22 Jonin, Pierre, 'L'espace et le temps de la nuit dans les romans de Chrétien de Troyes,' *Mélanges Planche*, pp. 235–46. (XXXVII.89)

See Md36 Lloyd.

23 Ménard, Philippe, 'Le monde médiéval: les curiosités profanes,' in *Le Merveilleux: l'imaginaire et les croyances en Occident*, ed. Michel Meslin (Paris: Bordas, 1984), pp. 30–34. (XXXVII.102)

24 Stanesco, Michel, '"Entre sommeillant et esveillé": un jeu d'errance du chevalier médiéval,' *MA*, 90 (1984), 401–32. (XXXVII.12)
On the *Charrette*, pp. 404–11.

See Ma29 Schmid.

See Pa178 Bertolucci Pizzorusso.

See Fb67 Press.

25   Stanesco, Michel, 'Le conte de fées et le merveilleux romanesque,' in *Réception*, pp. 11–19. (XL.58)

26   Cerquiglini, Bernard, 'De la syntaxe au topos: une figure de la souffrance féminine,' in *Souffrance*, pp. 227–42 (discussion pp. 263–67).

27   Kał ałr, Małgorzata, 'L'épreuve douloureuse comme étape initiatique dans quelques lais et romans des XIIe et XIIIe siècles,' in *Souffrance*, pp. 205–17 (discussion pp. 219–23).

28   Limentani, Alberto, '"Nessun maggior dolore...": mémoire et souffrance dans *Girart de Roussillon* et dans quelques textes épiques et narratifs,' in *Souffrance*, pp. 121–29 (discussion pp. 131–34).
See pp. 126–27.

29   Ménard, Philippe, 'Rires et sourires dans le roman du *Chevalier au lion*,' in *Chevalier au lion*, pp. 7–29; repr. in Dc29. (XLI.74)
Cf. Gf7 and Gf33.

30   Santucci, Monique, 'La folie dans le *Chevalier au lion*,' in *Chevalier au lion*, pp. 153–72. (XLI.88)

31   Zink, Michel, 'L'angoisse du héros et la douleur du saint: souffrance endurée, souffrance contemplée dans la littérature hagiographique et romanesque (XIIe–XIIIe siècles),' in *Souffrance*, pp. 85–98 (discussion pp. 99–106); repr. in Dc18.

See Lb2 Hult.

See Hf7 7 Santucci.

32   Dallapiazza, Michael, 'Emotionalität und Geschlechterbeziehung in Chrétien, Hartman[n] und Wolfram,' in *Liebe Triest*, pp. 167–84.

See Kd111 Gallais.

33   *Le Rire au Moyen Age dans la littérature et dans les arts: Actes du Colloque International des 17, 18 et 19 novembre 1988*, ed. Thérèse Bouché and Hélène Charpentier (Bordeaux: Presses Universitaires de Bordeaux, 1990).
   A.   Philippe Ménard, 'Le rire et le sourire au Moyen Age dans la littérature et dans les arts: essai de problématique,' pp. 7–30. (XLIV.41)
   B.   Marie-Françoise Notz, 'Tel est pris qui croyait prendre ou: les auteurs médiévaux nous font-ils rire malgré eux?' pp. 227–35. (XLIV.44)

See Kc93 Rychner.

See Sa132 Wack.

34 Wolfzettel, Friedrich, 'Liebe als Krankheit in der altfranzösischen Literatur: Überlegungen zu einer Funktionalisierung des Topos,' in *Liebe als Krankheit: 3. Kolloquium der Forschungsstelle für europäische Lyrik des Mittelalters*, ed. Theo Stemmler (Mannheim: Forschungsstelle für europäische Lyrik des Mittelalters an der Universität Mannheim, 1990), pp. 151–86.

35 Aguiriano, Begoña, 'Le cœur dans Chrétien,' in *Cuer*, pp. 9–25. (XLIV.17)

See Gd.b44 Villena.

See Fb83(G) Ferroul.

36 Freixe, Alain, 'Emotion, musement et poésie,' *Courrier du Centre International d'Etudes Poétiques*, 199 (July–Sept. 1993), 15–22.
On *Perceval*'s blood drops in the snow episode.

37 Wolf, Alois, 'Die "große Freude": vergleichende Betrachtungen zur Eros-*exsultatio* in Minnekanzonen, im *Erec* und im *Tristan*,' *LJG*, 34 (1993), 49–79; repr. in Dc31.

38 Dybeł, Katarzyna, 'Une double connaissance: le regard des yeux et le regard du cœur dans les romans de Chrétien de Troyes,' *PRIS-MA*, 10 (1994), 127–36. (XLVII.265)

39 Dottori, Daniela, 'L'aspetto spirituale nel *Cligès* di Chrétien de Troyes,' *QMacerata*, ser. 3, 10 (1995), 43–64. (XLIX.331)

40 Walter, Philippe, 'Mélancoliques solitudes: le roi Pêcheur (Chrétien de Troyes) et Amfortas (Wolfram von Eschenbach),' in *Solitudes, écriture et représentation*, ed. André Siganos (Grenoble: ELLUG, Université Stendhal, 1995), pp. 21–30.
Theory of Humors and the melancholy of Perceval and the Fisher King.

See Gb153(B) Callahan.

41 Derrien, Ève, 'Le sang et la saignée dans le roman médiéval en vers,' *LR*, 51 (1997), 3–18. (L.3)

42 Akkari, Hatem, '"Moult grant duel demener" ou le rituel de la mort,' in *Geste*, pp. 11–24.

43 Baudry, Robert, 'Et l'absence, éloquente, de geste...,' in *Geste*, pp. 41–50.

44 Greene, Virginie, 'Le deuil, mode d'emploi, dans deux romans de Chrétien de Troyes,' *FS*, 52 (1998), 257–78. (LI.375)
On Enide's and Laudine's grief.

45 Jeay, Madeleine, 'Consuming Passions: Variations on the Eaten Heart Theme,' in *Violence against Women in Medieval Texts*, ed. Anna Roberts (Gainesville: University Press of Florida, 1998), pp. 75–96.

46 Ferroul, Yves, 'Le mythe du courage individuel et de l'exploit singulier,' in *Mélanges Suard*, vol. 1, pp. 251–60. (LII.232)

47 Gingras, Francis, 'Le sang de l'amour dans le récit médiéval (XIIe-XIIIe siècle),' in *Sang*, pp. 207–16. (LII.236)

48 Noacco, Cristina, '"Horribile visu"? Aspects narratifs de l'horreur dans l'œuvre de Chrétien de Troyes,' in *L'Horreur au moyen âge*, Travaux du Groupe de Recherche 'Lectures Médiévales', Université de Toulouse II: Collection Moyen Age (Toulouse: Editions Universitaires du Sud, 1999), pp. 127–43. (LIII.267)

49 Boutet, Dominique, 'Le comique arthurien,' *BBSIA*, 52 (2000), 323–51.

50 Brainerd, Madeleine, 'Stolen Pain: Romance and the Redistribution of Suffering,' in *One Hundred Years of Masochism: Literary Texts, Social and Cultural Contexts*, ed. Michael C. Finke and Carl Niekerk, Psychoanalysis and Culture, 10 (Amsterdam: Rodopi, 2000), pp. 71–90.

51 Krass, Andreas, 'Die Mitleidfähigkeit des Helden: zum Motiv der *compassio* im höfischen Roman des 12. Jahrhunderts ("Eneit" – "Erec" – "Iwein"),' *W-S*, 16 (2000), 282–304. (LIII.91)

g: Indexes that Include Chrétien's Works

1 Frenzel, Elisabeth, *Motive der Weltliteratur: ein Lexikon dichtungsgeschichtlicher Längsschnitte*, 3rd revised and enlarged ed., Körners Taschenausgabe, 301 (Stuttgart: Körner, 1988).

2 Ruck, E. H., *An Index of Themes and Motifs in Twelfth-Century French Arthurian Poetry*, AS, 25 (Cambridge: Brewer, 1991). (XLV.271)

3 Guerreau-Jalabert, Anita, *Index des motifs narratifs dans les romans arthuriens français en vers (XIIe–XIIIe siècles) [Motif-Index of*

French Arthurian Verse Romances (XIIth–XIIIth Cent.)], PRF, 202 (Geneva: Droz, 1992). (XLV.182, 613)

See Vb3 Doss-Quinby.

4   Jonin, Pierre, *L'Europe en vers au Moyen Age: essai de thématique*, NBMA, 35 (Paris: Champion, 1996). (LI.2)

H: ROMANCE NARRATIVE: FORM – STRUCTURE – CHARACTERIZATION – GENRE

The general observations on items in this section in the 1976 Bibliography still hold by and large. Genre has been added because of the increase in the number of publications devoted to the topic, with respect both to Chrétien and to romance writing in the twelfth and thirteenth centuries. Questioning received opinion has been on the rise – for example, whether *Perceval* is incomplete or whether Godefroi de Lagny actually wrote the last thousand lines of the *Charrette*. Much of this reflects greater uncertainty about composition in earlier periods, an uncertainty that allows for greater latitude to test or question received or authoritative interpretations. Similarly, there is less agreement on which social or moral standards Chrétien may actually have fostered in his romances, and more emphasis on perceived problematic or debatable implications of his narratives (He55). Matters of intertextuality (see L) have made his relations with other romances or other works a growing factor in interpretation, and this is likely to continue as interest grows in his influence on subsequent French writing (see Pa). As the cross-references suggest, interpretation is often influenced more by diverse modern methodologies and theoretical positions (U) than by earlier, medieval conceptions (F).

a: General Studies

13 Köhler, Erich, *Ideal und Wirklichkeit* […]

Italian trans.: *L'avventura cavalleresca: ideale e realtà nei poemi della Tavola Ritonda*, trans. G. Baptist, introduction by Mario Mancini (Bologna: Il Mulino, 1985) (XXXVIII.407); Spanish trans.: *La aventura caballeresca: ideal y realidad en la narrativa cortés*, trans. Blanca Garí (Barcelona: Sirmio, 1990). (XLVI.255)

A French resumé: Mathias Waltz, 'Les romans de Chrétien de Troyes,' in *Problèmes d'une sociologie du roman*, a special issue of *La Revue de sociologie*

(Brussels: Institut de Sociologie, Université Libre de Bruxelles, 1963.2), pp. 271–84.

15 (IV) Jauss, Hans Robert, 'Chanson de geste […]'; German trans.: 'Epos und Roman – eine vergleichende Betrachtung an Texten des 12. Jahrhunderts,' in his *Alterität und Modernität der mittelalterlichen Literatur: gesammelte Aufsätze 1956–76* (Munich: Fink, 1977), pp. 310–26. (XXXI.26)

18 Brinkmann, Hennig, 'Wege der epischen Dichtung […]'; repr. in his *Studien zur Geschichte der deutschen Sprache und Literatur*, 2 vols (Düsseldorf: Schwann, 1965–66), vol. 2, pp. 106–36.

23 Vinaver, Eugène, *Form and Meaning* […] Repr. in his *On Art and Nature and Other Essays*, ed. W. R. J. Barron (Whitstable: Elizabeth Vinaver, 2000). (LIII.559)

30 Haug, Walter, 'Vom Imram […]' Repr. in Dc15.

36 Riquer, Martín de, 'La influencia de la transmisión […]' Correct as follows: in *Historia y estructura de la obra literaria: Coloquios celebrados del 28 al 31 de marzo 1967*, Anejos de *Revista de Literatura*, 31.

42 Haug, Walter, 'Struktur und Geschichte […]' Repr. in Dc15.

49 Haidu, Peter, ed., *Approaches* […]
  I. Dembowski, Peter F., 'Monologue […]' (XXVIII.121)
  II. Gallais, Pierre, 'Hexagonal and Spiral Structure […]' (XXVIII.126)
  III. Haidu, Peter, 'Narrativity and Language […]' (XXVIII.129)
  IV. Jackson, W. T. H., 'The Nature of Romance […]' Repr. in Dc12. (XXVIII.131)
  V. Lacy, Norris J., 'Spatial Form […]' (XXVIII.138)

50 Ollier, Marie-Louise, 'Discours […]' Repr. in Dc32.

51 Ollier, Marie-Louise, 'Demande sociale […]' (XXVIII.142). Repr. in Dc32.

53 Gallais, Pierre, 'L'Hexagone logique […]' (XXVIII.254)

See Kd32 Voelker.

54 Weston, Jessie L., *King Arthur and his Knights: A Survey of Arthurian Romance*, Popular Studies in Mythology, Romance and Folklore, 4 (London: Nutt, 1899).

55 Comfort, William Wistar, 'The Essential Difference between a *chanson de geste* and a *roman d'aventure*,' *PMLA*, 19 (1904), 64–74.

56   Cohen, Gustave, *Le roman courtois au XIIe siècle* (Paris: Centre de Documentation Universitaire, [1934]).
See pp. 83–100.

57   Hatzfeld, Helmut A., *Literature through Art: A New Approach to French Literature* (New York: Oxford University Press, 1952).

58   Robson, C. A., 'The Technique of Symmetrical Composition in Medieval Narrative Poetry,' in *Studies Ewert*, pp. 26–75. (XVI.68)
Pp. 38–40 on *Yvain*.

59   Hanning, Robert W., 'Uses of Names in Medieval Literature,' *Names*, 16 (1968), 325–38.

60   Lange, Hanne, 'Om middelalderlig talkomposition og talsymbolik: metoder og fortolkningsproblemer,' in *Romanproblemer: Teorier og Analyser. Festskrift til Hans Sørensen den 28. September 1968*, ed. Merete Gerlach-Nielsen, Hans Hertel and Morten Nøjgaard (Odense: Odense Universitets-forlag, 1968), pp. 106–27.

61   Le Goff, Jacques, 'Naissance du roman historique au XIIe siècle?', *Nouvelle Revue française*, 238 (1972), 163–73.

See Pg9 Durán.

62   Frappier, Jean, 'A propos du lai de *Tydorel* et de ses éléments mythiques,' *TLL*, 11:1 (1973), 561–87. Repr. in Dc2. (XXVI.119)
See pp. 586–87.

63   Pearsall, Derek, 'The Story and Its Setting,' in *Mediaeval World*, pp. 371–46.

See Sc13 Gallais.

64   García Gual, Carlos, *Primeras novelas europeas* (Madrid: Istmo, 1974; 2nd ed. 1988). (XXVIII.221, XLI.241).

65   Mauritz, Hans-Dieter, *Der Ritter im magischen Reich: Märchenelemente im französischen Abenteuerroman des 12. und 13. Jahrhunderts*, EH:F, 23 (Bern: H. Lang, Frankfurt/M.: P. Lang, 1974).

66   Hume, Kathryn, 'Romance: A Perdurable Pattern,' *College English*, 36 (1974–75), 129–46.

67   Jameson, Fredric, 'Magical Narratives: Romance as Genre,' *NLH*, 7 (1975), 135–63.

68 Jauss, Hans Robert, 'Ästhetische Erfahrung als Zugang zur mittelalterlichen Literatur,' *GRM*, 25 (1975), 385–401.

69 Meneghetti, Maria Luisa, 'L'*Estoire des Engleis* di Geffrei Gaimar fra cronaca genealogica e romanzo cortese,' *MedR*, 2 (1975), 232–46. (XXVIII.396)

70 Ollier, Marie-Louise, 'Le roman courtois: manifestation du dire créateur,' in *Lecture*, pp. 175–88.

71 Payen, J.-C., and F. N. M. Diekstra, *Le Roman*, TMA, 12 (Turnhout: Brepols, 1975).

72 Roach, Eleanor, 'Les termes "roman" et "gothique" dans le domaine littéraire: essai de définition,' *LR*, 29 (1975), 59–65. (XXVIII.92)

See Gb35 Uitti.

73 Zumthor, Paul, 'Roman et histoire: à l'origine d'un univers narratif (XIIᵉ siècle),' in *Lecture*, pp. 103–14.
Also printed as 'Roman et histoire: aux sources d'un univers narratif' in Fa56.

See Fa87 Freeman.

74 Fukui, Yoshio, and under the supervision of Eleven Professors, *Romance I, Course in French Literature I* (Tokyo: Taishûkan, 1976). (XXXI.461)
In Japanese. See Chap.1: 'Appearance and Evolution of Romance,' by E. Kamizawa (pp. 11–39); Chap. 2: 'Transformation of Romance (I),' by T. Amazawa (pp. 40–71).

See Pb187 Gürttler.

75 Михайлов, А. Д., 'Французский рыцарский роман и вопросы типологии жанра в средневековой литературе,' Академия наук СССР (Moskow: Nauka, 1976). (XXXI.510)

76 Payen, J. C., 'Structure et sens d'*Yonec*,' *MA*, 82 (1976), 263–87. (XXIX.161)
For Chrétien, see themes 6 and 7 (pp. 279–81).

77 Zumthor, Paul, 'Romanzo e storia,' *Saggi e Ricerche di Letteratura Francese*, 15 (1976), 9–24.

See La26 Boklund.

See Qe6 Boklund.

78 Duggan, Joseph J., 'Ambiguity in Twelfth-Century French and Provençal Literature: A Problem or a Value?' in *Misrahi Volume*, pp. 136–49. (XXXII.168)

See Ga18 Hanning.

79 Osland, Dianne, 'The Rationalization of Romance from Chrétien to Gottfried and Wolfram,' *Southern Review*, 10 (1977), 59–74.

See Pd34 Strohm.
See pp. 3–5.

80 Poirion, Daniel, 'L'écriture romanesque,' *PerM*, 3 (1977), 3–6. (XXX.288)

See Pa102 Adams.

See Uc12 Bozóky.

81 Brewer, Derek, 'The Nature of Romance,' *Poetica* (Tokyo), 9 (1978), 9–48.

82 Cavendish, Richard, *King Arthur and the Grail: The Arthurian Legends and their Meaning* (London: Weidenfeld & Nicolson, 1978; New York: Taplinger, 1979; London: Paladin, 1980). (XXXI.359)

83 Cockcroft, Robert, 'Castle Hautdesert: Portrait or Patchwork?' *Neophil*, 62 (1978), 459–77.
See pp. 461–62.

84 Payen, Jean-Charles, 'L'enracinement folklorique du roman arthurien,' in *Mélanges Rychner*, pp. 427–37. (XXXI.297)

See Jb26 Ribard.

85 Sklute, Larry M., 'The Ambiguity of Ethical Norms in Courtly Romance,' *Genre*, 11 (1978), 315–32. (XXXII.221)

86 Jauss, Hans Robert, 'Cinq modèles d'identification esthétique: complément à la théorie des genres littéraires au Moyen Age,' in *Congresso Napoli*, vol. 1, pp. 145–64.

87 Mikhailov, André D., 'Les genres narratifs dans la littérature française médiévale: particularités de leur évolution et voies à suivre dans leur étude,' in *Congresso Napoli*, vol. 5, pp. 343–52 (with discussion).

88 Ollier, Marie-Louise, 'Le roman courtois: l'exaltation de la connaissance ou le triomphe de "clergie",' in *Congresso Napoli*, vol. 5, pp. 361–69. Repr. in Dc32.

89 Uitti, Karl D., 'Foi littéraire et création poétique: le problème des genres littéraires en ancien français,' in *Congresso Napoli*, vol. 1, pp. 165–76.

90 Bloomfield, Morton W., 'Episodic Juxtaposition or the Syntax of Episodes in Narration,' in *Studies in English Linguistics for Randolph Quirk*, ed. S. Greenbaum, G. Leech, and J. Svartvik (London: Longman, 1979), pp. 210–20.

See Uc14 Cormeau.

91 Gier, Albert, 'Zum altfranzösischen Artusroman: literarisches Spiel und Aufhebung der Zeitgesetze,' *Lendemains*, 4 (Nov. 1979), 11–24. (XXXIII.25)

92 Haug, Walter, 'Erec, Enite und Evelyne B.,' in *Festschrift Ruh*, pp. 139–64; repr. in Dc15. (XXXII.34)

93 Haug, Walter, 'Strukturalistische Methoden und mediävistische Literaturwissenschaft,' *W-S*, 5 (1979), 8–21.

94 Jackson, W. T. H., 'The Arthuricity of Marie de France,' *RR*, 70 (1979), 1–18. (XXXII.90)
Includes comparisons with Chrétien.

95 Kellogg, Robert, 'Varieties of Tradition in Medieval Narrative', in *Symposium Odense*, pp. 120–29.

96 Shepherd, G. T., 'The Emancipation of Story in the Twelfth Century,' in *Symposium Odense*, pp. 44–57 (discussion p. 132).

97 Warning, Rainer, 'Formen narrativer Identitätskonstitution im höfischen Roman,' in *Identität*, ed. O. Marquard and Karlheinz Stierle, PH, 8 (Munich: Fink, 1979), pp. 553–89; repr. in *GRLMA*, vol. 4:1, pp. 25–59. (XXXII.80)
See also Hb20 Warning.

See Gd.b21 Bloch.

98 Bruckner, Matilda Tomaryn, 'Repetition and Variation in Twelfth-Century French Romance,' in *ICLS Athens*, pp. 95–114. (XXXII.161)

99 Grigsby, John L., 'The Ontology of the Narrator in Medieval French Romance,' in *Nature*, pp. 159–71. (XXXIII.146)

100 Kjær, Jonna, *Structure mythique et fonction magique: essai sur le roman courtois*, RIDS, 75 (Copenhagen: Romansk Institut, Københavns Universitet, 1980). (XXXIV.550)

101 Schulze, Joachim, 'Guigemar, der höfische Roman und die allegorische Psychologie des Mittelalters,' *AStnSpr*, 217 (1980), 312–26.

On two-part structure.

See Pa118 Stierle.

See Gb62 Vinaver.

102 Amazawa, Taijirô, *A Reading of Fantasy* (Tokyo: Chikuma-shobô, 1981). (XXXIV.482).
In Japanese. See esp. Chap. I. – 1. 'On the Theme of the Quest in the Middle Ages – The Grail Legend' (pp. 9–38) ; Chap. I – 2. 'A Hypothesis Concerning the Fisher King in the *Conte du Graal*' (pp. 39–58) ; Chap. III – 4. 'Nerval, Perceval – *Aurélia* and the *Conte del Graal*' (pp. 185–91).

103 Benton, John F., 'Collaborative Approaches to Fantasy and Reality in the Literature of Champagne,' in *ICLS Liverpool*, pp. 43–57; repr. in Dc16. (XXXIV.293)

See Qa53 Bloch.

104 Evans, Dafydd, 'Wishfulfilment: The Social Function and Classification of Old French Romances,' in *ICLS Liverpool*, pp. 129–34. (XXXIV.309)

105 Grigsby, John L., 'Narrative in Three Garbs: *roman courtois, lai, chanson de toile*,' *RPh*, 34, Special Issue (1981), *73–*87. (XXXIV.125)

106 Hanning, R. W., 'The Audience as Co-Creator in the First Chivalric Romances,' *Yearbook of English Studies*, 11 (1981), 1–28.

107 Haug, Walter, 'Transzendenz und Utopie: Vorüberlegungen zu einer Literarästhetik des Mittelalters,' in *Literaturwissenschaft und Geistesgeschichte: Festschrift für Richard Brinkmann*, ed. Jürgen Brummack [et alii] (Tübingen: Niemeyer, 1981), pp. 1–22; repr. in Dc15. (XXXV.31a)

108 Jeffrey, David L., 'Literature in an Apocalyptic Age; or, How to End a Romance,' *DR*, 61 (1981), 426–46. (XXXVII.403)
On closure; treats *Erec*.

109 Schmolke-Hasselmann, Beate, 'Untersuchungen zur Typik des arthurischen Romananfangs,' *GRM*, 31 (1981), 1–13. (XXXIV.44)

110 Zink, Michel, 'Une mutation de la conscience littéraire: le langage romanesque à travers des exemples français du XIIe siècle,' *CCM*, 24 (1981), 3–27. (XXXIV.261)

111 Gier, Albert, 'Skatologische Komik in der französischen Literatur des Mittelalters,' *W-S*, 7 (1982), 154–83. (XXXV.24)
See pp. 176–77.

112 Meneghetti, Maria Luisa, '"Fonte" e "modello culturale" nei romanzi cortesi,' in *La parola ritrovata: fonti e analisi letteraria*, ed. Costanzo Di Girolamo and Ivano Paccagnella (Palermo: Sellerio, 1982), pp. 65–81. (XXXV.468)

113 Nykrog, Per, 'The Rise of Literary Fiction,' in *Renaissance and Renewal in the Twelfth Century*, ed. Robert L. Benson and Giles Constable (Cambridge, MA: Harvard University Press, Oxford: Clarendon Press, 1982), pp. 593–612. (XXXVI.447, XXXVII.435)

114 Poirion, Daniel, *Le Merveilleux dans la littérature française du Moyen Age*, Que sais-je? 1938 (Paris: Presses Universitaires de France, 1982). (XXXIV.243)
See pp. 69–81.

115 Стебин-Каменский, М. И., 'От Саги к Роману,' Известия Академии Наук СССР: Серия Литературы и Языка, 41:1 (1982), 18–27.

116 Vinaver, Eugène, 'The Shaping Spirit in Medieval Verse and Prose,' *Sewanee Mediaeval Colloquium: Occasional Papers*, 1 (1982), 9–18. (XXXV.193)

See La32 Zumthor.

117 Baumgartner, Emmanuèle, and Charles Méla, 'La mise en roman,' chap. 3 in *Précis de littérature française du Moyen Age*, ed. Daniel Poirion (Paris: Presses Universitaires de France, 1983); repr. in Dc20.
See also Chap. 7:3: 'Romans et merveilles,' by Charles Méla.

118 Calin, William, *A Muse for Heroes: Nine Centuries of the Epic in France* (Toronto: University of Toronto Press, 1983). (XXXVII.349)
See Chap. 4: 'Chrétien de Troyes' (pp. 83–112).

119 Carmona, Fernando, *Narrativa románica medieval: introducción y textos* (Murcia: Departamento de Literaturas Románicas, Universidad de Murcia, 1983).
See Chap. 3: 'Chrétien de Troyes y sus continuadores.'

120 Gumbrecht, Hans Ulrich, 'Wie fiktional war der höfische Roman?' in *Funktionen des Fiktiven*, ed. Dieter Henrich and Wolfgang Iser, PH, 10 (Munich: Fink, 1983), pp. 433–40.

See Ke8 Haidu.

121 Bozóky, Edina, 'En attendant le héros... (pour une typologie de l'orientation de l'itinéraire du héros dans le roman arthurien),' in *Courtly Romance*, pp. 23–45. (XXXVII.347)

122 *Epische Stoffe des Mittelalters*, ed. Volker Mertens and Ulrich Müller, Kröners Taschenausgabe, 483 (Stuttgart: Kröner, 1984).
    A.   Volker Mertens, 'Artus,' pp. 290–340.
    B.   Dieter Welz, 'Gralromane,' pp. 341–64.

See Pb289 Haug.

123 Kelly, Douglas, 'The Rhetoric of Adventure in Medieval Romance,' in *Essays Topsfield*, pp. 172–85. (XXXVII.170)

See Pa147 Kelly.

124 Knape, Joachim, *'Historie' im Mittelalter und früher Neuzeit: begriffs- und gattungsgeschichtliche Untersuchungen im interdisziplinären Kontext*, Saecvla Spiritalis, 10 (Baden-Baden: Koerner, 1984).
See pp. 29–30.

See Db30 Marotta.
See pp. 16–20.

125 Meletinsky, Elizar M., 'The Typology of the Medieval Romance in the West and in the East,' *Diogenes*, 127 (1984), 1–22.

126 Roloff, Volker, 'Der Märchenwald als Traum: zur Interpretation von Märchenmotiven in der Artusepik ("Tristan" und "Lancelot en prose"),' in *Artusrittertum*, pp. 146–58. (XXXVII.660)

127 *Romance: Generic Transformation from Chrétien de Troyes to Cervantes*, ed. Kevin Brownlee and Marina Scordilis Brownlee (Hanover, NH: University Press of New England, 1985). (XXXVIII.473) See Hb34 Kelly.

128 Frakes, Jerold C., 'Metaphysical Structure as Narrative Structure in the Medieval Romance,' *Neophil*, 69 (1985), 481–89.

129 Gallais, Pierre, 'Prolégomènes à un manifeste. Première partie: du roman et de sa naissance,' *PRIS-MA*, 1 (1985), 45–49. (XXXVIII.210)

130 Halász, Katalin, 'A lukácsi esztétika és a középkori regény,' in *Lukács György irodalomelmélete* (Pécs: Pécsi Akadémiai Bizottság, 1985), pp. 115–22. (XL.202)

131 Kay, Sarah, 'The Tristan Story as Chivalric Romance, Feudal Epic and Fabliau,' in *ICLS Toronto*, pp. 185–95. (XXXVIII.323)

132 Kelly, Douglas, '*Disjointure* and the Elaboration of Prose Romance: The Example of the Seven Sages of Rome Prose Cycle,' in *ICLS Toronto*, pp. 208–16. (XXXVIII.325)
Compares with Chrétien's notion of *conjointure*; see also Ha213 Trachsler.

133 Sasu, Voichiţa, 'Le roman médiéval français – récit d'un apprentissage,' in *Problèmes des genres littéraires*, in *Zagadniania Rodzajów Literackich*, 26:2 (1985), 5–12.

134 Stanesco, Michel, 'Le secret de l'*estrange* chevalier: notes sur la motivation contradictoire dans le roman médiéval,' in *ICLS Toronto*, pp. 339–49. (XXXVIII.345)
Comparisons between Hue de Rotelande's *Ipomedon* and Chrétien's romances.

See Qa76 Stanesco.

135 Vàrvaro, Alberto, *Letterature romanze del medioevo*, Saggi, 282 (Bologna: Il Mulino, 1985).
See Chap. 5: 'L'esperienza narrativa.'

136 Zink, Michel, *La subjectivité littéraire: autour du siècle de Saint Louis*, Écriture (Paris: Presses Universitaires de France, 1985). (XXXVIII. 280)
See pp. 27–46.

137 Baumgartner, Emmanuèle, 'Le livre et le roman (XIIe-XIIIe siècles),' *Littérales*, 1 (1986), 7–19; repr. in Dc20. (XXXIX.631)

See Pd52 Crane.

See Ef7 Hunt, Chap. 1 and 2.

See La38 Lecco.

See Fa136 Maddox.

138 Poirion, Daniel, *Résurgences: mythe et littérature à l'âge du symbole (XIIe siècle)*, Écriture (Paris: Presses Universitaires de France, 1986). (XXXIX.666)
See pp. 135–215.

See Md37 Adams.

139 Spearing, A. C., *Readings in Medieval Poetry* (Cambridge: Cambridge University Press, 1987). (XL.137)

140 Urbina, Eduardo, 'Gigantes y enanos: de lo maravilloso a lo grotesco en el *Quijote*,' *RJ*, 38 (1987), 323–38.

See La41 Bruckner.

See Lc2 Calin.

See Pa198 Krueger.

141 Lacy, Norris J., 'The Typology of Arthurian Romance,' in *Legacy*, vol. 1, pp. 33–56. (XLII.222)

142 Zink, Michel, 'Chrétien et ses contemporains,' in *Legacy*, vol. 1, pp. 5–32. (XLII.249)

143 Helm, Joan, 'The Celestial Circle: Fées, Philosophy and Numerical Circularity in Medieval Arthurian Romance,' *AInt*, 3:1 (1988), 25–36. (XLII.313)

144 Janssens, Jozef D., *Dichter en publiek in creatief samenspel: over interpretatie van Middelnederlandse ridderromane*, Leuvense Studiën en Tekstuitgaven, n.s. 7 (Leuven: Acco, 1988). (XLI.7)

See Fa143 Marchello-Nizia.

145 Meneghetti, Maria Luisa, ed., *Il romanzo*, Problemi e Prospettive: Serie di Linguistica e Critica Letteraria – Strumenti di Filologia Romanza (Bologna: Il Mulino, 1988). (XLI.273)
The Introduction by Meneghetti treats romance's origins, scholarship, genre, and a historical survey emphasizing French romance (pp. 7–85). The remainder of the volume reprints a number of studies in whole or in part, most with some editorial changes. The bibliography points to future study.

Part One: 'Nome, luogo e data di nascita'
A. Aurelio Roncaglia, '"Romanzo": scheda anamnestica d'un termine chiave,' pp. 89–106.
B. Maurice Wilmotte, 'La fondazione del romanzo: nostalgia dell'antichità e attualità politica e culturale,' pp. 107–22. (Ha7)
Part Two: 'Fisionomia del genere'
C. Cesare Segre, 'I problemi del romanzo medievale,' pp. 125–45.
D. Erich Köhler, 'Forma e struttura nel romanzo arturiano,' pp. 147–69. (Ha13)
E. Peter Haidu, 'Il distanziamento estetico: ironia e commedia in Chrétien de Troyes,' pp. 171–82. (Fb18)
F. Rita Lejeune, 'Fra idillio e realismo: Jean Renart,' pp. 183–93.
G. Martín de Riquer, 'Il verosimile, il quotidiano e il comico nel *Tirant lo Blanc*,' pp. 195–205.
Part Three: 'Tecniche della narrazione'
H. Aurelio Roncaglia, 'L'*Alexandre* di Albéric e la separazione fra *chanson de geste* e romanzo,' pp. 209–27. (Ha15 III)
I. John L. Grigsby, 'Le voci del narratore,' pp. 229–49. (Hb22)
J. Karl D. Uitti, 'Il virtuosismo della buona costruzione,' pp. 251–67. (Ha48)
K. Alberto Limentani, 'L'*enchâssement* dei testi lirici nel tesssuto narrativo: il caso di *Flamenca*,' pp. 269–79. (Pi13)
L. Ilse Nolting-Hauff, 'La tecnica del dialogo,' pp. 281–97. (Ge7)
M. Ferdinand Lot, 'Il principio dell'*entrelacement*,' pp. 299–311. (Pa7)
Part Four: 'La tematica'
N. Alberto Vàrvaro, 'L'adulterio e il filtro,' pp. 315–31.
O. Jean Marx, 'Il Graal,' pp. 333–46. (Na.c14)
P. Jean Frappier, 'Il motivo del "don contraignant",' pp. 347–87. (Ge13)
Q. Philippe Ménard, 'L'incognito,' pp. 389–403. (Gf 7)
R. María Rosa Lida de Malkiel, 'Il palazzo sotterraneo dal *Merlin* all'*Estoria de dos amadores*,' pp. 405–12.
S. 'Indicazioni bibliografiche per ulteriori approfondimenti,' pp. 413–26. (cf. §§ 5 and 5:2)
T. See also: Gioia Zaganelli, Antonio Pioletti, Fabrizio Conla, and Maria Luisa Meneghetti, 'In margine a *Il romanzo*,' *Quaderni di Lingue e Letterature*, 14 (1989), 263–85. (XLII.132)

See Qg6 Morris.

146 Poirion, Daniel, 'Le roman d'aventure au Moyen Age: étude d'esthétique littéraire,' *CAIEF*, 40 (1988), 111–27. (XLI.81)

147 Wilson, Anne, *The Magical Quest: The Use of Magic in Arthurian Romance* (Manchester: Manchester University Press; New York: St Martin's Press, 1988). (XLI.161)
Treats *Yvain* (Chap. 1) and *Perceval* (Chap. 2) as illustrations of the 'magical plot'.

148 Haug, Walter, 'Literatur und Leben im Mittelalter: eine neue Theorie zur Entstehung und Entwicklung des höfischen Romans,' *Deutschunterricht*, 41 (1989), 12–26; repr. in Dc24. (XLII.541)

149 Haug, Walter, 'Wandlungen des Fiktionalitätsbewußtseins vom hohen zum späten Mittelalter,' in *Entzauberung der Welt: Deutsche Literatur 1200–1500*, ed. James F. Poag and Thomas C. Fox (Tübingen: Francke, 1989), pp. 1–17; repr. in Dc24. (XLII.550)

150 Morin, Lise, 'La naissance du roman médiéval,' *DFS*, 16 (1989), 3–14.

151 Peron, Gianfelice, 'Meraviglioso e verosimile nel romanzo francese medievale: da Benoît de Sainte-Maure a Jean Renart,' in *Meraviglioso*, pp. 293–323. (XLII.123)

152 Vitz, Evelyn Birge, *Medieval Narrative and Modern Narratology: Subjects and Objects of Desire*, New York University Studies in French Culture and Civilization (New York: New York University Press, 1989). (XLIII.604)
Although Chrétien appears only in passing, much of the book is useful for study of his narrative.

153 Almeida Ribeiro, Cristina, 'Changement d'espace et quête d'identité dans le roman arthurien,' in *Proceedings of the XIIth Congress of the International Comparative Literature Association – Actes du XIIᵉ Congrès de l'Association Internationale de Littérature comparée. München 1988 Munich, II: Space and Boundaries in Literature–Espace et frontières dans la littérature*, ed. Roger Bauer [et alii] (Munich: Iudicium, 1990), pp. 405–09.

154 Ashe, Geoffrey, *King Arthur: The Dream of a Golden Age* (New York: Thames & Hudson, 1990).

155 Cazelles, Brigitte, 'Outrepasser les normes: l'invention de soi en France médiévale,' *SFR*, 14 (1990), 69–92. (XLIII.507)
Includes *Yvain*.

156 Delcourt, Denyse, *L'éthique du changement dans le roman français du XIIᵉ siècle*, HICL, 276 (Geneva: Droz, 1990). (XLIII.448)
See Chap. 3: 'L'aventure et le changement dans *Erec et Enide* de Chrétien de Troyes: optimisme et souplesse,' and Chap. 4: 'Avancer "en esprit" ou le changement dans *Perceval ou le Conte du graal* de Chrétien de Troyes: à la recherche de nouveaux paradigmes.'

157 Fleischman, Suzanne, *Tense and Narrativity: From Medieval Performance to Modern Fiction*, Texas Linguistics Series (Austin: University of Texas Press, 1990).

158 Meletyinszkij, J. M., 'A. N. Veszelovszkij "Történeti poétikája" és az elbeszélő irodalom eredetének kérdésköre,' *Heli*, 1 (1990), 37–59. (XLIV.192)

159 Rubio Tovar, Joaquín, *La narrativa medieval: los orígenes de la novela*, Biblioteca Básica de Literatura (Madrid: Anaya, 1990). (XLVI.279)

160 Stanesco, Michel, 'A l'origine du roman: le principe esthétique de la nouveauté comme tournant du discours littéraire,' in *Styles et valeurs: pour une histoire de l'art littéraire au Moyen Age*, ed. Daniel Poirion, Moyen Age (Paris: SEDES, 1990), pp. 141–65.

161 Baumgartner, Emmanuèle. 'Retour des personnages et écriture du roman (XIIᵉ–XIIIᵉ siècles),' in *Personnage et histoire littéraire: Actes du Colloque de Toulouse 16/18 mai 1990*, ed. Pierre Glaudes and Yves Reuter (Toulouse: Presses Universitaires du Mirail, 1991), pp. 13–22.

162 Carmona, Fernando, 'Las transformaciones de la novela europea: I. Los siglos XII y XIII,' *EstRom*, 7 (1991), 9–14. (XLVI.237)

163 Dubost, Francis, *Aspects fantastiques de la littérature narrative médiévale (XIIème–XIIIème siècles): l'autre, l'ailleurs, l'autrefois*, 2 vols, NBMA, 15 (Paris: Champion, 1991). (XLIV.29)

See Pi25 Huchet, Chap. 8: 'Romans d'oïl et d'oc.'

164 Maddox, Donald, 'Specular Stories, Family Romance, and the Fictions of Courtly Culture,' *Exemplaria*, 3 (1991), 299–326. (XLIV.323)

165 Halász, Katalin, *Images d'auteur dans le roman médiéval (XIIᵉ–XIIIᵉ siècles)*, SRD, 17 (Debrecen: Kossuth Lajos Tudományegyetem, 1992). (XLV.310)

See Fa154 Kelly.

166 Stanesco, Michel, and Michel Zink, *Histoire européenne du roman médiéval: esquisse et perspectives*, Écriture (Paris: Presses Universitaires de France, 1992). (XLV.200)

See pp. 33–38.

167 Berthelot, Anne, 'The Romance as *Conjointure* of Brief Narratives,' *Esp*, 33 (1993), 51–60. (XLVII.678)

168 Bruckner, Matilda Tomaryn, *Shaping Romance: Interpretation, Truth, and Closure in Twelfth-Century French Fictions*, Middle Ages Series (Philadelphia: University of Pennsylvania Press, 1993).

See Ud8 Krueger.

169 Kelly, Douglas. *Medieval French Romance*, TWAS, 838 (New York: Twayne; Toronto: Macmillan, 1993). (XLVI.738)

170 Le Person, Marc, 'L'insertion de la "reverdie" comme ouverture ou relance narratives dans quelques romans des XIIème et XIIIème siècles,' in *Les Genres insérés dans le roman: Actes du Colloque International du 10 au 12 décembre 1992*, ed. Claude Lachet, CEIDC., 9 (Lyon: Université Jean Moulin–Lyon 3, [1993]), pp. 17–33.
Includes *Perceval*.

171 Maddox, Donald, 'Medieval Textualities and Intergeneric Form,' *Esp*, 33:4 (1993), 40–50. (XLVII.750)

172 Martin, Jean-Pierre, 'Remarques sur les récits rétrospectifs et les genres narratifs de la *Chanson de Roland* au *Tristan* en prose,' in *Hommage Dufournet*, vol. 2, pp. 910–23.(XLVI.342)
Treats *Erec* and *Yvain*.

173 Spearing, A. C., *The Medieval Poet as Voyeur: Looking and Listening in Medieval Love-Narratives* (Cambridge: Cambridge University Press, 1993). (XLVI.489)
See Chap. 4.

174 Sturm-Maddox, Sara, and Donald Maddox, '*Genre* and *Intergenre* in Medieval French Literature,' *Esp*, 33:4 (1993), 3–9. (XLVII.795)

175 Wild, Gerhard, '"Manuscripts Found in a Bottle?" Zum Fiktionalitätsstatus (post)arthurischer Schwellentexte,' in *Fiktionalität*, pp. 203–41 (XLVI.120).

176 Wyss, Ulrich, 'Fiktionalität — heldenepisch und arthurisch,' in *Fiktionalität*, pp. 242–56 (XLVI.122).

177 Pavel, Maria, 'Dénomination et référence dans le roman médiéval,' *ACLit*, 39–40 (1993–94), 29–33.

178 Baumgartner, Emmanuèle, 'Vers, prose et fiction narrative (1150–1240),' in *Festschrift Kennedy*, pp. 1–9. (XLVII.335)

179 Gavino, Enzo, 'L'eroe alla prova: i protagonisti di Gautier d'Arras tra etica e pratica dell'esistere,' *ImRif*, 3 (1994), 341–59. (XLVIII.548)
Compares Gautier's notion of 'adventure' with Chrétien's, pp. 343–46.

180 Haug, Walter, 'Lesen oder Lieben? Erzählen in der Erzählung vom "Erec" bis zum "Titurel",' *PBB*, 116 (1994), 302–23. (XLVII.100)

181 Kay, Sarah, 'Motherhood: The Case of the Epic Family Romance,' in *Festschrift Kennedy*, pp. 23–36.

182 Kennedy, Elspeth, 'The Narrative Techniques Used to Give Arthurian Romance a "Historical" Flavour,' in *Studies Kelly*, pp. 219–33. (XLVII.563)

183 *La letteratura romanza medievale: una storia per generi*, ed. Costanzo Di Girolamo (Bologna: Il Mulino, 1994).
See Chap. 3: 'Il romanzo,' by Maria Luisa Meneghetti.

184 Pardo García, Pedro Javier, 'Cervantes y Chrétien de Troyes: novela, *romance*, y realidad,' in *Actas Irvine–92, Asociación Internacional de Hispanistas. V: Lecturas y relecturas de textos españoles, latinoamericanos y US latinos* ([Irvine CA:] Asociación Internacional de Hispanistas, 1994), pp. 155–69.

185 Putter, Ad, 'Finding Time for Romance: Mediaeval Arthurian Literary History,' *MAe*, 63 (1994), 1–16. (XLVII.377)

186 Sturm-Maddox, Sara, '*Letres escrites i a*: The Marvelous Inscribed,' in *Studies Kelly*, pp. 515–28. (XLVII.595)

187 Sturm-Maddox, Sara, and Donald Maddox, 'Renoart in Avalon: Generic Shift in the *Bataille Loquifer*,' in *Festschrift Kennedy*, pp. 11–22. (XLVII.384)

188 Weimann, Robert, 'Memory, Fictionality, and the Issue of Authority: Author-Function and Narrative Performance in *Beowulf*, Chrétien and Malory,' in *Contexts of Pre-Novel Narrative: The European Tradition*, ed. Roy Eriksen, Approaches to Semiotics, 114 (Berlin: Mouton de Gruyter, 1994), pp. 83–100.

See Pi30 Wolfzettel.

189 Baumgartner, Emmanuèle, *Le récit médiéval XIIe–XIIIe siècles*, Contours littéraires (Paris: Hachette, 1995). (XLVIII.268)

190 Guerin, M. Victoria, *The Fall of Kings and Princes: Structure and Destruction in Arthurian Tragedy* (Stanford, CA: Stanford University Press, 1995). (XLVIII.693)

191 Kasten, Ingrid, 'Bachtin und der höfische Roman,' in *Festschrift Nellmann*, pp. 51–70. (XLVIII.110)

192 Rockwell, Paul Vincent, *Rewriting Resemblance in Medieval French Romance: 'Ceci n'est pas un graal'*, GSML, 13 (New York: Garland, 1995). (XLVII.772)

193 Stanesco, Michel, 'Chrétien de Troyes et le fondement du roman européen,' in *Amour Troyes*, pp. 361–68. (XLIX.191)

194 Burrichter, Brigitte, *Wahrheit und Fiktion: der Status der Fiktionalität in der Artusliteratur des 12. Jahrhunderts*, Beihefte zu Poetica, 21 (Munich: Fink, 1996). (XLIX.36)
See Chap. 5: 'Die nicht-historischen Artuserzählungen' and Chap. 6: 'Die Entwicklung der Fiktionalität nach Chrétien de Troyes.'

See Fe28 Haug.

195 Holzbacher, Ana-María, 'La narrativa de Chrétien de Troyes: este sutil juego con el lector,' in *Paisaje, juego y multilingüismo: Actas del X Simposio de la Sociedad Española de Literatura General y Comparada (Santiago de Compostela, 18–21 de octobre de 1994)*, ed. Darío Villanueva and Fernando Cabo Aseguinolaza, Cursos e Congresos da Universidade de Santiago de Compostela, 91, 2 vols (Santiago: Universidade de Santiago de Compostela, 1996), vol. 2, pp. 177–88. (LIII.819)
Treats incest motif.

196 Meletinsky, Eleazar, 'Sur les genres dans la littérature narrative médiévale,'in *Studi D'Arco Silvio Avalle*, pp. 321–28.
See pp. 325–28.

197 Neugart, Isolde, *Wolfram, Chrétien und das Märchen: Erzählstrukturen und Erzählweisen in der Gawan-Handlung*, EH:D, 1571 (Frankfurt/M.: P. Lang, 1996). (L.103)

See Uc44 Vincensini.

198 Dubost, Francis, *'"Quelque chose que l'on serait tenté d'appeler le fantastique…"* Remarques sur la naissance du concept,' *RLR*, 101:2 (1997), 3–21.

199 Dudley, Edward, *The Endless Text: 'Don Quixote' and the Hermeneutics of Romance*, SUNY Series The Margins of Literature (Albany: State University of New York Press, 1997).

See Fe30 *Gattungen*.

See Ge65 Lacy.

200 Segre, Cesare, 'What Bachtin Did Not Say: The Medieval Origins of the Novel,' *Russian, Croatian and Serbian, Czech and Slovak, Polish Literature*, 41 (1997), 385–409.

201 Voicu, Mihaela, 'Images d'auteur et naissance d'une stratégie narrative au XIIe siècle,' *ABLs*, 46 (1997), 67–84. (LI.713)

See Fa174 Marnette.

202 Ogurisu, Hitoshi, *The Concept of Discourse in Several Works of the Twelfth Century – Essay on Medieval Narratology* (Tokyo: Surugadai-shuppansha, 1998).
In Japanese.

203 Perret, Michèle, 'Typologie des fins dans les œuvres de fiction (XIe–XVe siècles),' *PRIS-MA*, 14 (1998), 155–74.

See Qb78 Boutet.

204 Dragonetti, Roger, 'L'inachevable,' *PRIS-MA*, 15 (1999), 173–85.

205 *Erzählstrukturen* (LII.66)
- A. Fritz Peter Knapp, 'Historiographisches und fiktionales Erzählen in der zweiten Hälfte des 12. Jahrhunderts,' pp. 3–22. (LII.91)
- B. Matthias Meyer, 'Struktur und Person im Artusroman,' pp. 145–63. (LII.97)
- C. Gerhard Wild, '(Pseudo-)arthurisches *recycling* oder: wie die Symbolstruktur des Artusromans im Spätmittelalter "aufgehoben" ward,' pp. 291–310.

See also Db75 Schmid, Hb53 Kullmann, Hb54 Wolfzettel, Hc78 Burrichter, Hf105 Haug, and Pb461 Unzeitig-Herzog.

206 Delcourt, Thierry, *La Littérature arthurienne*, Que sais-je? 3578 (Paris: Presses Universitaires de France, 2000). (LIII.218)

207 Dragonetti, Roger, 'Les sirènes du roman médiéval,' *RLR*, 104 (2000), 1–22. (LIII.220)

208 Haug, Walter, 'Für eine Ästhetik des Widerspruchs: neue Überlegungen zur Poetologie des höfischen Romans,' in *Hof und Kloster*, pp. 211–28. (LII.84)

209 *The Cambridge Companion to Medieval Romance*, ed. Roberta L. Krueger, Cambridge Companions to Literature (Cambridge: Cambridge University Press, 2000).

 A. Roberta L. Krueger, 'Introduction,' pp. 1–9.
 B. Matilda Tomaryn Bruckner, 'The Shape of Romance in Medieval France,' pp. 13–28.
 C. Christopher Baswell, 'Marvels of Translation and Crises of Transition in the Romances of Antiquity,' pp. 29–44.
 D. Simon Gaunt, 'Romance and Other Genres,' pp. 45–59.
 E. Sylvia Huot, 'The Manuscript Context of Medieval Romance,' pp. 60–77.
 F. Sarah Kay, 'Courts, Clerks, and Courtly Love,' pp. 81–96.
 G. Richard Kaeuper, 'The Societal Role of Chivalry in Romance: Northwestern Europe,' pp. 97–114.
 H. Jeff Rider, 'The Other Worlds of Romance,' pp. 115–31.
 I. Roberta L. Krueger, 'Questions of Gender in Old French Courtly Romance,' pp. 132–49.
 J. Sheila Fisher, 'Women and Men in Late Medieval English Romance,' pp. 150–64.
 K. Norris J. Lacy, 'The Evolution and Legacy of French Prose Romance,' pp. 167–82.
 L. Ann Marie Rasmussen, 'Medieval German Romance,' pp. 183–202.
 M. F. Regina Psaki, 'Chivalry and Medieval Italian Romance,' pp. 203–17.
 N. Thomas Hahn, 'Gawain and Popular Chivalric Romance in Britain,' pp. 218–34.
 O. Felicity Riddy, 'Middle English Romance: Family, Marriage, Intimacy,' pp. 235–52.
 P. Marina S. Brownlee, 'Romance at the Crossroads: Medieval Spanish Paradigms and Cervantine Revisions,' pp. 253–66.

See Gd.c 71 Grisgby.

210 Jewers, Caroline A., *Chivalric Fiction and the History of the Novel* (Gainesville: University Press of Florida, 2000).
See Chap. 2: 'Northern Exposure: Chivalry and Parody in the Old French Tradition.'

211 Maddox, Donald, *Fictions of Identity in Medieval France*, CSML, 43 (Cambridge: Cambridge University Press, 2000).
See Chap. 2: 'The Specular Encounter in Arthurian Romance.'

212 Sweeney, Michelle, *Magic in Medieval Romance from Chrétien de Troyes to Geoffrey Chaucer* (Dublin: Four Courts Press, 2000). (LIII. 550)

213 Trachsler, Richard, *Disjointures–Conjointures: étude sur l'interférence des matières narratives dans la littérature française du Moyen Age*, Romanica Helvetica, 120 (Tübingen: Francke, 2000).

See Uc57 Vincensini.

214 Combes, Annie, and Annie Bertin, *Écritures du Graal: (XIIe–XIIIe siècles)*, Etudes Littéraires: Recto-verso (Paris: Presses Universitaires de France, 2001).

    A.   Annie Combes, 'Approche littéraire: inventions du Graal,' pp. 11–70.
    B.   Annie Bertin, 'Approche linguistique: mutations du Graal,' pp. 71–123.

See Ue9 Pierreville.

See Ba34 Varvaro.

b: Chrétien's Narrative (General)

3   Guiette, Robert, '"Li conte de Bretaigne [...]"' Repr. in Dc6.

4   Ménard, Philippe, 'Le Temps [...]' Repr. in Dc29.

5   Pellegrini, Silvio, 'Tabù del nome [...]'; repr. in his *Varietà romanza*, ed. G. E. Sansone, Biblioteca di Filologia Romanza, 28 (Bari: Adriatica, 1977), pp. 325–31. (XXX.427)

7   Jackson, W. T. H., 'Problems of Communication [...]' Repr. in Dc12.

See Fe1 Titchener.

16   Stănescu, Mihail, 'Chrétien de Troyes – de la mitologia celtică la romanul european,' in his trans. *Chrétien de Troyes: Cavalerul Lancelot* (Bucarest: Editura Albatros, 1973), pp. 149–79. (XXVIII.482)

17   Carasso-Bulow, Lucienne, *The Merveilleux in Chrétien de Troyes' Romances*, HICL, 153 (Geneva: Droz, 1976). (XXIX.227)

18   Friedman, A., 'A Case for Béroul's *Tristan* as an *Embourgeoisement* of the Tristan Legend,' *CN*, 36 (1976), 9–32. (XXXI.454)
Includes numerous comparisons with Chrétien.

19   Green, Dennis Howard, 'Knightly Homicide in Chrétien,' in Pb209 *Approaches*, pp. 75–82.

20   Warning, Rainer, 'Heterogeneity of Plot – Homogeneity of Narration: On the Constitution of Chrétien de Troyes' Romances,' *Esp*, 18:3 (1978), 41–54. (XXII.233)
Briefer English version of Ha97 Warning; German trans. of this briefer version: 'Heterogenität des Erzählten – Homogenität des Erzählens: zur Konstitution des höfischen Romans bei Chrétien de Troyes,' *W-S*, 5 (1979), 79–95. (XXXII.79)

21   Voicu, Mihaela, 'Quelques remarques sur la catégorie du temps dans les romans de Chrétien de Troyes,' *ABLs*, 27:1 (1978), 95–100.

22   Grigsby, John L., 'Narrative Voices in Chrétien de Troyes: A Prolegomenon to Dissection,' *RPh*, 32 (1978–79), 261–73. (XXXII.180)

See Sb30 Accarie.

23   Adams, Alison, 'Chrétien de Troyes et l'art de la mystification,' *SN*, 51 (1979), 295–304.

See Fb47 Decrevel.

24   Liborio, Mariantonia, '"Qui petit semme petit quelt": l'itinerario poetico di Chrétien de Troyes,' *Quaderno di lingua e letteratura francese*, 1 (1979), 29–90; repr. in *Studi e ricerche di letteratura francese*, ed. G. C. Menichelli and G. C. Roscioni (Naples: Istituto Universitario Orientale, 1980), vol. 1, pp. 9–70. (XXXIII.533)

See Sb31 Thompson.

25   Halász, Katalin, *Structures narratives chez Chrétien de Troyes*, SRD, 7 (Debrecen: Kossuth Lajos Tudományegyetem, 1980). (XXXV.544)

26   Lacy, Norris J., *The Craft of Chrétien de Troyes: An Essay on Narrative Art*, Davis Medieval Texts and Studies, 3 (Leiden: Brill, 1980). (XXXIII.154)

27   Virdis, Maurizio, *Intreccio, strutture, narrazione e discorso nel romanzo: il caso di Chrétien de Troyes (analisi dell'"Erec et Enide" e dell'"Yvain")* (Cagliari: Istituto di Filologia Moderna della Facoltà di Lettere e Filosofia dell'Università degli Studi di Cagliari, 1980). (XXXIII.539)

See Db24(B) Jones.

See Db24(I) Maddox.

See Db24(J) Schenck.

28 Gallais, Pierre, *Dialectique du récit médiéval (Chrétien de Troyes et l'hexagone logique)*, Faux Titre, 9 (Amsterdam: Rodopi, 1982).

29 Voicu, Mihaela, 'O modalitate de implicare a autorului în text: prologurile romanelor lui Chrétien de Troyes,' *ABLs*, 31 (1982), 41–44.

30 Uitti, Karl D., 'Récit et événements: perspective et sens,' in *La Nouvelle: formation, codification et rayonnement d'un genre médiéval: Actes du Colloque International de Montréal (McGill University, 14–16 octobre 1982)*, ed. Michelangelo Picone, Giuseppe Di Stefano, and Pamela D. Stewart, Bibliotheca Romanica (Montréal: Plato, 1983), pp. 9–15. (XXXVIII.557)

31 Uitti, Karl D., 'Vernacularization and Old French Mythopoesis with Emphasis on Chrétien's *Erec et Enide*,' in *Sower*, pp. 81–115. (XXXV.192)

See Jb33 Accarie.

32 Ollier, Marie-Louise, 'Utopie et roman arthurien,' *CCM*, 27 (1984), 223–32. Repr. in Dc32. (XXXVII.105)

See Pa151 Owen.

33 Williamson, Edwin, 'The Art of Chrétien de Troyes,' in Pg16 Williamson, pp. 1–28.

34 Kelly, Douglas, 'Romance and the Vanity of Chrétien de Troyes,' in Ha127 Brownlee, pp. 74–90. (XXXVIII.512)

See Fb66 Monson.

35 Mullally, Evelyn, *The Artist at Work: Narrative Technique in Chrétien de Troyes*, TAPS, 78:4 (Philadelphia: American Philosophical Society, 1988). (XLII.336)
Chapters on all Arthurian romances except *Perceval*.

See Jb38 Nightingale.

See Kc86 Ollier.

See Sb47 Wunderli.

36   Helm, Joan, 'Examples of the Use of the Golden Ratio in Medieval Arthurian Literature,' *QetF*, 9:1–2 (1988–89), 7–14. (XLI.396)

See Lb3 Runte.

See Jb40 Szabics.

See Gb98 Vilella Morató.

See Gf35 Aguiriano.

37   Kay, Sarah, 'Commemoration, Memory and the Role of the Past in Chrétien de Troyes: Retrospection and Meaning in *Erec et Enide*, *Yvain* and *Perceval*,' *RMS*, 17 (1991), 31–50. (XLIV.107)

38   Maddox, Donald, *The Arthurian Romances of Chrétien de Troyes: Once and Future Fictions*, CSML, 12 (Cambridge: Cambridge University Press, 1991). (XLIV.116)

See Pg22 Williamson.

39   Greiner, Thorsten, 'Das Erzählen, das Abenteuer und ihre "sehr schöne Verbindung": zur Begründung fiktionalen Schreibens in Chrétiens de Troyes *Erec*-Prolog,' *Poetica*, 24 (1992), 300–16. (XLVI.67)

40   Helm, Joan, 'Golden Arthurian Symbolism in Twelfth-Century France,' in *In the Place of French: Essays on and around French Studies in Honour of Michael Spencer* ([St Lucia]: University of Queensland; Mount Nebo, Queensland: Boombana, 1992), pp. 51–68.

See Uc33 Aguiriano.

See Fb83(C) Blons-Pierre.

41   Staines, David, 'Chrétien de Troyes and his Narrator/s,' in *The Centre and its Compass: Studies in Medieval Literature in Honor of Professor John Leyerle*, ed. Robert A. Taylor, SMC, 33 (Kalamazoo: Medieval Institute, Western Michigan University, 1993), pp. 417–56. (XLVI.773)

42   Stierle, Karlheinz, 'Die Unverfügbarkeit der Erinnerung und das Gedächtnis der Schrift: über den Ursprung des Romans bei Chrétien de Troyes,' in *Memoria: Vergessen und Erinnern*, ed. Anselm Haverkamp and Renate Lachmann, with Reinhart Herzog, PH, 15 (Munich: Fink, 1993), pp. 117–59.

43   Voicu, Mihaela, 'La description chez Chrétien de Troyes: lectures des signes, "effet de reel" ou "effet de texte"?' in *Actes Zurich*, pp. 429–42. (XLVII.662)

See Qb70 Fourquet.

44   Notz, Marie-Françoise, 'La fin du récit chez Chrétien de Troyes: amour et chevalerie en quête de détermination,' in *Amour Troyes*, pp. 343–50. (XLIX.176)

45   Ribard, Jacques, 'Amour et oubli dans les romans de Chrétien de Troyes,' in *Amour Troyes*, pp. 83–91. (XLIX.183)

See Gb125(C) Rieger.

46   Runte, Hans R., 'True Lies: From Speaking Courtly to Courtspeak,' *RLA*, 7 (1995), 154–58.

47   Voicu, Mihaela, 'Ironie et dialogue, deux aspects de l'intertextualité chez Chrétien de Troyes,' *ABLs*, 44 (1995), 3–16.

48   Maddox, Donald, 'Cyclicity, Transtextual Coherence, and the Romances of Chrétien de Troyes,' in *Transtextualities: Of Cycles and Cyclicity in Medieval French Literature*, ed. Sara Sturm-Maddox and Donald Maddox, MRTS, 149 (Binghamton, NY: Medieval and Early Renaissance Texts and Studies, 1996), pp. 39–52.

49   Wieczorkiewicz, Anna, *Wędrowcy fikcyjnych światów: Pielgrzym, rycerz i włóczęga*, Idee (Gdańsk: wydawnictwo słowo/obraz terytoria, 1996).

50   *Panvini, Bruno, *'Matière' e 'sen' nei romanzi di Chrétien de Troyes* (Rome: Il Calamo, 1997).

51   *Demaules, Mireille, 'Chrétien de Troyes ou l'épanchement du rêve dans la fiction,' *SpecMA*, 3:1–2 (1998), 21–37.

52   Voicu, Mihaela, *Chrétien de Troyes: aux sources du roman européen*, Philologica Bucarestiensia, 2 (Bucarest: Editura Universităţii din Bucureşti, 1998). (LI.714)

See Hc78 Burrichter.

53   Kullmann, Dorothea, 'Frühe Formen der Parallelhandlung in Epos und Roman: zu den Voraussetzungen von Chrétiens *Conte du Graal*,' in *Erzählstrukturen*, pp. 23–45. (LII.93)

See Ge69 Noacco.

54 Wolfzettel, Friedrich, 'Doppelweg und Biographie,' in *Erzähl-strukturen*, pp. 119–41. (LII.125)
See also Db75 Schmid, Hc78 Burrichter.

55 Haug, Walter, 'Die neue Poetologie der vulgärsprachlichen Dichtung des 12. Jahrhunderts,' *W-S*, 16 (2000), 70–83. (LIII.78)

c: *Erec et Enide*

13 Frappier, Jean, 'Pour le commentaire [...]' Repr. in Dc2.

20 Plummer, J. F., '*Bien dire* [...]' (XXVII.253)

21 Pickens, Rupert T., '*Estoire, lai* [...]' (XXVIII.144)

22 Singer, Samuel, 'Erec,' in *Vom Werden des deutschen Geistes: Festgabe Gustav Ehrismann zum 8. Oktober 1925 dargebracht von Freunden und Schülern*, ed. Paul Merker and Wolfgang Stammler (Berlin: de Gruyter, 1925), pp. 61–65.

See Fa69(A) Bertau.

23 Huppé, Bernard F., 'The Gothic Hero: Chrétien's *Erec*,' in *Twelfth Century*, pp. 1–19.

24 Wolfzettel, Friedrich, 'Le rôle du père dans le procès d'arthurisation du sujet d'*Erec/Gereint*,' *MrR*, 25 (1975), 95–104. (XXIX.163)

See Gb38 Bender.

See Md31 Cormier.

See Jb23 Meneghetti.

25 Clark, S. L., and Julian N. Wasserman, 'Language, Silence, and Wisdom in Chrétien's *Erec et Enide*,' *MichA*, 9 (1976–77), 285–98. (XXX.128)

26 Mandel, Jerome, 'The Ethical Context of Erec's Character,' *FR*, 50 (1976–77), 421–28. (XXX.135)

See Gd.c12 Halász.

27 Maddox, Donald, 'Greimas in the Realm of Arthur: Toward an Analytical Model for Medieval Romance,' *Esp*, 17:3 (1977), 179–94. (XXXI.111 *bis*)

28 Maddox, Donald, 'Nature and Narrative in Chrétien's *Erec et Enide*,' *Mediaevalia*, 3 (1977), 59–82. (XXXI.112)

See Fb44 Maddox.

29 Maddox, Donald, *Structure and Sacring: The Systematic Kingdom in Chrétien's 'Erec et Enide'*, FFM, 8 (Lexington, KY: French Forum, 1978). (XXXI.113)

30 Maddox, Donald, 'The Structure of Content in Chrétien's *Erec et Enide*,' *Mélanges Wathelet-Willem*, pp. 381–94. (XXXI.193)

31 Suard, F., 'La réconciliation d'Erec et d'Enide: de la parole destructrice à la parole libératrice (*Erec*, 4879–4893),' *Bien dire*, 1 (1978), 86–105. (XXXI.305)
Cf. Hc51 Suard.

32 Coghlan, Maura, 'The Flaw in Enide's Character: A Study of Chrétien de Troyes' *Erec*,' *RMS*, 5 (1979), 21–37. (XXXII.409)

33 Gier, Albert, 'Zu einer neuen Interpretation von Chrétiens *Erec et Enide*,' *ZrP*, 95 (1979), 92–103.
On Hc 29 Maddox.

See Ua21 Leclercq.

See Pb228 Mayer.

34 Sargent-Baur, Barbara Nelson, 'Erec's Enide: "sa fame ou s'amie"?' *RPh*, 33 (1979–80), 373–87. (XXXIII.168)

35 Iyasere, Marla W. Mudar, 'The Tripartite Structure of Chrétien's *Erec et Enide*,' *Mediaevalia*, 6 (1980), 105–21. (XXXVII.400)

See Qa51 Luttrell.

36 Scully, Terence, 'The *Sen* of Chrétien de Troyes's *Joie de la cort*,' in *ICLS Athens*, pp. 71–94. (XXXII.218)

See Hb27 Virdis.

37 Nelson, Deborah, 'Enide: *Amie* or *Femme*?' *RomN*, 21 (1980–81), 358–63. (XXXIV.142)

See Db24(H) Sturm-Maddox.

38 Archambault, Paul J., 'Erec's Search for a New Language: Chrétien and Twelfth-Century Science,' *Symp*, 35:1 (1981), 3–17. (XXXIV.103)
Chrétien and the School of Chartres.

See Sb32 Bogdanow.

39 Burgess, Glyn S., 'The Theme of Beauty in Chrétien's *Philomena* and *Erec et Enide*,' in *Essays Thorpe*, pp. 114–28. (XXXIV.300)

40 Fassò, Andrea, 'Erec, lo sparviero e il cervo bianco,' *Lectures*, 7–8 (1981), 57–89. (XXXIV.439)

41 Hart, Thomas Elwood, 'The *quadrivium* and Chrétien's Theory of Composition: Some Conjunctures and Conjectures,' *Symp*, 35 (1981), 57–86. (XXXIV.130)
Numerical composition.

See Jf10 Murphy.

See Me21 Uitti.

See Qe15 Le Goff.

See Ga32 Ménage.

42 Mussetter, Sally, 'The Education of Chrétien's Enide,' *RR*, 73 (1982), 147–66. (XXXVII.432)

43 Sturm-Maddox, Sara, 'The *Joie de la Cort*: Thematic Unity in Chrétien's *Erec et Enide*,' *Rom*, 103 (1982), 513–28. (XXXVI.369)

44 Laidlaw, J. C., 'Rhyme, Reason and Repetition in *Erec et Enide*,' in *Studies Diverres*, pp. 129–37, 245–46. (XXXVI.443)

45 Sullivan, Penny, 'The Presentation of Enide in the *premier vers* of Chrétien's *Erec et Enide*,' *MAe*, 52 (1983), 77–89. (XXXVI.468)

See Hb31 Uitti.

See Uc23 Allard.

46 Bender, Karl-Heinz, 'Beauté, mariage, amour: la genèse du premier roman courtois,' in *Amour mariage*, pp. 173–83. (XXXVII.574)

See Gb73 Bender.

47   Collins, Frank, 'A Semiotic Approach to Chrétien de Troyes's *Erec et Enide*,' *AInt*, 15:2 (1984), 25–31. (XXXVII.355)

48   Gouttebroze, Jean-Guy, 'La chasse au blanc cerf et la conquête de l'épervier dans *Erec et Enide*,' *Mélanges Planche*, pp. 213–24. (XXXVII.84)

49   Mussetter, Sally, 'The Fairy Arts of *mesure* in Chrétien's *Erec*,' *KRQ*, 31 (1984), 9–22. (XXXVII.433)

50   Pérennec, René, 'La "faute" d'Enide: transgression ou inadéquation entre un projet poétique et des stéréotypes de comportement?' in *Amour mariage*, pp. 153–59. (XXXVII.651)

See Qc49 Salvini and Fassò.

See Kd97 Sargent-Baur.

See Fb58 Sturm-Maddox and Maddox.

51   Suard, François, 'Réconciliation d'Erec et Enide,' in *Chrétien Bruges*, pp. 27–44. (XXXVII.121)

52   Cropp, Glynnis M., 'Count Caloain's Courting of Enide,' *Parergon*, 3 (1985), 53–62.

See Hf59 Gier.

See Qa73 Gouttebroze.

See Ub26 Salinero.

See Ga53 Sullivan.

See Pb301 Fisher.

53   Panvini, Bruno, *L''Erec et Enide' di Chrétien de Troyes: 'conte d'aventure' e 'conjointure'*, Università di Catania: Collana di Studi di Filologia, 3 (Catania: CUECM, 1986).

See Uc25 Allard.

See Ga56 Armstrong.

See Me27 Firestone.

54   Owen, D. D. R., 'Reward and Punishment in Chrétien's *Erec* and Related Texts,' in *Rewards and Punishments in the Arthurian Romances* *and Lyric Poetry of Mediaeval France: Essays Presented to Kenneth Varty on the Occasion of His Sixtieth Birthday*, ed. Peter V. Davies and Angus J. Kennedy (Cambridge: Brewer, 1987), pp. 119–32. (XL.131)

See Md38 Patterson.

See Na.e45 Thomas.

See Fb69 Vance.

See Sb43 Aguiriano Barron.

55 Bradley-Cromey, Nancy, 'The "Recreantise" Episode in Chrétien's *Erec et Enide*,' in *Chivalry*, pp. 449–71.

56 Brumlik, Joan, 'Chrétien's Enide: Wife, Mistress and Metaphor,' *RomQ*, 35 (1988), 401–14. (XLI.356)

See Gd.c35 Halász.

57 Illingworth, R. N., 'Structural Interlace in *Li Premiers Vers* of Chrétien's *Erec et Enide*,' *NM*, 89 (1988), 391–405.

58 Nelson, Deborah, 'The Role of Animals in *Erec et Enide*,' *RomQ*, 35 (1988), 31–38. (XLI.422)

59 Goulden, Oliver, 'Erec et Enide: The Structure of the Central Section,' *AL*, 9 (1989), 1–24. (XLII.659)

See Ke11 Grimbert.

60 Katzenmeier, Ursula, *Das Schachspiel des Mittelalters als Strukturierungsprinzip der Erec-Romane*, Beiträge zur älteren Literaturgeschichte (Heidelberg: Winter, 1991). (XLII.556)

See Ga66 Bossy.

See Ud3 Stanbury.

61 Henwood, Dawn E., 'Le narrateur dans *Erec et Enide* de Chrétien de Troyes,' *Initiales*, 10–11 (1990–91), 3–9.

62 Aguiriano, Begoña, 'La iniciación del caballero en Chrétien: *Erec et Enide*,' in *Evolución*, pp. 35–57. (XLVI.220)

63 Middleton, Roger, 'Structure and Chronology in *Erec et Enide*,' *NFS*, 30:2 (1991), 43–80. (XLIV.118)

64 Brumlik, Joan, 'The Knight, the Lady, and the Dwarf in Chrétien's *Erec*,' *QetF*, 2:2 (1992), 54–72. (XLVI.692)

See Fa151 Clemente, Chap. 2: 'Chrétien de Troyes' Perfect Prince.'

See Fb82 Amtower.

65 Brumlik, Joan, 'Kinship and Kingship in Chrétien's *Erec*,' *RPh*, 47 (1993), 177–92. (XLVI.693)

66 Fourquet, Jean, 'L'épisode de Joie de la Cour dans l'*Erec* de Chrétien de Troyes: sa signification pour l'histoire littéraire médiévale,' in *Erec*, pp. 43–50. (XLVI.62)
Revised reprint of La7.

67 Gaudet, Minnette, 'The Denial of Feminine Subjectivity in Chrétien's Enide,' *RLA*, 5 (1993), 40–46.

68 McCracken, Peggy, 'Silence and the Courtly Wife: Chrétien de Troyes's *Erec et Enide*,' *AY*, 3 (1993), 107–26. (XLVI.751)

See Ud10 Ramey.

69 Dulac, Liliane, 'Peut-on comprendre les relations entre Erec et Enide?' *MA*, 100 (1994), 37–50. (XLVII.3)

70 Goulden, Oliver, '*Erec et Enide*: le masque de la courtoisie,' in *Le Monde des héros dans la culture médiévale*, ed. Danielle Buschinger and Wolfgang Spiewok, WODAN, 35: EG, 20–TS, 18 (Greifswald: Reineke, 1994), pp. 115–29. (XLVII.91)

71 Pintarič, Mitra, 'Le rôle de la violence dans le roman médiéval: l'exemple d'*Erec et Enide*,' in *Violence*, pp. 413–23. (XLVII.288)

72 Amor, Lidia, 'El protagonismo del *roman courtois* en la conformación de la narrativa medieval francesa,' in *'El cuento': Homenaje a María Teresa Maiorana: II Coloquio Internacional de Literatura Comparada, Buenos Aires, 12–15 de octubre de 1995*, 2 vols (Buenos Aires: Fundación María Teresa Maiorana, 1995), vol. 2, pp. 227–35.

73 Helm, Joan, 'Deus si beles ymages, une molt bele conjointure,' *AUMLA*, 84 (1995), 85–110.

74 Nightingale, Jeanne A., 'Erec in the Mirror: The Feminization of the Self and the Re-invention of the Chivalric Hero in Chrétien's First Romance,' in Gb125 *Arthurian Romance*, pp. 130–46.

75 Geninasca, Catherine, 'De l'usage de motifs de contes dans un roman "moderne": Erec de Chrétien de Troyes,' in *Folk Narrative and World View: Vorträge des 10. Kongresses der Internationalen Gesellschaft für Volkserzählungsforschung (ISFNR) Innsbruck 1992*, ed. Leander Petzoldt, 2 vols, Beiträge zur europäischen Ethnologie und Folklore, ser. B: Tagungsberichte und Materialien, 7 (Frankfurt/M.: P. Lang, 1996), vol. 1, pp. 199–208.

See Ga92 Murray.

76 Seebass-Linggi, Claudia, *Lecture d''Erec': traces épiques et troubadouresques dans le conte de Chrétien de Troyes*, EH:F, 211 (Bern: P. Lang, 1996). (XLIX.440)

77 Burrell, Margaret, 'The Specular Heroine: Self-Creation versus Silence in *Le Pèlerinage de Charlemagne* and *Erec et Enide*,' *Parergon*, 15:1 (1997), 83–99.

See Md49 Le Rider.

78 Burrichter, Brigitte, '"Ici fenist li premiers vers" (*Erec et Enide*) – noch einmal zur Zweiteilung des Chrétienschen Artusromans,' in *Erzählstrukturen*, pp. 87–98. (LII.66)

See Me40 Haas.

79 Houdeville, Michelle, 'Le beau et le laid: fonction et signification dans *Erec et Enide* de Chrétien de Troyes,' in *Beau et laid*, pp. 229–37. (LIII.244)

80 Noacco, Cristina, 'La dialectique du don dans la quête de la Joie d'*Erec et Enide*,' in *Mélanges Faucon*, pp. 299–311. (LIII.268)

d: *Cligés*

See Sc10 Hamel.

7 Levý, O., 'Psychologická analysa v "Cligésovi",' *Casopis*, 25 (1939), 63–70, 179–86.

8 Bergerfurth, Wolfgang, *Kommentar zu Chrétien de Troyes' Cligés*, diss. Mannheim (Mannheim: [s.p.], 1971). (XXIV.3)

See Sc15 Weber.

See Qd13 Shirt.

See Fb46 Haidu.

See Sc16 Kamizawa.

9 Micha, Alexandre, 'Cligès ou les folles journées,' in *Mélanges Wathelet-Willem*, pp. 447–54. (XXXI.196)

10 Freeman, Michelle A., *The Poetics of 'Translatio studii' and 'conjointure' in Chrétien de Troyes's 'Cligés'*, FFM, 12 (Lexington, KY: French Forum, 1979). (XXXII.178)

11 Kooijman, J. C., 'Cligès, héros ou anti-héros?' *Rom*, 100 (1979), 505–19. (XXXII.352)

12 Freeman, Michelle, 'Transpositions structurelles et intertextualité: le *Cligès* de Chrétien,' *Littérature*, 41 (1981), 50–61. (XXXV.316)

See Ma27 Hanning.

See Ga29 Nelson.

13 Stäblein, Patricia Harris, 'Transformation and Stasis in *Cligés*,' in *Essays Thorpe*, pp. 151–59. (XXXIV.378)

See He39 Burrell.

See Sc19 Freeman.

14 Maddox, Donald, 'Pseudo-Historical Discourse in Fiction: *Cligés*,' in *Essays in Early French Literature Presented to Barbara M. Craig*, ed. Norris J. Lacy and Jerry C. Nash (Columbia, SC: French Literature Publications Company, 1982), pp. 9–24. (XXXV.177)

See Qa61 Shirt.

See Gd.a18 Hanning.

15 Lacy, Norris J., '*Cligès* and Courtliness,' *AInt*, 15:2 (1984), 18–24. (XXXVII.413)

See Qc49 Salvini and Fassò.

16 Staines, David, '*Cliges*: Chrétien's Paradigmatic Experiment,' in *Courtly Romance*, pp. 251–72. (XXXVII.467)

See Lb1 Blumenfeld-Kosinski.

See Ub26 Salinero.

See Ga56 Armstrong.

See Pa191 Chase.

See Sc26 Curtis.

17 Enders, Jody, 'Memory and the Psychology of the Interior Monologue in Chrétien's *Cligés*,' *Rhetorica*, 10 (1992), 5–23.

See Ga82 Álvares.

See Qb67 Uitti.

18 Blons-Pierre, Catherine, 'Une lecture possible de l'amour et de la chevalerie dans *Cligés*: le baroque,' in *Amour Troyes*, pp. 221–29. (XLIX.130)

See Ud13 Over.

19 Toury, Marie-Noëlle, '"Courage, fuyons!" *Cligés* une écriture de l'antiphrase,' in *Amour Troyes*, pp. 191–201. (XLIX.195)

20 Voicu, Mihaela, '*Cligés* ou les miroirs de l'illusion,' in *Amour Troyes*, pp. 231–44. (XLIX.202)

See Fd6 Discenza.

See Qa119 Kinoshita.

21 Murphy, Diana L., 'Duelling Mirrors: Specularity in Chrétien de Troyes's *Cligès*,' *RLA*, 8 (1996), 74–78.

22 Álvares, Cristina, and Americo Diogo, 'La demande d'amour dans *Cliges* de Chrétien de Troyes,' *Bien dire*, 15 (1997), 109–17. (L.174)

See Md48 Zaganelli.

See Jb53 Wolfzettel.

23 Gingras, Francis, 'Les noces illusoires dans le récit médiéval (XIIe–XIIIe siècles),' in *Magie*, pp. 173–89. (LII.235)

See Bb79 Mulken.

e: *Le Chevalier de la charrette (Lancelot)*

15 Adams, Alison, 'Godefroi de Lagny's Continuation […]' (XXVII.276)

16 Mandel, Jerome, 'Proper Behavior […]' (XXVIII.140)

17   Shirt, David J., 'Godefroi de Lagny […]' (XXVIII.264)

18   Stuckey, William J., 'Chrétien de Troyes' Lancelot,' *Explicator*, 21 (1962–63), n° 38. (XVI.93)

See Sb28 Lyons.

19   Soudek, Ernst, 'The Origin and Function of Lancelot's Anonymity in Chrétien's *Le Chevalier de la charrette*,' *South Central Bulletin*, 30 (1970), 220–23.

20   Györy, Jean, 'La seconde naissance de Lancelot,' in *AnnBud*, 3 (1972), 53–79.

21   Györy, Jean, 'Esquisse d'une structure pour la *Charrette*,' in *AnnBud*, 4 (1973), 3–22.

22   Kamizawa, Eizô, 'Double Action in the *Chevalier de la charrette* by Chrétien de Troyes,' *JFLN*, 58 (1973), 109–22. (XXVII.386)
In Japanese.

23   Välikangas, Olli, 'A la recherche d'une identité: Godefroi de Leigni,' in *Actes Turku*, pp. 201–7.

24   Borsari, Anna Valeria, 'Il "sans" delle strutture sovrapposte nel *Chevalier de la charrete*,' *Atti dell'Accademia delle Scienze dell'Istituto di Bologna: Classe di Scienze Morali*, 68: *Rendiconti*, 62:2 (1973–74), 197–245. (XXVIII.391)

See Qd8 Brand.

25   Saly, Antoinette, 'Le cuens Guinables l'oï,' *Bulletin de la Faculté des Lettres de Mulhouse*, 6 (1974), 69–75.

26   Mickel, Emanuel J., Jr., 'The Theme of Honor in Chrétien's *Lancelot*,' *ZrP*, 91 (1975), 243–72. (XXVIII.57)

SeeQd11 Radulet.

See Gd.c9 Ribard.

27   Saly, Antoinette, 'Le pont de l'épée et la tour de Baudemagu,' *MedR*, 3 (1976), 51–65; repr. in Dc22. (XXIX.369)

28   Iker-Gittleman, Anne, 'Chrétien de Troyes, poète de la cour, dans *Le Chevalier de la charrette*,' *RPh*, 30 (1976–77), 152–58. (XXIX.115)

Court language in three episodes: the abduction of Guenevere, the Immodest Damsel, and the Tournament at Noauz.

See Bb29 Foulet.

See Gd.c12 Halász.

See Ra11 Kooijman.

29 White, Sarah Melhado, 'Lancelot on the Gameboard: The Design of Chrétien's *Charrette*,' *FF*, 2 (1977), 99–109. (XXX.147)

30 Deroy, Jean, 'Chrétien de Troyes et Godefroy de Leigni, conspirateurs contre la fin'amor adultère,' *CN*, 38 (1978), 67–78. (XXXII.476)

31 Fullman, Sally, '*Le jeu de miroirs*: The Role of the Secondary Women in *Le Chevalier de la charrete* of Chrétien de Troyes,' *Indiana Social Studies Quarterly*, 31 (1978), 18–28. (XXXI.96, XXXIII.143)

32 Haug, Walter, '*Das Land, von welchem niemand wiederkehrt':* Mythos, Fiktion und Wahrheit in Chrétiens 'Chevalier de la charrete', im 'Lanzelet' Ulrichs von Zatzikhoven und im 'Lancelot'-Prosaroman*, Untersuchungen zur deutschen Literaturgeschichte, 21 (Tübingen: Niemeyer, 1978). (XXXI.23)

33 Kooijman, J. C., 'Du conte au roman: recherches sur la structure du *Chevalier de la charrete* de Chrétien de Troyes,' *RR*, 69 (1978), 279–95. (XXXII.196)

See Kd84 Le Rider.

See Nb17 Saly.

See Db20 Shirt.

34 Williamson, Joan B., 'Suicide and Adultery in *Le Chevalier de la charrete*,' in *Mélanges Lods*, vol. 1, pp. 571–87. (XXXI.310)

See Ge31 Topsfield.

35 Tournon, André, 'Les masques de "senefiance" dans *Le Chevalier de la charette*,' in *Mélanges Jonin*, pp. 673–87. (XXXII.365)

See Ga22 Wolf.

36 Vinaver, Eugène, 'Landmarks in Arthurian Romance,' in *ICLS Athens*, pp. 17–31. (XXXII.232)

See Sb34 Morgan.

37   Ruiz Doménec, J. E., *El laberinto cortesano de la caballería. I: El juego como estructura de identidad en 'Le Chevalier de la charrete' de Chrétien de Troyes*, Medievalia: Monografias, 1 (Bellaterra: Instituto Universitario de Estudios Medievales, Universidad Autónoma de Barcelona, 1981). (XXXIV.210)
See Qc48 Ruiz Doménec.

38   Shirt, David J., '*Le Chevalier de la charrete*: A World Upside Down?' *MLR*, 76 (1981), 811–22. (XXXIV.375)

See Sb36 Topsfield.

39   Burrell, Margaret, 'From *Cliges* to *Le Chevalier de la charrete*: The Structural Uses of Treason, Treachery and Deceit,' *NZJFS*, 3 (1982), 5–20.

40   Lebsanft, Franz, 'Wer lacht über Lancelot? Zur Interpretation des Motivs der *demoiselle tentatrice* bei Chrétien de Troyes und im Prosa-*Lancelot*,' *RJ*, 33 (1982), 85–96. (XXXVI.50)

41   Verchère, Chantal, 'Du mépris à la méprise: l'impossible retour de Lancelot du Lac,' *CCM*, 25 (1982), 129–37.

See Ma28 Dornbush.

42   Borsari, Anna Valeria, *Lancillotto liberato: una ricerca intorno al 'fin amant' e all'eroe liberatore*, Università di Bologna: Pubblicazioni della Facoltà di Magistero, n. s. 12 (Florence: Nuova Italia, 1983). (XXXVI.520)
See also her 'Lancillotto liberato,' *Lectures*, 12 (1983), 55–76 (XXXVI.519) on the Godefroi de Lagny continuation.

See Ha118 Calin.

See Hf50 Krueger.

43   White, Sarah Melhado, 'Lancelot's Beds: Styles of Courtly Intimacy,' in *Sower*, pp. 116–26. (XXXV.195)

44   Beltrami, Pietro G., 'Racconto mitico e linguaggio lirico: per l'interpretazione del *Chevalier de la charrete*,' *SMV*, 30 (1984), 5–67. (XXXVIII.403)

See Ga42 Brewer.

45 Clark, Susan L., and Julian N. Wasserman, 'Putting the Cart before the Horse: Excess, Restraint, and Choices in Chrétien's *Chevalier de la charrete*,' *EsL*, 11 (1984), 127–35. (XXXVIII.482)

46 Gallais, Pierre, 'Meleagant et la contradiction,' in *Lancelot Picardie*, pp. 39–49.

See Fb56 Kelly.

47 Krueger, Roberta L., '"Tuit li autre": The Narrator and His Public in Chrétien de Troyes' *Le Chevalier de la charrete*,' in *Courtly Romance*, pp. 133–50. (XXXVII.412)

See Gd.c27 Molle.

48 Payen, Jean-Charles, 'Un auteur en quête de personnage: Chrétien de Troyes à la découverte de Lancelot,' in *Lancelot Picardie*, pp. 163–77.

49 Saly, Antoinette, 'L'épisode du Pré aux Jeux dans le *Chevalier de la charrette*,' in *Lancelot Picardie*, pp. 191–97; repr. in Dc22.

See Pa156 Schmolke-Hasselmann.

See Mf8 Walter.

50 Beltrami, Pietro G., 'Chrétien, l'amour, l'adultère: remarques sur le *Chevalier de la charrete*,' in *Actes Rennes*, vol. 1, pp. 59–69. (XXXVIII.185)

See Pk34 Boissinot and Lasserre.

51 Bruckner, Matilda Tomaryn, 'Essential and Gratuitous Inventions: Thomas' *Tristan* and Chrétien's *Lancelot*,' in *Actes Rennes*, vol. 1, pp. 120–41. (XXXVIII.195)

See Sb42 Burrell.

52 Chandès, Gérard, 'Le Pont de l'épée dans le *Chevalier de la charrete* et dans le *Lancelot* en prose,' *PRIS-MA*, 1 (1985), 37–43.

53 Janssens, Jan, 'L'obstacle dangereux dans le *Chevalier de la charrete*,' in *Actes Rennes*, vol. 1, pp. 346–53. (XXXVIII.230)
Use of irony.

See Bb51 Hult.

See Kd101 Janssens.

54   Maddox, Donald, 'Lancelot et le sens de la coutume,' *CCM*, 29 (1986), 339–53. (XXXIX.656)

55   Bruckner, Matilda Tomaryn, 'An Interpreter's Dilemma: Why Are There So Many Interpretations of Chrétien's *Chevalier de la charrette*?' *RPh*, 40 (1986–87), 159–80; repr. in Ga91. (XXXIX.223)

See Fb68 Sargent-Baur.

See Hf71 Sargent-Baur.

See Sb44 Citton.

See Fb71 Hult.

See Ud2 Krueger.

See Jb37 Moya.

See Bb55 Uitti.

See Lb2 Hult.

See Ub36 Álvares.

56   Beltrami, Pietro G., 'Lancelot entre Lanzelet et Eneas: remarques sur le sens du *Chevalier de la charrete*,' *ZfSL*, 99 (1989), 234–60. (XLII.499)

57   Benkov, Edith Joyce, 'Language and Women: From Silence to Speech,' in *Sign*, pp. 245–65.
Guenevere in the *Charrette*.

58   Brumlik, Joan, 'Illusory Duality in Chrétien's *Lancelot*,' *RomQ*, 36 (1989), 387–99. (XLVII.687)

59   Hult, David F., 'Author/Narrator/Speaker: The Voice of Authority in Chrétien's *Charrete*,' in *Discourses of Authority in Medieval and Renaissance Literature*, ed. Kevin Brownlee and Walter Stephens (Hanover, NH: University Press of New England, 1989), pp. 76–96, 267–69. (XLII.315)

See Bb56 Hult.

60   Janssens, Jan, 'Un "fin amant" et l'ironie romanesque: Lancelot et la chanson de change,' *AL*, 8 (1989), 29–78.

See Qc60 Sears.

61 Arden, Heather, 'Chrétien de Troyes's *Lancelot* and the Structure of Twelfth-Century French Romance,' in Da15 *King Arthur*, vol. 1, pp. 80–98. (XLIII.492)

62 Brownlee, Kevin, 'Transformations of the *Charrete*: Godefroi de Leigni Rewrites Chrétien de Troyes,' *SFR*, 14 (1990), 161–78. (XLIII.504)

63 García Gual, Carlos, 'El Caballero de la Carreta: Lanzarote,' pp. 17–23, 'El Caballero de la Carreta: temática y personajes,' pp. 25–44, and 'Amores de Lanzarote y de la reina Ginebra (consideraciones sobre el amor cortés),' pp. 45–59, in his *Lecturas y fantasías medievales* (Madrid: Mondadori España, 1990).

See Gc21 Salinero Cascante.

64 Brook, Leslie C., 'The Continuator's Monologue: Godefroy de Lagny and Jean de Meun,' *FS*, 45 (1991), 1–16. (XLIV.91)

65 Klüppelholz, Heinz, 'The Continuation *within* the Model: Godefroi de Lagny's "Solution" to Chrétien de Troyes' *Chevalier de la charrete*,' *Neophil*, 75 (1991), 637–40. (XLIV.263)

See Qa99 Stary.

See Pa234 Armstrong.

See Gb113 Rothschild.

66 Seaman, Gerald E., 'Sept questions à propos du *Chevalier de la charrette*,' *ZrP*, 108 (1992), 443–59. (XLVI.105)

67 Accarie, Maurice, 'Guenièvre et son Chevalier de la charrete: l'orgasme des anges,' in *Hommage Dufournet*, vol. 1, pp. 45–54. (XLVI.303)

See Ha168 Bruckner, Chap. 3: 'A Case for *mise en abyme*: Chrétien's *Chevalier de la charrete*.'

See Ud8 Krueger.

68 Steele, Stephen, 'Lancelot et Guinevere: l'amour dans l'oubli,' *Utah Foreign Language Review* (1993–94), pp. 81–85; repr. *LittéRéalité*, 7 (1995), 63–68.

69 Mickel, Emanuel J., Jr., 'The Conflict between *pitié* and *largesse* in the *Chevalier de la charrette*,' *NM*, 95 (1994), 31–36.

See Ub41–42 Salinero Cascante.

70   Brusegan, Rosanna. 'L'autre monde et le Chevalier de la charrette,' in *Recueil Micha*, pp. 77–85. (XLVIII.69)

See Ud11 Gaunt.
See pp. 91–103.

See Ha190 Guerin, Chap. 2.

See Sb53 Guerreau-Jalabert.

71   Williamson, Joan B., 'Le don contraignant et la coutume de Logres,' in *Recueil Micha*, pp. 389–99. (XLVIII.171)

72   Ferlampin-Acher, C., '*Le Chevalier de la charrette* de Chrétien de Troyes: *aventure* et *conjointure*,' *Bulletin de l'Association des Professeurs de Lettres*, 80 (Dec. 1996), 35–42.

73   Huchet, Jean-Charles, 'La loi de la Dame et le ravissement du roman,' in *Lancelot mythique*, pp. 101–24; repr. in Dc27.

74   Knepper, Wendy, 'Theme and Thesis in *Le Chevalier de la Charrete*,' *Arthuriana*, 6:2 (1996), 54–68. (XLIX.512)

See Fb92 Marchiori.

75   Sears, Theresa Ann, 'The Signifying System and the Crisis of Chivalry in *Le Chevalier de la Charette*,' *MedPer*, 11 (1996), 153–63.

See Uf2 Sturges.

See Ub47 Cohen.

76   Mathey-Maille, Laurence, 'Lancelot ou l'image du héros dans *Le Chevalier de la charrette*,' *InfLitt*, 49:5 (Nov.–Dec. 1997), 9–13.

See Rb34 Zemel.

77   Illingworth, R. N., 'Some Observations on the Structure of the Guiot *Charrete*,' *NM*, 100 (1999), 127–41.

See Ua22 Klassen.

See Jb57 Pipaprez.

See Jb59 Thomasset.

f: *Yvain (Le Chevalier au lion)*

See Ub5 Adler.

18 Jeschke, Hans, 'Ist Chrétiens *Yvain* ein Unterhaltungs- oder ein Thesenroman?' *ZrP*, 55 (1935), 673–81.

19 Snoy, Odette, *La structure et le sens du 'Chevalier au lion' de Chrétien de Troyes*, Mémoire Louvain (Louvain: Wouters, 1959).

See Qd8 Brand.

See Jb21 Györy.

See Uc9 Le Goff.

20 Ollier, Marie-Louise, 'Nom, désir, aventure: les structures latentes d'un roman courtois,' *Far-Western Forum*, 1 (1974), 221–32. Repr. in Dc32.

See Qd6 Combellack.

21 Edwards, Robert, 'The Problem of Closure in Chrétien's *Yvain*,' in *Twelfth Century*, pp. 119–29.

22 Hoek, Leo H., 'Contribution à une délimitation séquentielle du texte: l'exemple du *Chevalier au lion* (*Yvain*),' in *Mélanges de linguistique et de littérature offerts à Lein Geschiere par ses amis, collègues et amis* (Amsterdam: Rodopi, 1975), pp. 181–208. (XXVIII.476)

See Qd10 Pasero.

23 Lonigan, Paul R., 'Calogrenant's Journey and the Mood of the "Yvain",' *SF*, 58 (1976), 1–20. (XXIX.364)

See Qd12 Marazza.

24 Ménage, René, 'Sur un passage du *Chevalier au lion*: tentative d'explication de texte (vers 677 à 722),' *RT*, 13 (March 1976), 84–89.

25 Severin, Nelly H., 'The Function of the Magic Fountain in Chrétien's *Yvain*,' *Chimères* (Spring 1976), pp. 27–37.

26 Newstead, Helaine, 'Narrative Techniques in Chrétien's *Yvain*,' *RPh*, 30 (1976–77), 431–41. (XXX.139)

27 Forrer, Andreas, 'Gefühl und Verstand: eine Lebensgemeinschaft im *Chevalier au lion*,' in *Spaltung und Doppelung: Momente eines literarischen Motives* (Zürich: Juris, 1977), pp. 43–51.

See Gd.c12 Halász.

See Fd1 Hunt.

See Ra11 Kooijman.

See Qa45 Matthias.

28 Accarie, Maurice, 'La structure du *Chevalier au lion* de Chrétien de Troyes,' *MA*, 84 (1978), 13–34. (XXXI.183)

29 Fogg, Sarah, 'The Function of Split Personality in Chrétien's *Yvain*,' in *Selected Proceedings of the Twenty-Seventh Annual Mountain Interstate Foreign Language Conference, October 13–15, 1977* (Johnson City: East Tennessee State University, 1978), pp. 114–21.

30 Houdeville-Augier, Michelle, 'Le phénomène de l'exclusion dans l'épisode de la folie d'Yvain, le Chevalier au lion,' in *Exclus*, pp. 331–43. (XXX.276)

31 Lonigan, Paul R., *Chrétien's 'Yvain': A Study of Meaning through Style* (Ann Arbor, MI: University Microfilms for CUNY, 1978). (XXXII. 201)

32 Noble, P. S., 'Irony in *Le Chevalier au lion*,' *BBSIA*, 30 (1978), 196–208.

33 Assous, Joelle, 'Les trois triangles et la fontaine médiatrice dans *Yvain*,' *BF*, 8:1 (Fall 1979), 48–61.

34 Burrell, Margaret, 'The Fountain and Its Function in *Yvain*,' *AUMLA*, 52 (1979), 288–95.

35 Pioletti, Antonio, 'Lettura dell'episodio del "Chastel de Pesme-Aventure" (*Yvain*, vv. 5101–5805),' *MedR*, 6 (1979), 227–46. (XXXIII.537)

36 Schuh, Hans-Manfred, 'Epik,' esp. '*Yvain ou le Chevalier au lion* (um 1177),' in *Einführung in das Studium der französischen Literaturwissenschaft: Daten und Interpretationen*, ed. Wolf-Dieter Lange, Uni-Taschenbücher, 715 (Heidelberg: Quelle & Meyer, 1979), pp. 93–110.

37   Szabics, Imre, 'Motifs récurrents dans "Le Chevalier au lion" de Chrétien de Troyes,' in *AnnBud*, 10 (1979), 3–15.

See Qd15 Voisset.

38   Uitti, Karl D., 'Narrative and Commentary: Chrétien's Devious Narrator in *Yvain*,' *RPh*, 33 (1979–80), 160–67. (XXXII.230)

39   Brault, Gerard J., 'Fonction et sens de l'épisode du Château de Pesme Aventure dans l'*Yvain* de Chrétien de Troyes,' in *Mélanges Foulon*, vol. 1, pp. 59–64. (XXXIII.314)

See Fa106 Limentani.
Pp. 310–11 on *Yvain*.

40   Uitti, Karl D., 'Intertextuality in *Le Chevalier au lion*,' *DFS*, 2 (1980), 3–13. (XXXIV.152, XXXVI.194)

See Hb27 Virdis.

41   Zaddy, Z. P., 'Chrétien misogyne,' in *Mélanges Foulon*, vol. 2, pp. 301–7. (XXXIII.382)

42   Thorpe, Lewis, 'L'*Yvain* de Chrétien de Troyes et le jeu des topoi,' *OetC*, 5:2 (1980–81), 73–80. (XXXIV.255)

43   Clark, Susan L., and Julian N. Wasserman, 'Conflict and Resolution: Implications of Enclosure in Chrétien's *Yvain*,' *EsL*, 8 (1981), 63–72. (XXXVI.164)

See Me20 Diverres.

See Gb64 Ferran.

44   Runte, Hans R., 'Yvain: "Li chevaliers qui s'an fuioit",' *Incidences*, 5 (1981), 17–25. (XXXV.184)

45   Shirt, David J., 'Was King Arthur Really "Mad"? Some Comments on the *Charrete* References in *Yvain*,' in *Essays Thorpe*, pp. 187–202. (XXXIV.374).

See Sb37 Bogdanow.

46   Gyurcsik, Margareta, 'Chrétien de Troyes: *Yvain* ou *Le Chevalier au lion* – un modèle d'analyse,' in *La Littérature française du Moyen Age et de la Renaissance: choix de textes, plans d'analyse,* *commentaires critiques* (Timişoara: Tipografia Universității din Timişoara, 1982), pp. 22–27.

See Jb30 Heffernan.

47 Kratins, Ojars, *The Dream of Chivalry: A Study of Chrétien de Troyes's 'Yvain' and Hartmann von Aue's 'Iwein'* (Washington, DC: University Presses of America, 1982). (XXXVI.178)

48 Maraud, André, 'La lectrice dans le roman (*Yvain*, v. 5354–5395),' in *Le lecteur et la lecture dans l'œuvre: Actes du Colloque International de Clermont-Ferrand, décembre 1981*, ed. Alain Montandon, Publications de la Faculté des Lettres et Sciences Humaines de Clermont-Ferrand II, n. s. 15 (Clermont-Ferrand: Presses de l'Association de Publications de la Faculté des Lettres et Sciences Humaines de Clermont-Ferrand, 1982), pp. 155–62.

See Ge34 Pavel.

49 Ruiz Doménec, J. E., *El laberinto cortesano de la caballería. II: La diferencia como límite exterior del juego en el 'Chevalier au lion' de Chrétien de Troyes*, Medievalia: Monografias, 2 (Bellaterra: Instituto Universitario de Estudios Medievales, Universidad Autónoma de Barcelona, 1982).
See Qc48 Ruiz Doménec.

See Uc20 Verhuyck.

See Qe19 Haidu.

See Me23 Hunt.

See Qd17 Knight.

50 Krueger, Roberta L., 'Reading the *Yvain/Charrete*: Chrétien's Inscribed Audiences at Noauz and Pesme Aventure,' *FMLS*, 19 (1983), 172–87. (XXXVI.442)

See Ga39 Press.

See Fa123 Szabics.

51 Arrathoon, Leigh A., 'Jacques de Vitry, the Tale of Calogrenant, *La Chastelaine de Vergi* and the Genres of Medieval Narrative Fiction,' in *Craft*, pp. 281–368. (XXXVII.338)

See Ga42 Brewer.

52 Dubost, Francis, 'Le *Chevalier au lion*: une "conjointure" signifiante,' *MA*, 90 (1984), 195–222. (XXXVII.7)

See Bb44 Foulet and Uitti.

53 García Peinado, Miguel Ángel, 'Apuntes para una lectura de *Yvain, le Chevalier au lion*,' *Alfinge*, 2 (1984), 115–28.

54 Grimbert, Joan Tasker, 'Adversative Structure in Chrétien's *Yvain*: The Role of the Conjunction *mes*,' *MedR*, 9 (1984), 27–50. (XXXVII.276)

See Qe20 Haidu.

55 Hunt, Tony, 'Beginnings, Middles, and Ends: Some Interpretative Problems in Chrétien's *Yvain* and its Medieval Adaptations,' in *Craft*, pp. 83–117. (XXXVII.396)

56 Laidlaw, James, 'Shame Appeased: On the Structure and the *sen* of the *Chevalier au Lion*,' in *Essays Topsfield*, pp. 195–219. (XXXVII.171)

See Pb293 Rocher.

57 Santucci, Monique, 'Amour, mariage et transgressions dans le *Chevalier au lion* ou il faut transgresser pour progresser,' in *Amour mariage*, pp. 161–71. (XXXVII.665)

See Gb78 Krueger.

58 Lecco, Margherita, 'Livelli di cultura nel romanzo cortese: la modellizzazione spaziale nell'*Yvain*,' *FeS*, 5–8 (1984–87), 61–78. (XLI.270)

59 Gier, Albert, 'Leo est femina: Yvain, Enide und der Löwe,' pp. 269–88 in Sa109 Ruhe.

60 Grimbert, Joan Tasker, 'On the Prologue of Chrétien's *Yvain*: Opening Functions of Keu's Quarrel,' *PQ*, 64 (1985), 391–98. (XXXVIII.500)

61 Lock, Richard, *Aspects of Time in Medieval Literature*, Garland Publications in Comparative Literature (New York: Garland, 1985). (XXXIX.294)
See pp. 62–79, 186–206.

62 Szabics, Imre, 'La fonction poétique des structures syntaxiques récurrentes dans l'*Yvain* de Chrétien de Troyes,' in *Actes Rennes*, vol. 2, pp. 584–99. (XXXVIII.269)

See Mf9 Walter.

63 Figueiredo de Carvalho, Teresa, 'Le moi et les autres: l'aventure de la réconciliation dans *Le Chevalier au lion*,' *Ariane*, 4 (1986), 19–28.

64 Grimbert, Joan Tasker, 'Chrétien's *Yvain*: A Reflection on Romance Ideals,' *Avalon*, 2:3 (1986–87), 8–10.

See Fa136 Maddox.

65 Struyf, Marie-Claude, 'Les visages de Janus ou l'ambivalence de l'image de la forêt dans *Yvain* de Chrétien de Troyes,' *PRIS-MA*, 2 (1986), 41–50. (XXXIX.674)

See Jf13 Aguiriano.

See Ub31 Aubailly.

See Gd.b33 Colliot.

66 Gallais, Pierre, '*Yvain* et la logique "hexagonale" de l'imaginaire,' *PRIS-MA*, 3 (1987), 33–46; 4 (1988), 21–64. (XLI.60)

67 Glasser, Marc, 'Marriage and the Use of Force in *Yvain*,' *Rom*, 108 (1987), 484–502. (XLIII.178)

See Ke10 Haidu.

68 Notz, Marie-Françoise, 'Le dénouement d'Yvain: le seuil et le signe,' *PRIS-MA*, 3 (1987), 145–52. (XLI.78)

69 Ribard, Jacques, 'Calogrenant, Cahus et la Rose,' *PRIS-MA*, 3 (1987), 153–58; repr. in Dc25. (XLI.83)

70 Saly, Antoinette, 'Le *Chevalier au lion*: un jeu de cache-cache?' *PRIS-MA*, 3 (1987), 159–66; repr. in Dc22. (XLI.86)

See Fb68 Sargent-Baur.

71 Sargent-Baur, Barbara Nelson, 'With Catlike Tread: The Beginning of Chrétien's *Chevalier au lion*,' *Studies Woledge*, pp. 163–73.
Cf. Fb68 Sargent-Baur.

See Fb69 Vance.

72   Walter, Philippe, 'Yvain, "L'ogre et les trois jeunes filles" (autour d'un conte bulgare),' *PRIS-MA*, 3 (1987), 67–78. (XLI. 95)

See Qc54 Arthur.

73   Nicholson, Peter, 'The Adventures at Laudine's Castle in Chrétien de Troyes's *Yvain*,' *Allegorica*, 9 (1987–88), 195–219.

See Sb43 Aguiriano Barron.

See Gd.b35 Baumgartner.

74   Dubost, Francis, 'Merveilleux et fantastique dans *Le chevalier au lion*,' in *Chevalier au lion*, pp. 47–76. (XLI.56)

See Gc16 Dufournet.

75   Grimbert, Joan Tasker, *'Yvain' dans le miroir: une poétique de la réflexion dans le 'Chevalier au lion' de Chrétien de Troyes*, Purdue University Monographs in Romance Languages, 25 (Amsterdam: Benjamins, 1988). (XLI.388)

See Gd.c35 Halász.

See Fb72 Kelly.

76   Maddox, Donald, 'Yvain et le sens de la coutume,' *Rom*, 109 (1988), 1–17. (XLIV.40)

See Ge47 Marache.

See Gf29 Ménard.

See Uc27 Planche.

See Jb39 Ribard.

See Fb74 Sakari.

77   Santucci, Monique, 'La folie dans le *Chevalier au lion*,' in *Chevalier au lion*, pp. 153–72. (XLI.88).

78   Subrenat, Jean, 'Pourquoi Yvain et son lion ont-ils affronté les fils de Netun?' in *Chevalier au lion*, pp. 173–93. (XLI.91)

79   Walter, Philippe, 'Temps romanesque et temps mythique: éléments pour une recherche,' in *Chevalier au lion*, pp. 195–217. (XLI.94)

See Ga62 Zaddy.

80 Curtis, Renée L., 'The Perception of the Chivalric Ideal in Chrétien de Troyes's *Yvain*,' *AInt*, 3:2 (1989), 1–22.

81 Dubuis, Roger, 'L'art de la "conjointure" dans *Yvain*,' *Bien dire*, 7 (1989), 91–106. (XLIII.174)

82 Edwards, Robert R., *Ratio and Invention: A Study of Medieval Lyric and Narrative* (Nashville, TN: Vanderbilt University Press, 1989). (XLIV.304)
See Chap. 5: 'Invention and Closure in Chrétien's *Yvain*' (pp. 102–14).

See Nb43 Harf-Lancner.

See Ge48 Meneghetti.

See Qa91 Runte.

83 Dragonetti, Roger, 'Le vent de l'aventure dans *Yvain ou le Chevalier au lion* de Chrétien de Troyes,' *MA*, 96 (1990), 435–62. (XLIII.454)

84 Girard, René, 'Love and Hate in *Yvain*,' in Dd1, pp. 249–62. (XLIII.450)

See La42 Rockwell.

85 Cecchetti, Dario, 'Un innamoramento esemplare: Yvain e Laudine,' *AION*, 33 (1991), 317–401. (XLV.323)

See Ga70 Germain.

86 Godinho, Helder, 'Yvain ou le refus de l'autre monde,' *Arquivos do Centro Cultural Português*, 29 (1991), 87–105.

See Qc63 Hanning.

87 Lepage, Yvan G., 'Encore les trois cents pucelles (Chrétien de Troyes, *Yvain*, v. 5298–5324),' *CCM*, 34 (1991), 159–66. (XLIV.38)

88 McGuire, James R., 'L'onguent et l'initiative féminine dans *Yvain*,' *Rom*, 112 (1991), 65–82. (XLVII.280).

89 Wolf, Alois, '*Fol i allai – fol m'en revinc!* Der Roman vom Löwenritter zwischen *mançonge* und *mære*,' in *Festschrift Hoffmann*, pp. 205–25; repr. in Dc31. (XLIV.482; LIII.130)

90 Hawkins, Anne Hunsaker, 'Yvain's Madness,' *PQ*, 71 (1992), 377–97. (XLVII.727)

See Gb113 Rothschild.

91 Álvares, Cristina, and Américo Diogo, 'La demoiselle de Norison: la fin du monde où l'on croyait aux fées,' in *Fin du temps et temps de la fin dans l'univers médiéval*, Senefiance, 33 (Aix-en-Provence: CUER-MA, 1993), pp. 9–22. (XLVI.304)

See Fb83(A) Álvares and Diogo.

See Ud8 Krueger.

See Ga80 Suard.

92 Watanabe, Kôji, 'The Structure of the *Chevalier au lion* (*Yvain*) and Chrétien de Troyes's Irony (1)(2),' *NSH*, 22 (1993), 51–73; 23 (1994), 55–76. (XLIX.378)
In Japanese.

93 Chicote, Gloria Beatriz, 'El narrador y la materia narrada en *El caballero del león*,' *Medievalia* (Mexico City), 16 (April 1994), 8–15.

94 Matthews, David, 'Reading the Woman Reading: Culture and Commodity in Chrétien's Pesme Aventure Episode,' *FMLS*, 30 (1994), 113–23. (XLVII.370)

95 Munson, Marcella, 'Cil qui l'escrist: Narrative Authority and Intervention in Chrétien de Troyes's *Yvain*,' *Paroles*, 12 (1994), 27–45.

See Xb12 Neaman.

See Jb47 Rieger.

96 Brandsma, Frank, 'The Suggestion of Simultaneity in Chrétien de Troyes' *Yvain*, in the *Chanson de Roland*, and in the "Préparation à la Queste" Section of the *Lancelot en Prose*,' *AL*, 13 (1995), 133–44. (XLVII.338)

97 Deist, Rosemarie, 'Sun and Moon: Constellations of Character in Gottfried's *Tristan* and Chrétien's *Yvain*,' in Gb125 *Arthurian Romance*, pp. 50–65. (XLVI, p. 426)

98 Dubuis, Roger, 'Du bon usage du "double" et du "dédoublement" dans *Le Chevalier au lion* de Chrétien de Troyes,' in *Doubles et* *dédoublement en littérature*, ed. Gabriel-André Pérouse (Saint-Étienne: Publications de l'Université de Saint-Etienne, 1995), pp. 15–25.

See Gb125(E) Ihring.

99 Rousse, Michel, 'Le *Chevalier au lion*: de la fable au roman,' in *Amour Troyes*, pp. 203–19. (XLIX.185)

100 Grinnell, Natalie, 'The Other Woman in Chrétien de Troyes's *Yvain*,' *Critical Matrix*, 10 (1996), 36–57.
On Lunete.

See Jb51 Ruhe.

101 Szabics, Imre, 'Az Oroszlános Lovag,' in *Huszonöt fontos francia regény* (Budapest: Maecenas-Lord, 1996), pp. 5–15. (XLIX.319)

102 Dubost, Francis, 'Merveilleux, fantastique et ironie dans *Le Chevalier au lion* de Chrétien de Troyes,' in *Poétique du fantastique en hommage à Jean Fabre*, ed. Michèle Soriano and Christiane Tarroux, Co*textes, 33 (Montpellier: CERS, 1997), pp. 25–45.

See Ga95 Hostetler.

103 Picherit, Jean-Louis, 'La Domesticité féminine dans quelques œuvres médiévales,' *MA*, 104 (1998), 257–73. (LI.10)

See Gb150 Allen.

104 Álvares, Cristina, 'Gauvain et l'impossible dénouement romanesque,' *PRIS-MA*, 15 (1999), 1–15. (LII.194)

105 Haug, Walter, 'Das Spiel mit der arthurischen Struktur in der Komödie von *Yvain/Iwein*,' in *Erzählstrukturen*, pp. 99–118. (LII.82)

See Gc34 Hüe.

106 Sasu, Maria-Voichiţa, 'Chrétien de Troyes, *Yvain*,' Chap. 8 in her *Voix du texte* (Sibiu: Editura Societăţii Academice din România, 1999), pp. 37–43.

107 Watanabe, Kôji, 'Yvain's Madness and "Mythical Time",' *BEFC*, 32 (2000), 1–18.
In Japanese.

g: *Perceval (Le Conte du Graal)*

7   Frappier, Jean, 'Sur la composition [...]' Repr. in Dc5.

9   Frappier, Jean, 'Note complémentaire [...]' Repr. in Dc 5.

12   Hatzfeld, Helmut A., 'Deuten Stilelemente [...]'; Italian trans.: 'Nel "Perceval" di Chrétien gli elementi stilistici indicano una unità strutturale?' in his *Analisi e interpretazioni stilistiche* (Bari: Adriatica, 1971), pp. 56–81.

See Sb28 Lyons.

16   Frappier, Jean, 'Féerie du château [...]' Repr. in Dc5.

22   Delbouille, Maurice, 'Réalité du Château du Roi-Pêcheur dans le *Conte del Graal*,' in *Mélanges offerts à René Crozet à l'occasion de son 70 anniversaire par ses amis, ses collègues et ses élèves*, ed. Pierre Gallais and Yves-Jean Riou, 2 vols (Poitiers: Société d'Etudes Médiévales, 1966), vol. 2, pp. 903–13. (XIX.163)

23   Kakurai, Shukushi, 'Narrative Time in *Li Contes del Graal* (*Perceval*) by Chrétien de Troyes,' *RBN*, 15 (1971), 146–68.
In Japanese.

See Fa69(D-F) Bertau.

See Ga12 Imbs.

See Pb168 Ehlert and Meissburger.

See Jd18 Ribard.

24   Salmeri, Filippo, '"Bataille" e "solaz" nell'episodio di Belrepaire,' *SiG*, 28 (1975), 203–19.

See Ke3 Adam.

25   Colliot, Régine, 'Le voyage de Gauvain à la Roche Champguin chez Chrétien de Troyes et Wolfram d'Eschenbach,' in *Voyage*, pp. 323–38. (XXIX.231)

26   Gouttebroze, J. G., 'Sur l'étendue chronologique du premier mouvement du *Conte du graal* (vv. 69 à 4602),' *MA*, 82 (1976), 5–24. (XXIX.165)

See Eg12 Ribard.

See Gd.c9 Ribard.

27   Saly, Antoinette, 'L'itinéraire intérieur dans le *Perceval* de Chrétien de Troyes et la structure de la quête de Gauvain,' in *Voyage*, pp. 353–60 (discussion p. 361). (XXIX.256)

28   Baumgartner, Emmanuèle, 'Le défi du *chevalier rouge* dans *Perceval* et *Jaufré*,' *MA*, 83 (1977), 239–54. (XXX.209)

29   Frappier, Jean, and Philippe Ménard, 'La blessure du Roi Pêcheur dans le *Conte du graal*,' in *Misrahi Volume*, pp. 181–96. (XXXII.177)

30   Gallais, Pierre, 'La "maison" du Roi-Pêcheur,' in *Mélanges offerts à Henry Corbin*, ed. Seyyed Hossein Nasr, Wisdom of Persia, 9 (Teheran: Offset Press, 1977), pp. 629–49.

31   Gallais, R. [sic = Pierre], 'Le mythe du graal chez Chrétien de Troyes,' in *Formation et survie des mythes: travaux et mémoires: Colloque de Nanterre, 19–20 avril 1974* (Paris: Belles Lettres, 1977), pp. 81–89.

See Gd.c13 Larmat.

32   Méla, Charles, 'Perceval,' *YFS*, 55–56 (1977), 253–79; repr. in Dc19. (XXX.137 *bis*)

33   Pickens, Rupert T., *The Welsh Knight: Paradoxicality in Chrétien's 'Conte del graal'*, FFM, 6 (Lexington, KY: French Forum, 1977). (XXX.140)

See Gd.a6 Poirion.

See Jd19 Potters.

34   Toja, Gianluigi, 'L'"aventure humaine" nel *Perceval* di Chrétien de Troyes,' *Spicilegio Moderno*, 7 (1977), 3–21. (XXX.428)

See Uc11 Verhuyck.

See Jd20 Williams.

35   Foulon, Charles, 'Les quatre repas de Perceval,' *Mélanges Wathelet-Willem*, pp. 165–74. (XXXI.187)

See Ub11 Gallais.

36   Green, Dennis Howard, '*Avanture* in Chrétien's *Perceval*,' in Pb209 *Approaches*, pp. 158–61.

37 Groupe de Linguistique Romane de Paris VII [= Bernard Cerquiglini, Jacqueline Cerquiglini, Christiane Marchello-Nizia, and Michèle Perret], 'D'une quête à l'autre: de Perceval à Gauvain, ou la forme d'une différence,' in *Mélanges Lods*, vol. 1, pp. 269–96. (XXXI.265)

38 Le Rider, Paule, *Le Chevalier dans le Conte du graal de Chrétien de Troyes* (Paris: CDU and SEDES, 1978; 2nd ed. 1996). (XXXI.284)

39 Lods, Jeanne, 'La pucelle as manches petites,' in *Mélanges Wathelet-Willem*, pp. 357–79. (XXXI.192)

40 Maddux, John S., 'La pénitence de Perceval,' *Communio*, 3:5 (Sept.–Oct. 1978), 59–69.

41 Rohr, Rupprecht, 'Zur "Schuld" Percevals,' in *Mélanges Camproux*, vol. 1, pp. 459–68.

42 Saly, Antoinette, 'Beaurepaire et Escavalon,' in *Mélanges Rychner*, pp. 469–81; repr. in Dc22. (XXXI.303)

43 Méla, Charles, *Blanchefleur et le saint homme ou la semblance des reliques: étude comparée de littérature médiévale*, Au champ freudien: Connexions (Paris: Seuil, 1979). (XXXI.291 *bis*).
See pp. 11–46. Cf. his
    A. 'Blanchefleur et le saint homme,' *Ornicar?*, 17–18 (1979), 225–27; repr. in Dc19.
    B. 'La reine et le graal,' *Ornicar?*, 22–23 (1981), 301–4; repr. in Dc19.

44 Mohr, Wolfgang, 'Politische Hintergründe in Chrétiens Perceval-roman,' in his *Wolfgang von Eschenbach: Aufsätze*, GAG, 275 (Göppingen: Kümmerle, 1979), pp. 178–87. (XXXII.51)

45 Pioletti, Antonio, 'Cavalleria e racconto popolare nel *Contes del graal* di Chrétien de Troyes,' *SiG*, 32 (1979), 243–59. (XXXIII.536)

46 Sturm-Maddox, Sara, 'King Arthur's Prophetic Fool: Prospection in the *Conte du graal*,' *MrR*, 29:3–4 (1979), 103–8. (XXXIV.529)

47 Braet, Herman, 'Le lai de *Tyolet*: structure et signification,' in *Etudes Horrent*, pp. 41–46. (XXXIII.241)
Includes comparisons with the *Conte du graal*.

48 Buettner, Bonnie, 'The Good Friday Scene in Chrétien de Troyes' *Perceval*,' *Trad*, 36 (1980), 415–26. (XXXIV.110)

49   Dragonetti, Roger, *La Vie de la lettre au Moyen Age: Le Conte du graal*, Au champ freudien: Connexions (Paris: Seuil, 1980). (XXXII. 339)

See also Louis Marin, 'Les aventures d'une coupe dans une marge,' *Critique*, 37 (1981), 40–53.

See Fb49 Ollier.

50   Pioletti, Antonio, 'Peredur e Perceval: la vendetta, il lignaggio, il paradiso. I: Il *Peredur*: racconto di vendetta e di reconquista,' *QCatania*, 1 (1980), 65–152, and 'II: Lignaggio, cavalleria e "Paradis" nel *Contes del Graal*,' 2 (1980), 7–78. (XXXIV.445–46)

See Ub13 Rey-Flaud.

51   Salmeri, Filippo, 'Due studi sul *Perceval*. I: Le tre gocce di sangue nella neve (valore e funzione dell'episodio nella struttura del romanzo). II: "Perchevax li Galois",' *QCatania*, 1 (1980), 7–64. (XXXIV. 448–49)

52   Freeman, Michelle A., 'Jean Frappier et le mythe du graal,' *OetC*, 5:2 (1980–81), 129–34. (XXXIV.226)

See Db24(G) Rutledge.

See Db24(K) Williams.

See Ub14 Braet.

53   Hayart-Neuez, Gérard, *Structure narrative du Conte du graal* (Valenciennes: Bavay, 1981).

54   Stanesco, Michel, 'Le chemin le plus long: de la parole intempestive à l'économie du dire dans *Le Conte du graal*,' in *Essays Thorpe*, pp. 287–98. (XXXIV.379)

See Kd92 Baird and Pensom.

55   Burns, E. Jane, 'The Doubled-Question Text: Mystic Discourse in Chrétien's *Perceval*,' *RomN*, 23 (1982), 57–64. (XXXV.151)

See Pb262 Dubuis.

See Ub15 Rapaport.

See Na.d54 Foulon.

56 Lacy, Norris J., 'Gauvain and the Crisis of Chivalry in the *Conte del graal*,' in *Sower*, pp. 155–64. (XXXV.173)

See Fb55 Luttrell.

57 Saly, Antoinette, 'La récurrence des motifs en symétrie inverse et la structure du *Perceval* de Chrétien de Troyes,' *TLL*, 21:2 (1983), 21–41; repr. in Dc22. (XXXVI.368)

See Db29 Williams.

See Jd28 Bogdanow.

58 Busby, Keith, 'Reculer pour mieux avancer: l'itinéraire de Gauvain dans le *Conte du Graal*,' in *Chrétien Bruges*, pp. 17–26. (XXXVII.69)

See Ub21 Méla.

59 Ménard, Philippe, 'Problèmes et mystères du *Conte du Graal*: un essai d'interprétation,' in *Chrétien Bruges*, pp. 61–76. (XXXVII.101)

See Qf3 Payen.

60 Pioletti, Antonio, *Forme del racconto arturiano: 'Peredur', 'Perceval', 'Bel Inconnu', 'Carduino'*, Romanica Neapolitana, 16 (Naples: Liguori, 1984). (XXXIX.153)
See chap. 2.

See Ga45 Ribard.

See Qa70 Stiennon.

See Qa71 Sturm-Maddox.

See Hc51 Suard.

61 Voicu, Mihaela, 'Dialogue et discours dans le *Conte du graal* de Chrétien de Troyes,' *ABLs*, 33 (1984), 14–17.

62 Baudry, Robert, '"Gauvain au Château des Merveilles" dans le *Perceval* de Chrétien de Troyes,' in *Actes Rennes*, Supplément.

63 Halász, Katalin, 'Le narrateur et sa fonction interprétative: le *Conte du graal* et *Perlesvaus*,' in *Analyses de romans*, SRD, 11 (Debrecen: Kossuth Lajos Tudományegyetem, 1985), pp. 3–25. (XXXIX.700)

64   Houstin, Françoise, 'Le drame de la mère de Perceval: Chrétien de Troyes, *Le Conte du Graal*,' *PRIS-MA*, 1 (1985), 72–78. (XXXVIII. 226)

See Ub25 Ringger.

See Ub26 Salinero.

65   Sasaki, Shigemi, 'Arthur's Shadow and his "Swoon",' *Gengo*, 3 (1985), 21–35. (XXXIX.191).
In Japanese.

66   García Gual, Carlos, 'El héroe de la búsqueda del Grial como anticipo del protagonista novelesco (reflexiones sobre un tema medieval),' *Epos*, 2 (1986), 103–13; repr. in his *Lecturas y fantasías medievales* (Madrid: Mondadori España, 1990), pp. 115–28.

See Jd31 Houstin-Krempp.

See Ge43 Schmid.

67   Verstraete, Daniel, 'La fonction littéraire du silence de Perceval dans le *Conte du graal*,' *RLR*, 90 (1986), 99–110. (XXXIX.678)

68   Williams, Harry F., 'The Hidden Meaning of Chrétien's *Conte du graal*,' in *Diakonia: Studies in Honor of Robert T. Meyer*, ed. Thomas Halton and Joseph P. Williman (Washington, DC: Catholic University of America Press, 1986), pp. 145–57. (XXXIX.323)

69   Amazawa, Taijirô, 'Typology of the Fisher King's Castle in the *Conte du Graal*,' *MGRS*, 411 (1987), 3–22. (XL.216)
In Japanese.

70   Benedetti, Roberto, 'La morfologia dell'avventura e le pulzelle dell'albero nel *Perceval* di Chrétien de Troyes,' *SF*, 31 (1987), 59–63.

71   Chaurand, Jacques, 'Lenteur et douceur dans le conte du graal,' in *Etudes Matoré*, pp. 123–40. (XL.37)

See Jd33 Clej.

72   Burns, E. Jane, 'Quest and Questioning in the *Conte du graal*,' *RPh*, 41 (1987–88), 251–66. (XL.265)

See Fb72–73 Kelly.

73   Kinoshita, Sharon, 'Les échecs de Gauvain ou l'utopie manquée,' *Littérature*, 71 (1988), 108–19.

74 Maruyama, Masayoshi, 'An Incomplete or Double Tale,' *RH*, 6 (1988), 177–91.
In Japanese.

See Ub35 Virdis.

75 Williams, Harry F., 'The Unasked Questions in the Conte du Graal,' *MedPer*, 3 (1988), 292–302. (XLIII.608)

76 Colliot, Régine, 'Un rapport dramatique mère/enfant dans le récit médiéval: la mère dénonciatrice du crime,' in *Relations*, pp. 161–76. (XLII.52)
See pp. 169–70.

See Ke11 Grimbert.

77 Hirashima, Hitomi, 'The Bipartite Structure of *Perceval ou le conte del graal*,' *SGS*, 8 (1989), 77–94.
In Japanese.

78 Sargent-Baur, Barbara Nelson, '"Avis li fu": Vision and Cognition in the *Conte du graal*,' in *Essays Grigsby*, pp. 133–44. (XLII.346)

See Uc30 Vincensini.

79 Cazelles, Brigitte, 'Genèse de la violence institutionnalisée: le *Conte du graal* de Chrétien de Troyes,' in Dd1 *Modernité*, pp. 263–88. (XLIII.450)

80 Dubost, Francis, 'Procédures d'initialité dans la littérature du Graal,' in *Vers un 'thesaurus' informatisé: topique des ouvertures narratives avant 1800. Actes du Quatrième Colloque International SATOR, Université Paul Valéry–Montpellier III, 25–27 octobre 1990*, ed. Pierre Rodriguez and Michèle Weil (Montpellier: Presses de l'Imprimerie de Recherche–Université Paul-Valéry Montpellier III, 1990), pp. 15–33.

81 Hirashima, Hitomi, 'Three Levels in *Perceval ou le conte du graal*,' *SGS*, 9 (1990), 53–69.
In Japanese.

82 Suzuki, Tetsuya, 'Illumination for Chrétien de Troyes – On the "Interruption" of the *Conte du Graal*,' *BEng*, 21 (1990), 319–38.
In Japanese.

See Qa94 Voicu.

83 Aronstein, Susan, 'Chevaliers Estre Deüssiez: Power, Discourse and the Chivalric in Chrétien's *Conte du graal,*' *Assays*, 6 (1991), 3–28. (XLIV.294)

See Ge51 Callay.

84 Saccone, Antonio, 'La parola di Dio e la parola di Chrétien nel *Conte du graal*: la vera storia di Perceval,' *AION*, 33 (1991), 103–43. (XLIV.208)

85 Sargent-Baur, Barbara Nelson, 'Perceval and the Adventure Within,' in *Arturus rex*, pp. 120–33. (XL, p. 359)

See Ke13 Steele.

86 Watanabe, Kôji, '"Counterpoint Perceval/Gauvain": On the Structure of the *Conte du graal* by Chrétien de Troyes,' *BLFC*, 15 (1991), 2–15.
In Japanese.

See Ga74 Álvares.

87 Bonet, Jean-Michel, 'La magie dans le *Conte du graal* de Chrétien de Troyes: le Lit de la Merveille,' in *Le merveilleux et la magie dans la littérature*, ed. Gérard Chandès, CERMEIL, 2 (Amsterdam: Rodopi, 1992), pp. 39–62. (XLV.401)

88 Dubost, Francis, 'Le conflit des lumières: lire *"tot el"* la dramaturgie du graal chez Chrétien de Troyes,' *MA*, 98 (1992), 187–212. (XLV.627)

89 Sargent-Baur, Barbara N., 'Love in Theory and Practice in the *Conte du graal,*' *AY*, 2 (1992), 179–89. (XLVII.779)

90 Suárez, María Pilar, 'El espacio como soporte de la acción: el episodio de Gauvain en *Le Conte du graal,*' in *Investigaciones semi-óticas: IV. Describir, inventar, transcribir el mundo: Actas del IV simposio internacional: Asociación Española de Semiótica: Sevilla 3–5 diciembre de 1990*, Biblioteca Filológica Hispana, 9 (Madrid: Visor, 1992), pp. 251–58.

See Ke14 Voicu.

See Ub40 Balsamo.

See Gf36 Freixe.

91 Simons, Penny, 'Pattern and Process of Education in *Le Conte du graal*,' *NFS*, 32:2 (1993), 1–11. (XLVI.488)

92 Vincensini, Jean-Jacques, 'Procédés d'"esthétisation" et formes de l'"esthétique" dans la narration médiévale,' in *Actes Zurich*, pp. 413–26. (XLVII.661)

See Uc35 Holzbacher.

93 Berchtold, Jacques, 'L'échiquier absent: à propos d'une disparition signifiante dans le *Conte du graal* de Chrétien de Troyes,' in *Désordres du jeu – poétiques ludiques: études d'histoire et de littérature*, ed. Jacques Berchtold, Christopher Lucken, and Stefan Schoettke, RRG, 6 (Geneva: Droz, 1994), pp. 97–124. (L.401)

94 Detcherry, Chantal, 'Chrétien de Troyes: le graal ou la découverte manquée,' *Eidôlon*, 42 (1994), 79–90.

95 Kelly, Douglas, 'Le nom de Perceval,' in *Recueil Fourquet*, pp. 123–29. (XLVIII.112)

See Qa112 Knight.

96 Marchiori, Marina, 'Per una "rilettura" del *Perceval*,' *Letterature*, 17 (1994), 15–18.

See Jd43 Saly.

97 Goulden, Oliver, 'Gauvain's Imitatio Lanceloti in the *Conte du graal*,' in *Recueil Micha*, pp. 167–75. (XLVIII.99)

See Ha190 Guerin, Chap. 3.

98 *Maninchedda, Paolo, *I nemici immemori: Perceval e Gauvain nel 'Conte du Graal'* (Cagliari: CUEC, 1995). (L.336)

99 Ménard, Philippe, 'La révélation du nom pour le héros du *Conte du graal*,' in *Amour Troyes*, pp. 47–59; repr. in Dc29. (XLIX.171)

100 *Salmeri, Filippo, *Il 'Perceval' di Chrétien de Troyes: mito, cortesia, religiosità* (Catania: CUECM, 1995).

101 Saly, Antoinette, 'Gauvain, Clarissant et le château des reines,' in *Amour Troyes*, pp. 135–45; repr. in Dc22. (XLIX.187)

102 Saly, Antoinette, 'Masculin-féminin dans *Le Conte du graal*,' in Gb125 *Arthurian Romance*, pp. 160–64; repr. in Dc30. (XLVI, pp. 448–49)

See Ga88 Santucci.

See Ga89 Sargent-Baur.

103 Schwartz, Debora B., '"A la guise de Gales l'atorna": Maternal Influence in Chrétien's *Conte du Graal*,' *Essays in Medieval Studies*, 12 (1995), no. 7.
At http://www.luc.edu/publications/medieval/

104 Cazelles, Brigitte, *The Unholy Grail: A Social Reading of Chrétien de Troyes's 'Conte du Graal'*, Figurae (Stanford, CA: Stanford University Press, 1996). (XLIX.475)

See Pc25 Oliver.

105 Sargent-Baur, Barbara N., 'Alexander and the *Conte du graal*,' *AL*, 14 (1996), 1–18. (XLIX.261)

106 Zemel, Roel, 'Perceval en geen einde,' *Voortgang*, 16 (1996), 7–26. (L.392)

107 Divorne, Françoise, 'Un héros abstrait: à propos du *Perceval* de Chrétien de Troyes,' *L'Atelier du Roman*, 12 (Autumn 1997), 162–69.

See Jd51 Hausmann.

See Tb23 Stanesco.

108 Amazawa, Taijirô, 'La *devineuse* du nom de Perceval,' in *Mélanges Ménard*, vol. 1, pp. 33–36. (LI.202)

109 Blons-Pierre, Catherine, *Le Conte du Graal de Chrétien de Troyes: matière, sen et conjointure*, Lectures d'une Œuvre (Paris: Editions du Temps, 1998). (LI.214)

110 Bretel, Paul, 'La conversion de Perceval: lecture de l'épisode de l'ermite dans le *Conte du Graal* de Chrétien de Troyes,' *InfLitt*, 50:5 (Nov.–Dec. 1998), 3–12. (LI.220)

111 Combarieu du Grès, Micheline de, 'Perceval et les péchés de la langue,' *Littératures* (Toulouse), 39 (1998), 5–29.

112 Döffinger-Lange, Erdmuthe, *Der Gauvain-Teil in Chrétiens 'Conte du Graal': Forschungsbericht und Episodenkommentar*, StR, 95 (Heidelberg: Winter, 1998). (LI.67)

113 Donà, Carlo, '*Par le nom conoist en l'ome*: nome, conoscenza iniziatica e genealogia nel *Conte du Graal* di Chrétien de Troyes,' in *Tradizione letteraria, iniziazione, genealogia*, ed. Carlo Donà and Mario Mancini, BM:S, 2 (Milan: Luni, 1998), pp. 11–45. (LII.593)

114 Dubost, Francis, *Le Conte du Graal ou l'art de faire signe*, Unichamp, 71 (Paris: Champion, 1998). (LI.235)

See Db70 Gracia.

115 James-Raoul, Danièle, 'La parole empêchée dans le *Conte du Graal* de Chrétien de Troyes,' *Op. cit.*, 11 (1998), 15–27. (LII.244)

See Gd.a40 Kowalski.

116 Maninchedda, Paolo, 'I nemici immemori: Perceval e Gauvain nel *Conte du Graal*,' in *Studi Melli*, vol. 2, pp. 477–92.

117 Pickens, Rupert T., 'Courtesy and *Vasselage* in Chrétien de Troyes's *Conte del graal*,' in *Studies Brault*, pp. 189–221. (LIII.973)

See Ub49 Rey-Flaud.

118 Rider, Jeff, 'The Perpetual Enigma of Chrétien's Grail Episode,' *Arthuriana*, 8:1 (1998), 6–21. (LI.801)

See Uc50 Vincensini.

See Qf9 Almanza Ciotti.

119 Amazawa, Taijirô, 'The *devineuse* of Perceval's Name,' *Plume*, 4 (1999), 9–11.
In Japanese. See also Hg108 Amazawa.

See Kc109 Garnier.

See Fb100 Guidot.

See Uc53 McCracken.

See Ub51 Rey-Flaud.

See Gd.b61 Szkilnik.

120 Guézennec, Sophie, 'Violences dans le *Conte du Graal*: la mise en question d'une notion ambivalente,' in *Violence et société en Bretagne et dans les pays celtiques: Actes du Colloque International, Brest 18–20 mars 1999*, ed. Jean-Yves Carlver (Brest: Centre de Recherche Bretonne et Celtique, Université de Bretagne Occidentale, 2000), pp. 69–104.

121 Sargent-Baur, Barbara N., *La destre et la senestre: étude sur le 'Conte du graal' de Chrétien de Troyes*, Faux Titre, 185 (Amsterdam: Rodopi, 2000).

See Ha214 Combes and Bertin, pp. 17–30.

See Kb9 Sargent-Baur.

J: ALLEGORY AND SYMBOLISM

Examination of the allegorical potential of Chrétien's romances has continued, but without the major controversies characteristic of such scholarship in Jc and Jd in the 1976 Bibliography. It appears that the allegorical contexts for medieval reading or listening audiences depended on whether one is concerned with whether Chrétien intended such contexts when he wrote his romances, or whether his audiences perceived them in reflecting on their meaning. A less controversial area has been the allegorization of his narratives in later romances, most notably in the *Lancelot-Grail* cycle (see Pa). This leaves open the possibility for moral or spiritual allegory as a factor in audience reception, whatever the author's intention may have been. Modern symbolism (Jf) is linked to a number of topics in U.

a: General Studies

7   Ohly, Friedrich. 'Vom geistigen Sinn […]'; repr. in his *Schriften zur mittelalterlichen Bedeutungsforschung* (Darmstadt: Wissenschaftliche Buchgesellschaft, 1977), pp. 1–31. (XXX.56)

18   Haug, Walter, 'Die Symbolstruktur […]' Repr. in Dc15.

23   Beaujouan, Guy, 'Le symbolisme des nombres à l'époque romane,' *CCM*, 4 (1961), 159–69.

24   Frappier, Jean, 'Aspects de l'hermétisme dans la poésie médiévale,' *CAIEF*, 15 (1963), 9–24; repr. in Dc2.
Treats *Perceval* pp. 15–17.

25   Payen, Jean-Charles, 'Genèse et finalités de la pensée allégorique au Moyen Age,' *Revue de métaphysique et de morale*, 78 (1973), 466–79.
Chrétien's use of personifications.

26 Kuhn, Hugo, 'Allegorie und Erzählstruktur,' in *Formen und Funktionen der Allegorie*, Symposion Wolfenbüttel 1978, ed. Walter Haug, Germanistische Symposien: Berichtsbände, 3 (Stuttgart: Metzler, 1979), pp. 206–18 (XXXII.44); repr. in his *Liebe und Gesellschaft*, ed. Wolfgang Walliczek (Stuttgart: Metzler, 1980). (XXXIII.45)
Treats the *Joie de la cort* episode.

27 Ladner, Gerhart B., 'Medieval and Modern Understanding of Symbolism: A Comparison,' *Spec*, 54 (1979), 223–56.

28 Ribard, Jacques, 'L'interprétation symbolique des œuvres littéraires médiévales,' *MrR*, 29:3–4 (1979), 5–14. (XXXIV.527)

29 Brinkmann, Hennig, *Mittelalterliche Hermeneutik* (Darmstadt: Wissenschaftliche Buchgesellschaft, 1980).
Suite to Fa7.

30 Ribard, Jacques, 'Espace romanesque et symbolisme dans la littérature arthurienne au XIIe siècle,' in *Espaces romanesques*, ed. Michel Crouzet (Paris: Presses Universitaires de France, 1982), pp. 73–82.

31 Wells, David, 'The Medieval Nebuchadnezzar: The Exegetical Tradition of Daniel IV and Its Significance for the Ywain Romances and for German Vernacular Literature,' *FMSt*, 16 (1982), 380–432. (XXXV.83)

32 Ribard, Jacques, *Le Moyen Age: littérature et symbolisme* (Geneva: Slatkine, 1984). (XXXVII.114)

See Gd.b34 Vermette.

See Pb317(G) Combridge.

See Gd.c41 Benedetti.

See Ke13 Steele.

33 Wells, David A., 'Die Allegorie als Interpretationsmittel mittelalterlicher Texte: Möglichkeiten und Grenzen,' in *Bildhafte Rede im Mittelalter und früher Neuzeit: Probleme ihrer Legitimation und ihrer Funktion*, ed. Wolfgang Harms, Klaus Speckenbach, and Herfried Vögel (Tübingen: Niemeyer, 1992), pp. 7–23. (XLV.85)

See Gd.a36 Lerchner.

34   Takatô, Mako, 'A Critique of the Doctrine of "Twelfth-Century Symbolism",' in *Mélanges Teruo Satô*, Part II (Tokyo: France Tosho, 1993), pp. 179–91 (XLVII.649).
In Japanese.

35   Grünkorn, Gertrud, *Die Fiktionalität des höfischen Romans um 1200*, PSQ, 129 (Berlin: Schmidt, 1994). (XLVII.95)

36   *Lange, Hanne, 'Den mytisk-symbolske rejse: den dobbelttydige "vej" i fransk og latinsk middelalderlitteraturer,' in *Romanske Rejser: en tematisk rundfart i de romanske litteraturer. Fem Essays*, ed. John Pedersen (Copenhagen: Museum Tusculanums Forlag, Københavns Universitet, 1995), pp. 35–67.

37   Ribard, Jacques, 'Pour une lecture allégorique et religieuse des œuvres littéraires médiévales,' in *Littérature et religion au Moyen Age et à la Renaissance*, ed. Jean-Claude Vallecalle (Lyon: Presses Universitaires de Lyon, 1997), pp. 15–26.

See Qd21 Accarie.

b: Chrétien's Romances

2   Bezzola, Reto R., *Le Sens de l'aventure* [...]; repr. Paris: Champion, 1998.

5   Rychner, Jean, 'Le Sujet [...]' Repr. in Dc13.

6   Rychner, Jean, 'Le Prologue [...]' Repr. in Dc13.

10   Wolf, Alois, 'Erzählkunst [...]' Repr. in Dc31.

18   Kooijman, Jacques-Cornélis, '*Le Chevalier de la charrette* [...]' (XXVIII.188)

19   Schweitzer, E. C., 'Pattern and Theme [...]' (XXVII.29)

20   Gale, J. E., '*Le Chevalier au lion* [...]' (XXVIII.125)

See Ha60 Lange.

See He20–21 Györy.

21   Györy, Jean, 'Le temps dans le *Chevalier au lion*,' in *Études de civilisation médiévale (IXe–XIIe siècles): mélanges offerts à Edmond-René Labande à l'occasion de son départ à la retraite et du XXe* *anniversaire du CÉSCM par ses amis, ses collègues, ses élèves* (Poitiers: CÉSCM, 1974), pp. 385–93.

22   Eichmann, Raymond, 'Yvain's Lion: A Recapitulation,' *Publications of the Arkansas Philological Association*, 2:2 (1976), 26–32.

23   Meneghetti, Maria Luisa, '"Joie de la cort": intégration individuelle et métaphore sociale dans *Erec et Enide*,' *CCM*, 19 (1976), 371–79. (XXX.286 *ter*)

24   Ribard, Jacques, 'Les romans de Chrétien de Troyes sont-ils allégoriques?' *CAIEF*, 28 (1976), 7–20.

25   Stănescu, Mihail, 'Dimensiunea simbolică a romanului medieval,' in his trans. *Chrétien de Troyes – Cavalerul cu leul* (Bucarest: Editura Albatros, 1977), pp. 87–99. (XXIX.403)

See Db18 Grigsby.

26   Ribard, Jacques, 'La littérature médiévale d'origine celtique et le mythe,' in *Problèmes du mythe et de son interprétation: Actes du Colloque de Chantilly (24–25 avril 1976)*, ed. Jean Hani (Paris: Belles-Lettres, 1978), pp. 119–31; repr. in Dc25.

See He35 Tournon.

27   Voicu, Mihaela, 'L'espace courtois et le mythe du centre – littérature et mythologie chez Chrétien de Troyes,' *Colloques*, 1 (1979), 43–50.

See Hc35 Iyasere.

See Me20 Diverres.

28   Hart, Thomas Elwood, 'Chrestien, Macrobius, and Chartrean Science: The Allegorical Robe as Symbol of Textual Design in the Old French *Erec*,' *MS*, 43 (1981), 250–96. (XXXIV.127)

29   Malaxecheverria, I., 'El león de *Yvain* y la degradación del símbolo,' *RomN*, 22 (1981–82), 102–6. (XXXIV.139)
On Jf5.

30   Heffernan, Carol F., 'Chrétien de Troyes's *Yvain*: Seeking the Fountain,' *ResPL*, 5:1 (1982), 109–21. (XXXVI.174)

See He42 Borsari.

See Me23 Hunt.

31 Ribard, Jacques, 'Le symbolisme des quatre éléments dans le tournoi d'Osenefort du *Cligés* de Chrétien,' in *Quatre éléments*, pp. 163–83; repr. in Dc25. (XXXVI.67)

See La33 Rider.

32 Varty, Kenneth, 'On Birds and Beasts, "Death" and "Resurrection", Renewal and Reunion in Chrétien's Romances,' in *Studies Diverres*, pp. 194–212, 253. (XXXVI.472)

33 Accarie, Maurice, 'L'éternel départ de Lancelot: roman clos et roman ouvert chez Chrétien de Troyes,' *Mélanges Planche*, pp. 1–20. (XXXVII.54)

See He46 Gallais.

34 Ribard, Jacques, 'Pour une interprétation théologique de la "coutume" dans le roman arthurien,' in *Mittelalterstudien Köhler*, pp. 241–48; repr. in Dc25. (XXXVII.656)

See Mf8 Walter.

See Gc12 Williams.

See Hf59 Gier.

See Mf16 Walter.

35 Gicquel, Bernard, 'Montage et symbolique du voyage dans *Erec et Enide*,' in *Métamorphoses du récit: Actes du Colloque de la Sorbonne et du Sénat (2 mars 1985)*, ed. François Moureau, Littérature de Voyages, 1 (Paris: Champion-Slatkine, 1986), pp. 145–51.

36 Raabe, Pamela, 'Chrétien's *Lancelot* and the Sublimity of Adultery,' *UTQ*, 57 (1987–88), 259–69. (XLI.432)

37 Moya, Marie-Hélène, 'Les couleurs dans la structure narrative du *Lancelot*,' in *Couleurs*, pp. 273–83. (XL.52)

38 Nightingale, Jeanne A., 'The Romances of Chrétien de Troyes as Adventures in Interpretation,' *CRR*, 7 (1988), 11–28. (XLIII.584)

39 Ribard, Jacques, 'Yvain et Gauvain dans *Le Chevalier au lion*: essai d'interprétation symbolique,' in *Chevalier au lion*, pp. 139–52. (XLI.84)

40 Szabics, Imre, 'La symbolique des noms dans les romans de Chrétien de Troyes,' in *AnnBud*, 19 (1989–90), 169–77. (XLIV.194)

41 Nolan, Edward Peter, *Now through a Glass Darkly: Specular Images of Being and Knowing from Virgil to Chaucer* (Ann Arbor: University of Michigan Press, 1990).
See Chap. 6: 'Toads in the Garden: Chrétien de Troyes, Anagnorisis, and Epithalamion,' pp. 133–69.

See Gd.c41 Benedetti.

42 Helm, Joan, 'Nature's Marvel: Enide as Earth Measure in an Early Arthurian Manuscript,' *QetF*, 1:3 (1991), 1–24.

43 Le Rider, Paule, 'Le dépassement de la chevalerie dans *Le Chevalier de la charrette*,' *Rom*, 112 (1991), 83–99. (XLVII.279)

44 Hogetoorn, Corry, 'Onzalige paradijzen: tuinen in het werk van Chrétien de Troyes,' in *Tuinen in de middeleeuwen*, ed. R. E. V. Stuip and C. Vellekoop, UBM, 11 (Hilversum: Verloren, 1992), pp. 131–41. (XLV.411)

45 Nolin-Benjamin, Corinne, 'La fonction charnière de l'ermite dans la quête de l'identité,' *RomQ*, 39 (1992), 387–97.

See Gb114 Salinero Cascante.

46 Strubel, Armand, 'Littérature et pensée symbolique au Moyen Age (Peut-on échapper au "symbolisme médiéval"?),' in *Ecriture*, pp. 27–45. (XLVI.368)

See Hc69 Dulac.

47 Rieger, Dietmar, '"Il est a moi et je a lui": Yvains Löwe – ein Zeichen und seine Deutung,' in *Ritter mit dem Löwen*, pp. 245–85 (XLVII.590); rev. version in French: '"Il est à moi et je à lui": le lion d'Yvain – un symbole et son champ sémantique,' in *Mélanges Jung*, vol. 1, pp. 349–69. (L.339)

48 Fouillade, Claude, 'El papel de transición de la naturaleza en los romances medievales de Chrétien de Troyes,' *La palabra y el hombre*, ser. 2, 96 (1995), 99–109.

49 Stanesco, Michel, 'Cligès, le chevalier coloré,' in *Etudes Poirion*, pp. 391–402. (XLVIII.340)

See Qf8 Sutherland.

50 Ley, Marianne and Klaus, 'Yvains Nacktheit: zur spirituellen Deutung von Chrétiens Roman,' in *Text und Tradition: Gedenkschrift Eberhard Leube*, ed. Klaus Ley, Ludwig Schrader, and Winfried Wehle (Frankfurt/M.: P. Lang, 1996), pp. 253–80. (LI.92)

51 Ruhe, Ernstpeter, 'Conjointures apocryphes: la fontaine sous le pin d'Yvain,' in *Mélanges Jung*, vol. 1, pp. 371–85. (L.340)

See Rb33 Kay.

52 Rieger, Dietmar, '"Il ne set que ce senefie" – "Si panse tant que il s'oblie": sull'interpretazione della realtà in Chrétien de Troyes,' in *Festschrift Mölk*, pp. 251–64. (L.108)

53 Wolfzettel, Friedrich, '*Cligès*, roman "épiphanique",' in *Mélanges Ménard*, vol. 2, pp. 1489–1507. (LI.320)

54 Le Rider, Paule, 'Lions et dragons dans la littérature, de Pierre Damien à Chrétien de Troyes,' *MA*, 104 (1998), 9–52. (LI.7)
See also Peter Haidu, pp. 647–49, and Le Rider, p. 649.

55 Noacco, Cristina, 'Lumière et éclairage dans les romans de Chrétien de Troyes,' in *Feu*, pp. 181–97. (LI.281)

56 Vié, Stéphanie, 'Le feu merveilleux arthurien,' in *Feu*, pp. 199–218. (LI.315)

See Pa313 Armstrong.

57 Pipaprez, Delphine, 'Chrétien de Troyes, allégoriste malgré lui? Amour et allégorie dans *Le Roman de la rose* et *Le Chevalier de la charrette*,' in *Conjointure*, pp. 83–94.

58 Ribard, Jacques, 'L'énigme Calogrenant,' *Essays Lacy*, pp. 425–34.

59 Thomasset, Claude, 'Du pont de l'épée au pouvoir royal,' *Bien dire*, 18 (2000), 171–83.

c: Robertsonian Interpretations of Chrétien

2 Robertson, D. W., Jr., 'Chrétien's *Cliges* […]' Repr. in Dc10.

7 Robertson, D. W., Jr., 'The Idea of Fame […]' Repr. in Dc10.

9   Artin, T., *The Allegory of Adventure* […] (XXVIII.116)

10   Robertson, D. W., Jr., 'The Doctrine of Charity in Medieval Literary Gardens: A Topical Approach through Symbolism and Allegory,' *Spec*, 26 (1951), 24–49; repr. in Dc10.
Includes *Cligés*.

See Hc25 Clark and Wasserman.

11   Calin, William, 'Defense and Illustration of *Fin'amor*: Some Polemical Comments on the Robertsonian Approach,' in *ICLS Athens*, pp. 32–48 (XXXII.162); and *SFR*, 2 (1978), 247–57.

See He39 Burrell.

See Sc26 Curtis.

d: Perceval and Grail Allegory

13   Frappier, Jean, 'Le *Conte du graal* […]' Repr. in Dc5.

See Mc39 Duval.

18   Ribard, Jacques, 'L'écriture romanesque de Chrétien de Troyes d'après le Perceval,' *PerM*, 1 (1975), 38–51 (XXVIII.262); repr. in *MrR*, 25:1 (1975), 38–51, and in Dc25. (XXIX.167)

See Eg12 Ribard.

See Me13 Weinraub.

19   Potters, Susan, 'Blood Imagery in Chrétien's *Perceval*,' *PQ*, 56 (1977), 301–9. (XXXII.214)

20   Williams, Harry F., 'The Numbers Game in Chrétien's *Conte du Graal* (*Perceval*),' *Symp*, 31 (1977), 59–73. (XXX.148)

See Hg38 Le Rider.

21   Gicquel, Bernard, 'Aux origines du Graal: quelques sources de Chrétien de Troyes et de Wolfram von Eschenbach,' *Recherches Germaniques*, 10 (1980), 3–17. (XXXIII.332)

22   Ribard, Jacques, 'La symbolique du nom dans Le *Conte du Graal*,' in *Mythe – symbole – roman: Actes du Colloque d'Amiens, Université de*

Picardie, Centre d'Etudes du Roman et du Romanesque, ed. Jean Bessière (Paris: Presses Universitaires de France, 1980), pp. 5–17.

See Hg52 Freeman.

23 Ribard, Jacques, 'Ecriture symbolique et visée allégorique dans *Le Conte du Graal*,' *OetC*, 5:2 (1980–81), 103–9; repr. in Dc25. (XXXIV.244)

24 Keimeul, Léon, *Le Conte du Graal: symbolisme maçonnique* (Paris: Pensée Universelle, 1982).

25 Bayer, Hans, *Gral: die hochmittelalterliche Glaubenskrise im Spiegel der Literatur*, Monographien zur Geschichte des Mittelalters, 28:1–2 (Stuttgart: Hiersemann, 1983). (XXXVI.13)

26 Markale, Jean, 'Le nom, la parole et la magie,' *Corps Écrit*, 8 (1983), 29–39.

27 Méla, Charles, '"La lettre tue": cryptographie du Graal,' *CCM*, 26 (1983), 209–21; repr. in Dc19. (XXXVI.359)

See Db29 Williams.

28 Bogdanow, Fanni, 'The Mystical Theology of Bernard of Clairvaux and the Meaning of Chrétien de Troyes' *Conte du Graal*,' in *Essays Topsfield*, pp. 249–82. (XXXVII.159)

See Qf3 Payen.

29 Accarie, Maurice, 'Une lance est une lance: critique et fascination de la chevalerie dans le *Conte du Graal*,' in *Hommage Richer*, pp. 9–19. (XLI.40)

30 Bonnet, Jacques, 'L'énigme de la lance saignante,' *Etudes Traditionnelles,* 86 (1985), 180–86.

31 Houstin-Krempp, Françoise, 'Les images liées aux quatre éléments dans la partie "Perceval" du *Conte du Graal*,' *PRIS-MA*, 2 (1986), 27–34. (XXXIX.645)

See Hg67 Verstraete.

See Hg68 Williams.

32 Chocheyras, J., 'Trois gouttes de sang: une source historique et son symbole,' *PerM*, 13 (1987), 57–59.

33 Clej, Alina, 'La parole et le royaume: une variation romanesque sur un thème évangélique dans *Li Contes del Graal* de Chrétien de Troyes,' *RR*, 78 (1987), 271–90. (XL.268)

34 Vauthier, Michèle, 'Les âges d'Arthur dans le *Conte du Graal* de Chrétien de Troyes: le mirage de la vieillesse,' in *Vieillesse*, pp. 337–63. (XXXIX.677)
Interpreted according to the *Hortus deliciarum*.

35 Lange, Hanne, 'Symbolisme, exégèse, littérature profane: intertextualité et intratextualité dans le *Conte du Graal* de Chrétien de Troyes,' in *Actes Trèves*, vol. 6, pp. 289–307. (XLI.619)

36 Vauthier, Michèle, 'Le paradoxe des fenêtres colorées dans le *Conte du Graal*: une introduction possible à la lecture des couleurs chez Chrétien de Troyes,' in *Couleurs*, pp. 423–48. (XL.61)

37 Ribard, Jacques, *Du philtre au Graal: pour une interprétation théologique du 'Roman de Tristan' et du 'Conte du Graal'*, Essais, 12 (Paris: Champion, 1989). (XLII.75)

38 Strubel, Armand, *La rose, Renart et le Graal: la littérature allégorique en France au XIIIe siècle*, NBMA, 11 (Paris: Champion, 1989). (XLII.79)
See pp. 245–63.

39 Vauthier, Michèle, 'Les aventures de Gauvain dans la seconde partie du *Conte du Graal* de Chrétien de Troyes: une apologie de la croisade,' in *La Croisade: réalités et fictions: Actes du Colloque d'Amiens, 18–22 mars 1987*, ed. Danielle Buschinger, GAG, 503 (Göppingen: Kümmerle, 1989), pp. 219–49.

40 Diverres, Armel, 'The Grail and the Third Crusade: Thoughts on *Le Conte del Graal* by Chrétien de Troyes,' *AL*, 10 (1990), 13–104. (XLIII.246)

See Hg88 Dubost.

See Qf4 Guerreau-Jalabert.

41 Vauthier, Michèle, 'Le lit de la merveille dans *Le Conte du Graal* de Chrétien de Troyes: le jeu des images,' in *Image*, pp. 303–26.

42 Maruyama, Masayoshi, 'Blood on the Snow, or the Allegory of the "Bird" – A Reading of the *Conte du Graal* by Chrétien de Troyes,' *G-k*, 63 (1993), 230–43.
In Japanese.

See Ta37 Rohr.

43 Saly, Antoinette, 'Sur quelques vers du *Perceval*: la biche manquée (vv. 5656–5702),' in *Recueil Fourquet*, pp. 259–69; repr. in Dc30. (XLVIII.146)

44 Vauthier, Michèle, 'Vers la figure de la "Cité" au château du Roi Pescheor dans le *Conte du Graal* de Chrétien de Troyes: étude topographique en situation,' in *König Artus*, pp. 269–88. (XLVII.152)

45 Vauthier, Michèle, 'Du manoir maternel au château de Carduel dans le *Conte du Graal*: les avatars de la *Synagoga*, images de l'amour falsifié,' in *Amour Troyes*, pp. 61–82. (XLIX.198)

46 Marache, Bernard, 'Gornemant et Perceval entre rivière et mer,' in *Etudes Poirion*, pp. 277–84. (XLVIII.318)

47 Ribard, Jacques, 'Le Graal: symbole chrétien dès l'origine?' in Pk72 *Graal*, pp. 53–63.

48 Vauthier, Michèle, 'Quelques éléments de transposition de la légende d'Alexandre à la Borne de Galvoie dans le *Conte du Graal*,' *Bien dire*, 14 (1996), 79–99. (XLIX.199)

49 Vauthier, Michèle, 'The "Roi Pescheor" and Iconographic Implications in the *Conte del Graal*,' in *Word and Image*, pp. 320–38. (L.580)

50 Giannini, Fabio Giovanni, *I frammenti del Graal* (Milan: New Style, 1997).

51 Hausmann, Frank-Rutger, 'Blancheflor und die "Drei Blutstropfen im Schnee" – erneute Lektüre einer bekannten Episode in Chrétiens *Perceval ou le Conte du Graal*,' in *Festschrift Mölk*, pp. 265–76. (L.83)

See Hg110 Bretel.

52 Ardizio Visconti, Marie, *Le Conte du graal ou les clefs de l'éveil*, Brocéliande (Monaco: du Rocher, 2000).

e: The Holmes–Klenke Interpretation of *Perceval*

23 Holmes, Urban T., Jr, 'The Arthurian Tradition in Lambert d'Ardres,' *Spec*, 25 (1950), 100–03. (III.55)

24 Mahoney, John F., 'The Conte del Graal and the Praemonstratensian Order?' *Analecta Praemonstratensia*, 31 (1955), 166–67.

25   Klenke, Sister M. Amelia, *Chrétien de Troyes and 'Le Conte del Graal': A Study of Sources and Symbolism* (Potomac, MD: Studia Humanitatis, 1981). (XXXVII.409)

26   Helm, Joan, 'Erec, the Hebrew Heritage: Urban Tigner Holmes Vindicated?' *QetF*, 2:1 (1992), 1–15.

f: Modern Conceptions of Symbolism and Allegory

6   Guiette, Robert, 'Lecteur de romans, lecteur de symboles,' *RG*, 8 (1960), 50–56; repr. in Dc6.
An introduction to the subject.

7   Lindenberg, Christoph, 'Zur Wirklichkeit des Grals: Gestalten, Bilder und Bilderfolge bei Chrétien de Troyes,' *Die Drei*, 45 (1975), 345–50.

8   Borne, Gerhard von dem, *Der Gral in Europa: Wurzeln und Wirkungen* (Stuttgart: Urachhaus, 1976). (XXIX.8)

9   Sansonetti, Paul-Georges, 'Images mythiques dans la littérature arthurienne,' in *Le Retour du mythe* (Grenoble: Presses Universitaires de Grenoble, 1980), pp. 49–82.

10   Murphy, Margueritte S., 'The Allegory of "Joie" in Chrétien's *Erec et Enide*,' in *Allegory, Myth, and Symbol*, ed. Morton W. Bloomfield, Harvard English Studies, 9 (Cambridge, MA: Harvard University Press, 1981), pp. 109–27. (XXXIV.141, XXXVII.431)

11   Régnier-Bohler, Danielle, 'Le corps mis à nu: perception et valeur symbolique de la nudité dans les récits du Moyen Age,' *Europe*, 654 (Oct. 1983), 51–62.
Includes *Yvain*.

12   Pavel, Maria, 'Stratificare şi symbol,' in *Lingvistică, poetică, stilistică* (Iaşi: Universitatea Al. I. Cuza, 1986), pp. 159–62. (XL.498)

13   Aguiriano, Begoña, 'Yvain: chaman occidental du XIIe siècle,' *PRIS-MA*, 3 (1987), 79–91. (XLI.41)

See Gd.a27 Méla.

See Uc30 Vincensini.

See Hf84 Girard.

See Gc21 Salinero Cascante.

14 Ridoux, Charles, 'Trois exemples d'une approche symbolique (le tombeau de Camille, le nain Frocin, le lion),' in *Hommage Dufournet*, vol. 3, pp. 1217–21. (XLVI.360)

See Hg107 Divorne.

15 Ducluzeau, Francis, *Le Monde du Graal: les racines initiatiques de l'imaginaire chevaleresque*, La Pierre Philosophale (Monaco: du Rocher, 1997).
See Part II: '*Perceval le Gallois ou le Conte du Graal* d'après le roman de Chrétien de Troyes: la quête de la lucidité et de la connaissance de soi par l'action,' pp. 81–168.

16 Barbieri, Alvaro, 'Lo specchio liquido e il passaggio paradossale: l'avventura della Sorgente meravigliosa nell'*Yvain* di Chrétien de Troyes,' *AnticoModerno* (*I Numeri*), 4 (1999), 193–216.

See Hb53 Kullmann.

See Uc53 McCracken.

K: LANGUAGE AND LINGUISTICS

I have attempted to enlarge this section, given the importance of Chrétien's language for editing, interpretation, and reception. There have been very few studies devoted solely to his works, and even in these cases evidence has been drawn by and large from the CFMA edition or its base manuscript, BNF fr. 794, despite the controversy about this manuscript (see Bb). Included here are not only publications that emphasize Chrétien, but also those that use evidence from his works along with others. The scholar must in all cases check the edition and/or manuscript that is the source of evidence. Works in Ke may also belong more properly in a separate section under U. Kf has been added. There are fewer cross-references to *BBSIA*, where this topic is under-represented.

a: Dictionaries

1 Delcourt, Christian, and Gilles Mersch, 'Cluster Analysis and the Taxonomy of Words in Old French,' in *Computing in the Humanities: Papers from the Fifth International Conference on Computing in the Humanities, Ann Arbor, Michigan, May 1981*, ed. Richard W. Bailey (Amsterdam: North-Holland, 1982), pp. 111–22.
Based on *Yvain.* .

b: Proper Names (see also Na.f)

4 Seiffert, Fritz, *Ein Namenbuch zu den altfranzösischen Artusepen*, diss. Greifswald (Greifswald: Abel, 1882; rev. and expanded version, 1885).

5 Hoepffner, Ernest, '"Graëlent" ou "Lanval",' in *Recueil de travaux offerts à M. Clovis Brunel, membre de l'Institut, directeur honoraire de l'Ecole des Chartes, par ses amis, collègues et élèves*, Mémoires et

Documents Publiés par la Société de l'Ecole des Chartes, 12, 2 vols (Paris: Société de l'Ecole des Chartes, 1955), vol. 2, pp. 1–8. (VIII.108) Includes *Erec.*

6 Williams, Harry F., 'Allusions à la légende de Tristan,' *BBSIA*, 12 (1960), 91–96.

See Gd.b10 Elizalde.

See Lc3 Saly.

See Eh10 Bruce.

7 Schlyter, Börje, '"Tristanz qui onques ne rist",' *NM*, 100 (1999), 125–26.

8 Sims-Williams, Patrick, 'A Turkish-Celtic Problem in Chrétien de Troyes: The Name *Cligés*,' in *Ildánach Ildírech: A Festschrift for Proinsias Mac Cana*, ed. John Carey, John T. Koch, and Pierre-Yves Lambert (Andover, MA: Celtic Studies Publications, 1999), pp. 215–30.

9 Sargent-Baur, Barbara N., 'Le jeu des noms de personnes dans le *Conte du graal*,' *Neophil*, 85 (2001), 485–99.

c: Grammar: Phonology, Morphology, Syntax

14 *Le Coultre, Jean Jules, *De l'ordre des mots dans Crestien de Troyes*, diss. Leipzig (Dresden: [n.p.], 1875).

15 Svenonius, Thure Leonard, *Om bruket af subjonctif hos Chrestien de Troyes: ett bidrag till det franska språkets historiska grammatik*, diss. Uppsala (Uppsala: Berling, 1880).

16 Bischoff, Fritz, *Der Conjunctiv bei Chrestien* (Halle/S.: Niemeyer, [1881]).

17 Schiller, Hugo, *Der Infinitiv bei Chrestien*, diss. Leipzig (Breslau: Korn, 1883).

18 Roitzsch, Max, *Das Particip bei Chrestien*, diss. Leipzig (Leipzig: Sturm und Roppe, 1885, Fock, 1886).

19 Ellinger, Johann, *Syntax der Pronomina bei Chrestien de Troies*, Fünfzehntes Jahresbericht über die K. K. Oberrealschule in dem II. Bezirke von Wien 1885/86 (Vienna: K. K. Oberrealschule im II. Bezirke, 1886).

20   Schwieder, Adolphe, *Le Discours indirect dans Crestien de Troyes*, Wissenschaftliche Beilage zum Programm des Andreas-Realgymnasiums zu Berlin (Ostern 1890), 93 (Berlin: Gaertner, 1890).

21   Menshausen, Werner, *Die Verwendung der betonten und unbetonten Formen des Personal- und Possessiv-Pronomens bei Wace, Beneeit und Crestien v. Troyes*, diss. Halle-Wittenberg (Halle/S.: Hohmann, 1912).

22   Wacker, Gertrud, *Über das Verhältnis von Dialekt und Schriftsprache im Altfranzösischen*, Beiträge zur Geschichte der romanischen Sprachen und Literaturen, 11 (Halle/S.: Niemeyer, 1916).

23   Biller, Gunnar, *Remarques sur la syntaxe des groupes de propositions dans les premiers romans français en vers (1150–75)*, Göteborgs Högskolas Årsskrift 1920, i (Göteborg: Elander, 1920).

24   Foulet, L., 'Les noms féminins et la déclinaison en ancien français,' in *Studies Kastner*, pp. 264–74.

See Ta24 Spitzer.

25   Imbs, Paul, *Les Propositions temporelles en ancien français: la détermination du moment: contribution à l'étude du temps grammatical français*, Publications de la Faculté des Lettres de l'Université de Strasbourg, 120 (Paris: Belles Lettres, 1956).

26   Jansen-Beck, Lydia I., *Possessive Pronouns and Adjectives in 'Garin le Loheren' and 'Gerbert de Mez': Etymology, Morphology, Syntax and Comparison with Five Old French Epic Poems and Five Old French Courtly Romances* (Brooklyn, NY: the author, 1961).
Comparison with *Cligés*, *Charrette*, *Yvain*, and *Perceval*.

27   Rickard, P., '*Tanz* and *Fois* with Cardinal Numbers in Old and Middle French,' in *Studies Ewert* (Oxford: Clarendon Press, 1961), pp. 194–213.

28   Stéfanini, Jean, *La Voix pronominale en ancien et en moyen français*, Publications de la Faculté des Lettres, Aix-en-Provence, n. s. 31 (Gap: Ophrys, 1962).

29   Morimoto, Hideo, 'Tense System in *Guillaume d'Angleterre*,' *ELLF*, 2 (1963), 42–45.
In Japanese.

30   Morimoto, Hideo, 'Study of the French Verb (3) – The Subjunctive in *Erec et Enide* (I),' *JK*, 17:3 (1966), 71–81.
In Japanese.

31   Morimoto, Hideo, '*Sussiez* and *sauriez* in *Erec et Enide*,' *CEMN*, 4 (1966), 5–17.
In Japanese.

32   Pohoryles, Bernard M., *Demonstrative Pronouns and Adjectives in 'Garin le Loheren' and 'Gerbert de Mez': Etymology, Morphology, Syntax, and Comparison with Five Old French Epic Poems and Five Old French 'Romans'*, diss. New York University (New York: Pace College, 1966).
Romances include *Cligés*, *Charrette*, *Yvain*, and *Perceval*.

33   Morimoto, Hideo, 'Study of the French Verb (4) – The Subjunctive in *Erec et Enide* (II),' *JK*, 18:3 (1967), 33–46.
In Japanese.

34   Vogel, Irmgard, *Die affektive Intensivierung der adjektiva mit Hilfe des Vergleichs im Altfranzösischen*, StR, 12 (Heidelberg: Winter, 1967).

35   Wunderli, Peter, 'Indikativ, Konjunktiv oder Imperativ? Zum Problem des Imperativs im Teilsatz,' *VR*, 26 (1967), 213–48.

36   Morimoto, Hideo, 'The Meaning of Temporal Adverbs and Verb Tenses – Analytic Study of *Erec et Enide*,' *JK*, 19:11(1968), 58–73.
In Japanese.

37   Morimoto, Hideo, 'Phrases and their Temporal Meaning – Analytic Study of *Erec et Enide*,' *JK*, 21:3 (1969), 234–69.
In Japanese.

38   Woledge, B., 'Notes on the Syntax of Indeclinable Nouns in 12th-Century French,' in *The French Language: Studies Presented to Lewis Charles Harmer*, ed. T. G. S. Combe and P. Rickard (London: Harrap, 1970), pp. 38–52. (XXIV.243)

39   Currie, M., 'La proposition substantive en tête de phrase dans la langue française: aperçu historique,' *SN*, 43 (1971), 31–71.

40   Jonas, Pol, *Les Systèmes comparatifs à deux termes en ancien français*, Université Libre de Bruxelles: Travaux de la Faculté de Philosophie et Lettres, 45 (Brussels: Editions de l'Université de Bruxelles, 1971).

41   Morimoto, Hideo, 'Descriptive Study of the Relationships among Verb Tenses and their System in Chrétien de Troyes's *Cligès*,' *JK*, 24:1 (1972), 58–70.
In Japanese.

42   Honda, Tadao, 'The Terms of Negation in *Erec et Enide* – Compared with Marie de France,' *LLF*, 8 (1975), 171–90.
In Japanese.

43   Cerquiglini, Bernard, 'Un phénomène d'énonciation: a. fr. *mar*,' *Rom*, 97 (1976), 23–62. (XXIX.229)

44   Offord, Malcolm, 'Réflexions sur la construction du français médiéval Démonstratif + phrase relative avec adverbe locatif,' *Rom*, 97 (1976), 195–217. (XXIX.247)

45   Offord, Malcolm H., 'Sur l'imparfait de l'indicatif et le futur du verbe *estre* en français médiéval,' *TLL*, 14:1 (1976), 161–228.

46   Probes, Christine McCall, 'L'influence germanique sur la syntaxe de *Yvain* de Chrétien de Troyes,' in *Actes Laval*, vol. 2, pp. 491–98.

47   Moignet, Gérard, 'Ancien français *si/se*, ' *TLL*, 15:1 (1977), 267–89.
Based on first 3676 lines in Guiot.

48   Palm, Lars, *La Construction 'li filz le rei' et les constructions concurrentes avec 'a' et 'de' étudiées dans les œuvres littéraires de la seconde moitié du XIIᵉ siècle et du premier quart du XIIIᵉ siècle*, ActaUpsa, 17 (Uppsala: Almqvist & Wiksell, 1977).

49   Shirt, David J., '*Penser* Infinitive Constructions in the Old French Period,' in *Beiträge ZrP*, pp. 306–32.

50   Cerquiglini, Bernard, 'La parole étrange,' *LF*, 40 (1978), 83–98.

51   Hilty, Gerold, 'Dialektale Züge in Chrétiens *Erec*?' in *Festschrift Schon*, pp. 80–90. (XXXIII.33)

52   Monsonégo, Simone, and Roberte Tomassone, 'Déterminer un état de l'ancien français par la comparaison statistique de textes voisins?' *LF*, 40 (1978), 5–17.

53   Nordahl, Helge, 'La détermination bi-adverbiale du SV en ancien français,' *VR*, 37 (1978), 151–59.

54 Nordahl, Helge, 'Merveille, a merveille et a grant merveille: petite étude sur la syntaxe séquentielle de trois déterminants quantitatifs en ancien français,' *RLR*, 83 (1978), 105–21.

55 Nordahl, Helge, 'Superlatif absolu et structures séquentielles en ancien français,' in *Mélanges Camproux*, vol. 1, pp. 439–50.

See Fa96 Ollier.

See Ba9 Tekaat.

56 Wigger, Marianne, *Tempora in Chrétiens 'Yvain': eine text-linguistische Untersuchung*, Studia Romanica et Linguistica, 6 (Frankfurt/M.: P. Lang, 1978).

57 Woledge, Brian, 'Apostrophe et déclinaison chez Chrétien de Troyes,' in *Mélanges Lods*, vol. 1, pp. 588–603. (XXXI.311)

58 Woledge, Brian, '*La flors* et *la flor*: la déclinaison des féminins chez Chrétien de Troyes,' in *Mélanges Wathelet-Willem*, pp. 717–40. (XXXI.204)

59 Wunderli, Peter, 'Strukturen des Possessivums im Altfranz-ösischen,' *VR*, 36 (1977), 38–66.

60 Morimoto, Hideo, *Descriptive Method for Verb Tenses in French: Analysis of Tenses in Chrétien de Troyes's 'Cligès'* (Tokyo: Surugadai-shuppansha, 1979).
In Japanese.

61 Nordahl, Helge, 'La conjonction disjointe ... *se* – *non* ... en ancien français: constructions amplectives et bi-amplectives,' *ZfSL*, 89 (1979), 41–52.

62 Woledge, Brian, *La Syntaxe des substantifs chez Chrétien de Troyes*, PRF, 149 (Geneva: Droz, 1979). (XXXII.368)

63 Aragón Fernández, Mª Aurora, 'La calificación adjetiva en las novelas de Chrétien de Troyes,' *Archivum*, 29–30 (1979–80), 459–80.

64 Ménard, Philippe, 'Le subjonctif présent dans les propositions hypothétiques en ancien français,' *TLL*, 18:1 (1980), 321–32.

65 Pavel, Maria, 'La détermination-épithète chez Chrétien de Troyes,' *ACLin*, 26 (1980), 94–102.

66 Cerquiglini, Bernard, *La Parole médiévale: discours, syntaxe, texte* (Paris: Minuit, 1981).

67 Ndoye-Sarre, Nguissaly, 'Le complément de nom de parenté, de possession et de dépendance dans *Le Conte du graal* ou *Perceval*,' *Annales de la Faculté des Lettres et Sciences Humaines de Dakar*, 11 (1981), 135–56.

68 Szabics, Imre, 'Procédés de syntaxe expressive dans les chansons de geste et romans courtois du XIIe siècle,' in *AnnBud*, 12 (1981), 3–24.

See Fa116 Nordahl.

69 Herslund, Michael, 'La construction réfléchie en ancien français,' in *Actes Odense*, pp. 153–61.

70 Löfstedt, Leena, '*Facere/faire* + adj. et *reddere/rendre* + adj.,' in *Actes Odense*, pp. 237–46.

See Fc15 Woledge.

See Hf54 Grimbert.

71 Kleiber, Georges, 'L'opposition déterminé/indéterminé: les articles en ancien français,' *Mélanges Planche*, pp. 247–61.

72 Pavel, Maria, 'La détermination spatiale chez Chrétien de Troyes,' *Bulletin du Centre de Romanistique et de Latinité Tardive* (Université de Nice), 2 (1984), 15–19.

73 Queffélec, A., 'Les subordonnées d'exclusion en ancien français,' *Mélanges Planche*, pp. 379–92.

74 Linthorst, P., 'L'absence de concordance entre temps simples et composés en ancien et en moyen français et les implications de cette absence pour l'établissement du système verbal,' *Rapports*, 55 (1985), 124–35.

75 Love, Nathan, 'The Vocative Adjectives *Biaus*, *Dous* and *Chiers* in Old French,' *LingI*, 9:2 (1985), 307–19.

76 Marchello-Nizia, Christine, '*Si* + *faire* (*avoir/estre*),' in *Actes Moyen Français*, pp. 201–12 (discussion pp. 213–15).
See also Kd98 Marchello-Nizia.

77   Pavel, Maria, 'Les actualisations corrélatives en ancien français,' *Razo*, 5 (1985), 79–84.

78   Pavel, Maria, 'La modalisation véridictoire chez Chrétien de Troyes,' *ACLit*, 31 (1985), 43–46. (XL.496)

79   Roques, Gilles, 'La conjugaison du verbe *vouloir* en ancien français,' in *Actes Moyen Français*, pp. 227–65 (discussion pp. 266–68).

See Fa135 Trimborn.

80   Pavel, Maria, 'Métataxes et métasèmes en ancien français,' in *Stylistique, rhétorique et poétique dans les langues romanes: Actes du XVIIe Congrès International de Linguistique et de Philologie Romanes* (Marseille: Publications de l'Université de Provence-Jean Laffitte, 1986), vol. 8, pp. 353–66.

81   Pavel, Maria, 'Modalité et visée virtuelle chez Chrétien de Troyes,' *ACLin*, 32 (1986), 74–79. (XL.497)

See Bb52 Woledge.

82   Eskénazi, André, 'Le complément déterminatif dans les romans de Chrétien de Troyes – Guyot (BN 794),' *TLL*, 25:1 (1987), 207–41.

83   Kawaguchi, Yuji, 'Systèmes distincts, fluctuations ou variantes graphiques en ancien champenois,' *La Linguistique*, 23:2 (1987), 87–98. Based on BNF fr. 794.

84   Love, Nathan, 'Why *Tu*, Rather than *Vous*, in Chrétien de Troyes' *Le Chevalier de la Charrete?*', *LingI*, 11:1 (1987), 115–27.

85   Herslund, Michael, 'La construction causative en ancien français,' in *Mélanges d'études médiévales offerts à Helge Nordahl à l'occasion de son soixantième anniversaire*, ed. Kirsten Broch Flemestad, Tove Jacobsen, and Terje Selmer (Oslo: Solum, 1988), pp. 80–93.

86   Ollier, Marie-Louise, 'Discours intérieur et temporalité: l'adverbe OR en récit,' in *Hommage Zumthor*, pp. 201–17. Repr. in Dc32.

87   Rychner, Jean, 'Messages et discours double,' in *Studies Woledge*, pp. 145–61.

88   Beck, Jonathan, 'On Functional Multiplicity of Tense-Aspect Forms in Old French Narrative,' *RPh*, 42 (1988–89), 129–43. (XLI.346)

89   Ollier, Marie-Louise, 'La séquence *or si* en ancien français: une stratégie de persuasion,' *Rom*, 110 (1989), 289–330, and 101 (1990), 1–36.
Examples from the *Charrette*, *Philomena*, and *Guillaume d'Angleterre*.

90   Queffélec, Ambroise, 'La négation et l'exception dans l'*Yvain* de Chrétien de Troyes,' *InfGram*, 41 (March 1989), 22–27.

See Fa146 Rychner.

91   Zink, Gaston, 'L'ordre des mots dans *Yvain*, de Chrétien de Troyes (éd. Mario-Roques, v. 1–2477),' *InfGram*, 41 (March 1989), 16–21.

See Ha157 Fleischman.

92   Kunstmann, Pierre, *Le relatif-interrogatif en ancien français*, PRF, 191 (Geneva: Droz, 1990).

93   Rychner, Jean, *La Narration des sentiments, des pensées et des discours dans quelques œuvres des XIIe et XIIIe siècles*, PRF, 192 (Geneva: Droz, 1990). (XLIII.451)

94   Englebert, Annick, 'Un emploi partitif de *de* chez Chrétien de Troyes,' *Rom*, 112 (1991), 45–64. (XLVII.266)

95   Eskénazi, André, 'Le complément du comparatif d'inégalité dans les romans de Chrétien de Troyes (BN 794),' *RLingR*, 56 (1992), 385–425. (XLV.174)

96   Soutet, Olivier, *Études d'ancien et de moyen français*, Linguistique Nouvelle (Paris: Presses Universitaires de France, 1992). (XLVIII.339)

97   Epp, Anthony R., 'A Medieval Perspective on Agreement Patterns with *Gens*,' *Rom*, 113 (1992–95), 1–13.

98   Matsuura, Junko, 'On the Use of Tense in *Yvain* and *Iwein* (1)(2),' *SLCN*, 14:1 (1992), 169–85; 14:2 (1993), 137–52.
In Japanese.

99   Ôtaka, Yorio, 'Les Substantifs inanimés à deux genres en français médiéval,' in *Mélanges Teruo Satô*, Part II (Tokyo: France Tosho, 1993), pp. 63–100. (LI.670)

100   Ponchon, Thierry, *Sémantique lexicale et sémantique grammaticale: le verbe 'faire' en français médiéval*, PRF, 211 (Geneva: Droz, 1994).

101 Andrieux-Reix, Nelly, '*Lors veïssiez*, histoire d'une marque de diction,' *LINX*, 32 (1995), 133–45.

102 Epp, Anthony R., 'Les règles sur l'accord des participes passés d'après Chrétien de Troyes,' *RevR*, 30 (1995), 279–93.

103 Bauer, Brigitte L. M., 'The Verb in Indirect Speech in Old French: System in Change,' in *Reported Speech: Forms and Functions of the Verb*, ed. Theo A. J. M. Janssen and Wim van der Wurff, Pragmatics and Beyond, 43 (Amsterdam: Benjamins, 1996), pp. 75–96.
Examples from *Erec*.

104 Bertin, Annie, *L'Expression de la cause en ancien français*, PRF, 219 (Geneva: Droz, 1997). (XLIX.129)

105 Baril, Agnès, *Chrétien de Troyes: Perceval ou Le Conte du Graal (d'après l'édition de Félix Lecoy): commentaire grammatical et philologique des vers 1301 à 3407; préparation à l'épreuve d'ancien français* (Paris: Ellipses, 1998).

106 Gouttebroze, Jean-Guy, 'Pour une approche syntaxique de la prédicativité en ancien français: les particules adverbiales *non* et *ne* dans le *Conte du Graal* et dans d'autres textes médiévaux,' *Bulletin du Centre de Romanistique*, 11 (1998), 1–9.

107 Soutet, Olivier, 'La notion de mécanisme compensatoire en grammaire de l'ancien français,' in *Mélanges Ménard*, vol. 2, pp. 1253–66.

108 Bellon, Roger, 'La construction du complément déterminatif dans *Le Conte du Graal*,' *InfGram*, 81 (March 1999), 19–23.

109 Garnier, Bruno, 'Syntaxe de l'article et subjectivité littéraire dans le *Conte du Graal* (vv. 1301–3407),' *InfGram*, 81 (March 1999), 14–18.

110 Quereuil, Michel, 'La voix pronominale dans *Le Conte du Graal* (vers 1301 à 3407),' *InfGram*, 81 (March 1999), 10–13.

See Wb54 Ogawa.

111 Oppermann, Evelyne, *Les emplois injonctifs du futur en français médiéval*, PRF, 225 (Geneva: Droz, 2000).

112 Ollier, Marie-Louise, 'Linguistique de l'énonciation et langue morte: analyse de – *Or avez vos folie dite*,' in Dc32, pp. 433–59.

d: Lexicology

3   Frappier, Jean, 'Le Tour *je me sui* […]' Repr. in Dc1.

30   Sargent, Barbara Nelson, 'Mediæval *rire* […]' (XXVII.300)

See Qa26 Hiedsiek.

31   Kadler, Alfred, *Sprichwörter und Sentenzen der altfranzösischen Artus- und Abenteuerromane*, AA, 49 (Marburg: Elwert, 1886).

32   Voelker, P., 'Die Bedeutungsentwicklung des Wortes Roman,' *ZrP*, 10 (1886), 485–525.

33   Galpin, Stanley Leman, *'Cortois' and 'Vilain': A Study of the Distinctions Made between them by the French and Provençal Poets of the 12th, 13th and 14th Centuries*, diss. Yale (New Haven: Ryder's, 1905).

34   Stowell, William Averill, *Old-French Titles of Respect in Direct Address*, diss. Johns Hopkins (Baltimore: Furst, 1908).

35   Schumann, Hermann, 'Zu Yvain v. 304 (*ros*),' *ZrP*, 34 (1910), 373.

36   Fuchs, Philipp, 'Das altfranzösische Verbum *errer* mit seinen Stammesverwandten und das Aussterben dieses Wortes,' *RF*, 38 (1919), 335–91.

37   Goddard, Eunice Rathbone, *Women's Costume in French Texts of the Eleventh and Twelfth Centuries*, The Johns Hopkins Studies in Romance Literatures and Languages, 7 (Baltimore: Johns Hopkins Press, Paris: Presses Universitaires de France, 1927; repr. New York: Johnson, 1973).
A glossary with commentary.

38   Johnston, Oliver M., 'Old French *enui* Applied to Persons,' *MLN*, 45 (1930), 32–34.
On two examples in *Cligés*.

39   Kuttner, Max, 'Was bedeutet Guillaume d'Angleterre, v. 637: *N'i a ne borre ne garmos*,' *ZfSL*, 55 (1932), 219–21.

40   Braun, George M., 'Old French "Dangier": A New Interpretation of Its Semantic Origin,' *FR*, 7 (1934), 481–85.

41   Glasser, Richard, *Studien zur Geschichte des französischen Zeitbegriffs*, Münchner romanistische Arbeiten, 5 (Munich: Hueber, 1936).

42   Sneyders de Vogel, K., 'Or est venuz qui aunera,' *Neophil*, 21 (1936), 263–64.

43   Wagner, Robert-Léon, *'Sorcier' et 'magicien': contribution à l'histoire du vocabulaire de la magie* (Paris: Droz, 1939).
See pp. 78–86.

44   Wigand, Ruth, *Zur Bedeutungsgeschichte von · 'prud'homme'*, Marburger Beiträge zur romanischen Philologie, 24 (Marburg/Lahn: Michaelis-Braun, 1939).

45   Nitze, William A., '*"Or est venuz qui aunera"*: A Medieval Dictum,' *MLN*, 56 (1941), 405–9.

46   Lecoy, F., 'Anc. fr. *a la forclose*,' *Rom*, 68 (1944–45), 157–68; repr. in Dc14.

47   Holmes, Urban T., Jr, 'Old French *Grifaigne* and *Grifon*,' *SP*, 43 (1946), 586–94.

48   Foulet, Lucien, '*Sire, messire*,' *Rom*, 71 (1950), 1–48 and 180–221, 72 (1951), 31–77, 324–67, and 479–528. (III.133)

49   Greene, Marion A., 'A Note on the Word *Fauve* in Old French,' in *Romance Studies Presented to William Morton Dey on the Occasion of his Seventieth Birthday by his Colleagues and Former Students*, ed. Urban T. Holmes, Jr, Alfred G. Engstrom, and Sturgis E. Leavitt, UNCSRL, 12 (Chapel Hill: University of North Carolina, 1950), pp. 75–77. (III.54)

50   Taylor, Archer, '"Or est venuz qui aunera" and the English Proverbial Phrase "To Take His Measure",' *MLN*, 65 (1950), 344–45. (III.72)

51   Roques, Mario, 'Chrétien de Troyes, *Erec et Enide*,' *AIBL* (1953), pp. 193–94.

See Qa32 Bakos.

52   Lecoy, Félix, 'Notes de lexicographie française,' in *Recueil de travaux Clovis Brunel*, Mémoires et Documents Publiés par la Société de l'Ecole des Chartes, 12, 2 vols (Paris: Société de l'Ecole des Chartes, 1955), vol. 2, pp. 114–22; repr. in Dc14.
See pp. 118–20 on *de manieres*.

53   Simon, Hans Joachim, *Die Wörter für Gemütsbewegungen in den altfranzösischen Wortfeldern des Rolandsliedes und des Yvain-Romanes*, diss. Erlangen ([n.p.: n.p.], 1958).

54   Winkler, Maria, *Der kirchliche Wortschatz in der Epik Chrétiens von Troyes*, diss. Munich ([Munich: Maria Winkler], 1958.

55   Lipton, Wallace S., 'Imposed Verb Prenominalization in Medieval French and Provençal,' *RPh*, 14 (1960–61), 111–37. (XIII.40)
On Kd3.

56   Schleyer, Johannes Dietrich, *Der Wortschatz von List und Betrug im Altfranzösischen und Altprovenzalischen*, Romanistische Versuche und Vorarbeiten, 10 (Bonn: Romanisches Seminar der Universität Bonn, 1961).

57   Renson, Jean, *Les Dénominations du visage en français et dans les autres langues romanes: étude sémantique et onomasiologique*, BFPLUL, 162 (Paris: Belles Lettres, 1962).

58   Gougenheim, G., '"Meschine",' *MA*, 69 (1963), 359–64.

59   Stefenelli, Arnulf, *Der Synonymenreichtum der altfranzösischen Dichtersprache*, Österreichische Akademie der Wissenschaften: Philosophisch-historische Klasse, Sitzungsberichte 251:5 (Graz: Böhlaus, 1967).

60   Lecoy, Félix, 'Note sur le vocabulaire dialectal ou régional dans les œuvres littéraires au Moyen Age,' *RLingR*, 32 (1968), 48–69. Repr. in *Les Dialectes de France au Moyen Age et aujourd'hui: domaines d'oïl et domaine franco-provençal: colloque organisé par le Centre de Philologie et de Littérature Romanes de l'Université des Sciences Humaines de Strasbourg du 22 au 25 mai 1967*, ed. Georges Straka, Actes et Colloques, 9 (Paris: Klincksieck, 1972), pp. 59–80 (including discussion); and in Dc14.

61   Apostolides, Diana S., 'Old French "Bonet",' *RomN*, 11 (1969–70), 210–14.
Perceval v. 937, 2796 (ed. Roach).

62   Boulengier-Sedyn, R., *Le Vocabulaire de la coiffure en ancien français étudié dans les romans de 1150 à 1300*, Académie Royale de Belgique: Classe des Lettres et des Sciences Morales et Politiques, Mémoires, 2nd ser., 60:1 (n° 1829) (Brussels: Palais des Académies; Gembloux: Duculot, 1970).

63   Davis, J. Cary, 'Si m'aït Deus : se Deus m'aït,' *USFLQ*, 8:3–4 (Summer 1970), 1–6.

64   Aspland, Clifford, '*Aller* + the *-ant* Form in 12th Century Old French Verse: A Grammatical and Stylistic Analysis,' *SN*, 43 (1971), 3–30.

65   Ineichen, Gustav, 'Zur linguistischen Interpretation mittelalterlicher Glossen (afr. *estinc*, afr. *barbelote*),' in *Interlinguistica: Sprachvergleich und Übersetzung: Festschrift zum 60. Geburtstag von Mario Wandruszka* (Tübingen: Niemeyer, 1971), pp. 55–59.
See note 8.

66   Gorog, Ralph Paul de, 'The Medieval French Prepositions and the Question of Synonymy,' *PQ*, 51 (1972), 345–64.
Examples from *Erec*.

See Va6 Lavis.

67   Laugesen, Anker Teilgård, 'Quelques formules de salutation en ancien français,' *RevR*, 8 (1973), 143–50.

68   Lavis, Georges, 'La concurrence entre *penser*, *cuidier* et *croire* chez Chrétien de Troyes,' in *Hommage au Professeur Maurice Delbouille*, *MrR*, Special Issue (1973), pp. 147–68. (XXXVI.294)

69   Moignet, Gérard, 'Ancien français *ne tant ne quant*,' in *Mélanges Teruo Sato: partie I*, *CEMN*, Special Number (1973), pp. 91–96.

See Qc34 Flori.
On *bacheler*.

See Fb39 Hilty.
In the *Erec* Prologue.

70   Reid, T. B. W., 'Dahez et qui vos oï onques Ne vit' onques, que je soie!' in *Philologica Lommatzsch*, pp. 317–22. (XXIX.45)
On the expression 'Que je soie!'

71   Venckeleer, Theo, *Rolant li proz: contribution à l'histoire de quelques qualifications laudatives en français au Moyen Age* (Lille: Atelier des Thèses Université de Lille III; Paris: Champion, 1975).

72   Ducháček, Otto, 'Esquisse du champ conceptuel de la beauté dans le français du XIIe siècle,' *KN*, 23 (1976), 105–18.
Cf. his *Le Champ conceptuel de la beauté en français moderne*, Opera Universitatis Brunensis: Facultas Philosophica–Spisy University v Brně:

Filisifická Fakulta, 71 (Prague: Státní Pedagogické Nakladatelství, 1960), and 'Esquisse du champ conceptuel de la beauté dans le français du XIIIe siècle,' *Mélanges Camproux*, vol. 1, pp. 287–98.

73 Holden, A. J., 'Ancien français *tresoïr*, "entendre bien", "entendre mal", ou autre chose?' *Rom*, 97 (1976), 107–15, 268–71. (XXIX.236)
Examples from *Erec*. See also Félix Lecoy's 'Note additionnelle sur *tresoïr*,' pp. 115–17.

74 Baum, Richard, 'Eine neue Etymologie von frz. *lai* und apr. *lais*. Zugleich: ein Plädoyer für die Zusammenarbeit von Sprach- und Literaturwissenschaft,' in *Beiträge ZrP*, pp. 17–78.

75 Burgess, Glyn S., 'Old French *contenance* and *contenant*,' in *Essays Powell-Hodgins*, pp. 21–41.

See Ge27 Collins.

See Hg29 Frappier and Ménard.
On *parmi* and *hanches*.

76 Gier, Albert, 'Das Verwandtschaftsverhältnis von afr. *sens* und *sen*,' *RJ*, 28 (1977), 54–72.

77 Lavis, Georges, 'Note sur la synonymie des verbes a. fr. *penser*, *apenser*, *porpenser*, *trespenser*,' *MrR*, 27:3–4 (1977), 5–23.

78 Liver, Ricarda, 'Moderne Definitionsversuche des Sprichworts und Sprichwortbezeichnungen im Altfranzösischen,' in *Beiträge ZrP*, pp. 339–57.

79 Löfstedt, Leena, '*Chapiaus a IIII pertuis*,' *NM*, 78 (1977), 165–70.
On *Erec* v. 1639 (ed. Roques).

80 Roques, Gilles, 'Fantaisie maritime,' *TLL*, 15:1 (1977), 245–53.
See pp. 249–50.

81 Burgess, Glyn S., '*Sen(s)*, "Meaning", in Twelfth-Century French,' *Rom*, 99 (1978), 389–95. (XXXI.263)
On Fb17 and 24.

See Gb49 Dubost.

82 Green, Dennis Howard, '*Avanture* in Chrétien's *Perceval*,' in Pb209 *Approaches*, pp. 158–61.

83 Kleiber, Georges, *'Le mot 'ire' en ancien français (XIe–XIIIe siècles): essai d'analyse sémantique*, BFR, A41 (Paris: Klincksieck, 1978).

84 Le Rider, Paule, '*Or est venuz qui l'aunera* ou la fortune littéraire d'un proverbe,' in *Mélanges Lods*, vol. 1, pp. 393–409. (XXXI.285)

85 Riquer, Martín de, 'El *haubert* francés y la *loriga* castellana,' in *Mélanges Wathelet-Willem*, pp. 545–68.

See Qa49 Subrenat.

86 Brucker, Charles, *Sage et son réseau lexical en ancien français (des origines au XIIIème siècle: étude historique, sémantique, stylistique et comparative du vocabulaire intellectuel et moral*, diss. Nancy II, 2 vols (Lille: Atelier Reproduction des Thèses Université de Lille III, Paris: Champion, 1979).
Besides *sagesse*, there are sections on *sage, sené, sen(s), savoir, sapience/sagesse, fol, folie*, and 'marginal words' like *preu, preudome, proece, cortois*. Cf. Kd103.

87 Offord, M. H., 'Etude comparative du vocabulaire de *Cligès* de Chrétien de Troyes et d'*Ille et Galeron* de Gautier d'Arras,' *Cahiers de Lexicologie*, 34 (1979), 36–52.

88 Schwake, Helmut Peter, *Der Wortschatz des 'Cligés' von Chrétien de Troyes*, Beihefte zur *ZrP*, 149 (Tübingen: Niemeyer, 1979). (XXXIII.67)

89 Legros, Huguette, 'Le vocabulaire de l'amitié, son évolution sémantique au cours du XIIe siècle,' *CCM*, 23 (1980), 131–39. (XXXIII.345)

90 Matoré, Georges, 'Remarques sur Beau et Beauté en ancien français,' *Etudes Lanly*, pp. 225–32.

See Bb38 Woledge.

91 Torii, Masafumi, 'On the Words *sen* and *sens* in Old French,' *Flambeau* (Bulletin de la Section de Français de l'Université des Langues Étrangères de Tokyo), 9 (1981), 1–14.
In Japanese.

92 Baird, J. W. R., and R. M. Pensom, '*Pechié* in *Perceval*,' *FSB*, 4 (1982), 1–4. (XXXV.374)

93 Queffélec, Ambroise J. M., 'Des énoncés traduisant l'imminence contrecarrée en ancien français,' in *Mélanges Larmat*, pp. 239–68. (XXXVI.364)

94 Chaurand, Jacques, 'Les verbes-supports en ancien français: "*doner*" dans les œuvres de Chrétien de Troyes,' *LingI*, 7 (1983), 11–46.

95 Derval, Bernard, and Charles Doutrelepont, 'A Computer-Aided System of Text Lemmatization Applied to the Romances of Chrétien de Troyes,' in *Computer Applications to Medieval Studies*, ed. Anne Gilmour-Bryson, SMC, 17 (Kalamazoo: Medieval Institute Publications, Western Michigan University, 1984), pp. 31–44. (XXXVII.363)

96 Mölk, Ulrich, 'Remarques philologiques sur *tornoi(ement)* dans la littérature française des XIIe et XIIIe siècles,' in *Symposium in honorem Prof. M. de Riquer* (Barcelona: Universitat de Barcelona and Quaderns Crema, 1986), pp. 277–87.

97 Sargent-Baur, Barbara Nelson, '*Erec*, "novel seignor", à nouveau,' *Rom*, 105 (1984), 552–58. (XXXIX.672)

See Bb47 Uitti.

See Gd.c28 Grigsby.

98 Marchello-Nizia, Christiane, *Dire le vrai: l'adverbe 'si' en français médiéval: essai de linguistique historique*, PRF, 168 (Geneva: Droz, 1985). (XXXVIII.241)

99 Mölk, Ulrich, 'Philologische Aspekte des Turniers,' in *Turnier*, pp. 163–74.

See Fa134 Schulze-Busacker.

See Ha137 Baumgartner.

100 Gallais, Pierre, 'La terre chez quelques romanciers des XIIe et XIIIe siècles: étude statistique,' *PRIS-MA*, 2 (1986), 17–26, 73–87. (XXXIX.644)
Includes *Perceval, Guillaume d'Angleterre, Philomena*.

101 Janssens, Jan, 'Le prologue du *Chevalier de la charrette*: une clef pour l'interprétation du roman?' *Bien dire*, 4 (1986), 29–51. (XL.46)

See Bb52 Woledge.

102 Andrieux-Reix, Nelly, *Ancien français: fiches de vocabulaire*, Etudes littéraires (Paris: Presses Universitaires de France, 1987).
Includes bibliography and short essays on the history and semantic range of significant Old French words. Many examples from Chrétien.

103 Brucker, Charles, *Sage et sagesse au Moyen Age (XIIe et XIIIe siècles): étude historique, sémantique et stylistique*, PRF, 175 (Geneva: Droz, 1987). (XL.34)

104 Burgess, Glyn S., 'The Term *courtois* in Twelfth-Century French,' in *Etudes Matoré*, pp. 105–22. (XL.35)

105 Holden, A.-J., 'Ancien français *ferir (de)manois, ferir (de) maintenant*,' *Rom*, 108 (1987), 345–53.
Example from *Perceval*.

106 Eskénazi, André, '*Eglise* et *Mostier* dans les romans de Chrétien de Troyes (BN 794),' *RLingR*, 52 (1988), 121–37. (XLI.58)

See Gd.a25–26 Gallais.

107 Katô, Kyôko, 'Adjectives in the Works of Chrétien de Troyes,' *FFRSH*, 23 (1988), 21–28. (XLII.148).
In Japanese.

See Fb72 Kelly.

108 Lebsanft, Franz, *Studien zu einer Linguistik des Grußes: Sprache und Funktion der altfranzösischen Grußformeln*, Beihefte zur *ZrP*, 217 (Tübingen: Niemeyer, 1988).

See Sa120 MacBain.

See Ge47 Marache.

See Gc19 Burgess.

See Qc58 Chandès.

109 Eskénazi, André, '*Cheval* et *destrier* dans les romans de Chrétien de Troyes (BN 794),' *RLingR*, 53 (1989), 397–433. (XLII.54)

110 Gregory, Stewart, 'La description de la fontaine dans l'*Yvain* de Chrétien de Troyes: un problème d'interprétation,' *Rom*, 110 (1989), 539–41. (XLV.180)
Boz au v. 425 (ed. Foerster-Reid).

See Qa91 Runte.

111 Gallais, Pierre, 'Sémantique du bonheur chez les romanciers du XIIᵉ siècle,' in *Bonheur*, pp. 189–204.

See Gd.b41 Ménard.

112 Picoche, Jacqueline, 'Le bonheur ou le bon eür,' in *Bonheur*, pp. 347–54.
Examples from *Perceval* and *Guillaume d'Angleterre*.

113 Copeland, Rita, 'Between Romans and Romantics,' *TSLL*, 33 (1991), 215–24.

See Qa98 Gravdal.

See Hf87 Lepage.
On the meaning of *gaeignier*.

114 Bec, Pierre, *Vièles ou violes? variations philologiques et musicales autour des instruments à archet du Moyen Age (XIᵉ–XVᵉ siècle)*, Sapience (Paris: Klincksieck, 1992). (XLVI.308)

See Gb108 Burgess.

See Qc67 Ménard.

115 Ménard, Philippe, 'La ville dans les romans de chevalerie en France aux XIIᵉ et XIIIᵉ siècles,' in *50 rue de Varenne*, Supplemento Italo-Francese di Nuovi Argomenti, 43 (Paris: Istituto Italiano di Cultura, 1992), pp. 96–109. (XLV.190)

See Qa105 Akehurst.

116 Burgess, Glyn S., 'Etude sur le terme *cortois* dans le français du XIIᵉ siècle,' *TLL*, 31:2 (1993), 195–209. (XLVI.316)

117 Eskénazi, André, '*Tref, pavellon, tante* dans les romans de Chrétien de Troyes (BN 794),' in *Hommage Dufournet*, vol. 2, pp. 549–62. (XLVI.325)

See Qc70 Flori.

118 Harano, Noboru, 'Expression of Time in the Middle Ages – The Hours in a Day,' *The Hiroshima University Studies* (Faculty of Letters), 53 (1993), 163–81.
In Japanese.

119 Katô, Kyôko, '"Courtois" and "Amour" in Chrétien de Troyes's *Erec et Enide*,' in *Mélanges Teruo Satô*, Part II (Tokyo: France Tosho, 1993), pp. 125–36. (XLVII.634).
In Japanese.

120 Seto, Naohiko, 'Observation on the Meaning of "Melancholy" in Some Courtly Romances of the Twelfth and Thirteenth Centuries,' in *Mélanges Teruo Satô*, Part II (Tokyo: France Tosho, 1993), pp. 151–63 (XLVII.646).
In Japanese.

121 Burgess, Glyn S., 'The Term "Chevalerie" in Twelfth-Century French,' in *Studies Sinclair*, pp. 343–58. (XLVII.534)

See Qc71 Corradetti.

122 Crespo, Roberto, '"Merchi desert qui la prie" (R. 1206, v. 33),' *CN*, 54 (1994), 53–64. (XLVII.460)
On *Yvain* v. 5680–82 (ed. Foerster).

See Pb388 Wis.

See Qc74 Corradetti.

123 Lagorgette, Dominique, '"*Avoir a non*": étude diachronique de quelques expressions qui prédiquent le nom,' *LINX*, 32 (1995), 113–32.

124 Lignereux, Marielle, '*Jurer* est-il déjà un verbe performatif en ancien français?' *LINX*, 32 (1995), 97–111.

125 Ollier, Marie-Louise, '*Or*, opérateur de rupture,' *LINX*, 32 (1995), 13–31.

126 Oppermann, Evelyne, 'Les énoncés au futur comportant l'adverbe *mar* et l'expression de l'interdiction en ancien français,' *LINX*, 32 (1995), 77–95.

127 Raffaelli, Ida, 'Polisemičnost Leksema koji Označavaju Fizički Izgled (Krije li se Iza Ljepote Debrota) – La polysénie des lexèmes qui désignent l'appearance physique,' [sic] *Suvremena Lingvistika*, 39 (1995), 39–51.
French summary.

128 Rodríguez Somolinos, Amalia, '*Certes*, *voire*: l'évolution sémantique de deux marqueurs assertifs de l'ancien français,' *LINX*, 32 (1995), 51–76.

See Qc78 Corradetti.

See Rb32 Gouttebroze.

129 Luttrell, Claude, 'La *boz* de la fontaine dans *Le Chevalier au lion* de Chrétien de Troyes,' *Rom*, 114 (1996), 521–24. (XLIX.167)

See Kc104 Bertin.

See Gb133 Faaborg, Chap. 9 and 10.

130 Kunstmann, Pierre, '*Faire que sage(s), faire que fol(s)*: prudence!' in *Les formes du sens: études de linguistique française, médiévale et générale offertes à Robert Martin à l'occasion de ses 60 ans*, ed. Georges Kleiber and Martin Riegel, Champs Linguistiques (Louvain-la-Neuve: Duculot, 1997), pp. 233–40. (L.205)

131 Lagerqvist, Hans, 'Langue et société: l'exemple de *entor* en ancien français,' *RLingR*, 61 (1997), 41–78.

See Gd.c63 Ménard.

See Kc105 Baril.

See Gd.b57(A) Blons-Pierre.

See Gd.b57(B) Akkari.

132 Andrieux-Reix, Nelly, '*Il convient, il fault, il affiert a ung honme… estre ung escolier*: approche d'une synonymie occasionnelle dans l'histoire du français,' in *Mélanges Suard*, vol. 1, pp. 23–33.

133 Lemaire, Jacques, 'A propos d'*esveillier* au v. 538 du *Chevalier de la charrete*,' in *Mélanges Suard*, vol. 1, pp. 537–46. (LII.249)

See Nb51 Walter.

134 Van Emden, Wolfgang, 'Quelques hapax de mes connaissances,' *Ce nous dist li escris… Che est la verite: études de littérature médiévale André Moisan*, ed. Miren Lacassagne, Senefiance, 45 (Aix-en-Provence: CUER-MA, 2000), pp. 289–303.
See *espaarz* (v. 280, *Yvain*, ed. Reid), pp. 289–90, and *lois* (v. 818, *Perceval*, ed. Roach), pp. 292–93.

135 Crespo, Roberto, 'Conon de Béthune (R. 303, 19–24) e Gautier de Dargies (R. 1290, 21–22); Chrétien de Troyes, *Yvain*, 2533–2534,' in *Convergences médiévales: épopée, lyrique, roman: mélanges Madeleine*

Tyssens, Bibliothèque du moyen âge, 19 (Brussels: De Boeck Université, 2001), pp. 133–38.

e: Semiotics

2   Engler, Rudolf, 'Semiologische Lese (Betrachtungen zu Saussure, Salviati und Chrétien de Troyes),' in *Linguistique contemporaine: hommage à Eric Buyssens* (Brussels: Editions de l'Institut de Sociologie de l'Université Libre, 1970), pp. 61–73.

3   Adam, Jean-Michel, 'La logique du signifiant (Chrétien de Troyes, *Perceval ou Le Conte du Graal* [1]),' pp. 71–82, and 'L'isotopie du contexte arthurien (Chrétien de Troyes, *Perceval ou Le Conte du Graal* [2]),' pp. 108–20, in *Linguistique et discours littéraire: théorie et pratique des textes*, by Jean-Michel Adam and Jean-Pierre Goldstein, Collection L (Paris: Larousse, 1976).
The first article treats *Perceval* v. 1–6, 34–68; the second, v. 69–363.

4   Adam, Jean-Michel, with A.-M. Boulanger, D. Marzal, N. Delanos, M.-H. Deniel, and J.-P. Vidal, 'Pour une analyse macro-textuelle: l'exemple du *Conte du Graal*,' *Pratiques*, 9 (1976), 15–52.

5   Olsen, Michel, *Les transformations du triangle érotique* (Copenhagen: Akademisk Forlag, 1976).
See the Introduction, pp. 5–60.

See Fa84 Vance.

See La26 Boklund.

See Hc27 Maddox.

6   Grigsby, John L., 'Sign, Symbol and Metaphor: Todorov and Chrétien de Troyes,' *Esp*, 18:3 (1978), 28–40. (XXXII.181)

7   Corti, Maria, 'Models and Antimodels in Medieval Culture,' *NLH*, 10 (1978–79), 339–66.

See Va13 Haidu.

See Fb52 Haidu.

See Uc21 Bloch.

8   Haidu, Peter, 'The Episode as Semiotic Module in Twelfth-Century Romance,' *Poetics Today*, 4 (1983), 655–81.
See pp. 673–81.

9   Härmä, Juhani, 'La séquence du don contraignant: essai d'examen dans le cadre du dialogue,' in *Actes Odense*, pp. 163–73.

See Hc47 Collins.

See Hf52 Dubost.

10   Haidu, Peter, 'La valeur: sémiotique et marxisme,' in *Sémiotique en jeu: à partir et autour de l'œuvre d'A. J. Greimas: Actes de la Décade Tenue au Centre Culturel International de Cerisy-la-Salle du 4 au 14 août 1983*, ed. Michel Arrivé and Jean-Claude Coquet, Actes Sémiotiques, 5 (Paris: Hadès-Benjamins, 1987), pp. 247–63.
Treats *Yvain*.

11   Grimbert, Joan Tasker, 'Misrepresentation and Misconception in Chrétien de Troyes: Nonverbal and Verbal Semiotics in *Erec et Enide* and *Perceval*,' in *Sign*, pp. 50–79. (XLI.387)

12   Reiss, Edmund, 'Ambiguous Signs and Authorial Deceptions in Fourteenth-Century Fictions,' in *Sign*, pp. 113–37. (XLI.433)

13   Steele, Stephen, 'Resisting Chrétien's Grail: Some Analytic Footing,' *MIFLC Review*, 1 (1991), 68–77.

14   Voicu, Mihaela, '"Semblance" et "senefiance" ou de la lecture des signes dans *Le Conte du graal*,' *RRL*, 37 (1992), 79–87. (XLV.610)

15   Mendoza Ramos, María del Pilar, 'Laudine, Enide y Guenièvre: tres modelos femeninos del mundo cortés,' in *Actas Almagro*, pp. 219–24.

16   Edeline, Francis, 'Le roi Arthur et la sémiotique visuelle,' in *Text and Visuality*, ed. Martin Heusser [et alii], Word & Image Interactions, 3 – Textxet: Studies in Comparative Literature, 22 (Amsterdam: Rodopi, 1999), pp. 207–18.

f: Concordances

1   Andrieu, G., and J. Piolle, *Perceval ou Le Conte du Graal de Chrétien de Troyes: concordancier complet des formes graphiques occurrentes d'après l'édition de M. Félix Lecoy* (Aix-en-Provence: CREL-CUERMA, Paris: Champion, 1976). (XXVIII.242)

2   Bonnefois, Pascal, and Marie-Louise Ollier, *Yvain ou Le Chevalier au lion: concordance lemmatisée*, Collection ERA 642 (UA 04 1028)

(Paris: Laboratoire de Linguistique Formelle, and Département de Recherches Linguistiques, Université Paris 7, 1988).

3 Ollier, Marie-Louise, *Lexique et concordance de Chrétien de Troyes d'après la copie Guiot, avec introduction, index et rimaire*, Traitement informatique par Serge Lusignan, Charles Doutrelepont et Bernard Derval (Montréal: Institut d'Etudes Médiévales, Université de Montréal; Paris: Vrin, 1986; 2nd ed. revised and corrected, 1989). (XXXIX. 303)

4 *Léonard, Monique, *Concordancier du 'Conte du graal' de Chrétien de Troyes* (Paris: Champion électronique, 1998), CD-ROM

L: ADAPTATION AND INTERTEXTUALITY

Interest in medieval approaches to narrative invention, adaptation, and reception of romance has inspired investigation of the methods and expectations of composition in the time Chrétien wrote. The goal is to design critical approaches that reflect, insofar as possible, Chrétien's art and to use that knowledge to interpret his romances. Thus, in many ways, this central section of the Bibliography looks back to the work in the preceding sections as well as to much in the following sections. Inclusion here rather than in those sections is determined largely by emphasis on medieval theoretical presuppositions and efforts to theorize these in critically useful ways, including their relationship to modern theoretical and terminological concerns.

a: Analysis and Methodology

7   Fourquet, Jean, 'Le Rapport [...]' Repr. in Dc8.

19   Fourquet, Jean, 'Hartmann von Aue [...]' Repr. in Dc8.

21   Luttrell, Claude, *The Creation* [...] (XVIII.299)

22   Kooijman, Jacques-Cornélis, 'Le Motif [...]' (XXVIII.49)

23   Raible, Wolfgang, 'Vom Autor als Kopist zum Leser als Autor: Literaturtheorie in der literarischen Praxis,' *Poetica*, 5 (1972), 133–51. See pp. 134–38.

24   Diverres, A. H., 'Chrétien de Troyes and his Sources,' *FMLS*, 9 (1973), 298–300. On Hb12.

See Pf18 Barnes, pp. 407–16.

25 Fourquet, Jean, 'Nouvelles perspectives sur la littérature d'adaptation courtoise,' in *Actes du Colloque sur 'l'adaptation courtoise' en littérature médiévale allemande des 9 et 10 avril 1976*, ed. Danielle Buschinger, Centre d'Etudes Médiévales de l'Université de Picardie (Paris: Champion, 1976), pp. 7–18; repr. in Dc8.

See Qe6 Boklund.

26 Boklund, Karin M., 'On the Spatial and Cultural Characteristics of Courtly Romance,' *Semiotica*, 20 (1977), 1–37. Repr. in *Semiotics and Dialectics: Ideology and the Text*, ed. Peter V. Zima, Linguistic & Literary Studies in Eastern Europe (LLSEE), 5 (Amsterdam: Benjamins, 1981), pp. 387–443 + 1 foldout. (XXXII.514)

27 Kelly, Douglas, '*Translatio studii*: Translation, Adaptation, and Allegory in Medieval French Literature,' *PQ*, 57 (1978), 287–310. (XXXII.193)

See Fa97 Zumthor.

See Pb230 Pastré.

28 Hunt, Tony, 'The Medieval Adaptations of Chrétien's *Yvain*: A Bibliographical Essay,' in *Essays Thorpe*, pp. 203–13. (XXXIV.325)

29 Poirion, Daniel, 'Ecriture et ré-écriture au Moyen Age,' *Littérature*, 41 (1981), 109–18; repr. in Dc21. (XXXV.344)

30 Riffaterre, Michael, 'L'intertexte inconnu,' *Littérature*, 41 (1981), 4–7.
See also Marie-Rose Logan, 'L'intertextualité au carrefour de la philologie et de la poétique,' pp. 47–49; Matilda Tomaryn Bruckner, 'En guise de conclusion,' pp. 104–8.

31 Zumthor, Paul, 'Intertextualité et mouvance,' *Littérature*, 41 (1981), 8–16.

32 Zumthor, Paul, 'Le champ romanesque,' *Europe*, 642 (Oct. 1982), 27–36. (XXXV.349)

33 Rider, Jeff, 'The Eiron, the Critic, and the Elsewhere of Allegory,' in *CLAM Chowder: Proceedings of the Second Midwest Comparative Literature Graduate Student Conference*, ed. Mark Axelrod [et alii] (Minneapolis: Comparative Literature Association of Minnesota, 1983), pp. 141–49.

34 Baumgartner, Emmanuèle, 'Texte de prologue et statut du texte,' in *Essor et fortune de la chanson de geste dans l'Europe et l'Orient latin: Actes du IXe Congrès International de la Société Rencesvals pour l'Étude des Épopées Romanes, Padoue-Venise, 29 août–4 septembre 1982* (Modena: Mucchi, 1984), pp. 465–73.
See pp. 470–73.

See Pb292 Pérennec, vol. 1, pp. 1–29.

35 Baumgartner, Emmanuèle, 'L'écriture romanesque et son modèle scripturaire: écriture et réécriture du graal,' in *L'Imitation: aliénation ou source de liberté? Rencontres de l'Ecole du Louvre* (Paris: Documentation Française, 1985), pp. 129–43. (XXXVIII.182)

36 Busby, Keith, 'The Reception of Chrétien's Calogrenant Episode,' in *Studies Gerritsen*, pp. 25–40. (XXXVIII.680)

37 Worstbrock, Franz Josef, 'Dilatatio materiae: zur Poetik des *Erec* Hartmanns von Aue,' *FMSt*, 19 (1985), 1–30. (XXXIX.555)

38 Lecco, Margherita, 'Note su intertestualità e romanzo cortese,' in *Intertestualità: materiali di lavoro del Centro di Ricerche in Scienza della Letteratura*, ed. Massimo Bonafin (Genoa: il melangolo, 1986), pp. 45–56. (XXXIX.152)

39 Haupt, Barbara, 'Prinzipien literarischer Kulturvermittlung im Hochmittelalter,' *AStnSpr*, 224 (1987), 1–13.
See pp. 8–13.

40 Shitanda, Sô, 'Die "adaptation courtoise" in Wolframs *Parzival*,' *DB*, 20 (1987), 53–63. (XL.230).

41 Bruckner, Matilda Tomaryn, 'Intertextuality,' in *Legacy*, vol. 1, pp. 223–65. (XLII.179)

See Jd35 Lange.

42 Rockwell, Paul Vincent, 'Writing the Fountain: The Specificity of Resemblance in Arthurian Romance,' *BBSIA*, 42 (1990), 267–82. (XLIII.591)

See Db38 Wolfzettel.

See Pb351 Pérennec.

43 Kamizawa, Eizô, 'On the "Adaptation courtoise": the Case of Hartmann von Aue,' *JFLN*, 112 (1992), 87–96. (LI.656).
In Japanese.

44   Florence, Melanie J., 'Description as Intertextual Reference: Chrétien's *Yvain* and Hartmann's *Iwein*,' *FMLS*, 29 (1993), 1–17. (XLVI.440)

See Ha171 Maddox.

See Pb360(B) Meletinsky.

45   *The Medieval 'Opus': Imitation, Rewriting, and Transmission in the French Tradition: Proceedings of the Symposium Held at the Institute for Research in Humanities, October 5–7 1995, The University of Wisconsin-Madison*, ed. Douglas Kelly, Faux Titre, 116 (Amsterdam: Rodopi, 1996).
Articles dealing with Chrétien:
    A.   C. Stephen Jaeger, 'Patrons and the Beginnings of Courtly Romance,' pp. 45–58. (XLIX.402)
    B.   Donald Maddox, 'Inventing the Unknown: Rewriting in *Le Bel Inconnu*,' pp. 101–23. (XLIX.409)
    C.   Norris J. Lacy, 'Motif Transfer in Arthurian Literature,' pp. 157–68. (XLIX.406, L.508)
    D.   Matilda Tomaryn Bruckner, 'Rewriting Chrétien's *Conte du graal* – Mothers and Sons: Questions, Contradictions, and Connections,' pp. 213–44. (XLIX.393)
    E.   Frank Brandsma, 'The Presentation of Direct Discourse in Arthurian Romance: Changing Modes of Performance and Reception?' pp. 245–60. (XLIX.392)

See Uf2(B) Schwartz.

46   *Text and Intertext in Medieval Arthurian Literature*, ed. Norris J. Lacy , GRLH, 1997 (New York: Garland, 1996).
The following articles make use of Chrétien's romances: Gb131 Brandsma, Gd.a39 Sturm-Maddox, Gd.c59 Maddox, Lc5 Kennedy, and Lc6 Sargent-Baur.

47   Pickens, Rupert T., 'Transmission et *translatio*: mouvement textuel et variance,' *FF*, 23 (1998), 133–45. (LI.795)

See Fa181 Kelly.

b: Reading

See Pa 118 Stierle.

1   Blumenfeld-Kosinski, Renate, 'Chrétien de Troyes as a Reader of the *romans antiques*,' *PQ*, 64 (1985), 398–405. (XXXVIII.469)

2   Hult, David F., 'Lancelot's Shame,' *RPh*, 42 (1988–89), 30–50. (XLI.401)

3   Runte, Hans R., 'Initial Readers of Chrétien de Troyes,' in *Essays Grigsby*, pp. 121–32. (XLII.344)

4   Sturges, Robert S., *Medieval Interpretation: Models of Reading in Literary Narrative, 1100–1500* (Carbondale: Southern Illinois University Press, 1991).
On *Charrette*, see Chap. 1; on *Perceval*, see chap. 2.

5   Kennedy, Elspeth, 'The Knight as Reader of Arthurian Romance,' in *Essays Lagorio*, pp. 70–90. (XLIX.507)

See Hf94 Matthews.

See Ba34 Varvaro.

c: Influences

1   Uitti, Karl D., 'Chrétien de Troyes and his Vernacular Forebears: The City of Women (I),' *FF*, 11 (1986), 261–88. (XL.324)

2   Calin, William, 'The Exaltation and Undermining of Romance: *Ipomedon*,' in *Legacy*, vol. 2, pp. 111–24. (XLII.185)

3   Saly, Antoinette, 'Peredur, Perceval, Parzival, Parceval, Percyvell, Perlesvaus,' in *L'Unité de la culture européenne au Moyen Age: XXVIII. Jahrestagung des Arbeitskreises Deutsche Literatur des Mittelalters, Straßburg, 23.–26. Sept. 1993*, ed. Danielle Buschinger and Wolfgang Spiewok, WODAN, 38: EG, 23–TS, 21 (Greifswald: Reineke, 1994), pp. 143–50; repr. in Dc30. (XLVII.136)

4   Kay, Sarah, *The 'Chanson de Geste' in the Age of Romance: Political Fictions* (Oxford: Clarendon Press, 1995). (LII.406)

5   Kennedy, Elspeth, 'Intertextuality between Genres in the *Lancelot-Grail*,' in La46 *Text*, pp. 71–90.

6   Sargent-Baur, Barbara N., 'Veraces historiae aut fallaces fabulae?' in La46 *Text*, pp. 25–39. (XLIX.548)

See Db71 Hult.

7 Rollo, David, 'Three Mediators and Three Venerable Books: Geoffrey of Monmouth, Mohammed, Chrétien de Troyes,' *Arthuriana*, 8:4 (1998), 100–14. (LI.804)

d: Text and Manuscript Lay-out

1 Bruns, Gerald L., 'The Originality of Texts in a Manuscript Culture,' *CL*, 32 (1980), 113–29. (XXXIII.135)
See pp. 121–22.

2 Walters, Lori, 'Le rôle du scribe dans l'organisation des manuscrits des romans de Chrétien de Troyes,' *Rom*, 106 (1985), 303–25. (XL.62)

3 Huot, Sylvia, *From Song to Book: The Poetics of Writing in Old French Lyric and Lyrical Narrative Poetry* (Ithaca, NY: Cornell University Press, 1987). (XL.286)
See Chap. 1: 'Scribal Practice and Poetic Process in Didactic and Narrative Anthologies,' pp. 11–45.

4 *Mise en page et mise en texte du livre manuscrit*, ed. Henri-Jean Martin and Jean Vezin (Paris: Cercle de la Librairie-Promodis, 1990). (XLIII.180)
See Geneviève Hasenohr, 'VIII. Traductions et littérature en langue vulgaire,' especially 'Les romans en vers,' pp. 245–65.

5 Masters, Bernadette A., *Esthétique et manuscripture: le 'moulin à paroles' au Moyen Age*, Beiträge zur älteren Literaturgeschichte (Heidelberg: Winter, 1992).

6 Walters, Lori J., 'Parody and Moral Allegory in Chantilly MS 472,' *MLN*, 113 (1998), 937–50. (LII.833)

7 Busby, Keith, 'Rubrics and the Reception of Romance,' *FS*, 53 (1999), 129–41. (LII.358)

M: LEARNED SOURCES

Although scholars still seek to recover specific sources for Chrétien in learned traditions, the greater awareness of medieval invention and original adaptation, together with the implications of intertextuality, has made us more aware through recent studies of how Chrétien may have adapted or rewritten his presumed sources to new purposes in original composition.

a: Classical Antiquity

12   Micha, Alexandre, 'L'Épreuve […]' Repr. in D3.

23   Laurie, Helen C. R., 'Further Notes […]' (XXVII.250)

24   Ogle, M. B., 'The Sloth of Erec,' *RR*, 9 (1918), 1–20.

See Gd.c5 Schmitt-von Mühlenfels.

See Hc23 Huppé.
The *Aeneid* and *Erec*.

25   Schnell, Rüdiger, 'Ovids *Ars amatoria* und die höfische Minnetheorie,' *Euph*, 69 (1975), 132–59. (XXVIII.67)
See pp. 154–58. ·

See Fa87 Freeman.

26   Laurie, Helen C. R., 'Some New Sources for Chrétien's *Conte du graal*,' *Rom*, 99 (1978), 550–54. (XXXI.279)

27   Hanning, R. W., 'Courtly Contexts for Urban *Cultus*: Responses to Ovid in Chrétien's *Cligès* and Marie's *Guigemar*,' *Symp*, 35 (1981), 34–56. (XXXV.161)

See Wa22–23 Benkov.

28   Dornbush, Jean, 'Ovid's *Pyramus and Thisbe* and Chrétien's *Le Chevalier de la charrete,' RPh*, 36 (1982–83), 34–43. (XXXV.155)

See Fb55 Luttrell.

29   Schmid, Elisabeth, 'Augenlust und Spiegelliebe: der mittelalterliche Narciß, '*DVj*, 59 (1985), 551–71. (XXXVIII.51)
Treats *Cligés.*

See Ef7 Hunt, Chap. 4.

30   Laurie, Helen C. R., 'Chrétien at Work on the *Conte du graal,' Rom*, 107 (1986), 38–54. (XLI.66)

See Mf10 Laurie.

See Sb48 Laurie.

31   Nightingale, Jeanne A., 'From Mirror to Metamorphosis: Echoes of Ovid's *Narcissus* in Chrétien's *Erec et Enide,'* in *The Mythographic Art: Classical Fable and the Rise of the Vernacular in Early France and England*, ed. Jane Chance (Gainesville: University of Florida Press, 1990), pp. 47–82. (XLIII.583)

See Wa29 Keller.

32   Okken, Lambertus, 'Chrétien/Hartmann and Seneca, *De beneficiis,' ABäG*, 35 (1992), 21–36. (XLV.420)

33   Rollo, David, 'From Apuleius's Psyche to Chrétien's Erec and Enide,' in *The Search for the Ancient Novel*, ed. James Tatum (Baltimore: Johns Hopkins University Press, 1994), pp. 347–69.

34   Rossi, Luciano, 'I trovatori e l'esempio ovidiano,' in *Ovidius Redivivus: von Ovid zu Dante*, ed. Michelangelo Picone and Bernhard Zimmermann (Stuttgart: M & P, 1994), pp. 105–48.
See pp. 138–48.

See Ha195 Holzbacher.
On Hyginus.

35   Bianchini, Simonetta, 'Chrétien de Troyes lettore di Virgilio,' in *Atti del XXI Congresso Internazionale di Linguistica e Filologia romanza: Centro di Studi Filologici e Linguistici Siciliani, Università di Palermo, 18–24 settembre 1995*, ed. Giovanni Ruffino (Tübingen: Niemeyer, 1998), vol. 6, pp. 531–42.

36 Bertolucci Pizzorusso, Valeria, 'Orfeo "englouti" nelle letterature romanze dei secc. XII e XIII: prime attestazioni,' in *Le metamorfosi di Orfeo: Convegno Internazionale Verona, 28–30 maggio 1998: Atti*, ed. Anna Maria Babbi, Medioevi: Studi, 3 (Verona: Fiorini, 1999), pp. 135–54. (LIII.720)
See pp. 137, 150–51.

37 Bladh, Camilla, 'Ovide et l'héritage antique dans quelques œuvres du XIIe siècle,' in *Festskrift Swaton*, pp. 335–43.

38 Saccone, Antonio, 'Le "metamorfosi" di Chrétien de Troyes,' *Critica del Testo*, 2 (1999), 655–76. (LII.602)

b: Hagiography

3 Frappier, Jean, 'Du "graal [...]"]' Repr. in Dc5.

10 Kölbing, Eugen, 'Christian von Troyes Yvain und die Brandanuslegende,' *ZvL*, 11 (1897), 442–48.

11 Hurley, Margaret, 'Saints' Legends and Romance Again: Secularization of Structure and Motif,' *Genre*, 8 (1975), 60–73.

12 Legge, M. Dominica, 'Anglo-Norman Hagiography and the Romances,' *M&H*, 6 (1975), 41–49.

13 Pecoraro, Vincenzo, 'Dal romanzo di *Barlaam e Josaphat* all'*Erec et Enide*, ovvero di una fonte "bizantina" di Chrétien de Troyes,' *Quaderni di Lingue e Letterature Straniere*, 2 (1977), 111–34.

See Fa101 Lacy.

See Je25 Klenke.

14 Harley, Marta Powell, 'A Note on Chrétien de Troyes's Fénice and Wace's St Margaret,' *MAe,* 51 (1982), 225–26. (XXXV.393)

See Mf8 Walter.

15 Mori, Setsuko, 'Studies in Medieval Irish Saint's Lives (1)(2)', *JCSC*, 33 (1998), 123–44; 38 (2000), 73–100.
In Japanese.

c: History, including Oriental

30 Gallais, Pierre, *Perceval et l'initiation* [...] 2nd ed., Medievalia , 27 (Orléans: Paradigme, 1998).

33   Adolf, Helen, 'G. W. F. Hegel [...]' (XXVII.132)

34   Baist, G., 'Die Todtenbrücke,' *ZrP*, 14 (1890), 159–60.

35   Gaidoz, H., 'Le Chevalier au lion,' *Mélusine*, 5 (1890–91), col. 217–24, 241–44; 6 (1892–93), col. 74–75.

See Na.b15 Baist.

36   Richthofen, Erich von, *Nuevos estudios épicos medievales*, Biblioteca Románica Hispánica: II. Estudios y Ensayos, 138 (Madrid: Editorial Gredos, 1970). (XXIII.152)

37   Corbin, Henry, 'Une liturgie shî 'ite du Graal,' *Mélanges d'histoire des religions offerts à Henri-Charles Puech* (Paris: Presses Universitaires de France, 1974), pp. 81–99.

See Sc13 Gallais.

38   Polak, L., '*Tristan* and *Vis and Ramin*,' *Rom*, 95 (1974), 216–34. (XXVII.254)
Includes comparisons with *Cligés*.

39   Duval, Paulette, *Recherches sur les structures ('Gestalten') de la pensée alchimique, leurs correspondances dans le 'Conte du graal' de Chrétien de Troyes et l'influence de l'Espagne mozarabe de l'Ebre sur la pensée symbolique de l'œuvre*, diss. Paris I 1975 (Lille: Atelier Reproduction des Thèses, Université de Lille III; Paris: Champion, 1975). Repr. as *La Pensée alchimique et le 'Conte du graal': recherches sur les structures ('Gestalten') de la pensée alchimique, leurs correspondances dans le 'Conte du graal' de Chrétien de Troyes et l'influence de l'Espagne mozarabe de l'Ebre sur la pensée symbolique de l'œuvre* (Paris: Champion, 1979). (XXXII.342)

See Nb13 Fauth.

40   Blaess, Madeleine, 'Perceval et les "Illes de mer",' in *Mélanges Lods*, vol. 1, pp. 69–77. (XXXI.260)

41   Leckie, R. William, Jr, *The Passage of Dominion: Geoffrey of Monmouth and the Periodization of Insular History in the Twelfth Century* (Toronto: University of Toronto Press, 1981). (XXXIV.138)
Treats Arthur in the Latin, French, and English chronicles.

See Qb47 Lecouteux.

See Hd14 Maddox.

42 Reichert, Hermann, 'Les origines du motif de la Table Ronde dans le *Brut* de Wace,' in *La Représentation de l'antiquité au Moyen Age: Université de Picardie–Centre d'Etudes Médiévales, Actes du Colloque des 26, 27 et 28 mars 1981*, ed. Danielle Buschinger and André Crépin, Wiener Arbeiten zur germanischen Altertumskunde und Philologie, 20 (Vienna: Halosar, 1982), pp. 243–58. (XXXV.60a)

43 Aoyama, Yoshinobu, *Arthurian Legend, in History and Romance* (Tokyo: Iwanami-shoten, 1985). (XXXIX.184).
In Japanese.

44 Aoyama, Yoshinobu, 'Was Arthur a Real Man?' *Gengo*, 3 (1985), 1–10. (XXXIX.186)
In Japanese.

45 Goodrich, Norma Lorre, *King Arthur* (New York: Franklin Watts, 1986). (XXXIX.265)

See Jd32 Chocheyras.
Gregory of Tours.

See Qa89 Ciggaar.

See Jd40 Diverres.

46 Furtado, Antonio L., 'Geoffrey of Monmouth: A Source of the Grail Stories,' *QetF*, 1:1 (1991), 1–14.

47 Legros, Huguette, 'Connaissance, réception et perceptions des automates orientaux au XIIe siècle,' in *Le Merveilleux et la magie dans la littérature*, ed. Gérard Chandès, CERMEIL, 2 (Amsterdam: Rodopi, 1992), pp. 103–36. (XLV.416)

48 Mandach, André de, *Le 'Roman du graal' originaire: I. Sur les traces du modèle commun 'en code transpyrénéen' de Chrétien de Troyes et Wolfram von Eschenbach*, GAG, 581 (Göppingen: Kümmerle, 1992) (XLV.58). New version: *Auf den Spuren des heiligen Gral: die gemeinsame Vorlage 'im pyrenäischen Geheimkode' von Chrétien de Troyes und Wolfram von Eschenbach: neue Version*, GAG, 596 (Göppingen: Kümmerle, 1995). (XLVIII.123)

49 Yokoyama, Ayumi, '"Translatio imperii" and the Grail Romances,' *RLLF*, 8 (1992), 3–25. (XLIX.382).
In Japanese.

See Hg93 Berchtold.

See Xa18–19 Hindman.

See Ha185 Putter.

50 Ciggaar, Krijnie, 'Encore une fois Chrétien de Troyes et la "matière Byzantine": la révolution des femmes au palais de Constantinople,' *CCM*, 38 (1995), 267–74. (XLVIII.284)

See Gd.b54 Milin.

51 Pioletti, Antonio, 'Filologie e medioevi: limiti e prospettive del comparativismo,' in *Filologia Verona*, pp. 43–59. (LI.570)

d: Romance and Lyric

7 Micha, Alexandre, '*Eneas* et *Cliges* […]' Repr. in Dc3.

8 Micha, Alexandre, 'Sur les sources […]' Repr. in Dc3.

13 Viscardi, Antonio, 'Le origini romanze […]'. Repr. in his *Ricerche e interpretazioni mediolatine e romanze* (Milan: Cisalpino, 1970), pp. 763–82.

22 Witte, Rudolf, *Der Einfluß von Benoît's Roman de Troie auf die altfranzösische Litteratur*, diss. Göttingen (Göttingen: Dieterich, 1904). Treats *Erec* and *Cligés*.

23 Dreßler, Alfred, *Der Einfluß des altfranzösischen Eneas-Romanes auf die altfranzösische Literatur*, diss. Göttingen (Borna-Leipzig: Noske, 1907).

24 *Otto, Gustav, *Der Einfluß des Roman de Thèbes auf die altfranzösische Literatur*, diss. Göttingen (Göttingen: [n.p.], 1909).

25 Hoepffner, E., 'La chanson de geste et les débuts du roman courtois,' *Mélanges de linguistique et de littérature offerts à M. Alfred Jeanroy par ses élèves et ses amis* (Paris: Droz, 1928), pp. 427–37.

26 Levý, O., 'Marie de France a Chrétien de Troyes,' *Casopis*, 18 (1932), 178–85.

27 Remy, Paul, 'Le sentiment amoureux dans *Jaufre*,' in *Actes et Mémoires du 1ᵉʳ Congrès International de langue et littérature du Midi de la France*, Publications de l'Institut Méditerranéen du Palais du

Roure, Avignon (Fondation Flandreysy-Espérandieu), 3 (Avignon: Palais du Roure, 1957), pp. 28–33. (X.93)
Cf. Md9.

28 Kahane, Henry and Renée, 'Herzeloyde,' in *Mélanges Delbouille*, vol. 2, pp. 329–35. (XVII.91)
The fabliau *Richeut*.

29 Jodogne, Omer, 'Observations sur la tradition et l'originalité littéraires au Moyen Age,' *CAIEF*, 20 (1968), 9–17.

30 Legge, M. D., 'Quelques allusions littéraires,' in *Mélanges Le Gentil*, pp. 479–83.
Influence of *chansons de geste* on *Erec*.

See Gd.c6 Lyons.

31 Cormier, Raymond J., 'Remarques sur le *Roman d'Eneas* et l'*Erec et Enide*,' *RLR*, 82 (1976), 85–97. (XXIX.232)

See Qd13 Shirt.
Wace's *Brut*.

32 Kamizawa, Eizô, 'Courtly Romance,' *K-f*, 8:12 (1979), 32.
In Japanese.

33 Niikura, Shun'ichi, 'Lyric Poetry in the Middle Ages,' in *Poetry, A Course in French Literature III* (Tokyo: Taihûkan, 1979), pp. 30–71.
In Japanese.

See Ga23 Busby.

See Sb32 Bogdanow.

See Sb36 Topsfield.

See Sb37 Bogdanow.

34 Höfner, Eckhard, 'Zum Verhältnis von Tristan- und Artusstoff im 12. Jahrhundert,' *ZfSL*, 92 (1982), 289–323. (XXXV.34)
See pp. 301, 303–23.

35 Huchet, Jean-Charles, *Le Roman médiéval*, Littératures Modernes (Paris: Presses Universitaires de France, 1984).
Focuses on the *Roman d'Eneas* as precursor of and in comparison with Chrétien.

36   Lloyd, Heather, 'Chrétien's Use of the Conventions of Grief Depiction in a Passage from *Cligés*,' *FMLS*, 20 (1984), 317–22. (XXXVII.172)
Mourning for Alexandre by his Greek comrades.

See Sb41 Szabics.

See He50 Beltrami.

See Lb1 Blumenfeld-Kosinski.

See Hc52 Cropp.

See Ef7 Hunt, Chap. 4.

See Lc1 Uitti.

37   Adams, Alison, 'The Old French Tristan Poems and the Tradition of Verse Romance,' *Tris*, 12 (1986–87), 60–68. (XL.257)

38   Patterson, Lee, *Negotiating the Past: The Historical Understanding of Medieval Literature* (Madison: University of Wisconsin Press, 1987). (XLI.428)
See Chap. 5: 'Virgil and the Historical Consciousness of the Twelfth Century: the *Roman d'Eneas* and *Erec et Enide*'; and Chap. 6: 'The Romance of History and the Alliterative *Morte Arthure*,' repr. in *Medieval English Poetry*, ed. Stephanie Trigg, Longman Critical Readers (London: Longman, 1993), pp. 217–49. (XLVII.375)

See Va16 Rossi.

39   Kasten, Ingrid, 'Herrschaft und Liebe: zur Rolle und Darstellung des "Helden" im *Roman d'Eneas* und in Veldekes *Eneasroman*,' *DVj*, 62 (1988), 227–45. (XLI.608)

40   Bendinelli Predelli, Maria, 'La tradizione dei temi narrativi: criteri per la costruzione di uno stemma,' *YIS*, 8 (1989), 81–94.

See Sb48 Laurie.

See Sb49 Aletti.

See Ph8 Bendinelli Predelli.

41   Bendinelli Predelli, Maria, 'Un cantare italiano come chiave dell'intertestualità intorno al *Lancelot* di Chrétien de Troyes,' *ItC*, 8 (1990), 239–49.

See Hc63 Middleton.

See Gd.a32 Rosenstein.

42 Zambon, Francesco, 'L'amante onirica di Guglielmo IX,' *RZLG*, 15 (1991), 247–61; repr. in **Immaginario e follia*, ed. Fabio Rosa (Trento: UCT, 1991), pp. 49–62. (XLVI.574)

43 Laurie, Helen C. R., 'Chrétien in Debt to Benoît de Sainte Maure,' *RF*, 104 (1992), 377–87. (XLVI.82)

44 Mora, Francine, 'De Bernard Silvestre à Chrétien de Troyes: résurgences des enfers virgiliens au XIIe siècle,' in *Diesseits*, pp. 129–46.

See Gf37 Wolf.

See Uc35 Holzbacher.

45 Luttrell, Claude, '*Le Conte del graal* and Precursors of Perceval,' *BBSIA*, 46 (1994), 291–323.

46 Suzuki, Tetsuya, 'Trial Translation of "La partie arthurienne du Roman de *Brut*" by Robert Wace (I) (II) (III) (IV) (V) (VI),' *Bulletin of Teikyo Women's Junior College*, 14 (1994), 223–52; 15 (1995), 71–98; 16 (1996), 147–71; 17 (1997), 23–47; 19 (1999), 41–65; 20 (2000), 65–88. (XLIX.363, L.359)
In Japanese.

See Ha192 Rockwell.

47 Zambon, Francesco, '"*Neant tient, a neant parole*": il sogno erotico nel *Cligès* di Chrétien de Troyes,' in *Geografia, storia e poetiche del fantastico*, ed. Monica Farnetti, BArR, 262 (Florence: Olschki, 1995), pp. 75–82. (LI.576)

See Jb51 Ruhe.

See Hc76 Seebass-Linggi.

48 Zaganelli, Gioia, 'Alessandro Magno, Tristano, Cligés e una camicia tessuta sul Tamigi,' in *Percorsi intertestuali*, ed. Giovanni Bogliolo, Daniela da Agostini, and Paola Desideri, Peregre: Collana della Facoltà di Lingue e Letterature Straniere dell'Università degli Studi di Urbino (Fasano: Schena, 1997), pp. 13–31 (L.343); repr. in *Studi Melli*, vol. 2, pp. 897–909.

See Jb54 Le Rider.

See Gd.c67 Ásdís R. Magnúsdóttir.

49 Le Rider, Paule, 'L'épisode de l'épervier dans *Erec et Enide*,' *Rom*, 116 (1998), 368–93. (LI.267)

50 Eley, Penny, and Penny Simons, '*Partonopeus de Blois* and Chrétien de Troyes: A Re-Assessment,' *Rom*, 117 (1999), 316–41. (LII.229)

51 Huot, Sylvia, 'Troubadour Lyric and Old French Narrative,' in *The Troubadours: An Introduction*, ed. Simon Gaunt and Sarah Kay (Cambridge: Cambridge University Press, 1999), pp. 263–78. (LII.401)

See Hb53 Kullmann.

See Gb165 Schwartz.

52 Zotz, Nicola, 'Programmatische Vieldeutigkeit und verschlüsselte Eindeutigkeit: das Liebesbekenntnis bei Thomas und Gottfried von Straßburg (mit einer neuen Übersetzung des Carlisle-Fragments),' *GRM*, 50 (2000), 1–19.
See pp. 11–12.

e: Scholarly and Learned Traditions

7 Hamilton, George L., 'Storm-Making Springs: Rings of Invisibility – Studies on the Sources of the *Yvain* of Chrétien de Troies,' *RR*, 2 (1911), 355–75.
See Md3 Hamilton.

8 Peebles, Rose Jeffries, *The Legend of Longinus in Ecclesiastical Tradition and in English Literature, and its Connection with the Grail*, diss. Bryn Mawr (Baltimore: Furst, 1911).

9 Gelzer, Heinrich, *Nature: zum Einfluss der Scholastik auf den altfranzösischen Roman*, Stilistische Forschungen, 1 (Halle/S: Niemeyer, 1917).

See Ma24 Ogle.

10 Anitchkof, Eugène, *Joachim de Flore et les milieux courtois* (Rome: Collezione Meridionale, 1931).

11 Legge, Mary Dominica, 'Gautier Espec, Ailred de Rievaulx et la matière de Bretagne' in *Mélanges Frappier*, vol. 2, pp. 619–23.

See Gd.c4 Dronke.

12 Gewehr, Wolf, 'Der Topos "Augen des Herzens" – Versuch einer Deutung durch die scholastische Erkenntnistheorie,' *DVj*, 46 (1972), 626–49.
See pp. 641–45.

13 Weinraub, Eugene J., *Chrétien's Jewish Grail: A New Investigation of the Imagery and Significance of Chrétien de Troyes's Grail Episode Based upon Medieval Hebraic Sources*, UNCSRL: Essays, 2 (Chapel Hill: UNC Department of Romance Languages, 1976). (XXIX.125)

See Qa44 Green.

14 Itô, Yasuharu, 'The Wounds of the Grail King Anfortas – Natural Science in the Middle Ages,' *RBN*, 21 (1977), 85–102.
In Japanese.

See Hc28 Maddox.

15 Hunt, Tony, 'Chrestien and the *Comediae*,' *MS*, 40 (1978), 120–56. (XXXII.189)

See Ra18 Hunt.

See Gf15 Neaman.

16 Fiedler, Leslie A., 'Why Is the Grail Knight Jewish? A Passover Meditation,' in *Aspects of Jewish Culture in the Middle Ages: Papers of the Eighth Annual Conference of the Center for Medieval and Early Renaissance Studies, State University of New York, Binghamton, 3–5 May 1974*, ed. Paul E. Szarmach (Albany: State University of New York Press, 1979), pp. 151–70; see also 'Discussion,' pp. 186–88 (Alice Colby-Hall) and 'Rejoinder,' pp. 204–6 (Leslie A. Fiedler). (XXXIII. 141)

17 Hurst, Peter W., 'The Encyclopaedic Tradition, the Cosmological Epic, and the Validation of the Medieval Romance,' *Comparative Criticism*, 1 (1979), 53–71.

18 Bothorel, Nicole, and Francine Dugast-Portes, 'De l'écho à la résonance (nouveau roman et tradition médiévale),' *Mélanges Foulon*, vol. 1, pp. 29–35. (XXXIII.312)

See Gb60 Lecouteux.

19 Luttrell, Claude, 'Chrestien de Troyes and Alan of Lille,' *BBSIA*, 32 (1980), 250–75.

See Hc38 Archambault.

20 Diverres, Armel H., 'Yvain's Quest for Chivalric Perfection,' in *Essays Thorpe*, pp. 214–28. (XXXIV.308)
Prudentius's *Psychomachia*.

See Hc41 Hart.

See Jb28 Hart.

21 Uitti, Karl D., 'A propos de philologie,' *Littérature*, 41 (1981), 30–46. (XXXV.346)
Influence of Martianus Capella's *De nuptiis* on *Erec*.

22 Hunt, Tony, 'Chrestien and Macrobius,' *C&M*, 33 (1981–82), 211–27.

See Jb29 Malaxecheverria.

See Hc42 Mussetter.

23 Hunt, T., 'The Lion and Yvain,' in *Studies Diverres*, pp. 86–98, 237–40. (XXXVI.430)

See Fb54 Kelly.

See Jb31 Ribard.

See Jd28 Bogdanow.

See Fd3 Bradley-Cromey.

See Kd97 Sargent-Baur.

24 Laurie, H. C. R., 'Chrétien's "bele conjointure",' in *Actes Rennes*, vol. 1, pp. 379–96. (XXXVIII.235)

25 Okken, L., 'Ein Fass mit siedendkaltem Wasser: zu Chrétiens *Yvain* Vers 380–477,' in *Studies Gerritsen*, pp. 190–97. (XXXVIII.698)
Chrétien's knowledge of Byzantine machines that produce artificial storms.

See Ef7 Hunt, Chap. 5 on dialectic.

26 Laurie, Helen C. R., 'The "Letters" of Abelard and Heloïse: A Source for Chrétien de Troyes?' *SM*, ser. 3, 27 (1986), 123–46.

See Ta35 Barthélémy.

27 Firestone, Ruth H., 'Chrétien's Enide, Hartmann's Enite and Boethii *Philosophiae consolatio*,' *ABäG*, 26 (1987), 69–106. (XLII.196)

28 Hill, Thomas D., 'Enide's Colored Horse and Salernitan Color Theory: *Erec et Enide*, lines 5268–81,' *Rom*, 108 (1987), 523–27. (XLIII.181)

See Qb53 Stanesco.

See Sb45 Dahlberg.

See Ha143 Helm.

See Jb38 Nightingale.

See Pb324 Graf.

See Sb48 Laurie.

29 Nightingale, Jeanne A., 'Chrétien de Troyes and the Mythographical Tradition: The Couple's Journey in *Erec et Enide* and Martianus' *De Nuptiis*,' in Da15 *King Arthur*, vol. 1, pp. 56–79. (XLIII. 582)

30 Pegg, Mark Gregory, 'Le corps et l'autorité: la lèpre de Baudouin IV,' *Annales*, 45 (1990), 265–87. (XLIII.193)
See pp. 265–66 on the Fisher King in *Perceval*.

31 Laurie, Helen C. R., '*Cligés* and the Legend of Abelard and Heloise,' *ZrP*, 107 (1991), 324–42. (XLIV.449)

32 Laurie, Helen C. R., *The Making of Romance: Three Studies*, HICL, 290 (Geneva: Droz, 1991). (XLIV.402)
Influence of philosophical, theological, and medical treatises as well as of the correspondence of Heloise and Abelard.

See Wb48 Löfstedt.

See Hf90 Hawkins.

See Mc48 Mandach.

See Jd41 Vauthier.

33   Laurie, Helen C. R., 'The Letters of Abelard and Heloise: Classical, Patristic and Medieval Models: A Reconsideration,' *Mittellateinisches Jahrbuch*, 28:2 (1993), 35–45.

See Gb118 McCracken.

34   Méla, Charles, "*Jocosa materia*, ou la joie mise en jeu: de la *Comedia* et de la *Poetria* au fabliau et au roman," in Dc19, pp. 432–52.

See Hc73 Helm.

35   Luttrell, Claude, 'The Heart's Mirror in *Cligés*,' *AL*, 13 (1995), 1–18. (XLVII.365)

See Gf40 Walter.

36   Lutz, Eckart Conrad, 'Verschwiegene Bilder – geordnete Texte: mediävistische Überlegungen,' *DVj*, 70 (1996), 3–47. (XLIX.50)

See Jb51 Ruhe.

See Hg105 Sargent-Baur.

37   Derrien, Ève, 'Le sang et la saignée dans le roman médiéval en vers,' *LR*, 51 (1997), 3–18. (L.3)

See Gd.b54 Milin.

See Gd.b55 Queille.

38   Echard, Siân, *Arthurian Narrative in the Latin Tradition*, CSML, 36 (Cambridge: Cambridge University Press, 1998). (LI.364)

39   Löfstedt, Leena, 'Chrétien de Troyes et le Décret de Gratien,' *NM*, 99 (1998), 5–16.

See Ga98 Merceron.

40   Haas, Kurtis B., 'Erec's Ascent: The Politics of Wisdom in Chrétien's *Erec et Enide*,' *RomQ*, 46 (1999), 131–40.

41   Kelly, Douglas, *The Conspiracy of Allusion: Description, Rewriting, and Authorship from Macrobius to Medieval Romance*, Studies in the History of Christian Thought, 97 (Leiden: Brill, 1999). (LII.682)

42 Fritz, Jean-Marie, *Paysages sonores du moyen âge: le versant épistémologique*, Sciences, Techniques et Civilisations du Moyen Âge à l'Aube des Lumières, 5 (Paris: Champion, 2000). (LIII.230)

See Pa335 Séguy.

f: The Bible, including Apocrypha

6 Grill, P. Leopold, 'Château du graal: Clairvaux,' *Analecta Sacri Ordinis Cisterciensis*, 17 (1961), 115–26.
Bernard of Clairvaux's influence on Chrétien.

See Pa95 Larmat.

See Ma26 Laurie.

See Gd.b14 Saly.

See Hc40 Fassò.

7 Muir, Lynette R., 'Perceval's Religious Education and the Secret Prayer of the Names of God,' *Hebrew University Studies in Literature*, 9:1 (Spring 1981), 16–27.

8 Walter, Philippe, 'Lancelot, l'archange apocryphe (réminiscences et ré-écriture dans le *Chevalier de la charrette*),' in *Lancelot Picardie*, pp. 225–38.

See Ga50 Boutet.

9 Walter, Philippe, 'Moires et mémoires du réel chez Chrétien de Troyes: la complainte des tisseuses dans *Yvain*,' *Littérature*, 59 (1985), 71–84. (XXXVIII.274)

See Ma30 Laurie.

See Jd33 Clej.

10 Laurie, Helen C. R., 'Beasts and Saints: A Key to the Lion in Chrétien's *Yvain*,' *BBSIA*, 39 (1987), 297–306. (XLI.139)

See Jd34 Vauthier.

See Rb29 Bayer.

See Jd35 Lange.

See Sb48 Laurie.

See Sb49 Aletti.

11 Matsubara, Hideichi, *Christianity as a Foreign Religion* (Tokyo: Heibonsha, 1990).
In Japanese.

12 Laurie, Helen C. R., 'The Psychomachia of *Yvain*,' *NFS*, 30:2 (1991), 13–23. (XLIV.109)

See Hg84 Saccone.

13 Ferrante, Joan M., 'The Bible as Thesaurus for Secular Literature,' in *The Bible in the Middle Ages: Its Influence on Literature and Art*, ed. Bernard S. Levy, MRTS, 89 (Binghamton: Medieval and Renaissance Texts and Studies, 1992), pp. 23–49.

See Xa14 Mentré.

See Jd41 Vauthier.

14 Nightingale, Jeanne A., 'De l'épithalame au roman courtois: l'exégèse ad litteram du Cantique des Cantiques comme modèle heuristique pour la "conjointure" de Chrétien de Troyes,' in *Erec*, pp. 75–87. (XLVI.90)

See Gf38 Dybeł.

See Fb90 Gouttebroze.

See Gb125(F) Gouttebroze.

See Hc74 Nightingale.

15 Herzfeld, Claude, 'Un Graal cathare? Tentatives modernes de récupération,' in Pk72 *Graal*, pp. 99–107.

16 Walter, Philippe, 'L'intertextualité liturgique chez Chrétien de Troyes: étude de cas,' in *Aspects du classicisme et de la spiritualité: mélanges offerts à Jacques Hennequin*, ed. Alain Cullière (Metz: Centre Michel Baude 'Littérature et Spiritualité', Faculté des Lettres et Sciences Humaines, Université de Metz; Paris: Klincksieck, 1996), pp. 615–24.

See Gd.b55 Queille.

See Qf10 Moisan.

See Pa335 Séguy.

g: Arabic Literary Sources (see also Mc)

1   Barry, Michael, 'La Table Ronde et le folklore musulman,' in *Actes Rennes*, vol. 1, pp. 16–43. (XXXVIII. 180)

2   Barry, Michaël, 'La Table Ronde du roi Arthur et les Mille et une nuits,' in *Normandie*, pp. 161–212.

3   Furtado, Antonio L., 'The *Arabian Nights*: Yet Another Source of the Grail Stories?' *QetF*, 1:3 (1991), 25–40. (XLV.466)

4   Furtado, Antonio L., 'A Source in Babylon,' *QetF*, 3:1 (1993), 38–59. (XLVII.711)

N: NON-LEARNED SOURCES

Scholars working in Celtic and/or folklore studies continue to use evidence from Chrétien's romances to elucidate the origins and transmission of their material, whether lost or extant. In 1976 this topic seemed to be in decline among Chrétien scholars; however, psychoanalytic and anthropological approaches to issues of mythopoetics (see Ub and c) have signalled a return to earlier scholarship in interpreting Chrétien's romances, albeit in new theoretical contexts. The topic has certain affinities with studies of medieval orality.

a: Celtic Sources

a.a: Background

17 Golther, Wolfgang, 'Zur Frage nach der Entstehung der bretonischen oder Artus-Epen,' *ZvL*, 3 (1890), 211–19.

18 *Nutt, Alfred Trüdner, *Celtic and Mediaeval Romances*, Popular Studies in Mythology, Romance and Folklore, 1 (London: Nutt, 1899).

19 Huet, G., 'Le témoignage de Wace sur les "fables" arthuriennes,' *MA*, 19 (1916), 234–49.
Compares with statements by Chrétien.

20 Bromwich, Rachel, 'Dwy chwedl a thair rhamant,' in *Y Traddodiad rhyddiaith yn yr Oesau Canol*, ed. Geraint Bowen (Llandysul: Gwasg Gomer, 1974), pp. 143–75. (XXVII.282)

21 Jones, Bedwyr Lewis, *Arthur y Cymry/The Welsh Arthur* (Cardiff: University of Wales Press, 1975). (XXVIII.321)
In Welsh and English.

22 Roberts, Brynley F., 'Tales and Romances,' in *A Guide to Welsh Literature*, ed. A. O. H. Jarman and Gwilym Rees Hughes, 2 vols

(Swansea: Davies, 1976–79), vol. 1, pp. 203–43; rev. ed., 7 vols (Cardiff: University of Wales Press, 1992–98), vol. 1, pp. 203–43; repr. in Dc17. (XXIX.299, XLV.305)

See Nb12 *Enzyklopädie.*

23 Greene, David, 'Tabu in Early Irish Narrative,' in *Symposium Odense*, pp. 9–19.
On *geis.*

24 Gruffydd, R. Geraint, 'The Early Court Poetry of South West Wales,' *StC*, 14–15 (1979–80), 95–105.

25 Jarman, A. O. H., *The Cynfeirdd: Early Welsh Poets and Poetry* (Cardiff: University of Wales Press, 1981). (XXXV.396)
Includes bibliography.

26 Jarman, A. O. H., 'The Delineation of Arthur in Early Welsh Verse,' in *Essays Thorpe*, pp. 1–21. (XXXIV.331)

See Na.c76 Lozachmeur.

27 Jarman, A. O. H., 'La tradition galloise d'Arthur,' *MrR*, 32:2–4 (1982), 43–60. (XXXVIII.141)

28 Wais, Kurt, 'Volkssprachliche Erzähler Alt-Irlands im Rahmen der europäischen Literaturgeschichte,' in *Die Iren und Europa im frühen Mittelalter*, Veröffentlichungen des Europa Zentrums Tübingen: Kulturwissenschaftliche Reihe, 2 vols (Stuttgart: Klett-Cotta, 1982), vol. 1, pp. 639–85. (XXXV.79a)

29 Imura, Kimie, *Celtic Myth* (Tokyo: Chikuma-shobô, 1983). (XXXVI.544)
In Japanese.

30 Nakaki, Yasuo, *The Knight and the Fay – In Search of Celtic Civilization in Brittany* (Tokyo: Ongaku-no-tomo-sha, 1984).
In Japanese.

See Ta35 Barthélémy.

31 **Histoire littéraire et culturelle de la Bretagne*. Vol. I: *Héritage celtique et captation française*, ed. Jean Fleuriot and Auguste-Pierre Ségalen, 3 vols (Paris: Champion, Geneva: Slatkine, 1987; Paris: Champion, Spezed: Breizh, 1997). (LI.251)

32 Imura, Kimie, *The Romance of King Arthur* (Tokyo: Chikuma-shobô, 1987). (XL.219)
In Japanese.

See Nb36 Lozachmeur.

33 Ashe, Geoffrey, 'The Historical Origins of the Arthurian Legend,' in *Vitality*, pp. 25–43.

34 Nakaki, Yasuo, 'On the Structure of Celtic Society in Armorican Brittany in its First Period,' *StCJ*, 1 (1988), 49–70.
In Japanese.

35 Roberts, Brynley F., 'Dosbarthu'r chwedlau Cymraeg Canol,' *YB*, 15 (1988), 19–46. (XLII.677)

36 Tsuruoka, Mayumi, *The Celts/Decorative Thought* (Tokyo: Chikuma-shobô, 1989).
In Japanese.

37 *The Arthur of the Welsh: The Arthurian Legend in Medieval Welsh Literature*, ed. Rachel Bromwich, A. O. H. Jarman, and Brynley F. Roberts (Cardiff: University of Wales Press, 1991). (XLIV.88)
Contents:
   A.   Editors with Daniel Huws, 'Introduction,' pp. 1–14.
   B.   Thomas Charles-Edwards, 'The Arthur of History,' pp. 15–32. (XLIV.96)
   C.   Patrick Sims-Williams, 'The Early Welsh Arthurian Poems,' pp. 33–71. (XLIV.130)
   D.   Brynley F. Roberts, '*Culhwch ac Olwen*, The Triads, Saints' Lives,' pp. 73–95. (XLIV.126)
   E.   Brynley F. Roberts, 'Geoffrey of Monmouth, *Historia Regum Britanniae* and *Brut y Brenhinedd*,' pp. 97–116. (XLIV.127)
   F.   A. O. H. Jarman, 'The Merlin Legend and the Welsh Tradition of Prophecy,' pp. 117–45. (XLIV.105)
   G.   Roger Middleton, '*Chwedl Geraint ab Erbin*,' pp. 147–57. (XLIV.117)
   H.   R. L. Thomson, '*Owain: Chwedl Iarlles y Ffynnon*,' pp. 159–69. (XLIV.133)
   I.   Ian Lovecy, '*Historia Peredur ab Efrawg*,' pp. 171–82. (XLIV.113)
   J.   Ceridwen Lloyd-Morgan, '*Breuddwyd Rhonabwy* and Later Arthurian Literature,' pp. 183–208. (XLIV.110)
   K.   Rachel Bromwich, 'The *Tristan* of the Welsh,' pp. 209–28. (XLIV.90)
   L.   O. J. Padel, 'Some South-Western Sites with Arthurian Associations,' pp. 229–48. (XLIV.122)
   M.   J. E. Caerwyn Williams, 'Brittany and the Arthurian Legend,' pp. 249–72. (XLIV.135)
   N.   Rachel Bromwich, 'First Transmission to England and France,' pp. 273–98. (XLIV.89)

38 *The Celts: Tradition and Folk Imagination*, ed. The Institute of Cultural Science (Chuo University) (Tokyo: Chuo University Press, 1991).
In Japanese.

39 Mori, Setsuko, *The Religion and Culture of Ireland – A History of the Adaptation of Christianity* (Tokyo: The Board of Publications, The United Church of Christ in Japan, 1991).
In Japanese.

40 Katô, Kyôko, *Travel in the Arthurian Highlands* (Tokyo: Chûôkôron, 1992). (XLV.386).
In Japanese.

41 Darrah, John, *Paganism in Arthurian Romance* (Woodbridge: Boydell, 1994). (XLVII.347)

42 Griffen, Toby D., *Names from the Dawn of British Legend: Taliesin, Aneurin, Myrddin/Merlin, Arthur* (Felinfach: Llanerch, 1994). (XLVIII.416)

43 *The Celtic Sources for the Arthurian Legend*, ed. Jon B. Coe and Simon Young (Felinfach: Llanerch, 1995. (LI.336)
Collection of major sources in Welsh, Latin and Irish with English translations.

44 Pontfarcy, Yolande de, 'Archétypes indo-européens et celtiques du Graal,' in Pk72 *Graal*, pp. 17–30

45 Tanaka, Hitohiko, *Celtic Myth and the Arthurian Cycle – Travel in the Otherworld* (Tokyo: Chûôkôron, 1995). (XLIX.376)
In Japanese. See Chap. 3: 'The Otherworld in the Arthurian Cycle' – 2. 'Chrétien de Troyes' (pp. 190–226).

46 Tsuruoka, Mayumi, *Introduction to Celtic Art* (Tokyo: Chikuma-shobô, 1995).
In Japanese.

47 *The Celts : Transformation of Life and Death*, ed. The Institute of Cultural Science (Chuo University) (Tokyo: Chuo University Press, 1996).
In Japanese.

48 Mori, Setsuko, 'Irish Church Reform in the Twelfth Century (1)(2)(3)', *ÉIRE* (Irish Studies) (Japan-Ireland Society), 16 (1996), 22–44; 17 (1997), 1–24; 18 (1998), 86–110.
In Japanese.

49 Mori, Setsuko, 'Irish Monastic Culture – Sanctity and Secularity,' *JCSC*, 26 (1996), 55–87.
In Japanese.

50 Breeze, Andrew, *Medieval Welsh Literature* (Dublin: Four Courts, 1997).

51 Tanabe, Tamotsu, *The Forest of Brocéliande* (Tokyo: Seidosha, 1998) (LI.673).
In Japanese.

See Pc26 Lloyd-Morgan.

52 Mori, Setsuko, 'Irish Church Reform and the Cistercian Order', *ÉIRE* (Irish Studies) (Japan-Ireland Society), 19 (1999), 1–22.
In Japanese.

See Qb82 Takamiya.

53 Tsuruoka, Mayumi, and Kazuo Matsumura, *Illustrated History of the Celts : Reading Their Culture, Arts, and Myths* (Tokyo: Kawade-shobô-shinsha, 1999).
In Japanese.

54 *Canhwyll Marchogyon: Cyd-destunoli Peredur*, ed. Sioned Davies and Peter Wynn Thomas (Cardiff: University of Wales Press, 2000).
Contents:
    A. Daniel Huws, 'Y pedair llawysgrif ganoloesol,' pp. 1–9.
    B. Peter Wynn Thomas, 'Cydberthynas y pedair fersiwn ganoloesol,' pp. 10–49.
    C. Brynley F. Roberts, 'Y cysyniad o destun,' pp. 50–64.
    D. Sioned Davies, 'Cynnydd *Peredur vab Efrawc*,' pp. 65–90.
    E. Morfydd E. Owen, 'Arbennic milwyr a blodeu marchogyon: cymdeithas *Peredur*,' pp. 92–112.
    F. Ceridwen Lloyd-Morgan, 'Y cyd-destun Ewropeaidd,' pp. 114–27.
    G. Stephen Knight, 'Resemblance and Menace: A Post-Colonial Reading of *Peredur*,' pp. 128–47.

55 Padel, O. J., *Arthur in Medieval Welsh Literature* (Cardiff: University of Wales Press, 2000).

a.b: Transmission

15 Baist, G., 'Arthur und der Gral,' *ZrP*, 19 (1895), 326–47.

16 Williams, Mary Rh., *Essai sur la composition du roman gallois de Peredur*, diss. Paris (Paris: Champion, 1909).
See Part II, Chap. 1: 'Peredur et les poèmes français' on *Peredur*'s relation to Chrétien (contested) and other French poems.

17   Delbouille, Maurice, 'Le témoignage de Wace sur la légende arthurienne,' *Rom*, 74 (1953), 172–99. (VI.85)

18   Loomis, Roger Sherman, 'Did Gawain, Perceval, and Arthur Hail from Scotland?' *EtCelt*, 11 (1964–65), 70–82. (XVIII.155)

19   Piette, J. R. F., 'Yr agwedd Lydewig ar y chwedlau Arthuraidd,' *LlC*, 8 (1965), 183–90. (XX.163)

See Na.c71 Lozachmeur.

20   Lewis, Ceri W., 'The Court Poets: Their Function, Status and Craft,' in *Guide to Welsh Literature*, ed. A. O. H. Jarman and Gwilym Rees Hughes, 2 vols (Swansea: Davies, 1976–79), vol. 1, pp. 123–56. Rev. ed., 7 vols (Cardiff: University of Wales Press, 1992–98), vol. 1, pp. 123–56.

21   Lloyd, D. Myrddin, 'The Poets of the Princes,' in *Guide to Welsh Literature*, ed. A. O. H. Jarman and Gwilym Rees Hughes, 2 vols (Swansea: Davies, 1976–79), vol. 1, pp. 157–88. Rev. ed., 7 vols (Cardiff: University of Wales Press, 1992–98), vol. 1, pp. 157–88.

22   Williams, J. E. Caerwyn, *The Poets of the Welsh Princes*, Writers of Wales (Cardiff: University of Wales Press, 1978).

23   Casagrande, Carla, and Silvana Vecchio, 'Clercs et jongleurs dans la société médiévale (XIIᵉ et XIIIᵉ siècles),' *Annales*, 34 (1979), 913–28.

See Nb19 Littleton.

24   Lozachmeur, Jean-Claude, 'Le problème de la transmission des thèmes arthuriens à la lumière de quelques correspondances onomastiques,' in *Mélanges Foulon*, vol. 1, pp. 217–25. (XXXIII.350)
The names Perceval and Corbenic.

25   Markale, Jean, 'Brocéliande: mythe et réalité,' in *Mélanges Foulon*, vol. 2, pp. 185–92. (XXXIII.357)

See Na.a28 Wais.

26   Roberts, Brynley F., 'From Traditional Tale to Literary Story: Middle Welsh Narratives,' in *Craft*, pp. 211–30; repr. in Dc17. (XXXVII.448)

27   Lloyd-Morgan, Ceridwen, 'Continuity and Change in the Transmission of Arthurian Material: Later Mediaeval Wales and the Continent,' in *Actes Rennes*, vol. 2, pp. 397–405. (XXXVIII.238)

28   Jones, R. M., 'Narrative Structure in Medieval Welsh Prose Tales,' in *Proceedings of the Seventh International Congress of Celtic Studies Held at Oxford, from 10th to 15th July, 1983* (Oxford: Cranham Press, 1986), pp. 171–98. (XXXIX.65)

29   Roberts, Brynley F., 'Oral Tradition and Welsh Literature: A Description and Survey,' *Oral Tradition*, 3 (1988), 61–87; repr. in Dc17.

See Fe20 Duggan.

30   Fleuriot, Léon, 'Traduction et bilinguisme dans le monde brittonique médiéval,' in *Traduction et traducteurs au Moyen Age: Actes du Colloque International du CNRS Organisé à Paris, Institut de Recherche et d'Histoire des textes les 26–28 mai 1986*, ed. Geneviève Contamine (Paris: Editions du Centre National de la Recherche Scientifique, 1989), pp. 209–23.

31   *Sages, Saints and Storytellers: Celtic Studies James Carney*, ed. Donuchadh Ó Corráin, Liam Breatnach, and Kim McCone, Maynooth Monographs, 2 (Maynooth: An Segart, St Patrick's College, 1989).
   A.   Patrick Sims-Williams, 'The Irish Geography of *Culhwch and Olwen*,' pp. 412–26. (XLII.678)
   B.   Hildegard L. C. Tristram, 'Early Modes of Insular Expression,' pp. 427–48.

32   Baumgartner, Emmanuèle, 'Robert de Boron et l'imaginaire du livre du Graal,' in *Arturus rex*, pp. 259–68; repr. in Dc20. (XL, p. 310)
Discusses the *Perceval* 'livre'.

33   Gowans, Linda M., 'The Modena Archivolt and Lost Arthurian Tradition,' in *Arturus rex*, pp. 79–86. (XL, pp. 328–29)

34   Carey, John, 'The Narrative Setting of *Baile Chuinn Chétchathaig*,' *EtCelt*, 32 (1996), 189–201. (LI.226)
See pp. 199–201 on *Perceval*.

35   Bezerra Gomes Waddington, Claudius, 'L'imaginaire celte et le renversement de l'ordre féodal chez Chrétien de Troyes,' in *Mélanges de Mandach*, pp. 221–30.

36   Merdrignac, Bernard, '*Ut uulgo refertur*: tradition orale et littérature hagiographique en Bretagne au Moyen Age,' in *Mondes de l'Ouest et villes du monde: regards sur les sociétés médiévales. Mélanges en l'honneur d'André Chédeville* (Rennes: Presses Universitaires de Rennes, 1998), pp. 105–14. (LI.275)

37 Sims-Williams, Patrick, 'Did Itinerant Breton *Conteurs* Transmit the *Matière de Bretagne*?' *Rom*, 116 (1998), 72–111. (LI.302)

38 Shinoda, Chiwaki, 'Oral Literature and Romanticism in France,' *JFLN*, 136 (2000), 235–50.
In Japanese.

a.c: Special Problems: Themes – Images – Figures

30 Cormier, Raymond J., 'Cú Chulainn […]' (XXVIII.119)

31 San Marte (A. Schulz), *Die Arthur-Sage und die Mährchen des Rothen Buches von Hergest*, BdNL, 2:2 (Quedlinburg: Basse, 1842).

32 San-Marte (A. Schulz), *Beiträge zur bretonischen und celtisch-germanischen Heldensage*, BdNL, 2:3 (Quedlinburg: Basse, 1847).

33 *Osterwald, Wilhelm, *Iwein: ein keltischer Frühlingsgott. Ein Beitrag zur comparativen Mythologie* (Halle/S.: Pfeffer, 1853).

See Mc34 Baist.

34 Golther, Wolfgang, 'Beziehungen zwischen französischer und keltischer Literatur im Mittelalter,' *ZvL*, 3 (1890), 409–25.
See 'Perceval und der Gral,' pp. 417–25.

35 Rhŷs, John, *Studies in the Arthurian Legend* (Oxford: Clarendon Press, 1891; repr. New York: Russell & Russell, 1966).

36 Lot, Ferdinand, 'Celtica,' *Rom*, 24 (1895), 321–38.

See Qg1 Bellamy.

37 Lot, Ferdinand, 'Études sur la provenance du cycle arthurien. III,' *Rom*, 25 (1896), 1–32.
See pp. 7–14.

38 Weston, Jessie L., *The Legend of Sir Gawain: Studies upon Its Original Scope and Significance*, Grimm Library, 7 (London: Nutt, 1897; repr. New York: AMS Press, 1972).
See Chap. 3 and 8.

39 Wechssler, Eduard, *Die Sage vom heiligen Gral in ihrer Entwicklung bis auf Richard Wagners Parsifal* (Halle/S.: Niemeyer, 1898).
A. See also his 'Untersuchungen zu den Gralromanen,' *ZrP*, 23 (1899), 135–73.

40 Lot, Ferdinand, 'Nouveaux essais sur la provenance du cycle arthurien III' and 'VI,' *Rom*, 28 (1899), 321–47; 'V,' 46 (1920), 39–45.

41 Brown, Arthur C. L., 'The Round Table before Wace,' *[Harvard] Studies and Notes in Philology and Literature*, 7 (1900), 183–205.

42 Brugger, E., 'Beiträge zur Erklärung der Arthurischen Geographie,' *ZfSL*, 27 (1904), 69–116; 28 (1905), 1–71.

43 Ehrismann, Gustav, 'Märchen im höfischen Epos,' *PBB*, 30 (1905), 14–54.

44 Nitze, Wm. A., 'The Fisher King in the Grail Romances,' *PMLA*, 24 (1909), 365–418.

45 Brown, Arthur C. L., 'The Bleeding Lance,' *PMLA*, 25 (1910), 1–59.

46 Nitze, William A., 'The Castle of the Grail – An Irish Analogue,' in *Studies in Honor of A. Marshall Elliott*, 2 vols (Baltimore: Johns Hopkins University Press; Paris: Champion; Leipzig: Harrassowitz, [1911?]), vol. 1, pp. 19–51.

47 Brown, Arthur C. L., 'Notes on Celtic Cauldrons of Plenty and the Land-Beneath-the-Waves,' in *Papers Kittredge*, pp. 235–49.

48 Brown, Arthur C. L., 'From Cauldron of Plenty to Grail,' *MP*, 14 (1916), 385–404.

49 Pace, Roy Bennett, 'The Death of the Red Knight in the Story of Perceval,' *MLN*, 31 (1916), 53–55.

50 Dunn, Esther C., 'The Drawbridge of the Grail Castle,' *MLN*, 33 (1918), 399–405.

51 Taylor, Archer, 'The Motif of the Vacant Stake in Folklore and Romance,' *RR*, 9 (1918), 21–28.

See Pd15 Brown.

52 Brown, Arthur C. L., 'The Grail and the English Perceval,' *MP*, 22 (1924), 79–96 and 113–32.

53 Loomis, Roger Sherman, 'Medieval Iconography and the Question of Arthurian Origins,' *MLN*, 40 (1925), 65–70.
Cf. Arthur C. L. Brown, [Note], p. 70.

54 Krappe, Alexander Haggerty, *Balor with the Evil Eye: Studies in Celtic and French Literature*, Publications of the Institut des Etudes Françaises (New York: Institut des Etudes Françaises, 1927).
See 'The Drawbridge of the Grail Castle,' pp. 106–13; 'Perceval, the "Widow's Son",' pp. 126–31; and 'The Resuscitation of the Slain in the *Conte du Graal* and the Hilde Legend,' pp. 132–53.

55 Chambers, E. K., 'Some Points in the Grail Legend,' *Arthuriana*, 1 (1928–29), 7–20.

56 Krappe, Alexandre Haggerty, 'Lancelot et Guenièvre: à propos d'un livre récent,' *Revue Celtique*, 48 (1931), 94–123.
On Sb6 Cross and Nitze.

57 Chotzen, Th. M. Th., 'Le lion d'Owein (Yvain) et ses prototypes celtiques,' *Neophil*, 18 (1933), 51–58, 131–36.

58 Brown, Arthur C. L., 'Arthur's Loss of Queen and Kingdom,' *Spec*, 15 (1940), 3–11.

59 Nitze, William A., 'Who Was the Fisher King? A Note on Halieutics,' *RR*, 33 (1942), 97–104.

60 Nitze, William A., 'The Waste Land: A Celtic Arthurian Theme,' *MP*, 43 (1945), 58–62.

61 Newstead, Helaine, 'The Traditional Background of *Partonopeus de Blois*,' *PMLA*, 61 (1946), 916–46.

62 Williams, Mary, 'Some Aspects of the Grail Problem,' *Folklore*, 71 (1960), 85–103. (XIII.156)

63 Bromwich, Rachel, 'Celtic Dynastic Themes and the Breton Lays,' *EtCelt*, 9 (1961), 439–74. (XIV.133)

64 Marx, Jean, 'La vie et les aventures de la reine Guenièvre et la transformation de son personnage,' *JS* (1965), pp. 332–42.

65 Wais, Kurt, 'Morgan amante d'Accalon et rivale de Guenièvre,' *BBSIA*, 18 (1966), 137–49.

66 Charvet, Louis, 'Avalon et la quête du Graal,' *Cahiers du Sud*, 63, 387–88 (1967), 296–305.

67 Mandel, Jerome, 'Lancelot and Tristan: "The Prince as Bird",' *SMC*, 4:1 (1973), 141–46.

See Ga15 Noble.

68 Dumville, David N., '*Echtrae* and *Immram*: Some Problems of Definition,' *Ériu*, 27 (1976), 73–94. (XXIX.284)
Important terminological distinction.

69 Kelly, Susan, 'A Note on Arthur's Round Table and the Welsh *Life of Saint Carannog*,' *Folklore*, 87 (1976), 223–25. (XXIX.302)

70 Markale, Jean, *Le Roi Arthur et la société celtique* (Paris: Payot, 1976). (XXX.283)
English trans: *King of the Celts: Arthurian Legends and Celtic Tradition*, trans. Christine Hauch (London: Deep Books; Rochester, VT: Inner Traditions, 1977). (XXX.351)

71 Lozachmeur, Jean-Claude, 'Le motif du "Passage périlleux" dans les romans arthuriens et dans la littérature orale bretonne,' *EtCelt*, 15 (1976–78), 291–301. (XXIX.242)

72 Ó Riain-Raedel, Dagmar, *Untersuchungen zur mythischen Struktur der mittelhochdeutschen Artusepen: Ulrich von Zatzikhoven, 'Lanzelet' – Hartmann von Aue, 'Erec' und 'Iwein'*, PSQ, 91 (Berlin: Schmidt, 1978). (XXXI.37)

See Ga23 Busby.

See Ga26 Busby.

73 Darrah, John, *The Real Camelot: Paganism and the Arthurian Romances* (London: Thames and Hudson, 1981). (XXXIV.115, 303)

74 Gier, Albert, '"Il ne creoit pas en Artur": *Roman des sept sages*, v. 2875,' *RF*, 93 (1981), 367–71. (XXXV.25)
Reference to Arthur's death.

75 Gillies, William, 'Arthur in Gaelic Tradition. Part I: Folktales and Ballads,' *CMCS*, 2 (1981), 47–72; 'Part II: Romances and Learned Lore,' *CMCS*, 3 (1982), 41–75. (XXXIV.315, XXXV.391)

See Ga28 Jennings.

76 Lozachmeur, Jean-Claude, 'De la tête de Bran à l'hostie du Graal: pour une théorie des origines celtiques du mythe,' in *Essays Thorpe*, pp. 275–86. (XXXIV.343)

77 Wallbank, Rosemary E., 'Heinrichs von dem Türlîn "Crône" und die irische Sage von Etain und Mider,' in Pb253 *Kärnten*, pp. 251–68. (XL.609)

78   Campbell, Joseph, 'Indian Reflections in the Castle of the Grail,' in *The Celtic Consciousness*, ed. Robert O'Driscoll (Toronto: McClelland and Stewart, 1981; New York: Braziller, 1982), pp. 3–30.

79   Lozac'hmeur, Jean-Claude, and Shigemi Sasaki, 'A propos de deux hypothèses de R. S. Loomis: éléments pour une solution de l'énigme du Graal,' *BBSIA*, 34 (1982), 207–21.

See Mc42 Reichert.

80   Bromwich, Rachel, 'Celtic Elements in Arthurian Romance: A General Survey,' in *Studies Diverres*, pp. 41–55, 230–33. (XXXVI.405)

81   Sasaki, Shigemi, and Jean-Claude Lozachmeur, 'Researches on the Mystery of the Grail, Part I: The Enigma of the Grail Legend,' *Avalon*, 1:3 (1983), 19–22.

82   Sasaki, Shigemi, and Jean-Claude Lozachmeur, 'Researches on the Mystery of the Grail, Part II: Modern Critical Approaches,' *Avalon*, 1:4 (1984) 20–23.

83   Sterckx, Claude, 'Perceval le Gallois, Brân le Méhaigné et le symbolisme du Graal,' *RBPH*, 62 (1984), 463–73. (XXXVII.13)

84   Markale, Jean, *Lancelot et la chevalerie arthurienne* (Paris: Imago, 1985). (XXXVIII.242)

See Pc15 Rejhon.

85   Sterckx, Claude, 'Les têtes coupées et le Graal,' *StC*, 20–21 (1985–86), 1–42. (XL.138)

See Nb35 Lozachmeur.

See Ga59 Gowans.

86   Noble, Peter, 'The Heroic Tradition of Kei,' *RMS*, 14 (1988), 125–37. (XLII.670)

See Na.a35 Roberts.

See Nb42 Boutet.

87   Cassard, Jean-Christophe, 'Arthur est vivant! jalons pour une enquête sur le messianisme royal au Moyen Age,' *CCM*, 32 (1989), 135–46. (XLII.49)

88 Dunn, Vincent A., *Cattle-Raids and Courtships: Medieval Narrative Genres in a Traditional Context*, Garland Monographs in Medieval Literature, 2 (New York: Garland, 1989). (XLII.296)
See pp. 132–46.

89 Matthews, Caitlín, *Arthur and the Sovereignty of Britain: King and Goddess in the Mabinogion* (London: Arkana, 1989).

90 Miller, D. A., 'The Twinning of Arthur and Cei: An Arthurian Tessera,' *JIES*, 17 (1989), 47–76. (XLII.331)

91 Stone, Alby, 'Bran, Odin and the Fisher King: Norse Tradition and the Grail Legends,' *Folklore*, 100 (1989), 23–38. (XLII.680)

92 Wood, Juliette, 'Bran and the Fisher King,' *Folklore*, 101 (1990), 121–22. (XLIII.285)

93 Fife, Graeme, *Arthur the King* (London: BBC Books, 1990; New York: Sterling, 1991).

94 Hemmi, Yôko, 'Morgain le Fée's Water Connection,' *Studies in Medieval English Language and Literature*, 6 (1991), 19–36.

95 Hemmi, Yôko, 'Morgan le Fée's Zoomorphic Images,' *Eureka*, 23:10 (1991), 138–47.
In Japanese.

96 Bik, Elisabeth J., 'Le forgeron lacustre, "An Inconsistent Legend"?' *CCM*, 35 (1992), 3–25. (XLV.168)

97 Findon, Joanne, 'The Function of Cei in Welsh Arthurian Literature,' in *Celtic Languages and Celtic Peoples: Proceedings of the Second North American Conference of Celtic Studies*, ed. Cyril L. Byrne, Margaret Harry, and Padraig a Siadhail (Halifax, NS: D'Arcy McGee Chair of Irish Studies, 1992), pp. 405–23.

98 Lozachmeur, Jean-Claude, 'Pour une nouvelle herméneutique des mythes: essai d'interprétation de quelques thèmes celtiques,' in *Bretagne et pays celtiques: langues, histoire, civilisation: mélanges offerts à la mémoire de Léon Fleuriot*, ed. Gwennolé Le Menn and Jean-Yves Le Moing (Saint-Brieuc: Skol; Rennes: Presses Universitaires de Rennes, 1992), pp. 389–401. (XLV.185)
See pp. 398–401.

99 Morino, Satoko, 'Arthur in British Mythology,' *Reports of Faculty of Liberal Arts, Shizuoka University, Humanities and Social Sciences*, 28:1 (1992), 86–108.
In Japanese.

100 Roberts, Brynley F., 'Characterization in *The Four Branches of the Mabinogi*,' in Dc17 Roberts, pp. 105–13.

See Pb358 Antonini.

See Tb21 Doner.

See Ga78 Fulton.

101 Mori, Setsuko, '*The Book of Invasions*: (1) A Traditional, Biblical, and Historical Interpretation; (2) The Genealogical Theory of Sovereignty and Historical Background,' *ÉIRE* (Irish Studies) (Japan-Ireland Society), 13 (1993), 57–77; 14 (1994), 32–54.
In Japanese.

See Na.a41 Darrah.

102 Lühr, Rosemarie, 'Die Herkunftsbezeichnung Leonois und das Motif des dankbaren Löwen im *Mabinogion* und bei Chrétien von Troyes,' in *Ritter mit dem Löwen*, pp. 219–43. (XLVII.573)

103 Morino, Satoko, 'The Journey across the Wilderness: Structural Analysis of Three Welsh Arthurian Romances (I) (II),' *StCJ*, 6 (1994), 1–11; 7 (1995), 27–43.

104 Nøjgaard, Morten, 'La source d'Yvain: remarques sur quelques traits archaïques dans Le Chevalier au lion,' in *Michelanea: humanisme, litteratur og kommunikation. Festskrift til Michel Olsen i anledning af hans 60–årsdag den 23. april 1994*, ed. Inge Degn, Jens Høyrup, and Jan Scheel, Sprog og Multurmøde, 7 (Aalborg: Aalborg Universitetsforlag, 1994), pp. 163–67.

105 Pastré, Jean-Marc, '*Perceval* et *Parzival*: les données mélusiennes d'un roman médiéval,' *Bien dire*, 12 (1994), 191–201. (XLVII.285)

See Ga85 Pontfarcy.

106 Sterckx, Claude, 'Nûtons, Lûtuns et dieux celtes,' *ZcP*, 46 (1994), 39–79.

107 Brouland, Marie Thérèse, 'La souveraineté de Gwenhwyfar-Guenièvre,' in *Recueil Micha*, pp. 53–64. (XLVIII.65)

108 Lambert, Pierre-Yves. 'La vraie nature de Peredur fils d'Evrawc: roi ou guerrier?' in *Recueil Micha*, pp. 243–52. (XLVIII.120)
Treats *Owein* and *Gereint* also.

109 Even, Yann-Glaoda, and Maria Kernivinenn, *Emgaan Karaes: La bataille de Carohaise, Brocéliande et la source du Graal. Essai d'analyse et de résolution d'un chapitre des Romans de la Table Ronde* (Lannuon: Jean Claude Even, 1996).

110 Lacy, Norris J., 'King Arthur,' in *Le héros dans la réalité, dans la légende et dans la littérature médiévale–Der Held in historischer Realität, in der Sage und in der mittelalterlichen Literatur,* ed. Danielle Buschinger and Wolfgang Spiewok, WODAN: EG, 63–TS, 35 (Greifswald: Reineke, 1996), pp. 67–80. (XLIX.48)

111 Lozac'hmeur, Jean-Claude, 'Du héros civilisateur à Perceval ou les transpositions successives d'un mythe,' *Bien dire*, 13 (1996), 133–43. (XLIX.166)

112 Saly, Antoinette, 'Les "Enfances Perceval",' *PRIS-MA*, 12 (1996), 221–35; repr. in Dc30. (XLIX.186)

113 Benozzo, Francesco, 'L'origine di Lancillotto (mitologia gaelica e romanzo),' *FeS*, 11 (1996), 43–60. (LI.548)

114 Bromwich, Rachel, 'The Triads of the Horses,' in *The Horse in Celtic Culture*, ed. Sioned Davies and Nerys Ann Jones (Cardiff: University of Wales Press, 1997), pp. 102–20. (LI.351)

115 Hemmi, Yôko, 'The Mingling Regions of the Celtic Fairyland and the Land of the Dead,' *Kitasato Journal of Liberal Arts and Sciences*, 2 (1997), 10–23.
In Japanese.

116 Hemmi, Yôko, 'The Orientation of the Celtic Happy Otherworld,' in *Medieval Heritage: Essays Tadahiro Ikegami* (Tokyo: Yushôdô Press, 1997), pp. 427–40.
In Japanese.

117 Hemmi, Yôko, 'The Promised Land of the Saints in the *Navigatio Sancti Brendani*.' *G-k*, 73 (1997), 48–67.

118 Matsumura, Ken'ichi, *The Voyage of Bran* (Tokyo: Chuo University Press, 1997), with 'Appendix : Oisín and the Urashima Legend.'
In Japanese.

119 Milin, Gaël, 'Un entre-deux-mondes? L'imaginaire littéraire du marais au Moyen Age,' *KREIZ*, 8 (1997), 85–135. (LI.277)

120 Nakazawa, Shin'ichi, Mayumi Tsuruoka, and Kazuo Tsukikawa, *Druidism: Celtic Religion* (Tokyo: Iwanami-shoten, 1997).
In Japanese.

See Gd.b55 Queille.

121 Arita, Tadao, 'The Legend of the City of Ys and Brittany,' *ES-G*, 37 (1998), 1–32. (LI.646).
In Japanese.

122 Gouttebroze, Jean-Guy, 'Illusion de l'histoire, vérité du mythe: la mort du roi Crimthann,' *Razo*, 15 (1998), 35–43. (LI.244)

123 Hemmi, Yôko, 'The Wild Hunt and the Celtic Fairy Rade,' *Celtic Forum* (The Annual Report of the Japan Celticists' Society), 3 (1998), 2–20.

124 Lozac'hmeur, Jean-Claude, 'Le Forgeron, le Roi-Pêcheur et la libération des eaux ou l'arrière-plan mythologique d'une légende,' in *Mélanges Ménard*, vol. 2, pp. 917–31. (LI.270)

125 Baudry, Robert, 'Quelques "héros" hybrides: signes de leur lien avec un Autre Monde,' in *PRIS-MA*, 15 (1999), 187–98. (LII.198)

See Qb79 Gouttebroze.

126 Gouttebroze, Jean-Guy, 'De la reine à son fils, du roi à son épouse: pour une bonne actualisation de la dévolution de la souveraineté en milieu celtique et arthurien,' *Bien dire*, 17 (1999), 131–41.

127 Hemmi, Yôko, 'La "cavalcade des fées" celtique et la Chasse sauvage,' *Iris*, 18 (1999), 85–94.
Translated from the Japanese by Kôji Watanabe.

128 Hemmi, Yôko, 'King Arthur's Hunt of the Nightmare,' *Plume*, 4 (1999), 72–81.
In Japanese.

129 Hemmi, Yôko, 'Merlin in Celtic Traditions,' in *Mythologie comparée: les Vieux sages, Merlin eurasiatique: Actes du Colloque de Mythologie Comparée, Nagoya, septembre 1999* (Nagoya: University of Nagoya, 1999), pp. 115–18.

130 Nakano, Setsuko, 'On the Welsh Arthur (1) (2),' *Annual Report, Humanities and Social Studies (Otsuma Women's University)*, 31 (1999), 119–130; 32 (2000), 1–14.
In Japanese.

131 Watanabe, Kôji, 'Le défilé de femmes mortes dans le *Lai du Trot*,' *Iris*, 18 (1999), 73–83.

132 Watanabe, Kôji, 'The Procession of the Dead in the *Lai du Trot* and the Wild Hunt Myth,' *JCSC*, 35 (1999), 19–53.
In Japanese.

See Ga103 Whetter.

See Ga105 Gouttebroze.

133 Hemmi, Yôko, 'Celtic Heroes, "Changelings", and the Mothers,' *The Hiyoshi Review of English Studies* (Keio University), 37 (2000), 93–116.

See Ue8 Watanabe.

a.d: Stress on Chrétien's Romances

39 Goossens, Heinrich, *Über Sage, Quelle und Komposition des 'Chevalier au Lyon' des Crestien de Troyes*, diss. Münster (Paderborn: Schöningh, 1883); repr. in *Neuphilologische Studien*, 1 (1883), 1–61.

See Nb5 Ahlström.

40 Baist, G., 'Die Quellen des Yvain,' *ZrP*, 21 (1897), 402–5.

41 Johnston, O. M., 'The Fountain Episode in Chrétien de Troies's *Yvain*,' *Transactions and Proceedings of the American Philological Association*, 33 (1902), Proceedings for December 1901, pp. lxxxiii–lxxxiv.

42 Huet, G. Busken, 'De Graalsage bij Chrétien de Troies,' *De Beweging*, 3 (1907), 245–68.

See Pc2 Brown.

See Hc22 Singer.

43 Brown, Arthur C. L., 'A Note on the *Nugae* of G. H. Gerould's "King Arthur and Politics",' *Spec*, 2 (1927), 449–55.

44 Mühlhausen, Ludwig, 'Neue Beiträge zum Perceval-Thema,' *ZcP*, 17 (1927), 1–30.

45 Brown, Arthur C. L., 'Another Analogue to the Grail Story,' in *Studies Kastner*, pp. 85–93.

46 Loomis, Roger Sherman, 'Irish *Imrama* in the *Conte del Graal*,' *Rom*, 59 (1933), 557–64.

47 Nitze, William A., 'Count Philip's Book and the *Graal*,' *MLN*, 59 (1944), 559–62.

48 Newstead, Helaine, 'Perceval's Father and Welsh Tradition,' *RR*, 36 (1945), 3–31.

49 Brown, Arthur C. L., 'Irish Fabulous History and Chrétien's *Perceval*,' *MLQ*, 8 (1947), 419–25.

50 Amazawa, Taijirô, '"Question" in the *Conte del Graal* by Chrétien de Troyes,' *MGRS*, 125 (1967), 111–41.
In Japanese.

See Pc8 Goetinck.

51 Lozac'hmeur, Jean-Claude, 'A propos des sources du *mabinogi* d'Owein et du *Roman d'Yvain*,' *EtCelt*, 15 (1976–78), 573–75. (XXXI.288)

52 Roberts, Brynley F., '*Owein* neu *Iarlles y Ffynnawn*,' *YB*, 10 (1977), 124–43. (XXX.357)

See Hf39 Brault.

53 Sasaki, Shigemi, 'Observation on an Enigma of *Erec et Enide* (la Joie de la Cort),' *TATE*, 9 (1981), 98–114. (XXXIV.485).
In Japanese.

54 Foulon, C., 'Un personnage mystérieux du Roman de *Perceval le gallois*: l'*eschacier* dans la seconde partie du *Perceval*,' in *Studies Diverres*, pp. 67–75, 234–35. (XXXVI.424)

55 Lozac'hmeur, Jean-Claude, 'Origines celtiques des aventures de Gauvain au pays de Galvoie dans le *Conte du Graal* de Chrétien de Troyes,' in *Actes Rennes*, vol. 1, pp. 406–22. (XXXVIII.240)

See Ha142 Zink.

See Ga59 Gowans.

56 Sasaki, Shigemi, 'Perceval and his "Way" or the Onomastic Function in *Le Conte du graal*,' *TATE*, 21 (1988), 73–99. (XLI.308). In Japanese.

57 Szabics, Imre, 'Az Artur-legenda és az ófrancia udvari regény,' in *A nő az irodalomban* (Zalaegerszeg: Zala Megyei Könyvtár, 1988), pp. 156–66. (XLI.256)

58 Lozac'hmeur, Jean-Claude, 'Les origines armoricaines de la légende d'Erec et d'Enide,' *KREIZ*, 2 (1991–92), 145–62. (XLVI.341)

59 Hirashima, Hitomi, 'On "l'aventure à la fontaine" in *Yvain*,' *FBR*, 27 (1992), 39–50. In Japanese.

60 Mandach, André de, 'Erec et Enide: le clair-obscur de leur préhistoire,' in *Recueil Micha*, pp. 133–36. (XLVIII.122)

See Pc25 Oliver.

61 *Ystorya Gereint uab Erbin*, ed. Robert L. Thompson (Dublin: Dublin Institute of Advanced Studies, School of Celtic Studies, 1997). (LI.347)

See Uc56 Walter.

62 Watanabe, Kôji, 'The Mythic Subjects in *Le Chevalier au Lion* (*Yvain*) – On the "Myth of Barenton",' *Plume*, 3 (1999), 22–33. In Japanese.

See Na.a54 *Canhwyll*.

63 Walter, Philippe, *Fisher King or Salmon King? On a Character in the Conte du Graal by Chrétien de Troyes*, Jinbunken Booklet, 12 (The Institute of Cultural Science, Chuo University, 2000). In Japanese. Lecture introduced and translated by K. Watanabe.

a.e: The 'Mabinogionfrage'

7, 10 Zenker, Rudolf, 'Weiteres zur Mabinogionfrage [...]' Add *ZfSL*, 41 (1913), 131–65; 43 (1915), 11–73, and Na.e30, pp. 225–54.

See Pb69 Rauch.

20 Carruth, William H., 'Förster's *Chevalier au Lion* and the Mabinogi,' *MLN*, 4 (1889), cols. 326–32.

21 *Othmer, Karl, *Das Verhältnis von Christian's von Troyes 'Erec et Enide' zu dem Mabinogion des Roten Buches von Hergest 'Geraint ab Erbin'*, diss. Bonn (Cologne: Du Mont-Schauberg, 1889).

See Na.c34 Golther, 'Die Mabinogion,' pp. 410–17.

22 Hagen, Paul, 'Parzivalstudien. II,' *Germania*, 37 (1892), 121–45.

23 Foerster, W., 'Noch einmal die sogenannte Mabinogionfrage aus Anlaß einer neuen Veröffentlichung,' *ZfSL*, 38 (1911), 149–95.

24 Nitze, William A., 'The Sister's Son and the Conte del Graal,' *MP*, 9 (1912), 291–322.

25 Zenker, Rudolf, *Zur Mabinogionfrage: eine Antikritik* (Halle/S: Niemeyer, 1912).

26 Gaede, Wilhelm, *Die Bearbeitungen von Chrestiens Erek und die Mabinogionfrage*, diss. Münster (Berlin: Trenkel, 1913).

27 Greiner, Walter, *Owein-Ivain: neue Beiträge zur Frage nach der Unabhängigkeit der kymrischen Mabinogion von den Romanen Chrestiens*, diss. Leipzig (Halle/S: Karras, 1917).

28 Mühlhausen, L., 'Ein Beitrag zur Mabinogionfrage,' *GRM*, 10 (1922), 367–72.

29 Zenker, Rudolf, 'Ivain im Torverlies,' *ZfdA*, 62 (1925), 49–66.
See also Hermann Schneider, 'Schlußwort (zu Ivains torverlies),' *ZfdA*, 61 (1925), 112.

30 Zenker, Rudolf, 'Weiteres zur Mabinogionfrage,' *ZfSL*, 51 (1928), 225–54.

31 Sparnaay, H., 'Noch immer Ivain-Owein,' *ZfSL*, 52 (1929), 267–73.

32 Zenker, R., 'James Douglas Bruce und die Mabinogionfrage,' *ZfSL*, Supplementheft 13 (1929), 218–30.

33 Jones, Robert M., 'Y Rhamantau Cymraeg a'u cysylltiad â'r rhamantau Ffrangeg,' *LlC*, 4 (1957), 208–27. (XI.122)

See Na.b19 Piette.

34 *Owein or Chwedyl Iarlles y Ffynnawn*, ed. R. L. Thomson, Medieval and Modern Welsh Series, 4 (Dublin: Dublin Institute for Advanced Studies, 1968). (XXI.183)
See pp. xxii–xcvii.

35 Hunt, Tony, 'The Art of *Iarlles y Ffynnawn* and the European *Volksmärchen*,' *StC*, 8–9 (1973–74), 106–20. (XXVII.293)

See Na.a20 Bromwich.

36 Hunt, Tony, 'Some Observations on the Textual Relationship o[f] *Li Chevaliers au Lion* and *Iarlles y Ffynnawn*,' *ZcP*, 33 (1974), 93–113. (XXVII.153)

See Pc8 Goetinck.

37 Pioletti, Antonio, 'Note sul Peredur,' *SiG*, 28 (1975), 557–72.

See Pb185 Blosen.

38 Jones, Glyn E., 'Early Prose: The Mabinogi,' in *Guide to Welsh Literature*, ed. A. O. H. Jarman and Gwilym Rees Hughes, 2 vols (Swansea: Davies, 1976–79), vol. 1, pp. 189–202. Rev. ed., 7 vols (Cardiff: University of Wales Press, 1992–98), vol. 1, pp. 189–202.

See Na.d52 Roberts.

39 Lovecy, I. C., 'The Celtic Sovereignty Theme and the Structure of *Peredur*,' *StC*, 12–13 (1977–78), 133–46. (XXXI.375)

40 Lloyd-Morgan, Ceridwen, 'Narrative Structure in *Peredur*,' *ZcP*, 38 (1981), 187–231. (XXXIV.28)

See Pc10 Diverres.

41 Edel, Doris, 'Rhai sylwadau ar arddull *Peredur* a pherthynas y chwedl Gymraeg â *Perceval* Chrétien,' *LlC*, 14 (1983), 52–63. (XXXVI.418)

42 Nakano, Setsuko, 'The Tale of *Culhwch and Olwen* – The Welsh Arthur and Fairies,' *Bulletin of Children's Literature*, 14 (1983), 25–33.
In Japanese.

43 De Caluwé-Dor, Juliette, 'Prolégomènes à une étude comparée de La Dame à la Fontaine, Yvain et Ywain et Gawain,' in *Lancelot Wégimont*, pp. 43–61. (XXXVIII.204)

44 Nakano, Setsuko, 'A Study of *Y Mabinogi* (1) (2) (3) (4) (5) (6) (7) (8) (9) (10) (11),' *Journal of Yamanashi Eiwa Junior College*, 19 (1985), 56–76; 20 (1986), 18–39; 21 (1987), 1–17; 22 (1988), 281–302; 23 (1989), 229–48; 24 (1990), 85–105; *Annual Report, Humanities and Social Sciences (Otsuma Women's University)*, 24 (1992), 1–12; 25 (1993), 1–9; 26 (1994), 1–20; 27 (1995), 1–32; 28 (1996), 1–26. In Japanese.

45 Thomas, Neil, '*Gereint* and *Erec*: A Welsh Heroic Text and Its Continental Successors,' *Trivium*, 22 (1987), 37–48. (XL.140)

46 Thomas, Neil, 'Sir Gawein's Interpretation of Iwein's Transgression and the *Mabinogion* Controversy,' *RMS*, 13 (1987), 57–69. (XLI.158)

See Ga59 Gowans.

See Na.c89 Matthews.

47 Roberts, Brynley F., 'Sylwadau ar "ramant" *Gereint ac Enid*,' *YB*, 18 (1992), 29–42. (XLV.267)

See Md45 Luttrell.

48 Salberg, Trond Kruke, 'The Origins of the Arthurian Legend and of the Matter of Britain/Brittany,' in *Om Arthur- og Gralsromanen*, ed. Reinhold Schröder, MSFM, 12 (Odense: Odense Universitet, 1994), pp. 9–21. On *Owein* and *Yvain*.

See Pc24 Edel.

49 Morino, Satoko, 'The Sense of Ending in the Four Branches of the Mabinogi,' *ZcP*, 49–50 (1997), 341–48.

See Na.d61 *Ystorya*.

50 Jones, Robert M., *Tair Rhamant Arthuraidd* (Caernarfon: Gwasg Pantycelyn, 1998). (LI.383)

51 Nakano, Setsuko, 'A Portrait of a Victorian Lady (1) – Lady Charlotte Guest: An English Lady Living in Wales,' *Journal of Department of Literature of Otsuma Women's University in Celebration of the 30th Anniversary* (1998), pp. 31–49. In Japanese.

52   Nakano, Setsuko, 'A Portrait of a Victorian Lady (2) – Lady Charlotte Schreber: Seaching after the Life of "noblesse oblige",' *Annual Report, Humanities and Social Studies (Otsuma Women's University)*, 30 (1998), 9–21.
In Japanese.

See Pc26 Lloyd-Morgan.

See Na.a54(F) Lloyd-Morgan.

a.f: Arthurian Names

10   Zimmer, H., 'Beiträge zur Namenforschung in den altfranzösischen Arthurepen,' *ZfSL*, 13 (1891), 1–117.

11   Pütz, Franz, *Zur Geschichte der Entwicklung der Artursage*, diss. Bonn (Oppeln: Raabe, 1892).

12   Brugger, E., 'Ueber die Bedeutung von Bretagne, Breton in mittelalterlichen Texten,' *ZfSL*, 20 (1898), 79–162.

13   Lot, Ferdinand, 'L'origine du nom de Lancelot,' *Rom*, 51 (1925), 423.

14   Brugger, E., 'The Hebrides in the French Arthurian Romances,' *Arthuriana*, 2 (1929–30), 7–19.

15   Loomis, Roger Sherman, 'Baudemaguz,' *Rom*, 63 (1937), 383–93.

16   Smith, Roland M., 'Guinganbresil and the Green Knight,' *JEGP*, 45 (1946), 1–25.

17   Delbouille, Maurice, 'Le nom et le personnage d'Equitan,' *MA*, 69 (1963), 315–23. (XVI.112)
Equitan = 'sires des nains' in *Erec* 1941–42.

18   Goetinck, Glenys W., '*Gwalchmai, Gauvain* a *Gawain*,' *LlC*, 8 (1965), 234–35. (XX.149)

See Na.b19 Piette.

19   Lozachmeur, Jean-Claude, 'Origine du nom du héros dans le *Lai de Désiré*,' *EtCelt*, 15 (1976–78), 289–90. (XXIX.243)
Yvain's name.

See Nb13 Fauth.

20 Lozac'hmeur, Jean-Claude, 'Bendigeit vran et Corbenic,' *EtCelt*, 16 (1979), 283–85. (XXXI.290)

21 Lozac'hmeur, Jean-Claude, 'Guinglain et Perceval,' *EtCelt*, 16 (1979), 279–81. (XXXI.289)

22 Musès, Charles, 'Celtic Origins and the Arthurian Cycle: Geographic-Linguistic Evidence,' *JIES*, 7 (1979), 31–48.

23 Lozachmeur, Jean-Claude, 'A propos de l'origine du nom de *Mabonagrain*,' *EtCelt*, 17 (1980), 257–62. (XXXII.356 *bis*)

24 Lozac'hmeur, Jean-Claude, 'A propos des origines de l'expression "La Joie de la cour" dans *Erec et Enide*,' *EtCelt*, 18 (1981), 245–48. (XXXIII.351)

See Na.c80 Bromwich.

25 Lozac'hmeur, Jean-Claude, 'D'Yvain à Désiré: recherches sur les origines de la légende d'Yvain,' *EtCelt*, 21 (1984), 257–63. (XXXVII.96)

26 Woledge, Brian, 'Un o ffynonellau Cymreig Chrétien de Troyes, Laudune de Landuc, merch Landunet,' trans. A. O. H. Jarman, *LlC*, 15 (1984–86), 18–22. (XXXIX.86)

27 Ovazza, Maud, 'D'Apollon-Maponos à Mabonagrain: les avatars d'un dieu celtique,' in *Actes Rennes*, vol. 2, pp. 465–72. (XXXVIII.249)

See Kb8 Sims-Williams.

28 Breeze, Andrew, '*Gryngolet*, the Name of Sir Gawain's Horse,' *English Studies*, 81 (2000), 100–1.

a.g: Criticism of Celtic Theories

12 Golther, [W.], 'Chrestiens conte del Graal in seinem verhältnis zum wälschen Peredur und zum englischen Sir Perceval,' *Sitzungsberichte der philosophisch-philologischen und historischen Classe der königlichen bayerischen Akademie der Wissenschaften zu München* (1890), fasc. 2, pp. 174–217.

See Ma24 Ogle.

See Na.c55 Chambers.

13 Lewis, C. S., 'The Anthropological Approach,' in *English and Medieval Studies Presented to J. R. R. Tolkien on the Occasion of his Seventieth Birthday*, ed. Norman Davis and C. L. Wrenn (London: Allen & Unwin, 1962), pp. 219–30.

See Pa88 Tyssens.

14 Bell, Michael J., 'The Relation of Mentality to Race: William Wells Newell and the Celtic Hypothesis,' *JAF*, 92 (1979), 25–43. (XXXII.158)

See Gd.b16 Chênerie.

See Db24(C) Luttrell.

See Je25 Klenke.

15 Lovecy, Ian, 'Exploding the Myth of the Celtic Myth: A New Appraisal of the Celtic Background of Arthurian Romance,' *RMS*, 7 (1981), 3–18. (XXXIV.342)

See Nb44 Stone.

See Nb48 Malcor.

See Na.b37 Sims-Williams.

16 *The Celts and Japan*, ed. Tôji Kamata and Mayumi Tsuruoka (Tokyo: Kadokawa-shoten, 2000).
In Japanese.

b: Non-Celtic or Folklore Theories

5 Ahlström, Axel, 'Sur l'origine du *Chevalier au lion*,' in *Mélanges de philologie romane dédiés à Carl Wahlund à l'occasion du cinquantième anniversaire de sa naissance (7 janvier 1896)* (Mâcon: Protat, 1896; repr. Geneva: Slatkine, 1972), pp. 289–303.

6 Weston, Jessie L., *The Three Days' Tournament: A Study in Romance and Folk-Lore, Being an Appendix to the Author's 'Legend of Sir Lancelot'*, Grimm Library, 15 (London: Nutt, 1902).
See Na.a3 Weston.

7 Nitze, William A., 'A New Source of the *Yvain*,' *MP*, 3 (1905), 267–80.

See Me7 Hamilton.

8   Weston, Jessie L., *The Quest of the Holy Grail* (London: Bell, 1913; repr. London: Frank Cass, 1964).

9   Barto, P. S., 'The *Schwanritter-Sceaf* Myth in *Perceval le Gallois ou le Conte du Graal*,' *JEGP*, 19 (1920), 190–200.

See Na.c56 Krappe.

10   Renaut [de Beaujeu], *Le lai d'Ignaure ou Lai du prisonnier*, ed. Rita Lejeune, Académie Royale de Langue et de Littérature Françaises de Belgique: Textes Anciens, 3 (Brussels: Palais des Académies; Liège: Vaillant-Carmanno, 1938). (I.57)
See pp. 30–34.

See Na.e35 Hunt.

11   *Nickel, Helmut, 'Wer waren König Artus' Ritter? Über die geschichtliche Grundlage der Artussagen,' *Waffen und Kostümkunde: Zeitschrift der Gesellschaft für historische Waffen- und Kostümkunde*, ser. 3, 17 (1975), 1–18 + 23 plates. (XXVIII.58)
On the Sarmatian influence.

12   *Enzyklopädie des Märchens: Handwörterbuch zur historischen und vergleichenden Erzählforschung*, ed. Kurt Ranke [et alii] (Berlin: de Gruyter. 1977–)
- A.   'Artustradition,' by Karl Otto Brogsitter, vol. 1, col. 828–49. (XXIX.11)
- B.   'Chrétien de Troyes,' by Karl Otto Brogsitter, vol. 2, col. 1366–80. (XXXV.13)
- C.   'Erek,' by Karl Otto Brogsitter, vol. 4, col. 166–74. (XXXV.14)
- D.   'Gawein,' by Nikolaus Henkel, vol. 5, col. 780–82.
- E.   'Gral,' by Walter Haug, vol. 6, col. 86–91.
- F.   'Iwein,' by Nikolaus Henkel, vol. 7, col. 374–78.
- G.   'Lancelot,' by Walter Haug, vol. 8, col. 747–60.
- H.   'Parzival,' forthcoming.

13   Fauth, Wolfgang, 'Fata Morgana,' in *Beiträge ZrP*, pp. 417–54. (XXX.25)

See Hg30 Gallais.

See Ub11 Gallais.

14   Grisward, Joël H., 'Ider et le tricéphale: d'une "aventure" arthurienne à un mythe indien,' *Annales*, 33 (1978), 279–93. (XXXII.345)

15 Littleton, C. Scott, and Ann C. Thomas, 'The Sarmatian Connection: New Light on the Origin of the Arthurian and Holy Grail Legends,' *JAF*, 91 (1978), 513–27. (XXXI.111)

16 Luttrell, Claude, 'From Traditional Tale to Arthurian Romance: *Le Chevalier au lion*,' *NMS*, 22 (1978), 36–57. (XXXI.376)

17 Saly, Antoinette, 'Motifs folkloriques dans le *Lancelot* de Chrétien de Troyes,' *BBSIA*, 30 (1978), 187–95; repr. in Dc22.
On vv. 209–11, 1344–1499.

18 Friedman, Albert B., 'Folklore and Medieval Literature: A Look at Mythological Considerations,' *Southern Folklore Quarterly*, 43 (1979), 135–48. (XXXIV.122)

19 Littleton, C. Scott, 'The Holy Grail, the Cauldron of Annwn, and the Nartyamonga: A Further Note on the Sarmatian Connection,' *JAF*, 92 (1979), 326–33. (XXXII.200)

20 Rosenberg, Bruce A., 'Folkloristes et médiévistes face au texte littéraire: problèmes de méthode,' *Annales*, 34 (1979), 943–55.

21 Bretèque, François Amy de la, 'L'épine enlevée de la patte du lion: récit médiéval et conte populaire (essai d'analyse morphologique),' *RLR*, 84 (1980), 53–72. (XXXIII.365)

See Pb238 Green.

22 Luttrell, Claude, 'Folk Legend as Source for Arthurian Romance: The Wild Hunt,' in *Essays Thorpe*, pp. 83–100. (XXXIV.344)

23 Stanesco, Michel, 'Le chevalier au lion d'une déesse oubliée: Yvain et "Dea Lunae",' *CCM*, 24 (1981), 221–32. (XXXIV.250)

24 Payen, Jean-Charles, 'La légende arthurienne et la Normandie,' *BBSIA*, 34 (1982), 185–96.

25 Payen, Jean-Charles, 'Les romans arthuriens et la Basse-Normandie (Benoïc et Gaunes en pays domfrontais),' in *Recueil d'études offert en hommage au doyen Michel de Boüard*, 2 vols, Annales de Normandie: numéro spécial (Caen: Imprimerie Régionale, 1982), pp. 467–508. (XXXV.340 *bis*)

See Ge35 Boutet.

26 Grisward, Joël H., 'Des Scythes aux Celtes: le Graal et les talismans royaux des Indo-Européens,' *Artus*, 14 (1983), 15–22. (XXXVI.346 *bis*)

27 Grisward, Joël, 'Uter Pendragon, Artur et l'idéologie royale des Indo-Européens: structure trifonctionnelle et roman arthurien,' *Europe*, 654 (Oct. 1983), 111–20. (XXXVI.347)

28 Guerreau, Anita, 'Romans de Chrétien de Troyes et contes folkloriques: rapprochements thématiques et observations de méthode,' *Rom*, 104 (1983), 1–48. (XXXVI.348)

See Hc48 Gouttebroze.

29 Harf-Lancner, Laurence, 'Lancelot et la Dame du lac,' *Rom*, 105 (1984), 16–33. (XXXVIII.222)

See Gb75 Harf-Lancner.

See Qg3 *Légende*.

30 Andersson, Theodore M., '"Helgakviða Hjǫrvarðssonar" and European Bridal-Quest Narrative,' *JEGP*, 84 (1985), 51–75. (XXXIX.212)
Includes *Cligés*.

See Hg62 Baudry.

31 Kamizawa, Eizô, 'Chrétien de Troyes and Magical Folklores,' *Gengo*, 3 (1985), 11–20. (XXXIX.188).
In Japanese.

32 Tavera, Antoine, 'D'Indra à Perceval: en quête des origines du Graal,' in *Hommage Richer*, pp. 363–75.

33 Peterson, Linda A., 'The Alans and the Grail, or the Theft, the Swindle, and the Legend,' *F&MS*, 10 (1986), 27–41.
See also her 'The Alan of Lot: A New Interpretation of the Legends of Lancelot,' *F&MS*, 9 (1985), 31–49. Cf. Nb48.

See Hg70 Benedetti.

34 Bertin, Georges, 'La fête des lances dans l'ancien diocèse du Mans,' in *Normandie*, pp. 85–100.

See Pa179 Chênerie.

35 Lozachmeur, Jean-Claude, 'Du mythe au roman, I (essai d'archéologie arthurienne) – II (mythe, folklore et roman),' *PRIS-MA*, 3 (1987), 61–66, 137–44. (XLI.68)

36 Lozachmeur, Jean-Claude, 'Recherches sur les origines indo-européennes et ésotériques de la légende du Graal,' *CCM*, 30 (1987), 45–63. (XL.48)

37 Payen, Jean-Charles, 'A la recherche d'un "folklorisme medieval",' in *Normandie*, pp. 39–42.

38 Stanesco, Michel, 'Le conte de fées et le merveilleux romanesque,' in *Réception*, pp. 11–19. (XL.58)

39 Susong, Gilles, 'Personnages et paysages normands dans les derniers romans de Chrétien de Troyes,' in *Normandie*, pp. 51–72.

40 Wadge, Richard, 'King Arthur: A British or Sarmatian Tradition?' *Folklore*, 98 (1987), 204–15. (XL.142)

See Hf72 Walter.

41 Gier, Albert, 'Elementos populares y cultos en la narrativa breve románica medieval,' in *Narrativa breve medieval románica*, ed. Jesús Montoya Martínez, Aurora Juárez Blanquer, and Juan Paredes Núñez, Colección Romania: Biblioteca Universitaria de Estudios Románicos, número 0 (Granada: Ediciones TAT, 1988), pp. 63–86.

See Uc28 Walter.

42 Boutet, Dominique, 'Lancelot: préhistoire d'un héros arthurien,' *Annales*, 44 (1989), 1229–44. (XLII.46)

43 Harf-Lancner, Laurence, '*Le Chevalier au lion*, un conte morgan-ien,' *Bien dire*, 7 (1989), 107–16. (XLIII.179)

44 Stone, Alby, 'Bran, Odin, and the Fisher King: Norse Tradition and the Grail Legends,' *Folklore*, 100 (1989), 25–38. (XLII.680)

See Na.c96 Bik.

45 Littleton, C. Scott, and Linda A. Malcor, *From Scythia to Camelot: A Radical Reassessment of the Legends of King Arthur, the Knights of the Round Table, and the Holy Grail*, GRLH, 1795 (New York: Garland, 1994). (XLVII.751, XLVIII.711)

46 Vàrvaro, Alberto, *Apparizioni fantastiche: tradizioni folcloriche e letteratura nel medioevo: Walter Map* (Bologna: Il Mulino, 1994). (XLVII. 468)

See Uf2(C) Furtado and Veloso.

47 Littleton, C. Scott, 'King Arthur and the "Sarmatian Connection": An Overview and Update,' in *Medieval West*, pp. 121–29.

48 Malcor, Linda A., 'The Alan of Lot: A New Interpretation of the Legends of Lancelot,' in *Medieval West*, pp. 130–38. Cf. Nb33.

See Ha196 Meletinsky.

49 Wright, A. E., '"Le voir ne l'en osa dire": An Aesopic Reminiscence in Chrétien de Troyes?' *RomN*, 36 (1996), 125–30. (XLVIII.735)

50 Airò, Anna, 'Tracce sciamaniche nel *Chevalier de la Charrete* di Chrétien de Troyes,' *ImRif*, 7 (1998), 169–211. (LII.588)

See Uc51 Walter.

51 Walter, Philippe, 'Erec et la *cocadrille*: note de philologie et de folklore médiéval,' *ZrP*, 115 (1999), 56–64. (LII.120)

See Eh11 Lindahl.

52 Saly, Antoinette, 'Roi hermite, roi ascète,' *PRIS-MA*, 16 (2000), 289–301.

See Uc58 Walter.

c: Oral Sources (see also Fe)

See Md25 Hoepffner.

1 Carpenter, Dwayne E., 'Descriptive Modes of Physical Beauty in Hispano-Arabic *Muwaššahat* and Romance Models,' *CLS*, 16 (1979), 294–306.

2 Owen, D. D. R., 'Chrétien and the *Roland*,' in *Essays Thorpe*, pp. 139–50. (XXXIV.356)

3 Gilet, Peter, 'Le conte folklorique et le *Conte du Graal*: utilisation d'une forme orale dans l'analyse de la littérature écrite du Moyen Age,' *InfLitt*, 44:3 (1992), 3–5.

P: INFLUENCES

Scholars in Middle High German and Middle English have long been aware of the extent and importance of Chrétien's influence. In recent years the subject has attracted more attention by scholars working in other languages, notably Dutch and Scandinavian, so that the volume of published work on his influence has greatly increased – most strikingly, in the number of studies devoted to post-Chrétien Arthurian romances in French. These have evolved from traditional source study to reflect new awareness of original adaptation, intertextuality, *mouvance*, and the generic changes that might occur as Chrétien's influence extends to modes outside those of medieval romance.

'Influence' supposes some direct or indirect connection between or among works, even in modern or contemporary writings (Pk). But comparative studies have also appeared in which the connection first occurs when the scholar makes the comparison, and where actual influence is very unlikely; for these, see U, especially the new section Ue.

a: French Literature

20 Jauss, Hans Robert, *Untersuchungen* [...]; partly repr. in his *Alterität und Modernität der mittelalterlichen Literatur: gesammelte Aufsätze 1956–76* (Munich: Fink, 1977), pp. 50–124. (XXXI.26)

34 Raynaud de Lage, Guy, 'Sur quelques images [...]' Repr. in Dc4.

36 Baudry, Robert, 'De Chrétien de Troyes [...]' (XXVII.240)

38 Rochat, Alfred, *Über einen bisher unbekannten Parcheval li Galois* (Zürich: Kiesling, 1855).

See Pb69 Rauch.

39   Kirchrath, Leonhard, *Li romans de Durmart le Galois in seinem Verhaeltnisse zu Meraugis de Portlesguez und den Werken Chrestiens de Troies*, AA, 21 (Marburg: Elwert, 1884).

See Na.e22 Hagen.

See Na.c39 Wechssler.

40   Gröber, Gustav, 'Ein Marienmirakel,' in *Beiträge zur romanischen und englischen Philologie: Festgabe für Wendelin Foerster* (Halle/S: Niemeyer, 1902); repr. as *Festgabe für Wendelin Foerster* (Geneva: Slatkine, 1977), pp. 421–42.

See Eg6 Newell.

41   Rohde, Richard, *La Vengeance Raguidel: eine Untersuchung über ihre Beeinflussung durch Christian von Troyes und über ihren Verfasser*, diss. Göttingen (Hannover: Riemschneider, 1904).

42   Marquardt, Wilhelm, *Der Einfluß Kristians von Troyes auf den Roman 'Fergus' des Guillaume le Clerc*, diss. Göttingen (Heidelberg: Hörning & Berkenbusch, 1906).

43   Habemann, Cäsar, *Die literarische Stellung des Meraugis de Portlesguez in der französischen Artusepik*, diss. Göttingen (Göttingen: Haensch, 1908).

44   Thedens, Robert, *Li Chevaliers as deus espees in seinem Verhältnis zu seinen Quellen, insbesondere zu den Romanen Crestiens von Troyes*, diss. Göttingen (Göttingen: Hubert, 1908).

45   Carter, Charles Henry, 'Ipomedon, An Illustration of Romance Origin,' in *Haverford Essays: Studies in Modern Literature Prepared by Some Former Pupils of Professor Francis B. Gummere in Honor of the Completion of the Twentieth Year of his Teaching in Haverford College* (Haverford: Haverford College, 1909), pp. 235–70.
See pp. 250–52 on three-days' tournament.

46   Critchlow, F. L., 'Arthur in Old French Poetry not of the Breton Cycle,' *MP*, 6 (1909), 477–86.

47   Doutrepont, Georges, *La Littérature française à la cour des ducs de Bourgogne: Philippe le Hardi–Jean sans Peur–Philippe le Bon–Charles le Téméraire*, Bibliothèque du XVe Siècle, 8 (Paris: Champion, 1909).
See Chap. 1: 'Épopées et romans d'inspiration médiévale.'

48   Patterson, Shirley Gale, 'A Note on a Borrowing from Chrétien de Troyes,' *MLN*, 26 (1911), 73–74.
In *Guillaume le Faucon*.

49   Schultz-Gora, O., 'Eine neue Stelle für Crestien de Troies,' *ZrP*, 37 (1913), 464–65.
In *Foulque de Candie*.

50   Besch, Emile, 'Les adaptations en prose des chansons de geste au XVᵉ et au XVIᵉ siècles,' *Revue du Seizième Siècle*, 3 (1915), 155–81.
Treats as well the influence of some romances by Chrétien.

51   Wilmotte, M., 'L'auteur des branches II et Va du *Renard* et Chrétien de Troyes,' *Rom*, 44 (1915–17), 258–60.

52   Klose, Martin, *Der Roman von Claris und Laris in seinen Beziehungen zur altfranzösischen Artusepik des XII. und XIII. Jahrhunderts, unter besonderer Berücksichtigung der Werke Crestiens von Troyes*, Beihefte zur *ZrP*, 63 (Halle/S.: Niemeyer, 1916).

53   Gay, Lucy M., 'Hue de Rotelande's *Ipomédon* and Chrétien de Troyes,' *PMLA*, 32 (1917), 468–91.

54   Bruce, J. D., 'The Composition of the Old French Prose Lancelot: The So-Called *Charete*,' *RR*, 10 (1919), 57–66.

55   Hoepffner, E., 'Die Anspielung auf Chrestien de Troyes in *Hunbaut*,' *ZrP*, 40 (1919), 235–38.

56   Lot-Borodine, Myrrha, 'Les deux conquérants du Graal: Perceval et Galaad,' *Rom*, 47 (1921), 41–97.

57   Reinhard, John R., '*Amadas et Ydoine*. I. – Mediaeval Conventions; II. – Celtic Remains,' *RR*, 15 (1924), 179–265.

58   Foulet, Lucien, '*Galeran* et les dix compagnons de Bretagne,' *Rom*, 51 (1925), 116–21.
Includes *Perceval*.

59   Wilmotte, M., 'Marie de France et Chrétien de Troyes,' *Rom*, 52 (1926), 353–55.

60   Reinhard, John Revell, *The Old French Romance of 'Amadas et Ydoine': An Historical Study* (Durham, NC: Duke University Press, 1927).

61 Wilmotte, Maurice, 'Un curieux cas de plagiat littéraire: le poème de *Galeran*,' *BulLSMP*, ser. 5, 14 (1928), 269–309.

See Tb16 Anitchkof.

62 Murrell, E. S., 'An Old French Prose Romance of *Yvain*?' *Arthuriana*, 2 (1930), 46–57.
National Library of Wales Additional 444–D.

63 Thompson, Albert Wilder, ed., *The Elucidation: A Prologue to the 'Conte del Graal'* (New York: Institute of French Studies, 1931).
See pp. 34–85.

See Ra4 Heinermann.

64 Doutrepont, Georges, *Les Mises en prose des épopées et des romans chevaleresques du XIVe au XVIe siècle*, Académie Royale de Belgique: Classes des Lettres et des Sciences Morales et Politiques, Mémoires in-8°, 40 (Brussels: Palais des Académies, 1939).

65 Henry, Albert, ed., *Sarrasin: Le Roman du Hem*, Travaux de la Faculté de Philosophie et Lettres de l'Université de Bruxelles, 9 (Paris: Belles Lettres, 1939). (III.96)
See 'Chrétien de Troyes, Sarrazin et la fête du Hem,' pp. lii–lvi.

66 Adler, Alfred, 'The Themes of the "Handsome Coward" and of the "Handsome Unknown" in *Meraugis de Portlesguez*,' *MP*, 44 (1947), 218–24.

See Pb106 Adolf.

67 Fox, John Howard, *Robert de Blois, son œuvre didactique et narrative: étude linguistique et littéraire suivie d'une édition critique avec commentaire et glossaire de l''Enseignement des princes' et du 'Chastoiement des dames'* (Paris: Nizet, 1950).
See Chap. 5.

68 Beaulieux, Charles, 'L'orthographe de Ronsard.–Sa destinée,' in *Mélanges d'histoire littéraire de la Renaissance offerts à Henri Chamard, Professeur honoraire à la Sorbonne* (Paris: Nitze, 1951), pp. 125–35.

69 West, G. D., 'Gerbert's *Continuation de Perceval* (ll. 1528–1543) and the Sparrow-Hawk Episode,' *BBSIA*, 7 (1955), 79–87.

70   Adler, Alfred, 'The Education of Lancelot: "Grammar" – "Grammarye",' *BBSIA*, 9 (1957), 101–7. (X.85)

71   Lee, A. van der, *Zum literarischen Motiv der Vatersuche*, VerKA, n.s. 63:3 (Amsterdam: Noord-Holland, 1957). (XI.176)
See pp. 83–100.

72   Bérier, François, 'Renart et Tibert ou comment le goupil "ses moz retorne en autre guise" (Branche II, v. 699),' *RT*, 55 (1960), 33–53.
See pp. 48–51.

73   Pickford, Cedric Edward, *L'Évolution du roman arthurien en prose vers la fin du Moyen Age d'après le manuscrit 112 du fonds français de la Bibliothèque Nationale* (Paris: Nizet, 1960). (XII.238)
Includes illustrations from and comparisons with Chrétien's romances.

74   Togeby, Knud, *Litterære Renæssancer i Frankrigs Middelalder*, Studier fra Sprog- og Oldtidsforskning, 243 (Copenhagen: Gads, 1960). (XIII.90)
See pp. 36–43.

75   Frappier, Jean, 'Sur le *Perceval en prose* de 1530,' in *Fin du Moyen Age et Renaissance: mélanges de philologie française offerts à Robert Guiette* (Antwerp: Nederlandse Boekhandel, 1961), pp. 233–47; repr. in Dc5. (XVI.111)

76   Muir, Lynette, 'An Arthurian Enthusiast in the 16th Century: Pierre Sala,' *BBSIA*, 13 (1961), 111–16.

77   Pickford, C. E., 'Les éditions imprimées de romans arthuriens en prose antérieures à 1600,' *BBSIA*, 13 (1961), 99–109.

78   Cocito, Luciana, *Gerbert de Montreuil e il Poema del Graal* (Geneva: Bozzi, 1964). (XVIII.232)
See Chap. 7: 'Reminiscenze letterarie.'

79   Muir, Lynette R., 'A Reappraisal of the Prose *Yvain* (National Library of Wales MS. 444–D),' *Rom*, 85 (1964), 355–65. (XVII.115)

80   Frappier, Jean, 'Les romans de la Table Ronde et les lettres en France au XVIe siècle,' *RPh*, 19 (1965), 178–93; repr. in *Actes Poitiers*, pp. 83–102. (XVIII.67)

81   Lyons, Faith, *Les Éléments descriptifs dans le roman d'aventure au XIIIe siècle (en particulier 'Amadas et Ydoine', 'Gliglois', 'Galeran',*

'L'Escoufle', 'Guillaume de Dole', 'Jehan et Blonde', 'Le Castelain de Couci'), PRF, 84 (Geneva: Droz, 1965). (XVIII.269)

82 Lyons, Faith, 'The Literary Originality of *Galeran de Bretagne*,' in *Medieval Miscellany Presented to Eugène Vinaver by Pupils, Colleagues and Friends*, ed. F. Whitehead, A. H. Diverres, and F. E. Sutcliffe (Manchester: Manchester University Press; New York: Barnes & Noble, 1965), pp. 206–19. (XVIII.205)

See Na.c64 Marx.

83 Bogdanow, Fanni, *The Romance of the Grail: A Study of the Structure and Genesis of a Thirteenth-Century Arthurian Prose Romance* (Manchester: Manchester University Press; New York: Barnes and Noble, 1966) (XIX.217).
See the Introduction.

84 Charvet, Louis, *Des vaus d'Avalon à la Queste du Graal* (Paris: Corti, 1967). (XX.261)

85 Frappier, Jean, 'De Chrétien de Troyes au *Lancelot en prose*,' *CEMN*, 5 (1967), 5–16.

86 Micha, Alexandre, '"Matière" et "sen" dans l'*Estoire dou Graal* de Robert de Boron,' *Rom*, 89 (1968), 457–80. (XXI.148)

87 Pickford, Cedric E., 'Benoist Rigaud et le *Lancelot du Lac* de 1591,' in *Mélanges Frappier*, vol. 2, pp. 903–11.

88 Tyssens, Madeleine, 'Les sources de Renaut de Beaujeu,' in *Mélanges Frappier*, vol. 2, pp. 1043–55.

89 Cocco, Marcello, 'L'inedito *Roman de Cardenois* e la fortuna di Guillaume de Machaut,' *CN*, 31 (1971), 125–53.
See pp. 129–30.

90 West, G. D., 'Grail Problems, I: Silimac the Stranger,' *RPh*, 24 (1970–71), 599–611; 'II: The Grail Family in the Old French Verse Romances,' 25 (1971–72), 53–73. (XXIV.80–81)

91 Bogdanow, Fanni, 'The Treatment of the Lancelot-Guenevere Theme in the *Prose Lancelot*,' *MAe*, 41 (1972), 110–20. (XXV.235)

92 Bogdanow, Fanni, 'The Transformation of the Role of Perceval in Some Thirteenth Century Prose Romances,' in *Studies in Medieval Literature and Languages in Memory of Frederick Whitehead*, ed. W.

Rothwell et al (Manchester: Manchester University Press; New York: Barnes and Noble, 1973), pp. 47–65. (XXVI.185)

See Gd.c6 Lyons.

See Ub6 Roubaud.

93 Thiry-Stassin, Martine, 'Interventions d'auteur dans le *Cligès* en prose de 1454,' in *Hommage Maurice Delbouille*, = *MrR*, Special Issue (1973), pp. 269–77.

94 Baker, M.-J., 'France's First Sentimental Novel and Novels of Chivalry,' *BHR*, 36 (1974), 33–45. (XXVII.239)

See Pg10 Bruneti.

95 Larmat, Jean, 'Le péché de Perceval dans la *Continuation* de Gerbert,' in *Mélanges Rostaing*, vol. 1, pp. 541–57. (XXVII.101)

See Ga14 Barnett.

96 Baumgartner, Emmanuèle, 'A propos du *Mantel mautaillié*,' *Rom*, 96 (1975), 315–32. (XXVIII.243)

97 Baumgartner, Emmanuèle, *Le 'Tristan en prose': essai d'interprétation d'un roman médiéval*, PRF, 133 (Geneva: Droz, 1975). (XXVIII.244)
See pp. 134–38, 145–46.

98 Bakelaar, Bette Lou, 'Certain Characteristics of the Syntax and Style in the Fifteenth-Century *mises en prose* of Chrestien's *Erec* and *Cligès*,' *Semasia*, 3 (1976), 61–73.

See Fa87 Freeman.

See Gd.c9 Ribard.

See He27 Saly.

99 Wolfgang, Lenora D., ed., *'Bliocadran': A Prologue to the 'Perceval' of Chrétien de Troyes – Edition and Critical Study*, Beihefte zur *ZrP*, 150 (Tübingen: Niemeyer, 1976). (XXIX.64)
See pp. 1–52.

100 Vesce, Thomas E., 'The Return of the *Chevalier du papegau*,' *RomN*, 17 (1976–77), 320–27. (XXX.146)

101 Keen, Maurice, 'Huizinga, Kilgour and the Decline of Chivalry,' *M&H*, 8 (1977), 1–20.

102 Adams, Alison, 'La conception de l'unité dans le roman médiéval en vers,' *SN*, 50 (1978), 101–12.

See Ha83 Cockcroft.

103 De Paepe, Norbert, 'Le *Fergus* et le *Ferguut*: remaniement d'une tradition courtoise,' in *Literature and Translation: New Perspectives in Literary Studies*, ed. James S. Holmes, José Lambert, and Raymond van den Broeck (Leuven: Acco, 1978), pp. 204–13.

See He32 Haug.

104 Kennedy, Elspeth, 'Royal Broodings and Lovers' Trances in the First Part of the Prose *Lancelot*,' in *Mélanges Wathelet-Willem*, pp. 301–14. (XXXI.190)

105 Pickford, Cedric E., 'La transformation littéraire d'*Erec* le fils *Lac*,' in *Mélanges Wathelet-Willem*, pp. 477–84. (XXXI.199)

106 Yamamoto, Jun'ichi, 'The Transformation of Romance – On *Meraugis de Portlesguez* by Raoul de Houdenc,' *Hum*, 24 (1978), 56–82. (XXXI.466)
In Japanese.

See Ea30 *Roman*.

107 Amazawa, Taijirô, 'Nerval, Perceval – *Aurélia* and the *Conte del Graal*,' *Cahiers*, 2 (1979), 170–73.
In Japanese.

108 Leupin, Alexandre, 'Les enfants de la Mimésis: différence et répétition dans la "Première Continuation du *Perceval*",' *VR*, 38 (1979), 110–26. (XXXIII.607)

109 Lods, Jeanne, '"Le baiser de la reine" et "Le cri de la fée": étude structurale du *Bel Inconnu* de Renaud de Beaujeu,' in *Mélanges Jonin*, pp. 413–26. (XXXII.356)

110 Rossi, Luciano, '*Trubert*: il trionfo della scortesia e dell'ignoranza: considerazioni sui *fabliaux* e sulla parodia medievale,' *Romanica vulgaria quaderni: studi francesi e portoghesi 79*, 1 (1979), 5–49.

111 Bozóky, Edina, 'Quêtes entrelacées et itinéraire rituel (regard sur la structure de la *Deuxième Continuation* du *Perceval*),' in *Mélanges Foulon*, vol. 1, pp. 49–57. (XXXIII.312 *ter*)

112 Braet, Herman, 'Un thème celtique dans le roman de *Gui de Warewik*,' *Mélanges Foulon*, vol. 2, pp. 19–25. (XXXIII.313)

See Ga23 Busby.

See Gd.a11 Connochie-Bourgne.

113 Cremonesi, Carla, 'Le lion reconnaissant: *Yvain* et *Le Roman de la Dame à la lycorne et du Biau Chevalier au lyon*,' in *Mélanges Foulon*, vol. 2, pp. 49–53; repr. in Dc11. (XXXIII.324)

114 Gumbrecht, Hans Ulrich, 'Literarische Gegenwelten, Karneval-struktur und die Epochenschwelle vom Spätmittelalter zur Renaissance,' in *Literatur in der Gesellschaft*, pp. 95–144.
See pp. 114–15 on Chrétien and 'unreliable narrator.'

See Ga24 Larmat.

115 Morse, Ruth, 'Historical Fiction in Fifteenth-Century Burgundy,' *MLR*, 75 (1980), 48–64.

116 Schmolke-Hasselmann, Beate, *Der arthurische Versroman von Chrestien bis Froissart: zur Geschichte einer Gattung*, Beihefte zur *ZrP*, 177 (Tübingen: Niemeyer, 1980). (XXXIII.64)
English trans. updated with Foreword by Keith Busby, *The Evolution of Arthurian Romance: The Verse Tradition from Chrétien to Froissart*, trans. Margaret and Roger Middleton, CSML, 35 (Cambridge: Cambridge University Press, 1998). (LI.400)

117 Serper, Arié, 'La demoiselle au char des deux côtés du Rhin,' in *Mélanges Foulon*, vol. 1, pp. 357–62. (XXXIII.374)
The episode at Belrepaire.

118 Stierle, Karlheinz, 'Die Verwilderung des Romans als Ursprung seiner Möglichkeit,' in *Literatur in der Gesellschaft*, pp. 253–313. (XXXIV.51)

119 Thorpe, Lewis, *The 'Lancelot' in the Arthurian Prose Vulgate*, The Wheaton College Monographs, 1 (Wheaton, IL: Department of English, Wheaton College; Cambridge: Heffers, 1980). (XXXIII.172, 458)

See He36 Vinaver.

120 Sweetser, Frank, 'La réincarnation de Lancelot dans le roman en prose,' *OetC*, 5:2 (1980–81), 135–39. (XXXIV.254)

See Ga25 Wolfgang.

121 Wolfgang, Lenora D., 'Prologues to the *Perceval* and Perceval's Father: The First Literary Critics of Chrétien Were the Grail Authors Themselves,' *OetC*, 5:2 (1980–81), 81–90. (XXXIV.259)

122 Bakelaar, Bette Lou, 'Interpolations rolandiennes dans les mises-en-prose de *Glices* [sic = *Cligés*] et *Blancandin et Orgueilleuse d'amour*,' in *VIII Congreso de la Société Rencesvals* (Pamplona: Institución Príncipe de Viana, 1981), pp. 37–42.

See Gd.c20 Delcourt-Angélique.

See La28 Hunt.

123 O'Sharkey, Eithne M., 'The Character of Lancelot in *La Queste del saint Graal*,' in *Essays Thorpe*, pp. 328–41. (XXXIV.355)

124 Pickford, C. E., 'The Good Name of Chrétien de Troyes,' in *Essays Thorpe*, pp. 389–401. (XXXIV.363)

125 Rigolot, François, 'La "conjointure" du *Pantagruel*: Rabelais et la tradition médiévale,' *Littérature*, 41 (1981), 93–103.

126 Schmolke-Hasselmann, Beate, 'Der französische höfische Roman,' in *Neues Handbuch der Literaturwissenschaft*, vol. 7: *Europäisches Hochmittelalter*, ed. Henning Krauss (Wiesbaden: Athenaion, 1981), pp. 283–322. (XXXV.67)

127 Schmolke-Hasselmann, Beate, 'Le roman de *Fergus*: technique narrative et intention politique,' in *Essays Thorpe*, pp. 342–53. (XXXIV.371)

See Ha109 Schmolke-Hasselmann.

128 Wolfzettel, Friedrich, 'Arthurian Adventure or Quixotic "Struggle for Life"? A Reading of Some Gauvain Romances in the First Half of the Thirteenth Century,' in *Essays Thorpe*, pp. 260–74. (XXXIV.391)

See Ha110 Zink.

129 Corley, Corin, 'Réflexions sur les deux premières Continuations de *Perceval*,' *Rom*, 103 (1982), 235–58. (XXXVI.335)

See He40 Lebsanft.

130 Lecouteux, Claude, 'Note sur Isabras (*Bataille Loquifer I*),' *Rom*, 103 (1982), 83–87. (XXXV.328)

131 Leupin, Alexandre, 'La faille et l'écriture dans les continuations du *Perceval*,' *MA*, 88 (1982), 237–69. (XXXV.249)
See pp. 256–69.

See Ha112 Meneghetti.

See Ga34 Ruh.

132 Wallen, Martha, 'Significant Variations in the Burgundian Prose Version of *Erec et Enide*,' *MAe*, 51 (1982), 187–96. (XXXV.418)

See Ub16 Wolfzettel.

133 Alvar, Carlos, 'El *Lancelot* en prosa: reflexiones sobre el éxito y la difusión de un tema literario,' in *Serta philologica F. Lázaro Carreter natalem diem sexagesimum celebranti dicata*, 2 vols (Madrid: Cátedra, 1983), vol. 2, pp. 1–12. (XXXVII.264)

See Ga35 Brewer.

134 Busby, Keith, 'Plagiarism and Poetry in the *Tournoiement Antéchrist* of Huon de Mery,' *NM*, 84 (1983), 505–21.

135 Busby, Keith, 'Der *Tristan Menestrel* des Gerbert de Montreuil und seine Stellung in der altfranzösischen Artustradition,' *VR*, 42 (1983), 144–56. (XXXVII.561)

136 Freeman, Michelle A., '*Fergus*: Parody and the Arthurian Tradition,' *FF*, 8 (1983), 197–215. (XXXVI.170)

137 Kelly, Douglas, '*Tout li sens du monde* dans *Claris et Laris*,' *RPh*, 36 (1983), 406–17. (XXXV.169)

138 Palermo, Joseph, 'The Arthurian Element in the Cycle of the *Sept Sages de Rome*,' *Society of the Seven Sages Newsletter*, 10 (1983), 9–16. (XXXVI.184)

139 Pastoureau, Michel, *Armorial des chevaliers de la Table Ronde* (Paris: Léopard d'Or, 1983). (XXXV.338)

140 Schmolke-Hasselmann, Beate, 'Der französische Artusroman in Versen nach Chrétien de Troyes,' *DVj*, 57 (1983), 415–30. (XXXVI.72)

141 Spilsbury, S. V., 'Traditional Material in the *Artus de Bretaigne*,' in *Studies Diverres*, pp. 183–93, 250–52. (XXXVI.467)

142 Atanassov, Stoyan, 'Gauvain: malheur du nom propre et bonheur du récit,' in *Le Récit amoureux*, Colloque de Cerisy, ed. Didier Coste and Michel Zéraffa, L'Or d'Atalante (Seyssel: Champ Vallon, 1984), pp. 11–21.

143 Busby, Keith, '"Li buens chevaliers" ou "uns buens chevaliers"? Perlesvaus et Gauvain dans le *Perlesvaus*,' *RevR*, 19 (1984), 85–97.

144 Busby, Keith, 'Fabliau et roman breton: le cas de Berengier au long cul,' *Cahiers d'Études Médiévales*, 2–3 (1984), 121–32.

145 Corley, Corin, 'Wauchier de Denain et la deuxième continuation de *Perceval*,' *Rom*, 105 (1984), 351–59. (XXXVIII.201)

See Nb29 Harf-Lancner.

146 Keller, Hans-Erich, 'The *Mise en prose* and the Court of Burgundy,' *FCS*, 10 (1984), 91–105.

147 Kelly, Douglas, 'L'invention dans les romans en prose,' in *Craft*, pp. 119–42. (XXXVII.407)
Conjointure and *disjointure* from Chrétien to prose romance.

See Fa124 Kelly.

148 Kennedy, Elspeth, 'Etudes sur le *Lancelot* en prose: I. Les allusions au *Conte Lancelot* et à d'autres contes dans le *Lancelot* en prose,' *Rom*, 105 (1984), 34–46. (XXXVIII.232).

149 Kennedy, Elspeth, 'Le rôle d'Yvain et de Gauvain dans le *Lancelot* non cyclique,' in *Lancelot Wégimont*, pp. 19–27. (XXXVIII.233)

150 Lacy, Norris J., 'The Form of the Prose *Erec*,' *NM*, 85 (1984), 169–77.

See Hb32 Ollier.

151 Owen, D. D. R., 'The Craft of Guillaume Le Clerc's *Fergus*,' in *Craft*, pp. 47–81. (XXXVII.437)
See also his 'The Craft of *Fergus*: Supplementary Notes,' *FSB*, 25 (1987–88), 1–5. (XL.130)

152 Owen, D. D. R., 'Chrétien, *Fergus*, *Aucassin et Nicolette* and the Comedy of Reversal,' in *Essays Topsfield*, pp. 186–94. (XXXVII.178)

153 Pickens, Rupert T., '"*Mais de çou ne parole pas Crestiens de Troies*": A Re-Examination of the Didot-*Perceval*,' *Rom*, 105 (1984), 492–510. (XXXIX.664)

See Hg60 Pioletti.

See Ha126 Roloff.

See Ga46 Santoni-Rozier.

154 Sasaki, Shigemi, 'Observations on Two Motifs in the Three *Continuations* of the *Conte du Graal*,' *TATE*, 14 (1984), 92–120. (XXXVII. 321).
In Japanese.

155 Schmolke-Hasselmann, Beate, 'Ausklang der altfranzösischen Artusepik: *Escanor* und *Meliador*,' in *Artusliteratur*, pp. 41–52. (XXXVII. 671)

156 Schmolke-Hasselmann, Beate, 'Der Ritter mit dem Herz aus Holz: zur Gestaltung des Bösen in den Lancelotromanen,' in *Artusrittertum*, pp. 177–84. (XXXVII.672)
On Meleagant.

157 Zambon, Francesco, *Robert de Boron e i segreti del Graal*, BArR, 189 (Florence: Olschki, 1984). (XXXVII.280)
See pp. 28–39: 'Robert de Boron e Chrétien de Troyes.'

See Ha127 *Romance*.

See La36 Busby.

See He52 Chandès.

158 Chênerie, Marie-Luce, 'Le thème du nom dans la carrière héroïque de Lancelot du Lac. Deuxième partie: la révélation du nom et du lignage,' *Littératures*, 12 (1985), 15–30.

See Hg63 Halász.

159 Hanning, Robert W., 'Arthurian Evangelists: The Language of Truth in Thirteenth-Century Prose Romances,' *PQ*, 64 (1985), 347–65. (XXXVIII.501)

See Na.c84 Markale.

160 Sasaki, Shigemi, 'Le Mystère de la lance et la chapelle à la main noire dans les trois *Continuations de Perceval*,' *Actes Rennes*, vol. 2, pp. 536–57. (XXXVIII.263)

161 Wolfzettel, Friedrich, 'Idéologie chevaleresque et conception féodale dans *Durmart le Galois*: l'altération du schéma arthurien sous l'impact de la réalité politique du XIIIe siècle,' in *Actes Rennes*, vol. 2, pp. 668–86. (XXXVIII.277)

162 Zemel, Roel, 'Fergus en Schotland,' *Bzzletin*, 124 (March 1985), 51–57. (XXXVIII.710)

163 Peron, Gianfelice, 'Décor arthurien, idéal chevaleresque et esprit monastique dans le *Tournoiement de l'Antéchrist* de Huon de Méry,' in *Homenaje a Álvaro Galmés de Fuentes*, 3 vols (Oviedo: Universidad de Oviedo; Madrid: Editorial Gredos, 1985–87), vol. 3, pp. 535–49.

164 Burgwinkle, William, '"L'écriture totalizante" de Robert de Boron,' *Constructions* (1986), pp. 87–101. (XLII.279)

165 Busby, Keith, 'Courtly Literature and the Fabliaux: Some Instances of Parody,' *ZrP*, 102 (1986), 67–87.

See Ge42 Colliot.

166 Curtis, Renée L., 'Tristan *forsené*: The Episode of the Hero's Madness in the *Prose Tristan*,' in *Essays Pickford*, pp. 10–22. (XXXIX.55)
Adaptation from *Yvain*.

See Hg66 García Gual.

167 Gier, Albert, '*Cil dormi et cele veilla*: ein Reflex des literarischen Gesprächs in den Fabliaux,' *ZrP*, 102 (1986), 88–93. (XXXIX.481)

168 Grant, Marshal S., 'The Question of Integrity in the First Continuation of Chrétien de Troyes' *Conte du Graal*,' *Proceedings of the PMR Conference: Annual Publication of the Patristic, Medieval and Renaissance Conference*, 11 (1986), 101–25. (XLI.384)

169 Kennedy, Elspeth, *Lancelot and the Grail: A Study of the Prose 'Lancelot'* (Oxford: Clarendon Press, 1986). (XXXIX.66)
See the Index s. v. Chrétien de Troyes, p. 385.

170 Kennedy, Elspeth, 'Lancelot und Perceval: zwei junge unbekannte Helden,' *W-S*, 9 (1986), 228–41. (XXXIX.506)

171 Kennedy, Elspeth, 'The Re-writing and Re-reading of a Text: The Evolution of the *Prose Lancelot*,' in *Essays Pickford*, pp. 1–9. (XXXIX.67)

See Pb305 Knapp.

172 Lacy, Norris J., 'Chivalry in *Le chevalier à l'épée* and *La mule sans frein*,' *VR*, 45 (1986), 150–56. (XL.503)

173 Okada, Machio, 'On Robert de Boron's Trilogy,' *JG*, 182 (1986), 1–64.
In Japanese.

174 Roussel, Claude, 'L'art de la suite: Sagremor et l'intertexte,' *Annales*, 41 (1986), 27–42. (XXXIX.668)

See Pi21 Saly.

175 Saly, Antoinette, 'Perceval-Perlesvaus: la figure de Perceval dans le "Haut Livre du Graal",' *TLL*, 24:2 (1986), 7–18; repr. in Dc22. (XXXIX.671)

See Md37 Adams.

176 *Stafford, Greg, 'Yvain's Fountain: Centuries of Storytelling,' *Avalon*, 2:3 (1986–87), 20–22.

177 Baumgartner, Emmanuèle, 'Le lion et sa peau ou les aventures d'Yvain dans le *Lancelot* en prose,' *PRIS-MA*, 3 (1987), 93–102; repr. in Dc20. (XLI.45)

178 Bertolucci Pizzorusso, Valeria, 'Il motivo del "lieto e dolente" nella prosa del *Lancelot*,' *MedR*, 12 (1987), 329–36 (XL.236); repr. in her *Morfologie del testo medievale* (Bologna: Il Mulino, 1989), pp. 67–74. (XLII.114)

179 Chênerie, Marie-Luce, 'Un recueil arthurien des contes populaires au XIIIᵉ siècle? *Les Merveilles de Rigomer*,' in *Réception*, pp. 39–49. (XL.38)

180 Corley, Corin F. V., *The Second Continuation of the Old French 'Perceval': A Critical and Lexicographical Study*, MHRATD, 24 (London: Modern Humanities Research Association, 1987). (XL.106)

181 Gowans, Linda M., 'New Perspectives on the *Didot-Perceval*,' *AL*, 7 (1987), 1–22. (XL.114)

See Sc24 Martineau-Genieys.

182 Pastoureau, Michel, 'L'"enromancement" du nom: enquête sur la diffusion des noms de héros arthuriens à la fin du Moyen Age,' in *Normandie*, pp. 73–84; repr. as 'L'"enromancement" du nom: étude sur la diffusion des noms de héros arthuriens à la fin du Moyen Age,' in his *Couleurs, images, symboles: études d'histoire et d'anthropologie* (Paris: Léopard d'Or, [1989]), pp. 111–24. (XLII.69)

See Hf69 Ribard.

183 Vial, Guy, '*Le Conte du Graal': sens et unité: la Première Continuation: textes et contenue*, PRF, 178 (Geneva: Droz, 1987). (XL. 507)

184 Adams, Alison, 'The *Roman d'Yder*: The Individual and Society,' in *Legacy*, vol. 2, pp. 71–77. (XLII.159)

185 Adams, Alison, 'The Shape of Arthurian Verse Romance (to 1300),' in *Legacy*, vol. 1, pp. 141–65. (XLII.160)

186 Ainsworth, Peter F., 'The Art of Hesitation: Chrétien, Froissart and the Inheritance of Chivalry,' in *Legacy*, vol. 2, pp. 187–206. (XLII.161)

187 Baumgartner, Emmanuèle, 'Les techniques narratives dans le roman en prose,' in *Legacy*, vol. 1, pp. 167–90; repr. in Dc20. (XLII.163)

188 Blumenfeld-Kosinski, Renate, 'Arthurian Heroes and Convention: *Meraugis de Portlesguez* and *Durmart le Galois*,' in *Legacy*, vol. 2, pp. 79–92. (XLII.174)

See La41 Bruckner.

189 Burns, E. Jane, '*La voie de la voix*: The Aesthetics of Indirection in the Vulgate Cycle,' in *Legacy*, vol. 2, pp. 151–67. (XLII.180)

190 Busby, Keith, 'Diverging Traditions of Gauvain in Some of the Later Old French Verse Romances,' in *Legacy*, vol. 2, pp. 93–109 (XLII.184).
Addition to Ga23 Busby.

See Ga57 Busby.

191 Chase, Carol J., 'Double Bound: Secret Sharers in *Cligés* and the *Lancelot-Graal*,' in *Legacy*, vol. 2, pp. 169–85. (XLII.187)

192 Coolput, Colette-Anne van, 'La réaction de quelques romanciers postérieurs,' in *Legacy*, vol. 1, pp. 91–114. (XLII.189)

193 Coolput, Colette-Anne van, 'Références, adaptations et emprunts directs,' in *Legacy*, vol. 1, pp. 333–42. (XLII.190)

194 Gier, Albert, 'Chrétien de Troyes et les auteurs de fabliaux: la parodie du roman courtois,' in *Legacy*, vol. 2, pp. 207–14. (XLII.200)

195 Grigsby, John L., 'Heroes and their Destinies in the Continuations of Chrétien's *Perceval*,' in *Legacy*, vol. 2, pp. 41–53. (XLII.203)

196 Grigsby, John L., 'Remnants of Chrétien's Æsthetics in the Early *Perceval* Continuations and the Incipient Triumph of Writing,' *RPh*, 41 (1987–88), 379–93. (XLI.386)

197 Huchet, Jean-Charles, 'Le nom et l'image: de Chrétien de Troyes à Robert de Boron,' in *Legacy*, vol. 2, pp. 1–16; repr. in Dc27. (XLII.207)

See Fa141 Kelly.

198 Krueger, Roberta L., 'The Author's Voice: Narrators, Audiences, and the Problem of Interpretation,' in *Legacy*, vol. 2, pp. 115–40. (XLII.219)

See Ha141 Lacy.

199 Meneghetti, Maria Luisa, 'Signification et fonction réceptionnelle de l'*Élucidation* du *Perceval*,' in *Legacy*, vol. 2, pp. 55–69. (XLII.227)

200 Noble, Peter S., 'Chrétien de Troyes and Girard d'Amiens,' in *Legacy*, vol. 2, pp. 143–50. (XLII.229)

201 Pickens, Rupert T., 'Histoire et commentaire chez Chrétien de Troyes et Robert de Boron: Robert de Boron et le livre de Philippe de Flandre,' in *Legacy*, vol. 2, pp. 17–39. (XLII.233)

202 Taylor, Jane H. M., 'The Fourteenth Century: Context, Text and Intertext,' in *Legacy*, vol. 1, pp. 267–332. (XLII.241)

203 Uitti, Karl D., with Michelle A. Freeman, 'Christine de Pisan and Chrétien de Troyes: Poetic Fidelity and the City of Ladies,' in *Legacy*, vol. 2, pp. 229–53. (XLII.242)

204 Wolfzettel, Friedrich, 'Le *Roman d'Erec* en prose du XIIIᵉ siècle: un anti-*Erec et Enide*?' in *Legacy*, vol. 2, pp. 215–28. (XLII.244)

See Ha142 Zink.

205 Colliot, Régine, 'Ambiguïté de l'aventure dans *le Chevalier aux deux épées*: un monde étrange,' in *De l'étranger à l'étrange, ou la 'conjointure' de la merveille (en hommage à Marguerite Rossi et Paul Bancourt)*, Senefiance, 25 (Aix-en-Provence: CUER-MA, 1988), pp. 71–88. (XLI.52)
Relation to *Perceval*.

See Ga61 Lazard.

See Ba15 Short.

206 Ueda, Hiroshi, 'L'entrée en scène du héros dans le *Perlesvaus*,' *ELLF*, 52 (1988), 1–12.

207 Ueda, Hiroshi, 'King Arthur and the Grail in Two Grail Romances in Prose,' *JFLN*, 103 (1988), 165–177 and *RTr*, B (March 1990), pp. 45–56. (XLIII. 409)
In Japanese.

208 Zink, Michel, 'Vieillesse de Perceval: l'ombre du temps,' in *Hommage Zumthor*, pp. 285–94; repr. in Dc18.

209 Gallais, Pierre, *L'Imaginaire d'un romancier français de la fin du XIIᵉ siècle: description raisonnée, comparée et commentée de la 'Continuation-Gauvain' (première suite du 'Conte du Graal' de Chrétien de Troyes)*, Faux Titre, 33, 34, 36, 39, 4 vols (Amsterdam: Rodopi, 1988–89).

See Lb2 Hult.

See Pe29 Zemel.

210 Busby, Keith, '*Cristal et Clarie*: A Novel Romance?' in *Convention and Innovation in Literature*, ed. Theo D'haen, Rainer Grübel, and Helmut Lethen, UPGC, 24 (Amsterdam: Benjamins, 1989), pp. 77–103. (XLV.403)
See also Hermann Breuer, ed., *Cristal und Clarie, nach Friedrich Apfelstedt's Abschrift der einzigen Arsenal-Handschrift (3516) und Hugo von Feilitzen's Entlehnungsnachweisen*, Gesellschaft für romanische Literatur, 36 (Dresden: Gesellschaft für romanische Literatur-Niemeyer, 1915), pp. xlix–lix.

211 Busby, Keith, '"Je fout savoir bon lai breton": Marie de France contrefaite?' *MLR*, 84 (1989), 589–600. (XLII.656)

212 Calin, William, '*Amadas et Ydoine*: The Problematic World of an Idyllic Romance,' in *Essays Grigsby*, pp. 39–49.
Relation to *Cligés*.

213 Gravdal, Kathryn, *Vilain and Courtois: Transgressive Parody in French Literature of the Twelfth and Thirteenth Centuries*, Regents Studies in Medieval Culture (Lincoln: University of Nebraska Press, 1989). (XLII.304)
Includes *Fergus*.

See Gb94 Grigsby.

214 Kibler, William W., 'The Prologue to the Lyon Manuscript of the *Chanson de Roland*,' in *Essays Grigsby*, pp. 217–28.

215 Picherit, Jean-Louis, 'Le motif du tournoi dont le prix est la main d'une riche et noble héritière,' *RomQ*, 36 (1989), 141–52. (XLII.339)

216 Rieger, Dietmar, 'Le motif de la jalousie dans le roman arthurien: l'exemple du roman d'*Yder*,' *Rom*, 110 (1989), 364–82. (XLV.197)

See Jd38 Strubel.

217 Torrini-Roblin, Gloria, 'Oral or Written Model?: Description, Length, and Unity in the *First Continuation*,' in *Essays Grigsby*, pp. 145–61. (XLII.351)

See Gb96 Uitti.

See Pe37 Zemel.

218 Baumgartner, Emmanuèle, '*Del Graal cui l'an an servoit*: variations sur un pronom,' in *The Editor and the Text*, ed. Philip E. Bennett and Graham A. Runnalls (Edinburgh: Edinburgh University Press, 1990), pp. 137–44; repr. in Dc20. (XLIV.84)

See Ph8 Bendinelli Predelli.

See He62 Brownlee.

See Hg80 Dubost.

219 Fernández Vuelta, María del Mar, '*Meraugis de Portlesguez*: el *jeu-parti* y la ficción novelesca,' *AnFil*, 13 (1990), 51–68. (XLVI.245)

220 Lacy, Norris J., '*Perlesvaus* and the *Perceval* Palimpsest,' *PQ*, 69 (1990), 263–71. (XLIII.567)

221 Macdonald, Aileen Ann, *The Figure of Merlin in Thirteenth Century French Romance*, SML, 3 (Lewiston, NY: Mellen, 1990). (XLV.499)

See La42 Rockwell.

222 Unzeitig-Herzog, Monika, *Jungfrauen und Einsiedler: Studien zur Organisation der Aventiurewelt im 'Prosalancelot'*, Beiträge zur älteren Literaturgeschichte (Heidelberg: Winter, 1990).
See pp. 19–36.

223 Baumgartner, Emmanuèle, 'Retour des personnages et mise en prose de la fiction arthurienne au XIIIᵉ siècle,' *BBSIA*, 43 (1991), 297–314; repr. in Dc20. (XLIV.296)

224 Berthelot, Anne, *Figures et fonction de l'écrivain au XIIIᵉ siècle*, Publications de l'Institut d'Etudes Médiévales, Université de Montréal, 25 (Montreal: Institut d'Etudes Médiévales, Paris: Vrin, 1991).

See Ga69 Brugger-Hackett.

225 Busby, Keith, 'Chrétien de Troyes and Raoul de Houdenc: "Romancing the *conte*",' *FF*, 16 (1991), 133–48. (XLIV.299)

226 Busby, Keith, 'L'intertextualité du *Livre d'Artus*,' in *Arturus rex*, pp. 306–19. (XL, p. 318)

227 Chase, Carol J., 'Remaniement et le personnage de Gauvain dans le *Lancelot* en prose,' in *Arturus rex*, pp. 278–93. (XL, p. 321)

228 Cirlot, Victoria, 'La estética postclásica en los *romans* artúricos en verso del siglo XIII,' in *Studia de Riquer*, vol. 4, pp. 381–400. (XLVI.240)

229 Dover, Carol, 'The Split-Shield Motif in the Old French Prose *Lancelot*,' *AY*, 1 (1991), 43–61. (XLIV.302)

See Pg20 Gracia.

230 Halász, Katalin, 'Aventure arthurienne en dehors de Bretagne,' in *Arturus rex*, pp. 155–63. (XL, pp. 331–32)

See Xa11 Hindman.

See He65 Klüppelholz.

231 Morris, Rosemary, 'King Arthur and the Growth of French Nationalism,' in *France and the British Isles in the Middle Ages and Renaissance: Essays by Members of Girton College, Cambridge, in Memory of Ruth Morgan*, ed. Gillian Jondorf and D. N. Dumville (Woodbridge: Boydell, 1991), pp. 115–29. (XLIV.120)

232 Muratori, Emilia, 'A proposito di uno studio sulla *Terza Continuazione* del *Perceval* di Chrétien de Troyes,' *QBologna*, 8 (1991), 95–104. (XLV.339)

See Ba19 Walters.

233 Willard, Charity Cannon, 'The Misfortunes of *Cligès* at the Court of Burgundy,' in *Arturus rex*, pp. 397–403. (XL, p. 374)

See Ga74 Álvares.

234 Armstrong, Grace M., 'Rescuing the Lion: From *Le Chevalier au lion* to *La Queste del saint Graal*,' *MAe*, 61 (1992), 17–34. (XLV.241)

235 Bauschke, Ricarda, 'Auflösing des Artusromans und Defiktionalisierung im *Bel Inconnu*: Renauts de Beaujeu Auseinandersetzung mit Chrétien de Troyes,' *ZfSL*, 102 (1992), 42–63 (XLV.10); slightly expanded version in *Fiktionalität*, pp. 84–116. (XLVI.39)

236 Jefferson, Lisa, 'Don-don contraignant-don contraint: A Motif and its Deployment in the French Prose Lancelot,' *RF*, 104 (1992), 27–51. (XLV.44)

237 Lachet, Claude, *Sone de Nansay et le roman d'aventures en vers au XIIIe siècle*, NBMA, 19 (Paris: Champion, Geneva: Droz, 1992). (XLV.183)

238 Mazzoni Peruzzi, Simonetta, 'Tematica cortese ed elementi folclorici nel *Dit dou levrier* di Jean de Condé,' in *ICLS Salerno*, pp. 387–407. (XLV.337)

239 Peron, Gianfelice, 'Image et amour dans *Gelaran de Bretagne*,' in *Image*, pp. 243–55.

240 Susong, Gilles, 'A propos de deux récits arthuriens du XIVe siècle: *Erec*, *Perceforest*,' *MF*, 30 (1992), 19–25. (XLVI.776)

See Tb20 Zambon.

241 Séguy, Mireille, 'L'ordre du discours dans le désordre du monde: la recherche de la transparence dans la *Quatrième Continuation*,' *Rom*, 113 (1992–95), 175–93. (XLVIII.337)

242 Angeli, Giovanna, 'Entre mémoire et dialogue: les *Lais* de Marie de France,' in *Actes Zurich*, pp. 165–80. (XLVII.653)

See Fb83(B) Baudry.

243 Berthelot, Anne, 'La carrière avortée du "Chevalier qui jamais ne mentit",' in *Erec*, pp. 1–9. (XLVI.44)

244 Berthelot, Anne, 'Reconstitution d'un archétype littéraire: Merlin correcteur de Chrétien,' in *What Is Literature?*, pp. 181–96.
On the *Livre d'Artus*.

245 Bruckner, Matilda Tomaryn, 'The Poetics of Continuation in Medieval French Romance: From Chrétien's *Conte du Graal* to the *Perceval* Continuations,' *FF*, 18 (1993), 133–49. (XLVI.691)

See Qb61 Busby.

See Tb21 Doner.

246 Lacy, Norris J., 'Convention and Innovation in *Le Chevalier du papegau*,' in *Studies Keller*, pp. 237–46. (XLVI.742)

247 Lacy, Norris J., '*Les Merveilles de Rigomer* and the Esthetics of "Post-Chrétien" Romance,' *AY*, 3 (1993), 77–90. (XLVI.743)

248 Noble, Peter S., '*Partonopeu de Blois* and Chrétien de Troyes,' in *Studies Keller*, pp. 195–211.

249 Noble, Peter, 'Wace and Renaut de Beaujeu,' *FS*, 47 (1993), 1–5. (XLVI.469)

250 Pearcy, Roy J., 'Intertextuality and *La Damoiselle qui n'ot parler de foutre qu'i n'aust mal au cuer*,' *ZrP*, 109 (1993), 526–38.

251 Peron, Gianfelice, 'Il "simbolismo" degli animali nel *Tournoiement Antéchrist* di Huon de Méry,' in *Omaggio Folena*, vol. 1, pp. 247–62. (XLVI.570)

252 Simó, Meritxell, 'Literatura y sociedad en el siglo XIII: *Le Tournoi de Chauvency*,' in *Cantar*, pp. 493–503.

253 Sturm-Maddox, Sara, '*Tout est par senefiance*: Gerbert's *Perceval*,' *AY*, 2 (1993), 191–207. (XLVII.794)

254 Wild, Gerhard, *Erzählen als Weltverneinung: Transformation von Erzählstrukturen im Ritterroman des 13. Jahrhunderts*, FORA: Studien zu Literatur und Sprache, 1 (Essen: Die blaue Eule, 1993). (XLVI.119)

See Pe42 Zemel, pp. 188–91.

255 Baumgartner, Emmanuèle, 'From Lancelot to Galahad: The Status of Filiation,' in *The Lancelot-Grail Cycle: Text and Transformations*, ed. William W. Kibler (Austin: University of Texas Press, 1994), pp. 14–30. (XLIX.458)

256 Berthelot, Anne, 'Du chevalier "nice" au chevalier sauvage: Perlesvaus, variante sanglante de Perceval,' in *Recueil Fourquet*, pp. 15–23. (XLVIII.54)

257 Bouché, Thérèse, 'De Chrétien de Troyes à la *Mort le roi Artu*: le personnage d'Arthur ou la désagrégation progressive d'un mythe,' *op. cit.*, 3 (November 1994), 5–13.

258 Busby, Keith, '*Hunbaut* and the Art of Medieval French Romance,' in *Studies Kelly*, pp. 46–68. (XLVII.536)

259 Ferlampin-Acher, Christine, 'Epreuves, pièges et plaies dans *Artus de Bretagne*: le sourire du clerc et la violence du chevalier,' in *Violence*, pp. 201–17. (XLVII.267)

260 Gaucher, Elisabeth, *La Biographie chevaleresque: typologie d'un genre (XIIIe–XVe siècle)*, NBMA, 29 (Paris: Champion, 1994).
See pp. 137–48.

See Qb65 Grossel.

261 Klüppelholz, Heinz, 'Die Idealisierung und Ironisierung des Protagonisten in den altfranzösischen Gauvain-Romanen,' *GRM*, 44 (1994), 18–36. (XLVII.111)

262 Lacy, Norris J., 'Guinevere's Kidneys, or The Lancelot-Grail Cycle and the Rise of Realism,' *JRMMRA*, 15 (1994), 17–33. (XLIX.514)

263 Lacy, Norris J., 'Motivation and Method in the Burgundian *Erec*,' in *Studies Kelly*, pp. 271–80. (XLVII.569)

264 Maddox, Donald, 'Coutumes et "conjointure" dans le *Lancelot* en prose,' in *Studies Kelly*, pp. 293–309. (XLVII.575)

265 Morin, Lise, 'Etude du personnage de Gauvain dans six récits médiévaux,' *MA*, 100 (1994), 333–51. (XLVII.5)

266 Ribard, Jacques, '*Jehan et Blonde*: mythe ou réalité?' in *Studies Kelly*, pp. 481–86. (XLVII.588)
Relation to the *Charrette*.

267 Susong, Gilles, 'Les impressions arthuriennes françaises (1488–1591) et la grande rhétorique,' *MF*, 34 (1994), 189–96 + 9 plates. (XLVIII.730)
Includes *Perceval en prose* (1530).

268 Taylor, Jane H. M., 'The Parrot, the Knight and the Decline of Chivalry,' in *Studies Kelly*, pp. 529–44. (XLVII.597)

See Ba26 Trachsler.

269 Walters, Lori, 'The Formation of a Gauvain Cycle in Chantilly Manuscript 472,' *Neophil*, 78 (1994), 29–43. (XLVII.604)

See Pe47 Winkelman.

270 Zemel, Roel, 'The New and Old Perceval: Guillaume's *Fergus* and Chrétien's *Conte du Graal*,' *BBSIA*, 46 (1994), 324–42.

271 Baumgartner, Emmanuèle, 'Lancelot et la Joyeuse Garde,' in *Recueil Micha*, pp. 7–14. (XLVIII.52)

272 Berthelot, Anne, 'Bohort, Blanor, Blihoberis …: à quoi sert le lignage de Lancelot?' in *Recueil Micha*, pp. 15–26. (XLVIII.55)

273 Brandsma, Frank, 'Opening Up the Narrative: The Insertion of New Episodes in Arthurian Cycles,' *Queeste*, 2 (1995), 31–39. (XLVIII.612)
Includes discussion of insertions into *Perceval*.

274 Busby, Keith, 'The Intertextual Coordinates of *Floriant et Florete*,' *FF*, 20 (1995), 261–77.

275 Colliot, Régine, 'Lancelot-guerrier d'après le *Roman de Laurin*,' in *Recueil Micha*, pp. 101–9. (XLVIII.79)

276 Combarieu, Micheline de, '*Matiere, san* et *conjointure* dans deux versions du *Conte de la Charrette* (Chrétien de Troyes et *Lancelot* en prose),' in *Amour Troyes*, pp. 261–77. (XLIX.142)

277 Di Febo, Martina, 'Erec e Tristano, interazione e conflittualità di modelli nel *Bel Inconnu* di Renaut de Beaujeu,' *Carte romanze: Serie I,*

Università degli Studi di Milano, Faccoltà di Lettere e Filosofia: Quaderni di Acme, 23 (Bologna: Cisalpino, 1995), 63–88. (XLVIII.545)

See Ud11 Gaunt, pp. 103–21.

278 Grossel, M. G., 'Narcisse, Pirame, Tristan ... et Lancelot: images du *fin amant* dans la poésie lyrique de Thibaut de Champagne,' in *Recueil Micha*, pp. 177–86.

279 Kennedy, Elspeth, 'Chrétien de Troyes comme intertexte du *Lancelot en prose*,' in *Amour Troyes*, pp. 279–86. (XLIX.162)

See Gb129 Mikhaïlova.

See Ha192 Rockwell.

280 Suard, François, 'La réécriture du *Chevalier au lion* par Pierre Sala,' in *Amour Troyes*, pp. 329–41. (XLIX.193)

281 Thomas, Neil, 'The Old French *Durmart le Galois*: A Demystified Version of the Perceval Story?' *Parergon*, 13 (1995), 117–28.

282 Baumgartner, Emmanuèle, 'L'enfant du Lac,' in *Lancelot mythique*, pp. 33–49.

283 Bogdanow, Fanni, 'Robert de Boron's Vision of Arthurian History,' *AL*, 14 (1996), 19–52. (XLIX.234)

284 Bouchet, Florence, 'De la lecture à l'écriture: quelques modes de transfert dans le *Chevalier errant* de Thomas de Saluces,' *Bien dire*, 13 (1996), 217–35. (XLIX.132)
See pp. 218–20 on *Perceval*.

See La45(D) Bruckner.

See Pk71 Busby.

285 Combarieu, Micheline de, 'Un exemple de réécriture: le franchissement du pont de l'épée dans le *Chevalier de la Charrete* de Chrétien de Troyes et dans le *Lancelot en prose*,' *Bien dire*, 13 (1996), 113–31. (XLIX.141)

See Xa22 Doner.

286 Gally, Michèle, 'Sous le feu des regards ou la beauté captive,' in *Lancelot mythique*, pp. 51–64.

287 Kennedy, Elspeth, 'The Figure of Lancelot in the *Lancelot-Graal*,' in Ga91 *Lancelot*, pp. 79–104.

See Pb413 Knapp.

See La45(C) Lacy.

288 MacCornack, Katharine G., *Mental Representation Theory in Old French Allegory from the Twelfth and Thirteenth Centuries*, SFL, 26 (Lewiston, NY: Mellen, 1996).

See La45(B) Maddox.

See Sa144 Reil.

289 *Le Roman chevaleresque tardif*, ed. Jean-Philippe Beaulieu, Études Françaises, 32:1 (Montreal: Les Presses de l'Université de Montréal, 1996).
> A. Jean-Philippe Beaulieu, 'Présentation: le roman chevaleresque tardif: permanence, contamination, dissolution,' pp. 3–5.
> B. Michel Stanesco, 'Les lieux de l'aventure dans le roman français du Moyen Age flamboyant,' pp. 21–34. See also Qe22.
> C. Pierre Servet, 'Les romans chevaleresques de la fin du Moyen Age et de la Renaissance: éléments de bibliographie,' pp. 109–13.

290 Séguy, Mireille, 'D'armes et d'amour, à corps perdu,' in *Lancelot mythique*, pp. 7–32.

291 Servet, Pierre, ed., *Pierre Sala: Le Chevalier au lion* (Paris: Champion, 1996). (XLIX.118)
See 'Le manuscript B. N. f. fr. 1638 et les manuscrits du *Chevalier au lion* de Chrétien de Troyes' (pp. 21–24), and 'Etude littéraire' (pp. 24–75).

292 Simons, Penny, 'The Squire, the Dwarf and the Damsel in Distress: Minor Characters in *Le Bel Inconnu*?' *FMLS*, 32 (1996), 27–36. (XLIX.264)

293 Stephens, Louise D., 'Gerbert and Manessier: The Case for a Connection,' *AL*, 14 (1996), 53–68. (XLIX.268)

294 Thomas, Neil, 'The Secularisation of Myth: *Les Merveilles de Rigomer* as a *contrafactura* of the French Grail Romances,' in *Myth and its Legacy in European Literature*, ed. Neil Thomas and Françoise Le Saux, Durham Modern Language Series, GM 6 (Durham: University of Durham, 1996), pp. 159–69. (LI.405)

295 Brault, Gerard J., 'The Names of the Three Isolts in the Early Tristan Poems,' *Rom*, 115 (1997), 22–49. (L.183)
See pp. 26–28.

296 Colombo Timelli, Maria, 'Entre *histoire* et *compte*: de l'*Erec* de Chrétien de Troyes à la prose du XVe siècle,' in *'A l'heure encore de mon escrire': aspects de la littérature de Bourgogne sous Philippe le Bon et Charles le Téméraire*, ed. Claude Thiry (Louvain-la-Neuve: Les Lettres Romanes, 1997), pp. 23–30. (LI.4)

297 Denda, Kuniko, 'Desire of Possession in the Marriage of Humans and Non-Humans – The Case of the Anonymous Lays of the Twelfth and Thirteenth Centuries,' *ELLF*, 71 (1997), 3–13. (LI.648)
In Japanese.

298 Ménard, Philippe, 'La réception des romans de chevalerie à la fin du Moyen Age et au XVIe siècle,' *BBSIA*, 49 (1997), 234–73.

299 *L'Œuvre de Chrétien de Troyes dans la littérature française: réminiscences, résurgences et réécritures*, Actes du Colloque (23 et 24 mai 1997), ed. Claude Lachet, CEIDC, 13 (Lyon: APRIME, 1997).
- A. Jean Dufournet, 'Introduction,' pp. 9–17. (L.193)
- B. Corinne Pierreville, 'Réminiscences de Chrétien de Troyes dans le *Chevalier à l'épée*,' pp. 19–32. (L.223)
- C. Jean Subrenat, 'Lecture du *Lai de l'ombre* à la lumière de Chrétien de Troyes,' pp. 33–44. (L.232)
- D. Michel Rousse, 'De Chrétien de Troyes à Philippe de Rémy: la joie d'amour,' pp. 45–57. (L.228)
- E. Marie-Luce Chênerie, 'Sagremor, encore …,' pp. 59–72. (L.187)
- F. Claude Lachet, 'A la griffe on reconnaît le lion: quelques échos du *Chevalier au lion* dans les romans en vers des XIIIe et XIVe siècles,' pp. 73–86. (L.206)
- G. Monique Léonard, 'Du *roman* au *dit*: *Le Chevalier au lion* et *le Tournoi de l'Antéchrist*,' pp. 87–97. (L.211)
- H. Marcel Faure, 'A propos des voix dans *Le Haut Livre du Graal*,' pp. 99–105. (L.194)
- I. Marc Le Person, 'Les métamorphoses du cimetière: de la tombe prophétique au terrain d'aventure (comparaison entre *Le Chevalier de la charrette* et *le Lancelot propre*),' pp. 107–25. (L.210)
- J. Jean-René Valette, 'Ecriture et réécriture de la merveille dans le *Conte de la charrette* (de Chrétien de Troyes au *Lancelot en prose*),' pp. 127–48. (L.234)
- K. Danielle Quéruel, 'D'un manuscrit à l'autre: variations autour du personnage de Gauvain dans le roman de *Tristan en prose*,' pp. 149–68. (L.226)
- L. Marylène Possamaï-Pérez, 'Chrétien de Troyes au début du XIVe siècle: *Philomena* "moralisé",' pp. 169–85. (L.225)

M. Roger Dubuis, '*Saintré* ou les illusions perdues de Lancelot,' pp. 187–96. (L.192)

N. Pierre Servet, 'D'un Perceval l'autre: la mise en prose du *Conte du Graal* (1530),' pp. 197–210. (L.229)

O. Philippe Ménard, 'Conclusions,' pp. 247–50. (L.214)

See also Pk75 Baudry, Pk77 Debreuille, and Pk78 Lavorel.

300 Owen, D. D. R., 'Calogrenant and the Dreamer: the Inspiration for the *Roman de la rose*,' *FMLS*, 33 (1997), 328–40. (L.275)

301 Taylor, Jane H. M., 'Perceval/Perceforest: Naming as Hermeneutic in the *Roman de Perceforest*,' *RomQ*, 44 (1997), 201–14. (L.568)

302 Thomas, Neil, 'Gauvain's Guilt in *L'Âtre périlleux*: The Subtext of Sexual Abuse,' *RMS*, 23 (1997), 107–19. (L.282)

See Cb27 Trachsler.

See Db67 Zambon.

See Qd21 Accarie.

See Pk79 Baudry, pp. 23–25.

303 Bromiley, Richard [*sic* Geoffrey], 'Stylistic Aspects of Proper Names in Some Late French Arthurian Verse Romances,' in *RMS*, 24 (1998), 3–24. (LI.350)

304 Busby, Keith, '"Estrangement se merveille": l'autre dans les *Continuations* de *Perceval*,' in *Mélanges Ménard*, vol. 1, pp. 279–97. (LI.223)

305 Col[o]mbo Timelli, Maria, 'De l'*Erec* de Chrétien de Troyes à la prose du XVe siècle: le traitement des proverbes,' *MF*, 42 (1998), 87–113.

306 Colombo Timelli, Maria, 'Syntaxe et technique narrative: titres et attaques de chapitre dans l'*Erec* bourguignon,' *FCS*, 24 (1998), 208–30.

307 Karczewska, Kathryn, *Prophecy and the Quest for the Holy Grail: Critiquing Knowledge in the Vulgate Cycle*, Studies in the Humanities: Literature–Politics–Society, 37 (New York: P. Lang, 1998).

308 Lacy, Norris J., 'Adaptation as Reception: The Burgundian *Cligès*,' *FCS*, 24 (1998), 198–207. (LI.778, LII.789)

309 Legros, Huguette, 'La "*Folie Tristan*" dans le *Tristan en prose*: aboutissement de traditions antérieures et réécriture,' in *Mélanges Ménard*, vol. 2, pp. 869–78. (LI.269)

See Ga97 Luttrell.

310 Sargent-Baur, Barbara N., 'Echos de Chrétien de Troyes dans les romans de Philippe de Remi,' in *Mélanges Ménard*, vol. 2, pp. 1193–1201. (LI.300)

311 Taylor, Jane H. M., 'The Significance of the Insignificant: Reading Reception in the Burgundian *Erec* and *Cligès*,' *FCS*, 24 (1998), 183–97. (LI.817)

312 Wolfzettel, Friedrich, 'L'autre dans le *Lancelot do Lac*,' in Pb437 *Chevaliers errants*, pp. 327–38. (LI.124)

313 Armstrong, Grace M., 'Questions of Inheritance: *Le Chevalier au lion* and *La Queste del saint Graal*,' *YFS*, 95 (1999), 171–92. (LII.729)

314 Bruckner, Matilda Tomaryn, 'Knightly Violence and Grail Quest Endings: Conflicting Views from the Vulgate Cycle to the *Perceval* Continuations,' *M&H*, 26 (1999), 17–32. (LII.376)

315 Burch, Sally L., 'The Lady, the Lords and the Priests: The Making and Unmaking of Marriage in *Amadas et Ydoine*,' *RMS*, 25 (1999), 17–31.

316 Colombo Timelli, Maria, 'Expressions de temps et progression de l'histoire dans l'*Histoire d'Erec*, roman en prose du XVème siècle,' in *Temps et histoire dans le roman arthurien* (Toulouse: Editions Universitaires du Sud, Paris: Champion, 1999), pp. 75–82.

317 Krause, Virginia, 'The End of Chivalric Romance: Barthélemy Aneau's *Alector* (1560),' *Renaissance and Reformation/Renaissance et Réforme*, 23:2 (1999), 45–60.

See Gb154 Krueger.

See Ga102 Markale.

318 Okada, Machio, ' "Avalon": The Transfer of the Grail to the West and the Succession of its Gardien – On a Passage in the *Roman de l'Estoire dou Graal* by Robert de Boron,' *Plume*, 3 (1999), 42–47. (LII.642)
In Japanese.

See Ha205 *Erzählstrukturen*.

319 Wolf-Bonvin, Romaine, 'Amadas, Ydoine et les *Faes* de la dort-veille,' in *Magie*, pp. 601–16.

320 Bruckner, Matilda Tomaryn, 'Looping the Loop through a Tale of Beginnings, Middles and Ends: from Chrétien to Gerbert in the *Perceval* Continuations,' in *Essays Lacy*, pp. 33–51.

321 Colombo Timelli, Maria, 'L'*Histoire d'Erec* en prose du manuscript Paris, B. N., fr. 363 (ff. 193r°b–222r°b): quelques remarques,' in *Essays Lacy*, pp. 149–61.

322 Kelly, Douglas, 'The Name Topos in the *Chevalier aux deux épées*,' in *Essays Lacy*, pp. 257–68.

323 Kibler, William W., 'Sagremor dans le *Méliador* de Froissart,' in *Mélanges Subrenat*, 307–11.

See Ga106 Kibler.

See Ha209(K) Lacy.

324 Lacy, Norris J., 'Perceval's Sister in the Prose *Yvain*,' in *Mélanges Faucon*, pp. 255–63.

325 Maddox, Donald, 'Épreuves et ambiguïté dans *Le Bel Inconnu*,' in *Conjointure*, pp. 67–82.

See Jb57 Pipaprez.

326 Rockwell, Paul Vincent, '*Appellation contrôlée*: Motif Transfer and the Adaptation of Names in the *Chevalier as deus espees*,' in *Essays Lacy*, pp. 435–52.

See Nb52 Saly.

327 Sturm-Maddox, Sara, 'Arthurian Evasions: The End(s) of Fiction in *Floriant et Florete*,' in *Essays Lacy*, pp. 475–89.

328 Sturm-Maddox, Sara, 'The Arthurian Romance in Sicily: *Floriant et Florete*,' in *Conjointure*, pp. 95–107.

See Ha213 Trachsler.

329 Walters, Lori, 'Parody and the Parrot: Lancelot References in the *Chevalier du papegau*,' in *Essays Uitti*, pp. 331–44.

330 Walters, Lori J., 'Resurrecting Gauvain in *L'Atre périlleux* and the Middle Dutch *Walewein*,' in *Essays Lacy*, pp. 509–37.

331 Watanabe, Kôji, 'Gauvain or the Image of the "Eternal Celibate" in *La Mule sans frein*,' *Bulletin d'Etudes de Langue et Littérature Françaises* (Société de Langue et Littérature Françaises du KANTO), 9 (2000), 1–10.

See Ga108(A) Berthelot.

332 Carapezza, Francesco, 'Le fragment de Turin du *Rigomer*: nouvelles perspectives,' *Rom*, 119 (2001), 76–112.
See pp. 106–10.

333 Combes, Annie, *Les Voies de l'aventure: réécriture et composition romanesque dans le 'Lancelot' en prose*, NBMA, 59 (Paris: Champion, 2001).

See Ha214 Combes and Bertin.

See Kd135 Crespo.

334 Mora, Francine, 'Remploi et sens du jeu dans quelques textes medio-latins et français des XIIᵉ et XIIIᵉ siècles: Baudri de Bourgueil, Hue de Rotelande, Renaut de Beaujeu,' in *Auctor*, pp. 219–30.
See pp. 227–30 on the *Bel Inconnu*.

335 Séguy, Mireille, *'Les romans du Graal' ou le signe imaginé*, NBMA, 58 (Paris: Champion, 2001).

b: German Literature

18 Fourquet, Jean, 'Les Noms propres […]' Repr. in Dc8.

23 Fourquet, Jean, 'La Structure […]' Repr. in Dc8.

24 Hatto, Arthur T., 'Y a-t-il un Roman […]' Repr. in Dc9.

28 Schröder, Walter Johannes, 'Horizontale […]' Repr. in Dc 7.

44 Fourquet, Jean, 'La Composition […]' Repr. in Dc8.

53 Bertau, Karl, 'Versuch […]'; repr. in his *Wolfram von Eschenbach: Neun Versuche über Subjektivität und Ursprünglichkeit in der Geschichte* (Munich: Beck, 1983), pp. 24–58. (XXXVI.17)

59 Kuhn, Hugo, *Tristan* […]; repr. in his *Liebe und Gesellschaft*, ed. Wolfgang Walliczek (Stuttgart: Metzler, 1980), pp. 12–35. (XXXIII.45)

63 Salmon, Paul, '"âne zuht" […]' (XXVII.305)

64 Peters, Ursula, 'Artusroman […]' (XXVIII.61)

65 Shaw, Frank, 'Die Ginoverentführung […]' (XXVIII.74)

See Pa38 Rochat.

66 Holland, Wilhelm Ludwig, 'Zu Hartmanns Iwein,' *Germania*, 2 (1857), 163.

67 Rochat, Alfred, 'Wolfram von Eschenbach und Chrestiens de Troyes,' *Germania*, 3 (1858), 81–120.

68 Rochat, Alfred, 'Der deutsche Parzival, der Conte del Graal und Chrestiens Fortsetzer,' *Germania*, 4 (1859), 414–20.

69 Rauch, Christian, *Die wälische, französische und deutsche Bearbeitung der Iweinsage*, diss. Göttingen (Berlin: Schade, 1869).

70 Güth, Dr., 'Das Verhältnisz des Hartmann'schen Iwein zu seiner altfranzösischen Quelle,' *AStnSpr*, 46 (1870), 251–92.

71 Settegast, Franz, *Hartmanns 'Iwein' verglichen mit seiner altfranzösischen Quelle*, diss. Marburg (Marburg: Pfeil, 1873).

72 Gärtner, Gustaf, *Der 'Iwein' Hartmanns von Aue und der 'Chevalier au lyon' des Crestien von Troies*, diss. Breslau (Breslau: Graß, Barth, 1875).

See Wb20 Toischer.

73 Blume, Ludwig, *Über den Iwein des Hartmann von Aue* (Vienna: Hölder, 1879).

74 Martin, Ernst, *Zur Gralsage*, Quellen und Forschungen zur Sprach- und Culturgeschichte der germanischen Völker, 42 (Strassburg: Trübner, 1880).

75 Hertz, Wilhelm, *Die Sage von Parzival und dem Gral* (Breslau: Schottlaender, 1882).

76 Muret, Ernest, 'Eilhart d'Oberg et sa source française,' *Rom*, 16 (1887), 288–363.
See pp. 356–63.

77 Roetekken, Hubert, *Die Behandlung der einzelnen Stoffelemente in den Epen Veldekes und Hartmanns* (Halle/S.: Karras, 1887).

78 Bachmann, Albert, 'Bruchstücke eines mhd. Cliges,' *ZfdA*, 32 (n. s. 20) (1888), 123–28.

79 *Dreyer, Karl, *Hartmanns von Aue Erec und seine altfranzösische Quelle* (Königsberg: Hartung, 1893).

80 Heinzel, Richard, *Ueber Wolframs von Eschenbach Parzival*, Sitzungsberichte der philosophisch-historischen Classe der kaiserlichen Akademie der Wissenschaften [Wien], 130:1 (Vienna: Tempsky, 1894).

81 Hagen, Paul, 'Zum Erec,' *ZdP*, 27 (1895), 463–74.

82 Gaster, Bernhard, *Vergleich des Hartmannschen Iwein mit dem Löwenritter Crestiens*, diss. Greifswald (Greifswald: Kunike, 1896).

83 Rosenhagen, G., 'Die Episode vom Raube der Königin in Hartmanns Iwein,' *Philologische Studien: Festgabe Eduard Sievers* (Halle/S: Niemeyer, 1896), pp. 231–36.

84 Wechssler, Eduard, 'Zur Beantwortung der Frage nach den Quellen von Wolframs Parzival,' *Philologische Studien: Festgabe für Eduard Sievers zum 1. Oktober 1896* (Halle/S: Niemeyer, 1896), pp. 237–51.

85 Lichtenstein, Julius, 'Zur Parzivalfrage,' *PBB*, 22 (1897), 1–93.

86 Reck, Oskar, *Das Verhältnis des Hartmannschen Erec zu seiner französischen Vorlage*, diss. Greifswald (Greifswald: Abel, 1898).

See Na.c39 Wechssler.

87 Gruhn, Albert, 'Erek und Lanzelet,' *ZfdA*, 43 (1899), 265–302.
See also Pb89 Jellinek and Zwierzina.

88 *Jahncke, Ernst, *Studien zum Wilhelm von Wenden Ulrichs von Eschenbach*, diss. Göttingen (Goslar: [n.p.], 1903).

89 Jellinek, M. H., and K. Zwierzina, 'Erek und Lanzelet,' *ZfdA*, 47 (1904), 267–71.

90 Ehrismann, Gustav, 'Wolframprobleme,' *GRM*, 1 (1909), 657–74.

91 *Reimer, P. Jakob, *Die Abhängigkeitsverhältnisse der Überlieferung des 'Erec'*, Programm des Gymnasiums in Seitenstetten (Linz: [n.p.], 1909).

See Ga8 Strucks.

92 Sparnaay, H., 'Über die Laudinefrage,' *Neophil*, 3 (1918), 122–29.

93 Sparnaay, H., 'Laudine bei Crestien und bei Hartmann,' *Neophil*, 4 (1919), 310–19.

94 Heller, Edmund Kurt, 'Studies on the Story of Gawain in Crestien and Wolfram,' *JEGP*, 24 (1925), 463–503.

95 Heller, Edmund K., 'Wolfram's Relationship to the Chrestien MSS,' *MLN*, 41 (1926), 520–23.

96 Schröder, Franz Rolf, *Die Parzivalfrage* (Munich: Beck, 1928). See pp. 70–80.

97 Walker, Emil, *Der Monolog im höfischen Epos: stil- und literaturgeschichtliche Untersuchungen*, TgA, 5 (Stuttgart: Kohlhammer, 1928).

98 Drube, Herbert, *Hartmann und Chrétien*, FdSD, 2 (Münster: Aschendorff, 1931).

99 Lichtenberg, Heinrich, *Die Architekturdarstellungen in der mittelhochdeutschen Dichtung*, FdSD, 4 (Münster: Aschendorff, 1931).

100 Paetzel, Martin, *Wolfram von Eschenbach und Crestien von Troyes: 'Parzival, Buch 7–13 und seine Quelle'*, diss. Berlin (Berlin: Funk, 1931).

101 Richey, Margaret F., 'Ither von Gaheviez,' *MLR*, 26 (1931), 315–29.

102 Wilmotte, M., 'Wolfram, imitateur de Chrétien de Troyes,' *BulLSMP*, ser. 5, 1 (1932), 433–55.

103 Rachbauer, Mary Aloysia, *Wolfram von Eschenbach: A Study of the Relation of the Content of Books III–VI and IX of the 'Parzival' to to* [sic] *the Chrestien Manuscripts* (Washington, DC: The Catholic University of America, 1934).

104 Kohler, Erika, *Liebeskrieg: zur Bildersprache der höfischen Dichtung des Mittelalters*, TgA, 21 (Stuttgart: Kohlhammer, 1935).

105 Scheunemann, Dr., 'Hartmann von Aue und Chrétien de Troyes,' *Jahres-Bericht der schlesischen Gesellschaft für vaterländische Kultur*, 108 (1935), 156–57.

See Gb27 Woelker.

106 Adolf, Helen, 'New Light on Oriental Sources for Wolfram's *Parzival* and Other Grail Romances,' *PMLA*, 62 (1947), 306–24.

107 Hatto, A. T., 'Two Notes on Chrétien and Wolfram,' *MLR*, 42 (1947), 243–46; 44 (1949), 380–85; repr. in Dc9. (I.164, II.208)

108 Schneider, Hermann, *Parzival-Studien*, Sitzungsberichte der Bayerischen Akademie der Wissenschaften: Philosophisch-historische Klasse, Jahrgang 1944–46, 4 (Munich: Bayerische Akademie der Wissenschaften, 1947).

109 Kuhn, Hugo, 'Erec,' in *Festschrift Paul Kluckhohn und Hermann Schneider gewidmet zu ihrem 60. Geburtstag* (Tübingen: Mohr, 1948), pp. 122–47; repr. in his *Dichtung und Welt im Mittelalter* (Stuttgart: Metzler, 1959), pp.133-50.

110 Walshe, M. O'C., 'Some *Parzival* Problems,' *MLR*, 43 (1948), 514–19. (I.189)
On Kyot.

111 Hatto, A. T., 'On Wolfram's Conception of the "grael",' *MLR*, 43 (1948), 216–22; repr. in Dc9. (I.165)

112 Scholte, J. H., 'Kyot von Katelangen,' *Neophil*, 33 (1949), 23–36.

113 Springer, Otto, 'The "Âne stegreif" Motif in Medieval Literature,' *GR*, 25 (1950), 163–77. (III.70)

114 Frank, Istvan, 'Le manuscrit de Guiot entre Chrétien de Troyes et Wolfram von Eschenbach,' *Annales Universitatis Saraviensis: Philosophie-Lettres*, 1 (1952), 169–83. (V.205)

115 Schröder, Walter Johannes, 'Der dichterische Plan des Parzivalromans,' *PBB*, 74 (1952), 160–92, 409–53; repr. in Dc7.

116 Mohr, Wolfgang, 'Parzival und die Ritter: von einfacher Form und Ritterepos,' *Fabula*, 1 (1958), 201–13.

See Pd18 Renoir.

117 Ruh, Kurt, 'Lancelot,' *DVj*, 33 (1959), 269–82. (XII.28)

118 Schröder, Franz Rolf, 'Parzivals Schuld,' *GRM*, 9 (1959), 1–20. (XII.31)

119 Schröder, Walter, 'Kyot,' *GRM*, 9 (1959), 329–50; repr. in Dc7. (XII.33)

120 Salmon, Paul, 'Ignorance and Awareness of Identity in Hartmann and Wolfram: An Element of Dramatic Irony,' *PBB*, 82 (1960), 95–115. (XIII.18)

See Wa17 Kolb.

See Pj1 Szövérffy.

121 Wapnewski, Peter, *Hartmann von Aue*, Sammlung Metzler, M 17 (Stuttgart: Metzler, 1962). (XV.26, XXV.50, XXXII.78)
Numerous re-editions.

122 Bindschedler, Maria, 'Guot und Güete bei Hartmann von Aue,' in *Die Wissenschaft von der deutschen Sprache und Dichtung: Methoden–Probleme–Aufgaben. Festschrift für Friedrich Maurer zum 65. Geburtstag* (Stuttgart: Klett, 1963), pp. 352–65. (XVI.15)

123 Kolb, Herbert, *Munsalvaesche: Studien zum Kyotproblem* (Munich: Eidos, 1963). (XVI.30)

124 Stockum, Th. C. van, *Hartmann von Ouwes 'Iwein': sein Problem und seine Probleme*, Mededelingen der Koninklijke Nederlandse Akademie van Wetenschappen, Afd. Letterkunde, n.s. 26:3 (Amsterdam: Noord-Hollandsche Uitgever, 1963). (XVI.220)

See Fa66 Brinkmann.

125 Bumke, Joachim, *Wolfram von Eschenbach*, Sammlung Metzler, 36 (Stuttgart: Metzler, 1964; rev. ed. 1991). (XXXIV.10, XLIV.422)

126 Kôzu, Haruhisa, '*Iwein*, A Courtly Romance by Hartmann von Aue,' *Hum*, 10 (1964), 56–79.
In Japanese.

127 Fourquet, Jean, 'La composition des Livres III à VI du *Parzival*,' in *Mediaeval German Studies Presented to Frederick Norman by his Students, Colleagues and Friends on the Occasion of his Retirement* (London: Institute for Germanic Studies, 1965), pp. 138–56; repr. in Dc8. (XX.146)

128 Mohr, Wolfgang, 'Landgraf Kingrimursel: zum VIII. Buch von Wolframs *Parzival*,' in *Festschrift Henzen*, pp. 21–38.

129 Ruh, Kurt, 'Zur Interpretation von Hartmanns *Iwein*,' in *Festschrift Henzen*, pp. 39–51. (XVIII.271)

130 Schröder, Walter Johannes, 'Die Parzivalgestalt Wolframs von Eschenbach,' in *Der Menschenbild in der Dichtung*, ed. Albert Schaefer (Munich: Beck, 1965), pp. 83–102; repr. in Dc7. (XIX.32)

131 Blamires, David, *Characterization and Individuality in Wolfram's 'Parzival'* (Cambridge: Cambridge University Press, 1966). (XIX.218)

132 Kakurai, Shukushi, 'The Question of Sources for Wolfram's Parzival: Arthurian Romance, Chrétien, Kyot …,' *RBN*, 11 (1967), 78–90.
In Japanese.

133 Kôzu, Haruhisa, 'On Wolfram's Creative Shaping of Traditional Matter in *Parzival* – A Comparison with Chrétien's *li contes del graal*,' *Hum*, 13 (1967), 35–56.
In Japanese.

134 Stavenhagen, Lee, 'A Legendary Backdrop for Gahmuret,' *Rice University Studies*, 53:4 (1967), 43–56. (XX.71)

135 Ruh, Kurt, *Höfische Epik des deutschen Mittelalters: Erster Teil: Von den Anfängen bis zu Hartmann von Aue. Zweiter Teil: 'Reinhart Fuchs', 'Lanzelet', Wolfram von Eschenbach, Gottfried von Straßburg*, Grundlagen der Germanistik, 7, 25 (Berlin: Schmidt, 1967–80). (XXX.64)

136 Groos, Arthur B., Jr., '"Sigune auf der Linde" and the Turtledove in *Parzival*,' *JEGP*, 67 (1968), 631–46. (XXIII.39)

137 Leckie, R. William, Jr., 'Psychological Allegory in Middle High German Translations of Old French Romances,' *Colloquia Germanica*, 2 (1968), 258–71.

138 Linke, Hansjürgen, *Epische Strukturen in der Dichtung Hartmanns von Aue: Untersuchungen zur Formkritik, Werkstruktur und Vortragsgliederung* (Munich: Fink, 1968). (XXI.33)

139 Wolff, Ludwig, 'Hartmann von Aue: vom Büchlein und Erec bis Iwein,' *Deutschunterricht*, 20:2 (1968), 43–59. (XXI.49)

140 Zatočil, Leopold, 'Prager Bruchstück einer bisher unbekannten mittelfränkischen Übertragung der mittelniederländischen Versarbeitung von Chrétiens de Troyes Percevalroman (Le Contes del Graal),' in his *Germanistische Studien und Texte I: Beiträge zur deutschen und niederländischen Philologie des Spätmittelalters*, Opera Universitatis Purkynianae Brunensis: Facultas Philosophica – Spisy University J. E.

Purkyně v Brně: Filosofická Fakulta, 131 (Brno: Universita J. E. Purkyně, 1968), pp. 247–81.

See Pe7 Draak.

141 Vizkelety, András, 'Neue Fragmente des mhd. Cligès-Epos aus Kalocsa (Ungarn),' *ZdP*, 88 (1969), 409–32. (XXII.24)

142 Carne, Eva-Maria, *Die Frauengestalten bei Hartmann von Aue: ihre Bedeutung im Aufbau und Gehalt der Epen*, Marburger Beiträge zur Germanistik, 31 (Marburg: Elwert, 1970). (XXIV.8)
See final chapter.

143 Eroms, Hans-Werner, *'Vreude' bei Hartmann von Aue*, Medium Aevum: Philologische Studien, 20 (Munich: Fink, 1970). (XXIII.7)

144 Jackson, W. H., 'Some Observations on the Status of the Narrator in Hartmann von Aue's *Erec* and *Iwein*,' *FMLS*, 6 (1970), 65–82. (XXIII.211)

145 Ruberg, Uwe, 'Bildkoordination im "Erec" Hartmanns von Aue,' in *Gedenkschrift für William Foerste*, Niederdeutsche Studien, 18 (Cologne: Böhlau, 1970), pp. 477–501. (XXIV.29)

146 Hatto, Arthur T., 'Wolfram von Eschenbach and the Chase,' in *Et multum et multa: Beiträge zur Literatur, Geschichte und Kultur der Jagd. Festgabe Kurt Lindner* (Berlin: de Gruyter, 1971), pp. 101–12; repr. in Dc9. (XXV.16)

147 Huby, Michel, 'Veldekes Bedeutung für die Entwicklung der Bearbeitung des französischen höfischen Romans,' in *Heinric van Veldeken: Symposion Gent 23–24 Oktober 1970*, ed. A. R. de Smet (Antwerp: Nederlandse Boekhandel, 1971), pp. 160–79. (XXVII.98).

148 Andersson, Theodore M., 'Chrétien's *Cligés* as a Source for the *Nibelungenlied* II–IV,' in *Saga og Språk: Studies in Language and Literature*, ed. John M. Weinstock (Austin, TX: Jenkins, 1972), pp. 153–64.

149 Baba, Katsuya, 'A Study of Wolfram's Parzivâl (1) (2) (3) (4) (5),' *RBN*, 16 (1972), 124–38; 19 (1975), 124–33; 21 (1977), 183–95; 23 (1979), 279–90; *SLCN*, 9:2 (1988), 93–113.
In Japanese.

See Gd.c4 Dronke.

150 Lofmark, Carl, 'Wolfram's Source References in *Parzival*,' *MLR*, 67 (1972), 820–44. (XXV.260)

151 Ruh, Kurt, 'Wolfram von Eschenbach heute,' *W-S*, 3 (1972), 9–19. (XXVIII.65)

152 Störmer, Wilhelm, 'König Artus als aristokratisches Leitbild während des späteren Mittelalters, gezeigt an Beispielen der Ministerialität und des Patriziats,' *Zeitschrift für bayerische Landesgeschichte*, 35 (1972), 946–71. (XXXI.43)

153 Wiehl, Peter, 'Zur Komposition des *Erec* Hartmanns von Aue,' *WW*, 22 (1972), 89–107. (XXV.52)

154 Wolf, Alois, 'Literarhistorische Aspekte von Parzivals Schweigen,' in *Zeiten und Formen in Sprache und Dichtung: Festschrift für Fritz Tschirch zum 70. Geburtstag*, ed. Karl-Heinz Schirmer and Bernhard Sowinski (Cologne: Böhlau, 1972), pp. 74–95; repr. in Dc31. (XXV.53)

155 Zimmermann, Gisela, 'Untersuchungen zur Orgeluseepisode in Wolfram von Eschenbachs *Parzival*,' *Euph*, 66 (1972), 128–50. (XXV.55)

See Fa69 Bertau.

156 Cometta, Marina, 'La "Bahrprobe" e la sua rappresentazione nel *Nibelungenlied* e in altri poemi epici medievali,' *Acme*, 26 (1973), 331–57. (XXVII.365)

157 Kratz, Bernd, 'Zur Kompositionstechnik Heinrichs von dem Türlin,' *ABäG*, 5 (1973), 141–53. (XXVII.402)
Includes the *Conte du Graal*.

158 Schnell, Rüdiger, 'Literarische Beziehungen zwischen Hartmanns *Erec* und Wolframs *Parzival*,' *PBB*, 95 (1973), 301–32. (XXVI.373)

159 Schröder, Franz Rolf, '*Cundrîe*,' in *Festschrift für Ingeborg Schröbler zum 65. Geburtstag*, ed. Dietrich Schmidtke and Helga Schüppert, Beiträge zur Geschichte der deutschen Sprache und Literatur: Sonderheft, 95 (Tübingen: Niemeyer, 1973), pp. 187–95. (XXVI.375)

160 Benkert, Renate L., 'Wolfram von Eschenbach's Kyot,' *Philological Papers: West Virginia University Bulletin*, 21 (1974), 3–8.

161 Green, Dennis H., *Der Weg zum Abenteuer im höfischen Roman des deutschen Mittelalters: als öffentlicher Vortrag der Joachim Jungius-Gesellschaft der Wissenschaften, gehalten am 25.6.1974 in Hamburg,*

Veröffentlichung der Joachim Jungius-Gesellschaft der Wissenschaften (Göttingen: Van den Hoeck & Ruprecht, 1974) (XXVIII.31); expanded English-language version: 'The Pathway to Adventure,' *Viator*, 8 (1977), 145–88. (XXX.131)

162 Harroff, Stephen C., *Wolfram and his Audience: A Study of the Themes of Quest and of Recognition of Kinship Identity*, GAG, 120 (Göppingen: Kümmerle, 1974). (XXVII.148)
See Appendix B: 'Chrétien and His Audience,' pp. 97–108.

163 Hatto, Arthur T., 'Die Höflichkeit des Herzens in der Dichtung der mittelhochdeutschen Blütezeit,' in *Strukturen und Interpretationen: Studien zur deutschen Philologie gewidmet Blanka Horacek zum 60. Geburtstag*, Philologica Germanica, 1 (Vienna: Braumüller, 1974), pp. 85–101. (XXVII.149)

164 Höhler, Gertrud, 'Der Kampf im Garten: Studien zur Brandigan-Episode in Hartmanns *Erec*,' *Euph*, 68 (1974), 371–419. (XXVII.151)

165 Huby, Michel, 'Adaptation courtoise et société ou "La réalité dépasse la fiction",' *EtGerm*, 29 (1974), 289–301. (XXVII.247)
Criticism of Pb61.

See Gc4 Lewis.

See Rb25 Müller.

166 Nölle, Marie Theres, *Formen der Darstellung in Hartmanns 'Iwein'*, EH:D, 89 (Bern, Frankfurt/M.: H. Lang, 1974). (XXVII.420)

See Fb37 Wiehl.

167 Curschmann, Michael, 'The French, the Audience, and the Narrator in Wolfram's *Willehalm*,' *Neophil*, 59 (1975), 548–62.

168 Ehlert, Trude, and Gerhard Meissburger, '*Perceval* et *Parzival*: valeur et fonction de l'épisode dit "des trois gouttes de sang sur la neige",' *CCM*, 18 (1975), 197–227. (XXVIII.249)

169 Fourquet, Jean, 'Die Entstehung des *Parzival*,' *W-S*, 3 (1975), 20–27; repr. in Dc8. (XXVIII.25)

170 Goebel, Ulrich, 'Concerning the Promotion of Hartmann's *Erec*,' *Semasia*, 2 (1975), 75–81.

171 Green, D. H., 'Hartmann's Ironic Praise of Erec,' *MLR*, 70 (1975), 795–807. (XXVIII.311)

See Fa77–78 Green.

172 Groos, Arthur, 'Parzival's *swertleite*,' *GR*, 50 (1975), 245–59. (XXVIII.128)

173 Groos, Arthur, 'Time Reference and the Liturgical Calendar in Wolfram von Eschenbach's *Parzival*,' *DVj*, 49 (1975), 43–65. (XXVII.145)
Cf. Hg3.

174 Haug, Walter, 'Der aventiure meine,' in *Würzburger Prosastudien II: Untersuchungen zur Literatur und Sprache des Mittelalters: Kurt Ruh zum 60. Geburtstag*, ed. Peter Kesting, Medium Aevum, 31 (Munich: Fink, 1975), pp. 93–111; repr. in Dc15. (XXVIII.34)
Hartmann and the Prologue to Chrétien's *Erec*.

175 Heinzle, Joachim, 'Gralkonzeption und Quellenmischung: forschungskritische Anmerkungen zur Entstehungsgeschichte von Wolframs "Parzival" und "Titurel",' *W-S*, 3 (1975), 28–39. (XXVIII.37)

176 Hennig, Ursula, 'Die Gurnemanzlehren und die unterlassene Frage Parzivals,' *PBB*, 97 (1975), 312–32. (XXIX.23)

177 Huby, Michel, 'Wolframs Bearbeitungstechnik im *Parzival* (Buch III),' *W-S*, 3 (1975), 40–51. (XXVIII.40)

178 Kolb, Herbert, 'Chanson-de-geste-Stil im *Parzival*,' *W-S*, 3 (1975), 189–216. (XXVIII.47)

179 Kutzner, Patricia L., *The Use of Imagery in Wolfram's 'Parzival': A Distributional Study*, Stanford German Studies, 8 (Bern: H. Lang, Frankfurt/M.: P. Lang, 1975).
See pp. 171–72.

See Gd.c7 Peil.

180 Ruh, Kurt, 'Der "Lanzelet" Ulrichs von Zatzikhofen: Modell oder Kompilation?' in *Deutsche Literatur des späten Mittelalters: Hamburger Kolloquium 1973*, ed. Wolfgang Harms and L. Peter Johnson, Publications of the Institute of German Studies, University of London, 22 (Berlin: Schmidt, 1975), pp. 47–55. (XXVIII.64)

181 Schröder, Franz Rolf, 'Kyot und das Gralproblem,' *PBB*, 97 (1975), 263–311. (XXIX.52)

182 Schröder, Walter Johannes, 'Bemerkungen zum Heilsgedanken in Chrétiens *Perceval* und Wolfgangs *Parzival*,' in *Teilnahme und Spiegelung: Festschrift für Horst Rüdiger* (Berlin: de Gruyter, 1975), pp. 112–19; repr. in Dc7. (XXVIII.69)

183 Schupp, Volker, 'Kritische Anmerkungen zur Rezeption des deutschen Artusromans anhand Hartmanns *Iwein*: Theorie–Text–Bildmaterial,' *FMSt*, 9 (1975), 405–42. (XXVIII.72)
Critique of Qe3 Kaiser.

184 Thoran, Barbara, 'Diu ir man verrâten hat – zum problem von Enîtes schuld im *Erec* Hartmanns von Aue,' *WW*, 25 (1975), 255–68. (XXVIII.79)

185 Blosen, Hans, 'Noch einmal: zu Enites Schuld in Hartmanns *Erec*. Mit Ausblicken auf Chrétiens Roman und das Mabinogi von *Gereint*,' *OrL*, 31 (1976), 81–109. (XXIX.207)

See Hg25 Colliot.

186 Cormeau, Christoph, 'Zur Rekonstruction der Leserdisposition am Beispiel des deutschen Artusromans,' *Poetica*, 8 (1976), 120–33. (XXXI.470)

See La25 Fourquet.

187 Gürttler, Karin R., *'Künec Artus der guote': das Artusbild der höfischen Epik des 12. und 13. Jahrhunderts*, SGAK, 52 (Bonn: Bouvier, 1976). (XXIX.22)

188 Hirao, Kôzô, '*The Lady of the Fountain* (Mabinogi), *Yvain* (Chrestien), *Iwein* (Hartmann) – Forays through Arthur's Court and Kalogrenant's *aventiure* at the Beginning of these Works,' *JDLA*, 9 (1976), 37–63.
In Japanese.

189 Hirschberg, Dagmar, *Untersuchungen zur Erzählstruktur von Wolframs 'Parzival': die Funktion von erzählter Szene und Station für den doppelten Kursus*, GAG, 139 (Göppingen: Kümmerle, 1976). (XXIX.26)

190 Huby, Michel, 'Hat Hartmann von Aue im *Erec* das Eheproblem neu gedeutet?' *Recherches germaniques*, 6 (1976), 3–17. (XXIX.237)

See Ga17 Huby.

191 Knapp, Fritz Peter, 'Enites Totenklage und Selbstmordversuch in Hartmanns *Erec*: eine quellenkritische Analyse,' *GRM*, 26 (1976), 83–90. (XXIX.31)

See Sc14 Mohr.

192 Pérennec, René, 'Un aspect de l'adaptation d'*Erec et Enide* en terre d'Empire: l'analogie entre la carrière des héros et la destinée du chrétien,' in *L'Adaptation courtoise en littérature médiévale allemande: Actes du Colloque des 9 et 10 avril 1976* (Paris: Champion, 1976), pp. 67–105. (XXX.297)

193 Reinitzer, Heimo, 'Über Beispielfiguren im *Erec*,' *DVj*, 50 (1976), 597–639. (XXIX.44)

194 Selbmann, Rolf, 'Strukturschema und Operatoren in Hartmanns *Iwein*,' *DVj*, 50 (1976), 60–83. (XXIX.55)

195 Welz, Dieter, 'Episoden der Entfremdung in Wolframs *Parzival*: Herzeloydentragödie und Blutstropfenszene im Verständigungsrahmen einer psychoanalytischen Sozialisationstheorie,' *Acta Germanica*, 9 (1976), 47–110.

196 Pickering, F. P., 'The "Fortune" of Hartmann's Erec,' *GLL*, 30 (1976–77), 94–109; repr. in his *Essays on Medieval German Literature and Iconography* (Cambridge: Cambridge University Press, 1980), pp. 110–29. (XXX.353)

197 Wynn, Marianne, 'Orgeluse: Persönlichkeitsgestaltung auf chrestienschem Modell,' *GLL*, 30 (1976–77), 127–37. (XXX.365)

See Qa41 Blumstein.

198 Boesch, Bruno, *Lehrhafte Literatur: Lehre in der Dichtung und Lehrdichtung im deutschen Mittelalter*, Grundlagen der Germanistik, 21 (Berlin: Schmidt, 1977). (XXX.15)

199 Delcourt-Angélique, Janine, '"Lapsit exillîs": le nom du Graal chez Wolfram d'Eschenbach (*Parzival* 469, 7): histoire d'un problème et tentative de solution,' *MrR*, 27: 3–4 (1977), 55–126. (XXXI.186)

200 Fourquet, Jean, 'Les adaptations allemandes de romans chevaleresques français: changement de fonction sociale et changement de vision,' *EtGerm*, 32 (1977), 97–107; repr. in Dc8. (XXX.273)

See Fa91 Haug.

201 Hrubý, Antonín, 'Moralphilosophie und Moraltheologie in Hartmanns *Erec*,' in *The Epic in Medieval Society: Aesthetic and Moral Values*, ed. Harald Scholler (Tübingen: Niemeyer, 1977), pp. 193–213. (XXX.32)

See Qa45 Matthias.

202 Mertens, Volker, 'Imitatio Arthuri: zum Prolog von Hartmanns *Iwein*,' *ZfdA*, 106 (1977), 350–58. (XXX.47)

See Cb12 Neubuhr.

See Fa92 Pastré.

203 Schusky, Renate, 'Lunete – eine "kupplerische Dienerin?",' *Euph*, 71 (1977), 18–46. (XXX.72)

204 Wolf, Alois, 'Die "adaptation courtoise": kritische Anmerkungen zu einem neuen Dogma,' *GRM*, 27 (1977), 257–83; repr. in Dc31. (XXX.83)

Critical discussion of Pb40. See also: Michel Huby, 'Zur Definition der "adaptation courtoise": kritische Antwort auf kritische Anmerkungen,' *GRM*, 33 (1983), 301–22; and Alois Wolf, 'Kurze Schlußreplik,' *GRM*, 33 (1983), 323–24.

205 Buschinger, Danielle, 'Hartmann von Aue, adaptateur du *Chevalier au lion* de Chrétien de Troyes,' in *Littérature et société au Moyen Age: Actes du Colloque des 5 et 6 mai 1978, Université de Picardie*, ed. Danielle Buschinger (Paris: Champion, [1978]), pp. 371–91.

206 Dick, Ernst S., '*Katabasis* and the Grail Epic: Wolfram von Eschenbach's *Parzival*,' *ResPL*, 1 (1978), 57–87. (XXXIII.137)

207 Freytag, Wiebke, 'Zu Hartmanns Methode der Adaptation im *Erec*,' *Euph*, 72 (1978), 227–39. (XXXI.20)

208 Gnädinger, Louise, 'Rois Peschiere/Anfortas: der Fischerkönig in Chrestiens und Wolframs Graldichtung,' in *Mélanges Bezzola*, pp. 127–48.

209 *Approaches to Wolfram von Eschenbach: Five Essays*, ed. Dennis Howard Green and Leslie Peter Johnson, Mikrokosmos, 5 (Bern: P. Lang, 1978). (XXXI.486)

See He32 Haug.

210 Kuttner, Ursula, *Das Erzählen des Erzählten: eine Studie zum Stil in Hartmanns 'Erec' und 'Iwein'*, SGAK, 70 (Bonn: Bouvier, 1978). (XXXI.30)

211 Markey, T. L., 'The *ex lege* Right of Passage in Hartmann's *Iwein*,' *Colloquia Germanica*, 11 (1978), 97–110. (XXXI.495)

See Gd.a7 Mellen.

212 Mertens, Volker, *Laudine: soziale Problematik im 'Iwein' Hartmanns von Aue*, Beihefte zur *ZdP*, 3 (Berlin: Schmidt, 1978). (XXXI. 32)

213 Milde, Wolfgang, '"daz ih minne an uch suche": neue Wolfenbütteler Bruchstücke des Erec,' in *Wolfenbütteler Beiträge: aus den Schätzen der Herzog August Bibliothek*, ed. Paul Raabe, 3 (1978), 43–58. (XXXI.33)
Comparisons with Chrétien MSS.

See Na.c72 Ó Riain-Raedel.

See Gd.c15 Ruberg.

See Qe10 Schnell.

214 Tobin, Frank, 'Hartmann's *Erec*: The Perils of Young Love,' *Seminar*, 14 (1978), 1–14.

215 Adolf, Helen, 'Structure and Character Delineation in the *Parzival*,' *W-S*, 5 (1979), 166–82. (XXXII.9)

216 Clark, S. L., 'Changing One's Mind: Arenas of Conflict and Resolution in Hartmann's *Îwein*,' *Euph*, 73 (1979), 286–303. (XXXII.19)

217 Cormeau, Christoph, '*Joie de la curt*: Bedeutungssetzung und ethische Erkenntnis,' in *Formen und Funktionen der Allegorie: Symposion Wolfenbüttel 1978*, ed. Walter Haug, Germanistische Symposien: Berichtsbände, 3 (Stuttgart: Metzler, 1979), pp. 194–205. (XXXII.20)

See Uc14 Cormeau.

218 Ehrismann, Otfrid, 'Enite: Handlungsbegrundungen in Hartmanns von Aue *Erec*,' *ZdP*, 98 (1979), 321–44. (XXXII.25)

219 Fourquet, Jean, *Parzival: Cours d'agrégation de 1963–64*, ed. Jean-Paul Vernon, GAG, 283 (Göppingen: Kümmerle, 1979). (XXXII.30)

220 Fromm, Hans, 'Zur Karrenritter-Episode im Prosa-Lancelot: Struktur und Geschichte,' in *Festschrift Ruh*, pp. 69–97. (XXXII.32)

221 Hart, Thomas Elwood, 'Twelfth Century Platonism and the Geometry of Textual Space in Hartmann's *Iwein*: A "Pythagorean" Theory,' *ResPL*, 2 (1979), 81–107. (XXXIV.128)

222 *Herlem, Brigitte, and Claire Santoni-Rozier, 'La fidèle traduction infidèle des adaptateurs allemands du Moyen Age: 2. Du roman en prose *Lancelot du Lac* au *Prosa-Lancelot;* traduction et adaptation dans l'épisode de la "*Charrette*": *Der Karrenritter*,' in *La Traduction: un art, une technique: Actes du XIe Congrès de l'Association des Germanistes de l'Enseignement Supérieur (Nancy, 28–30 avril 1978)* (Nancy: Bureau de l'AGES, 1979), pp. 226–56 (discussion pp. 257–59).

223 Hrubý, Antonín, 'Hartmann als artifex, philosophus und praeceptor der Gesellschaft,' in *Kuhn Gedenken*, pp. 254–75. (XXXIII.35)

224 Huby, Michel, 'La "faute" d'Iwein,' *EtGerm*, 34 (1979), 129–40. (XXXII.348)

225 Huby, Michel, 'L'interprétation des romans courtois de Hartmann von Aue,' *CCM*, 22 (1979), 23–38. (XXXII.350)

226 Huby, Michel, 'Réflexions sur *Parzivâl* et le *Conte del Graal*: "Schildes ambet ist mîn art",' *EtGerm*, 34 (1979), 390–403; 'II. Comment Wolfram a-t-il résolu les problèmes que lui posait le *Conte del Graal*?' *EtGerm*, 35 (1980), 1–17. (XXXII.349, XXXIII. 337)

See Gd.c16 Knapp.

227 Kraft, Karl Friedrich O., *Iwein's Triuwe: zu Ethos und Form der Aventiurenfolge in Hartmanns 'Iwein': eine Interpretation*, APSL, 42 (Amsterdam: Rodopi, 1979).

See Ja26 Kuhn.

228 Mayer, Hartwig, '*ein vil vriuntlîchez spil*: Erecs und Enites gemeinsame Schuld,' in *Analecta Helvetica et Germanica: ein Festschrift zu Ehren von Hermann Boeschenstein*, SGAK, 85 (Bonn: Bouvier, 1979), pp. 8–19. (XXXIII.49)

229 Mohr, Wolfgang, 'König Artus und die Tafelrunde: politische Hintergründe in Chrétiens *Perceval* und Wolframs *Parzival*,' in his

Wolfram von Eschenbach: Aufsätze, GAG, 275 (Göppingen: Kümmerle, 1979), pp. 170–222. (XXXII.51)

230 Pastré, Jean-Marc, *Rhétorique et adaptation dans les œuvres allemandes du Moyen-Age*, PUR, 50 (Paris: Presses Universitaires de France, 1979). (XXXII.359 *bis*)

231 Pastré, Jean-Marc, 'Rhétorique et adaptation: l'*Erec* de Hartmann von Aue et l'*Erec et Enide* de Chrétien de Troyes,' *Cahiers d'Etudes Médiévales*, 1 (1979), 109–32.

232 Ragotzky, Hedda, and Barbara Weinmayer, 'Höfischer Roman und soziale Identitätsbildung: zur soziologischen Deutung des Doppelwegs im *Iwein* Hartmanns von Aue,' in *Kuhn Gedenken*, pp. 211–53. (XXXIII.59)

233 Schnell, Rüdiger, 'Wolframs *Parzival* und der *Roman de Thèbes*,' *Neophil*, 63 (1979), 88–94. (XXXII.521)

234 Zutt, Herta, *König Artus, Iwein, der Löwe: die Bedeutung des gesprochenen Worts in Hartmanns 'Iwein'*, Untersuchungen zur deutschen Literaturgeschichte, 23 (Tübingen: Niemeyer, 1979). (XXXII.87)

235 Brandt, Wolfgang, 'Die Entführungsepisode in Hartmanns *Iwein*,' *ZdP*, 99 (1980), 321–54. (XXXIII.13)

236 Dubuis, Roger, '*Yvain* et *Iwein*: variations sur le motif du "don contraignant",' in *Mélanges Foulon*, vol. 2, pp. 81–91. (XXXIII.329)

See Jd21 Gicquel.

237 Green, Dennis, 'The Art of Namedropping in Wolfram's *Parzival*,' *W-S*, 6 (1980), 84–150. (XXXIII.28)

238 Green, Dennis, '*Parzival*'s Departure – Folklore and Romance,' *FMSt*, 14 (1980), 352–409. (XXXIV.18)

239 Keller, Thomas L., 'Iwein and the Lion,' *ABäG*, 15 (1980), 59–75. (XXXIII.585)

240 Mohr, Wolfgang, 'Chrétiens und Hartmanns *Erec*: ein Vergleich,' in his *Hartmann von Aue: Erec*, GAG, 291 (Göppingen: Kümmerle, 1980), pp. 239–312.

241 Pérennec, René, 'Le discours arthurien,' *EtGerm*, 35 (1980), 441–43. (XXXIII.363)

Compares *Yvain* and *Iwein*.

242 Smits, Kathryn, 'Einige Beobachtungen zu gemeinsamen Motiven in Hartmanns *Erec* und Wolframs *Parzival*,' in *Festschrift for E. W. Herd* (Dunedin: Department of German, University of Otago, 1980), pp. 251–62.

See Pa121 Wolfgang.

243 Christoph, Siegfried Richard, *Wolfram von Eschenbach's Couples*, APSL, 44 (Amsterdam: Rodopi, 1981).

244 Clark, Susan L., 'Hartmann's *Êrec*: Language, Perception, and Transformation,' *GR*, 56 (1981), 81–94. (XXXIV.113)

245 Cramer, Thomas, 'Der deutsche höfische Roman und seine Vorläufer,' in *Neues Handbuch der Literaturwissenschaft*, vol. 7: *Europäisches Hochmittelalter*, ed. Henning Krauss (Wiesbaden: Athenaion, 1981), pp. 323–56. (XXXV.17)

See Gd.c20 Delcourt-Angélique.

246 Green, Dennis H., 'The Young Parzival – Naming and Anonymity,' in *Festschrift Asher*, pp. 103–18. (XXXIV.19)

247 Hänsch, Irene, '*Parzivâl. der nam ist rehte enmitten durch*: zum Problem von Namen und Identität in Wolframs *Parzival*,' *Euph*, 75 (1981), 260–74. (XXXV.30)

248 Heine, Thomas, 'Shifting Perspectives: The Narrative Strategy in Hartmann's *Erec*,' *OrL*, 36 (1981), 95–115.

249 Hennig, Beate, *'Maere' und 'werk': zur Funktion von erzählerischem Handeln im 'Iwein' Hartmanns von Aue*, GAG, 321 (Göppingen: Kümmerle, 1981). (XXXIV.23)

See La28 Hunt.

250 Jillings, Lewis, 'The Rival Sisters Dispute in *Diu Crone* and Its French Antecedents,' in *Essays Thorpe*, pp. 248–59. (XXXIV.333)

251 Lofmark, Carl, *The Authority of the Source in Middle High German Narrative Poetry*, Bithell Series of Dissertations, 5 (London: Institute of Germanic Studies, 1981). (XXXIV.341)

252 Mertens, Volker, 'Iwein und Gwigalois – der Weg zur Landesherrschaft,' *GRM*, 31 (1981), 14–31. (XXXIV.29)

253 *Die mittelalterliche Literatur in Kärnten: Vorträge des Symposions in St Georgen/Längsee vom 8. bis 13.9.1980*, ed. Alexander Cella and Peter Krämer, Wiener Arbeiten zur germanischen Altertumskunde und Philologie, 16 (Vienna: Halosar, 1981).

The following treat Chrétien's influence:

    A.   Danielle Buschinger, 'Burg Salîe und Gral: zwei Erlösungstaten Gaweins in der *Crône* Heinrichs von dem Türlîn,' pp. 1–32; repr. in Dc23.

    B.   Alfred Ebenbauer, 'Gawein als Gatte,' pp. 33–66.

    C.   Fritz Peter Knapp, 'Heinrich von dem Türlîn: literarische Beziehungen und mögliche Auftraggeber, dichterische Selbstein-schätzung und Zielsetzung,' pp. 145–87.

254 Parshall, Linda B., *The Art of Narration in Wolfram's 'Parzival' and Albrecht's 'Jüngerer Titurel'*, Anglica Germanica: ser. 2 (Cambridge: Cambridge University Press, 1981). (XXXIV.359)

255 Sauer, Margret, *Parzival auf der Suche nach der verlorenen Zeit: ein Beitrag zur Ausbildung einer formkritischen Methode*, GAG, 323 (Göppingen: Kümmerle, 1981). (XXXIV.42)

256 Sinka, Margit M., '"Der höfschte man": An Analysis of Gawein's Role in Hartmann von Aue's *Iwein*,' *MLN*, 46 (1981), 471–87. (XXXIV. 149)

257 Smits, Kathryn, 'Enite als christliche Ehefrau,' in *Festschrift Asher*, pp. 13–25. (XXXIV.48)

258 Thomas, Neil, 'Sense and Structure in the Gawan Adventures of Wolfram's *Parzival*,' *MLR*, 76 (1981), 848–56. (XXXIV.384)

See Na.c77 Wallbank.

See Xa4 Wells.

259 Willson, H. B., '"Ordo amoris" and the Character of Hartmann's *Erec*,' in *Essays Thorpe*, pp. 129–38. (XXXIV.390)

260 Yeandle, David N., 'Herzeloyde: Problems of Characterization in Book III of Wolfram's *Parzival*,' *Euph*, 75 (1981), 1–28. (XXXIV.61)

261 Blosen, Hans, '"Assumptions about Lost Manuscripts"? – zur *Erec*-Diskussion,' *OrL*, 37 (1982), 367.

On Pb185 Blosen and Pb248 Heine.

262 Dubuis, Roger, 'La première rencontre de Perceval avec le Graal, dans le *Conte du Graal* de Chrétien de Troyes et le *Parzival* de Wolfram d'Eschenbach,' *GRM*, 32 (1982), 129–55. (XXXV.19)

263 Gärtner, Kurt, 'Der Text der Wolfenbütteler Erec-Fragmente und seine Bedeutung für die Erec-Forschung,' *PBB*, 104 (1982), 207–30, 359–430. (XXXV.23)

See: 'III. Das Verhältnis der neuen Fragmente zu Chrétiens *Erec* und den übrigen Bearbeitungen des Erec-Stoffes' (pp. 369–415). Cf. also Wolfgang Milde, 'Zur Kodikologie der neuen und alten Wolfenbütteler Erec-Fragmente und zum Umfang des darin überlieferten Erec-Textes,' pp. 190–206. (XXXV.48)

264 Green, Dennis H., 'Advice and Narrative Action: Parzival, Herzeloyde and Gurnemanz,' in *From Wolfram and Petrarch to Goethe and Grass: Studies in Literature in Honour of Leonard Forster*, ed. D. H. Green et al., Saecvla Spiritvalia, 5 (Baden-Baden: Koerner, 1982), pp. 33–81. (XXXV.29)

265 Green, D. H., *The Art of Recognition in Wolfram's 'Parzival'* (Cambridge: Cambridge University Press, 1982). (XXXV.392)

See Db26 Hrubý.

266 Johnson, Leslie Peter, 'The Grail-Question in Wolfram and Elsewhere,' in *From Wolfram and Petrarch to Goethe and Grass: Studies in Literature in Honour of Leonard Forster*, ed. D. H. Green et al., Saecvla Spiritvalia, 5 (Baden-Baden: Koerner, 1982), pp. 83–102. (XXXV.38)

See Hf47 Kratins.

267 Nellmann, Eberhard, 'Ein zweiter Erec-Roman? zu den neu-gefundenen Wolfenbütteler Fragmenten,' *ZdP*, 101 (1982), 28–78; 'Diplomatischer Abdruck der neuen Erec-Fragmente: Berichtigung zum Abdruck in *ZfdPh* 101, 5.35–40,' *ZdP*, 101 (1982), 436–41. (XXXV. 54)

268 Ranawake, Silvia, 'Zu Form und Funktion der Ironie bei Hartmann von Aue,' *W-S*, 7 (1982), 75–116. (XXXV.60)

See Ga34 Ruh.

269 Schirok, Bernd, *Parzivalrezeption im Mittelalter*, Erträge der Forschung, 174 (Darmstadt: Wissenschaftliche Buchgesellschaft, 1982). (XXXV.65)

Treats differences between reception of Chrétien's and Wolfram's romances.

270 Schröder, Werner, *Die Namen im 'Parzival' und im 'Titurel'*
Wolframs von Eschenbach (Berlin: de Gruyter, 1982). (XXXIV.47)

271 Smits, Kathryn, 'Die Schönheit der Frau in Hartmanns *Erec*,' *ZdP*,
101 (1982), 1–28. (XXXV.74)

272 Voß, Rudolf, 'Handlungsschematismus und anthropologische
Konzeption – zur Ästhetik des klassischen Artusromans am Beispiel des
Erec und *Iwein* Hartmanns von Aue,' *ABäG*, 18 (1982), 95–114.

See Ja31 Wells.

273 Poag, James F., 'The Quest of Narrator, Hero and Audience in
Wolfram von Eschenbach's *Parzival*,' *Renascence: Essays on Value in
Literature*, 35 (1982–83), 247–57.

See Jd25 Bayer.

274 Brall, Helmut, *Gralsuche und Adelsheil: Studien zu Wolframs
Parzival*, Germanische Bibliothek, ser. 3: Untersuchungen (Heidelberg:
Winter, 1983). (XXXVI.21)

275 Buschinger, Danielle, 'Un roman arthurien allemand post-classique:
la *Couronne* de Heinrich von dem Türlin,' *MA*, 89 (1983), 381–95.
(XXXVI.288)

276 Francke, Walter K., 'Orgeluse's Predicament,' *MGS*, 9 (1983), 18–
32. (XXXVII.374)

277 Green, Dennis H., 'Über die Kunst des Erkennens in Wolframs
Parzival,' *PBB*, 105 (1983), 48–65. (XXXVI.40)

278 Jillings, Lewis, 'The Ideal of Queenship in Hartmann's *Erec*,' in
Studies Diverres, pp. 113–28, 242–45. (XXXVI.435)

279 Schultz, James A., *The Shape of the Round Table: Structures of
Middle High German Arthurian Romance* (Toronto: University of
Toronto Press, 1983). (XXXVII.457)

280 Schulze, Ursula, '*Âmîs unde man*: die zentrale Problematik in
Hartmanns *Erec*,' *PBB*, 105 (1983), 14–47. (XXXVI.76)

281 Voss, Rudolf, *Die Artusepik Hartmanns von Aue: Untersuchungen
zum Wirklichkeitsbegriff und zur Ästhetik eines literarischen Genres im
Kräftefeld von soziokulturellen Normen und christlicher Anthropologie*,
Literatur und Leben, n. s. 25 (Cologne: Böhlau, 1983). (XXXV.79)

282 Waldmann, Bernhard, *Natur und Kultur im höfischen Roman um 1200: Überlegung zu politischen, ethnischen und ästhetischen Fragen epischer Literatur des Hochmittelalters*, Erlanger Studien, 38 (Erlangen: Palm & Enke, 1983). (XXXVI.83)

See Uc23 Allard.

283 Borck, Karl Heinz, 'Lanzelets adel,' in *Festschrift für Siegfried Grosse*, ed. Werner Besch, Klaus Hufeland, Volker Schupp, and Peter Wiehl, GAG, 423 (Göppingen: Kümmerle, 1984), pp. 337–53. (XXXVII.580)

284 Brogsitter, Karl Otto, 'Der Held im Zwiespalt und der Held als strahlender Musterritter: Anmerkungen zum Verlust der Konfliktträgerfunktion des Helden im deutschen Artusroman,' in *Artusrittertum*, pp. 16–27. (XXXVII.583)

285 Buschinger, Danielle, 'La nourriture dans les romans arthuriens allemands entre 1170 et 1210,' in *Manger et boire au Moyen Age: Actes du Colloque de Nice (15–17 octobre 1982)*, Publications de la Faculté des Lettres et Sciences Humaines de Nice, 27 – 1ᵉ série: Centre d'Etudes Médiévales de Nice, 2 vols (Paris: Belles Lettres, 1984), vol. 1, pp. 377–89. (XXXVII.70)

286 Buschinger, Danielle, 'Le personnage de Lancelot dans la littérature allemande du Moyen Age (à l'exception du *Lanzelet* et du *Prosa-Lancelot*),' in *Lancelot Picardie*, pp. 17–28.

287 Cormeau, Christoph, 'Zur Gattungsentwicklung des Artusromans nach Wolframs *Parzival*,' in *Artusliteratur*, pp. 119–31. (XXXVII.591)

288 Delcourt-Angélique, Janine, 'Le Graal de Chrétien de Troyes: pour Wolfram von Eschenbach, un "objet non identifié" au livre V; au livre IX, une pierre baptisée lapsit exillîs. Au terme de quelle évolution?' in *Chrétien Bruges*, pp. 89–105. (XXXVII.78)

289 Haug, Walter, 'Das Fantastische in der späteren deutschen Artusliteratur,' in *Artusliteratur*, pp. 133–49. (XXXVII.615)

See Hf55 Hunt.

290 Karnein, Alfred, 'Minne, Aventiure und Artus-Idealität in den Romanen des späten 13. Jahrhunderts,' in *Artusrittertum*, pp. 114–25. (XXXVII.626)
Transformation of Chrétien's romance model.

291 Kern, Peter, 'Reflexe des literarischen Gesprächs über Hartmanns *Erec* in der deutschen Dichtung des Mittelalters,' in *Artusrittertum*, pp. 126–37. (XXXVII.629)

See Qa67 Matthias.

292 Pérennec, René, *Recherches sur le roman arthurien en vers en Allemagne aux 12ᵉ et 13ᵉ siècles*, GAG, 393:1–2, 2 vols (Göppingen: Kümmerle, 1984). (XXXVII.650)

293 Rocher, Daniel, 'Stratégie matrimoniale, réalités politiques et sentiments romanesques dans l'*Yvain* et l'*Iwein*,' in *Lancelot Wégimont*, pp. 63–75. (XXXVIII.257)

See Ga46 Santoni-Rozier.

See Ga48 Schopf.

294 Wynn, Marianne, *Wolfram's 'Parzival': On the Genesis of Its Poetry*, Mikrokosmos, 9 (Frankfurt/M.: P. Lang, 1984). (XXXVII. 568, 691)

See Jd30 Bonnet.

See Gb80 Brandt.

295 Cormeau, Christoph, and Wilhelm Störmer, *Hartmann von Aue: Epoche – Werk – Wirkung*, Beck'sche Elementarbücher: Arbeitsbücher zur Literaturgeschichte (Munich: Beck, 1985). (XXXVIII.14)
See pp. 166–78, 198–201, 218–22.

296 Dallapiazza, Michael, 'Häßlichkeit und Individualität: Ansätze zur Überwindung der Idealität des Schönen in Wolframs von Eschenbach *Parzival*,' *DVj*, 59 (1985), 400–21. (XXXVIII.15)

297 Green, Dennis, 'The Aesthetic Consequence of Literacy: An Aspect of the Twelfth-Century Renaissance in Germany,' *ResPL*, 8 (1985), 83–92. (XXXVIII.498)
Pp. 89–90 on the 'Prologue' in *Yvain* and *Iwein*.

See Fa130 Haug.

See Ub24 *Psychologie*.

See Gd.b26 Santoni-Rozier.

298 Spiewok, Wolfgang, 'Wolframs von Eschenbach *Parzival*: Voraussetzungen, Ansätze und Probleme einer Interpretation,' *ZfG*, 6 (1985), 165–79 (XXXVIII.58); repr. in his *Mittelalter-Studien II*, GAG, 499, ed. Danielle Buschinger (Göppingen: Kümmerle, 1987), pp. 138–56. (XL.688)

See Fa135 Trimborn.

299 Wolf, Alois, '*Ein maere will ich niuwen, daz saget von grôzen triuwen*: vom höfischen Roman Chrétiens zum Meditationsgeflecht der Dichtung Wolframs,' *LJG*, 26 (1985), 9–73; repr. in Dc31.

See La37 Worstbrock.

See Qa78 Bumke.

300 Dick, Ernst S., 'The Hero and the Magician: On the Proliferation of Dark Figures from *Li Contes del Graal* and *Parzival* to *Diu Crône*,' in *The Dark Figure in Medieval German and Germanic Literature*, ed. Edward R. Haymes and Stephanie Cain Van D'Elden, GAG, 448 (Göppingen: Kümmerle, 1986), pp. 128–50. (XL.535)

301 Fisher, Rodney, 'Räuber, Riesen und die Stimme der Vernunft in Hartmanns und Chrétiens *Erec*,' *DVj*, 60 (1986), 353–74. (XXXIX. 476)

302 Gottzmann, Carola L., *Deutsche Artusdichtung*. Vol. 1: *Rittertum, Minne, Ehe und Herrschertum: die Artusepik der hochhöfischen Zeit*, Information und Interpretation, 2 (Frankfurt/M.: P. Lang, 1986). (XL. 502)

303 Groos, Arthur, 'Perceval and Parzival Discover Knighthood,' in *Studies Kaske*, pp. 117–37. (XXXIX.269)

304 Heinen, Hubert, 'The Concepts of *hof*, *hövesch*, and the Like in Hartmann's *Iwein*,' in Qa81 *Medieval Court*, pp. 41–57. (XXXIX.275)

305 Knapp, Fritz Peter, *'Chevalier errant' und 'fin'amor': das Ritterideal des 13. Jahrhunderts in Nordfrankreich und im deutschsprachigen Südosten: Studien zum 'Lancelot en prose', zum 'Moriz von Craûn', zur 'Krone' Heinrichs von dem Türlin, zu Werken des Strickers und zum 'Frauendienst' Ulrichs von Lichtenstein*, Schriften der Universität Passau: Reihe Geisteswissenschaften, 8 (Passau: Passavia, 1986). (XXXIX.510)

306 Morrison, Susan S., 'Displaced Rivalry in Hartmann von Aue's *Iwein*,' *ABäG*, 25 (1986), 45–62.

See Uc25 Allard.

307 Eichholz, Birgit, *Kommentar zur Sigune- und Ither-Szene im 3. Buch von Wolframs 'Parzival' (138,9–161,8)*, Helfant Studien, S3 (Stuttgart: Helfant, 1987).

See Me27 Firestone.

See La39 Haupt.

308 Huby, Michel, 'Les procédés descriptifs de Hartmann von Aue, adaptateur de Chrétien de Troyes (*Yvain-Iwein*), I–II,' *PRIS-MA*, 3 (1987), 47–60, 103–27. (XLI.62)

309 McConeghy, Patrick M., 'Women's Speech and Silence in Hartmann von Aue's *Erec*,' *PMLA*, 102 (1987), 772–83.

See Hc54 Owen.

310 Pastré, Jean-Marc, 'Gregorius: le portrait d'un homme vieilli chez Hartmann von Aue,' *Vieillesse*, pp. 243–63. (XXXIX.663)

See Na.e45 Thomas.

See Pa193 Coolput.

311 Buschinger, Danielle, 'Réécriture et écriture dans la littérature médiévale allemande (XIIe–XIIIe siècles),' in *Théories*, pp. 87–99.

312 Classen, Albrecht, 'Keie in Wolframs von Eschenbach *Parzival*: "Agent provocateur" oder Angeber?' *JEGP*, 87 (1988), 382–405. (XLI.368)

313 *Deutsche Literatur: eine Sozialgeschichte. 1: Aus der Mündlichkeit in die Schriftlichkeit: höfische und andere Literatur 750–1320*, ed. Ursula Liebertz-Grün (Reinbek bei Hamburg: Rowohlt, 1988).
    A.   Klaus Grubmüller, 'Artus- und Gralromane,' pp. 216–35.
    B.   Ulrich Müller, 'Wolfram von Eschenbach,' pp. 239–44.

314 Ehrismann, Otfrid, 'Laudine – oder: Hartmanns *Iwein* postmodern,' in *Sammlung–Deutung–Wertung: Ergebnisse, Probleme, Tendenzen und Perspektiven philologischer Arbeit: Mélanges de littérature médiévale et de linguistique allemande offerts à Wolfgang Spiewok à l'occasion de* *son soixantième anniversaire par ses collègues et amis*, ed. Danielle Buschinger (Stuttgart: Sprint, 1988), pp. 91–100. (XLII.514)

315 Firestone, Ruth H., 'Boethian Order in Hartmann's *Erec* and *Iwein*,' *EsL*, 15 (1988), 117–30. (XLI.378)

316 Haase, Gudrun, *Die germanistische Forschung zum 'Erec' Hartmanns von Aue*, EH:D, 1103 (Frankfurt/M.: P. Lang, 1988). (XLI. 598, XLII.472)
See pp. 72–83, 102–14, 250–80.

317 *Hartmann von Aue: Changing Perspectives: London Hartmann Symposium 1985*, ed. Timothy McFarland and Silvia Ranawake, GAG, 486 (Göppingen: Kümmerle, 1988). (XLI.601)
The following articles refer in important ways to Chrétien:
  A. Nigel F. Palmer, 'Poverty and Mockery in Hartmann's *Erec*, v. 525ff.: A Study of the Psychology and Aesthetics of Middle High German Romance,' pp. 65–92. (XLI.626)
  B. Silvia Ranawake, 'Erec's *verligen* and the Sin of Sloth,' pp. 93–115. (XLI.629)
  C. Alan Robertshaw, 'Ambiguity and Morality in *Iwein*,' pp. 117–28. (XLI.635)
  D. Timothy McFarland, 'Narrative Structure and the Renewal of the Hero's Identity in *Iwein*,' pp. 129–57. (XLI.622)
  E. William Henry Jackson, 'The Tournament in the Works of Hartmann von Aue: Motifs, Style, Functions,' pp. 233–51. (XLI.606)
  F. George T. Gillespie, 'Real and Ideal Images of Knightly Endeavour and Love in the Works of Hartmann von Aue,' pp. 253–70. (XLI.592)
  G. Rosemary Combridge, 'The Use of Biblical and Other Learned Symbolism in the Narrative Works of Hartmann von Aue,' pp. 271–84. (XLI.586)

318 Kamizawa, Eizô, '*Yvain* and *Iwein*: Two Different Universes,' *JFLN*, 103 (1988), 125–142, and *RTr*, B (March 1990), pp. 1–17. (XLII.147; XLIII.404).
In Japanese.

See Md39 Kasten.

319 Pastré, Jean-Marc, 'Pour une esthétique du portrait: les couleurs du visage dans la littérature médiévale allemande,' in *Couleurs*, pp. 285–300. (XL.53)

See Gc18 Weiss.

See Ha147 Wilson.

320 Bertau, Karl, 'Zum System der arthurischen Symbolisation,' *EtGerm*, 44 (1989), 271–83. (XLII.45)

321 Brackert, Helmut, '"der lac an riterschefte tôt": Parzival und das Leid der Frauen,' in *Ist zwîvel herzen nâchgebûr: Günther Schweikle zum 60. Geburtstag*, ed. Rüdiger Krüger, Jürgen Kühnel, and Joachim Kuolt, Helfant Studien, S 5 (Stuttgart: Helfant, 1989), pp. 143–63.

322 Christoph, Siegfried, 'Guenevere's Abduction and Arthur's Fame in Hartmann's *Iwein*,' *ZfdA*, 118 (1989), 17–33. (XLII.509)

323 Clark, Susan L., *Hartmann von Aue: Landscapes of the Mind* (Houston, TX: Rice University Press, 1989). (XLIII.510)

See Pe30 Duijvestijn.

324 Graf, Michael, *Liebe-Zorn-Trauer-Adel: die Pathologie in Hartmann von Aues 'Iwein': eine Interpretation auf medizinhistorischer Basis*, Deutsche Literatur von den Anfängen bis 1700, 7 (Bern: P. Lang, 1989). (XLII.470, 528)

325 Grosse, Siegfried, 'Die Erzählperspektive der gestaffelten Wiederholung: Kalogreants *âventiure* in Hartmanns *Iwein*,' in *Festschrift Rupp*, pp. 82–96. (XLII.471, 529)

326 Haferland, Harald, *Höfische Interaktion: Interpretationen zur höfischen Epik und Didaktik um 1200*, FGädL, 10 (Munich: Fink, 1989). (XLII.532)

See Ha148–49 Haug.

327 Haupt, Barbara, 'Literaturgeschichtsschreibung im höfischen Roman: die Beschreibung von Enites Pferd und Sattelzeug im *Erec* Hartmanns von Aue,' *Festschrift für Herbert Kolb zu seinem 65. Geburtstag* (Bern: P. Lang, 1989), pp. 202–19. (XLII.473, 551)

See Hc60 Katzenmeier.

328 Oguri, Tomokazu, '*Perceval* and *Parzival* – Representation of the Hero's Childhood in Both Works,' in *Französische mittelalterliche höfische Romane: Rezeption und Bearbeitung in Deutschland (Forschungstitel Nr. 63450062)*, Staatliches Forschungsproject des Jahrgangs Heisei 1 (1989), Allgemeine Forschung (B), Forschungsbericht März, Heisei 2 (1990), pp. 38–44. (XLIII. 406).
In Japanese.

329 Okamoto, Mamiko, '"der ist genuoc getân" – On the Motivation for Departure in Hartmann's *Erec*,' *JDLA*, 22 (1989), 105–14.
In Japanese.

330 Pratt, Karen, 'Direct Speech – A Key to the German Adaptor's Art?', in *Medieval Translators and their Craft*, ed. Jeanette Beer, SMC, 25 (Kalamazoo: Medieval Institute Publications, Western Michigan University, 1989), pp. 213–46. (XLI.431)

331 Schirok, Bernd, '*Artûs der meienbære man*: zum Stellenwert der "Artuskritik" im klassischen deutschen Artusroman,' in *Festschrift Rupp*, pp. 58–81. (XLII.476, 575)

332 Schmid-Cadalbert, Christian, 'Der wilde Wald: zur Darstellung und Funktion eines Raumes in der mittelhochdeutschen Literatur,' in *Festschrift Rupp*, pp. 24–47. (XLII.577)

333 Shitanda, Sô, 'Perspektiven in Chrétiens *Le Conte du Graal* und in Wolframs *Parzival*,' *Nishinihon Doitsu Bungaku* (Gesellschaft für Germanistik-Westjapan), 1 (1989), 27–36.

See Gd.b38 Studer.

334 Wehrli, Max, 'Zur Identität der Figuren im frühen Artusroman,' in *Festschrift Rupp*, pp. 48–57. (XLII.480, 586)

335 Zutt, Herta, 'Gawan und die Geschwister Antikonie und Vergulaht,' in *Festschrift Rupp*, pp. 97–117. (XLII.481, 592)

336 Buschinger, Danielle, 'Französisch-deutsche Literaturbeziehungen im Mittelalter,' *ZfG*, 11 (1990), 172–83; repr. in Dc23. (XLIII.15)

See Gf32 Dallapiazza.

337 Haug, Walter, 'Von *aventiure* und *minne* zu Intrige und Treue: die Subjektivierung des hochhöfischen Aventürenromans im *Reinfrid von Braunschweig*,' in *Liebe Triest*, pp. 7–22; repr. in Dc24.

338 Simon, Ralf, *Einführung in die strukturalistische Poetik des mittelalterlichen Romans: Analysen zu deutschen Romanen der matière de Bretagne*, Epistemata. Würzburger wissenschaftliche Schriften: Literaturwissenschaft, 66 (Würzburg: Königshausen & Neumann, 1990). (XLIII.61)

339 Singer, Johannes, '"nû swîc, lieber Hartman: ob ich ez errâte?" Beobachtungen zum fingierten Dialog und zum Gebrauch der Fiktion in Hartmanns *Erec*-Roman (7493–7766),' in *Dialog: Festschrift für*

Siegfried Grosse, ed. Gert Rickheit and Sigurd Wichter (Tübingen: Niemeyer, 1990), pp. 59–74.

See Qa97 Brall.

340 Brall, Helmut, 'Imaginationen des Fremden: zu Formen und Dynamik kultureller Identitätsfindung in der höfischen Dichtung,' in *Grenzen*, pp. 115–65.

See Ga69 Brugger-Hackett.

341 Brunner, Horst, 'Von Munsalvaesche wart gesant / der den der swane brahte: Überlegungen zur Gestaltung des Schlusses von Wolframs *Parzival*,' *GRM*, 41 (1991), 369–84. (XLIV.419)

342 Egerding, Michael, 'Konflikt und Krise im *Gauriel von Muntabel* des Konrad von Stoffeln,' *ABäG*, 34 (1991), 111–25. (XLIV.255)

343 Ertzdorff, Xenja von, 'Über die Liebe in den deutschen Artusromanen,' *BBSIA*, 43 (1991), 332–56. (XLIV.305)

344 Gärtner, Kurt, 'Stammen die französischen Lehnwörter in Hartmanns *Erec* aus Chrétiens *Erec et Enide*?' *ZLiLi*, 83 (1991), 76–88.

345 Grubmüller, Klaus, 'Der Artusroman und sein König: Beobachtungen zur Artusfigur am Beispiel von Ginovers Entführung,' in *Positionen*, pp. 1–20. (XLIV.435)

346 Haug, Walter, 'Hat Wolfram von Eschenbach Chrétiens *Conte du Graal* kongenial ergänzt?' in *Arturus rex*, pp. 236–58; repr. in Dc24. (XL, pp. 333–34)

347 Haug, Walter, 'Über die Schwierigkeiten des Erzählens in "nachklassischer" Zeit,' in *Positionen*, pp. 338–65; repr. in Dc24. (XLIV.440)

348 Masser, Achim, '"Ir habt den künec Ascalon erslagen",' in *Festschrift Hoffmann*, pp. 183–204. (XLIV.455)

349 Matejovski, Dirk, 'Selbstmord: Rezeptionstypen eines tabuisierten Motivs,' in *Grenzen*, pp. 237–63.

350 Miklautsch, Lydia, *Studien zur Mutterrolle in den mittelhochdeutschen Großepen des zwölften und dreizehnten Jahrhunderts*, Erlanger Studien, 88 (Erlangen: Palm & Enke, 1991). (XLIV.459)
See 'Das Wunderschloßabenteuer bei Wolfram und Chrestien,' pp. 14–25, and 'Herzeloydes Tod und Parzivals Schuld,' pp. 69–75.

351 Pérennec, René, 'Les romans de Chrétien de Troyes vus à travers leurs adaptations allemandes,' in *Arturus rex*, pp. 230–35. (XL, pp. 353–54)

352 Rider, Jeff, 'De l'énigme à l'allégorie: l'adaptation du "merveilleux" de Chrétien de Troyes par Hartmann von Aue,' *Rom*, 112 (1991), 100–28. (XLVII.293)

353 Schmid, Elisabeth, 'Obilot als Frauengeber,' *GRM*, 41 (1991), 46–60. (XLIV.469)

354 Shitanda, So, 'Wissensrahmen und Handlungslogik in Chrétiens *Le Conte du Graal* und in Wolframs *Parzival*: kontrastive Textanalysen der kognitiven Strukturen in der höfischen Bearbeitung,' in *Begegnung mit dem Fremden: Grenzen, Traditionen, Vergleiche: Akten des VIII. Germanisten-Kongresses, Tokyo 1990*, ed. Eijiro Iwasaki and Yoshinori Schichiji, 11 vols (Munich: Iudicium, 1991), vol. 5, pp. 249–58. (XLV.391)

See Hf89 Wolf.

355 Kellermann, Karina, '"Exemplum" und "historia": zu poetologischen Traditionen in Hartmanns *Iwein*,' *GRM*, 42 (1992), 1–27. (XLV.45)

See Mc48 Mandach.

356 Oguri, Tomokazu, '*Gauvain et la pucelle aux Petites Manches* and *Gawan und Obilot*: On the Reception of Chrétien de Troyes by Wolfram von Eschenbach,' *SLCN*, 13:2, (1992), 3–15.
In Japanese.

357 Pastré, Jean-Marc, 'Les montures de Parzival: quatre images de la carrière du héros de Wolfram von Eschenbach,' in *Cheval*, pp. 385–99. (XLV.193)

358 Antonini, Lucia, 'Fâmurgân nell'Erec di Hartmann von Aue e i suoi legami con le divinità dell'"altro mondo" celtico,' in *Epica arturiana*, pp. 65–76. (XLVI.545)

See Fb83(B) Baudry.

359 Buschinger, Danielle, 'Hartmann von Aue, adapteur de Chrétien de Troyes,' in *Erec*, pp. 11–23. (XLVI.51)

360 *Chrétien de Troyes and the German Middle Ages: Papers from an International Symposium*, ed. Martin H. Jones and Roy Wisbey, AS,

26/Publications of the Institute of Germanic Studies, 53 (Cambridge: Brewer; London: Institute of Germanic Studies, 1993). (XLVI.456)

Contents:

A. 'Introduction,' pp. viI–xxi.

B. E. M. Meletinsky, 'L'œuvre de Chrétien de Troyes dans une perspective comparatiste,' pp.1–8. (XLVI.465)

C. Michael Batts, 'National Perspectives on Originality and Translation: Chrétien de Troyes and Hartmann von Aue,' pp. 9–18. (XLVI.414)

D. Silvia Ranawake, '*verligen* and *versitzen*: das Versäumnis des Helden und die Sünde der Trägheit in den Artusromanen Hartmanns von Aue,' pp. 19–35. (XLVI.478)

E. William Henry Jackson, 'Aspects of Knighthood in Hartmann's Adaptations of Chrétien's Romances and in the Social Context,' pp. 37–55. (XLVI.452)

F. Bernard Willson, 'The Heroine's Loyalty in Hartmann's and Chrétien's *Erec*,' pp. 57–65. (XLVI.497)

G. Karen Pratt, 'Adapting Enide: Chrétien, Hartmann, and the Female Reader,' pp. 67–84. (XLVI.477)

H. Martin H. Jones. 'Chrétien, Hartmann, and the Knight as Fighting Man: On Hartmann's Chivalric Adaptation of *Erec et Enide*,' pp. 85–109. (XLVI.455)

I. Daniel Rocher, '*Cligés* in Deutschland,' pp. 111–19. (XLVI.480)

J. Walter Blank, 'Zu den Schwierigkeiten der Lancelot-Rezeption in Deutschland,' pp. 121–36. (XLVI.416)

K. Klaus Grubmüller, 'Die Konzeption der Artusfigur bei Chrestien und in Ulrichs *Lanzelet*: Misverständnis, Kritik oder Selbständigkeit? Ein Diskussionsbeitrag,' pp. 137–49. (XLVI.446)

L. Tony Hunt, '*Iwein* and *Yvain*: Adapting the Love Theme,' pp. 151–63. (XLVI.448)

M. Wiebke Freytag, '*rehte güete* als wahrscheinlich *gewisse lêre*: topische Argumente für eine Schulmaxime in Hartmanns *Iwein*,' pp. 165–217. (XLVI.442)

N. Michael Curschmann, '*Der aventiure bilde nemen*: The Intellectual and Social Environment of the Iwein Murals at Rodenegg Castle,' pp. 219–27. (XLVI.427)

O. René Pérennec, 'Wolfram von Eschenbach vor dem *Conte du Graal*,' pp. 229–40. (XLVI.474)

P. Adrian Stevens, 'Heteroglossia and Clerical Narrative: On Wolfram's Adaptation of Chrétien,' pp. 241–55. (XLVI.490)

Q. Arthur Groos, 'Dialogic Transpositions: The Grail Hero Wins a Wife,' pp. 257–76. (XLVI.445)

R. Timothy McFarland, 'Clinschor: Wolfram's Adaptation of the *Conte du Graal*: The Schastel Marveile Episode,' pp. 277–94. (XLVI.462)

S. Jean-Marc Pastré, 'Versuch einer vergleichenden Ästhetik: die Kunst des Porträts bei Chrétien und einigen deutschen Bearbeitern des 12. und 13. Jahrhunderts,' pp. 295–309. (XLVI.472)

T.   Volker Honemann, '*Guillaume d'Angleterre*, *Gute Frau*, *Wilhelm von Wenden*: zur Beschäftigung mit dem Eustachius-Thema in Frankreich und Deutschland,' pp. 311–29.

361 Draesner, Ulrike, *Wege durch erzählte Welten: intertextuelle Verweise als Mittel der Bedeutungskonstitution in Wolframs 'Parzival'*, Mikrokosmos, 36 (Frankfurt/M.: P. Lang, 1993).

See La44 Florence.

362 Grassi, Sabrina, 'L'importanza della bellezza di Enite dell'*Erec* di Hartmann von Aue,' in *Epica arturiana*, pp. 77–84. (XLVI.561)

363 Knapp, Fritz Peter, 'Theorie und Praxis der Fiktionalität im nachklassischen deutschen Artusroman,' in *Fiktionalität*, pp. 160–70; repr. in Dc26. (XLVI.80).

364 Mertens, Volker, 'Enide-Enite: Projektionen weiblicher Identität bei Chrétien und Hartmann,' in *Erec*, pp. 61–74. (XLVI.85)

See Va18 Mertens.

365 Okken, Lambertus, *Kommentar zur Artusepik Hartmanns von Aue: im Anhang: Die Heilkunde und Der Ouroboros*, by Bernhard Dietrich Haage, APSL, 103 (Amsterdam: Rodopi, 1993). (XLVI.639)

366 Pastré, Jean-Marc, 'L'éducation et l'initiation d'un héros: le *Parzival* de Wolfram von Eschenbach,' in *Éducation*, pp. 359–68. (LII. 261)

367 Pastré, Jean-Marc, 'Erec, ou l'oubli des armes,' in *Erec*, pp. 89–100. (XLVI.95)

368 Pastré, Jean-Marc, 'La topologie d'un mythe: les lieux et leurs fonctions dans le *Perceval* de Chrétien et le *Parzival* de Wolfram von Eschenbach,' in *Provinces*, pp. 291–97. (XLVI.353)

369 Peeters, J., 'Cundrie *la surziere* en Malcreatiure: twee monsters uit Indië in de *Parzival* van Wolfram von Eschenbach,' *Millenium*, 7 (1993), 131–46. (XLVI.642)

370 Peil, Dietmar, 'Beobachtungen zur Kleidung in der Dichtung Hartmanns unter besonderer Berücksichtigung der Artus-Epen,' in *Les 'Realia' dans la littérature de fiction au Moyen Age: Actes du Colloque du Centre d'Etudes Médiévales de l'Université de Picardie-Jules Verne, Chantilly 1er–4 avril 1993*, ed. Danielle Buschinger and Wolfgang

Spiewok, WODAN 25: EG, 10–TS, 12 (Greifswald: Reineke, 1993), pp. 119–39. (XLVII.132)

371 Pérennec, René, 'Adaptation et société: l'adaptation par Hartmann von Aue du roman de Chrétien de Troyes, *Erec et Enide,*' in *Erec*, pp. 101–15. (XLVI.96)
Revision of Pb61.

372 Pol, Roberto De, *Der aventiure meine: proposte di approccio filologico a testi medievali* (Genoa: La Quercia, 1993).
See Chap. 2: '"Triuwe" e "dienst" nel *Parzival*: ipotesi sul pubblico di un romanzo cortese.'

373 Rocher, Daniel, 'Erec selbdritt?' in *Erec*, pp. 117–26. (XLVI.99)

374 Spiewok, Wolfgang, 'La composition de l'*Erec* chez Chrétien de Troyes et chez Hartmann von Aue,' in *Erec*, pp. 127–34. (XLVI.108)

375 Spiewok, Wolfgang, 'Zur Minneproblematik im "Lanzelet" des Ulrich von Zazikhoven,' in *Fiktionalität*, pp. 135–45. (XLVI.109)

376 Strasser, Ingrid, 'Fiktion und ihre Vermittlung in Hartmanns *Erec*-Roman,' in *Fiktionalität*, pp. 63–83 (XLVI.114).

377 Thomas, Heinz, 'Zeitgeschichtliche Komponenten in Chrétiens *Perceval* und Wolframs *Parzival,*' ZdP, 112 (1993), 420–26. (XLVI. 116)

See Gf37 Wolf.

See Ha176 Wyss.

See Hg93 Berchtold.

See Fb85 Bertau.

378 Buschinger, Danielle, 'La tradition du Graal en Allemagne au Moyen Age,' in *König Artus*, pp. 89–106. (XLVII.69)

379 Ertzdorff, Xenja von, 'Hartmann von Aue: Iwein und sein Löwe,' in *Ritter mit dem Löwen*, pp. 287–311. (XLVII.547)

See Ub43(B) Firestone.

380 Fourquet, Jean, 'Une adaptation singulièrement créatrice: le livre IX du *Parzival; Le Conte du Graal*, œuvre de commande,' in *Europäische Literaturen im Mittelalter: mélanges en l'honneur de Wolfgang Spiewok à* *l'occasion de son 65ᵉᵐᵉ anniversaire*, ed. Danielle Buschinger, WODAN: EG, 30–TS, 15 (Greifswald: Reineke, 1994), pp. 165–75. (XLVIII.91)

See Fe24 Green.

See Ja35 Grünkorn.

381 Haage, Bernhard Dietrich, 'Der Ritter Gawan als Wundarzt (*Parzival* 506, 5ff.),' in *Die Funktion außer- und innerliterarischer Faktoren für die Entstehung deutscher Literatur des Mittelalters und der frühen Neuzeit*, ed. Christa Baufeld, GAG, 603 (Göppingen: Kümmerle, 1994), pp. 193–216. (XLVII.96)

See Ha180 Haug.

382 Hirao, Kôzô, 'On the Development of Arthurian Romance (A Lecture),' *Goethe Jahrbuch* (Goethe-Gesellschaft in Japan), 36 (1994), 1–14. (XLVIII.589)
In Japanese.

383 Hurst, Peter William, 'Ênîte's Dominion over the Horses: Notes on the Coalescence of Platonic and Hagiographic Elements in an Episode from Hartmann's *Êrec*,' *MAe*, 73 (1994), 211–21. (XLVII.355)

384 Jackson, W. H., *Chivalry in Twelfth-Century Germany: The Works of Hartmann von Aue*, AS, 34 (Cambridge: Brewer, 1994). (XLVII.357)

385 Jones, Martin H., 'Changing Tact or Showing Tact? Erec's Self-Criticism on the Second Encounter with Guivreiz in Hartmann von Aue's *Erec*,' in *German Narrative Literature of the Twelfth and Thirteenth Centuries: Studies Presented to Roy Wisbey on his Sixty-Fifth Birthday*, ed. Volker Honemann [et alii] (Tübingen: Niemeyer, 1994), pp. 229–43. (XLVII.106)

See Qe25 Liebertz-Grün.

See Gc30 Pastré.

See Na.c105 Pastré.

386 Schmid, Elisabeth, 'Text über Texte: zur *Crône* des Heinrich von dem Türlîn,' *GRM*, 44 (1994), 266–87. (XLVII.137)

387 Thierry, Christophe, 'Wolfram von Eschenbach et l'héritage de Chrétien de Troyes: le Livre VIII du *Parzival*: composition numérique et adaptation,' in *König Artus*, pp. 217–55. (XLVII.147)

388 Wis, Marjatta, '*Mîn her, mîn vrou* gegenüber *Monsieur, Madame*: zur Verwendung des französischen Titels im Mittelhochdeutschen,' *NM*, 95 (1994), 147–66.

389 Wright, Aaron E., 'Hartmann and the Fable: *Erec* 9049ff.,' *PBB*, 116 (1994), 28–36. (XLVII.158)

See Gb124 Zanoner.

390 Buschinger, Danielle, 'Amour et chevalerie dans l'*Erec* et l'*Iwein* de Hartmann von Aue,' in *Amour Troyes*, pp. 313–25. (XLIX.135)

391 Buschinger, Danielle, 'L'inceste dans la littérature médiévale allemande,' in *Conformité et déviances au Moyen Age: Actes du Deuxième Colloque International de Montpellier Université Paul-Valéry (25–27 novembre 1993)*, Les Cahiers du CRISIMA, 2 (Montpellier: Université Paul-Valéry, Montpellier III, 1995), pp. 65–75. (XLVIII.280, LII.210)

392 Butzer, Günter, 'Das Gedächtnis des epischen Textes: mündliches und schriftliches Erzählen im höfischen Roman des Mittelalters,' *Euph*, 89 (1995), 151–88. (XLVIII.74)

See Hf97 Deist.

393 Feistner, Edith, '*er nimpt ez allez zeime spil*: der *Lanzelet* Ulrichs von Zatzikhofen als ironische Replik auf den Problemhelden des klassischen Artusromans,' *AStnSpr*, 232 (1995), 241–54. (XLVIII.87)

394 Groos, Arthur, *Romancing the Grail: Genre, Science, and the Quest in Wolfram's 'Parzival'* (Ithaca, NY: Cornell University Press, 1995).

395 Herzog, Urs, 'Ein geheimes anderes Bethlehem: zum Eingang von Hartmanns *Erec*,' in *Contemplata aliis tradere: Studien zum Verhältnis von Literatur und Spiritualität*, ed. Claudia Brinker, Urs Herzog, Niklaus Largier, and Paul Michel (Bern: P. Lang, 1995), pp. 217–23. (XLVIII.662)

396 Hoffmann, Werner, 'Die *vindaere wilder maere*,' *Euph*, 89 (1995), 129–50. (XLVIII.106)
Gottfried von Straßburg and Chrétien's *Charrette*.

397 Ichijô, Mamiko, 'God's Role in *Erec* and *Gregorius*,' *PFLT*, 43:1 (1995), 1–29. (XLIX. 366).
In Japanese.

See Ha191 Kasten.

398 Müller, Maria E., *Jungfräulichkeit in Versepen des 12. und 13. Jahrhunderts*, FGädL, 17 (Munich: Fink, 1995).

399 Pastré, Jean-Marc, 'Amour, mariage et chevalerie: structures littéraires et tripartition fonctionnelle dans le *Perceval* de Chrétien et le *Parzival* de Wolfram,' in *Amour Troyes*, pp. 305–11. (XLIX.177)

See Ge61 Pastré.

400 Pérennec, René, '*dâ heime niht erzogen* – Translation und Erzählstil: "Rezeptive Produktion" in Hartmanns *Erec*,' in *Interregionalität*, pp. 107–26.

401 Remakel, Michèle, *Rittertum zwischen Minne und Gral: Untersuchungen zum mittelhochdeutschen 'Prosa-Lancelot'*, Mikrokosmos, 432 (Frankfurt/M.: P. Lang, 1995). (XLVIII.139)

402 Ruberg, Uwe, 'Die Königskrönung Erecs bei Chrétien und Hartmann im Kontext arthurischer Erzählschlüsse,' *ZLiLi*, 99 (1995), 69–82. (XLVIII.144)

403 See, Geoffrey, '"Wes möhten si langer bîten?" Narrative Digressions in Hartmann von Aue's *Erec*,' *NM*, 96 (1995), 335–43.

404 Spiewok, Wolfgang, 'Discussion sur l'amour dans le *Parzival* de Wolfram von Eschenbach,' in *Amour Troyes*, pp. 289–304. (XLIX.189)

405 Volkmann, Berndt, '*Costumiers est de dire mal*: Überlegungen zur Funktion des Streites und zur Rolle Keies in der Pfingstfestszene in Hartmanns *Iwein*,' in *Festschrift Nellmann*, pp. 95–108. (XLVIII.168)

See Va21 Willaert.

See Gd.c58 Brunner.

406 Campbell, Ian R., 'An Act of Mercy: The Cadoc Episode in Hartmann von Aue's *Erec*,' *Monatshefte*, 88 (1996), 4–16.

407 Dallapiazza, Michael, 'Plippalinots Tochter,' *Prospero*, 3 (1996), 85–95.

408 Eikelmann, Manfred, '*Schanpfanzun*: zur Entstehung einer offenen Erzählwelt im *Parzival* Wolframs von Eschenbach,' *ZfdA*, 125 (1996), 245–63. (L.75)

409 Fisher, R. W., 'The Courtly Hero Comes to Germany: Hartmann's Erec and the Concept of Shame,' *ABäG*, 46 (1996), 119–30. (XLIX.397)

410 Hasty, Will, *Adventures in Interpretation: The Works of Hartmann von Aue and their Critical Reception*, Studies in German Literature, Linguistics and Culture: Literary Criticism in Perspective (Columbia, SC: Camden House, 1996). (XLIX.497)

411 Huber, Christoph, 'Ritterideologie und Gegnertötung: Über-legungen zu den *Erec*-Romanen Chrétiens und Hartmanns und zum *Prosa-Lancelot*,' in *Spannungen*, pp. 59–73.

412 Jones, Martin H., 'Schutzwaffen und Höfischheit: zu den Kampf-ausgängen im *Erec* Hartmanns von Aue,' in *Spannungen*, pp. 74–90.

413 Knapp, Fritz Peter, 'Der Gral zwischen Märchen und Legende,' *PBB*, 118 (1996), 49–68; repr. in Dc26. (XLIX.45)

414 Knapp, Fritz Peter, 'Von Gottes und der Menschen Wirklichkeit: Wolframs fromme Welterzählung *Parzival*,' *DVj*, 70 (1996), 351–68. (XLIX.46)

415 Kugler, Hartmut, 'Fenster zum Hof: die Binnenerzählung von der Entführung der Königin in Hartmanns *Iwein*,' in *Erzählungen in Erzählungen: Phänomene der Narration im Mittelalter und Früher Neu-zeit*, ed. Harald Haferland and Michael Mecklenburg, FGädL, 19 (Munich: Fink, 1996), pp. 115–24. (XLIX.47)

See Me36 Lutz.

416 McDonald, William C., 'King Arthur and the Round Table in the *Erec* and *Iwein* of Hartmann von Aue,' in *King Arthur: A Casebook*, ed. Edward Donald Kennedy, ACT, 1/GRLH, 1915 (New York: Garland, 1996), pp. 45–70.

417 Nellmann, Eberhard, 'Produktive Mißverständnisse: Wolfram als Übersetzer Chrétiens,' *W-S*, 14 (1996), 134–48. (L.101)

418 Nellmann, Eberhard, 'Zu Wolframs Bildung und zum Literatur-konzept des *Parzival*,' *Poetica*, 28 (1996), 327–44. (L.100)

See Ha197 Neugart.

419 Pastré, Jean-Marc, 'Terres d'exil et romans du Graal: le *Perceval* de Chrétien de Troyes et le *Parzival* de Wolfram von Eschenbach,' in *L'Exil*, ed. Alain Niderst, Actes et Colloques, 48 (Paris: Klincksieck, 1996), pp. 19–30.

See Sa144 Reil.

420 Schröder, Werner, *Irrungen und Wirrungen um den Text von Hartmanns 'Erec'*, AMainz 1996, 11 (Stuttgart: Steiner, 1996). (XLIX.61)

421 Spiewok, Wolfgang, 'Wolfram von Eschenbach, maître queux aux visages de Janus ou faim et abondance dans le *Parzival* de Wolfram von Eschenbach,' in Tb22 *Banquets*, pp. 479–92. (XLIX.190)

422 Wandhoff, Haiko, *Der epische Blick: eine mediengeschichtliche Studie zur höfischen Literatur*, PSQ, 141 (Berlin: Schmidt, 1996). (XLIX.69)
See Chap. 4:4.

423 Wandhoff, Haiko, 'Gefährliche Blicke und rettende Stimmen: eine audiovisuelle Choreographie von Minne und Ehe in Hartmanns *Erec*,' in *Aufführung*, pp. 170–89. (XLIX.68)

See Sa146 Wolf.

424 Clifton-Everest, John M., 'Wolfram und Statius: zum Namen "Antikonie" und zum VIII. Buch von *Parzival*,' *ZdP*, 116 (1997), 321–51. (L.72)

425 Dallapiazza, Michael, 'Antikonie, Bene, Obilot: immagini della donna in Wolfram e Chrétien,' in *Filologia Verona*, pp. 73–84. (LI.556)

426 Ehrismann, Otfrid, 'Jeschute, or, How to Arrange the Taming of a Hero: The Myth of Parzival from Chrétien to Adolf Muschg,' in *Medievalism in Europe II*, ed. Leslie J. Workman and Kathleen Verduin, StMed, 8 (Cambridge: Brewer, 1997), pp. 46–71. (LII.378)

427 Fuchs, Stephan, *Hybride Helden: Gwigalois und Willehalm. Beiträge zum Heldenbild und zur Poetik des Romans im frühen 13. Jahrhundert*, Frankfurter Beiträge zur Germanistik, 31 (Heidelberg: Winter, 1997). (L.76)

428 Gibbs, Marion E., and Sidney M. Johnson, *Medieval German Literature: A Companion*, GRLH, 1774 (New York: Garland, 1997). (LII.765)
See pp. 129–32.

See Fb97 Haupt.

429 Haymes, Edward R., 'The Sexual Stranger: The Sexual Quest in Wolfram's *Parzival*,' in *Stranger*, pp. 80–91.

430 Lynch, James A., 'Tapestries Viewed from Behind: *Parzival* as Intertext for *Don Quixote*,' *RLA*, 9 (1997), 588–92.

431 Margetts, John, '"*si enredete im niht vil mite*": einige Bemerkungen zum *Erec* Hartmanns von Aue,' in *Der fremdgewordene Text: Festschrift für Helmut Brackert zum 65. Geburtstag*, ed. Silvia Bovenschen [et alii] (Berlin: de Gruyter, 1997), pp. 11–23. (LI.94)

432 Pérennec, René, 'L'étude des adaptations allemandes d'œuvres narratives françaises (fin XIIe–début XIIIe siècle): un trait d'union entre les deux philologies?' in *Filologia Verona*, pp. 61–71. (LI.567)

433 Schröder, Werner, *Laudines Kniefall und der Schluß von Hartmanns 'Iwein'*, AMainz 1997, 2 (Mainz: Akademie der Wissenschaften und der Literatur, Stuttgart: Steiner, 1997). (LII.110)

434 Wand-Wittkowski, Christine, 'Die Zauberin Feimurgan in Hartmanns *Erec*: ein Beispiel für phantastisches Erzählen im Mittelalter,' *Fabula*, 38 (1997), 1–13. (L.112)
See p. 2 n. 4.

435 Wetzlmair, Wolfgang, *Zum Problem der Schuld im 'Erec' und im 'Gregorius' Hartmanns von Aue*, GAG, 643 (Göppingen: Kümmerle, 1997). (L.113)

See Db67 Zambon.

See Gd.c68 Bein.

436 Buschinger, Danielle, 'Le mythe de l'au-delà celtique dans le *Conte del Graal* de Chrétien de Troyes et le *Parzival* de Wolfram von Eschenbach,' in *Mélanges Demarolle*, pp. 295–311. (LI.225)

437 *Chevaliers errants, demoiselles et l'Autre: höfische und nach-höfische Literatur im europäischen Mittelalter: Festschrift für Xenja von Ertzdorff zum 65. Geburtstag*, ed. Trude Ehlert, GAG, 644 (Göppingen: Kümmerle, 1998). (LI.59)

    A. Monika Unzeitig-Herzog, 'Vom Sieg über den Drachen: alte und neue Helden,' pp. 41–61.
    B. Herta Zutt, 'Die unhöfische Lunete,' pp. 103–20. (LI.135)
    C. Michael Dallapiazza, 'Noch einmal: Fräulein Obilot,' pp. 121–30.
    D. Marianne Wynn, 'The Abduction of the Queen in German Arthurian Romance,' pp. 131–44. (LI.125)
    E. Ulrich Ernst, 'Liebe und Gewalt im *Parzival* Wolframs von Eschenbach: literaturpsychologische Befunde und mentalitäts-geschichtliche Begründungen,' pp. 215–43.

F.   Peter Kern, 'Text und Prätext: zur Erklärung einiger Unterschiede von Hartmanns *Iwein* gegenüber Chrétiens *Yvain*,' pp. 363–73. (LI.85)

438 Eikelmann, Manfred, 'Autorität und ethischer Diskurs: zur Verwendung von Sprichwort und Sentenz in Hartmanns von Aue *Iwein*,' in *Autor*, pp. 73–100.

439 Fisher, Rodney, 'Aspects of Madness in Hartmann's *Erec*,' *Seminar*, 34 (1998), 221–34.

440 Fritsch-Rößler, Waltraud, 'Motivgirlanden: zur Technik der Motiv-Verknüpfung in Hartmanns *Erec*,' *AStnSpr*, 235 (1998), 344–49. (LI.73)

See Cb12 Hörner.

See Gd.b58 James-Raoul.

441 *Kultureller Austausch und Literaturgeschichte im Mittelalter–Transferts culturels et histoire littéraire au Moyen Age: Kolloquium im Deutschen Historischen Institut Paris–Colloque tenu à l'Institut Historique Allemand de Paris 16.–18.3.1995*, ed. Ingrid Kasten, Werner Paravicini, and René Pérennec, Beihefte der Francia, 43 (Sigmaringen: Thorbecke, 1998).
On Chrétien, see:
A.   Walter Haug, 'Kulturgeschichte und Literaturgeschichte: einige grundsätzliche Überlegungen aus mediävistischer Sicht,' pp. 23–33.
B.   Thomas Heinz, 'Zum Wandel zeitgeschichtlicher Funktion romanischer Literatur bei ihrer Rezeption im deutschen Sprachraum: *Maurice de Craon/Moriz von Craûn* und *Perceval/Parzival*,' pp. 103–14. (LI.115)
C.   Ingrid Strasser, 'Übernahme von Literatur. Zwei Fallbespiele: Hartmanns *Erec* und *Der kluge Knecht* des Strickers,' pp. 185–99. (LI.112)
D.   Christoph Huber, 'Lachen im höfischen Roman: zu einigen komplexen Episoden im literarischen Transfer,' pp. 345–58. (LI.81)
See also Pe56 Winkelman.

See Ga97 Luttrell.

442 McDonald, William C., 'Wolfram's Grail,' *Arthuriana*, 8:1 (1998), 22–34. (LI.787)

443 Mertens, Volker, *Der deutsche Artusroman*, Universal-Bibliothek, 17609 (Stuttgart: Reclam, 1998). (LI.96)

444 Ridder, Klaus, 'Autorbilder und Werkbewußtsein im *Parzival* Wolframs von Eschenbach,' *W-S*, 15 (1998), 168–94.

445 Ridder, Klaus, 'Die Inszenierung des Autors im *Reinfried von Braunschweig*: Intertextualität im späthöfischen Roman,' in *Autor*, pp. 239–54.

446 Siewerts, Ute, '*sam das holz under der rinden, alsam sît ir verborgen*: Verborgenheit und Erkenntnis in Hartmanns *Iwein*,' in *Hartmann von Aue: mit einer Bibliographie 1976–1997*, ed. Petra Hörner, Information und Interpretation, 8 (Frankfurt/M.: P. Lang, 1998), pp. 91–122. (LII.112)

See Gd.b57(D) Touber.

447 Unzeitig-Herzog, Monika, '*Artus mediator*: zur Konfliktlösung in Wolframs *Parzival* Buch XIV,' *FMSt*, 32 (1998), 196–217.

448 Young, Christopher, 'The Character of the Individual in Hartmann von Aue's *Erec*,' *AL*, 16 (1998), 1–21. (L.413)

449 Althoff, Gerd, 'Spielen die Dichter mit den Spielregeln der Gesellschaft?' in *Hof und Kloster*, pp. 53–71. (LII.60)

450 Baisch, Martin, 'Orgeluse – Aspekte ihrer Konzeption in Wolframs von Eschenbach *Parzival*,' in *Schwierige Frauen*, pp. 15–33. (LI.52)

451 Dohi, Yumi, 'From Iwein to Daniel: The Genre-Specific Representation of King Arthur and His Knights in the Manner of Der Stricker,' *Plume*, 4 (1999), 50–60.
In Japanese.

See Ga101 Feistner.

452 Fritsch-Rößler, Waltraud, *Finis amoris: Ende, Gefährdung und Wandel von Liebe im hochmittelalterlichen deutschen Roman*, Mannheimer Beiträge zur Sprach- und Literaturwissenschaft, 42 (Tübingen: Narr, 1999). (LII.76)

453 Fritsch-Rößler, Waltraud, 'Zur Beziehung zwischen Hartmanns *Iwein* und *Erec*,' *GRM*, 49 (1999), 241–47. (LII.77)

454 Hasty, Will, ed., *A Companion to Wolfram's 'Parzival'*, Studies in German Literature, Linguistics, and Culture (Columbia, SC: Camden House, 1999). (LII.773)

See Hf105 Haug.

455 Heckel, Susanne, '"*die wîbes missewende vlôch*" (113, 12): Rezeption und Interpretation der Herzeloyde,' in *Schwierige Frauen*, pp. 35–52. (LI.77)

See Ha205(B) Meyer.

456 Nakamura, Yukari, 'On *Perceval, Parzival* und *Parsifal*,' *Bulletin of Musashino Academia Musicae*, 31 (1999), 35–52.
In Japanese.

See Uc54 Pastré.

457 Pastré, Jean-Marc, 'Logique narrative et cohérence mythique dans le dénouement du *Parzival* de Wolfram von Eschenbach,' *PRIS-MA*, 15 (1999), 125–35. (LII.263)

See Qa128 Peters.

458 Ridder, Klaus, 'Parzivals schmerzliche Erinnerung,' *ZLiLi*, 114 (1999), 21–41. (LII.102)

459 Schirok, Bernd, '*Ein Rîter, der gelêret was*: literaturtheoretische Aspekte in den Artusromanen Hartmanns von Aue,' in *Festschrift Schepp*, pp. 184–211. (LII.105)

See Db75 Schmid.

460 Steppich, Christoph J., 'Parzivals "Absage an die Freude" als Moment der Gralsuche,' *JEGP*, 98 (1999), 40–77.

461 Unzeitig-Herzog, Monika, 'Überlegungen zum Erzählschluß im Artusroman,' in *Erzählstrukturen*, pp. 233–53. (LII.117)

462 Wandhoff, Haiko, 'Iweins guter Name: zur medialen Konstruktion von adliger Ehre und Identität in den Artusromanen Hartmanns von Aue,' in *Mittelalter: neue Wege durch einen alten Kontinent*, ed. Jan-Dirk Müller and Horst Wenzel (Stuttgart: Hirzel, 1999), pp. 111–26. (LII.122)

See Ha205(C) Wild.

See Fa182 Wolf.

See Jd52 Ardizio Visconti.

463 *The Arthur of the Germans: The Arthurian Legend in Medieval German and Dutch Literature*, ed. W. H. Jackson and S. A. Ranawake (Cardiff: University of Wales Press, 2000). (LIII.449)
See esp.:
   A.   Ingrid Kasten, 'The Western Background,' pp. 21–37.
   B.   Silvia Ranawake, 'The Emergence of German Arthurian Romance: Hartmann von Aue and Ulrich von Zatzikhoven,' pp. 38–53.
   C.   Timothy McFarland, 'The Emergence of the German Grail Romance: Wolfram von Eschenbach, *Parzival*,' pp. 54–68.
   See also Pe60 Besamusca.

464 Dieterich, Barbara S., 'Das venushafte Erscheinungsbild der Orgeluse in Wolframs von Eschenbach *Parzival*,' *LJG*, 41 (2000), 9–65.

465 Galloway, Helen, '"Ich wil mich schuldic ergeben": The Inner Life and Penitential Practice in Hartmann's *Erec*,' *FMLS*, 36 (2000), 33–48.

466 Haug, Walter, '*Joie de la curt*,' in *Festschrift Johnson*, pp. 271–90. (LIII.77)

See Hb55 Haug.

467 Jones, Martin H., '*Durch schœnen list er sprach*: Empathy, Pretence, and Narrative Point of View in Hartmann von Aue's *Erec*,' in *Festschrift Johnson*, pp. 291–307. (LIII.85)

468 Kartschoke, Dieter, 'Erzählte Zeit in Versepen und Prosaromanen des Mittelalters und in der frühen Neuzeit,' *ZfG*, 10 (2000), 477–92.

See Gf51 Krass.

See Ha209(L) Rasmussen.

469 Nitsche, Barbara, 'Die literarische Signifikanz des Essens und Trinkens im *Parzival* Wolframs von Eschenbach: historisch-anthropologische Zugänge zur mittelalterlichen Literatur,' *Euph*, 94 (2000), 245–70.

470 Schulz-Grobert, Jürgen, '*Von quâdrestein geworhte...* Bautechnische "Detailrealismen" in Architekturphantasien der höfischen Epik?' *ZfdA*, 129 (2000), 275–95.

c: Celtic Literature

See Na.c31 San Marte.

See Pa38 Rochat.

See Pb69 Rauch.

See Na.g12 Golther.

2 Brown, Arthur C. L., 'On the Independent Character of the Welsh *Owain*,' *RR*, 3 (1912), 143–72.

See Na.d44 Mühlhausen.

See Na.e33 Jones.

3 Marx, Jean, 'Le cortège du Château des merveilles dans le roman gallois de Peredur,' *EtCelt*, 9 (1960–61), 92–105. (XIII.113)

4 Goetinck, Glenys W., 'Peredur a'r Dafnau Gwaed,' *LlC*, 7 (1962), 54–61. (XVIII.199)

5 Marx, Jean, 'Observations sur la structure du roman gallois de Peredur,' *EtCelt*, 10 (1962–63), 88–108. (XV.108)

6 Goetinck, Glenys Witchard, 'Sofraniaeth yn y Tair Rhamant,' *LlC*, 8 (1965), 168–82. (XX.148).

See Na.e34 *Owein*.

7 Thomson, R. L., ed., '*Iarlles y Ffynnon*: The Version in Llanstephan MS. 58,' *StC*, 6 (1971), 57–89. (XXIV.224)
Edition and translation of this late variant MS that includes the lion episodes, which the other late copies omit.

See Na.e35 Hunt.

See Na.a20 Bromwich.

See Na.e36 Hunt.

8 Goetinck, Glenys, *Peredur: A Study of Welsh Tradition in the Grail Legends* (Cardiff: University of Wales Press, 1975). (XXVIII.310)
See pp. 41–128.

See Na.e37 Pioletti.

See Hc24 Wolfzettel.

See Na.e38 Jones.

See Na.d52 Roberts.

See Na.e39 Lovecy.

See Nb16 Luttrell.

9 Pennar, Meirion, 'Tynghedfen Peredur,' *YB*, 11 (1979), 52–62. (XXXVII.182)

See Hg50 Pioletti.

See Gc10 De Caluwé-Dor.

See La28 Hunt.

10 Diverres, A. H., '*Iarlles y Ffynnawn* and *Le Chevalier au lion*: Adaptation or Common Source?' *StC*, 16–17 (1981–82), 144–62. (XXXVI.414)

11 Heffernan, Carol F., 'Combat at the Fountain: the Early Irish *Pursuit of the Gilla Decair* and the Old French *Yvain*,' *Éire-Ireland: A Journal of Irish Studies*, 17:4 (1982), 41–57.

12 Williams, Patricia, 'Y gwrthdaro rhwng serch a milwriaeth yn y Tair Rhamant,' *YB*, 12 (1982), 40–56. (XXXV.420)

See Na.e41 Edel.

13 Roberts, Brynley F., 'The Welsh Romance of the *Lady of the Fountain* (*Owein*),' in *Studies Diverres*, pp. 170–82, 250. (XXXVI.458)

See Na.e43 De Caluwé-Dor.

See Hg60 Pioletti.

14 McCann, W. J., 'Adeiledd y Tair Rhamant: Gereint, Owein, Peredur,' *YB*, 13 (1985), 123–33.

15 Rejhon, Annalee C., 'The "Mute Knight" and the "Knight of the Lion": Implications of the Hidden Name Motif in the Welsh *Historia Peredur vab Efrawc* and Chrétien de Troyes's *Yvain ou le Chevalier au lion*,' *StC*, 20–21 (1985–86), 110–22. (XL.133)

See Na.b28 Jones.

16 Lloyd-Morgan, Ceridwen, 'Perceval in Wales: Late Medieval Welsh Grail Traditions,' in *Essays Pickford*, pp. 78–91. (XXXIX.69)

17 Lloyd-Morgan, Ceridwen, 'Tradition et individualité dans le conte gallois d'*Owein*,' *PRIS-MA*, 3 (1987), 129–35.

See Hc54 Owen.

See Pa193 Coolput.

18 Goetinck, Glenys, '*Peredur*... Upon Reflection,' *EtCelt*, 25 (1988), 221–32. (XLII.58)

See Ga59 Gowans.

See Na.a35 Roberts.

See Na.a37(J) Lloyd-Morgan.

19 Lloyd-Morgan, Ceridwen, 'French Texts, Welsh Translators,' in *The Medieval Translator II*, ed. Roger Ellis, Westfield Publications in Medieval Studies, 5 (London: Centre for Medieval Studies, Queen Mary and Westfield College, University of London, 1991), pp. 45–63. (XLIV.111)

See Na.a37(I) Lovecy.

See Na.a37(G) Middleton.

See Na.a37(H) Thomson.

See Na.e47 Roberts.

See Ga78 Fulton.

20 Aronstein, Susan, 'When Arthur Held Court in Caer Llion: Love, Marriage, and the Politics of Centralization in Gereint and Owein,' *Viator*, 25 (1994), 215–28. (XLVII.674)

21 Brouland, Marie Thérèse, 'Peredur ab Efrawg,' in *Recueil Fourquet*, pp. 59–70. (XLVIII.67)

22 Lloyd-Morgan Ceridwen, 'Lancelot in Wales,' in *Festschrift Kennedy*, pp. 169–79. (XLVII.364)

See Hc72 Amor.

See Na.c108 Lambert.

23 Echard, Sian, 'Of Parody and Perceval: Middle Welsh and Middle English Manipulations of the Perceval Story,' *NMS*, 40 (1996), 63–79. (LI.365)

24   Edel, Doris, 'The "Mabinogionfrage": Arthurian Literature between Orality and Literacy,' in *(Re)Oralisierung*, ed. Hildegard L. C. Tristram, ScriptOralia, 84 (Tübingen: Narr, 1996), pp. 311–33. (LI.69, LII.71)

25   Oliver, Lisi, 'Spilled Wine and Lost Sovereignty in Chrétien's *Perceval*,' *NM*, 97 (1996), 91–102.

See Na.d61 *Ystorya*.

See Gd.c68 Bein.

See Na.e50 Jones.

See Ga97 Luttrell.

26   Lloyd-Morgan, Ceridwen, 'The Celtic Tradition,' in *The Arthur of the English: The Arthurian Legend in Medieval English Life and Literature*, ed. W. R. J. Barron, Arthurian Literature in the Middle Ages, 2 (Cardiff: University of Wales Press, 1999), pp. 1–9, 268–69. (LII.416)

27   Bollard, John K., 'Theme and Meaning in *Peredur*,' *Arthuriana*, 10:3 (2000), 73–92.

See Na.a54(E) Owen, 54(F) Lloyd-Morgan, and 54(G) Knight.

28   Lindahl, Carl, 'Yvain's Return to Wales,' *Arthuriana*, 10:3 (2000), 44–56.

29   Roberts, Brynley F., '*Peredur Son of Efrawg*: A Text in Transition,' *Arthuriana*, 10:3 (2000), 57–72.

d: English Literature

9   Steinbach, Paul, *Über den Einfluss des Crestien de Troies auf die altenglische Literatur*, diss. Leipzig (Leipzig: Metzger & Wittig, 1885).

10   Schleich, Gustav, *Über das Verhältnis der mittelenglischen Romanze Ywain and Gawain zu ihrer altfranzösischen Quelle*, Wissenschaftliche Beilage zum Programm des Andreas-Realgymnasiums zu Berlin, Ostern 1889: Programm Nr. 91 (Berlin: Gaertner, 1889).

See Na.g12 Golther.

See Na.c39 Wechssler, p. 143.

11   Weston, Jessie L., '*Ywain and Gawain* and *Le Chevalier au Lion,*' *Modern Quarterly of Language and Literature*, 1 (1898), 98–107, 194–202.

12   Maynadier, Howard, *The Arthur of the English Poets* (Boston: Houghton Mifflin, 1907).
See Chap. 5: 'Chrétien de Troies and the Romances.'

See Ga8 Strucks.

13   Griffith, Reginald Harvey, *Sir Perceval of Galles: A Study of the Sources of the Legend*, diss. Chicago (Chicago: University of Chicago Press, 1911).

14   Woods, George B., 'A Reclassification of the Perceval Romances,' *PMLA*, 27 (1912), 524–67.

See Wa15 Lowes.

15   Brown, Arthur C. L., 'The Grail and the English *Sir Perceval*,' *MP*, 16 (1919), 553–68; 17 (1919), 361–82; 18 (1920–21), 201–28 and (1921), 661–73; 22 (1924), 79–96 and 113–32.

16   Ven-Ten Bensel, Elise Francisca Wilhelmina van der, *The Character of King Arthur in English Literature* (Amsterdam: H. J. Paris, 1925; repr. New York: Haskell House, 1966).

17   App, August J., *Lancelot in English Literature: His Rôle and Character*, diss. Catholic University of America (Washington, DC: Catholic University of America, 1929).

See Ba6 Ketrick.

18   Renoir, Alain, 'Gawain and Parzival,' *SN*, 31 (1959), 155–58.

19   Friedman, Albert B., and Norman T. Harrington, ed., *Ywain and Gawain*, Early English Text Society: Original Series, 254 (London: Oxford University Press, 1964).
See Chap. 3: 'Relation to Chrétien's *Yvain, le Chevalier au lion*.'

20   Shimizu, Aya, *A Study of the Medieval Arthurian Legends* (Tokyo: Kenkyûsha-shuppan, 1966). (L.367).
In Japanese.

21   Baugh, Albert C., 'The Middle English Romance: Some Questions of Creation, Presentation, and Preservation,' *Spec*, 42 (1967), 1–31. (XX.48)

22 Mehl, Dieter, *Die mittelenglischen Romanzen des 13. und 14. Jahrhunderts*, Anglistische Forschungen, 93 (Heidelberg: Winter, 1967). English trans.: *The Middle English Romances of the Thirteenth and Fourteenth Centuries* (London: Routledge & Kegan Paul, 1967 [1969]). (XXII.166)

23 Finlayson, John, '*Ywain and Gawain* and the Meaning of Adventure,' *Anglia*, 87 (1969), 312–37. (XXII.9)

24 Harrington, Norman T., 'The Problem of Lacunae in *Ywain and Gawain*,' *JEGP*, 69 (1970), 659–65. (XXIII.43)

25 Baron, F. Xavier, 'Mother and Son in *Sir Perceval of Galles*,' *PLL*, 8 (1972), 3–14. (XXIV.50)

26 Eckhardt, Caroline D., 'Arthurian Comedy: The Simpleton-Hero in *Sir Perceval of Galles*,' *ChauR*, 8 (1973–74), 205–20. (XXVII.9)

27 Pearcy, Roy J., 'Chaucer's Franklin and the Literary Vavasour,' *ChauR*, 8 (1973–74), 33–59. (XXVII.26)

28 Barron, W. R. J., '*Golagrus and Gawain*: A Creative Redaction,' *BBSIA*, 26 (1974), 173–85. (XXVII.278)
Based on 'Chastel Orguelleus' in the *Conte du Graal*.

29 Brewer, D. S., 'Chaucer and Chrétien and Arthurian Romance,' in *Chaucer and Middle English Studies in Honour of Rossell Hope Robbins* (London: Allen & Unwin, 1974), pp. 255–59. (XXVIII.300)

See Ga14 Barnett.

30 Fowler, David C., '*Le Conte du Graal* and *Sir Perceval of Galles*,' *CLS*, 12 (1975), 5–20. (XXVIII.124)

31 Hexter, Ralph J., *Equivocal Oaths and Ordeals in Medieval Literature,* The LeBaron Russell Briggs Prize Honors Essays in English 1974 (Cambridge, MA: Harvard University Press, 1975). Treats the *Charrette*, pp. 37–44.

32 Hamilton, Gayle J., 'The Breaking of the Troth in *Ywain and Gawain*,' *Mediaevalia*, 2 (1976), 111–35. (XXXII.184)

33 Robbins, Rossell Hope, 'The Vintner's Son: French Wine in English Bottles,' in *Eleanor*, pp. 147–72.

34 Strohm, Paul, 'The Origin and Meaning of Middle English *Romaunce*,' *Genre*, 10 (1977), 1–28. See pp. 3–5.

35 Busby, Keith, '*Sir Perceval of Galles*, *Le Conte du Graal* and *La Continuation-Gauvain*: The Methods of an English Adaptor,' *EtAngl*, 31 (1978), 198–202.

36 Barron, W. R. J., 'Arthurian Romance: Traces of an English Tradition,' *English Studies*, 61 (1980), 2–23. (XXXIV.492)

37 Finlayson, John, 'Definitions of Middle English Romance,' *ChauR*, 15 (1980), 44–62 and 168–81. (XXXIV.118)

38 Jesmok, Janet, 'Malory's "Knight of the Cart",' *MichA*, 13 (1980–81), 107–15. (XXXIII.151)

See Gc10 De Caluwé-Dor.

See La28 Hunt.

39 Veldhoen, N. H. G. H., 'I Haffe Spedde Better þan I Wend: Some Notes on the Structure of the M. E. *Sir Perceval of Galles*,' *Dutch Quarterly Review of Anglo-American Letters*, 11 (1981), 279–86.

40 Barron, W. R. J., 'Alliterative Romance and the French Tradition,' in *Middle English Alliterative Poetry and its Literary Background*, ed. David Lawton (Cambridge: Brewer, 1982), pp. 70–87. (XXXV.375)
See pp. 83–85 on *Perceval* and *Golagrus and Gawain*.

41 Hamel, Mary, 'The *Franklin's Tale* and Chrétien de Troyes,' *ChauR*, 17 (1982–83), 316–31. (XXXVII.385)

See Ga35 Brewer.

42 Dean, Christopher, 'Sir Kay in Medieval English Romances: An Alternative Tradition,' *ESC*, 9 (1983), 125–35. (XXXVII.360)

43 Fichte, Jörg O., 'The Middle English Arthurian Romance: The Popular Tradition in the Fourteenth Century,' in *Literature in Fourteenth-Century England: The J. A. W. Bennett Memorial Lectures, Perugia, 1981–1982*, ed. Piero Boitani and Anna Torti, Tübinger Beihefte zur Anglistik, 5 (Tübingen: Narr; Cambridge: Brewer, 1983), pp. 137–53. (XXXVI.35)

44 Pickering, James D., 'Malory's *Morte Darthur*: The Shape of Tragedy,' *FCS*, 7 (1983), 307–28. (XXXVII.440)

45 Ramsey, Lee C., *Chivalric Romances: Popular Literature in Medieval England* (Bloomington: Indiana University Press, 1983). (XXXVII.444)

46 Bergner, Heinz, 'Gauvain dans la littérature anglaise du Moyen Age,' in *Lancelot Wégimont*, pp. 141–55. (XXXVIII.186)

47 Bergner, Heinz, 'Gawain und seine literarischen Realisationen in der englischen Literatur des Spätmittelalters,' in *Artusrittertum*, pp. 3–15. (XXXVII.576)

See Na.e43 De Caluwé-Dor.

48 Fichte, Jörg O., 'Geschichte wird Geschichte: Überlegungen zum Realitätsbezug der homiletischen Artusromanze,' in *Artusliteratur*, pp. 69–83. (XXXVII.604)

See Hf55 Hunt.

See Ga48 Schopf.

49 Praga, Inés, 'Romances medievales ingleses,' in *Estudios literarios ingleses: Edad Media*, ed. J. F. Galván Reula, Crítica y Estudios Literarios (Madrid: Cátedra, for the Instituto de Estudios Ingleses, 1985), pp. 237–52.

50 Reiss, Edmund, 'Romance,' in *The Popular Literature of Medieval England*, ed. Thomas J. Heffernan, Tennessee Studies in Literature, 28 (Knoxville: University of Tennessee Press, 1985), pp. 108–30. (XXXIX.304)

51 Bennett, J. A. W., and Douglas Gray, *Middle English Literature*, in *The Oxford History of English Literature*, vol. 1:2 (Oxford: Clarendon Press, 1986). (XL.99)
See Chap. 5: iv (pp. 170–87).

52 Crane, Susan, *Insular Romance: Politics, Faith, and Culture in Anglo-Norman and Middle English Literature* (Berkeley: University of California Press, 1986). (XXXIX.240)

53 Jost, Jean E., *Ten Middle English Arthurian Romances: A Reference Guide* (Boston: Hull, 1986). (XXXIX.286)
Includes *Sir Percyvelle of Galles* (pp. 65–77) and *Ywain and Gawain* (pp. 77–85).

54 Lyons, Faith, 'Malory's *Tale of Sir Gareth* and French Arthurian Tradition,' in *Essays Pickford*, pp. 137–47. (XXXIX.71)

55 Barron, W. R. J., *English Medieval Romance*, Longman's Literature in English Series (London: Longman, 1987). (XL.98)

56   Busby, Keith, 'Chrétien de Troyes English'd,' *Neophil*, 71 (1987), 596–613. (XLII.183)

See Md38 Patterson.

57   Rice, Joanne A., *Middle English Romance: An Annotated Bibliography, 1955–85*, GRLH, 545 (New York: Garland, 1987). (XLI.434)

See: 'Arthurian Literature' (pp. 85–114), 'Influence Studies' (pp. 135–39), '*Sir Cleges*' (pp. 407–08), '*Sir Perceval of Galles*' (pp. 503–06), and '*Ywain and Gawain*' (pp. 547–52).

58   Barron, W. R. J., 'Chrétien and the *Gawain*-Poet: Master and Pupil or Twin Temperaments?' in *Legacy*, vol. 2, pp. 255–84. (XLII.162)

See Pa193 Coolput.

See Gd.b36 Botterill.

59   Ikegami, Tadahiro, *Gawain and the Arthurian Legend* (Tokyo: Shûbun International, 1988). (XLI. 305).
In Japanese.

See Gc18 Weiss.

See Ha147 Wilson.
On *Ywain and Gawain*.

60   Eckhardt, Caroline D., 'Chaucer's Franklin and Others of the Vavasour Family,' *MP*, 87 (1990), 239–48. (XLIII.529)

61   Fichte, Joerg Otto, 'Arthurische und nicht-arthurische Texte im Gespräch, dargestellt am Beispiel der mittelenglischen Romanze *Sir Perceval of Galles*,' in *Artusroman*, pp. 19–34. (XLIII.23)

62   Gosman, Martin, 'The French Background,' in *Companion to Middle English Romance*, ed. Henk Aertsen and Alasdair A. MacDonald (Amsterdam: VU University Press, 1990), pp. 1–27. (XLIV.257)

63   Dirscherl, Ulrike, *Ritterliche Ideale in Chrétiens 'Yvain' und im mittelenglischen 'Ywain and Gawain': von 'amour courtois' zu 'trew luf', vom 'frans chevaliers deboneire' zum 'man of mekyl myght'*, Sprache und Literatur: Regensburger Arbeiten zur Anglistik und Amerikanistik, 33 (Frankfurt/M.: P. Lang, 1991). (XLIV.428)

64   Field, P. J. C., 'Malory and Chrétien de Troyes,' *RMS*, 17 (1991), 19–30 (XLIV.99); repr. in his *Malory: Texts and Sources*, AS, 40 (Cambridge: Brewer, 1998), pp. 236–45. (LI.368)

65   Matthews, David, 'Translation and Ideology: The Case of *Ywain and Gawain*,' *Neophil*, 76 (1992), 452–63. (XLV.419)

66   Wilson, Anne D., 'The Critic and the Use of Magic in Narrative,' *Yearbook of English Studies*, 22 (1992), 81–94. (XLV.277)

67   Dallapiazza, Michael, 'Zur Sprache der Gewalt im mittelenglischen *Sir Perceval of Gales*,' in *Epica arturiana*, pp. 7–25. (XLVI.556)

68   Pheifer, J. D., 'Malory's Lancelot,' in *Noble and Joyous Histories: English Romances, 1375–1650*, ed. Eiléan Ní Cuilleanáin and J. D. Pheifer (Dublin: Irish Academic Press, 1993), pp. 157–93. (XLVI.475)

69   Bergner, Heinz, 'Chrétiens Löwenritter und der mittelenglische *Ywain and Gawain*,' in *Ritter mit dem Löwen*, pp. 369–81. (XLVII.524)

70   Bollard, John K., '*Hende Wordes*: The Theme of Courtesy in *Ywain and Gawain*,' *Neophil*, 78 (1994), 655–70. (XLVII.530)

71   Calin, William, *The French Tradition and the Literature of Medieval England*, University of Toronto Romance Series (Toronto: University of Toronto Press, 1994).

72   Crépin, André, 'La fine construction de *The Romance off Sir Percyvelle of Gales*,' in *Recueil Fourquet*, pp. 79–87. (XLVIII.83)

73   Wallace, Joy, 'Transposing the Enterprise of Adventure: Malory's "Take the Adventure" and French Tradition,' in *Festschrift Kennedy*, pp. 151–67. (XLVII.389)

74   Calf, Berenice-Eve S., 'The Middle English *Ywain and Gawain*: A Bibliography, 1777–1995,' *Parergon*, 13:1 (1995), 1–24.

75   Putter, Ad, *'Sir Gawain and the Green Knight' and French Arthurian Romance* (Oxford: Oxford University Press, 1995). (XLVIII.434)

See Pc23 Echard.

See Pk72(H) Marigny.

76   Bidard, Josseline, and Arlette Sancery, *L'Angleterre et les légendes arthuriennes*, Lectures en Sorbonne, 7 (Paris: Presses de l'Université de Paris-Sorbonne, 1997). (L.181)
Pp. 49–58.

77   *A Companion to the 'Gawain'-Poet*, ed. Derek Brewer and Jonathan Gibson, AS, 38 (Cambridge: Brewer, 1997). (L.276)
Comparisons with Chrétien's romances in various articles; see Index s.v. 'Chrétien de Troyes.'

78   Crane, Susan, 'Knights in Disguise: Identity and Incognito in Fourteenth-Century Chivalry,' in *Stranger*, pp. 63–79.

79   Barnes, Geraldine, 'The Age of Innocence: Childhood and Chastity in Some Middle English Romances,' in Pb437 *Chevaliers errants*, pp. 293–315.

See Ga97 Luttrell.

80   Yoshida, Mizuho, 'A Study of the Grail Quest in Malory,' *JHum*, 2 (1998), 1–24. (LI.677).

81   Batt, Catherine, and Rosalind Field, 'The Romance Tradition,' in *The Arthur of the English: The Arthurian Legend in Medieval English Life and Literature*, ed. W. R. J. Barron, Arthurian Literature in the Middle Ages, 2 (Cardiff: University of Wales Press, 1999), pp. 59–70, 294–98. (LII.345)

82   Mills, Maldwyn, Elizabeth Williams, Flora Alexander, Rosamund Allen, and W. R. J. Barron, 'Chivalric Romance,' in *The Arthur of the English: The Arthurian Legend in Medieval English Life and Literature*, ed. W. R. J. Barron, Arthurian Literature in the Middle Ages, 2 (Cardiff: University of Wales Press, 1999), pp. 113–83, 313–44. (LII.432)

83   Shôji, Kuniko, 'The Art of the *Ywain* Poet,' *Plume*, 3 (1999), 34–41.
In Japanese.

See Qb82 Takamiya.

84   Yoshida, Mizuho, 'Percival in Malory – The Knight of the Holy Grail,' *Plume*, 4 (1999), 82–89.
In Japanese.

See Ha209(G) Kaeuper, 209(J) Fisher, 209(N) Hahn, and 209(O) Riddy.

e: Dutch and Flemish Literature

1 Fuehrer, Sister M. R., *A Study of the Relation* [...]; repr. New York: AMS Press, 1970.

3 Veerdeghem, F. van, 'Een paar fragmenten van den Roman van Perchevael,' *Académie Royale de Belgique: Bulletins de l'Académie Royale des Sciences, des Lettres et des Beaux-Arts de Belgique*, 3rd ser., 20 (1890), 637–88.
'Rapports' by Pierre Willems (pp. 630–32), L. Roersch (pp. 632–36), and J. Stecher (p. 636).

See Na.c39 Wechssler, pp. 143–45.

4 Draak, A. M. E., 'The Second Part of the Dutch *Ferguut* and its French Sources,' *Neophil*, 19 (1934), 107–11; repr. in *Arturistiek*, pp. 89–93.

5 Mierlo, J. van, 'Oorspronkelijk Dietse Arthur-literatuur in de twaalfde eeuw ook voorbeeld van Franse,' *Koninklijke Vlaamse Academie voor Taal- en Letterkunde: Verslagen en mededelingen* (1956), pp. 177–212; repr. in *Arturistiek*, pp. 13–48.
French resumé.

See Pa71 Lee.

6 *Asselbergs, W. J. M. A., 'Ferguut,' *SpL*, 8 (1964), 1–9; repr. in *Nijmeegse colleges*, Zwolse reeks van taal- en letterkundige studies, 19 (Zwolle: Tjeenk Willinke, 1967), pp. 34–42; and in *Arturistiek*, pp. 95–103.

See Pb140 Zatočil.

7 Draak, Maartje, 'Een onbekend Praags Perchevael-fragment,' *NTg*, 62 (1969), 175–76. (XXII.232)
On Pb140 Zatočil.

8 Spahr, Blake Lee, 'Ferguut, Fergus, and Chrétien de Troyes,' in *Traditions and Transitions: Studies in Honor of Harold Jantz* (Baltimore: Department of German, Johns Hopkins University; Munich: Delp, 1972), pp. 29–36; repr. in *Arturistiek*, pp. 129–36.

See Pb156 Cometta, pp. 342–43 and 347–49.

9 Joye, M., 'De Middelnederlandse graalromans: overzicht en enkele vaststellingen,' *Leuvense Bijdragen*, 63 (1974), 151–64; repr. in *Arturistiek*, pp. 209–22. (XXVII.100)

10 De Haan, M. J. M., 'Is Ferguut's geluk spreekwoordelijk?' in *Gastenboek van Es*, pp. 211–17. (XXVIII.475)

11 Draak, A. M. E., *Onderzoekingen over de Roman van Walewein (met aanvullend hoofdstuk over 'Het Walewein onderzoek sinds 1936')* (Groningen: Bouma; Amsterdam: Hagen, 1975). (XXVIII.473)

12 Kazemier, G., 'Lanseloet van Denemerken,' in *Gastenboek van Es*, pp. 229–36. (XXVIII.477)

13 Kazemier, G., 'Der Dichter des mittelniederländischen *Lanseloet van Denemerken* und seine Quellen,' in *Akten des V. Internationalen Germanisten-Kongresses Cambridge 1975*, 4 vols, Jahrbuch für Internationale Germanistik. Reihe A: Kongreßberichte, 2 (Bern: H. Lang; Frankfurt/M: P. Lang, 1976), pp. 389–95.

14 Janssens, J. D., 'De *Fergus* en de *Ferguut*: Marginalia bij de nieuwe *Ferguut*-editie,' *SpL*, 19 (1977), 280–88. (XXX.480)

15 Oostrom, F. P. van, 'Een curieus type kopiistenfout: de associatieve verwisseling van persoonsnamen,' *SpL*, 20 (1978), 187–90.

See Pa103 De Paepe.

16 Janssens, J. D., 'Nieuwe en oude wegen binnen de Middelnederlandse arturistiek,' *Handelingen der Koninklijke Zuidnederlandse Maatschappij voor Taal- en Letterkunde: geschiedenis*, 35 (1981), 177–86. (XXXV.246)

17 Besamusca, Bart, 'Ende Walewein, een ridder van prise: de bewerker van de *Ferguut* en de Middelnederlandse Arturroman,' *SpL*, 24 (1982), 225–29. (XXXVI.285)

18 Janssens, J. D., 'Oude en nieuwe wegen in "het woud zonder gnade" (terreinverkenning voor verder onderzoek van de Mnl. niet-historische Arturroman),' *NTg*, 75 (1982), 291–312. (XXXV.535)

See Fa118 Willaert.

19 Hogenhout-Mulder, Maaike Janna, *Proeven van tekstkritiek: een onderzoek betreffende de tekstgeschiedenis van de 'Renout van Montalbaen' en de 'Perceval'* (Groningen: Rijksuniversiteit Groningen, 1984). (XXXVIII.686)

20 Besamusca, Bart, *Repertorium van de Middelnederlandse Arturepiek: een beknopte Beschrijving van de handschriftlijke en gedrukte overlevering* (Utrecht: HES, 1985). (XXXVIII.673)

21 Janssens, J. D., ed., *Koning Artur in de Nederlanden: Middelnederlandse Artur- en Graalromans* (Utrecht: HES, 1985). (XXXVIII.664)
See pp. 18–21.

See Eb14 Janssens.

22 Stufkens, R. D. H., '*Perchevael*: de rode ridder,' *Bzzletin*, 124 (March 1985), pp. 58–63. (XXXVIII.702)

23 Gumbert, J. P., 'Le corpus du moyen-néerlandais ancien,' *Scriptorium*, 40 (1986), 126–28. (XXXIX.4)

24 *Arturus rex.* Vol. 1: *Catalogus: Koning Artur en de Nederlanden – La matière de Bretagne et les anciens Pays-Bas: Exposition Organisée au Musée Municipal L. Vander Kelen-Mertens à Leuven du 25 juillet au 25 octobre 1987*, ed. Werner Verbeke, Jozef Janssens, and Maurits Smeyers, MedL: Studia, 16 (Leuven: Leuven University Press, 1987), with 24 illustrations. (XL.5)
Contains:
- A. Jozef Janssens, 'Koning Artur en de Tafelrunde,' pp. 1–102.
- B. Jozef Janssens, 'Artushof in de Nederlanden,' pp. 103–43.
- C. Gilbert Tournoy, 'De latijnse Artur en de Nederlanden,' pp.145–88.
- D. Willy Van Hoecke, 'La littérature française d'inspiration arthurienne dans les anciens Pays-Bas,' pp. 189–260.
- E. Jozef Janssens, 'De middelnederlandse Arturroman,' pp. 261–300.
- F. Jozef Janssens, 'Het naleven van Koning Artur,' pp. 303–10, and Michèle Goyens, 'La survivance de la matière arthurienne,' pp. 310–22.

Vol. 2 contains the proceedings of the 1987 Congress of the International Arthurian Society; the articles in the Proceedings that treat Chrétien are listed in the appropriate places in this Bibliography.
See also P. Avonds, *Koning Artur in Brabant (12de–14de eeuw): Studies over riddercultuur en vorstenideologie*, Verhandelingen van de Koninklijke Vlaamse Academie van België voor Wetenschappen en Kunsten: Klasse der Letteren, 61:167 (Brussels: Paleis der Akademiën, 1999).

25 Berg, E. van den, 'Genre en gewest: de geografische spreiding van de ridderepiek,' *TNTL*, 103 (1987), 1–36. (XLII.165)

26 Janssens, J. D., 'The Influence of Chrétien de Troyes on Middle Dutch Arthurian Romances: A New Approach,' in *Legacy*, vol. 2, pp. 285–306. (XLII.211)

See Pa193 Coolput.

27 Gerritsen, W.P., 'Vertalingen van Oudfranse litteraire werken in het Middelnederlands,' in *Franse Literatuur van de middeleeuwen*, ed. R. E. V. Stuip (Muiderberg: Coutinho, 1988), pp. 184–207. (XLII.199)

See Ha144 Janssens.

28 Kienhorst, Hans, *De hantschriften van de Middelnederlandse ridderepiek: een codicologische beschrijving*, Deventer Studiën, 9, 2 vols (Deventer: *Sub Rosa*, 1988). (XLII.214)

29 Zemel, R. M. T., 'Het vergeten vergrijp van Galiene,' *Spektator*, 18 (1988–89), 262–82. (XLII.247)

30 Duijvestijn, Bob W. Th., 'Middelnederlandse literatuur in Duitse overlevering: een arbeidsveld voor neerlandici,' in *Symposium Antwerpen*, pp. 153–68 (with report on discussion by Margreet Rierink). (XLII.192)

31 Gijsen, Johanna Elisabeth van, *Liefde, kosmos en verbeelding: mens- en wereldbeeld in Colijn van Rijsseles 'Spiegel der Minnen'* (Groningen: Wolters-Noordhoff/Forsten, 1989). (XLII.201)
Chrétien, esp. *Yvain*, as source; see pp. 41–43, 247–53. English summary pp. 263–66.

32 Hage, A. L. H., *Sonder favele, sonder lieghen: Onderzoek naar vorm en functie van de Middelnederlandse rijmkroniek als historiografisch genre*, Historische Studies, 48 / Bijdragen van het Instituut voor Middeleeuwse Geschiedenis, 49 (Groningen: Wolters-Noordhoff/Forsten, 1989). (XLII.204)

33 Janssens, J. D., 'De Middelnederlandse, "niet-historische" Arturroman: vertaling of oorspronkelijke schepping?' in *Symposium Antwerpen*, pp. 121–34 (with report on discussion by Veerle Uyttersprot); see also Pe38. (XLII.212)

34 Kossen, Wilma, 'Moriaen en de Graalheld,' in *Opstellen Schenkeveld*, pp. 95–108. (XLII.218)

35 Smith, Simon, 'Van koning tot kroonprins: over de structuur van de *Roman van den riddere metter mouwen*,' in *Opstellen Schenkeveld*, pp. 109–41. (XLII.237)

36 Winkelman, J. H., 'Eschatologie als dieptestruktuur: over oorsprong en interpretatie van de oudfranse Florisroman en zijn Middelnederlandse bewerkingen,' in *Symposium Antwerpen*, pp. 135–51. (XLII. 243)

37 Zemel, Roel, 'Fergus, Ferguut en de Graalheld,' in *Opstellen Schenkeveld*, pp. 75–94. (XLII.245)

See Ga69 Brugger-Hackett.

38 Janssens, Jozef D., 'Le roman arthurien "non historique" en moyen néerlandais: traduction ou création originale?' in *Arturus rex*, pp. 330–51.

39 Zemel, R. M. T., *Op zoek naar Galiene: over de Oudfranse 'Fergus' en de middelnederlandse 'Ferguut'*, Thesaurus, 3 (Amsterdam: Schiphouwer en Brinkman, 1991), vol. 1. (XLIV.275)
French resumé pp. 357–67.

40 *De ongevalliche Lanceloet: Studies over de 'Lancelotcompilatie'*, ed. Bart Besamusca and Frank Brandsma, MSB, 28 (Hilversum: Verloren, 1992). (XLV.399)
See Bart Besamusca and W. P. Gerritsen, 'De Studie van de *Lanceloet-compilatie*,' pp. 9–21. (XLV.400)

41 Besamusca, Bart, *Walewein, Moriaen en de Ridder metter mouwen: intertekstualiteit in drie Middelnederlandse Arturromans*, MSB, 39 (Hilversum: Verloren, 1993). (XLVI.619)

42 Zemel, R. M. T., 'Ene behagele coninginne: over de heldin van de *Ferguut* en haar voorgangsters,' *Spektator*, 22 (1993), 181–97. (XLVI.652)

43 Besamusca, Bart, 'Die Rezeption von Chrétiens *Yvain* in den Niederlanden,' in *Ritter mit dem Löwen*, pp. 353–68. (XLVII.529)

44 Hogenbirk, Marjolein, '"Die coenste die ie werd geboren": over *Walewein ende Keye*,' *NTg*, 87 (1994), 57–75. (XLVII.558)

45 Lie, Orlanda S. H., 'What Is Truth? The Verse-Prose Debate in Medieval Dutch Literature,' *Queeste*, 1 (1994), 34–65. (XLVII.571)

46 *Medieval Dutch Literature in Its European Context*, ed. Erik Kooper, CSML, 21 (Cambridge: Cambridge University Press, 1994).
    A.   Bart Besamusca and Orlanda S. H. Lie, 'The Prologue to *Arturs doet*, the Middle Dutch Translation of *La Mort le Roi Artu* in the *Lancelot Compilation*,' pp. 96–112. (XLVII.336)

B.   J. D. Janssens, 'The *Roman van Walewein*, an Episodic Arthurian Romance,' pp. 113–28. (XLVII.358)

47   Winkelman, J. H., 'In margine: Lanceloet in de problemen: opmerkingen bij een recentelijk verschenen boek,' *SpL*, 36 (1994), 181–207. (XLIX.9)
On Pe40 De ongevelliche.

See Pa273 Brandsma.

48   Janssens, J. D., 'Een geschiedenis van de Middelnederlandse epiek. Van publiek naar dichter: terug naar af...?' in *Grote Lijnen*, pp. 83–98, 193–200. (XLVIII.627)

See Ba28 Klein.

49   Sonnemans, Gerard, *Functionele aspecten van Middelnederlandse versprologen* (Boxmeer: G. Sonnemans, 1995). (XLVIII.645)

See Va21 Willaert.

50   Besamusca, Bart, 'Lancelot and Guinevere in the Middle Dutch *Lancelot* Compilation,' in Ga 91 *Lancelot*, pp. 105–24.

51   *De kunst van het zoeken: studies over 'aventuur' en 'queeste' in de middeleeuwse literatuur*, ed. Bart Besamusca and Frank Brandsma, Uitgaven Stichting Neerlandistiek VU, 22 (Amsterdam: Stichting Neerlandistiek VU Amsterdam, Münster: Nodus, 1996).
The following articles treat Chrétien:
   A.   Frank Brandsma, 'Avonturen: de quintessens van de queeste,' pp. 9–47. (XLIX.390)
   B.   Johan Winkelman, 'Over Heinrich von Melk, Chrétien de Troyes en de begrippen "aventure" en "queeste" in de *Queeste vanden Grale*,' pp. 75–88. (XLIX.420)
   C.   Marjolein Hogenbirk, '*Walewein ende Keye*: hoogmoed ten val gebracht,' pp. 89–111. (XLIX.401)
   D.   Lieve de Wachter, 'Twee fasen in de avonturen van Heinric en Echites in de *Roman van Heinric en Margriete van Limborch*,' pp. 113–41. (XLIX.418)

52   Willaert, Frank, 'La littérature moyen-néerlandaise replacée dans son contexte européen,' *Septentrion*, 25 (1996), 26–33. (LI.15)

53   Zemel, Roel, 'Moriaen en Perceval in "Waste Land",' *TNTL*, 112 (1996), 297–319. (XLIX.424)

54 *Op avontuur: middeleeuwse epiek in de Lage Landen*, ed. Jozef Janssens, Nederlandse Literatuur en Cultuur in de Middeleeuwen, 18 (Amsterdam: Prometheus, 1998). (LI.688)
- A. Jozef D. Janssens, 'Subtiel vertellen: middeleeuwse epiek in de Lage Landen,' pp. 9–35. (LI.689)
- B. Piet Avonds, 'Waar blijven dan toch Bohort, Galaad, Perceval en de anderen? De verspreiding van de Arturepiek in Brabant (twaalfde-begin veertiende eeuw),' pp. 37–49. (LI.682)

55 Oppenhuis de Jong, Soetje, '".V.c. merchis, biax tres dols sire": een episode in de Lancelotcompilatie, de Luikse fragmenten en de Oudfranse *Perceval*,' *Madoc*, 12 (1998), 195–201. (LI.696)

56 Winkelman, Johan H., 'Chrétien de Troyes, Perceval, und die Niederlande: Adaptation als didaktisches Verfahren,' in Pb441 *Kultureller Austausch*, pp. 245–58. (LI.122)

57 Zemel, Roel, 'Evax en Sibilie: een verhaal over liefde en ridderschap in de *Roman van Limborch*,' *SpL*, 40 (1998), 1–24. (LII.12)

58 Oppenhuis de Jong, Soetje, '*Perchevael*: Walewein en het duel te Scaveloen,' in *Jeesten van rouwen ende van feesten: een bloemlezing uit de 'Lancelotcompilatie'*, ed. Bart Besamusca, Middelnederlandse Tekstedities, 6 (Hilversum: Verloren, 1999), pp. 89–114. (LII.667)

59 *Originality and Tradition in the Middle Dutch 'Roman van Walewein'*, ed. Bart Besamusca and Erik Kooper, AL 17 (Cambridge: Brewer, 1999).
Listed below are the contributions that give significant attention to Chrétien as source, model, or comparative text. Other articles not listed here deal primarily with German and English texts that are related to the *Walewein*. See the Introduction for summaries.
- A. Bart Besamusca and Erik Kooper, 'Introduction: The Study of the *Roman van Walewein*,' pp. 1–16. (LII.346)
- B. Douglas Kelly, 'The Pledge Motif in the *Roman van Walewein*: Original Variant and Rewritten Quest,' pp. 29–46. (LII.408)
- C. Norris J. Lacy, 'Convention and Innovation in the Middle Dutch *Roman van Walewein*,' pp. 47–62. (LII.412)
- D. Ad Putter, 'Walewein in the Otherworld and the Land of Prester John,' pp. 79–99. (LII.446)
- E. Jane H. M. Taylor, 'The *Roman van Walewein*: Man into Fox, Fox into Man,' pp. 131–45. (LII.463)
- F. Bart Veldhoen, 'The *Roman van Walewein* Laced with Castles,' pp. 147–67. (LII.465)
- G. Lori J. Walters, 'Making Bread from Stone: The *Roman van Walewein* and the Transformation of Old French Romance,' pp. 189–207. (LII.471)

60 Besamusca, Bart, 'The Medieval Dutch Arthurian Material,' in Pb463 *Arthur*, pp. 187–228.

61 Coolput-Storms, Colette-Anne van, '"Walsche boucken" voor het hof,' in *Medioneerlandistiek*, pp. 39–52.

62 Hogenbirk, Marjolein, 'Walewein en Gringalet: trouwe kameraden,' in *Opstellen Gerritsen*, pp. 85–90.

63 Oostrom, Fritz van, 'De Lage Landen en het hooggebergte: Middelnederlandse ridderromans in Europese context,' *Literatuur*, 17 (2000), 3–11. (LIII.883)

See Pa330 Walters.

f: Scandinavian Literatures

6 Kölbing, Eugen, 'Die nordische Parzivalsaga und ihre Quelle,' *Germania*, 14 (1869), 129–81, and 'Nachtrag zur Parzivalssaga,' *Germania*, 15 (1870), 89–94.

7 Kölbing, Eugen, 'Die nordische Erexsaga und ihre Quelle,' *Germania*, 16 (1871), 381–414.

8 Kölbing, Eugen, ed., *'Riddarasögur': 'Parcevals saga', 'Valvers þáttr', 'Ivents saga', 'Mirmans saga'* (Strassburg: Trübner, 1872).
See 'Die Quelle der *Parcevals saga* und des *Valvers þáttr*,' pp. iv–v, and 'Die Quelle der *Ívents Saga* und das Verhältniss der Saga zum altschwedischen Herr Ivan Lejon-Riddaren,' pp. xii–xxxviii.

9 Cederschiöld, Gustaf, ed., *'Erex Saga' efter handskrifterna utgifven* (Copenhagen: Møller, 1880).
See pp. iii–viii.

10 Kölbing, Eugen, ed., *Ívens saga*, Altnordische Saga-Bibliothek, 7 (Halle/S: Niemeyer, 1898).
See 'Die französische quelle der saga,' pp. vi–xi; and 'Die schwedische Herra Iwan Lejon-riddaren und anspielungen Iwein-stoff in der späteren isländischen dichtung,' pp. xvi–xxiii.

11 Jónsson, Finnur, *Den oldnorske og oldislandske Litteraturs Historie*, 2 vols (Copenhagen: Gad, 1898–1901).
See vol. 2, pp. 963–82: 'Romantiske sagaer og andre dermed beslægtede frembringelser.'

P: INFLUENCES

12   Leach, Henry Goddard, *Angevin Britain and Scandinavia*, Harvard Studies in Comparative Literature, 6 (Cambridge, MA: Harvard University Press, 1921).
See Chap. 9: 'Arthur and Charlemagne'.

13   Frandsen, Ernst, *Folkevisen: Studier i middelalderens poetiske litteratur* (Copenhagen: Levin & Munksgaard, 1935; 2nd ed. Gyldendal: Glydendals Uglebøkers, 1969).
On Swedish *Herr Ivan*.

14   Blaisdell, Foster W., Jr., 'Names in the *Erex saga*,' *JEGP*, 62 (1963), 143–54.

15   Loomis, R. S., 'The Grail in the *Parcevals saga*,' *GR*, 39 (1964), 97–100. (XVII.46).

16   Schlauch, Margaret, 'Arthurian Material in Some Late Icelandic Sagas,' *BBSIA*, 17 (1965), 87–91.
See also her 'A Bibliographical Note,' *BBSIA*, 19 (1967), 139–40. (XXI.209)

17   Kalinke, Sister Jane A., 'The Structure of the *Erex Saga*,' *SS*, 42 (1970), 343–55. (XXIII.47)

18   Barnes, Geraldine, 'The *Riddarasögur*: A Medieval Exercise in Translation,' *Saga-Book of the Viking Society*, 19 (1974–77), 403–41.
Pp. 432–37 on *Ívens saga*.

19   Kratz, Henry, '*Textus*, *Braull* and *Gangandi Greiði*,' *Saga-Book of the Viking Society*, 19 (1974–77), 371–82.
On Grail in the *Parcevals saga*, the Norse version of the *Conte du Graal*.

20   Barnes, Geraldine, 'The *riddarasögur* and Mediaeval European Literature,' *MedS*, 8 (1975), 140–58.

21   Hunt, Tony, 'Herr Ivan Lejonriddaren,' *MedS*, 8 (1975), 168–86. (XXX.344)
On Swedish adaptation of *Yvain*.

22   Kalinke, Marianne E., 'Characterization in *Erex saga* and *Ivens saga*,' *Modern Language Studies*, 5:1 (1975), 11–19.

23   *Les Relations littéraires franco-scandinaves au Moyen Age: Actes du Colloque de Liège (avril 1972)*, BFPLUL, 208 (Paris: Belles Lettres, 1975).
   A.   Georges Zink, 'Les poèmes arthuriens dans les pays scandinaves,' pp. 77–95.
   B.   Paul Schach, 'Some Observations on the Translations of Brother Róbert,' pp. 117–35.

427

C. Knud Togeby, 'La chronologie des versions scandinaves des anciens textes français,' pp. 183–91.
D. Eyvind Fjeld Halvorsen, 'Problèmes de la traduction scandinave des textes français du Moyen Age,' pp. 247–74.
E. Jónas Kristjánsson, 'Text Editions of the Romantic Sagas,' pp. 275–88.
F. Knud Togeby, 'Les relations littéraires entre le monde roman et le monde scandinave: relevé bibliographique,' pp. 299–329.

All but item E include discussion.

24 Boklund Coffer, Karin, '*Herr Ivan*: A Stylistic Study,' *SS*, 48 (1976), 299–315.

25 Blaisdell, Foster W., Jr, and Marianne E. Kalinke, trans., *'Erex Saga' and 'Ívens Saga': The Old Norse Versions of Chrétien de Troyes's 'Erec' and 'Yvain'* (Lincoln: University of Nebraska Press, 1977). (XXX.120)
See pp. ix–xxiii.

26 Kalinke, Marianne E., '*Erex saga* and *Ívens saga*: Medieval Approaches to Translation,' *ANF*, 92 (1977), 125–44.

27 Kratz, Henry, 'Names in *Parcevals saga* and *Valvers Þáttr*,' *Names*, 25 (1977), 63–77.

28 Kratz, Henry, 'The *Parcevals saga* and *Li contes del Graal*,' *SS*, 49 (1977), 13–47. (XXXI.109)

29 Kalinke, Marianne E., 'Alliteration in *Ívens saga*,' *MLR*, 74 (1979), 871–83. (XXXII.423)

30 Skårup, Povl, 'Forudsætter Rémundar saga en norrøn Lancelots saga kerrumanns?' *Gripla*, 4 (1980), 76–80. (XXXIV.551)

See La28 Hunt.

31 Kalinke, Marianne E., *King Arthur North-by-Northwest: The 'Matière de Bretagne' in Old Norse-Icelandic Romances*, Bibliotheca Arnamagnæana, 37 (Copenhagen: Reitzel, 1981).

32 Patron-Godefroit, Annette, 'La transmission scandinave d'*Yvain*,' in *Essays Thorpe*, pp. 239–47. (XXXIV.360)

33 Clover, Carol J., *The Medieval Saga* (Ithaca, NY: Cornell University Press, 1982). (XXXVII.353)

34 Kalinke, Marianne E., 'Scribes, Editors, and the *riddarasögur*,' *ANF*, 97 (1982), 36–51.

35 Kretschmer, Bernd, *Höfische und altwestnordische Erzähltradition in den 'Riddarasögur': Studien zur Rezeption der altfranzösischen Artusepik am Beispiel der 'Erex saga', 'Ívens saga' und 'Parcevals saga'*, Wissenschaftliche Reihe, 4 (Abteilung Literaturwissenschaft) (Hattingen: Kretschmar, 1982). (XXXV.43)

36 Simek, Rudolf, trans., *Die Saga von Perceval und die Geschichte von Valver: 'Parcevals saga' ok 'Valvers þáttr'*, Wiener Arbeiten zur germanischen Altertumskunde und Philologie, 19 (Vienna: Halosar, 1982). (XXXV.7)
See pp. vii–xiv.

37 Schosmann, Rémy, 'De la France à l'Islande: la métamorphose des chevaliers,' *EtGerm*, 38 (1983), 454–62.

38 Álfrún Gunnlaugsdóttir, 'Um Parcevals sögu,' *Gripla*, 6 (1984), 218–40.

39 Barnes, Geraldine, '*Parcevals Saga*: Riddara Skuggsjá?' *ANF*, 99 (1984), 49–62.

40 Patron-Godefroit, Annette, 'L'adaptation suédoise d'*Yvain*,' in *Lancelot Wégimont*, pp. 125–32. (XXXVIII. 251)

41 Skårup, Povl, 'Tre marginalnoter om *Erex saga*,' *Gripla*, 6 (1984), 49–63. (XXXVIII.172)
Resumé in French.

42 Clover, Carol J., and John Lindow, *Old Norse-Icelandic Literature: A Critical Guide*, Islandica, 45 (Ithaca, NY: Cornell University Press, 1985). (XXXIX.235)
See Marianne Kalinke, 'Norse Romance (*Riddarasögur*),' pp. 316–63.

43 Kalinke, Marianne E., and P. M. Mitchell, comp., *Bibliography of Old Norse-Icelandic Romances*, Islandica, 44 (Ithaca, NY: Cornell University Press, 1985). (XXXVIII.509)
See pp. 39–41 (*Erex saga*), 56–60 (*Ívens saga*), 87–90 (*Parcevals saga*), and 126–27 (*Valvens þáttr*).

44 *Les Sagas de chevaliers (Riddarasögur): Actes de la Ve Conférence Internationale sur les Sagas (Toulon, Juillet 1982)*, ed. Régis Boyer, Civilisations, 10 (Paris: Presses de l'Université de Paris-Sorbonne, 1982). (XXXVIII.261)
On Chrétien's influence, see:
    A. Paul Bibire, 'From *Riddarasaga* to *Lygisaga*: The Norse Response to Romance,' pp. 55–74.

B. Marianne E. Kalinke, '*Riddarasögur, Fornaldarsögur*, and the Problem of Genre,' pp. 77–91.

C. Jürg Glauser, 'Erzähler–Ritter–Zuhörer: das Beispiel der *Riddarasögur*: Erzählkommunikation und Hörergemeinschaft im mittelalterlichen Island,' pp. 93–119.

D. Hermann Reichert, 'Soziologische Voraussetzungen für die Rezeption der arturischen Tafelrunde in Skandinavien,' pp. 121–42.

E. Olivier Gouchet, 'Die altislandische Bearbeitung von Chrétiens *Erec et Enide*,' pp. 145–55.

F. Edith Marold, 'Von Chrestiens *Yvain* zur *Ivenssaga*: die *Ivenssaga* als rezeptionsgeschichtliches Zeugnis,' pp. 157–92.

G. Rémy Schosmann, '*Yvain – Yvenssaga*: Translation or Travesty?' pp. 193–203.

H. Rudolf Simek, 'Lancelot in Iceland,' pp. 205–16.

I. Álfrún Gunnlaugsdóttir, 'Quelques aspects de *Parcevals Saga*,' pp. 217–33.

45 *Structure and Meaning in Old Norse Literature: New Approaches to Textual Analysis and Literary Criticism*, ed. John Lindow, Lars Lönnroth, and Gerd Wolfgang Weber, The Viking Collection: Studies in Northern Civilization, 3 (Odense: Odense University Press, 1986).

A. Hermann Reichert, 'King Arthur's Round Table: Sociological Implications of its Literary Reception in Scandinavia,' pp. 394–414. (XXXIX.532)

B. Gerd Wolfgang Weber, 'The Decadence of Feudal Myth – Towards a Theory of *riddarasaga* and Romance,' pp. 415–54.

46 Barnes, Geraldine, 'Arthurian Chivalry in Old Norse,' *AL*, 7 (1987), 50–102. (XL.97)

47 Boyer, Régis, '*Ívens saga*: présentation de l'œuvre,' *PRIS-MA*, 3 (1987), 15–22. (XLI.49)

See Pa193 Coolput.

48 Almazan, Vincent, 'Translations at the Castilian and Norwegian Courts in the Thirteenth Century: Parallels and Patterns,' *MedS*, 12 (1988), 213–32.

49 Gad, Tue and Bodil, *Ved Kilden under Træt...: Kapitler af Paradisdrømmens Historie* (Copenhagen: Reitzel, 1988).
See chap. 3: 'Tryllekilden.'

See Gc18 Weiss.

50 Barnes, Geraldine, 'Some Current Issues in *riddarasögur* Research,' *ANF*, 104 (1989), 73–88.

51   Campbell, Ian, 'Medieval *Riddarasögur* in Adaptation from the French: *Flóres saga ok Blankiflúr* and *Parcevals saga*,' *Parergon*, 8:2 (1990), 23–35.

52   Farrier, Susan E., '*Erex saga* and the Reshaping of Chrétien's *Erec et Enide*,' *AInt*, 4:2 (1990), 1–11.

53   Kjær, Jonna, 'Censure morale et transformations idéologiques dans deux traductions de Chrétien de Troyes: *Ívens saga* et *Erex saga*,' in *The Audience of the Sagas: Preprints: The Eighth International Saga Conference, August 11–17, 1991, Gothenburg University*, ed. Lars Lönnroth ([n.p.: n.p.], 1991), pp. 287–96; English version: 'Franco-Scandinavian Literary Transmission in the Middle Ages: Two Old Norse Translations of Chrétien de Troyes – *Ívens saga* and *Erex saga*,' *AY*, 2 (1992), 113–34. (XLV.2; XLVII.740)

54   Barnes, Geraldine, 'The Lion-Knight Legend in Old Norse Romance,' in *Ritter mit dem Löwen*, pp. 383–99. (XLVII.520)

See Gd.c68 Bein.

55   Glauser, Jürg, 'Textüberlieferung und Textbegriff im spätmittelalterlichen Norden: das Beispiel der Riddarasögur,' *ANF*, 113 (1998), 7–27.

56   Gottzmann, Carola L., 'Die Sinnstruktur der *Erex saga* im Vergleich mit Chrétiens und Hartmanns *Erec*,' in *Hartmann von Aue: mit einer Bibliographie 1976–1997*, ed. Petra Hörner, Information und Interpretation, 8 (Frankfurt/M.: P. Lang, 1998), pp. 123–54. (LII.80)

57   Skårop, Povl, 'Traductions norroises de textes français: un aperçu,' *RLR*, 102:1 (1998), 3–6.

g: Spanish and Portuguese Literatures

5   Knust, Germán, *Dos obras didácticas y dos leyendas sacadas de manuscritos de la Biblioteca del Escurial*, Sociedad de Bibliófilos Españoles, 17 (Madrid: M Ginesta, 1878).
See pp. 159–70.

6   Michels, Ralph J., 'Deux traces du *Chevalier de la charrete* observées dans l'*Amadís de Gaula*,' *Bulletin Hispanique*, 37 (1935), 478–80.

7   Bohigas, Pere, 'La Matière de Bretagne en Catalogne,' *BBSIA*, 13 (1961), 81–98.

8   Stegagno Picchio, Luciana, 'Fortuna iberica di un topos letterario: la corte di Costantinopoli dal *Cligès* al *Palmerín de Olivia*,' in *Studi sul Palmerín de Olivia*, vol. 3: *Saggi e ricerche*, Istituto di Letteratura Spagnola e Ispano-Americana dell'Università di Pisa, 13 (Pisa: Cursi, 1966), pp. 99–136.

9   Durán, Armando, *Estructura y técnicas de la novela sentimental y caballeresca*, Biblioteca Románica Hispánica, 2: Estudios y Ensayos, 184 (Madrid: Gredos, 1973). (XXVII.227)
See pp. 67–87.

10   Bruneti, Almir de Campos, *A lenda do Graal no contexto heterodoxo do pensamento português* (Lisbon: Sociedade de Expansão Cultural, 1974). (XXVII.226)

11   Rossi, Luciano, *A literatura novelística na Idade Média portuguesa*, trans. Carlos Moura, Biblioteca Breve (serie Literatura), 38 ([Lisbon]: Instituto de Cultura Portuguesa, 1979). (XXXIV.209)
See Chap. 2: 'Da recitação à leitura: A "Matéria de Bretanha".'

12   Fagundes, Francisco Cota, 'The Chivalric Tradition in Branquinho da Fonseca's *O Barão*,' *Revista de Estudios Hispánicos* (USA), 15 (1981), 199–210.

13   Schreiner, Elisabeth, 'Die "matière de Bretagne" im *Libro del Cavallero Cifar*: zur Rezeption der "matière de Bretagne" in zwei Episoden des *Libro del Cavallero Cifar*,' in *Romanisches Mittelalter: Festschrift zum 60. Geburtstag von Rudolf Baehr*, ed. Dieter Messner and Wolfgang Pöckl with Angela Birner (Göppingen: Kümmerle, 1981), pp. 269–83. (XXXV.69)

14   Eisenberg, Daniel, *Romances of Chivalry in the Spanish Golden Age*, Hispanic Monographs: Documentación Cervantina, 3 (Newark, DE: Juan de la Cuesta, 1982).

15   Paredes Núñez, Juan, 'El término "cuento" en la literatura románica medieval,' *Bulletin Hispanique*, 86 (1984), 435–51. (XXXIX.661)
See p. 443.

16   Williamson, Edwin, *The Half-Way House of Fiction: 'Don Quixote' and Arthurian Romance* (Oxford: Clarendon Press, 1984). (XXXVI.474)

See Ha127 *Romance*.

See Gc15 McGrady.

17 Urbina, Eduardo, 'Chrétien de Troyes y Cervantes: más allá de los libros de caballerías,' *Anales Cervantinos*, 24 (1986), 137–47.

See Ha140 Urbina.

18 Hatzfeld, Helmut, 'La Renaissance chevaleresque,' *Neohelicon*, 15:1 (1988), 167–85. (XLI.254)

See Gd.c40 Urbina.

19 Buescu, Maria Gabriela Carvalhão, *Perceval e Galaaz, cavaleiros do Graal*, Biblioteca Breve, 125 (Lisbon: Instituto de Cultura Portuguesa: Divisão de Publicações, 1991).

20 Gracia, Paloma, *Las señales del destino heroico*, Héroes y Dioses (Barcelona: Montesinos, 1991). (XLVI.250)

21 Infantes, Víctor, 'La narración caballeresca breve,' in *Evolución*, pp. 165–81. (XLVI.253)
See as well Nieves Baranda, 'Compendio bibliográfico sobre la narrativa caballeresca breve,' pp. 183–91, especially p. 186. (XLVI.227)

22 Williamson, Edwin, 'Cervantes y Chrétien de Troyes: la destrucción creadora de la narrativa caballeresca,' in *Evolución*, pp. 145–63. (XLVI.287)

23 Alvar, Carlos, 'Poesía gallego-portuguesa y Materia de Bretaña: algunas hipótesis,' in *Cantar*, pp. 31–51. (XLVI.225)

24 Harney, Michael, 'Economy and Utopia in Medieval Hispanic Chivalric Romance,' *HR*, 62 (1994), 381–403. (XLVII.723)

25 Rieger, Angelica, '"En esto sigo la antigua usanza de los andantes caballeros": zur Rezeption der Geschichte des Ritters mit dem Löwen bei Cervantes,' in *Ritter mit dem Löwen*, pp. 419–49. (XLVII.589)

26 Calvo, Florencia, '"Otros modos de llevar a los encantados": Cervantes y Chrétien de Troyes: el libro no leído ni visto ni oído por Don Quijote,' in *Actas del II Congreso Internacional de la Asociación de Cervantistas*, ed. Giuseppe Grilli, = *AION*, 37:2 (1995), 379–86.

27 Contreras Martín, Antonio M., 'El episodio de la carreta en el *Lanzarote del Lago* castellano (Ms. 9611 BN Madrid),' in *Actas Granada*, vol. 2, pp. 61–74.

28 Liffen, Shirley, 'The Transformation of a *passio* into a Romance: A Study of Two Fourteenth-Century Spanish Versions of the Legends of St Eustace and King William of England,' *Iberoromania*, ser. 2, no. 41 (1995), 1–16.

29 Meneghetti, Maria Luisa. 'Marie et Leonor, Lancelot et Amadís: histoire et fiction dans la *poïesis* romanesque,' in *Recueil Micha*, pp. 275–83. (XLVIII.126)

30 Deyermond, Alan, '¿Obras artúricas perdidas en la Castilla medieval?,' *Anclajes: Revista del Instituto de Análisis Semiótico del Discurso*, 1 (1997), 95–114.

See Ha199 Dudley.

31 *Riquer, Isabel de, 'La réception du *Graal* en Catalogne au Moyen Age,' in *Transferts de thèmes, transferts de textes: mythes, légendes et langues entre Catalogne et Languedoc* (Barcelona: PPU, 1997), pp. 49–60. (LI.642)

32 Toledo Neto, Sílvio de Almeida, 'Breve notícia da matéria arturiana anterior às traduções ibéricas da *Post-Vulgata*,' in *Textos medievais portugueses e suas fontes: matéria da Bretanha e cantigas com notação musical*, ed. Heitor Megale and Haquira Osakabe (São Paulo: Humanitas, 1999), pp. 129–56.

See Ha205(C) Wild.

See Ha209(P) Brownlee.

See Ha210 Jewers, Chap. 3: 'Romance into Novel: *Tirant lo blanc*.'

h: Italian Literature

1 Neri, Ferdinando, 'Sulle trace [...]'; repr. in his *Letteratura e leggende* (Turin: Chiantore, 1951), pp. 179–84.

2 Graf, A., 'Appunti per la storia del ciclo brettone in Italia,' *Giornale Storico della Letteratura Italiana*, 5 (1885), 80–130.
See pp. 102–16.

See Ga8 Strucks.

3 Comfort, W. W., 'Vita nova: 41 and *Cligés*: 5815 ff.,' *RR*, 2 (1911), 209–11.

4   Palgen, Rudolf, *Brandansage und Purgatorio* (Heidelberg: Winter, 1934).
See pp. 5–12.

5   Caldarini, Ernesta, 'Da Lancillotto al Petrarca,' *Lettere Italiane*, 27 (1975), 373–80. (XXVIII.392)

6   Roncaglia, Aurelio, 'Nascita e sviluppo della narrativa cavalleresca nella Francia medievale,' in *Ludovico Ariosto: Convegno Internazionale Roma-Lucca-Castelnuovo di Garfagnana-Reggio Emilia-Ferrara (27 settembre-5 ottobre 1974)*, Atti dei Convegni Lincei, 6 (Rome: Accademia Nazionale dei Lincei, 1975), pp. 229–50.

See Gd.c14 Caldarini.

7   Picone, Michelangelo, 'Dante e la tradizione arturiana,' *RF*, 94 (1982), 1–18. (XXXV.58)

See Hg60 Pioletti.

See Ha127 *Romance*.

See Gd.b36 Botterill.

See Ue3 Mancini.

8   Bendinelli Predelli, Maria, *Alle origini del 'Bel Gherardino'*, BArR, 236 (Florence: Olschki, 1990). (XLIII.335)

9   Winternitz De Vito, Rosella, 'Uno studio su Dante: ricerca tematica, I–II,' *Veltro*, 35 (1991), 77–99, 299–309.

10   Delcorno Branca, Daniela, 'Tradizione italiana dei testi arturiani: note sul *Lancelot*,' *MedR*, 17 (1992), 215–50. (XLV.328)

11   Ferrucci, Franco, 'Dante e Chrétien de Troyes: sublimazione classico-cristiana del romanzo cortese,' *Lectura Dantis*, 13 (1993), 3–21.

12   Heijkant, Marie-José, 'Der Ritter mit dem Löwen in der Tradition der ritterlichen Dichtung Italiens,' in *Ritter mit dem Löwen*, pp. 401–17. (XLVII.557)

13   Bianchini, Simonetta, *Cielo d'Alcamo e il suo contrasto: intertestualità romanze nella scuola poetica siciliana*, Medioevo Romanzo e Orientale, 6 (Soveria Mannelli: Rubbettino, 1996). (LI.550)

See Ga97 Luttrell.

14 Picone, Michelangelo, 'Theories of Love and the Lyric Tradition from Dante's *Vita nuova* to Petrarch's *Canzoniere*,' *RomN*, 39 (1998), 83–93. (LI.796)

See Ha209(M) Psaki.

i: Occitan Literature (this includes Catalan poets writing in Occitan)

1 Williams, Frances M., 'Arthurian Romance and *Flamenca*,' *Arthuriana*, 2 (1929–30), 70–80.

2 Pontecorvo, Aurelia, 'Una fonte del *Jaufré*,' *ArR*, 22 (1938), 399–401.

3 Jeanroy, A., 'Le roman de *Jaufré*,' *Annales du Midi*, 53 (1941), 363–90.
See pp. 373–80.

4 Cluzel, Irénée, 'A propos de l'*Ensenhamen* du troubadour catalan Guerau de Cabrera,' *BRABL*, 26 (1954–56), 87–93. (X.80)

See Md27 Remy.

5 Várvaro, Alberto, ed., *Rigaut de Barbezilh: liriche*, Biblioteca di Filologia Romanza, 4 (Bari: Adriatica, 1960).
See pp. 13–16 on 'Altressi con Persavaus,' Poem 3, and 'Tuit demandon qu'es devengu d'Amors,' Poem 9, in this edition.

6 Lejeune, Rita, 'Analyse textuelle et histoire littéraire: Rigaut de Barbezieux,' *MA*, 68 (1962), 331–77. (XV.86)
Denies Chrétien's influence in 'Altressi con Persavaus.'

7 Limentani, Alberto, 'Dalle nozze di Erec e Enide alle nozze di Archambaut e Flamenca,' in *Miscellanea di studi offerta a Armando Balduino e Bianca Bianchi per le loro nozze, Vicenza, 30 giugno 1962* (Padua: Seminario di Filologia Moderna dell'Università, 1962), pp. 9–14; repr. in Pi13 Limentani.

8 Limentani, Alberto, 'Due studî di narrativa provenzale: II. Il problema dell'umorismo nel *Jaufré* e una contraffazione del *Perceval*,' *Atti dell'Istituto Veneto di Scienze, Lettere ed Arti*, 121 (1962–63), 102–12. (XVI.191)

9 Cluzel, Irénée-Marcel, 'La culture générale d'un troubadour du XIIIe siècle,' *Mélanges Delbouille*, vol. 2, pp. 91–104. (XVII.87)

See Ra10 Lejeune.

10 Lefèvre, Yves, 'Bertran de Born et la littérature française de son temps,' in *Mélanges Frappier*, vol. 2, pp. 603–9.
Allusion to Chrétien.

11 Limentani, Alberto, 'L'elaborazione delle fonti nelle *Novas de Guillem de Nivers* (*Flamenca*),' in *Actele celui de-al XII-lea congres internaţional de lingvistică şi filologie romanică*, 2 vols (Bucharest: Editura Academiei Republicii Socialiste România, 1970–71), vol. 2, pp. 757–63.

12 Pirot, François, *Recherches sur les connaissances littéraires des troubadours occitans et catalans des XIIᵉ et XIIIᵉ siècles: les 'sirventes-ensenhamens' de Guerau de Cabrera, Guiraut de Calanson et Bertrand de Paris*, Memorias de la Real Academia de Buenas Letras de Barcelona, 14 (Barcelona: Real Academia de Buenas Letras, 1972).

See Hg28 Baumgartner.

13 Limentani, Alberto, *L'eccezione narrativa: la Provenza medievale e l'arte del racconto*, Nuova Biblioteca Scientifica Einaudi, 60 (Turin: Einaudi, 1977).

14 Tecchio, Donatella, 'Uc de Saint-Circ e il *Cligés* di Chrétien de Troyes,' *Atti e Memorie dell'Accademia Patavina di Scienze, Lettere ed Arti. Parte III: Classe di Scienze Morali, Lettere e Arti*, 91 (1978–79), 195–99. (XXXII.477)

15 De Caluwé, Jacques, 'Quelques réflexions sur la pénétration de la matière arthurienne dans les littératures occitanes et catalanes médiévales,' in *Essays Thorpe*, pp. 354–67. (XXXIV.304)

16 Fleischman, Suzanne, '*Jaufre* or Chivalry Askew: Social Overtones of Parody in Arthurian Romance,' *Viator*, 12 (1981), 101–29. (XXXIV.120)

17 Dragonetti, Roger, *Le gai savoir dans la rhétorique courtoise: 'Flamenca' et 'Joufroi de Poitiers'*, Connexions du Champ Freudien (Paris: Seuil, 1982).
See pp. 149–58.

See Ha112 Meneghetti.

18 Calin, William, 'Vers une nouvelle lecture de *Jaufré*: un dialogue avec Marc-René Jung,' *MrR*, 33 (1983), 39–47. (XXXIX.2)

19 Busby, Keith, '"Moseiner Galvain l'astrucz" (*Jaufré*, v. 488): le portrait de Gauvain d'après le roman de *Jaufré* et quelques troubadours de l'époque,' in *Studia Remy*, vol. 2, pp. 1–11. (XXXIX.226)

20 Harrison, Ann Tukey, 'Arthurian Women in *Jaufre*,' in *Studia Remy*, vol. 2, pp. 65–73. (XXXIX.273)

21 Saly, Antoinette, 'Jaufre, lo fil Dozon, et Girflet, fils de Do,' in *Studia Remy*, vol. 2, pp. 179–88; repr. in Dc22.

22 Wais, Kurt, 'Brunissen im *Jaufre* und die Tradition Brünhild/Brunehout,' in *Studia Remy*, vol. 2, pp. 211–32. (XXXIX.320)

23 Hunt, Tony, '*Texte* and *Prétexte*: *Jaufre* and *Yvain*,' in *Legacy*, vol. 2, pp. 125–41. (XLII.208)

24 Huchet, Jean-Charles, 'Le roman à nu: *Jaufré*,' *Littérature*, 74 (1989), 91–99.

25 Huchet, Jean-Charles, *Le Roman occitan médiéval*, Littératures Modernes (Paris: Presses Universitaires de France, 1991).

26 Jung, Marc-René, '*Jaufre*: "E aiso son novas rials",' in *Il miglior fabbro: mélanges de langue et de littérature occitanes en hommage à Pierre Bec par ses amis, ses collègues, ses élèves* (Poitiers: Université de Poitiers, Centre d'Études Supérieures de Civilisation Médiévale, 1991), pp. 223–34.

27 Bartoli, Renata A., 'Analisi rimica del *Jaufre* in rapporto con il *Conte du Graal* di Chrétien de Troyes,' in *Atti del Secondo Congresso Internazionale della 'Association Internationale d'Etudes Occitanes' Torino, 31 agosto-5 settembre 1987*, ed. Giuliano Gasca Queirazza, 2 vols (Turin: Dipartimento di Scienze Letterarie e Filologiche, Università di Torino, 1993), vol. 1, pp. 3–29. (XLVI.547)

28 Perugi, Maurizio, 'Il "Chastel d'Amour" e la maschera di Lancilotto: reperti oitanici nell'iconografia poetica di Arnaut Daniel,' in *Omaggio Folena*, vol. 1, pp. 147–63. (XLVI.571)

29 Huchet, Jean-Charles, '*Jaufré* et le Graal,' *VR*, 53 (1994), 156–73. (XLIX.436)

30 Wolfzettel, Friedrich, 'Artus en cage: quelques remarques sur le roman arthurien et l'histoire,' in *Studies Kelly*, pp. 575–88. (XLVII.607)

31   Busby, Keith, 'Hagiography at the Confluence of Epic, Lyric, and Romance: Raimon Feraut's *La Vida de Sant Honorat*,' *ZrP*, 113 (1997), 51–64. (L.69)

32   Jewers, Caroline, 'The Name of the Ruse and the Round Table: Occitan Romance and the Case for Cultural Resistance,' *Neophil*, 81 (1997), 187–200. (L.387)

33   Lorenzo Gradín, Pilar, '*Jaufre* o el orden ambiguo,' in *Mélanges de Mandach*, pp. 201–19.

See Ha205(C) Wild.

See Ha207 Jewers, Chap. 3: 'Going South: Courtliness and Comedy in the Occitan Tradition,' and Chap. 4: 'The Uses of Literacy: Parodic Fusion in the *Roman de Flamenca*.'

j: Medieval Latin and Byzantine Literatures

1   Szövérffy, Joseph, 'Deux héros féodaux: Perceval et saint Christophe: une légende médiévale et la poésie courtoise,' *Aevum* (Milan), 36 (1962), 258–67.

2   Bologna, Corrado, 'Lo sparviero, l'allodola e la quaglia (sulle "fonti" cortesi di Andrea Cappellano),' *ImRif*, 13 (1990), 113–57. (XLV.321)

3   Nadal Cañellas, Juan, 'Un *Parsifal* litúrgico bizantino,' *BRABL*, 44 (1993–94), 391–98.

4   Comes, Annalisa, 'Tra parodia e critica letteraria: *Cligès*, *Miles gloriosus* e la distinzione *cuer-cor*,' *SMV*, 42 (1996), 119–28. (L.333)

See Me38 Echard.

k: Modern Literatures, Cinema, and Other Arts (after the Sixteenth Century)

See Pa 36 Baudry.

1   Harper, George McLean, 'The Legend of the Holy Grail,' *PMLA*, 8 (1893), 77–140.

See Na.c39 Wechssler.

2 Curdy, A. E., 'Arthurian Literature,' *RR*, 1 (1910), 125–39, 265–78.

3 Nitze, William Albert, *Arthurian Romance and Modern Poetry and Music* (Chicago: University of Chicago Press, 1940).

4 Beringause, A. F., 'Melville and Chrétien de Troyes,' *AN&Q*, 2 (1963), 20–21.

5 Cadot, M., 'De Perceval à Candide ou la simplicité d'esprit dans la littérature,' in *Actes Poitiers*, pp. 113–22. (XX.260)

6 Leroy, Jean-Pierre, 'La littérature médiévale dans la *Bibliothèque française* de Charles Sorel,' in *Actes Poitiers*, pp. 103–12.

7 Baudry, Robert, 'L'itinéraire du Grand Meaulnes vers le domaine étrange,' *TLL*, 9:2 (1971), 145–57.

8 Baudry, Robert, 'Une lecture magique du Grand Meaulnes,' *TLL*, 11:2 (1973), 155–69. (XXVI.110)

9 García Gual, Carlos, and Luis Alberto de Cuenca, 'La herencia artúrica: de Chrétien al "comic",' *Cuadernos Hispanoamericanos*, 314–15 (1976), 559–69. (XXIX.213)

10 Hays, Peter L., 'Malamud's Yiddish-Accented Medieval Stories,' in *The Fiction of Bernard Malamud*, ed. Richard Astro and Jackson J. Benson, American Authors Series (Corvallis: Oregon State University Press, 1977), pp. 87–96.

11 Adair, Gilbert, 'Rohmer's *Perceval*,' *SandS*, 47 (1978), 230–34. Interview with Eric Rohmer.

12 Kratz, Bernd, 'Die Geschichte vom Maultier ohne Zaum: Paien de Maisières, Heinrich von dem Türlin und Wieland,' *Arcadia*, 13 (1978), 227–41. (XXXI.28)

13 Saurel, Renée, 'De Perceval à Abdallah: lectures théâtrales,' *Les Temps Modernes*, 34 (1978), 551–66.

14 Tesich-Savage, Nadja, 'Rehearsing the Middle Ages,' *Film Comment*, 14:5 (Sept.–Oct. 1978), 50–56. Interview with Eric Rohmer.

15 Larmat, Jean, 'Henri Bosco et l'esprit médiéval,' in *Hommage Onimus*, pp. 285–95.

16   Rohmer, Eric, 'Note sur la traduction et sur la mise en scène de *Perceval*,' *L'Avant-Scène Cinema*, 221 (Feb. 1979), 6–7.
The script for the film *Perceval*, pp. 9–62.

17   Baudry, Robert, 'La tradition du merveilleux et l'*Enchanteur pourrissant* ou de Chrétien de Troyes à Apollinaire,' *Essays in French Literature* (Australia), 17 (1980), 36–49.

18   Grimbert, Joan Tasker, 'Aesthetic Distance in Rohmer's *Perceval le Gallois*,' in *Purdue Film*, pp. 53–58.

19   Grimm, Reinhold R., 'Rezeptionsweisen des Romans in der Neuzeit,' in *Literatur in der Gesellschaft*, pp. 315–34.

20   Huchet, Jean-Charles, 'Mereceval,' *Littérature*, 40 (1980), 69–94.
On Rohmer's *Perceval*.

21   Zumthor, Paul, 'Le *Perceval* d'Eric Rohmer: note pour une lecture,' *RSH*, 177 (1980), 119–24.

22   Movshovitz, Howard P., 'Rohmer's *Perceval*: Narrative Time and Space in Medieval Literature and Film,' in *Purdue Film*, pp. 66–72.

23   Smith, Sarah W. R., 'Rohmer's *Perceval* as Literary Criticism,' in *Purdue Film*, pp. 59–65.

24   Baudry, Robert, 'Julien Gracq et la légende du Graal,' in *Julien Gracq: Actes du Colloque International d'Angers (21, 22, 23 mai 1981)* (Angers: Presses Universitaires d'Angers, 1981), pp. 244–63.

25   Cormier, Raymond J., 'Rohmer's Grail Story: Anatomy of a French Flop,' *SFR*, 5 (1981), 391–96.

26   Milne, Tom, 'Rohmer's Siege Perilous,' *SandS*, 50 (1981), 192–95.

27   Baigent, Michael, Richard Leigh, and Henry Lincoln, *The Holy Blood and the Holy Grail* (London: Cape, 1982; London: Arrow, 1996); *Dutch trans., *Het heilige bloed en de heilige graal*, trans. Minze bij de Weg (Baarn: Tirion, 1982).

28   Prédal, René, 'Lancelot, Perceval, Roland: chevalerie et littérature dans le cinéma français des années 70,' *Mélanges Larmat*, pp. 507–21. (XXXVI.363)

29   Thompson, Raymond H., 'Modern Fantasy and Medieval Romance: A Comprehensive Study,' in *The Aesthetics of Fantasy: Literature and*

Art, ed. Roger C. Schlobin (Notre Dame, IN: University of Notre Dame Press; Brighton: Harvester Press, 1982), pp. 211–25. (XXXV.191)

30 Delay, Florence, 'Entrée dans l'univers médiéval: l'expérience du *Graal théâtre*,' *PerM*, 9 (1983), 74–82.

31 Williams, Linda, 'Eric Rohmer and the Holy Grail,' *Literature/Film Quarterly*, 11 (1983), 71–82.

32 Attolini, Vito, 'Perceval, tra letteratura e sogno,' *Quaderni Medievali*, 17 (1984), 143–53.

33 Ryan, J. S., 'Uncouth Innocence: Some Links between Chrétien de Troyes, Wolfram von Eschenbach and J. R. R. Tolkien,' *Mythlore*, 11:2 (1984), 8–13; and *Inklings: Jahrbuch für Literatur und Äesthetik*, 2 (1984), 25–41.
Latter printing includes a German resumé.

34 Boissinot, Alain, and Marie-Martine Lasserre, 'Jeu de piste médiéval,' *Le Français Aujourd'hui*, 72 (Dec. 1985), 61–71.

35 Burns, E. Jane, 'Nostalgia Isn't What It Used to Be: The Middle Ages in Literature and Film,' in *Shadows of the Magic Lamp: Fantasy and Science Fiction in Film*, ed. George Slusser and Eric S. Rabkin (Carbondale: Southern Illinois University Press, 1985), pp. 86–97. (XXXVIII.477)

36 Buschinger, Danielle, 'Die Popularisierung epischer Stoffe des Mittelalters in Frankreich: die Epen-Reihen der Edition d'Art H. Piazza,' in *Mittelalter-Rezeption: ein Symposion*, ed. Peter Wapnewski, Germanistische Symposien: Berichtsbände, 6 (Stuttgart: Metzler, 1986), pp. 308–26; repr. in Dc23

37 Marty, Joseph, '*Perceval le Gallois*: une symbolique de l'alliance chrétienne,' *EtCin*, 149–152 (1986), 27–53.

38 Middleton, Roger, 'Chrétien's *Erec* in the Eighteenth Century,' in *Essays Pickford*, pp. 151–64. (XXXIX.74)

39 Middleton, Roger, 'Le Grand d'Aussy's *Erec et Enide*,' *NFS*, 25:2 (1986), 14–41. (XXXIX.38)

40 Tigoulet, Marie-Claude, 'Note sur *Perceval le Gallois*,' *EtCin*, 149–152 (1986), 17–26.

41 Harty, Kevin J., 'Cinema Arthuriana: Translations of the Arthurian Legend to the Screen,' *AInt*, 2:1 (1987), 95–113. (XLI.393)

42 Middleton, Roger, 'Le Grand d'Aussy's Unpublished *extraits*,' *NFS*, 26 (1987), 19–65. (XL.127)

43 Mitchell, Jerome, *Scott, Chaucer, and Medieval Romance: A Study in Sir Walter Scott's Indebtedness to the Literature of the Middle Ages* (Lexington: University Press of Kentucky, 1987). (XLI.418)

44 Crisp, C. G., *Eric Rohmer: Realist and Moralist* (Bloomington: Indiana University Press, 1988).
See Chap. 9: '*Perceval*.'

45 Middleton, Roger, 'Le Grand d'Aussy and the *Bibliothèque Universelle des romans*,' *NFS*, 27:1 (1988), 1–2. (XLI.143)

46 *Mittelalter-Rezeption III. Gesammelte Vorträge des 3. Salzburger Symposions: 'Mittelalter, Massenmedien, Neue Mythen'*, ed. Jürgen Kühnel [et alii], GAG, 479 (Göppingen: Kümmerle, 1988).
  A. Danielle Buschinger, 'Die Darstellung des Mittelalters im französischen Kinderbuch der Gegenwart,' pp. 147–64; repr. in Dc23
  B. Gérard Chandès, '*Ladyhawke*: die Neubelebung eines mittel-alterlichen Wandlungsmythos in einem Film und einem Roman aus dem Jahre 1984,' pp. 545–62.
  C. Willibald Kraml and Elizabeth Werner, 'Computer-Aventiure,' pp. 609–26.
  D. Brigitte Hochberg, '"Graal Théâtre: une molt bele conjointure": Die "Matière de Bretagne" im zeitgenössischen französischen Theater,' pp. 627–45. (XLI.602)
  E. Ulrich Müller, 'Schwerter, Motorräder und Raumschiffe: Versuch über eine Gruppe von epischen Universalien,' pp. 697–712.
  F. Linda Tarte Holley, 'Medievalism in Film: The Matter of Arthur, A Filmography,' pp. 713–16. (XLI.603)

47 Ward, Marvin J., 'Fabrice del Dongo et Perceval le Gallois; intertextualité?' *Stendhal-Club*, 30 (1988), 209–22.

48 Asmuth, Bernhard, 'Die Unterweisung des Simplicius: mit einem Hinweis auf Grimmelshausens Beziehung zu Wolframs *Parzival* und Chrétien de Troyes,' in *Dialoganalyse, II: Referate der 2. Arbeitstagung Bochum 1988*, ed. Edda Weigand and Franz Hundschnurscher, 2 vols, Linguistische Arbeiten, 229–30 (Tübingen: Niemeyer, 1989), vol. 2, pp. 97–113.

49 Bego, Marina, '*Wangbang wideya*: een middeljavaanse hofroman,' in *Opstellen Schenkeveld*, pp. 143–73. (XLII.164)

50 Harty, Kevin J., 'Cinema Arthuriana: A Bibliography of Selected Secondary Materials,' *AInt*, 3:2 (1989), 119–37. (XLII.311)
For Rohmer's *Perceval*, see pp. 131–32.

51   Owen, D. D. R., '*Yvain* and *The Magic Flute*,' *FMLS*, 25 (1989), 88–90. (XLII.672)

52   Goebel, Janet, 'The Hero as Artist: Arthur among the German Romantics,' in Da15 *King Arthur*, vol. 2, pp. 3–26. (XLIII.538)

53   Lacy, Norris J., 'Arthurian Film and the Tyranny of Tradition,' *AInt*, 4:2 (1990), 75–85. (XLIII.564)

54   Roman, Paola, 'La letteratura cortese-arturiana ed epico-carolingia nella *Bibliothèque Universelle des Romans* (1775–1789),' *Annali di Ca' Foscari*, 29:1–2 (1990), 185–220.

See Xa10 Whitaker.

55   Baudry, Robert, 'Avatars du Graal en littérature française des XVIIIe et XIXe siècles,' in *Moderne Artus-Rezeption 18.–20. Jahrhundert*, ed. Kurt Gamerschlag, GAG, 548 (Göppingen: Kümmerle, 1991), pp. 23–50. (XLV.9)

56   Baudry, Robert, 'Echos arthuriens dans les romans de Pierre Benoit,' in *Arturus rex*, pp. 491–508. (XL, pp. 309–10)

57   Glencross, M. J., 'La Matière de Bretagne dans l'érudition française à l'époque romantique,' *PerM*, 17 (1991), 95–105.

58   *Mittelalter-Rezeption: zur Rezeptionsgeschichte der romanischen Literaturen des Mittelalters in der Neuzeit*, ed. Reinhold R. Grimm, Begleitreihe zum *GRLMA*, 2 (Heidelberg: Winter, 1991).
   A.   Heinz Klüppelholz, 'Die Rezeption des Artus-Romans in der "Bibliothèque universelle des romans",' pp. 111–38.
   B.   Dietmar Rieger, 'Se assez miauz morir ne vuel / A enor, que a honte vivre: zur Rezeption mittelalterlicher Literatur in der Lyrik und im Roman der Résistance,' pp. 313–34.

59   Rider, Jeff, Richard Hull, and Christopher Smith, 'The Arthurian Legend in French Cinema: *Lancelot du Lac* and *Perceval le Gallois*,' in *Cinema Arthuriana: Essays on Arthurian Film*, ed. Kevin J. Harty, GRLH, 1426 (New York: Garland, 1991), pp. 41–56.

60   Speare, Mary Jean, 'Wagnerian and Arthurian Elements in Chausson's *Le roi Arthus*,' *AY*, 1 (1991), 195–214. (XLIV.335)

61   *Chevrie, Marc, 'La scène et le hors-champ (notes sur Rohmer et le théâtre),' in *Eric Rohmer: tout est fortuit sauf le hasard* (Dunkirk: Studio 43 M. J. C., 1992).
See pp. 39–41.

62 Kimsey, John, 'Dolorous Strokes, or, Balin at the Bat: Malamud, Malory, and Chrétien,' in *The Celebration of the Fantastic: Selected Papers from the Tenth Anniversary International Conference on the Fantastic in the Arts*, ed. Donald E. Morse, Marshall B. Tymn, and Csilla Bertha (Westport, CT: Greenwood, 1992), pp. 103–12.

See Fb83(B) Baudry.

63 Glencross, Michael, 'Le débat romantique et la littérature française du Moyen Age dans la critique littéraire de la Restauration,' *NFS*, 33 (1994), 10–20.

64 *La Quête du Graal chez les écrivains européens contemporains*, ed. Michel Bonté, Daniela Fabiani, and Monique Grandjean, Association Européenne François Mauriac (Nancy: Presses Universitaires de Nancy, 1994).

65 Steele, Stephen, 'Chrétien de Troyes avant le XIXe siècle: présentation d'une notice inédite de Lévesque de La Ravalière,' *MedR*, 19 (1994), 345–59. (XLVIII.554)

66 Angeli, Giovanna, '*Perceval le Gallois* d'Eric Rohmer et ses sources,' *CAIEF*, 47 (1995), 33–48. (XLVIII.264)

67 Baudry, Robert, 'De Chrétien de Troyes à Jean Cocteau ou les vengeances du mythe,' in *Amour Troyes*, pp. 351–60. (XLIX.123)

68 Glencross, Michael, *Reconstructing Camelot: French Romantic Medievalism and the Arthurian Tradition*, AS, 36 (Cambridge: Brewer, 1995). (XLVIII.413)

69 Joly, Jehanne, 'Les adaptations théâtrales du corpus arthurien au XXe siècle en France,' *CAIEF*, 47 (1995), 135–68. (XLVIII.307)

See Ha193 Stanesco.

70 Valle, Viviane, 'Manifestations de la légende arthurienne en pays breton,' *AION*, 37:1 (1995), 241–54. (XLIX.333)

71 Busby, Keith, 'The Public and Private Life of Chrétien de Troyes,' *MedPer*, 11 (1996), 1–22.

72 *Graal et modernité*, Cahiers de l'Hermétisme (Paris: Dervy, 1996). (XLIX.158)
   A. Silvia Chitimia, 'Traces du Graal dans le folklore roumain,' pp. 65–77.
   B. Antoine Faivre, 'Présence du Graal dans les courants ésotériques au XXe siècle,' pp. 81–97.

C. Emmanuelle Ceaux, 'Variation et dérive sur le Graal,' pp. 109–14.
D. Henriette Bessis, 'Retour d'un souvenir oublié: les héros du Graal dans la peinture du XIXe siècle,' pp. 117–38.
E. Christian Merlin, 'Le Graal, la musique, l'opéra,' pp. 139–49.
F. Gérard Chandès, 'La société de communication et ses Graals: panorama,' pp. 151–67.
G. Isabelle Cani, 'Le Graal aujourd'hui: pour une typologie des œuvres,' pp. 169–81.
H. Jean Marigny, 'Le Graal dans la littérature anglo-saxonne de Malory à Marion Zimmer Bradley,' pp. 185–96.
I. Jean-Marc Pastré, 'Le Graal dans la littérature allemande contemporaine,' pp. 197–209.
J. Robert Baudry, 'Un nouveau "Cycle du Graal" en France,' pp. 211–25.

See also Db61 Ridoux, Jd47 Ribard, Mf15 Herzfeld, and Na.a44 Pontfarcy.

73 *Tortajada, Maria, 'L'exception médiévale: *Perceval le Gallois* d'Eric Rohmer,' *Equinoxe*, 16 (1996), 115–30. (L.404)

74 Zanelli Quarantini, Franca, 'J.-J. Rousseau tra Brocéliande e Forez,' in *Miscellanea in onore di Liano Petroni: studi e ricerche sulle letterature di lingua francese*, Il Ventaglio: Miscellanee, 8 (Bologna: CLUEB, 1996), pp. 89–104.

75 Baudry, Robert, 'Les lois d'évolution du mythe selon les récits "arthuriens" anciens et modernes,' in Pa299 *Œuvre*, pp. 211–26. (L.175)

76 Baudry, Robert, '*Ou* l'amour *ou* le Graal! Déclarations et disqualifications amoureuses dans *L'Enchanteur* de René Barjavel,' *Bien dire*, 15 (1997), 157–66. (L.176)

77 Debreuille, Jean-Yves, '"Je maintiendrai, fors d'y croire": Chrétien de Troyes, Julien Gracq et André Frénaud,' in Pa299 *Œuvre*, pp. 227–35. (L.190)

See Pb426 Ehrismann.

78 Lavorel, Guy, 'Du *Chevalier à la Charrette* à "l'enlèvement de Guenièvre": la réécriture de J. Roubaud et F. Delay,' in Pa299 *Œuvre*, pp. 237–46. (L.209)

79 Baudry, Robert, *Graal et littérature d'aujourd'hui, ou les échos de la légende du Graal dans la littérature française contemporaine*, Essais (Rennes: Terre de Brume, 1998). (LI.206)

80 Busby, Keith, 'Roman breton et chanson de geste au XVIIIe siècle,' in *Studies Brault*, pp. 17–48.

81 Cardini, Franco, Massimo Introvigne, and Marina Montesano, *Il Santo Graal* (Florence: Giunti, 1998). (LI.554)

82 Ferrand, Françoise, 'La réception de la littérature française médiévale en Allemagne au XIXe siècle: l'exemple de Richard Wagner,' in *Mélanges Ménard*, vol. 1, pp. 529–41. (LI.240)

83 Murrell, Elizabeth, 'History Revenged: Monty Python Translates Chrétien de Troyes's *Perceval or The Story of the Grail* (Again),' *Journal of Film and Video*, 50 (1998), 50–62. (LI.792)

84 Vibert, Bertrand, 'Axël, fils de Perceval,' *RT*, 55 (1998), 143–67.

85 Baudry, Robert, 'Quelques figures du roi Arthur dans la littérature française moderne,' *Bien dire*, 17 (1999), 7–21.

86 Callahan, Leslie Abend, '*Perceval le Gallois*: Eric Rohmer's Vision of the Middle Ages,' *Film & History*, 29:3–4 (1999), 46–53. (LII.740)

87 Gally, Michèle, ed., *La Trace médiévale et les écrivains d'aujourd'hui*, Perspectives Littéraires (Paris: Presses Universitaires de France, 2000).
Chrétien receives attention in the following:
- A. Michèle Gally, 'Rémanences,' pp. 1–11.
- B. Yves Bonnefoy, 'L'attrait des romans bretons,' pp. 15–27.
- C. Florence Delay, 'Graal soixante-treize,' pp. 39–45.
- D. Vincent Ferré, 'Tolkien et le Moyen Age, ou l'arbre et la feuille,' pp. 121–41.
- E. Jean-Charles Huchet, 'Gracq et le Graal: de l'échec au renoncement,' pp. 195–213.
- F. Laurence Giavarini, 'Signes et symboles, spectacle et représentation: l'aura du Moyen Age au cinéma,' pp. 235–45.

88 Grimbert, Joan Tasker, 'Distancing Techniques in Chrétien de Troyes's *Li Contes del Graal* and Eric Rohmer's *Perceval li Gallois*,' *Arthuriana*, 10:4 (2000), 33–44.

89 Hoffman, Donald L., 'Re-Framing Perceval,' *Arthuriana*, 10:4 (2000), 45–56.

See Ue7 Jewers.

90 Lacy, Norris J., 'From Medieval to Post-Modern: The Arthurian Quest in France,' *South Atlantic Review*, 65:2 (2000), 114–33.

See Ec9 Carroll and Colombo Timelli.

Q: LITERARY HISTORY AND SOCIOLOGY

Influenced by the Annalist French historians as well as by Erich Köhler's sociology of literature, work on this topic has produced interesting studies of medieval mentalities, prejudices, and beliefs that Chrétien's romances seem to reflect. Equally revealing have been studies of the nobility and chivalry as these are reflected in his romances, as well as how Chrétien seems to correct or ignore historical realities – for example, the place of marriage, lineage, and feudalism in his imaginary Arthurian world.

a: Political, Economic, Social, and Legal History

1   Wilmotte, Maurice, *L'Evolution du roman français* [...]
See also 'L'évolution du roman français aux environs de 1150,' *Académie Royale de Belgique: Bulletins de la Classe des Lettres et des Sciences Morales et Politiques et de la Classe des Beaux-Arts* (1903), pp. 323–79, 475–83.

8   Bezzola, Reto R., *Les Origines* [...]
See also Payen, M., *Les Origines de la courtoisie dans la littérature française médiévale*, 2 vols (Paris: Centre de Documentation Universitaire, 1966–67). See vol. 1, pp. 24–25, and vol. 2, pp. 26–40.

15   Benton, John F., 'The Court of Champagne [...]' Repr. in Dc16.
See also Patricia Danz Stirnemann, 'Quelques bibliothèques princières et la production hors scriptorium au XIIe siècle,' *Bulletin Archéologique du Comité des Travaux Historiques et Scientifiques*, n. s. 17–18A (1984), 7–38, esp. 'La bibliothèque de Henri le Libéral, comte de Champagne (1127–1181),' pp. 21–29, and 'La bibliothèque de Marie, comtesse de Champagne, femme de Henri le Libéral (1138–1198),' pp. 31–36.

26   Hiedsiek, Wilhelm, *Die ritterliche Gesellschaft in den Dichtungen des Crestien de Troies*, diss. Greifswald (Greifswald: Abel, 1883).

27   Krick, Charles, *Les Données sur la vie sociale et privée des Français au XIIe siècle contenues dans les romans de Chrestien de Troyes*,

Kreuznach: Wissenschaftliche Beilage zum Programm des kgl. Gymnasiums (Brussels: Tulkens, 1885).

28 Doerks, Henry, *Haus und Hof in den Epen des Crestien von Troies*, diss. Greifswald (Greifswald: Abel, 1885).

29 Oschinsky, Hugo, *Der Ritter unterwegs und die Pflege der Gastfreundschaft im alten Frankreich*, diss. Halle-Wittenberg (Halle/S.: [n.p.], 1900).

30 Euler, Heinrich, *Recht und Staat in den Romanen des Crestien von Troyes*, diss. Marburg (Marburg: Bauer, 1906).

See Kd34 Stowell.

See Kd37 Goddard.

See Gd.b2 Baker.

31 Huganir, Kathryn, 'Equine Quartering in *The Owl and the Nightingale*,' *PMLA*, 52 (1937), 935–45.
Discusses the practice in *Cligés*.

See Kd44 Wigand, pp. 6–24 and 45–73.

32 Bakos, F., 'Contributions à l'étude des formules de politesse en ancien français: I,' *Acta Linguistica Academiae Scientiarum Hungaricae*, 5 (1955), 295–367.
Resumé in Russian.

See Gb28 Peters.

33 Satô, Teruo, 'The Family of Eleanor of Aquitaine and Courtly Literature in the European Middle Ages,' *Cours d'Iwanami: Histoire Universelle: Geppo* 14, vol. 10 Appendice (1970), 1–4.
In Japanese.

See Gd.c6 Lyons.

34 Parkes, Malcolm, 'The Literacy of the Laity,' in *Mediaeval World*, pp. 555–78.

See Sa61 Salter.

35 Gerritsen, W.P., 'Het beeld van feodaliteit en ridderschap in middeleeuwse litteratuur,' *Bijdragen en mededelingen betreffende de geschiedenis der Nederlanden*, 89 (1974), 241–61. (XXVII.397)
Abridged version in French: 'Le Poète médiéval et l'histoire,' *RBPH*, 54 (1976), 329–40. (XXIX.160)

See Gb33 Combridge.

36 Erickson, Carolly, and Kathleen Casey, 'Women in the Middle Ages: A Working Bibliography,' *MS*, 37 (1975), 340–59.

37 Evergates, Theodore, *Feudal Society in the Bailliage of Troyes under the Counts of Champagne, 1152–1284* (Baltimore: Johns Hopkins University Press, 1975).

See Gb40 Colliot.

38 Pastoureau, Michel, *La Vie quotidienne en France et en Angleterre au temps des chevaliers de la Table Ronde (XIIe–XIIIe siècles)* (Paris: Hachette, 1976, 1981).

39 Schmitt, Jean-Claude, 'Le suicide au Moyen Age,' *Annales*, 31 (1976), 3–28.
See pp. 17–18.

40 Bloch, R. Howard, *Medieval French Literature and Law* (Berkeley: University of California Press, 1977). (XXX.127 *bis*).

41 Blumstein, Andrée Kahn, *Misogyny and Idealization in the Courtly Romance*, SGAK, 41 (Bonn: Bouvier, 1977). (XXX.35)
Emphasis on German romances, but offers comparisons with Chrétien.

42 Bur, Michel, *La Formation du comté de Champagne v. 950–v. 1150*, Mémoires des Annales de l'Est, 54 (Nancy: Université de Nancy II, 1977).
Not on Chrétien, but useful 'pre-history' on the county of Champagne. Cf. Qa37 Evergates and Qb65 Grossel.

See Ge26 Chênerie.

43 *La Femme dans les civilisations des Xe–XIIIe siècles: Actes du Colloque tenu à Poitiers les 23–25 septembre 1976*, in *CCM*, 20 (1977), 93–263.
    A.   Robert Fossier, 'La femme dans les sociétés occidentales,' pp. 93–104.
    B.   Chiara Frugoni, 'L'iconographie de la femme au cours des Xe–XIIe siècles,' pp. 177–88.
    C.   Rita Lejeune, 'La femme dans les littératures française et occitane du XIe au XIIIe siècle,' pp. 201–17. (XXX.281)
    D.   Jean Verdon, 'Les sources de l'histoire de la femme en Occident aux Xe–XIIIe siècles,' pp. 219–51.

44 Green, Dennis, 'The King and the Knight in the Medieval Romance,' *Festschrift for Ralph Farrell*, Australisch-neuseeländische Studien zur deutschen Sprache und Literatur, 7 (Bern: P. Lang, 1977), pp. 175–83.

45 Matthias, Anna-Susanna, 'Yvains Rechtsbrüche,' in *Beiträge ZrP*, pp. 156–92. (XXX.46)

See Gb43 Ménard.

See Sa76 Métral.

46 Antoine, Gérald, 'La place de l'argent dans la littérature française médiévale,' *Mélanges Rychner*, pp. 17–31. (XXXI.256)

See Qd14 Barron.

47 Duby, Georges, *Medieval Marriage: Two Models from Twelfth-Century France*, Johns Hopkins Symposia in Comparative Literature, 11 (Baltimore: Johns Hopkins University Press, 1978); French version: *Le Chevalier, la femme et le prêtre: le mariage dans la France médiévale* (Paris: Hachette, 1981).

See Hc29 Maddox.

See Pb211 Markey.

48 Shell, Marc, 'The Economy of the Grail Legends,' *CRCL*, 5 (1978), 1–29.

49 Subrenat, Jean, 'La place de quelques petits enfants dans la littérature médiévale,' in *Mélanges Lods*, pp. 547–57. (XXXI.307)

50 Boutet, Dominique, and Armand Strubel, *Littérature, politique et société dans la France du Moyen Age*, Littératures Modernes, 18 (Paris: Presses Universitaires de France, 1979). (XXXV.305)
See pp. 85–94.

See Hg44 Mohr.

See Fa103 Schulze-Busacker.

51 Luttrell, Claude, 'La nouveauté significative dans *Erec et Enide*,' *Rom*, 101 (1980), 277–80. (XXXIII.354)
On *novel seignor*.

See Gd.c19 Peron.

52 Berkvam, Doris Desclais, *Enfance et maternité dans la littérature française des XIIe et XIIIe siècles*, Essais, 8 (Paris: Champion, 1981). (XXXIV.225)

53 Bloch, R. Howard, 'Money, Metaphor, and the Mediation of Social Differences in Old French Romance,' *Symp*, 35 (1981), 18–33.

See Ha104 Evans.

54 Foulon, Charles, 'Les vavasseurs dans les romans de Chrétien de Troyes,' in *Essays Thorpe*, pp. 101–13. (XXXIV.312)

See Pb252 Mertens.

See Ha88 Ollier.

55 Payen, Jean-Charles, 'La "mise en roman" du mariage dans la littérature française des XIIe et XIIIe siècles: de l'évolution idéologique à la typologie des genres,' in *Love Leuven*, pp. 219–35. (XXXV.251)

56 Schmolke-Hasselmann, Beate, 'Henry II Plantagenêt, roi d'Angleterre, et la genèse d'*Erec et Enide*,' *CCM*, 24 (1981), 241–46. (XXXIV.248)

57 Vilhena, Maria da Conceição, 'A mulher na poesia francesa do Séc. XII,' *Arquipélago*, 3 (1981), 315–59; 4 (1982), 321–47.
See vol. 3, pp. 339–40, and vol. 4, pp. 337–39.

58 Bouvier-Ajam, Maurice, 'Chrétien de Troyes dans son temps,' *Europe*, 642 (Oct. 1982), 16–26. (XXXV.307)

See Gd.c23 Esposito.

59 Gouttebroze, J. G., 'Famille et structures de la parenté dans l'œuvre de Chrétien de Troyes,' *Europe*, 642 (Oct. 1982), 77–95. (XXXV.317)

See Ha112 Meneghetti.

See Sb39 Noble.

See Gb69 Payen.

60 Shell, Marc, *Money, Language, and Thought: Literary and Philosophical Economies from the Medieval to the Modern Era* (Berkeley: University of California Press, 1982).
Contains preprint of 'The Blank Check: Accounting for the Grail,' *SFR*, 7 (1983), 5–25.

61   Shirt, David J., '*Cligés* – A Twelfth-Century Matrimonial Case-Book?' *FMLS*, 18 (1982), 75–89. (XXXV.411)

62   Sayers, William, 'The Jongleur Taillefer at Hastings: Antecedents and Literary Fate,' *Viator*, 14 (1983), 77–88. (XXXVI.187)
Some discussion of *Perceval*.

63   Accarie, Maurice, 'Classe de loisir et naissance de la littérature,' in *Matériaux*, pp. 7–16. (XXXVII.53)

See Cb17 Alford and Seniff.

See Gb73 Bender.

See Hc46 Bender.

64   Blaess, Madeleine, 'The Public and Private Face of King Arthur's Court in the Works of Chrétien de Troyes,' in *Essays Topsfield*, pp. 238–48. (XXXVII.157)

65   Buschinger, Danielle, 'Le viol dans la littérature allemande au Moyen Age,' in *Amour mariage*, pp. 369–88. (XXXVII.586)

See Pb285 Buschinger.

See Sb40 Evans.

66   Holzermayr, Katharina, 'Le "mythe" d'Arthur: la royauté et l'idéologie,' *Annales*, 39 (1984), 480–94. (XXXVII.88)

67   Matthias, Anna-Susanna, 'Ein Handhaftverfahren aus dem Perceval/Parzivalroman (der Proceß des Urjans),' *GRM*, 34 (1984), 29–43. (XXXVII.639)
Greoreas's trial for rape.

See Ge37 Niessen-Poutet.

68   Raybin, David, 'Social Strain and the Genesis of Literary Genre in Twelfth-Century France and England,' *Works and Days*, 2:1 (1984), 45–63.

See Pb293 Rocher.

69   Ruiz Doménec, José Enrique, *La memoria de los feudales* (Barcelona: Argot, 1984).

70   Stiennon, Jacques, 'Bruges, Philippe d'Alsace, Chrétien de Troyes et le Graal,' in *Chrétien Bruges*, pp. 5–15. (XXXVII.119)

71 Sturm-Maddox, Sara, '"Tenir sa terre en pais": Social Order in the *Brut* and in the *Conte del Graal*,' *SP*, 81 (1984), 28–41. (XXXVII.468)

See Sb42 Burrell.

72 Gold, Penny Schine, *The Lady and the Virgin: Image, Attitude, and Experience in Twelfth-Century France*, Women in Culture and Society (Chicago: University of Chicago Press, 1985). (XXXVIII.495)
See pp. 18–42.

73 Gouttebroze, J.-G., 'Le statut sociologique du mariage d'Erec et d'Enide,' in *Actes Rennes*, vol. 1, pp. 218–40. (XXXVIII.213)

74 McCash, June Hall, 'Marie de Champagne's "cuer d'ome et cors de fame": Aspects of Feminism and Misogyny in the Twelfth Century,' in *ICLS Toronto*, pp. 234–45. (XXXVIII.331)

See Sa110 Muir.

75 Régnier-Bohler, Danielle, 'Fictions: exploration d'une littérature,' in *Histoire de la vie privée*, ed. Philippe Ariès and Georges Duby, in vol. 2 of *De l'Europe féodale à la Renaissance* (Paris: Seuil, 1985), pp. 311–91.
English trans. 'Imagining the Self: Exploring Literature,' in *A History of Private Life*, trans. Arthur Goldhammer (Cambridge, MA: Harvard University Press, 1988), vol. 2, pp. 311–93.

See Gb84 Rousse.

76 Stanesco, Michel, 'Sous le masque de Lancelot: du comportement romanesque au Moyen Age,' in *Actes Rennes*, vol. 2, pp. 569–83. (XXXVIII.268), and *Poétique*, 61 (1985), 23–33. (XXXVIII.267)

See Gb85 Stanesco.

See Pa161 Wolfzettel.

77 Kellogg, Judith L., 'Economic and Social Tensions Reflected in the Romance of Chrétien de Troyes,' *RPh*, 39 (1985–86), 1–21. (XXXVIII.511)
Especially *Erec* and *Yvain*.

78 Bumke, Joachim, *Höfische Kultur: Literatur und Gesellschaft im hohen Mittelalter*, 2 vols (Munich: Deutscher Taschenbuch Verlag, 1986). (XL.527).

79   Ebenbauer, Alfred, and Ulrich Wyss, 'Der mythologische Entwurf der höfischen Gesellschaft im Artusroman,' in *Höfische Literatur, Hofgesellschaft, höfische Lebensformen um 1200: Kolloquium am Zentrum für Interdisziplinäre Forschung der Universität Bielefeld (3. bis 5. November 1983)*, ed. Gert Kaiser and Jan-Dirk Müller, Studia Humaniora, 6 (Düsseldorf: Droste, 1986), pp. 513–39. (XXXIX.472)

See Kd100 Gallais.

80   Haidu, Peter, 'Idealism *vs.* Dialectics in Some Contemporary Theory,' *CRCL*, 13 (1986), 424–49. (XL.282)
See pp. 432–41 on the *Conte du Graal.*

See Qb52(B) Labande.

81   *The Medieval Court in Europe*, ed. Edward R. Haymes, Houston German Studies, 6 (Munich: Fink, 1986). (XXXIX.274)
See Gd.b29 Ferrante, Gd.b31 Jackson, Gd.c31 Krueger, and Pb304 Heinen.

See Ge43 Schmid.

82   Vance, Eugene, 'Chrétien's *Yvain* and the Ideologies of Change and Exchange,' *YFS*, 70 (1986), 42–62 (XXXIX.315); repr. in his *Mervelous Signals: Poetics and Sign Theory in the Middle Ages* (Lincoln: University of Nebraska Press, 1986), Chap. 5. (XXXIX.316)

See Gd.c32 Varty.

83   Barbero, Alessandro, *L'aristocrazia nella società francese del medioevo: analisi delle fonti letterarie (secoli X–XIII)*, Studi e Testi della Storia Medioevale, 12–13 (Bologna: Cappelli, 1987).

84   Régnier-Bohler, Danièle, 'Lieux et rituels de la sociabilité dans les œuvres narratives de la littérature médiévale en langue vernaculaire,' in *Sociabilité, pouvoirs et société: Actes du Colloque de Rouen 24/26 novembre 1983*, ed. Françoise Thelamopu, PUR, 110 (Rouen: Université de Rouen, 1987), pp. 75–78.

85   *Les Soins de beauté: Moyen Age, début des temps modernes: Actes du IIIe Colloque International, Grasse (26–28 avril 1985)*, ed. Denis Menjot (Nice: Centre d'Etudes Médiévales de Nice, Faculté des Lettres et Sciences Humaines, Université de Nice, 1987).
    A.   Christine Martineau-Genieys, 'Modèles, maquillage et misogynie, à travers les textes littéraires français du Moyen Age,' pp. 31–50.
    B.   Jean Larmat, 'Les bains dans la littérature française du Moyen Age,' pp. 195–210.

See Wb45 Belletti.

See Sa119 Duby.

See Kd108 Lebsanft.

86 Rieger, Dietmar, 'Le motif du viol dans la littérature de la France médiévale entre norme courtoise et réalité courtoise,' *CCM*, 31 (1988), 241–67. (XLI.85)

87 Rieger, Dietmar, *'Par force sos moi la mis*: intertextualité et littérature médiévale: l'exemple de la pastourelle et du roman arthurien,' *SMV*, 34 (1988), 79–96. (XLIII.345)

88 Brooke, Christopher N. L., *The Medieval Idea of Marriage* (Oxford: Oxford University Press, 1989).
See pp. 180–83, 188–90.

89 Ciggaar, Krijnie, 'Chrétien de Troyes et la "matière byzantine": les demoiselles du Château de Pesme Aventure,' *CCM*, 32 (1989), 325–31. (XLII.51)

90 Ménard, Philippe, 'Les emblèmes de la folie dans la littérature et dans l'art (XIIe–XIIIe siècles),' in *Hommage Payen*, pp. 253–65. (XLII.65)
In *Yvain*.

91 Runte, Hans R., 'Lunete et Gaston Paris: note sur le terme "courtois",' *ALFA*, 2 (1989), 143–53.

See Ue4 Sasaki.

92 Moorman, Charles, 'Literature of Defeat and of Conquest: The Arthurian Revival of the Twelfth Century,' in Da15 *King Arthur*, vol. 1, pp. 22–43. (XLIII.577)

93 Schmitt, Jean-Claude, *La Raison des gestes dans l'Occident médiéval*, Bibliothèque des Histoires (Paris: Gallimard, 1990).
See pp. 207–24.

94 Voicu, Mihaela, 'Une émeute communale au XIIe siècle ou "le monde bestourné",' *ABLs*, 39 (1990), 62–68.

95 Voicu, Mihaela, 'Există revoltă în Evul Mediu?' *Verbum*, 2 (1990), 75–80.

96 Bloch, R. Howard, *Medieval Misogyny and the Invention of Western Romantic Love* (Chicago: University of Chicago Press, 1991).

97 Brall, Helmut, 'Geschlechtlichkeit, Homosexualität, Freundesliebe: über mann-männliche Liebe in mittelalterlicher Literatur,' *Forum Homosexualität und Literatur*, 13 (1991), 5–27.
See pp. 17–27.

98 Gravdal, Kathryn, *Ravishing Maidens: Writing Rape in French Literature and Law*, New Cultural Studies Series (Philadelphia: University of Pennsylvania Press, 1991).
See Chap. 2: 'The Poetics of Rape Law: Chrétien de Troyes's Arthurian Romance.'

See Xa11 Hindman.

99 Stary, J. M., 'Adultery as a Symptom of Political Crisis in Two Arthurian Romances,' *Parergon*, 9:1 (1991), 63–73.
Includes the *Charrette*.

100 Wis, Marjatta, 'Hartmanns Connelant und Chrétiens *Cligés*: der Dichter und der Stauferhof,' *NM*, 92 (1991), 269–80.
References to contemporary Byzantine history in *Cligés*.

See Gb107 Boutet.

See Gb111 Fritz.

See Ud5 Gravdal.

101 Kullmann, Dorothea, *Verwandtschaft in epischer Dichtung: Untersuchungen zu den französischen 'Chansons de geste' und Romanen des 12. Jahrhunderts,'* Beihefte zur *ZrP*, 242 (Tübingen: Niemeyer, 1992).
See Part III: 'Die Romane der zweiten Hälfte des 12. Jahrhunderts.'

102 Meyer, Kajsa, 'Pourquoi un Chevalier au lion? Remarques sur l'actualité du thème choisi par Crestien de Troyes,' *BBSIA*, 44 (1992), 241–44.

103 Mori, Setsuko, 'Women in Early Ireland (1) (2) (3),' *JCSC*, 15 (1992), 1–27; 18 (1993), 85–114; 20 (1994), 1–26.
In Japanese.

104 Owen, D. D. R., 'The Prince and the Churl: The Traumatic Experience of Philip Augustus,' *Journal of Medieval History*, 18 (1992), 141–44.

105 Akehurst, F. R. P., 'Murder by Stealth: *traïson* in Old French Literature,' in *Studies Keller*, pp. 459–73.
See pp. 467–70.

See Kd116 Burgess.

106 Crane, Susan, 'Brotherhood and the Construction of Courtship in Arthurian Romance,' *AY*, 3 (1993), 193–201. (XLVI.703)

107 Ferguson, Gary, 'Symbolic Sexual Inversion and the Construction of Courtly Manhood in Two French Romances,' *AY*, 3 (1993), 203–13. (XLVI.712)
Includes the *Charrette*.

See Hc68 McCracken.

108 Maddox, Donald, 'La représentation du droit coutumier dans les romans de Chrétien de Troyes,' in *Le Droit et sa perception dans la littérature et les mentalités médiévales: Actes du Colloque du Centre d'Etudes Médiévales de l'Université de Picardie Amiens 17–19 mars 1989*, ed. Danielle Buschinger, GAG, 551 (Göppingen: Kümmerle, 1993), pp. 133–44. (XLVI.84)

109 Abbott, Reginald, 'What Becomes a Legend Most?: Fur in the Medieval Romance,' *Dress*, 21 (1994), 4–16.

110 Baldwin, John W., *The Language of Sex: Five Voices from Northern France around 1200*, The Chicago Series on Sexuality, History, and Society (Chicago: University of Chicago Press, 1994).

111 Carroll, Carleton W., 'Quelques observations sur les reflets de la cour d'Henri II dans l'œuvre de Chrétien de Troyes,' *CCM*, 37 (1994), 33–39. (XLVII.259)

See Ga83 Diverres.

See Qb64 Ferrante.

See Xa19 Hindman.

112 Knight, Stephen, 'From Jerusalem to Camelot: King Arthur and the Crusades,' in *Studies Sinclair*, pp. 223–32. (XLVII.567)
Treats *Perceval*.

113 Roussel, Claude, 'Courtoisie et féminité: le jeu des dames,' in *Du goût, de la conversation et des femmes*, ed. Alain Montandon, LE.L (Clermont-Ferrand: Association des Publications de la Faculté des Lettres et Sciences Humaines de Clermont-Ferrand, 1994), pp. 149–65.

114 Roussel, Claude, 'Le legs de la rose: modèles et préceptes de la sociabilité médiévale,' in *Pour une histoire des traités de savoir-vivre en Europe*, ed. Alain Montandon, LE.L (Clermont-Ferrand: Association des Publications de la Faculté des Lettres et Sciences Humaines de Clermont-Ferrand, 1994), pp. 1–90.

115 Stierle, Karlheinz, 'Cortoisie: die literarische Erfindung eines höfischen Ideals,' *Poetica*, 26 (1994), 256–83.

See Qb69 Kullmann.

116 Putter, Ad, 'Knights and Clerics at the Court of Champagne: Chrétien de Troyes's Romances in Context,' in *Medieval Knighthood V: Papers from the Sixth Strawberry Hill Conference, 1994*, ed. Stephen Church and Ruth Harvey (Woodbridge: Boydell, 1995), pp. 243–66. (XLVIII.433)

117 Duby, Georges, *Dames du XIIe siècle*, Bibliothèque des Histoires, 3 vols (Paris: Gallimard, 1995–96).
English trans. *Women of the Twelfth Century*, trans. Jean Birrell, 3 vols (Cambridge: Polity, Blackwell; Chicago: University of Chicago Press, 1998) (LI.363). See vol. 1, pp. 151–67 (trans. pp. 90–100) and vol. 3, pp. 147–215 (trans. pp. 81–120).

118 Finke, Laurie A., 'Sexuality in Medieval French Literature: "Séparés, on est ensemble",' in *Handbook of Medieval Sexuality*, ed. Vern L. Bullough and James A. Brundage, GRLH, 1696 (New York: Garland, 1996), pp. 345–68.

119 Kinoshita, Sharon, 'The Politics of *Translatio*: French-Byzantine Relations in Chrétien de Troyes's *Cligés*,' *Exemplaria*, 8 (1996), 315–54. (XLIX.510; L.504)

See Sa145 Spiewok.

120 Cartlidge, Neil, *Medieval Marriage: Literary Approaches, 1100–1300* (Cambridge: Brewer, 1997). (LI.355)
See Chap. 2:3 on *Erec* and other Chrétien romances.

See Gf41 Derrien.

121 White, Stephen D., 'La traición en la ficción literaria: derecho, hecho y ordalías en la narrativa y la épica en francés antiguo,' *Hispania* (Madrid), 57 (1997), 957–80.

122 Coss, Peter, *The Lady in Medieval England 1000–1500* (Stroud: Sutton; Mechanicsburg, PA: Stackpole, 1998). (LII.366)

See Qc84 Guyon.

See Me39 Löfstedt.

123 McCracken, Peggy, *The Romance of Adultery: Queenship and Sexual Transgression in Old French Literature*, The Middle Ages Series (Philadelphia: University of Pennsylvania Press, 1998).

124 Sylvester, Louise, 'Reading Rape in Medieval Literature,' *StMed*, 10 (1998), 120–35.

See Rb34 Zemel.

125 Carreto, Carlos F. C., '*Ce est mervoille et deablie*: économie du désir et magie verbale dans quelques récits arthuriens en vers,' in *Magie*, pp. 89–109. (LII.216)

126 Cowell, Andrew, *At Play in the Tavern: Signs, Coins, and Bodies in the Middle Ages*, Stylus: Studies in Medieval Culture (Ann Arbor: University of Michigan Press, 1999).
See chap. 1: 'Charity, Hospitality, and Profit.'

See Me41 Kelly, Chap. 5: 'The Issue and Topics of Consent in *Eneas*, *Erec*, and the *Bel Inconnu*.'

127 Lops, Reiner, 'De dood in de middeleeuwen,' *Rapports*, 69 (1999), 96–112. (LII.689)

128 Peters, Ursula, *Dynastengeschichte und Verwandtschaftsbilder: die Adelsfamilie in der volkssprachigen Literatur des Mittelalters*, Hermaea, 85 (Tübingen: Niemeyer, 1999). (LII.99)

129 Burch, S. L., '*Amadas et Ydoine*, *Cligès*, and the Impediment of Crime,' *FMLS*, 36 (2000), 185–95. (LIII.354)

See Fb105 Heyworth.

130 Lutz, Eckart Conrad, 'Herrscherapotheosen: Chrestiens Erec-Roman und Konrads Karl-Legende im Kontext von Herrschafts-legitimation und Heilssicherung,' in *Geistliches in weltlicher und*

Weltliches in geistlicher Literatur des Mittelalters, ed. Christoph Huber, Burghart Wachinger, and Hans-Joachim Ziegeler (Tübingen: Niemeyer, 2000), pp. 89–104. (LIII.99)

See Ge70 Ménard.

b: Cultural History

16   Cremonesi, Carla, 'Spunti di realismo [...]' Repr. in Dc11.

18   Badel, Pierre-Yves, *Introduction à la vie littéraire* [...]; new ed. 1984. (XXXVII.61)

25 (II)   Brault, Gerard J., 'Isolt and Guenevere [...]' (XXVIII.118)

26   Réau, Louis, and Gustave Cohen, *L'Art au Moyen Âge: arts plastiques, art littéraire et la civilisation française*, L'Évolution de l'Humanité: Synthèse Collective, 40 (Paris: Renaissance du Livre, 1935).
See Part II, chap. 2: 'Les manifestations littéraires de l'esprit social courtois.'

27   Schirmer, Walter F., and Ulrich Broich, *Studien zum literarischen Patronat im England des 12. Jahrhunderts*, Wissenschaftliche Abhandlungen der Arbeitsgemeinschaft für Forschung des Landes Nordrhein-Westfalen, 23 (Cologne: Westdeutscher Verlag, 1962).

28   Tanabe, Jûji, *Literary History of Medieval Europe* (Tokyo: Hosei University Press, 1966).
In Japanese.

29   Jongkees, A. G., '*Translatio studii*: les avatars d'un thème médiéval,' in *Miscellanea mediaevalia in Memoriam Jan Frederik Niermeyer* (Groningen: Wolters, 1967), pp. 41–51.
Includes *Cligés*.

30   Burrow, J. A., 'Bards, Minstrels, and Men of Letters,' in *Mediaeval World*, pp. 347–70.

31   Togeby, Knud, 'La littérature du Moyen Age,' in *Actes du 5ème Congrès des Romanistes Scandinaves, Turku (Åbo), du 6 au 10 août 1972*, Turun Yliopiston Julkaisuja – Annales Universitatis Turkuensis, B 127 (Turku: Turun Yliopisto, 1973), pp. 7–15. (XXVII.116)

See Ge24 Gössmann.

See Pb162 Harroff.

32 Lofmark, Carl, 'On Mediaeval Credulity,' in *'Erfahrung und Über-lieferung': Festschrift for C. P. Magill*, in *Trivium*, Special Publications, 1 (Cardiff: University of Wales Press, 1974), pp. 5–21.

See Sa69 Lazar.

33 Pastoureau, Michel, *Les armoiries*, TMA, 20 (Turnhout: Brepols, 1976). (XXIX.166)
See also Qb21 Brault.

34 Batany, Jean, 'Rome dans un schéma narratif bipolaire au Moyen Age,' in *Influence de la Grèce et de Rome sur l'Occident moderne: Actes du Colloque des 14, 15, 19 décembre 1975*, ed. Raymond Chevallier, Caesarodunum, 12 *bis* (numéro spécial) (Paris: Belles Lettres, 1977), pp. 43–54.

See Qa41 Blumstein, Chap. 5: 'The Wicked Widows.'

35 Washida, Tetsuo, 'The Monastery,' in *Pensée, Cours de Littérature Française V*, directed by Y. Fukui and ten other professors (Tokyo: Taishûkan, 1977), pp. 1–17.
In Japanese.

36 Elwert, Wilhelm Theodor, 'Il "committente" nella letteratura medievale,' in *Mélanges Bezzola*, pp. 113–26.

37 Tokui, Yoshiko, 'The Depiction of Costume in Courtly Romance,' *Costume Aesthetics* (The Society of Costume Aesthetics), 7 (1978), 59–78.
In Japanese.

38 Washida, Tetsuo, 'Monks and the "Auctores" (1) (2) (3),' *ALC*, 14 (1978), 1–19; 18 (1982), 97–117; 36 (2000), 65–87.
In Japanese.

39 *Batany, Jean, 'Langage et identités culturelles dans la France médiévale: du Concile de Tours à la Touraine de Panurge,' in *Langue française et identités culturelles: Actes du VIIe Biennale de la langue française (Moncton, 1977)* (Dakar: Nouvelles Éditions Africaines, 1979), pp. 154–67; repr. in his *Approches langagières de la société médiévale*, Varia, 2 (Caen: Paradigme, 1992), pp. 77–94.

40 Bumke, Joachim, *Mäzene im Mittelalter: die Gönner und Auftraggeber der höfischen Literatur in Deutschland 1150–1300* (Munich: Beck, 1979). (XXXII.17)

41   McCash, June Hall Martin, 'Marie de Champagne and Eleanor of Aquitaine: A Relationship Reexamined,' *Spec*, 54 (1979), 698–711. (XXXII.202)

42   Tyson, Diana B., 'Patronage of French Vernacular History Writers in the Twelfth and Thirteenth Centuries,' *Rom*, 100 (1979), 180–222, 584.
Useful discussion of patronage, although Chrétien not treated.

43   Devailly, M., 'La formation d'un milieu favorable au développement de la littérature arthurienne,' *Mélanges Foulon*, pp. 69–71. (XXXIII.327)
The Plantagenet court in the twelfth century.

44   Hanada, Humio, 'The Development of the Awareness of the Individual in French Literature of the Twelfth Century (I)(II)(III),' *CUCJ*, 17:4 (1980), 85–106; 18:1 (1980), 103–21; 18:3 (1980), 59–82.
In Japanese.

45   Holmes, Urban T., Jr, *Medieval Man: His Understanding of Himself, his Society, and his World Illustrated from his Own Literature*, ed. Urban T. Holmes, III, UNCSRL, 212 (Chapel Hill: Department of Romance Languages, University of North Carolina, 1980).
Includes illustrations from Chrétien's romances.

See Fe6 Scholz.

46   Bumke, Joachim, *Literarisches Mäzenatentum: ausgewählte Forschungen zur Rolle des Gönners und Auftraggebers in der mittel-alterlichen Literatur*, WF, 598 (Darmstadt: Wissenschaftliche Buch-gesellschaft, 1982). (XXXV.46)
Contains an excerpt from Qa8 Bezzola pp. 326–91, Qa15 Benton, and excerpts from Qa40 Bumke pp. 409–18 and Qb27 Schirmer pp. 9–23 (all in German), as well as an Introduction pp. 1–31.

47   Lecouteux, Claude, 'Paganisme, christianisme et merveilleux,' *Annales*, 37 (1982), 700–16. (XXXVII.92)

See Uc21 Bloch.

48   Oostrom, F. P. van, 'Hoofse cultuur en litteratuur,' in *Hoofse Cultuur: Studies over een aspect van de middeleeuwse cultuur*, ed. R. E. V. Stuip and C. Vellekoop (Utrecht: HES, 1983), pp. 119–38. (XXXVIII.700)

See Ga38 Pastoureau.

49 Pastoureau, Michel, 'Arthur, Lancelot, Perceval et les autres,' *L'Histoire*, 53 (1983), 84–86; repr. in his *Figures et couleurs: études sur la symbolique et la sensibilité médiévales* (Paris: Léopard d'Or, 1986), pp. 177–82. (XXXIX.662)

50 Jaeger, C. Stephen, *The Origins of Courtliness: Civilizing Trends and the Formation of Courtly Ideals 939–1210* (Philadelphia: University of Pennsylvania Press, 1985). (XXXVIII.508)

See Qa78 Bumke.

51 Pastoureau, Michel, 'L'héraldique arthurienne: une héraldique normande,' in his *Figures et couleurs: études sur la symbolique et la sensibilité médiévales* (Paris: Léopard d'Or, 1986), pp. 183–91. (XXXIX.662)

52 *Y a-t-il une civilisation du monde Plantagenêt? Actes du Colloque d'histoire médiévale, Fontevraud, 26–28 avril 1984,* = *CCM*, 29 (1986). (XXXIX.680)
  A. Pascale Bourgain, 'Aliénor d'Aquitaine et Marie de Champagne mises en cause par André le Chapelain,' pp. 29–36. (XXXIX.634)
  B. Edmond-René Labande, 'Les filles d'Aliénor d'Aquitaine: étude comparative,' pp. 101–12.

53 Stanesco, Michel, 'Nigromance et université: scolastique du merveilleux dans le roman français du Moyen Age,' in *Milieux universitaires et mentalité urbaine au Moyen Age, Colloque du Département d'Etudes Médiévales de Paris-Sorbonne et de l'Université de Bonn*, ed. Daniel Poirion, CCMed, 6 (Paris: Presses de l'Université de Paris-Sorbonne, 1987), pp. 129–44. (XL.60)

54 Kelly, Douglas, 'Le patron et l'auteur dans l'invention romanesque,' in *Théories*, pp. 25–39.

55 Tamura, Hajime, 'The Temporal Structure of the Seasons in Medieval France – Images, Words, Mentality,' *Shisô*, 768 (1988), 4–28. In Japanese.

See Ge49 Mölk.

See Uc31 Walter.

56 *Curialitas: Studien zu Grundfragen der höfisch-ritterlichen Kultur*, ed. Josef Fleckenstein, VMPG, 100 (Göttingen: Vandenhoeck & Ruprecht, 1990).
Contents:
  A. 'Einleitung,' pp. 9–13.
  B. Paul Gerhard Schmid, 'Curia und curialitas: Wort und Bedeutung im Spiegel der lateinischen Quellen,' pp. 15–26.

C. Ulrich Mölk, 'Curia und curialitas – Wort und Bedeutung im Spiegel der romanischen Dichtung: zu fr. *cortois(ie)*/ pr. *cortes(ia)* im 12. Jahrhundert,' pp. 27–38.
D. Peter Ganz, '"hövesch"/ "hövescheit" im Mittelhochdeutschen,' pp. 39–54.
E. Lutz Fenske, 'Der Knappe: Erziehung und Funktion,' pp. 55–127.
F. Elsbet Orth, 'Formen und Funktionen der höfischen Rittererhebung,' pp. 128–70.
G. Werner Rösener, 'Die höfische Frau im Hochmittelalter,' pp. 171–230.
H. Rüdiger Schnell, 'Die "höfische" Liebe als "höfischer" Diskurs über die Liebe,' pp. 231–301.
I. Josef Fleckenstein, 'Miles und clericus am Königs- und Fürstenhof: Bemerkungen zu den Voraussetzungen, zur Entstehung und zur Trägerschaft der höfisch-ritterlichen Kultur,' pp. 302–25.
J. Sabine Krüger, '"Verhöflichter Krieger" und miles illitteratus,' pp. 326–49.
K. Thomas Szabó, 'Der mittelalterliche Hof zwischen Kritik und Idealisierung,' pp. 350–91.
L. Thomas Zotz, 'Urbanitas: zur Bedeutung und Funktion einer antiken Wortvorstellung innerhalb der höfischen Kultur des hohen Mittelalters,' pp. 392–451.
M. Josef Fleckenstein, 'Nachwort: Ergebnisse und Probleme,' pp. 452–87.

57 Pastoureau, Michel, '*De gueules plain*: Perceval et les origines héraldiques de la maison d'Albret,' *Revue Française d'Héraldique et de Sigillographie*, 60–61 (1990–91), 63–81.

58 Cingolani, Stefano Maria, 'Filologia e miti storiografici: Enrico II, la corte plantageneta e la letteratura,' *SM*, ser. 3, 32 (1991), 815–32. (XLVI.554)

See Gd.c45 Carré.

59 Itô, Yasuharu, 'The Twelfth-Century Renaissance as Reflected in German Literature,' *JCIS*, 8 (1992), 47–67.
In Japanese.

60 Noble, Peter, 'Music in the Twelfth-Century French Romance,' *RMS*, 18 (1992), 17–31. (XLV.262)

61 Busby, Keith, '"Neither Flesh nor Fish, nor Good Red Herring": The Case of Anglo-Norman Literature,' in *Studies Keller*, pp. 399–417.

62 *Literarische Interessenbildung im Mittelalter*, DFG-Symposion 1991, ed. Joachim Heinzle, Germanistische Symposien: Berichtsbände, 14 (Stuttgart: Metzler, 1993).

- A. L. Peter Johnson, 'Die Blütezeit und der neue Status der Literatur,' pp. 235–56.
- B. Peter von Moos, 'Was galt im lateinischen Mittelalter als das Literarische an der Literatur? Eine theologisch-rhetorische Antwort des 12. Jahrhunderts,' pp. 431–51.
- C. Christoph Huber, 'Herrscherlob und literarische Autoreferenz,' pp. 452–73.

63 Stirnemann, Patricia, 'Women and Books in France: 1170–1220,' in *Representations of the Feminine in the Middle Ages*, ed. Bonnie Wheeler, Feminea Medievalia, 1 (Dallas, TX: Academia, 1993), pp. 247–52.
On patronage and transmission of texts.

64 Ferrante, Joan, 'Whose Voice? The Influence of Women Patrons on Courtly Romance,' in *Literary Aspects of Courtly Culture: Selected Papers from the Seventh Triennial Congress of the International Courtly Literature Society, University of Massachusetts, Amherst, USA, 27 July–1 August 1992*, ed. Donald Maddox and Sara Sturm-Maddox (Cambridge: Brewer, 1994), pp. 3–18.

65 Grossel, Marie-Geneviève, *Le milieu littéraire en Champagne sous les Thibaudiens (1200–1270)*, Medievalia, 14–15, 2 vols (Orléans: Paradigme, 1994).

66 Ôtaka, Yorio, 'Couleurs d'écus et d'enseignes des chevaliers arthuriens – essai préliminaire,' in *Mélanges Minoru Matsuda* (Tokyo: Editions Surugadai-shuppansha, 1994), pp. 69–84.

67 Uitti, Karl D., 'Chrétien de Troyes's *Cligés*: Romance *Translatio* and History,' in *Studies Kelly*, pp. 545–57. (XLVII.601)

68 Walters, Lori J., 'Jeanne and Marguerite de Flandre as Female Patrons,' *DFS*, 28 (1994), 15–27.

69 Kullmann, Dorothea, 'Hommes amoureux et femmes raisonnables: *Erec et Enide* et la doctrine ecclésiastique du mariage,' in Gb125 *Arthurian Romances*, pp. 119–29. (XLVI, pp. 437–38)

See Gb125(D) Blons-Pierre.

70 Fourquet, Jean, 'Chrétien entre Philippe d'Alsace et Marie de Champagne: deux œuvres sur commande: *Lancelot* et *Perceval*,' in *Amour Troyes*, pp. 19–28. (XLIX.152)

See Gb125(A) Régnier-Bohler.

71 Tokui, Yoshiko, *The Middle Ages in Fashion* (Tokyo: Keisô-shobô, 1995). (L.374)
In Japanese.

72 Broadhurst, Karen M., 'Henry II of England and Eleanor of Aquitaine: Patrons of Literature in French?' *Viator*, 27 (1996), 53–84. (L.439)

73 García Gual, Carlos, 'Mecenas y escritores: tres apuntes,' *Revista de Occidente*, 180 (May 1996), 11–26.
See pp. 17–22: 'La condesa María y el amor cortés.'

74 Krämer, Ulrike, *Translatio imperii et studii: zum Geschichts- und Kulturverständnis in der französischen Literatur des Mittelalters und der frühen Neuzeit*, Anhandlungen zur Sprache und Literatur, 98 (Bonn: Romanistischer Verlag, 1996).

See La45(A) Jaeger.

75 Lecouteux, Claude, *Au-delà du merveilleux: des croyances au moyen-âge*, CCMed, 13 (Paris: Presses de l'Université de la Sorbonne, 1996); 2nd rev. ed. under title *Au-delà du merveilleux: essai sur les mentalités du Moyen Age* (1998).

76 Owen, D. D. R., *Eleanor of Aquitaine: Queen and Legend* (Oxford: Blackwell, 1993, 1996). (LIII.505)

See Uf2(F) Stone.

77 Tokui, Yoshiko, 'The Feeling for Colour in Medieval Costume in France,' in *History and Culture of Colour* (Tokyo: Meigensha, 1996), pp. 59–90. (L.375).
In Japanese.

See Pb437(E) Ernst.

78 Boutet, Dominique, *Formes littéraires et conscience historique aux origines de la littérature française (1100–1250)*, Moyen Age (Paris: Presses Universitaires de France, 1999). (LII.207)

79 Gouttebroze, Jean-Guy, 'De la dévolution du pouvoir en milieu celtique et arthurien: croyances, rituel, éthique,' *MA*, 105 (1999), 681–702. (LII.3)

80 Niikura, Shun'ichi, *Travelling in the Middle Ages – Miracles, Love, and Death* (Tokyo: Hakusuisha, 1999).
In Japanese.

See Db74 Riquer.

81 Sugizaki, Taiichirô, *Monasteries and Twelfth-Century Society* (Tokyo: Hara-shobô, 1999).
In Japanese.

82 Takamiya, Toshiyuki, *Charms of Arthurian Legends – From Celts to Soseki* (Tokyo: Shûbun International, 1999).
In Japanese.

83 Tokui, Yoshiko, 'Colour in Medieval Europe: Symbolism of Clothes,' *Proceedings of 'Constructing Japanese Studies in Global Perspectives II'* (Ochanomizu University, Graduate School of Humanities and Sciences, 2001), pp. 82–89.
In Japanese.

c: Knighthood, Chivalry, and Courtesy

6 Micha, Alexandre, 'Le *Perceval* […]' Repr. in Dc3.

9 Frappier, Jean, 'Le Graal […]' Repr. in Dc5.

15 Bumke, Joachim, *Studien zum Ritterbegriff* […]; 2nd ed. (Heidelberg: Winter, 1977). (XXX.19)
English trans. *The Concept of Knighthood in the Middle Ages*, trans. W. T. H. Jackson and Erika Jackson, AMS Studies in the Middle Ages, 2 (New York: AMS, 1982).

See Kd33 Galpin.

25 Webster, K. G. T., 'The Twelfth-Century Tourney,' in *Papers Kittredge*, pp. 227–34.

26 Hatto, A. T., 'Archery and Chivalry: A Noble Prejudice,' *MLR*, 35 (1940), 40–54. (I.162)
See pp. 48–50.

27   Melville, Marion, *La Vie des Templiers*, La Suite des Temps, 24 (Paris: Gallimard, 1951; 2nd rev. ed., 1974). (IV.99)
See Chap. 16: 'Un archevêque et deux trouvères.'

28   Russo, Vittorio, ' "Cavalliers e clercs",' *FiR*, 6 (1959), 305–32.
See pp. 308–10, 329–30.

29   Moorman, Charles, 'The First Knights,' *Southern Quarterly*, 1 (1962), 13–26. (XV.64)

30   Winter, J. M. van, *Ridderschap: ideaal en werkelijkheid*, Fibula-reeks, 11 (Bussum: van Dishoeck, 1965).
See pp. 65–77.

31   Washida, Tetsuo, 'The Knight and the Cleric (1),' *ALC*, 5 (1969), 313–36; '(2)–(3),' *YBK*, 19 (1971), 47–71; 23 (1975), 122–41; '(4)–(9),' *F-b*, 1 (1976), 131–44; 2 (1977), 114–29; 3 (1978), 128–41; 4 (1979), 132–45; 5 (1980), 118–37; 6 (1981), 109–22.
In Japanese.

32   Barber, Richard, *The Knight and Chivalry* (London: Longman; Totowa, NJ: Rowman and Littlefield, 1970; Woodbridge: Boydell, 1974; rev. ed. 1995).

33   Horigoshi, Kôichi, 'Knighthood in Epic Poetry in the Middle Ages,' in *Japanese Literature in the World* (Tokyo: Tôdai Shuppankai, 1973), pp. 227–46.
In Japanese.

See Gd.c6 Lyons.

34   Flori, Jean, 'Qu'est-ce qu'un *bacheler*: étude historique de vocabu-laire dans les chansons de geste du XIIe siècle,' *Rom*, 96 (1975), 289–314. (XXVIII.251)

See Gb39 Chênerie.

See Gb42 Ménard.

35   *Das Rittertum im Mittelalter*, ed. Arno Borst, WF, 349 (Darmstadt: Wissenschaftliche Buchgesellschaft, 1976). (XXIX.9)

See Pa101 Keen.

36   Flori, Jean, 'Chevalerie et liturgie: remise des armes et vocabulaire "chevaleresque" dans les sources liturgiques du IXe au XIVe siècle,' *MA*, 84 (1978), 247–78, 409–42.

See Hg38 Le Rider.

See Kd85 Riquer.

37 Brewer, Derek, 'The Arming of the Warrior in European Literature and Chaucer,' in *Chaucerian Problems and Perspectives: Essays Presented to Paul E. Beichner* (Notre Dame, IN: University of Notre Dame Press, 1979), pp. 221–43.

38 Flori, Jean, 'Les origines de l'adoubement chevaleresque: études des remises d'armes et du vocabulaire qui les exprime dans les sources historiques latines jusqu'au début du XIIIe siècle,' *Trad*, 35 (1979), 209–72.

39 Flori, Jean, 'Pour une histoire de la chevalerie: l'adoubement dans les romans de Chrétien de Troyes,' *Rom*, 100 (1979), 21–53. (XXXII.344)

See Hg45 Pioletti.

See Ga22 Wolf.

40 Barber, Richard, *The Reign of Chivalry* (Newton Abbot: David & Charles; New York: St Martin's Press, 1980). (XXXIII.433)

41 Benson, Larry D., 'The Tournament in the Romances of Chrétien de Troyes and *L'Histoire de Guillaume le maréchal*,' in *Chivalric Literature: Essays on Relations between Literature and Life in the Later Middle Ages*, ed. Larry D. Benson and John Leyerle, SMC, 14 (Kalamazoo: Medieval Institute, Western Michigan University, 1980), pp. 1–24, 147–52 (XXXIII.130); repr. in his *Contradictions – From 'Beowulf' to Chaucer: Selected Studies*, ed. Theodore M. Andersson and Stephen A. Barney (Aldershot: Scolar; Brookfield, VT: Ashgate, 1995), pp. 266–92.

42 Lénat, R., 'L'adoubement dans quelques textes littéraires de la fin du XIIe siècle: clergie et chevalerie,' *Mélanges Foulon*, vol. 1, pp. 195–203. (XXXIII.347)

See Gb62 Vinaver.

43 Hunt, Tony, 'The Emergence of the Knight in France and England 1000–1200,' *FMLS*, 17 (1981), 93–114. (XXXIV.326); repr. in *Knighthood in Medieval Literature*, ed. W. H. Jackson (Cambridge: Brewer, 1981), pp. 1–22. (XXXV.395)

See Gd.a13 Katô.

See He37 Ruiz Doménec.

See Hf49 Ruiz Doménec.

See Ge35 Boutet.

See Fa119 Busby.

See Hg56 Lacy.

44 Sargent-Baur, Barbara Nelson, 'Promotion to Knighthood in the Romances of Chrétien de Troyes,' *RPh*, 37 (1983–84), 393–408. (XXXVII.453)

45 Gies, Frances, *The Knight in History* (New York: Harper and Row, 1984). (XXXIX.261)
See Chap. 4: 'The Troubadours and the Literature of Knighthood.'

46 Keen, Maurice, *Chivalry* (New Haven, CT: Yale University Press, 1984). (XXXVII.406)

See Hd15 Lacy.

47 Ross, D. J. A., 'Breaking a Lance,' in *Guillaume d'Orange and the 'Chanson de geste': Essays Presented to Duncan McMillan in Celebration of his Seventieth Birthday by his Friends and Colleagues of the Société Rencesvals*, ed. Wolfgang van Emden, Philip E. Bennett, and Alexander Kerr (Reading: Société Rencesvals [British Branch], 1984), pp. 127–35.
Discusses *Cligés* vv. 4786–4816 (Micha ed.).

48 Ruiz Doménec, José Enrique, *La caballería o la imagen cortesana del mundo*, Collana Storica di Fonti e Studi, 40 (Genoa: Università di Genova, Istituto di Medievistica, 1984).
Includes slightly revised versions of He37 and Hf49.

49 Salvini, Michela, and Andrea Fassò, 'Alle origini del romanzo moderno: il sogno del cavaliere e il sacrificio dello sparviero,' *Quaderni Medievali*, 18 (Dec. 1984), 6–43.

See Jd29 Accarie.

See Gb79 Baumgartner.

See Gb82 Houstin.

50 Parisse, Michel, 'Le tournoi en France, des origines à la fin du XIIIe siècle,' in *Turnier*, pp. 175–211.

CHRÉTIEN DE TROYES

See Gb87 Chênerie.

51 Flori, Jean, *L'Essor de la chevalerie: XIe–XIIe siècles*, Travaux d'Histoire Éthico-Politique, 46 (Geneva: Droz, 1986).

See Pb303 Groos.

52 North, Sally, 'The Ideal Knight as Presented in Some French Narrative Poems, c. 1090–c. 1240: An Outline Sketch,' in *The Ideals and Practice of Medieval Knighthood: Papers from the First and Second Strawberry Hill Conferences*, ed. Christopher Harper-Bill and Ruth Harvey (Woodbridge: Boydell, 1986), pp. 111–32.

See Hf67 Glasser.

53 Lecouteux, Claude, 'Harpin de la Montagne (*Yvain*, v. 3770 et ss.),' *CCM*, 30 (1987), 219–25. (XL.47)

54 Arthur, Ross G., 'The Judicium Dei in the *Yvain* of Chrétien de Troyes,' *RomN*, 28 (1987–88), 3–12. (XLI.340)

See Pb317(E) Jackson.

55 Switten, Margaret, '*Chevalier* in Twelfth-Century French and Occitan Literature,' in *Chivalry*, pp. 403–47.

56 Takatô, Mako, 'Dirge for the "MASURAOS = Knights of God",' *ELF*, 10 (1988), 157–79.
In Japanese.

57 Zijlstra-Zweens, H. M., *Of His Array Telle I No Lenger Talle: Aspects of Costume, Arms and Armour in Western Europe, 1200–1400* (Amsterdam: Rodopi, 1988). (XLII.248)
Although Chrétien is not discussed specifically, the following chapters contain useful information on costume, arms, and armour in his romances: Chap. 2: 'A Short Survey of the Costume, Arms and Armour of the Period,' pp. 19–26, and Chap. 4: 'Kostüm und Waffen im Spiegel der höfischen Dichtung,' pp. 51–86. Summaries in English (pp. 125–26) and Dutch (pp. 127–28).

58 Chandès, Gérard, 'Observations sur le champ sémantique de la *recreantise*,' in *Hommage Payen*, pp. 123–31. (XLII.50)

59 *Forme dell'identità cavalleresca*, in *ImRif*, 12 (1989).
Articles that touch on Chrétien:
  A. Jean Flori, 'La lancia e il vessillo: tecnica militare e ideologia cavalleresca nei secoli XI e XII,' pp. 7–40.
  B. Ulrich Mölk, 'A proposito del senso di *cortois(ie)* nella letteratura del XII secolo,' pp. 41–54.

C. Andrea Fassò, 'La lotta col re-padre e il sogno della sovranità: gli
    eroi di Chrétien de Troyes,' pp. 55–90.
D. José Enrique Ruiz Doménec, 'Il grande anelito della cavalleria
    cortese,' pp. 133–46.
E. Mario Mancini, 'Onore cavalleresco e onore aristocratico,' pp. 147–
    91.
F. Corrado Bologna, 'La generosità cavalleresca di Alessandro Magno,'
    pp. 367–404 (esp. pp. 388–90).

See Pa215 Picherit.

60 Sears, Theresa Ann, 'Prisoners of Love: Love, Destiny, and
Narrative Control in *Le Chevalier de la charrette* and *Cárcel de Amor*,'
FCS, 15 (1989), 269–82. (XLII.347)

See Fa147 Stanesco.

61 Baldwin, John W., 'Jean Renart et le tournoi de Saint-Trond: une
conjonction de l'histoire et de la littérature,' *Annales*, 45 (1990), 565–88.
(XLIII.162)

62 Zaddy, Z. P., 'The Courtly Ethic in Chrétien de Troyes,' in *The
Ideals and Practice of Medieval Knighthood III: Papers from the Fourth
Strawberry Hill Conference 1988*, ed. Christopher Harper-Bill and Ruth
Harvey (Woodbridge: The Boydell Press, 1990), pp. 159–80.

See Hc62 Aguiriano.

See Pd63 Dirscherl.

See Gd.c42 *Feste*.

63 Hanning, R. W., 'Love and Power in the Twelfth Century, with
Special Reference to Chrétien de Troyes and Marie de France,' in *The
Olde Daunce: Love, Friendship, Sex, and Marriage in the Medieval
World*, ed. Robert R. Edwards and Stephen Spector, SUNY Series in
Medieval Studies (Binghamton: State University of New York Press,
1991), pp. 87–103.

64 Scaglione, Aldo, *Knights at Court: Courtliness, Chivalry, and
Courtesy from Ottonian Germany to the Italian Renaissance* (Berkeley:
University of California Press, 1991). (XLV.521)

See Ub39 Holzbacher.

65 Ailes, Adrian, 'The Knight, Heraldry and Armour: The Role of
Recognition and the Origins of Heraldry,' in *Knighthood IV*, pp. 1–21.

66 Cardini, Franco, *Guerre di primavera: studi sulla cavalleria e la tradizione cavalleresca*, Le Vie della Storia, 7 (Florence: Le Lettere, 1992). (XLVI.552)

67 Ménard, Philippe, '"Je sui encore bacheler de jovent" (*Aimeri de Narbonne*, v. 766): les représentations de la jeunesse dans la littérature française aux XIIe et XIIIe siècles: études des sensibilités et mentalités médiévales,' in *Les Âges de la vie au Moyen Âge: Actes du Colloque du Département d'Études Médiévales de l'Université de Paris-Sorbonne et de l'Université Friedrich-Wilhelm de Bonn, Provins, 16–17 mars 1990*, ed. Henri Dubois and Michel Zink, CCMed, 7 (Paris: Presses de l'Université de Paris Sorbonne, 1992), pp. 171–86. (XLV.189)

68 Noble, Peter, 'Perversion of an Ideal,' in *Knighthood IV*, pp. 177–86.

69 Coss, Peter, *The Knight in Medieval England 1000–1400* (Stroud: Sutton, 1993, 1995). (LII.365)

70 Flori, Jean, 'Les écuyers dans la littérature française du douzième siècle (pour une lexicologie de la société médiévale),' in *Hommage Dufournet*, vol. 2, pp. 579–92. (XLVI.329)

See Pb360(E) Jackson.

See Pa252 Simó.

See Kd121 Burgess.

71 Corradetti, Roberta, 'Le armi di lancio nei romanzi di Chrétien de Troyes,' *QMacerata*, ser. 3, 9 (1994), 61–95. (XLVII.459)

72 Fahrner, Rudolf, *West-östliches Rittertum: das ritterliche Menschenbild in der Dichtung des europäischen Mittelalters und der islamischen Welt*, ed. Stefano Bianca (Graz: Akademische Drucks- und Verlagsanstalt, 1994).
See Chap. 9: 'Alianor: Geistige Erhebung des westlichen Rittertums,' and Chap. 10: 'Der Karrenritter des Christian von Troyes.'

73 Hildebrand, Kristina, 'Society through a Visor: History and Arthurian Romance,' in *English Studies and History*, ed. David Robertson, Tampere English Studies, 4 (Tampere, Finland: University of Tampere Publications Sales Office, 1994), pp. 179–93.

See Xa19 Hindman.

74   Corradetti, Roberta, 'Le armi manesche nei romanzi di Chrétien de Troyes,' *QMacerata*, ser. 3, 10 (1995), 65–126. (XLIX.328)

See Gd.c54 Ferlampin-Acher.

See Sb52 Ferroul.

See Gd.c55 Flores Arroyuelo.

75   Flori, Jean, *La Chevalerie en France au Moyen Age*, Que sais-je? 972 (Paris: Presses Universitaires de France, 1995).
Japanese trans. by Shun'ichi Niikura (Tokyo: Hakusuisha, 1998). (LI.649)

76   Guerreau-Jalabert, Anita, 'Fées et chevalerie: observations sur le sens social d'un thème dit merveilleux,' in *Miracles, prodiges et merveilles au Moyen Age: XXVe Congrès de la SHMES (Orléans, juin 1994)*, Série Histoire Ancienne et Médiévale, 34 (Paris: Publications de la Sorbonne, 1995), pp. 133–50.

See Gd.c57 Nickel.

See Gb125(B) Putter.

See Db56 Ruiz Domènec.

See Ga89 Sargent-Baur.

77   Badellino, Enrico, *I templari* (Milan: Xenia, 1996).
See 'Il Santo Graal e lo spirito delle origini,' pp. 103–8.

See Hg104 Cazelles.

78   Corradetti, Roberta, 'L'abbigliamento del cavaliere nei romanzi di Chrétien de Troyes,' *QMacerata*, ser. 3, 11 (1996), 33–94. (XLIX.329)

79   Flori, Jean, 'La notion de chevalerie dans les romans de Chrétien de Troyes,' *Rom*, 114 (1996), 289–315. (XLIX.151)

80   Keen, Maurice, *Nobles, Knights and Men-at-Arms in the Middle Ages* (London: Hambledon, 1996).

81   Benoît, Louis, 'Famille et chevalerie dans *Le Conte du Graal* de Chrétien de Troyes,' *SLCO*, 24 (1998), 35–48.

82   Flori, Jean, *Chevaliers et chevalerie au Moyen Age*, La Vie Quotidienne (Paris: Hachette, 1998).

83 Gosman, Martin, 'De opkomst van de France kroniek,' in *Koningen en kronieken*, ed. R. E. V. Stuip and C. Vellekoop (Hilversum: Verloren, 1998), pp. 95–115. (LII.677)

84 Guyon, Gérard D., 'Essai de lecture juridique du roman médiéval: le champion du droit chez Chrétien de Troyes,' *Revue d'Histoire des Facultés de Droit et de la Science Juridique*, 10 (1998), 251–83. (LII.239)

85 Neumeyer, Martina, *Vom Kriegshandwerk zum ritterlichen Theater: das Turnier im mittelalterlichen Frankreich*, Abhandlungen zur Sprache und Literatur, 89 (Bonn: Romanistischer Verlag, 1998).

See Hg117 Pickens.

See Qf9 Almanza Ciotti.

86 Santina, Mary Arlene, *The Tournament and Literature: Literary Representations of the Medieval Tournament in Old French Works, 1150–1226*, Studies in the Humanities: Literature–Politics–Society, 49 (New York: P. Lang, 1999).

87 Janssens, Jozef, 'Beschaafde emoties: hoofsheid en hoofse liefde in de volkstaal,' in *Medioneerlandistiek*, pp. 141–53. (LIII.873)

See Ha209(G) Kaeuper.

See Gd.b62 Noble.

d: Realism

6 Combellack, C. R. B., 'The Entrapment [...]' (XXIX.110)

7 Hall, Robert A., Jr., 'The Silk-Factory in Chrestien de Troyes' *Yvain*,' *MLN*, 56 (1941), 418–22; repr. in his *Language, Literature, and Life: Selected Essays*, Edward Sapir Monograph Series in Language, Culture, and Cognition, 5 (Lake Bluff, IL: Jupiter, 1978), pp. 143–46.

8 Brand, Wolfgang, 'Das Wirklichkeitsbild im *Lancelot* und *Yvain*,' *VR*, 33 (1974), 186–213.

9 Kamizawa, Eizô, 'Secularization of Courtly Romance – from Chrétien de Troyes to Jean Renart,' *JFLN*, 55 (1972), 149–68.
In Japanese.

10 Pasero, Nicolò, 'Chrétien, la realtà, l'ideologia: ancora sul *Chastel de Pesme-Aventure* (*Yvain*, vv. 5179 ss.),' in *Studi in ricordo di Guido Favati* (Genoa: Istituto di Filologia Romanza e Ispanistica dell'Università degli Studi di Genova, 1975), pp. 145–69. (XXIX.366)

11 Radulet, Carmen M., 'Intorno al realismo cerimoniale del *Lancelot* di Chrétien de Troyes,' *CN*, 35 (1975), 9–30. (XXIX.367)

12 Marazza, Camillo, 'Immaginazione poetica e realtà sociale: il caso delle "tisseuses" di Chrétien de Troyes,' *Quaderni di Lingue e Letterature*, 1 (1976), 49–57.

13 Shirt, David, '*Cligès*: Realism in Romance,' *FMLS*, 13 (1977), 368–80. (XXX.360)

14 Barron, W. R. J., 'A propos de quelques cas d'écorchement dans les romans anglais et français du Moyen Age,' in *Mélanges Lods*, vol. 1, pp. 49–68. (XXXI.258)
See pp. 62–65.

See Hf35 Pioletti.

15 Voisset, Georges M., 'Ici, ailleurs, au-delà: topographie du réel et de l'irréel dans *Le 'Chevalier au Lion'*, in *Mélanges Jonin*, pp. 703–15. (XXXII. 366)

See Ha103 Benton.

16 Cremonesi, Carla, 'A proposito del realismo di Chrétien de Troyes,' in *Mélanges à la mémoire de Franco Simone: France et Italie dans la culture européenne. IV: Tradition et originalité dans la création littéraire*, Bibliothèque Franco Simone, 9 (Geneva: Slatkine, 1983), pp. 47–58.

17 Knight, Stephen, *Arthurian Literature and Society* (New York: St Martin's Press; London: Macmillan, 1983). (XXXVI.440, XXXVII.410)
See '"Prowess and Courtesy": Chrétien de Troyes' *Le Chevalier au lion*,' pp. 68–104.

See Gd.c27 Molle.

See Ha151 Peron.

18 Itô, Yasuharu, 'Courtly Epic and Courtly Life Styles, in which Literature and Reality Cross Paths,' *JCIS*, 7 (1991), 33–51.
In Japanese.

19   Maddox, Donald, 'La quotidienneté et le texte narratif courtois,' in *ICLS Salerno*, pp. 441–52.

See Pb377 Thomas.

See Pa262 Lacy.

20   Sodigné-Costes, Geneviève, 'Les blessures et leur traitement dans les romans en vers (XIIe–XIIIe siècles),' in *Violence*, pp. 499–514.

See Jb52 Rieger.

21   Accarie, Maurice, 'Vérité du récit ou récit de la vérité: le problème du réalisme dans la littérature médiévale,' *Razo*, 15 (1998), 5–34. (LI.199)

See Gf46 Ferroul.

22   Ferroul, Yves, 'Réalités sexuelles et fiction romanesque,' in *Les 'Realia' dans la littérature de fiction au moyen âge: Actes du Colloque du Centre d'Etudes Médiévales de l'Université de Picardie-Jules Verne, Saint-Valery-sur-Somme, 25–28 mars 1999*, ed. Danielle Buschinger, Médiévales, 9 (Amiens: Presses du Centre d'Etudes Médiévales, Université de Picardie-Jules Verne, 2000), pp. 40–49.

See Pb470 Schulz-Grobert.

e: Sociology

3   Kaiser, Gert, *Textauslegung* […] (XXVI.353)

See Gb25 Meyer.

See Ke2 Engler.

See Pb165 Huby.

5   Köhler, Erich, 'Il sistema sociologico del romanzo francese medievale,' *MedR*, 3 (1976), 321–44. (XXX.426)

6   Boklund, Karin, 'Socio-sémiotique du roman courtois,' *Semiotica*, 21 (1977), 227–56.

7   Brall, Helmut, 'Zur sozialgeschichtlichen Interpretation mittel-alterlicher Literatur: Anmerkungen zum Stand der Diskussion,' *ZLiLi*, 7, no. 26 (1977), 19–38. (XXX.17)

8   Nerlich, Michael, *Kritik der Abenteuer-Ideologie: Beitrag zur Erforschung der bürgerlichen Bewußtseinsbildung 1100–1750*, Literatur und Gesellschaft, 2 vols (Berlin: Akademie, 1977). (XXXI.35)

See Gb46 Batany.

9   Duby, Georges, *Les Trois Ordres ou l'imaginaire du féodalisme* (Paris: Gallimard, 1978).
See pp. 352–70.
See also Jean Batany, 'Du *bellator* au *chevalier* dans le schéma des "trois ordres" (étude sémantique),' in *La Guerre et la paix: frontières et violences au Moyen Age: Actes du 101e Congrès National des Sociétés Savantes, Lille, 1976: Section de Philologie et d'Histoire jusqu'à 1610* (Paris: Bibliothèque Nationale, 1978), pp. 23–34; repr. in his *Approches langagières de la société médiévale*, Varia, 2 (Caen: Paradigme, 1992), pp. 147–58.

See Ha84 Payen.

10   Schnell, Rüdiger, *Zum Verhältnis von hoch- und spätmittelalterlicher Literatur: Versuch einer Kritik*, PSQ, 92 (Berlin: Schmidt, 1978). (XXXI.41)

See Na.b23 Casagrande.

See Pa114 Gumbrecht, pp. 112–15.

11   Pioletti, Antonio, 'La condanna del lavoro: gli "ordines" nei romanzi di Chrétien de Troyes,' *FeS*, 1 (1980), 71–109. (XXXIV.444)

12   Poirion, Daniel, 'Histoire de la littérature médiévale et histoire sociale: perspectives de recherche,' in *Literatur in der Gesellschaft*, pp. 13–16.

13   Marchello-Nizia, Christiane, 'Amour courtois, société masculine et figures du pouvoir,' *Annales*, 36 (1981), 969–82. (XXXV.331)

14   Melli, Elio, 'Commercio, mercanti, prefigurazione di organizzazione industriale, nei romanzi di Chrétien de Troyes,' *QBologna*, 2 (1981), 55–80. (XXXIV.442)

See Gb66 Callay.

See Fb52 Haidu.

15   Le Goff, Jacques, 'Quelques remarques sur les codes vestimentaire et alimentaire dans *Erec et Enide*,' in *La Chanson de geste et le mythe carolingien: mélanges René Louis publiés par ses collègues, ses amis et* *ses élèves à l'occasion de son 75ᵉ anniversaire*, 2 vols (Saint-Père-sous-Vézelay: Musée Archéologique Régionale, 1982), vol. 2, pp. 1243–58; repr. in his *L'Imaginaire médiéval: essais* (Paris: Gallimard, 1985), pp. 188–207.

Italian trans. 'Osservazioni sui codici di abbigliamento e alimentari nell'*Erec et Enide*,' in *Il Meraviglioso e il quotidiano nell'Occidente medievale*, ed. Francesco Maiello, trans. Michele Sampaolo (Bari: Laterza, 1983; repr. 1988), pp. 81–100. (XLIII.340)

16 Ruiz-Doménec, J. E., 'Littérature et société médiévale: vision d'ensemble,' *MA*, 88 (1982), 77–114.

17 Sprandel, Rolf, *Gesellschaft und Literatur im Mittelalter*, Uni-Taschenbücher, 1218 (Paderborn: Schöningh, 1982). (XXXV.75)

18 Voicu, Mihaela, 'Text literar şi context social: de la *Tristan* la *Cligés*,' *LMS*, 2 (1982), 84–87.

19 Haidu, Peter, 'The Hermit's Pottage: Deconstruction and History in *Yvain*,' in *Sower*, pp. 127–45; repr. in *RR*, 74 (1983), 1–15. (XXXVII.383)

20 Haidu, Peter, 'Romance: Idealistic Genre or Historial Text?' in *Craft*, pp. 1–46. (XXXVII.384)

21 Meneghetti, Maria Luisa, 'Les modèles culturels: "ante rem," "in re," "post rem"?' in *Semiosis: Semiotics and the History of Culture in Honorem Georgii Lotman*, ed. Morris Halle [et alii], Michigan Slavic Contributions, 10 (Ann Arbor: University of Michigan, 1984), pp. 77–91. (XXXVIII.532)

See Ga50 Boutet.

22 Stanesco, Michel, *Jeux d'errance du chevalier médiéval: aspects ludiques de la fonction guerrière dans la littérature du Moyen Âge flamboyant*, Brill's Studies in Intellectual History, 9 (Leiden: Brill, 1988).

23 Kellogg, Judith, *Medieval Artistry and Exchange: Economic Institutions, Society, and Literary Form in Old French Narrative*, AUS:RL, 123 (New York: P. Lang, 1989). (XLIII.559)
See Chap. 2 'Chrétien de Troyes,' and pp. 148–50 '*Largesce* and *Mesure* in Chrétien's Romance.'

24   Larmat, Jean, *Les Pauvres et la pauvreté dans la littérature française du Moyen Age* (Nice: Centre d'Etudes Médiévales, Université de Nice, 1994). (XLVII.276)

25   Liebertz-Grün, Ursula, 'Kampf, Herrschaft, Liebe: Chrétiens und Hartmanns Erec- und Iweinromane als Modelle gelungener Sozialisation im 12. Jahrhundert,' in *Graph*, pp. 297–328. (XLVII.572)

See Qd21 Accarie.

26   Le Rider, Paule, 'A propos de costumes... De Giraud de Barri au *Conte du graal* et à *Fergus*,' *MA*, 107 (2001), 253–82.

f: Religious Practices

See Me10 Anitchkof.

See Qb26 Réau and Cohen, Part II, Chap. 4: 'Les manifestations littéraires de l'esprit religieux.'

See Je24 Mahoney.

See Kd54 Winkler.

1   Rousset, Paul, 'La notion de chrétienté aux XIe et XIIe siècles,' *MA*, 69 (1963), 191–203.
Useful material à propos of *Erec*, which is not cited.

See Hg40 Maddux.

See Gb57 Payen.

See Hg48 Buettner.

2   Bozóky, Edina, 'Les éléments religieux dans la littérature arthurienne,' *Cercle Ernest Renan: Cahiers*, 29, no. 122 (Nov.–Dec. 1981), 125–37.

See Jd25 Bayer.

3   Payen, Jean-Charles, 'Encore la pratique religieuse dans *Le Conte du Graal*,' in *Chrétien Bruges*, pp. 121–32. (XXXVII.109)

See Rb29 Bayer.

See Ue4 Sasaki.

4 Guerreau-Jalabert, Anita, 'Les nourritures comme figures symboliques dans les romans arthuriens,' in *La Sociabilité à table: commensalité et convivialité à travers les âges: Actes du Colloque de Rouen avec la participation de Jacques Le Goff, 14–17 novembre 1990*, ed. Martin Aurell, Olivier Dumoulin, and Françoise Thelamon, PUR, 178 (Rouen: Publications de l'Université de Rouen, 1992), pp. 35–40 (discussion p. 45).

See Tb20 Zambon.

5 Kullmann, Dorothea, 'Chrétien de Troyes et la doctrine ecclésiastique du mariage,' *QBologna*, 10 (1993), 33–74. (XLVII.463)

6 Baldwin, John W., 'The Crisis of the Ordeal: Literature, Law, and Religion around 1200,' *JMRS*, 24 (1994), 327–53. (XLVII.675)

7 Mandach, André de, 'A la recherche du *Conte du Graal* originaire: le modèle commun en code transpyrénéen de Chrétien de Troyes et de Wolfram von Eschenbach,' in *Granatapfel: Festschrift für Gerhard Bauer zum 65. Geburtstag*, ed. Bernhard Dietrich Haage, GAG, 580 (Göppingen: Kümmerle, 1994), pp. 137–48.

See Gb127 Bretel.

8 Sutherland, Ross, *'Cligès' et le mystère de Terre Sainte du Templier: l'hérésie sacrée du sépulcre de la 'Christe'*, Medieval Studies, 9 (Lewiston, NY: Mellen, 1995).

See Db72 Zambon.

9 Almanza Ciotti, Gabriella, 'Il cavaliere Perceval (elementi per una rilettura),' *QMacerata*, 3rd ser., 14 (1999), 5–22.

10 Moisan, André, 'Le chevalier chrétien à la lumière de la mystique de Saint Bernard,' in *Mélanges Subrenat*, pp. 393–408.

g: Geography

1 Bellamy, Félix, *La Forêt de Bréchéliant, la Fontaine de Bérenton, quelques lieux d'alentour, les principaux personnages qui s'y rapportent*, 2 vols (Rennes: J. Plihon & L. Hervé, 1896).
See vol. 1, pp. 463–594 on *Yvain*.

2 Bell, Alexander, 'Zu Perceval 3675: Cotöatre,' *ZrP*, 54 (1934), 753–55.

See Mf6 Grill.

See Gd.b11 Seidel.

See Rb28 Bullock-Davies.

3 *La Légende arthurienne et la Normandie (hommage à René Bansard)*, ed. Jean-Charles Payen (Condé-sur-Noireau: Corlet, 1983). (XXVI.362)
- A. Jean-Charles Payen, 'Culture normande et mythes arthuriens,' pp. 7–22.
- B. André Moisson, 'Héroïsme et sainteté: interférences entre deux types de l'idéal au Moyen Age,' pp. 45–71.
- C. Réjane Molina, 'La Chapelle Royale Saint-Frambourg de Senlis et le Graal,' pp. 127–49.
- D. André-Edgard Poëssel, 'Sur une piste '"normande"' du cycle arthurien,' pp. 151–61.
- E. Gilles Susong, 'Où situer la fontaine merveilleuse d'Yvain?' pp. 163–80.
- F. Jean-Charles Payen, 'Appendice: Quelques dossiers de René Bansard,' pp. 203–37.

4 Pickford, Cedric E., 'The River Humber in French Arthurian Romances,' in *Studies Diverres*, pp. 149–59, 247–48. (XXXVI.450)
See pp. 151–52.

5 Watson, Michael, 'British Geography in Arthurian Literature,' *Gengo*, 3 (1985), 52–87.

See Mc45 Goodrich.

See Wb37 Holden.

See Nb39 Susong.

See Gd.b34 Vermette.

6 Morris, Rosemary, 'Aspects of Time and Place in the French Arthurian Verse Romances,' *FS*, 42 (1988), 257–77. (XLI.145)

7 Foulon, Charles, 'Brocéliande et sa Fontaine dans la littérature latine médiévale,' in *Au miroir de la culture antique: mélanges offerts au Président René Marache* (Rennes: Presses Universitaires de Rennes, 1992), pp. 231–36. (XLV.177)

See Kd115 Ménard.

See Ge58 Zumthor, Chap. 10: 'Le Chevalier errant.'

See Gd.c50 Bromiley.

8   Ueda, Hiroshi, 'Medieval Romance and Geography: *Ipomedon*,' *JFLN*, 121 (1995), 131–46. (XLIX.377)
In Japanese.

See Ga96 Zink.

See Bb73 Luttrell.

9   Luttrell, Claude, 'Arthurian Geography: The Islands of the Sea,' *Neophil*, 83 (1999), 187–96. (LII.691)

R: BIOGRAPHY AND CHRONOLOGY

Recent attempts to delineate Chrétien's character, social status, and life have emphasized how little we know, rather than attempting to draw from his works some documentary evidence lacking in other sources. On the other hand, this great ignorance of his biography has opened the door to some speculation – the less we know, the more we can make of isolated material like names (Chrétien, Troyes) or allusions (Godefroy de Lagny). There have been no widely accepted advances in the chronology of Chrétien's romances, the two contrasting views represented by Rb12 and Rb17 still being most representative.

a: Problems of Chronology in Medieval French Literature, with Special Reference to Chrétien de Troyes

4   Heinermann, Th., 'Zur Zeitbestimmung der Werke Gautiers von Arras und zu seiner Stellung zu Chrétien von Troyes,' *ZfSL*, 59 (1935), 237–45.

5   Wilmotte, M., 'Problèmes de chronologie littéraire,' *MA*, 40 (1940), 99–114. (III.104)

6   Lejeune, Rita, 'La date du roman de *Jaufré*: à propos d'une édition récente,' *MA*, 54 (1948), 257–95. (II.158)
See pp. 278–95.

7   Delbouille, Maurice, 'A propos de la patrie et de la date de *Floire et Blanchefleur* (version aristocratique),' in *Mélanges de linguistique et de littérature romanes offerts à Mario Roques par ses amis, ses collègues et ses anciens élèves de France et de l'étranger*, 4 vols (Paris: Didier, 1952), vol. 4, pp. 53–98. (V.124)
See pp. 71 (*Philomena*) and 89–98 (*Erec*).

8   Delbouille, Maurice, 'Les "senhals" littéraires désignant Raimbaut d'Orange et la chronologie de ses témoignages,' *CN*, 17 (1957), 49–73. See pp. 59–60, 68–69.

9   Tiemann, Hermann, 'Noch einmal für eine kritische Chronologie der altfranzösischen Literatur,' *RJ*, 10 (1959), 53–58. On Ra3 Levy.

10   Lejeune, R., 'La datation du troubadour Rigaut de Barbezieux: questions de détail et question de méthode,' *MA*, 70 (1964), 397–417. (XIX.136)

11   Kooijman, Jacques-Cornélis, 'Temps réel et temps romanesque: le problème de la chronologie relative d'*Yvain* et de *Lancelot* de Chrétien de Troyes,' *MA*, 83 (1977), 225–37. (XXX.215)

12   Luttrell, Claude, 'King Arthur's Solemn Vow and the Dating of *Yvain*,' *FMLS*, 13 (1977), 285–87. (XXX.349)

13   Shirt, David J., 'How Much of the Lion Can we Put before the Cart? Further Light on the Chronological Relationship of Chrétien de Troyes's *Lancelot* and *Yvain*,' *FS*, 31 (1977), 1–17. (XXX.359)

14   Han, Françoise, 'Chronologie(s), bibliographie,' *Europe*, 642 (Oct. 1982), 135–37. (XXXV.321)

15   Kartschoke, Dieter, 'Eneas-Erec-Tristrant: zur relativen Chronologie der frühen höfischen Versromane,' in *Philologische Untersuchungen gewidmet Elfriede Stutz zum 65. Geburtstag*, PG, 7 (Vienna: Braumüller, 1984), pp. 212–22. (XXXVIII.34)

16   Mullally, Evelyn, 'The Order of Composition of *Lancelot* and *Yvain*,' *BBSIA*, 36 (1984), 217–29. (XXXVIII.337)

17   Engelhardt, Klaus, Volker Roloff, and Marie Engelhardt-Bayssade, *Daten der französischen Literatur. Bd. I: Von den Anfängen bis 1800*, 2 vols (Munich: Deutsches Taschenbuch, 1978).

18   Hunt, Tony, 'Redating Chrestien de Troyes,' *BBSIA*, 30 (1978), 209–37.

19   Sasaki, Shigemi, 'État présent de la chronologie de la légende du Graal,' *Kiyo: Bulletin of the University of Tokyo-Meisei*, 21 (March 20, 1985), 9–18.

20   Janssens, Jan, 'The "Simultaneous" Composition of *Yvain* and *Lancelot*: Fiction or Reality?' *FMLS*, 23 (1987), 366–76. (XL.117)

See Md50 Eley and Simons.

b: Chrétien's Biography

See Ea23 Emecke.

22 Ménard, Philippe, 'Note sur la date [...]' Repr. in Dc29.

24 Lejeune, Rita, 'Le troubadour Rigaut de Barbezieux,' in *Mélanges István Frank*, Annales Universitatis Saraviensis, 6 ([n.p.]: Universität des Saarlandes, 1957), pp. 269–95. (XI.185)

See Pi5 Várvaro.

See He23 Välikangas.

25 Müller, Karl Friedrich, *Hartmann von Aue und die Herzöge von Zähringen*, Oberrheinische Studien, 3 (Lahr: Schauenburg, 1974). (XXVII.169)
See pp. 16 and 26–27.

26 Katô, Kyôko, 'Who Was Chrétien de Troyes?' *Sophia*, 108 (1978), 76–78.
In Japanese.

27 Williams, Harry F., 'Godefroi de Leigni,' *USFLQ*, 18:1–2 (1979), 19, 22, and 26. (XXXIII.179)

28 Bullock-Davies, Constance, 'Chrétien de Troyes and England,' *AL*, 1 (1981), 1–61. (XXXIV.297)

See Qa56 Schmolke-Hasselmann.

See Nb24–25 Payen.

See Mc45 Goodrich.

See Va16 Rossi.

See Na.e45 Thomas.

29 Bayer, Hans, '"Vita cum Phoenice complice": Gottfried von Straßburg's "gotinne" Isolde, Chrétien's Fenice and neo-Platonic Mysticism in Alsace and Troyes,' *OrL*, 43 (1988), 20–31.
Cathar heresy and Chrétien.

30 Vitz, Evelyn Birge, 'Chrétien de Troyes: clerc ou ménestrel? Problèmes des traditions orale et littéraire dans les cours de France au XIIe siècle,' *Poétique*, 81 (1990), 21–42. (XLIII.204)
Cf. Fe34.

See Ge57 Steele.

See Qa111 Carroll.

31 Goldsmith-Rose, Nancy Helen, 'Languages at the Norman Court of England,' in *The Formation of Culture in Medieval Britain: Celtic, Latin, and Norman Influences on English Music, Literature, History, and Art*, ed. Françoise H. M. Le Saux (Lewiston, NY: Mellen, 1995), pp. 71–86. (XLVIII.414).

See Pk71 Busby.

32 Gouttebroze, Jean-Guy, '"Sainz Pos le dit, et je le lui", Chrétien de Troyes lecteur,' *Rom*, 114 (1996), 524–35. (XLIX.157)

33 Kay, Sarah, 'Who Was Chrétien de Troyes?' *AL*, 15 (1997), 1–35. (L.267)

34 Zemel, Roel, 'Maria van Champagne en Chrétien de Troyes,' *Madoc*, 12 (1998), 149–60. (LI.700)

35 Watanabe, Kôji, 'Who Was Chrétien de Troyes? – A Reexamination of the Attempt to Identify a Canon of the Abbey Saint-Loup with Chrétien,' *Welt*, 90 (1999), 8–17.
In Japanese.

See Jb59 Thomasset.

See Va23 Rossi.

S: PROBLEMS OF COURTLY LOVE

The problematic notion 'courtly love' and its medieval counterparts like *fin'amour* remain a controversial and much discussed feature of Chrétien scholarship. Recent developments include focus on women, misogyny, and social hierarchies (reflected in Q and Ud), as well as debate regarding perceived moral, social, satirical, or farcical features of love in his romances. The significance of the love of Tristan and Iseut for Chrétien still attracts attention, although the problematic character of that love in medieval Tristan romances in recent scholarship has complicated the reading of Chrétien's responses to it, as well as that of the characters in his romances.

a: General Studies

14   Jackson, W. T. H., 'The *De Amore* [...]' Repr. in Dc12.

30(II) Benton, John F., 'Clio and Venus [...]' Repr. in Dc16.

43   Ferrante, J. M., and G. D. Economou, ed., *In Pursuit of Perfection...* (XXVIII.122)
See Joan M. Ferrante, 'The Conflict of Lyric Conventions and Romance Form,' pp. 135–78.

45   Mott, Lewis Freeman, *The System of Courtly Love Studied as an Introduction to the 'Vita Nuova' of Dante* (Boston: Ginn, 1896; repr. New York: Haskell House, 1965).
See Chap. 4.

46   Neilson, William Allan, *The Origins and Sources of the 'Court of Love'*, [Harvard] Studies and Notes in Philology and Literature, 6 (Boston: Ginn, 1899; repr. New York: Russell & Russell, 1967).

47   Wilcox, John, 'Defining Courtly Love,' *Papers of the Michigan Academy of Science, Arts and Letters*, 12 (1929), 313–25.

48 Meader, William G., *Courtship in Shakespeare: Its Relation to the Tradition of Courtly Love* (New York: King's Crown, 1954; repr. New York: Octagon, 1971). (VIII.62)
See pp. 13–26.

49 Sutherland, D. R., 'The Language of the Troubadours and the Problem of Origins,' *FS*, 10 (1956), 199–215.

50 Kolb, Herbert, *Der Begriff der Minne und das Entstehen der höfischen Lyrik*, Hermaea, 4 (Tübingen: Niemeyer, 1958).

51 Hill, D. M., 'The Structure of *Sir Orfeo*,' *MS*, 23 (1961), 136–53.
Discusses love madness in *Yvain*.

See Fa63 Sutherland.

52 Askew, Melvin W., 'Courtly Love: Neurosis as Institution,' *Psychoanalytic Review*, 52 (1965), 19–29.

53 Matsubara, Hideichi, 'Women in Art and Literature (Medieval French Literature),' *G-k*, 19 (1965), 56–64.
In Japanese.

54 Koenigsberg, Richard A., 'Culture and Unconscious Fantasy: Observations on Courtly Love,' *Psychoanalytic Review*, 54 (1967), 36–50.

55 Moore, John C., 'Love in Twelfth-Century France: A Failure in Synthesis,' *Trad*, 24 (1969), 429–43.

56 Press, A. R., 'The Adulterous Nature of *fin'amors*: A Re-examination of the Theory,' *FMLS*, 6 (1970), 327–41.

57 Moore, John C., *Love in Twelfth-Century France* (Philadelphia: University of Pennsylvania Press, 1972).

58 Tobin, Frank, '*Concupiscentia* and Courtly Love,' *RomN*, 14 (1972), 387–93.

59 Utley, Francis Lee, 'Must We Abandon the Concept of Courtly Love?' *M&H*, 3 (1972), 299–324.

60 Baron, F. Xavier, and Judith M. Davis, '*Amour courtois*', the Medieval Ideal of Love: A Bibliography* (Louisville, KY: University of Louisville [1973]).

61   Salter, Elizabeth, 'Courts and Courtly Love,' in *Mediaeval World*, pp. 407–44.

62   Yamamoto, Jun'ichi, '"Fine amor" in the *Roman de Troie*,' *Hum*, 19 (1973), 73–103.
In Japanese.

63   Buridant, Claude, trans., *André le Chapelain: Traité de l'amour courtois*, BFR, ser. D, 9 (Paris: Klincksieck, 1974). (XXVIII.229)
See Introduction, pp. 7–44.

64   Miller, Robert P., 'The Wounded Heart: Courtly Love and the Medieval Antifeminist Tradition,' *WomS*, 2 (1974), 335–50.

65   Davidson, Clifford, 'The Love Mythos in the Middle Ages and Renaissance,' *Ball State University Forum*, 16:4 (1975), 3–14.

66   Kelly, Henry Ansgar, *Love and Marriage in the Age of Chaucer* (Ithaca, NY: Cornell University Press, 1975).
See Chap. 1: 'Guinevere, Marie de Champagne, and Heloise Revisited.'

67   Owen, D. D. R., *Noble Lovers* (New York: New York University Press, 1975).
See Chap. 3: 'Lancelot: Courtly Lover'.

See Ma25 Schnell.

68   Herlihy, David, 'The Medieval Marriage Market,' *Medieval and Renaissance Studies, 6: Proceedings of the Southeastern Institute of Medieval and Renaissance Studies, 1974*, ed. Dale B. J. Randall (Durham, NC: Duke University Press, 1976), pp. 3–27.

69   Lazar, Moshé, 'Cupid, the Lady, and the Poet: Modes of Love at Eleanor of Aquitaine's Court,' in *Eleanor*, pp. 35–59.

70   Niikura, Shun'ichi, 'Love: Europe's Invention,' in *Course in Comparative Culture 3: Northern Europe and the Japanese*, ed. S. Itô [et alii] (Tokyo: Kenkyûsha-shuppan, 1976), pp. 167–87.
In Japanese.

71   Niikura, Shun'ichi, 'Love: The Invention in the Twelfth Century,' in *The Search for the Occidental Mind*, ed. Y. Horigome (Tokyo: Nihonhôsô Kyôkai, 1976), pp. 181–204.
In Japanese.

See Qa41 Blumstein.

72 Boase, Roger, *The Origin and Meaning of Courtly Love: A Critical Study of European Scholarship* (Manchester: Manchester University Press; Totowa, NJ: Rowman and Littlefield, 1977). (XXX.337)

73 Chydenius, Johan, *Love and the Medieval Tradition*, Commentationes Humanarum Litterarum, 58 (Helsinki: Societas Scientiarum Fennica, 1977).

74 Foster, Kenelm, 'Courtly Love and Christianity,' in his *The Two Dantes and Other Studies* (London: Darton, 1977), pp. 15–36.

75 Liebertz-Grün, Ursula, *Zur Soziologie des 'amour courtois': Umrisse der Forschung*, Beihefte zum *Euph*, 10 (Heidelberg: Winter, 1977). (XXX.43)

76 Métral, Marie-Odile, *Le Mariage: les hésitations de l'Occident* (Paris: Aubier-Montaigne, 1977).

77 Morgan, Gerald, 'Natural and Rational Love in Medieval Literature,' *Yearbook of English Studies*, 7 (1977), 43–52.

78 Oka, Fumiko, 'Some Notes on "druery" (1) – "drut" and "drudaria" in the Provençal Tradition,' *Ronshû*, 18 (1977), 35–42. (XXXI. 381).

79 Press, A. R., 'The Theme of Concealed Love in Two French Poets of the Twelfth Century,' in *Essays Powell–Hodgins*, pp. 119–30. (XXXI. 118)

80 Taiana, Franz, *Amor purus und die Minne*, Germanistica Friburgensia, 1 (Freiburg Schweiz: Universitätsverlag, 1977).

81 Kelly, Douglas, *Medieval Imagination: Rhetoric and the Poetry of Courtly Love* (Madison: University of Wisconsin Press, 1978). (XXXI. 103)
See Chap. 2: 'Allegory of Love.'

See Gf15 Neaman.

82 Niikura, Shun'ichi, 'The *Tractatus de amore* by André le Chapelain,' *GS*, 6:1 (1978), 130–39.
In Japanese.

83 Oka, Fumiko, 'Some Notes on "Lemman" (1),' *TCE*, 51 (1978), 43–108 ; '(2)', *JA*, 20 (1978), 1–30.

See Ha85 Sklute.

84   Bowden, Betsy, 'The Art of Courtly Copulation,' *M&H*, 9 (1979), 67–85.

85   Cherchi, Paolo, 'Andreas' *De amore*: Its Unity and Polemical Origin,' in his *Andrea Cappellano, i trovatori e altri temi romanzi*, Biblioteca di Cultura, 128 (Rome: Bulzoni, 1979), pp. 83–111.

See Fd2 Hunt.

See Ua21 Leclercq.

86   Lerner, Laurence, *Love and Marriage: Literature and its Social Context* (London: Arnold, 1979).
See 'Tristan in Context,' pp. 11–14.

87   Loyd, James, and Virginia León de Vivero, 'The Artful Rejection of Love from Ovid to Andreas to Chartier,' *Modern Language Studies*, 9:2 (1979), 46–52.

88   Manzalaoui, M. A., 'Tragic Ends of Lovers: Medieval Islam and the Latin West,' *Comparative Criticism*, 1 (1979), 37–52.

89   Moore, John C., '"Courtly Love": A Problem of Terminology,' *Journal of the History of Ideas*, 40 (1979), 621–32.

See Gb58 Payen and Legros.

90   Reiss, Edmund, '*Fin'amors*: Its History and Meaning in Medieval Literature,' *Medieval and Renaissance Studies* (Duke University), 8 (1979), 74–99.

91   Burnley, J. D., '*Fine amor*: Its Meaning and Context,' *RES*, 31 (1980), 129–48. (XXXIII.437)

See Jc11 Calin.

92   Ferrante, Joan M., '*Cortes'Amor* in Medieval Texts,' *Spec*, 55 (1980), 686–95. (XXXIII.140)

93   Smith, Nathaniel B., and Joseph T. Snow, 'Courtly Love and Courtly Literature,' in *ICLS Athens*, pp. 3–14. (XXXII.222)

See Qb52(B) Labande.

94   Karnein, Alfred, '*Amor est passio* – A Definition of Courtly Love?' in *ICLS Liverpool*, pp. 215–21.

95 Karnein, Alfred, 'La réception du *De amore* d'André le Chapelain au XIIIe siècle,' *Rom*, 102 (1981), 324–51, 501–42.

96 Karnein, Alfred, 'Europäische Minnedidaktik,' in *Neues Handbuch der Literaturwissenschaft*, vol. 7: *Europäisches Hochmittelalter*, ed. Henning Krauss (Wiesbaden: Athenaion, 1981), pp. 121–44.

See Qe13 Marchello-Nizia.

See Qa55 Payen.

97 Leclercq, Jean, 'The Development of a Topic in Medieval Studies in the Eighties: An Interdisciplinary Perspective on Love and Marriage,' in *Literary and Historical Perspectives of the Middle Ages: Proceedings of the 1981 SEMA Meeting*, ed. Patricia W. Cummins, Patrick W. Conner, and Charles W. Connell (Morgantown: West Virginia University Press, 1982), pp. 20–37.

98 Leclercq, Jean, *Monks on Marriage: A Twelfth-Century View* (New York: Seabury, 1982); French trans.: *Le Mariage vu par les moines du XIIe siècle* (Paris: Le Cerf, 1983).
See Chap. 6: 'Cloisters, Literature, and Secular Writings.'

99 Liebertz-Grün, Ursula, 'Minne-Utopie im Mittelalter,' in *Literarische Utopie-Entwürfe*, ed. Hiltrud Gnüg, Suhrkamp taschenbuch, 2012 (Frankfurt/M: Suhrkamp, 1982), pp. 80–90. (XXXVI.52)

100 Schmolke-Hasselmann, Beate, 'Accipiter et chirotheca: die Artusepisode des Andreas Capellanus – eine Liebesallegorie?' *GRM*, 32 (1982), 387–417. (XXXV.66)
Includes some comparisons with Chrétien's romances.

101 Schnell, Rüdiger, *Andreas Capellanus: zur Rezeption des römischen und kanonischen Rechts in 'De amore'*, MMS, 46 (Munich: Fink, 1982). (XXXIX.405)

See Va14 Zaganelli.

102 Colman, Rebecca V., 'Mud Huts and Courtly Love,' *Revue de l'Université d'Ottawa*, 53 (1983), 147–53.

103 Keen, M. H., 'Chivalry and Courtly Love,' Denis Bethell Memorial Lecture, 1, *Peritia*, 2 (1983), 149–69. (LII.407)

See Ub18 Rey-Flaud.

104 Rocher, Daniel, 'L'amour, transgression du couple,' in *Amour mariage*, pp. 359–67. (XXXVI.657)

Includes passages from *Cligés*.

105 Singer, Irving, *The Nature of Love. 2: Courtly and Romantic* (Chicago: University of Chicago Press, 1984). (XXXIX.312)

See pp. 116–21.

106 Sullivan, Penny, 'Love and Marriage in Early French Narrative Poetry,' *Trivium*, 19 (1984), 85–102. (XXXVII.187)

Various models, including some from *Cligés*.

See He50 Beltrami.

107 Karnein, Alfred, *De amore in volkssprachlicher Literatur: Untersuchungen zur Andreas-Capellanus-Rezeption in Mittelalter und Renaissance*, GRM: Beihefte, 4 (Heidelberg: Winter, 1985). (XXXVII. 625)

108 Kelly, Henry Ansgar, 'Gaston Paris's Courteous and Horsely Love,' in *ICLS Toronto*, pp. 217–23. (XXXVIII.326)

See Qa74 McCash.

109 *Mittelalterbilder aus neuer Perspektive: Diskussionsanstöße zu amour courtois, Subjektivität in der Dichtung und Strategien des Erzählens: Kolloquium Würzburg 1984*, ed. Ernstpeter Ruhe and Rudolf Behrens, BRPMA, 14 (Munich: Fink, 1985).

Includes several contributions on courtly love which concern Chrétien directly or indirectly:

  A. Marie Benoît, 'Le *De amore*: dialectique et rhétorique,' pp. 13–21.
  B. Paolo Cherchi, 'New Uses of Andreas' *De amore*,' pp. 22–30.
  C. Alfred Karnein, 'Andreas, Boncompagno und andere: oder das Problem, eine Textreihe zu konstituieren,' pp. 31–42.
  D. Jean-Charles Payen, 'Un ensenhamen trop précoce: L'Art d'aimer d'André le Chapelain,' pp. 43–58.
  E. Bruno Roy, 'André le Chapelain, ou l'obscénité rendue courtoise,' pp. 59–74.
  F. Rüdiger Schnell, 'Kirche, Hof und Liebe: zum Freiraum mittelalterlicher Dichtung,' pp. 75–111.
  G. Hans Ulrich Gumbrecht, 'Auf gemeinsamer Suche nach der "höfischen Kultur" des Mittelalters? Antworten (und Fragen) an R. Schnell,' pp. 112–18.

See also Hf59 Gier, Ub27 Wolfzettel.

110 Muir, Lynette R., *Literature and Society in Medieval France: The Mirror and the Image 1100–1500* (Basingstoke: Macmillan; New York: St Martin's Press, 1985). (XXIX.77)

Chap. 3: 'The Quest of the Self,' pp. 47–85, treats Chrétien along with other twelfth-century authors and works.

111 Schnell, Rüdiger, *Causa amoris: Liebeskonzeption und Liebesdarstellung in der mittelalterlichen Literatur*, Bibliotheca Germanica, 27 (Bern: Francke, 1985). (XXXVIII.725)

112 Ayerbe-Chaux, Reinaldo, 'Las *Islas Dotadas*: texto y miniaturas del manuscrito de París, clave para su interpretación,' in *Hispanic Studies in Honor of Alan D. Deyermond: A North American Tribute*, ed. John S. Miletich (Madison: Hispanic Seminary of Medieval Studies, 1986), pp. 31–50. (XXXVIII.463)

See Qb52(A) Bourgain.

113 Moi, Toril, 'Desire in Language: Andreas Capellanus and the Controersy of Courtly Love,' in *Medieval Literature: Criticism, Ideology and History*, ed. David Aers (New York: St Martin's Press, 1986), pp. 11–33.

114 Wack, Mary F., 'Imagination, Medicine, and Rhetoric in Andreas Capellanus' *De amore*,' *Studies Kaske*, pp. 101–15. (XXXIX.318)

115 Kelly, Henry Ansgar, 'The Varieties of Love in Medieval Literature According to Gaston Paris,' *RPh*, 40 (1986–87), 301–27. (XXXIX.291)

116 Dinzelbacher, P., 'Pour une histoire de l'amour au Moyen Age,' *MA*, 93 (1987), 223–40.

See Ue2 Kimura.

117 Markale, Jean, *L'Amour courtois ou le couple infernal* (Paris: Imago, 1987). (XLI.72)

118 Méla, Charles, 'Aimer son désir: l'amour courtois,' in *Acquisitions récentes en sexologie clinique: Actes du XVIème Séminaire 14 et 15 mars 1986 organisé conjointement par les Facultés de Genève, Lyon, Marseille et sous l'égide de l'Association Inter–Hospitalo–Universitaire de Sexologie (AIHUS)*, ed. Willy Pasini (Geneva: Éditions Médecine et Hygiène, 1987), pp. 127–34; repr. in Dc19.

119 Duby, Georges, *Mâle Moyen Age: de l'amour et autres essais*, Nouvelle Bibliothèque Scientifique (Paris: Flammarion, 1988).

120 MacBain, William, 'Some Religious and Secular Uses of the Vocabulary of *fin'amor* in the Early Decades of the Northern French Narrative Poem,' *FF*, 13 (1988), 261–76. (XLI.409)

121 Monson, Don A., 'Andreas Capellanus and the Problem of Irony,' *Spec*, 63 (1988), 539–72. (XLI.419)

122 Thomas, Patrick A., 'The Split Double Vision: The Erotic Tradition of Medieval Literature,' *Neohelicon*, 15:1 (1988), 187–206. (XLI.257)

123 Zemel, Roel, 'Hoofse liefde in de literatuur van de twaalfde eeuw,' in *Herkennen wij de middeleeuwen?* ed. J. B. Weenink (Amsterdam: VU Uitgeverij, 1988), pp. 71–107. (XLII.246)

124 Classen, Albrecht, 'Erotik als Spiel, Spiel als Leben, Leben als Erotik: komparatistische Überlegungen zur Literatur des europäischen Mittelalters,' *Mediaevistik*, 2 (1989), 7–42. (XLV.25)

125 Keller, Hans-Erich, 'De l'amour dans le *Roman de Brut*,' in *Essays Grigsby*, pp. 63–81. (XLII.319)

126 Liebertz-Grün, Ursula, 'Satire und Utopie in Andreas Capellanus' Traktat *De amore*,' *PBB*, 111 (1989), 210–25.

127 Monson, Donald, '*Auctoritas* and Intertextuality in Andreas Capellanus' *De Amore*,' in *Poetics of Love in the Middle Ages: Texts and Contexts*, ed. Moshe Lazar and Norris J. Lacy (Fairfax, VA: George Mason University Press, 1989), pp. 69–79. (XLII.333)

128 Schnell, Rüdiger, 'L'amour courtois en tant que discours courtois sur l'amour,' *Rom*, 110 (1989), 72–126 and 331–63.

See Pj2 Bologna.

129 Calin, William, 'Contre la *fin'amor*? contre la femme? une relecture de textes du Moyen Age,' in *ICLS Dalfsen*, pp. 61–82.

See Qb56 *Curialitas*.

130 Katô, Kyôko, 'Love in the Works of Chrétien de Troyes's Contemporaries,' *FFRSH*, 25 (1990), 19–37. (XLIX. 367).
In Japanese.

131 McCash, June Hall, 'Mutual Love as a Medieval Ideal,' in *ICLS Dalfsen*, pp. 429–38. (XLIII.429)

132 Wack, Mary Frances, *Lovesickness in the Middle Ages: The 'Viaticum' and its Commentaries*, The Middle Ages Series (Philadelphia: University of Pennsylvania Press, 1990). (XLII.357)

See Qa96 Bloch.

See Qc63 Hanning.

133 Inoue, Tomie, 'Troubadours and Tristan Romances,' in *French Literature and Genres,* ed. K. Uemura and Y. Nishikawa (Tokyo: Keisô-shobô, 1991), pp. 1–17. (XLIV. 237)
In Japanese.

134 Schnell, Rüdiger, 'Die "hofische Liebe" als Gegenstand von Psychohistorie, Sozial- und Mentalitätsgeschichte,' *Poetica,* 23 (1991), 374–424. (XLIV.471)

135 Allen, Peter L., *The Art of Love: Amatory Fiction from Ovid to the 'Romance of the Rose',* Middle Ages Series (Philadelphia: University of Pennsylvania Press, 1992).

136 Dales, Richard C., *The Intellectual Life of Western Europe in the Middle Ages,* 2nd rev. ed. (Leiden: Brill, 1992).
See Chap. 9: 'The Romantic Love Literature of the Twelfth Century.'

137 Seto, Naohiko, 'On the Myth of the "Midi" – Some Courtly Romances,' *YBK,* 39 (1992), 27–40. (XLV.388).
In Japanese.

See Ha173 Spearing.

See Pb375 Spiewok.

138 Cherchi, Paolo, *Andreas and the Ambiguity of Courtly Love,* Toronto Italian Studies (Toronto: University of Toronto Press, 1994).

See Ma34 Rossi.

See Qa113 Roussel.

139 Schnell, Rüdiger, 'Liebesdiskurs und Ehediskurs im 15. und 16. Jahrhundert,' in *Graph,* pp. 77–119.
See pp. 85–88.

See Gd.c56 Kasper.

140 Kasten, Ingrid, 'Der *amour courtois* als "überregionales" Kulturmuster: Skizze zum Problem einer Begriffsbildung,' in *Interregionalität,* pp. 161–74.

141 Pulega, Andrea, *Amore cortese e modelli teologici: Guglielmo IX, Chrétien de Troyes, Dante,* Di fronte e attraverso, 379 (Milan: Jaca Book, 1995). (XLVIII.553)
See Part II: 'Chrétien de Troyes e l'*amour courtois*,' pp. 175–230.

142 Ragland, Ellie, 'Psychoanalysis and Courtly Love,' *Arthuriana*, 5:1 (1995), 1–20. (XLVII.767, XLVIII.722)

See Pb401 Remakel, Chap. 3:1.

See Qa117 Duby, vol. 3, pp. 147–215 (trans. pp. 81–120): 'De l'amour.'

See Ud16 Burns, Kay, Krueger, and Solterer.

See Qb73 García Gual.

143 Hult, David F., 'Gaston Paris and the Invention of Courtly Love,' in Dd10 *Medievalism*, pp. 192–224.

See Qc80 Keen, pp. 21–42.

144 Reil, Cornelia, *Liebe und Herrschaft: Studien zum altfranzösischen und mittelhochdeutschen Prosa-Lancelot*, Hermaea, 78 (Tübingen: Niemeyer, 1996).

145 Spiewok, Wolfgang, 'Ehe, Ehebruch und seine Folgen in mittelalterlicher Literatur und Wirklichkeit,' in *Sex, Love and Marriage in Medieval Literature and Reality: Thematische Beiträge im Rahmen des 31st International Congress on Medieval Studies an der Western Michigan University (Kalamazoo – USA), 8.–12. Mai 1996*, WODAN: EG, 69–TS, 40 (Greifswald:Reineke, 1996), pp. 73–78.

146 Wolf, Alois, *Das Faszinosum der mittelalterlichen Minne*, Wolfgang Stammler Gastprofessur für germanische Philologie – Vorträge, 5 (Freiburg: Universitätsverlag Freiburg Schweiz, 1996).

See Qa120 Cartlidge.

147 Taylor, Mark N., 'Servant and Lord/Lady and Wife: The *Franklin's Tale* and Traditions of Courtly and Conjugal Love,' *ChauR*, 32 (1997), 64–81. (L.569)

148 Camille, Michael, *The Medieval Art of Love: Objects and Subjects of Desire* (London: Calmann & King; New York: Abrams, 1998).

149 Haahr, Joan G., 'Justifying Love: The Classical *Recusatio* of Medieval Love Literature,' in *Desiring Discourse: The Literature of Love, Ovid through Chaucer* (Selinsgrove, PA: Susquehanna University Press; London: Associated University Presses, 1998), pp. 39–61.
Treats *Cligés*.

See Qa123 McCracken.

150 Voicu, Mihaela, 'Amie, ennemie ou douce sœur? Visages de la femme dans la littérature française médiévale,' *ABLs*, 57–58 (1998–99), 3–22.

See Gb152 Burns.

See Pb452 Fritsch-Rößler.

See Gf47 Gingras.

151 Jaeger, C. Stephen, *Ennobling Love: In Search of a Lost Sensibility*, The Middle Ages Series (Philadelphia: University of Pennsylvania Press, 1999). (LII.779)

152 Olsen, Michel, 'De l'obsession à la passion – et retour au point de depart?' in *Festskrift Swaton*, pp. 335–43.

See Qc87 Janssens.

See Ha209(F) Kay.

b: Chrétien

27 Mott, Lewis F., 'The Love Theories of Chrétien de Troies,' *PMLA*, 9 (1894), Appendix, pp. xxvii–xxix (discussion pp. xxix–xxxi).

28 Lyons, Nathan, 'Chrétien's *Lancelot* and *Perceval*: Some Contrasts in Method, Style, and the Nature of Love,' *University Review* [University of Missouri, Kansas City], 31 (1965), 313–18. (XVIII.77)

29 Kamizawa, Eizô, 'Love and Adventure in Chrétien de Troyes,' *France*, 46:5 (1971), 50–54.
In Japanese.

See Hb18 Friedman.

See He30 Deroy.

30 Accarie, Maurice, 'Faux mariage et vrai mariage dans les romans de Chrétien de Troyes,' in *Hommage Onimus*, pp. 25–35. (XXXV.301 *bis*)

See Hf37 Szabics.

31 Thompson, Raymond H., 'The Prison of the Senses: *Fin'Amor* as a Confining Force in the Arthurian Romances of Chrétien de Troyes,' *FMLS*, 15 (1979), 249–54. (XXXII.430)

See Hc36 Scully.

32 Bogdanow, Fanni, 'The Tradition of the Troubadour Lyrics and the Treatment of the Love Theme in Chrétien de Troyes' *Erec et Enide*,' in *ICLS Liverpool*, pp. 79–92. (XXXIV.294)

33 Calin, William C., 'Parenté et sexualité dans la littérature française du XIIe siècle,' *Lectures*, 7–8 (1981), 35–55. (XXXIV.438)
On the *Charrette* and *Yvain*, see pp. 42–55.

34 Morgan, Gerald, 'The Conflict of Love and Chivalry in *Le Chevalier de la charrete*,' *Rom*, 102 (1981), 172–201. (XXXIV.239)

35 Sakurai, Atsuko, 'Marriage and Courtesy in Chrétien de Troyes's *Yvain*,' *LiC*, 11 (1981), 37–50.
In Japanese.

36 Topsfield, Leslie T., '*Fin'amors* in Marcabru, Bernart de Ventadorn, and the *Lancelot* of Chrétien de Troyes,' in *Love Leuven*, pp. 236–49. (XXXV.255)

37 Bogdanow, Fanni, 'The Tradition of the Troubadours and the Treatment of the Love Theme in Chrétien de Troyes' *Chevalier au lion*,' *AL*, 2 (1982), 76–91. (XXXV.377)

38 Dauphiné, James, 'Le thème de l'amour dans *Le Conte du Graal*,' *Europe*, 642 (Oct. 1982), 114–20. (XXXV.314)

39 Noble, Peter S., *Love and Marriage in Chrétien de Troyes* (Cardiff: University of Wales Press, 1982). (XXXV.408)

See Va14 Zaganelli.

See Ga39 Press.

See He44 Beltrami.

See Hc46 Bender.

40 Evans, Dafydd, 'Marie de France, Chrétien de Troyes, and the *malmariée*,' in *Essays Topsfield*, pp. 159–71. (XXXVII.166)

See Hf57 Santucci 1984.
On Yvain.

41 Szabics, Imre, 'A trubadurköltészettől az udvari regényig (A *fin'amor* fejlődéstörténetéhez),' *FK*, 30:2–3 (1984), 140–48. (XL.204)

42 Burrell, Margaret, 'The *sens* of *Le Chevalier de la charrete* and the Court of Champagne,' *BBSIA*, 37 (1985), 299–308. (XLI.129)

See Hc52 Cropp.

See Ef7 Hunt 1986, Chap. 4.

43 *Aguiriano Barron, Begoña, 'Le lyrisme de l'amour naissant dans *Erec et Enide* et *Le Chevalier au lion*,' *Queste*, 4 (1988), 7–19.

44 Citton, Giuliana, 'L'eroe ingenuo: l'ironia nel *Chevalier de la charrette* di Chrétien de Troyes,' *MedR*, 13 (1988), 331–60. (XLI.264)

45 Dahlberg, Charles, *The Literature of Unlikeness* (Hanover, NH: University Press of New England, 1988). (XLII.290)
See Chap. 4: 'Love as Unlikeness: Andreas Capellanus, Chrétien de Troyes.'

46 Knight, Gillian, 'Chrétien de Troyes: His "Rhetoric of Love",' *RMS*, 14 (1988), 77–110. (XLII.665)

See Na.d57 Szabics.

47 Wunderli, Peter, '"Andere Welten" und "höfische Spekulation": zu den Romanen von Chrétien de Troyes,' in *Alternative Welten in Mittelalter und Renaissance*, ed. Ludwig Schrader, Studia Humaniora: Düsseldorfer Studien zu Mittelalter und Renaissance, 10 (Düsseldorf: Droste, 1988), pp. 111–59.

See Ga62 Zaddy.

See He56 Beltrami.

48 Laurie, Helen C., 'Chrétien de Troyes and the Love Religion,' *RF*, 101 (1989), 169–83. (XLII.567)

49 Aletti, Daniele, 'Bernart de Ventadorn, Bernardo di Chiaravalle e lo sviluppo dell'ideologia cavalleresco-cortese in Chrétien de Troyes,' *CN*, 50 (1990), 105–64. (XLV.317)

See He63 García Gual.

50 Szabics, Imre, 'Les visages de l'amour dans les romans de Chrétien de Troyes,' *Acta Litteraria Academiae Scientiarum Hungaricae*, 32 (1990), 221–32.

See Ga67 Faivre-Duboz.

See Hf85 Cecchetti.

See Pd63 Dirscherl.

See Me31 Laurie.

See Gd.a31 Paoli.

See Hg89 Sargent-Baur.

See He68 Steele.

See Qc72 Fahrner.

51 Holzbacher, Ana-María, 'Chrétien de Troyes: una forma soterrada de misoginia,' in *Actas Zaragoza*, pp. 207–14.

See Ke15 Mendoza Ramos.

52 Ferroul, Yves, 'La dérision de l'amour,' in *Amour Troyes*, pp. 149–59. (XLIX.150)

53 Guerreau-Jalabert, Anita, 'Traitement narratif et signification sociale de l'amour courtois dans le *Lancelot* de Chrétien de Troyes,' in *Amour Troyes*, pp. 247–59. (XLIX.159)

See Jb57 Pipaprez.

c: Chrétien and the Tristan Legend

5 Micha, Alexandre, 'Tristan et Cliges [...]' Repr. in Dc3.

9 Lonigan, Paul R., 'The *Cliges* [...]' (XXVII.367)

10 Hamel, A. G. van, 'Bijdrage tot de vergelijking van Cligès en Tristan,' *Taal en Letteren*, 14 (1904), 193–211.

11 Mergell, Bodo, *Tristan und Isolde: Ursprung und Entwicklung der Tristansage des Mittelalters* (Mainz: Kirchheim, 1949).
See Chaps. 2 and 3.

12 Fisher, John H., 'Tristan and Courtly Adultery,' *CL*, 9 (1957), 150–64. (X.31)

See Fa69(A) Bertau.

13 Gallais, Pierre, *Genèse du roman occidental: essais sur 'Tristan et Iseut' et son modèle persan* (Paris: Tête de Feuilles-Sirac, 1974). (XXVII. 245)
See Chap. 7: 'La hantise tristanesque de Chrétien de Troyes' (pp. 56–74).

See Va8 Zai.

See Ub8 Levine.

14 Mohr, Wolfgang, 'Tristan und Isolde,' *GRM*, 26 (1976), 54–83. (XXX.50)

15 Weber, Hubert, *Chrestien und die Tristandichtung*, EH:F, 32 (Bern: H. Lang, Frankfurt/M.: P. Lang, 1976).

16 Kamizawa, Eizô, 'The Tristan Myth in Chrétien de Troyes – *Cligès*,' *JFLN*, 73 (1978), 163–85. (XXXI.462).
In Japanese.

17 Delage, M.-J., 'Quelques notes sur Chrétien de Troyes et le roman de *Tristan*,' in *Mélanges Jonin*, pp. 211–19. (XXXII.338)

See Cb13 Shirt.

See Hd12 Freeman.

18 Gérard-Zai, Marie-Claire, 'La légende de Tristan et Iseut et Chrétien de Troyes: la chanson courtoise, *D'Amors, qui m'a tolu a moi* (R. 1664),' *Tris*, 7:1–2 (1981–82), 21–26. (XXXV.157)

See Md34 Höfner.

See Ed5 Polak, pp. 50–69.

19 Freeman, Michelle A., 'Structural Transpositions and Intertextuality: Chrétien's *Cligés*,' *M&H*, 11 (1982), 149–63.

20 Ertzdorff, Xenja von, 'Tristan und Lanzelot: zur Problematik der Liebe in den höfischen Romanen des 12. und frühen 13. Jahrhunderts,' *GRM*, 33 (1983), 21–52. (XXXVI.34)

See Qa66 Holzermayr.

21 Karnein, Alfred, 'Liebe, Ehe und Ehebruch im minnedidaktischen Schrifttum,' in *Liebe Gießen*, pp. 148–60.

22 Sargent-Baur, Barbara Nelson, 'Between Fabliau and Romance: Love and Rivalry in Béroul's *Tristran*,' *Rom*, 105 (1984), 292–311. (XXXVIII.262)
See pp. 294–95.

See He51 Bruckner.

See Ha131 Kay.

23 Deist, Rosemarie, *Die Nebenfiguren in den Tristanromanen Gottfrieds von Straßburg, Thomas' de Bretagne und im 'Cligès' Chrétiens de Troyes*, GAG, 435 (Göppingen: Kümmerle, 1986). (XL.533)

See Md37 Adams.

24 Martineau-Genieys, Christine, 'De Lancelot à Tristan, ou plutôt d'Iseut aux Blanches Mains à la demoiselle entreprenante: la preuve par la chair,' in *Tristan et Iseut, mythe européen et mondial: Actes du Colloque des 10, 11 et 12 janvier 1986*, ed. Danielle Buschinger, GAG, 474 (Göppingen: Kümmerle, 1987), pp. 252–61.

25 Pollmann, Leo, 'Tristan und Isolde im Kontext der hochhöfischen Literatur Frankreichs (*Folie* und szenische Gestaltung),' in *Studia de Riquer*, vol. 3, pp. 471–98.

26 Curtis, Renée L., 'The Validity of Fénice's Criticism of Tristan and Iseut in Chrétien's *Cligés*,' *BBSIA*, 41 (1989), 293–300. (XLIII.516)

27 Di Girolamo, Costanzo, *I trovatori* (Turin: Bollati Boringhieri, 1989).
See Chap. 5: 'Tristano e Carestia.'

See Sb48 Laurie.

See Ue4 Sasaki.

28 Haug, Walter, 'Der "Tristan" – eine interarthurische Lektüre,' in *Artusroman*, pp. 57–72; repr. in Dc24. (XLIII.29)

See Me31 Laurie.

See Va17 Meneghetti.

29 Rossi, Luciano, 'La "chemise" d'Iseut et l'amour tristanien chez les troubadours et les trouvères,' in *Contacts de langue, de civilisations et intertextualité: IIIème Congrès International d'Etudes Occitanes, Montpellier, 20–26 septembre [sic = août] 1990*, ed. Gérard Gouiran, 3 vols (Montpellier: Centre d'Etudes Occitanes de l'Université de Montpellier, and the Section Française de l'Association Internationale d'Etudes Occitanes, 1992), vol. 3, pp. 1119–32.
See pp. 1126–28.

30 Toury, Marie-Noëlle, 'Narcisse et Tristan: subversion et usure des mythes aux XIIe et XIIIe siècles,' in *ICLS Salerno*, pp. 421–37. (XLV.343)

31 Zaganelli, Gioia, 'Béroul, Thomas e Chrétien de Troyes (sull' amore, la morte, la gioia),' *FeS*, n.s. 4 (1992), 9–46. (XLVI.573)

See Va18 Mertens.

32 Chocheyras, Jacques, 'Le personnage d'Arthur dans le *Tristan* de Béroul,' *PRIS-MA*, 11 (1995), 159–63. (XLVIII.283)

See Pa277 Di Febo.

33 *Tristan and Isolde: A Casebook*, ed. Joan Tasker Grimbert, ACT, 2 / GRLH, 1514 (New York: Garland, 1995). (XLIX.494)
See the Introduction, pp. xxxii–xxxiii.

See Hd19 Toury.

34 Chocheyras, Jacques, 'Chrétien de Troyes et Tristan: une nouvelle approche,' in *Tristan-Tristrant: Mélanges en l'honneur de Danielle Buschinger à l'occasion de son 60ème anniversaire*, ed. André Crépin and Wolfgang Spiewok, WODAN 66: EG, 53– TS, 37 (Greifswald: Reineke, 1996), pp. 79–84.

See Pj4 Comes.

35 Deist, Rosemarie, 'The Description of Isolde and Iseut and their Confidantes in Gottfried von Straßburg and Thomas of Bretagne,' *BBSIA*, 48 (1996), 271–82. (XLIX.485)

36 Demaules, Mireille, 'Lancelot et l'envenimement: une rêverie tristanienne,' in *Lancelot mythique*, pp. 81–99.

See Pa295 Brault.

37 Brault, Gérard J., '*L'amer, l'amer, la mer*: la scène des aveux dans le Tristan de Thomas à la lumière du fragment de Carlisle,' in *Mélanges Ménard*, vol. 1, pp. 216–26. (LI.218)
See pp. 217–23.

38 Keck, Anna, *Die Liebeskonzeption der mittelalterlichen Tristanromane: zur Erzähllogik der Werke Bérouls, Eilharts, Thomas' und Gottfrieds*, Beihefte zu *Poetica*, 22 (Munich: Fink, 1998). (LI.83)

39 Moltó Hernández, Elena, 'La leyenda de *Tristan* y el amor cortés,' in *Literatura de caballerías y orígenes de la novela*, ed. Rafael Beltrán, Col·lecció Oberta (Valencia: Universitat de València, 1998), pp. 77–92. (LI.638)

40 Sahel, Claude, *Esthétique de l'amour: Tristan et Iseut* (Paris: L'Harmattan, 1999).

See Md52 Zotz.

41 Grimbert, Joan Tasker, 'On Fenice's Vain Attempts to Revise a Romantic Archetype and Chrétien's Fabled Hostility to the Tristan Legend,' in *Reassessing the Heroine in Medieval French Literature*, ed. Kathy M. Krause (Gainesville: University Press of Florida, 2001), pp. 87–106.

T: THE GRAIL

Chrétien's Grail continues to be examined principally in relation to the traditions it is made to derive from (M and N), its allegorical meaning (Jd), and its influence (P). His description of the object as a low-bottomed bowl is generally recognized, although there is less agreement on its use, the meaning of the procession it is part of, and the significance of the answer to the question Perceval failed to ask about it. For Tc in the 1976 Bibliography, or illustrations of the Grail and its procession, see now X.

a: The Object

2 Frappier, Jean, 'Sur l'interprétation [...]' Repr. in Dc5.

3 Frappier, Jean, 'Autres remarques [...]' Repr. in Dc5.

6 Micha, Alexandre, 'Encore le "Graal" [...]' Repr. in Dc 3.

8 Frappier, Jean, 'Du "graal [..."]' Repr. in Dc5.

10 Frappier, Jean, 'A propos [...]' Repr. in Dc5.

14 Frappier, Jean, 'Le Graal [...]' Repr. in Dc5.

See Tb15 Voicu.

23 Golther, Wolfgang, 'Der Gral in den französischen und deutschen Gedichten des Mittelalters,' *Der Türmer*, 25 (1923), 648–53, 733–39.

24 Spitzer, Leo, 'The Name of the Holy Grail,' *AJP*, 65 (1944), 354–63. Cf. William A. Nitze, 'Spitzer's Grail Etymology,' *AJP*, 66 (1945), 279–81.

25 Dronke, E. P. M., 'The Original Grail,' *N&Q*, 205 (n.s. 7) (1960), 4–5.

26   Cocheril, Maur, 'Le Saint Graal,' in *Dictionnaire de spiritualité: ascétique et mystique, doctrine et histoire* (Paris: Beauchesne, 1965, 1966, 1967), vol. 6, cols. 672–700.

See Mc39 Duval.

See Jf8 Borne.

See Hg31 Gallais.

27   Evans, Arthur R., Jr., 'Leonardo Olschki, 1865–1961,' *RPh*, 31 (1977–78), 17–54.
See pp. 51–53 on Olschki's Grail theories.

See Me16 Fiedler.

See Jd21 Gicquel.

28   Gripari, Pierre, 'Le roman arthurien et le mythe du Graal,' in his *Critique et autocritique*, Bibliothèque L'Age d'Homme (Lausanne: L'Age d'Homme, 1981), pp. 125–34.

29   *Payen, Jean-Charles, 'Le Graal, qu'est-ce que c'est au juste? Propos (cuistres) d'un médiéviste en quête de rigueur,' *Graal*, 2 (1981), 3–8; repr. as 'Propos d'un médiéviste en quête de rigueur,' in *Normandie*, pp. 19–23.

30   Markale, Jean, *Le Graal*, Questions de (Paris: Retz, 1982). (XXXV. 332)
See Chap. 1: 'Le Graal de Chrétien de Troyes'.

31   Sansonetti, Paul-Georges, *Graal et alchimie*, Ile verte (Paris: Besz, 1982).

See Na.c79 Lozac'hmeur and Sasaki.

32   Amazawa, Taijirô, 'In Search of the Sources for the Grail Legend,' *Gensô*, 4 (1983), 80–87.
In Japanese.

See Na.c81 Sasaki and Lozachmeur.

See Pb288 Delcourt-Angélique.

33   Rivière, Patrick, *Sur les sentiers du Graal*, Les Énigmes de l'Univers (Paris: Laffont, 1984).

See Na.c83 Sterckx.

See Pa157 Zambon.

34 Varenne, Jean-Michel, *Le Graal* (Paris: MA Editions, 1986).

35 Barthélémy, Docteur André, *Au XIIe siècle le Graal: sa première révélation* (Paris: Poliphile, 1987). (XL.28)

See Qc66 Cardini, 'La cerca del Graal: storia e tradizione di un "mistero",' pp. 137–57.

36 Goodrich, Norma Lorre, *The Holy Grail* (New York: Harper Collins, 1992, 1993).
Italian trans: *Il Santo Graal: la storia vera oltre la leggenda*, trans. Bruno Amato (Milan: Rusconi, 1996).

37 Rohr, Rupprecht, 'Über erklärte und unerklärte Wunder in französischen erzählenden Texten im 12. und 13. Jahrhundert,' in *Das Wunderbare in der mittelalterlichen Literatur*, ed. Dietrich Schmidtke, GAG, 606 (Göppingen: Kümmerle, 1994), pp. 7–14.

See Uc38 Vierne.

See Db65 Markale.

38 Sasu, Maria-Voichiţa, 'Cupa şi graalul,' in her *Constante*, pp. 66–76. (LI.712)

39 Yokoyama, Ayumi, 'The Development of the Holy Grail Legend in Medieval France,' *RSCL*, 14 (1997), 1–9.
In Japanese.

See Db67 Zambon.

See Pk81 Cardini, Introvigne, and Montesano.

See Pa307 Karczewska, pp. 14–16.

See Jb56 Vié.

40 *The Grail: A Casebook*, ed. Dhira B. Mahoney, ACT, 5 / GRLH, 1510 (New York: Garland, 2000).
    A. Dhira B. Mahoney, 'Introduction and Comparative Table of Medieval Texts,' pp. 10–13.
    B. Glenys Witchard Goetinck, 'The Quest for Origins,' pp. 117–47.
    C. Ub1 Jung and Franz, Chap. 7, pp. 149–73.
    D. Ea 11 Frappier, trans. Cormier, Chap. 7, pp. 175–200.

E.   Pa253 Sturm-Maddox, pp. 201–17.
F.   Ge52 Kennedy, pp. 279–99.
G.   Pk31 Williams, pp. 575–90.

See Db76 Wood.

See Pa335 Séguy.

b: The Ceremony

5   Frappier, Jean, 'Le Cortège […]' Repr. in Dc5.

6   Micha, Alexandre, 'Deux études [...]' Repr. in Dc3.

15   Voicu, Mihaela, 'Semnificația […]' (XXVIII.483)

See Ta23 Golther.

16   Anitchkof, Eugène, 'Le saint Graal et les rites eucharistiques,' *Rom*, 55 (1929), 174–94.

17   Amazawa, Taijirô, 'The Profound Meaning of the Grail in the *Conte del Graal* by Chrétien de Troyes,' *ELLF*, 5 (1964), 92.
In Japanese.

See Mc37 Corbin.

See Hg35 Foulon.

See Hg55 Burns.

See Pb262 Dubuis.

See Uc24 Gouttebroze.

18   Katô, Kyôko, 'The Enigma of *Perceval ou le Conte du Graal* by Chrétien de Troyes,' *Shunjû*, 255 (1984), 1–4.
In Japanese.

See Pa218 Baumgartner.

19   Baumgartner, Emmanuèle, 'Le Graal, le temps: les enjeux d'un motif,' in *Le Temps, sa mesure et sa perception au Moyen Age: Actes du Colloque Orléans 12–13 avril 1991*, ed. Bernard Ribémont (Caen: Paradigme, 1992), pp. 9–17.

See Hg88 Dubost.

20 Zambon, Francesco, 'Angelologia catara e mito del Graal,' in *L'angelo dell'immaginazione: Atti del Seminario di Antropologia Letteraria, Trento 21 marzo–25 aprile 1991*, ed. Fabio Rosa, Labirinti, 1 (Trento: Dipartimento di Scienze Filologiche e Storiche, Università degli Studi di Trento, 1992), pp. 175–93. (XLV.344)

21 Doner, Janet R., 'The Knight, the Centurion, and the Lance,' *Neophil*, 78 (1993), 19–29. (XLVI.626)

22 *Banquets et manières de table au Moyen Age*, Senefiance, 38 (Aix-en-Provence: CUER-MA, 1996).
    A.   Robert Baudry, 'La vertu nourricière du Graal,' pp. 433–50. (XLIX.125)
    B.   Anne Berthelot, 'Le Graal nourricier,' pp. 451–66. (XLIX.128)
    C.   Jean-Guy Gouttebroze, 'A quoi sert le repas du Graal? Remarques sur la liturgie du Graal dans *Le Conte du Graal*,' pp. 467–78. (XLIX.156)

See Gd.c60 Mühlethaler.

See Pb421 Spiewok.

See Uc43 Vincensini.

23 Stanesco, Michel, 'Le secret du Graal et la voie interrogative,' *TrL*, 10 (1997), 15–31. (L.230)

See Pa335 Séguy.

U: MODERN INTERPRETATIVE METHODOLOGIES
AND APPROACHES

New methodologies and approaches have required some additions to this section. Studies in Ua, b, and c help us appreciate why certain features of Chrétien's romances were perceived as marvellous. An active new topic has been Ud, which also has obvious connections to social and cultural studies like those in Q and Ub. See also Dd, Ke, and Qe. Uf takes 'comparative literature' not only in the traditional sense, but also as comparison of works that are totally divorced from any direct or indirect influence beyond the comparison itself.

a: Psychology

20 Anacker, Robert, 'Chrétien de Troyes: The First French Psychological Novelist,' *FR*, 8 (1935), 293–300.

See Hd7 Levý.

See Pb137 Leckie.

See Hg34 Toja.

See Hf29 Fogg.

21 Leclercq, Jean, *Monks and Love in Twelfth-Century France: Psycho-Historical Essays* (Oxford: Clarendon Press, 1979).
See pp. 129–32 on *Erec*. French trans.: **L'Amour vu par les moines au XIIᵉ siècle* (Paris: Le Cerf, 1983).

See Ha101 Schulze.

See Db24(D) Kelly.

22   Klassen, Norman, 'The Lover's *Largesce*: Agency and Selfhood in Chrétien's *Le Chevalier de la Charrette* (*Lancelot*),' *FF*, 24 (1999), 5–20.

See Gf50 Brainerd.

b: Psychoanalysis

5   Adler, Alfred, 'Yvain, der Löwenritter: ein Versroman von Crestien de Troyes (Mitte des 12. Jahrhunderts),' *Internationale Zeitschrift für Individualpsychologie*, 13 (1935), 185–89; repr. in *Psychoanalytische Literaturkritik*, ed. Reinhold Wolff (Munich: Fink, 1975), pp. 125–29, 392.

See Sa52 Askew.

See Sa54 Koenigsberg.

See Ke2 Engler.

6   Roubaud, Jacques, 'Généalogie morale des rois-pêcheurs: deuxième fiction théorique à partir des romans du Gral,' *Change*, 16–17 (1973), 228–47. (XXVI.145)
Incest dissimulation in Chrétien and his adaptors.

See Ha66 Hume.

7   Chandès, Gérard, 'Recherches sur l'imagerie des eaux dans l'œuvre de Chrétien de Troyes,' *CCM*, 19 (1976), 151–64. (XXIX.229 *bis*)
Image of the woman.

See Uc10 Gouttebroze.

8   Levine, Robert, 'Repression in *Cligés*,' *Sub-stance*, 15 (1976), 209–21. (XXXIII.155)

See Pb195 Welz.

9   Beutin, Wolfgang, 'Zum Lebensweg des "Helden" in der mittelhochdeutschen Dichtung (Erec, Iwein, Tristan, Parzival): Bemerkungen aus psychoanalytischer Sicht,' *ZLiLi*, 7 (1977), 39–57. (XXX.14)

See Hg30 Gallais.

10   Leclercq, Jean, 'Modern Psychology as an Approach to the Medieval Psyche,' *The Indiana Social Studies Quarterly*, 30 (1977), 5–26.

See Hg32 Méla.

11   Gallais, Pierre, 'Le sang sur la neige (le conte et le rêve),' *CCM*, 21 (1978), 37–42. (XXXI.273)

12   Robinson, Lewis S., 'Pao-yü and Parsifal: Personal Growth as a Literary Sub-structure,' *Tamkang Review*, 9 (1978–79), 407–26.

See Ha92 Haug.

See Hg43 Méla.

13   Rey-Flaud, Henri, 'Le sang sur la neige: analyse d'une image-écran de Chrétien de Troyes,' *Littérature*, 37 (1980), 15–24. (XXXII.362 *bis*)

See Uc18 Solié.

See Ha103 Benton.

14   Braet, Herman, 'Tyolet/Perceval: The Father Quest,' in *Essays Thorpe*, pp. 299–307. (XXXIV.295)

See Qe13 Marchello-Nizia.

15   Rapaport, Herman, 'The Disarticulated Image: Gazing in Wonderland,' *Enclitic*, 6:2 (Fall 1982), 57–77.

16   Wolfzettel, Friedrich, 'Lancelot et les fées: essai d'une lecture psychanalytique du *Lancelot en prose*,' *MrR*, 30:2–4 (1982), 25–42. (XXXVIII.146)

17   Chandès, Gérard, 'Les quatre éléments: symboles du processus d'individuation dans les romans de Chrétien de Troyes,' in *Quatre éléments*, pp. 153–61. (XXXVI.28)

18   Rey-Flaud, Henri, *La névrose courtoise*, Bibliothèque des Analytica (Paris: Navarin, 1983).

19   Virdis, Maurizio, *L'immagine della castrazione: un tema ricorrente nella letteratura francese del medioevo* (Cagliari: COOP.CUEC, 1983). (XXXVI.523)
See 'Perceval: al di là del mito,' pp. 55–72

See He43 White.
Oedipal complex in the *Charrette*.

20 Chandès, Gérard, 'Amour, mariage et transgressions dans le *Bel Inconnu* à la lumière de la psychologie analytique,' in *Amour mariage*, pp. 325–33. (XXXVII.587)

21 Méla, Charles, *La Reine et le Graal: la 'conjointure' dans les romans du Graal, de Chrétien de Troyes au 'Livre de Lancelot'* (Paris: Seuil, 1984). (XXXVII.98)

22 Carter, M. L., 'The Psychological Symbolism of the Magic Fountain and the Giant Herdsman in *Yvain*,' *Mythlore*, 11:3 (1985), 30–31.

See Ga51 Chauveau.

23 Huchet, Jean-Charles, 'Psychanalyse et littérature médiévale: rencontre ou méprise? (A propos de deux ouvrages récents),' *CCM*, 27 (1985), 223–33. (XXXVIII.228)
On Ub21 Méla and Ub18 Rey-Flaud.

24 *Psychologie in der Mediävistik: Gesammelte Vorträge des Steinheimer Symposions*, ed. Jürgen Kühnel [et alii], GAG, 431 (Göppingen: Kümmerle, 1985).
The following include some commentary on Chrétien's romances:
  A. Danielle Buschinger, 'Das Inzest-Motiv in der mittelalterlichen Literatur,' in pp. 107–40; repr. in Dc23. (XL.529)
  B. Wolfgang Schmitt, 'Der "Wahnsinn" in der Literatur des Mittelalters am Beispiel des *Iwein* Hartmanns von Aue,' pp. 197–214. (XL.589)
  C. Burkhardt Krause, 'Zur Psychologie von Kommunikation und Interaktion: zu Iweins "Wahnsinn",' pp. 215–42. (XL.567)

25 Ringger, Kurt, 'Perceval et les rêveries de l'eau,' *Corps Écrit*, 16 (1985), 57–64; repr. in his *Gedenkband Ringger*, pp. 23–28.

26 Salinero, Mª Jesús, 'Introducción a "l'imaginaire" de Chrétien de Troyes: la feminidad causa de "conflicto heroico" en Erec, Cliges, Perceval,' *CIF*, 11:1–2 (1985), 167–85.

27 Wolfzettel, Friedrich, 'Mediävistik und Psychoanalyse: eine Bestandsaufnahme,' in Sa109 *Mittelalterbilder,* pp. 210–39.

28 Chandès, Gérard, *Le Serpent, la femme et l'épée: recherches sur l'imagination symbolique d'un romancier médiéval: Chrétien de Troyes*, Faux Titre, 27 (Amsterdam: Rodopi, 1986).

29 Giani Gallino, Tilde, *La ferita e il re: gli archetipi femminili della cultura maschile*, Collana di Psicologia, 9 (Milan: Raffaello Cortina, 1986). (XXXVIII.406)

30 Giannini, John, 'Lancelot: The Wounded Child Aspect of Arthur,' *Avalon*, 2:2 (1986), 35–39.

31 Aubailly, Jean-Claude, 'Plaidoyer pour une mythanalyse: le cas d'*Yvain*,' *PRIS-MA*, 3 (1987), 3–14. (XLI.42)

32 Bojesen, Lars Bo, 'Skyggen og lykken,' *Dansk Udsyn*, 67 (1987), 275–94.

See Sa118 Méla.

33 Guerrero-Ricard, Dominique, 'Où est donc passée Blanche-Neige?' in *Couleurs*, pp. 119–40. (XL.45)

34 Nelson, Jan A., 'A Jungian Interpretation of Sexually Ambiguous Imagery in Chrétien's *Erec et Enide*,' in *The Arthurian Tradition: Essays in Convergence*, ed. Mary Flowers Braswell and John Bugge (Tuscaloosa: University of Alabama Press, 1988), pp. 75–89. (XLI.423)

35 Virdis, Maurizio, *'Perceval': per un'e(ste)tica del poetico: fra immaginario, strutture linguistiche e azioni* (Oristano: Editrice S'Alvure, 1988). (XLI.277)

36 Álvares, Cristina, 'Le conflit père-fils dans le *Chevalier de la charrette*,' in *Relations*, pp. 117–30. (XLII.44)

37 Huchet, Jean-Charles, *Littérature médiévale et psychanalyse: pour une clinique littéraire*, Ecriture (Paris: Presses Universitaires de France, 1990); repr. of Chap. One in Dc27.
See pp. 112–16, 187–88, 193–236.

38 Sturges, Robert S., '*La*(ca)*ncelet*,' *AInt*, 4:2 (1990), 12–23.

39 Holzbacher, Ana-María, 'Chrétien de Troyes et le thème de la recréantise,' *BRABL*, 43 (1991–92), 125–52.

See Gc24 Aguiriano.

See Gb112 Gallais.

40 Balsamo, Gian, 'Son, Knight, and Lover: Perceval's Dilemma at the Castle of Beaurepaire,' *Exemplaria*, 5 (1993), 263–81. (XLVI.682)
Lacanian approach.

See Sb51 Holzbacher.

41 Salinero Cascante, María Jesús, 'Guigemar y Lancelot, dos variantes de un mismo trayecto ontológico: el *animus* en busca del *anima*,' in *Actas Almagro*, pp. 225–32.

42 Salinero Cascante, Mª Jesús, 'El viaje de Lancelot du Lac o la iniciación al conocimiento de sí mismo,' in *Actas Zaragoza*, pp. 493–500.

43 *Sexuelle Perversionen im Mittelalter – Les perversions sexuelles au Moyen Age: XXIX. Jahrestagung des Arbeitskreises 'Deutsche Literatur des Mittelalters' – 29ème Congrès du Cercle de travail de la littérature allemande au Moyen-Age (Greifswald/Deutschland-Allemagne) (Brugge/ Belgien-Belgique, 22.–25. September 1994)*, WODAN: EG, 46–TS, 26 (Greifswald: Reineke, 1994).
> A. Danielle Buschinger, 'Quelques aspects du thème de l'inceste dans la littérature médiévale,' pp. 29–56. (XLVII.77)
> B. Ruth H. Firestone, 'Mabonagrin: Does a Happy Night in the Park Depend upon a Dead Knight on a Pole?' pp. 85–95. (XLVII.87)
> C. Sibusiso Hyacinth Mdluli, 'Le fantasme du clerc: écriture et perversion au Moyen Age,' pp. 143–52.

44 Lancaster, Susan Bahner, 'Most Anxious Now to Return: Language Learning in *Perceval*,' *Postscript*, 12 (1995), 69–78.

45 Olef-Krafft, F., 'Œdipe au château du Graal,' *MA*, 101 (1995), 227–57. (XLVIII.6)

See Sa142 Ragland.

46 Burgwinkle, William E., 'Sodomy and Social Control in the Grail Legends,' *RLA*, 9 (1997), 27–34.

47 Cohen, Jeffrey Jerome, 'Masach/Lancelotism,' *NLH*, 28 (1997), 231–60. (L.447)

See Uc49 Gouttebroze.

48 Jeay, Madeleine, 'Sanguine Inscriptions: Mythic and Literary Aspects of a Motif in Chrétien de Troyes's *Conte du Graal*,' in *Telling Tales*, pp. 137–54. (LII.403)

49 Rey-Flaud, Henri, *Le sphinx et le Graal: le secret et l'énigme*, BibSP (Paris: Payot & Rivages, 1998). (LI.293)

See Pa312 Wolfzettel.

See Hf104 Álvares.

50   Cohen, Jeffrey Jerome, *Of Giants: Sex, Monsters, and the Middle Ages*, Medieval Cultures, 17 (Minneapolis: University of Minnesota Press, 1999).

51   Rey-Flaud, Henri, *Le Chevalier, l'autre et la mort: les aventures de Gauvain dans 'Le Conte du Graal'*, BibSP (Paris: Payot & Rivages, 1999). (LII.274)

See Uf3 Kay.

52   Roberts, Anna, 'Queer Fisher King: Castration as Site of Queer Representation (*Perceval, Stabat Mater, The City of God*),' *Arthuriana*, 11:3 (2001), 49–88.

c: Anthropology and Mythopoetics

9   Le Goff, Jacques, and Pierre Vidal-Naquet, 'Lévi-Strauss en Brocéliande: esquisse pour une analyse d'un roman courtois (Yvain de Chrétien de Troyes),' *Critique*, 325 (1974), 541–71; expanded version in *Claude Lévi-Strauss: textes de et sur Claude Lévi-Strauss*, ed. Raymond Bellour and Catherine Clément (Paris: Gallimard, 1979), pp. 265–319; repr. in his *L'Imaginaire médiéval: essais* (Paris: Gallimard, 1985), pp. 151–87.
Italian trans.: 'Abbozzo di analisi di un romanzo cortese,' *Il Meraviglioso e il quotidiano nell'Occidente medievale*, ed. Francesco Maiello, trans. Michele Sampaolo (Bari: Laterza, 1983; repr. 1988), pp. 101–43. (XLIII.340)

10   Gouttebroze, Jean-Guy, 'L'arrière-plan psychique et mythique de l'itinéraire de Perceval dans le *Conte du Graal* de Chrétien de Troyes,' in *Voyage*, pp. 339–50 (discussion, pp. 351–52). (XXIX.235)

11   Verhuyck, Paul, 'Les deux ruptures du premier Perceval,' *RBPH*, 55 (1977), 751–59. (XXX.218)

12   Bozóky, Edina, 'Roman arthurien et conte populaire: les règles de conduite et le héros élu,' *CCM*, 21 (1978), 31–36. (XXXI.261)

See Nb14 Grisward.

See He33 Kooijman.
Proppian analysis.

See Hg38 Le Rider.

See Hc29 Maddox.

13 Sturm-Maddox, Sara, 'Lévi-Strauss in the Waste Forest,' *Esp*, 18:3 (1978), 82–94.

14 Cormeau, Christoph, 'Artusroman und Märchen: zur Beschreibung und Genese der Struktur des höfischen Romans,' *W-S*, 5 (1979), 63–78. (XXXII.21)
Cf. Uc8.

15 Grisward, J. H., 'Trois perspectives médiévales: des talismans fonctionnels des Scythes au Cortège du Graal,' in *Georges Dumézil à la découverte des Indo-Européens*, Maîtres à Penser (Paris: Copernic, 1979), pp. 205–11. (XXXIII.335)

16 Wyatt, Isabel, *From Round Table to Grail Castle* (Peredur, East Grinstead: Lanthorn, 1979). (XXXIII.460)

17 Göttner-Abendroth, Heide, 'Matriarchale Mythologie (ausgewählte Beispiele aus Mythos, Märchen, Dichtung),' in *Weiblich-Männlich: kulturgeschichtliche Spuren einer verdrängten Weiblichkeit*, ed. Brigitte Wartmann (Berlin: Ästhetik und Kommunikation, 1980), pp. 202–39. (XXXV.27)

18 Solié, Pierre, *La Femme essentielle: mythanalyse de la Grande-Mère et de ses Fils-Amants*, L'Esprit Jungien (Paris: Seghers, 1980).
See pp. 220–21.

19 Viseux, Dominique, *L'Initiation chevaleresque dans la légende arthurienne*, L'Œuvre Secrète (Paris: Dervy-Livres, 1980).

See Ha108 Jeffrey.

See Nb23 Stanesco.

See Qa59 Gouttebroze.

20 Verhuyck, Paul, and Anneli Vermeer-Meyer, 'Le temps divin d'Yvain,' *RBPH*, 60 (1982), 527–39. (XXXV.257)

21 Bloch, R. Howard, *Etymologies and Genealogies: A Literary Anthropology of the Middle Ages* (Chicago: University of Chicago Press, 1983). (XXXVII.343)
See also his 'Étymologies et généalogies: théories de la langue, liens de parenté et genre littéraire au XIIIᵉ siècle,' *Annales*, 36 (1981), 946–62.

22 Gouttebroze, J. G., *Qui perd gagne: le Perceval de Chrétien de Troyes comme représentation de l'Oedipe inversé*, Textes et Essais (Nice: Centre d'Etudes Médiévales de Nice, 1983). (XXXVI.346)

See Nb26–27 Grisward.

See Hb31 Uitti.

23   Allard, Jean-Paul, 'Les étapes et les épreuves de l'initiation d'Erec à la chevalerie et à la royauté: étude des structures symboliques des romans de Chrétien de Troyes et de Hartmann von Aue,' *EIn*, 8 (March 1984), 25–70, and 10 (Oct. 1984), 1–53.

24   Gouttebroze, Jean-Guy, 'Cousin, cousine, dévolution du pouvoir et sexualité dans le Conte du Graal,' in *Chrétien Bruges*, pp. 77–87. (XXXVII.85)

See Qa79 Ebenbauer.

25   Allard, Jean-Paul, *L'Initiation royale d'Erec, le chevalier*, EIn, 1 (Milan: Archë, 1987).

26   Edwards, Michael, 'La légende arthurienne et la lecture mythique de l'histoire,' *Storia della Storiografia*, 14 (1988), 23–35. (XLI.269)

27   Planche, Alice, 'Les taureaux et leur maître: sur un épisode discuté de l'*Yvain* de Chrétien de Troyes,' *PRIS-MA*, 4 (1988), 9–19. (XLI.80)

28   Walter, Philippe, *Canicule: essai de mythologie sur 'Yvain' de Chrétien de Troyes* (Paris: SEDES, 1988). (XLI.93)

See Hf79 Walter.

29   Ribémont, Bernard, and Geneviève Sodigné-Costes, 'A l'ombre de l'arbre: le poète et l'encyclopédiste,' *PRIS-MA*, 5 (1989), 71–80. (XLIII. 195)

30   Vincensini, Jean-Jacques, 'L'"allure" mythique du *Conte du Graal* (comment faire communiquer les mots, les actes et les êtres?),' in *Relations*, pp. 303–20. (XLII.83)

31   Walter, Philippe, *La mémoire du temps: fêtes et calendriers de Chrétien de Troyes à 'La Mort Artu'*, NBMA, 13 (Paris: Champion, 1989). (XLII.84)

See Hc62 Aguiriano.

32   Fassò, Andrea, 'Cortesie indoeuropee,' in *Medioevo romanzo e orientale: testi e prospettive storiografiche: Colloquio Internazionale Verona, 4–6 aprile 1990: Atti* (Messina: Rubbettino, 1992), pp. 184–203 (XLV.330); repr. in *Omaggio Folena*, vol. 1, pp. 87–107.

33   Aguiriano, Begoña, 'Les images de la mort-naissance initiatique dans les romans de Chrétien de Troyes,' in *Éducation*, pp. 9–22. (LII.192)

34   Stäblein, Patricia Harris, '*Erec et Enide*: l'ouverture du sacrifice arthurien,' in *Erec*, pp. 51–60. (XLVI.71)

35   Holzbacher, Ana María, 'L'ombre d'Œdipe dans le *Perceval* de Chrétien de Troyes,' *BRABL*, 44 (1993–94), 119–41.

36   Benoît, Louis, '*Le Conte du Graal*: la mère et le chevalier,' *SLCO*, 20 (1994), 289–300.

37   Maddox, Donald, 'Lévi-Strauss in Camelot: Interrupted Communication in Arthurian Feudal Fictions,' in *Essays Lagorio*, pp. 35–53. (XLVII.749)

38   Vierne, Simone, 'Les soupirs de la sainte et les cris de la fée: les femmes et le Graal, hier et aujourd'hui' *Cahiers Internationaux de Symbolisme*, 77–79 (1994), 151–69.

See Gd.c53 Vincensini.

39   Watanabe, Kôji, 'On the Mythological Approach to Literary Works of the Middle Ages – Analysis of Part Two of Chrétien de Troyes's *Cligès*,' *ELLF*, 65 (1994), 95.
In Japanese.

See Gb125(A) Régnier-Bohler.

40   Watanabe, Kôji, 'Arthurian Onomastics as Mythological Stakes (I): On Perceval's Name,' *BLFC*, 19 (1995), 7–19. (XLVIII.601).
In Japanese.

41   Watanabe, Kôji, 'The Four-Day Tournament and its Mythological Outline (*Cligès* by Chrétien de Troyes, vv. 4543–4919) (I)(II),' *BNFS*, 11 (1995), 127–145; 12 (1995), 90–111. (XLVIII. 602).
In Japanese.

42   Benoît, Louis, '*Le Conte du Graal*: au nom de la mère,' *SLCO*, 22 (1996), 195–228.

43   Vincensini, Jean-Jacques, 'Échange de mets, échange de mots, échange de corps dans *Le conte du Graal*,' in Tb22 *Banquets*, pp. 493–509. (XLIX.201)

44 Vincensini, Jean-Jacques, *Pensée mythique et narrations médiévales*, NBMA, 34 (Paris: Champion, 1996).

45 Watanabe, Kôji, 'The "Loi étiologique" and the "loi de distribution calendaire" as Keys to a Mythological Reading: Interpretative Essay on the Episode of the Lovers Discovered in Chrétien de Troyes's *Cligès*,' *JSFLN*, 14 (1996), 34–62. (XLIX.381).
In Japanese.

46 Dunton-Downer, Leslie, 'The Horror of Culture: East-West Incest in Chrétien de Troyes's *Cligés*,' *NLH*, 28 (1997), 367–81. (XLIX.487)

47 Smith, Evans Lansing, *The Hero Journey in Literature: Parables of Poesis* (Lanham, MD: University Press of America, 1997).
See 'Chrétien's Lancelot,' pp. 100–8; 'Chrétien's Yvain,' pp. 108–19; and 'Chrétien's and Wolfram's Parzival,' pp. 119–37.

48 Allen, Nick, 'Varnas, Colours, and Functions: Expanding Dumézil's Schema,' *Zeitschrift für Religionswissenshcaft*, 6 (1998), 163–77. (LII.59)
On *Cligés*.

49 Gouttebroze, Jean-Guy, 'Perceval héros structuraliste,' in *Motifs chiffrés et déchiffrés: mélanges offerts à Etienne Brunet*, ed. Sylvie Mellet and Marcel Vuillaume, Travaux de Linguistique Quantitative, 64 (Paris: Champion, Geneva: Slatkine, 1998), pp. 513–25.

50 Vincensini, Jean-Jacques, 'Impatience et impotence: l'étrangeté des rois du château du Graal dans le *Conte du Graal*,' *Rom*, 116 (1998), 112–30. (LI.316)

51 Walter, Philippe, 'Myth and Text in the Middle Ages: Folklore as Literary "Source",' in *Telling Tales*, pp. 59–75. (LII.469)

52 Benoît, Louis, 'La mère coupable dans *Le Conte du Graal* de Chrétien de Troyes,' *SLCO*, 25 (1999), 27–49.

See Gb151 Bucher.

See Qb79 Gouttebroze.

53 McCracken, Peggy, 'The Poetics of Sacrifice: Allegory and Myth in the Grail Quest,' *YFS*, 95 (1999), 152–68. (LII.801)

54 Pastré, Jean-Marc, 'Folklore, mythe et mythologie: Wolfram von Eschenbach et les gouttes de sang sur la neige,' in *Sang*, pp. 183–94. (LII.262)

55 *Billington, Sandra, *Midsummer: A Cultural Sub-Text from Chrétien de Troyes to Jean Michel*, Medieval Texts and Cultures of Northern Europe, 3 (Turnhout: Brepols, 2000).

56 Walter, Philippe, 'Un roman mythologique: *Le Chevalier au lion* de Chrétien de Troyes,' *Plume*, 4 (1999), 4–8.

57 Vincensini, Jean-Jacques, *Motifs et thèmes du récit médiéval* (Paris: Nathan Université, 2000).

58 Walter, Philippe, 'Perceval, fils du Roi des Poissons: Chrétien de Troyes et le conte-type AT303,' in *Enfant-Dieu, Est-Ouest depuis l'antiquité à nos jours: Actes du colloque de mythologie comparée, Nagoya septembre 2000* (Nagoya: [n.p.], 2000), pp. 87–91 and pp. 92–97. In French and in Japanese.

See Hf107 Watanabe.

d: Feminism and the Woman Reader

See Sa64 Miller.

See Qa57 Vilhena.

See Hf48 Maraud.

1 Ferrante, Joan M., 'Male Fantasy and Female Reality in Courtly Literature,' *WomS*, 11 (1984), 67–97. (XXXVII.371)

See Gb78 Krueger.

See Qa74 McCash.

See Sa113 Moi.

See Ue2 Kimura.

See Ga58 Armstrong.

2 Krueger, Roberta L., 'Desire, Meaning, and the Female Reader: The Problem in Chrétien's *Charrete*,' in *The Passing of Arthur: New Essays in Arthurian Tradition*, ed. Christopher Baswell and William Sharpe, GRLH, 781 (New York: Garland, 1988), pp. 31–51. (XLI.406)

3 Stanbury, Sarah, 'Feminist Film Theory: Seeing Chrétien's Enide,' *Literature and Psychology*, 36:4 (1990), 47–66.

See Qa98 Gravdal.

4   Heng, Geraldine, 'A Map of her Desire: Reading the Feminism in Arthurian Romance,' in *Perceiving Other Worlds*, ed. Edwin Thumboo (Singapore: Times Academic Press, 1991), pp. 250–60.

5   Gravdal, Kathryn, 'Chrétien de Troyes, Gratian, and the Medieval Romance of Sexual Violence,' *Signs*, 17 (1992), 558–85.

6   Burns, E. Jane, *Bodytalk: When Women Speak in Old French Literature*, New Cultural Studies (Philadelphia: University of Pennsylvania Press, 1993).

See Ga78 Fulton.

See Hc67 Gaudet.

7   Ishii, Michiko, 'Women and Courtly Literature in the Middle Ages,' *ELE*, 40 (1993), 78–90. (XLVII.630)
In Japanese.

8   Krueger, Roberta L., *Women Readers and the Ideology of Gender in Old French Verse Romance*, CSF, 43 (Cambridge: Cambridge University Press, 1993). (XLVI.460)
See Chap. 1: 'The Displaced Reader: The Female Audience of Old French Romance,' and Chap. 2: 'The Question of Women in *Yvain* and *Le Chevalier de la Charrete*.'

9   McCracken, Peggy, 'The Body Politic and the Queen's Adulterous Body in French Romance,' in *Feminist Approaches to the Body in Medieval Literature*, ed. Linda Lomperis and Sarah Stanbury, New Cultural Studies (Philadelphia: University of Pennsylvania Press, 1993), pp. 38–64.

See Pb360(G) Pratt.

10   Ramey, Lynn Tarte, 'Representations of Women in Chrétien's *Erec et Enide*: Courtly Literature or Misogyny?' *RR*, 84 (1993), 377–86. (XLVII.768)

See Hf94 Matthews.

See Ub42 Salinero Cascante.

See Qb68 Walters.

See Gb125 *Arthurian Romance*.

11   Gaunt, Simon, *Gender and Genre in Medieval French Literature*, CSF, 53 (Cambridge: Cambridge University Press, 1995). (XLVIII.412)

12 *Hellman, Dara, 'Interdiction and the Imperative Feminine Redress in *Gereint ab Erin* and *Erec et Enide,*' *Aestel*, 3 (1995), 19–33.

13 Over, Kristen Lee, 'Narrative Treason and Sovereign Form in Chrétien de Troyes's *Cligés,*' *Comitatus*, 26 (1995), 95–113. (XLVIII.721, L.532)

14 Steele, Stephen, 'Rape in the Eye of the Reader: Sexual Violence in Chrétien's *Yvain,*' *DFS*, 30 (1995), 11–16.

See Fb91 Watanabe.

15 *Arthurian Women: A Casebook*, ed. Thelma S. Fenster, ACT, 3/GRLH, 1499 (New York: Garland, 1996). (L.468)
Contains Gb78 Krueger, pp. 3–18, an extract from Ud6 Burns, pp. 19–40, and Gb110 Fries, pp. 59–73.

See Gb132 Cereceda.

16 Burns, E. Jane, Sarah Kay, Roberta L. Krueger, and Helen Solterer, 'Feminism and the Discipline of Old French Studies: *une bele disjointure,*' in Dd10 *Medievalism*, pp. 225–66.

17 Ferrante, Joan M., *To the Glory of her Sex: Women's Roles in the Composition of Medieval Texts*, Women of Letters (Bloomington: Indiana University Press, 1997). (L.461)
See Chap. 4: 'Courtly Literature.'

18 Potkay, Monica Brzezinski, and Regula Meyer Evitt, *Minding the Body: Women and Literature in the Middle Ages, 800–1500*, Twayne's Women and Literature Series (New York: Twayne, 1997). (L.540)
See Chap. 4: 'Love and Marriage: Women in the Family Romance.'

See Gb141 Arendt.

See Db68 Armstrong.

See Ha209(I) Krueger.

See Hf107 Watanabe.

e: Comparative Literature

1 Жкирмунский, В. М., 'Средневековые Литературы как Предмет Сравнительного Литературоведения,' Известия Академии Наук СССР: Серия Литературы и Языка, 30:3 (1971), 185–97.

2   Kimura, Nobuko, 'A Comparative Essay on Courtly Romance and the Courtly Literature of Japanese Women,' *Bungei-kenkyû [Etudes de littérature]* (Meiji University), 56 (1987), 83–104.
In Japanese.

3   Mancini, Mario, 'I "cavallieri antiqui": paradigmi dell'aristocratico nel *Furioso*,' *Intersezioni*, 8 (1988), 423–54. (XLI.272)

4   Sasaki, Shigemi, *Bateau ou chemin pour les 'lieux sacrés' dans la Légende Arthurienne – étude comparative entre les civilisations japon- aise et européenne au Moyen Age* (Tokyo: Chûôkôron-Jigyôshuppan, 1989) (XLII. 153)
See Chap. 2: 'Bed and Lodging, an Essay in Comparative Analysis of the *Conte du Graal* and *Notes from My Monk's Cabin* (Beginning of the Thirteenth Century),' pp. 61–86 (in Japanese); and Chap. 5: 'La *Fin'Amor* dans les romans français et japonais du Moyen Age – essai de rapprochement de la conception de la fin'amor dans le *Tristan* de Thomas et le *Dit de Genji*,' pp.159–85.

See Qc60 Sears.

See Mc51 Pioletti.

5   Inoue, Tomie, 'Voyage dans l'autre monde – comparaison de *Urashima-Tarô* avec les lais bretons et les romans en France,' *Memoirs of Beppu University*, 39 (1998), 1–10. (LI.652)

6   Fenster, Thelma, 'Christine at Carnant: Reading Christine de Pizan Reading Chrétien de Troyes's *Erec et Enide*,' in *Christine de Pizan 2000: Studies on Christine de Pizan in Honour of Angus J. Kennedy*, ed. John Campbell and Nadia Margolis, Faux Titre, 196 (Amsterdam: Rodopi, 2000), pp. 135–48.

7   Jewers, Caroline, 'Heroes and Heroin: From True Romance to Pulp Fiction,' *Journal of Popular Culture*, 33:4 (2000), 39–61.

8   Watanabe, Kôji, 'The Figure of the Old Sage in Japan and Europe – On Merlin and Sarutahiko,' *JCSC*, 39 (2000), 43–68.
In Japanese.

9   Pierreville, Corinne, *Gautier d'Arras: l'autre Chrétien*, NBMA, 55 (Paris: Champion, 2001).

f: (Post)Modern Theory

See Qe19 Haidu.

1   Grigsby, John L., 'Perceval devant l'herméneutique et la grammatologie,' *Esp*, 23:1 (1983), 25–37. (XXXVI.173)

2 Sturges, Robert S., *Chrétien's 'Knight of the Cart' and Critical Theory*, in part of *Arthuriana* 6:2 (1996).
- A. Robert S. Sturges, 'Chrétien's *Knight of the Cart* and Critical Theory,' pp. 3–10. (XLIX.555)
- B. Debora B. Schwartz, 'The Horseman before the Cart: Intertextual Theory and the *Chevalier de la Charrette*,' pp. 11–27. (XLIX.550)
- C. Antonio L. Furtado and Paulo A. S. Veloso, 'Folklore and Myth in *The Knight of the Cart*,' pp. 28–43. (XLIX.490)
- D. Theresa Ann Sears, '"And Fall Down at His Feet": Signifying Guinevere in Chrétien's *Le Chevalier de la charrete*,' pp. 44–53. (XLIX.551)
- E. Wendy Knepper, 'Theme and Thesis in *Le Chevalier de la Charrete*,' pp. 54–68.
- F. Gregory L. Stone, 'Chrétien de Troyes and Cultural Materialism,' pp. 69–87. (XLIX.553)

See Fa171 Halász.

See Na.a54(G) Knight.

3 Kay, Sarah, *Courtly Contradictions: The Emergence of the Literary Object in the Twelfth Century*, Figurae (Stanford, CA: Stanford University Press, 2001).

V: THE *CHANSONS*

The *trouvère* tradition continues to provide a broader context for reading the two lyrics commonly ascribed to Chrétien, especially because he was one of the earliest known *trouvères*. This in turn has inspired further investigation (related to Rb) of links he may have had with certain troubadours, perhaps through the Angevin court of Eleanor of Aquitaine. See Ae for editions.

a: Studies

6   Lavis, Georges, *L'Expression de l'affectivité dans la poésie lyrique française du Moyen Age (XIIe–XIIIe s.): étude sémantique et stylistique du réseau lexical 'joie'-'dolor'*, BFPLUL, 200 (Paris: Belles Lettres, 1972).

7   Bec, Pierre, 'Genres et registres dans la lyrique médiévale des XIIe et XIIIe siècles: essai de classement typologique,' *RLingR*, 38 (1974), 26–39.

8   Zai, Marie-Claire, 'Chrétien de Troyes, poète lyrique,' *RITL*, 24 (1975), 53–56.

9   Dembowski, Peter F., 'Vocabulary of Old French Courtly Lyrics – Difficulties and Hidden Difficulties,' *CI*, 2 (1975–76), 763–79.

10   Bec, Pierre, *La Lyrique française au Moyen Age (XIIe–XIIIe siècles): contribution à une typologie des genres poétiques médiévaux: études et textes*. Vol. 1: *Etudes* (Paris: Picard, 1977).

11   Allen, Judson Boyce, 'The *grand chant courtois* and the Wholeness of the Poem: The Medieval *assimilatio* of Text, Audience, and Commentary,' *Esp*, 18:3 (1978), 5–17.

12 Haidu, Peter, 'The Narrative of the Appropriated Self: Chrétien de Troyes, *D'amors qui m'a tolu a moi*, Stanza I,' *Esp*, 18:3 (1978), 19–27. (XXXII.183)

13 Haidu, Peter, 'Text and History: The Semiosis of Twelfth-Century Lyric as Sociohistorical Phenomenon (Chrétien de Troyes: "D'amors qui m'a tolu"),' *Semiotica*, 33 (1981), 1–62.
Cf. also his 'Semiotics and History,' *Semiotica*, 40 (1982), 187–228.

See Sc18 Gérard-Zai.

14 Zaganelli, Gioia, *Aimer, sofrir, joïr: i paradigmi della soggettività nella lirica francese dei secoli XII e XIII*, Università di Bologna: Pubblicazioni della Facoltà di Magistero, n. s. 9 (Florence: La Nuova Italia, 1982).
See Chap. 2: 'Chrétien de Troyes: la "fin'amors" occitanica e il desiderio,' pp. 26–65.

15 Di Girolamo, Costanzo, 'Tristano, Carestia e Chrétien de Troyes,' *MedR*, 9 (1984), 17–26. (XXXVII.275)

See Hf55 Hunt.

16 Rossi, Luciano, 'Chrétien de Troyes e i trovatori: Tristan, Linhaura, Carestia,' *VR*, 46 (1987), 26–62.

See Sc27 Di Girolamo.

See Sb49 Aletti.

17 Meneghetti, Maria Luisa, *Il pubblico dei trovatori: la ricezione della poesia cortese fino al XIV secolo*, Saggi, 759 (Turin: Einaudi, 1992).
See pp. 101–6.

See Sc29 Rossi.

See Pa242 Angeli.
Discusses 'Amors tençon et bataille.'

18 Mertens, Volker, 'Intertristanisches – Tristan-Lieder von Chrétien de Troyes, Bernger von Horheim und Heinrich von Veldeke,' in *Kultureller Wandel und die Germanistik in der Bundesrepublik: Vorträge des Augsburger Germanistentags 1991*, ed. Johannes Janota, vol. 3: *Methodenkonkurrenz in der germanistischen Praxis* (Tübingen: Niemeyer, 1993), pp. 37–55. (XLVI.86)

19   Tyssens, Madeleine, 'Les deux chansons de Chrétien de Troyes: propositions nouvelles,' in *Omaggio Folena*, vol. 1, pp. 195–206.

20   Formisano, Luciano, 'La lirica,' in Ha183 *Letteratura romanza*, Chap. 2.

See Qb65 Grossel.

See Ma34 Rossi.

21   Willaert, Frank, 'Van Luisterlied tot danslied: de hoofse lyriek in het Middelnederlands tot omstreeks 1300,' in *Grote Lijnen*, pp. 65–81, 183–93.

22   Tyssens, Madeleine, 'Lecture des chansons de Chrétien,' in *Mélanges Ménard*, vol. 2, pp. 1409–22. (LI.309)

23   Rossi, Luciano, '*Carestia, Tristan*, les troubadours et le modèle de saint Paul: encore sur *D'Amors qui m'a tolu a moi* (RS 1664),' in *Convergences médiévales: épopée, lyrique, roman: mélanges Madeleine Tyssens*, Bibliothèque du Moyen Âge, 19 (Brussels: De Boeck Université, 2001), pp. 403–19.

b: Bibliography

1   Raynaud, Gaston, *Bibliographie des chansonniers français des XIIIᵉ et XIVᵉ siècles*, 2 vols (Paris: Vieweg, 1884; repr. New York: Franklin, 1972).
See nos. 66, 121, 1380, 1664, and 2020.

2   Linker, Robert White, *A Bibliography of Old French Lyrics*, Romance Monographs, 31 (University, MS: Romance Monographs, 1979).
See pp. 120–21.

3   Doss-Quinby, Eglal, *The Lyric of the Trouvères: A Research Guide (1970–1990)*, Garland Medieval Bibliographies, 17/GRLH, 1423 (New York: Garland, 1994).
See pp. 188–91.

W: WORKS OF DISPUTED ATTRIBUTION

Philomena is still usually attributed to Chrétien. *Guillaume d'Angleterre* is not included in many recent collected editions (see A), and recent editions ascribe it only to 'Chrétien' without adding 'de Troyes', in conformity with the work's prologue (and all other romances ascribed to Chrétien except *Erec et Enide*; see Rb33 Kay), although an apparently single author of his works, with or without the 'de Troyes', continued in use though the thirteenth century (Pa193 Coolput). The works suggested in Wc have not won general acceptance; for editions, see Ad.

a: *Philomena*

13 Thomas, A., 'Chrétien de Troyes et l'auteur de l'*Ovide moralisé*,' *Rom*, 22 (1893), 271–74.

14 Gay, Lucy M., 'Notes on De Boer's Edition of *Philomena*,' *MLN*, 26 (1911), 77–78.

15 Lowes, John Livingston, 'Chaucer and the *Ovide moralisé*,' *PMLA*, 33 (1918), 302–5.

16 De Boer, C., 'Une hypothèse sur le nom de "Crestiien li Gois",' *Rom*, 55 (1929), 116–18.

See Ra7 Delbouille.

17 Kolb, Herbert, 'Über den Epiker Bligger von Steinach: zu Gottfrieds Tristan vv. 4691–4722,' *DVj*, 36 (1962), 507–20.

18 Cormier, Raymond J., *One Heart One Mind: The Rebirth of Virgil's Hero in Medieval French Romance*, Romance Monographs, 3 (University, MS: Romance Monographs, 1973). (XXVII.6)
See pp. 40–44.

19   Gérard-Zai, Marie-Claire, 'L'auteur de Philomena,' *RITL*, 25 (1976), 361–68.

20   Cormier, Raymond J., 'The Gift of Tears in Chrétien's *Philomena*,' in *Beiträge ZrP*, pp. 193–97.

21   Bertrand, Denis, and Jean-Jacques Vincensini, 'La vengeance est un plat qui se mange cuit (notes de travail: quelques réflexions sur le problème de la thématisation),' *Bulletin du Groupe de Recherches Sémio-Linguistiques de l'Ecole des Hautes-Etudes en Sciences Sociales*, 16 (1980), 30–43. (XXXIII.310)

See Hc39 Burgess.

22   Benkov, Edith Joyce, 'Hyginus' Contribution to Chrétien's *Philomène*,' *RPh*, 36 (1982–83), 403–6. (XXXVI.159)

23   Benkov, Edith Joyce, '*Philomena*: Chrétien de Troyes' Reinterpretation of the Ovidian Myth,' *CML*, 3 (1982–83), 201–9. (XXXVI.160)

24   Pfeffer, Wendy, *The Change of Philomel: The Nightingale in Medieval Literature*, AUS:CL, 14 (New York: P. Lang, 1985). (XL.307)
See pp. 137–40.

25   Dingley, R. J., 'The Misfortunes of Philomel,' *Parergon*, 4 (1986), 73–86.
See p. 76.

26   Schulze-Busacker, Elisabeth, '*Philomena*: une révision de l'attribution de l'œuvre,' *Rom*, 107 (1986), 459–85. (XLI.90)

27   Sansone, Giuseppe E., 'Chrétien de Troyes e Chrétien li Gois: un consuntivo,' *SMV*, 33 (1987), 117–34. (XLII.128)

28   Azzam, Wagih, 'Le printemps de la littérature: la "translation" dans *Philomena* de Crestiiens li Gois,' *Littérature*, 74 (1989), 47–62.

29   Keller, Hans-Erich, 'De l'amour dans *Philomena*,' in *ICLS Salerno*, pp. 361–70. (XLV.334)

See Pa239 Peron.

30   Cormier, Raymond J., 'Térée, le pécheur fatal dans *Philomena* de Chrétien de Troyes,' *DFS*, 24 (1993), 1–9.

31 Coolput-Storms, Colette-Anne van, 'Autoportraits de héros,' in *Studies Kelly*, pp. 97–111. (XLVII.543)

32 Van Vleck, Amelia E., 'Textiles as Testimony in Marie de France and *Philomena*,' *M&H*, 22 (1995), 31–60. (L.579)
See pp. 33–37.

33 Guéret-Laferté, Michelle, 'De Philomèle à Philomena,' *Bien dire*, 15 (1997), 45–56.

See Pa299(L) Possamaï-Pérez.

34 Baumgartner, Emmanuèle, 'Remarques sur la réception des mythes antiques dans la littérature française du XIIe au XIIIe siècle,' in *Antichità*, pp. 135–48.

35 Clier-Colombani, Françoise, 'La mère dans l'*Ovide moralisé*,' *Bien dire*, 16 (1998), 71–108.

36 Jeay, Madeleine, 'La cruauté de Philomèle: métamorphoses médiévales du mythe ovidien,' in *Violence et fiction jusqu'à la Révolution: Travaux du IXe Colloque International de la Société d'Analyse de la Topique Romanesque (SATOR) (Milwaukee-Madison, septembre 1995)*, ed. Martine Debaisieux and Gabrielle Verdier, Études Littéraires Françaises, 66 (Tübingen: Narr, 1998), pp. 111–19.

37 Peron, Gianfelice, 'L'anacronismo nella *Philomena* di Chrétien de Troyes,' in *Antichità*, pp. 81–91.

38 Peron, Gianfelice, 'La "mère amère": du *Fresne* de Marie de France à *Galeran de Bretagne*,' *Bien dire*, 16 (1998), 217–27. (LI.284)

See Gf48 Noacco, pp. 129–30.

39 Storms, Colette, 'Le mal dans *Philomena*,' in *Imaginaires du mal*, ed. Myriam Watthée-Delmotte and Paul-Augustin Deproost, Transversalités, 1 (Paris: Cerf; Louvain-la-Neuve: Université Catholique de Louvain, 2000), pp. 103–13.

b: *Guillaume d'Angleterre*

20 Toischer, Wendelin, ed., *Wilhelm von Wenden, ein Gedicht Ulrichs von Eschenbach*, Bibliothek der mittelhochdeutschen Litteratur in Bœhmen, 1 (Prag: Verein für Geschichte der Deutschen in Bœhmen, 1876).
See pp. xiv–xxiii.

See Pg5 Knust.

21 Wilmotte, M., 'Le conte de *Guillaume d'Engleterre*,' *MA*, 2 (1889), 188–91.

22 Müller, Rudolf, *Untersuchung über den Verfasser der altfranzösischen Dichtung Wilhelm von England* (Bonn: Röhrscheid u. Ebbecke, 1891).

23 Menzel, Wilhelm, *Sprachliche Untersuchung der Handschrift C des Wilhelm von England von Christian von Troyes*, diss. Bonn (Bonn: Georgi, 1900).

24 Ogden, Philip, *A Comparative Study of the Poem 'Guillaume d'Angleterre' with a Dialectic Treatment of the Manuscripts*, diss. Johns Hopkins (Baltimore: Murphy, 1900).

See Fa58 Stevenson, esp. 'B. Das Verhältnis des Eracle zum Gm. d'Angleterre,' pp. 65–69.

See Kd39 Kuttner.

25 Viscardi, Antonio, 'Narrativa cortese di tono realistico e le fonti bizantine,' *Acme*, 5 (1952), 29–40; repr. in Wb 17.

26 Legge, M. Dominica, *Anglo-Norman Literature and Its Background* (Oxford: Clarendon Press, 1963). (XVI.177)
See pp. 141–43.

See Kc29 Morimoto.

See Gb40 Colliot.

27 Buzzetti Gallarati, Silvia, ed., *'Dit de Guillaume d'Engleterre': edizione critica e commento linguistico-letterario*, Istituto di Lingue e Letterature Straniere Moderne: Sezione di Filologia Romanza, Facoltà di Lettere e Filosofia, Torino, 3 (Turin: Giappichelli, 1978; 2nd ed., Turin: dell'Orso, 1990). (XLV.312)
See Chap. 5.

28 Dees, A., and J. A. De Vries, 'Bepaling van de herkomst van Oudfranse literaire teksten aan de hand van oorkondengegevens,' *ForL*, 20 (1979), 497–508.

See Kc61 Nordahl.

See Gf18 Morrissey.

29   Colliot, Régine, 'Oiseaux merveilleux, dans *Guillaume d'Angleterre* et les *Lais* de Marie de France,' in *Mélanges Foulon*, vol. 1, pp. 115–26. (XXXIII.321)

30   Cremonesi, Carla, 'A proposito della paternità del *Guillaume d'Angleterre*,' in *Etudes Horrent*, pp. 77–83; repr. in Dc11.

See Hb26 Lacy, pp. 118–24.

31   Plouzeau, May, 'Vingt regards sur l'enfançonnet, ou fragments du corps puéril dans l'ancienne littérature française,' in *L'Enfant au moyen-âge (littérature et civilisation)*, Senefiance, 9 (Aix-en-Provence: CUER-MA, Paris: Champion, 1980), pp. 201–18 (discussion p. 218).

See Rb28 Bullock-Davies.

32   Larmat, Jean, 'Prières au cours des tempêtes en mer,' in *La Prière au moyen-âge (littérature et civilisation)*, Senefiance, 10 (Aix-en-Provence: CUER-MA, Paris: Champion, 1981), pp. 347–60. (XXXIII. 340)
See p. 350.

See Fb50 Lindvall.

See Qe14 Melli.

See Gb66 Callay.

33   Holzermayr, Katharina, 'La métamorphose du Roi Guillaume,' *Médiévales*, 4 (1983), 91–101.

34   Mickel, Emanuel J., Jr., 'Theme and Narrative Structure in *Guillaume d'Angleterre*,' in *Sower*, pp. 52–65. (XXXV.181)

35   Sturm-Maddox, Sara, '"Si m'est jugie et destinee": On *Guillaume d'Angleterre*,' in *Sower*, pp. 66–80. (XXXV.190)

36   Holzermayr, Katharina, *Historicité et conceptualité de la littérature médiévale: un problème d'esthétique*, diss. Salzburg, Salzburger romanistische Schriften, 9 (Salzburg: Institut für Romanistik der Universität Salzburg, 1984).
See Chap. 2: 'Chrétien de Troyes: *Guillaume d'Angleterre*.'

See Qa66 Holzermayr.

37   Holden, A. J., 'La géographie de *Guillaume d'Angleterre*,' *Rom*, 107 (1986), 124–29. (XLI.61)

38 Mickel, Emanuel J., Jr, 'Studies and Reflections on Chrétien's *Guillaume d'Angleterre*,' *RomQ*, 33 (1986), 393–406. (XXXIX.300)

39 D'Alessandro, Domenico, 'Guillaume d'Angleterre e Chrétien de Troyes: un'analisi comparata del descrittivo,' *AION*, 29 (1987), 349–56. (XLI.266)

40 Krauss, Henning, 'Der überschätzte Bürger und der unterschätzte König – Zu Michael Nerlichs Versuch, den *Guillaume d'Angleterre* postmodern zu deuten,' *Lendemains*, 12 (1987), 77–96.
Resumé in French.

41 Nerlich, Michael, 'Ein Hauch von Posthistoire? Antwort auf zwei Kenner des *Guillaume d'Angleterre*,' *Lendemains*, 12 (1987), 109–29.
Resumé in French.

42 Nerlich, Michael, 'Der Kaufmann von Galvaïde, oder die Sünden der Chrestien-Forschung: ein Essay über die Ursprünge der Moderne-Mentalität in der literarischen Gestaltung,' *Lendemains*, 12 (1987), 12–39.

43 Thomas, Heinz, 'Der König von England – Überlegungen zur Interpretation des *Guillaume d'Angleterre*,' *Lendemains*, 12 (1987), 97–108.
Resumé in French.

44 Williams, Harry F., 'The Authorship of *Guillaume d'Angleterre*,' *South Atlantic Review*, 52 (1987), 17–24. (XL.332)

45 Belletti, Gian Carlo, 'Per una lettura ideologica del *Guillaume d'Angleterre*,' *ImRif*, 11 (1988), 3–60. (XLII.113)

46 Gowans, Linda, '*Guillaume d'Angleterre*: Prologue and Authorship,' *FSB*, 35 (1990), 1–5. (XLIII.250)

47 Klüppelholz, Heinz, 'Zur Deutung der Jagdepisoden im *Guillaume d'Angleterre*,' *AStnSpr*, 227 (1990), 298–305.

See Kd112 Picoche.

See Pg21 Infantes, p. 186.

48 Löfstedt, Leena, 'De l'influence du *Décret* de Gratien et de la traduction française de ce texte sur la culture et la littérature françaises pendant la seconde moitié du XIIe siècle,' *NM*, 92 (1991), 129–44.
See pp. 135–40.

See Fa155 Melkersson.

49 Brandt, Rüdiger, *Enklaven-Exklaven: zur literarischen Darstellung von Öffentlichkeit und Nichtöffentlichkeit im Mittelalter. Interpretation, Motiv- und Terminologiestudien*, FGädL, 15 (Munich: Fink, 1993). (XLVII.67)
See pp. 193–97.

See Pb360(T) Honemann.

See Pg28 Liffen.

50 Mora, Francine, 'La *fabula* antique comme matrice des premières mises en roman: l'exemple du *Guillaume d'Angleterre*,' in *Etudes Poirion*, pp. 295–303.

51 Planche, Alice, 'Enfance et ressemblance: regards sur quelques textes médiévaux,' *PRIS-MA*, 12 (1996), 95–103.
See pp. 96–98.

52 Tomasek, Tomas, 'Über den Einfluß des Apolloniusromans auf die volkssprachliche Erzählliteratur des 12. und 13. Jahrhunderts,' in *Mediävistische Komparatistik: Festschrift für Franz Josef Worstbrock zum 60. Geburtstag*, ed. Wolfgang Harms and Jan-Dirk Müller, with Susanne Köbele and Bruno Quast (Stuttgart: Hirzel, 1997), pp. 221–37 (discussion pp. 238–39).

53 Garreau, Isabelle, 'Eustache et Guillaume ou les mutations littéraires d'une vie et d'un roman,' *Médiévales*, 35 (1998), 105–23.

See Qa125 Carreto, pp. 99–105.

54 Ogawa, Sadayoshi, 'Word Order in the Romance *Guillaume d'Angleterre* (I)(II)(III),' *FRLH*, 31:3 (1999), 2165–92; 31:4 (2000), 3033–60; 32:1 (2000), 487–515.
In Japanese.

c: Other Attributions

3 Wilmotte, Maurice, 'La part de Chrétien de Troyes dans la composition du plus ancien poème sur le Gral,' *BulLSMP*, 5th ser., 16 (1930), 40–64, 97–119.

4 Owen, D. D. R., 'Paien de Maisières – A Joke that Went Wrong,' *FMLS*, 2 (1967), 192–96.

5   Bianchini, Simonetta, 'Due brevi romanzi di Chrétien de Troyes?' *CN*, 33 (1973), 55–68. (XXVII.363)
Critique of Wc1.

6   Johnston, R. C., 'The Authorship of the *Chevalier* and the *Mule*,' *MLR*, 73 (1978), 496–98. (XXXI.372)

7   Williams, Harry F., 'The Authorship of Two Arthurian Romances,' *FR*, 61 (1987–88), 163–69. (XL.333)

8   Gallais, Pierre, 'Et si Chrétien était l'auteur de *Liétart*? L'argument de la versification,' *PRIS-MA*, 7 (1991), 229–55. (XLIV.31)

X: ILLUSTRATION

This new section recognizes the greater attention being paid to the manuscript as artifact, performance, or *objet d'art* itself. Xb is broader than Xa, since extra-manuscript illustration may still relate to reception of Chrétien's romance through intermediaries in other languages. On gestures in illustrations, see François Garnier, *Le Langage de l'image au Moyen Age: I. Signification et symbolique. II. Grammaire des gestes*, 2 vols (Paris: Léopard d'Or, 1982–89), as well as Ba and Ld.

a: In Manuscript and Text

1   Brown, Arthur C. L., [A note on Perceval's two javelins], *MLN*, 40 (1925), 70.

2   Frühmorgen-Voss, Hella, *Text und Illustration im Mittelalter: Aufsätze zu den Wechselbeziehungen zwischen Literatur und bildender Kunst*, Münchener Texte und Untersuchungen zur deutschen Literatur des Mittelalters, 50 (Munich: Beck, 1975). (XXVIII.26)
See the Introduction by Norbert H. Ott, 'Text und Illustration im Mittelalter' (pp. ix–xxi); and Chap. 1: 'Mittelhochdeutsche weltliche Literatur und ihre Illustration: ein Beitrag zur Überlieferungsgeschichte' (pp. 1–56).

See Pb183 Schupp.

3   Barber, Richard, *The Arthurian Legends: An Illustrated Anthology* (Woodbridge: Boydell, 1979), Chap. 6: '*Yvain or the Knight with the Lion* by Chrétien de Troyes: Yvain Wins Laudine.' (XXXII.150, 402).

4   Wells, David A., 'Die Ikonographie von Daniel IV und der Wahnsinn des Löwenritters,' in *Festschrift Asher*, pp. 39–57. (XXXIV.56)

See Ga36 Bullock-Davies.

See Qa70 Stiennon.

See Gc13 *Monde animal.*

5   Dinzelbacher, Peter, 'The Way to the Other World in Medieval Literature and Art,' *Folklore*, 97 (1986), 70–87. (XXXIX.56)

6   Mentré, Mireille, 'Note iconographique sur le Graal,' in Gd.b28 Bouyer, pp. 83–125.

7   Mentré, Mireille, 'Remarques sur l'iconographie des romans arthuriens à propos de quelques exemples,' *CCM*, 29 (1986), 231–42. (XXXIX.659)
Treats the *Conte du Graal* and its Continuations in Montpellier Bibl. Ec. Méd. H249.

8   Busby, Keith, 'The Illustrated Manuscripts of Chrétien's *Perceval*,' *ZfSL*, 98 (1988), 41–52. (XLI.582)

See Qa90 Ménard.

9   Rieger, Angelica, 'Neues über Chrétiens Illustratoren: Bild und Text in der ältesten Überlieferung von *Perceval-le-Vieil* (*T*),' *BBSIA*, 41 (1989), 301–11. (XLIII.590)

10   Whitaker, Muriel, *The Legends of King Arthur in Art*, AS, 22 (Cambridge: Brewer, 1990). (XLIV.340)

11   Hindman, Sandra. 'King Arthur, his Knights, and the French Aristocracy in Picardy,' in *Contexts: Style and Values in Medieval Art and Literature*, ed. Daniel Poirion and Nancy Freeman Regalado, *YF* Special Issue (New Haven, CT: Yale University Press, 1991), pp. 114–33. (XLIV.314).

12   Rushing, James A., Jr., 'The Adventures of the Lion Knight: Story and Picture in the Princeton *Yvain*,' *PLC*, 53 (1991), 31–49. (XLV.518)

13   Stones, Alison, 'Arthurian Art since Loomis,' in *Arturus rex*, pp. 21–78. (XL, pp. 363–65)
Includes 23 illustrations.

See Gd.c45 Carré.

See Mc48 Mandach.

14   Mentré, Mireille, 'Le voyage du Graal dans l'iconographie médiévale – iconographie du Graal et iconographie biblique,' in *Diesseits*, pp. 101–11, 245–47.

15 Ott, Norbert H., 'Zur Ikonographie des Parzival-Stoffs in Frankreich und Deutschland: Struktur und Gebrauchssituation von Handschriftenillustration und Bildzeugnis,' *W-S*, 12 (1992), 108–23. (XLV.66)

16 Van D'Elden, Stephanie Cain, 'Specific and Generic Scenes: A Model for Analyzing Medieval Illustrated Texts Based on the Example of *Yvain/Iwein*,' *BBSIA*, 44 (1992), 255–69.

17 Black, Nancy B., 'The Language of the Illustrations of Chrétien de Troyes's *Le Chevalier au lion* (*Yvain*),' *Studies in Iconography*, 15 (1993), 45–75.
On Princeton Garrett 125 and BNF fr. 1433.

See Ba22 *Manuscrits*.

See Ba23 Gehrke.

See Gd.a36 Lerchner.

18 Hindman, Sandra, 'Perceval à l'image de Saint Louis: vers une nouvelle lecture des manuscrits parisiens de Chrétien de Troyes,' *Bulletin du Bibliophile* (1994), pp. 249–72. (XLVII.272, XLVIII.305)
Treats BNF fr. 1453 and 12577.

19 Hindman, Sandra, *Sealed in Parchment: Rereadings of Knighthood in the Illustrated Manuscripts of Chrétien de Troyes* (Chicago: University of Chicago Press, 1994). (XLVII.700)
Treats Mons Bibl. Univ. 331/206; Paris BNF fr. 794, 1433, 1453, 12576, 12577, 24403; and Princeton Garrett 125.

See Xb13 Bruckner.

20 Joly, Jehanne, 'L'image du roi dans trois manuscrits de la Bibliothèque Nationale (mss. fr. 12576, 12577 et 1453),' *PRIS-MA*, 11 (1995), 175–84. (XLVIII.308)

See Xb14 Rushing.
Treats Princeton Garrett 125 and Paris BNF fr. 1433.

21 Carroll, Carleton W., 'Text and Image: The Case of *Erec et Enide*,' in *Word and Image*, pp. 58–78. (L.445)

22 Doner, Janet R., 'Scribal Whim and Miniature Allocation in the Illustrated Manuscripts of the *Continuation-Gauvain*,' *MAe*, 65 (1996), 72–95. (XLIX.243)

23   Stones, Alison, 'Illustrating Lancelot and Guinevere,' in Ga91 *Lancelot*, pp. 125–57.

See Jd49 Vauthier.

See Hg109 Blons-Pierre, 'Remarques sur l'iconographie des manuscrits du *Conte du Graal*,' pp. 179–86.

24   Doner, Janet R., 'Illuminating Romance: Narrative, Rubric, and Image in Mons, BU 331/206, Paris, BN, fr. 1453, and Paris, BN, fr. 12577,' *Arthuriana*, 9:3 (1999), 3–26. (LII.756)

See Uc55 Walter.

25   Walters, Lori J., 'Female Figures in the Illustrated Manuscripts of *Le Conte du Graal* and its *Continuations*: Ladies, Saints, Spectators, Mediators,' *BJRL*, 81:3 (1999), 7–54. (LII.470)

See Ha209(E) Huot.

b: In Other Media

1   Antoniewicz, Johann von, 'Ikonographisches zu Chrestien de Troyes,' *RF*, 5 (1890), 241–68.

2   Szklenar, Hans, 'Iwein-Fresken auf Schloß Rodeneck in Südtirol,' *BBSIA*, 27 (1975), 172–80. (XXVIII.332)

See Fa88 Ballet Lynn.

See Ta27 Evans, pp. 49–50, on the Modena archivolt.

3   *Lukman, Niels, 'Andlau, Elsass – Yvain, Löveridderen,' in *Gotlands Didirk*, ed. Armin Tuulse [et alii] (Copenhagen: [n.p.?], 1987), pp. 136–44. (XXXI.246)

4   *Friedrich Tiecks Kartenspiel der Sagenkreise Karls des Grossen, Arturs, der Tafelrunde und des Grales, Attilas, der Amelungen und Nibelungen*, commented by Detlef Hoffmann, Historische Kartenspiele (Leipzig: Edition Leipzig, 1982). (XXXVI.11)

5   Bonnet, Anne-Marie, *Rodenegg und Schmalkalden: Untersuchungen zur Illustration einer ritterlich-höfischen Erzählung und zur Entstehung profaner Epenillustration in den ersten Jahrzehnten des 13. Jahrhunderts*, tuduv-Studien: Kunstgeschichte, 22 (Munich: tuduv, 1986). (XLI.580)

See Xa5 Dinzelbacher.

6   Rushing, James A., Jr, 'The Enville Ywain Misericord,' *BBSIA*, 38 (1986), 279–84. (XLI.149)

7   *Rezak, Brigitte Bedos, 'The Knight and Lion Motif in Some Medieval Seals,' *Avalon*, 2:3 (1986–87), 30–34.

8   Le Bossé, Michel, 'Les motifs arthuriens d'un chapiteau de l'église Saint-Pierre de Caen: interprétation alchimique,' in *Normandie*, pp. 227–44.

9   Smith, Susan L., 'The Power of Women Topos on a Fourteenth-Century Embroidery,' *Viator*, 21 (1990), 203–28 + 8 plates.

See Xa10 Whitaker.

10   Rushing, James A., Jr., 'Adventure and Iconography: Ywain Picture Cycles and the Literarization of Vernacular Narrative,' *AY*, 1 (1991), 91–105 + 7 plates. (XLIV.333)

See Pb348 Masser.

11   Rushing, James A., 'Iwein as Slave of Woman: The "Maltererteppich" in Freiburg,' *Zeitschrift für Kunstgeschichte*, 55 (1992), 124–35. (XLV.519)

See Pb360(N) Curschmann.

12   Neaman, Judith S., 'Romanticizing the Past: Stasis and Motion in *Yvain* and Vézelay,' *Arthuriana*, 4 (1994), 250–70. (XLVII.760)

13   Bruckner, Matilda Tomaryn, 'Reconstructing Arthurian History: Lancelot and the Vulgate Cycle,' in *Memory and the Middle Ages*, ed. Nancy Netzer and Virginia Reinburg (Chestnut Hill, MA: Boston College Museum of Art, 1995), pp. 57–76.

14   Rushing, James A., Jr., *Images of Adventure: Ywain in the Visual Arts*, Middle Ages Series (Philadelphia: University of Pennsylvania Press, 1995).

15   Smith, Susan L., *The Power of Women: A 'Topos' in Medieval Art and Literature* (Philadelphia: University of Pennsylvania Press, 1995). See Chap. 5.

16   Schupp, Volker, and Hans Szklenar, *Ywain auf Schloß Rodenegg: eine Bildergeschichte nach dem 'Iwein' Hartmanns von Aue*, Kulturgeschichtliche Miniaturen (Sigmaringen: Thorbeke, 1996). (XLIX. 64)
Chaps. 1–4 by Volker Schupp, chaps. 5–8 by Hans Szklenar.

17   Walter, Philippe, 'Perceval en Grésivaudan: la découverte de fresques arthuriennes inconnues au château de Theys (Isère),' *MA*, 103 (1997), 349–61. (L.6)

18   *Le stanze di Artù: gli affreschi di Frugarolo e l'immaginario cavalleresco nell'autunno del Medioevo* (Milan: Electa, 1999). (LII.601)

19   Mühlemann, Joanna, 'Die *Erec*-Rezeption auf dem Krakauer Kronenkranz,' *PBB*, 122 (2000), 76–102 + 8 plates.

INDEX OF AUTHORS, EDITORS, AND TRANSLATORS

Cross-references are not included

Feinstein, Sandy, Gd.c69
Feistner, Edith, Ga101; Pb393
Fenske, Lutz, Qb56(E)
Fenster, Thelma, Ud15; Ue6
Ferguson, Gary, Qa107
Ferlampin-Acher, Christine, Eb18(E); Gd.c54; He72; Pa259
Fernández Vuelta, María del Mar, Pa219
Ferran, Marie-Hélène, Gb64
Ferrand, Françoise, Pk82
Ferrante, Joan M., Dc12; Gb24, 55; Gd.b29; Mf13; Qb64; Sa43, 92; Ud1, 17
Ferré, Vincent, Pk87(D)
Ferroul, Yves, Fb64, 83(G); Gf46; Qd22; Sb52
Ferrucci, Franco, Ph11
Fery-Hue, Françoise, Fb83(F)
Fichte, Joerg Otto, Gd.c42(B); Pd43, 48, 61
Fiedler, Leslie A., Me16
Field, P. J. C., Pd64
Field, Rosalind, Pd81
Fife, Graeme, Na.c93
Figueiredo de Carvalho, Teresa, Hf63
Findon, Joanne, Na.c97
Finke, Laurie A., Fa140; Qa118
Finke, Michael C., Gf50
Finlayson, John, Pd23, 37
Firestone, Ruth H., Me27; Pb315; Ub43(B)
Fisher, John H., Sc12
Fisher, Lizette Andrews, Ge17
Fisher, Rodney W., Pb301, 409, 439
Fisher, Sheila, Ha209(J)
Fleckenstein, Josef, Gd.b18; Qb56 (and I, M)
Fleischman, Suzanne, Ha157; Pi16
Flemestad, Kirsten Broch, Kc85
Fleuriot, Léon, Na.a31; Na.b30
Florence, Melanie J., La44
Flores Arroyuelo, Francisco J., Gd.c55
Flori, Jean, Qc34, 36, 38–39, 51, 59(A), 70, 75, 79, 82
Foehr-Janssens, Yasmina, Gb161
Foerster, Wendelin, Aa5; Gd.c2; Na.e23

Fogg, Sarah, Hf29
Ford, Boris, Ef6
Formisano, Luciano, Va20
Forrer, Andreas, Hf27
Fossier, Robert, Qa43(A)
Foster, Kenelm, Sa74
Fouillade, Claude, Jb48
Foulet, Alfred, Ac14; Bb29, 32, 44, 53(B), 55; Ea37(G-H)
Foulet, Lucien, Kc24; Kd48; Pa58
Foulon, Charles, Hg35; Na.d54; Qa54; Qg7
Fourquet, Jean, Bb20; Dc8; Hc66; La 7, 19, 25; Pb18, 23, 44, 127, 169, 200, 219, 380; Qb70
Fowler, David C., Pd30
Fox, John Howard, Pa67
Fox, Thomas C., Ha149
Frakes, Jerold C., Ha128
Francke, Walter K., Pb276
François, Charles, Ba7
Frandsen, Ernst, Pf13
Frank, Barbara, Fe22, 30(and A)
Frank, Istvan, Pb114
Frank, Roberta, Bb64
Frappier, Jean, Bb26; Da12; Dc1–2, 5; Ea11, 30; Eg4; Fc4–5; Gd9, 17; Ha62, 145(P); Hc13; Hg 7, 9, 16, 29; Ja24; Jd13; Kd3; Mb3; Pa75, 80, 85; Qc9; Ta2, 3, 8, 10, 14; Tb5
Freeman, Michelle A., Ea37(C), 42; Eh1; Fa87; Fb41; Hd10, 12; Hg52; Pa136, 203; Sc19
Freixe, Alain, Gf36
Frenzel, Elisabeth, Gg1
Freymond, E., Da7
Freytag, Wiebke, Pb207, 360(M)
Friedman, A., Hb18
Friedman, Albert B., Nb18; Pd19
Friedman, Lionel J., Bb53(C); Gb95
Friedrich, Ellen Lorraine, Ga108(C)
Fries, Maureen, Db44 (and B); Gb110, 143
Fritsch-Rößler, Waltraud, Pb440, 452–53
Fritz, Jean-Marie, Ah1; Cb28; Eb24(C); Eh7; Gb111; Me42
Froide, Amy M., Gb154

Gnädinger, Louise, Pb208
Gnüg, Hiltrud, Sa99
Goddard, Eunice Rathbone, Kd37
Godinho, Helder, Hf86
Goebel, Janet, Pk52
Goebel, Ulrich, Pb170
Goerke, Georg, Gc3
Goetinck, Glenys Witchard, Na.f18;
    Pc4, 6, 8, 18; Ta40(B)
Gold, Penny Schine, Qa72
Goldhammer, Arthur, Qa75
Goldsmith-Rose, Nancy Helen, Rb31
Goldstein, Jean-Pierre, Ke3
Golther, Wolfgang, Na.a17; Na.c34;
    Na.g12; Ta23
Gonthier, Nicole, Eg17(R)
González, Aurelio, Gb130
Goodrich, Norma Lorre, Mc45; Ta36
Goossens, Heinrich, Na.d39
Gorog, Ralph Paul de, Kd66
Gosman, Martin, Fa167; Pd62; Qc83
Gössmann, Elisabeth, Ge24
Göttner-Abendroth, Heide, Uc17
Gottzmann, Carola L., Da14; Pb302;
    Pf56
Gouchet, Olivier, Pf44(E)
Gougenheim, G., Kd58
Gouiran, Gérard, Sc29
Goulden, Oliver, Hc59, 70; Hg97
Gouttebroze, Jean-Guy, Fb90; Ga105;
    Gb125(F); Gd.b13; Hc48; Hg26;
    Kc106; Na.c122, 126; Qa59, 73;
    Qb79; Rb32; Tb22(C); Uc10, 22,
    24, 49
Gowans, Linda M., Ga59; Na.b33;
    Pa181; Wb46
Goyens, Michèle, Pe24(F)
Grabel, Lotte, Db60
Gracia, Paloma, Db70; Gd.c38; Pg20
Graevenitz, Gerhart von, Fa153
Graf, A., Ph2
Graf, Michael, Pb324
Graillat, Béatrice, Ef10(L); Eg17(U)
Grandjean, Monique, Pk64
Grant, Marshal S., Pa168
Grassi, Sabrina, Pb362
Gravdal, Kathryn, Pa213; Qa98; Ud5
Gray, Douglas, Pd51

Greco, Gina L., Bb69, 75; Db48, 63
Green, Dennis Howard, Fa77–78, 98;
    Fe10, 24; Gb41; Hb19; Hg36;
    Kd82; Pb161, 171, 209, 237–38,
    246, 264–66, 277, 297; Qa44
Greenbaum, S., Ha90
Greene, David, Na.a23
Greene, Marion A., Kd49
Greene, Virginie, Gf44
Greetham, D. C., Bb71
Gregory, Stewart, Af17–18; Ai1;
    Ba22(G); Kd110
Greiner, Thorsten, Hb39
Greiner, Walter, Na.e27
Griffen, Toby D., Na.a42
Griffith, Reginald Harvey, Pd13
Grigsby, John L., Db18, 31; Gb94;
    Gd.c28, 71; Ha99, 105, 145(I);
    Hb22; Ke6; Pa195–96; Uf1
Grill, P. Leopold, Mf6
Grilli, Giuseppe, Pg26
Grimbert, Joan Tasker, Db32; Hf54,
    60, 64, 75; Ke11; Pk18, 88; Sc33,
    41
Grimm, Reinhold R., Da12; Ea30;
    Pk19, 58
Grinnell, Natalie, Hf100
Gripari, Pierre, Ta28
Grisward, Joël H., Nb14, 26–27; Uc15
Gröber, Gustav, Pa40
Groos, Arthur B., Jr., Pb136, 172–73,
    303, 360(Q), 394
Gros, Gérard, Gd.a30
Grosse, Siegfried, Pb325
Grossel, Marie-Geneviève, Pa278;
    Qb65
Grossweiner, Karen A., Cb26
Groupe de linguistique romane de Paris
    VII, Hg37
Grübel, Rainer, Pa210
Grubmüller, Klaus, Pb313(A), 345,
    360(K)
Gruffydd, R. Geraint, Na.a24
Gruhn, Albert, Pb87
Grünkorn, Gertrud, Fa159; Ja35
Grunmann-Gaudet, Minnette, Hc67
Guéret-Laferté, Michelle, Wa33
Guerin, M. Victoria, Ha190

Haverkamp, Anselm, Hb42
Hawkins, Anne Hunsaker, Hf90
Hayart-Neuez, Gérard, Hg53
Haye, Thomas, Fe30
Haymes, Edward R., Pb300, 429; Qa81
Hayward, Rebecca, Gb153(A)
Heckel, Susanne, Pb455
Heffernan, Carol F., Jb30; Pc11
Heffernan, Thomas J., Pd50
Heijkant, Marie-José, Ph12
Heine, Thomas, Pb248
Heinen, Hubert, Pb304
Heinermann, Th., Ra4
Heinz, Thomas, Pb441(B); Wb43
Heinzel, Richard, Pb80
Heinzle, Joachim, Pb175; Qb62
Heitmann, Klaus, Ef4
Held, Claude, Eb12
Held, Jacqueline, Eb12
Hélix, Laurence, Eg18(C)
Heller, Edmund Kurt, Pb94–95
Hellman, Dara, Ud12
Helm, Joan, Ha143; Hb36, 40; Hc73;
    Jb42; Je26
Hemmi, Yôko, Na.c94–95, 115–17,
    123, 127–29, 133
Hendrix, Harald, Fe27
Heng, Geraldine, Ud4
Henkel, Nikolaus, Nb12(D, F)
Hennig, Beate, Pb249
Hennig, Ursula, Pb176
Henrich, Dieter, Ha120
Henry, Albert, Pa65
Henwood, Dawn E., Hc61
Herlem, Brigitte, Pb222
Herlihy, David, Sa68
Herman, Harold J., Ga64
Hernández Álvarez, Vicenta, Ga84
Herrmann, Michael, Fa165
Herslund, Michael, Kc69, 85
Hertel, Hans, Ha60
Hertz, Wilhelm, Pb75
Herzfeld, Claude, Mf15
Herzog, Reinhart, Hb42
Herzog, Urs, Pb395
Heusser, Martin, Ke16
Hexter, Ralph J., Pd31
Heyworth, G. G., Fb105

Hicks, Eric, Bb40
Hiedsiek, Wilhelm, Qa26
Hildebrand, Kristina, Qc73
Hilka, Alfons, Aa6; Da9; Fb2
Hill, D. M., Sa51
Hill, Thomas D., Me28
Hilty, Gerold, Fb39; Kc51
Hindman, Sandra, Xa11, 18–19
Hirao, Kôzô, Pb188, 382
Hirashima, Hitomi, Hg77, 81; Na.d59
Hirdt, Willi, Ge64
Hirhager, Ulrike, Gb149
Hirschberg, Dagmar, Pb189
Hochberg, Brigitte, Pk46(D)
Hoecke, Willy van, Pe24(D)
Hoek, Leo H., Hf22
Hoepffner, Ernest, Kb5; Md25; Pa55
Hoffman, Donald L., Pk89
Hoffmann, Detlef, Xb4
Hoffmann, Richard C., Gd.c29
Hoffmann, Werner, Pb396
Höfner, Eckhard, Md34
Hogenbirk, Marjolein, Pe44, 51(C), 62
Hogenhout-Mulder, Maaike Janna,
    Pe19
Hogetoorn, Corry, Db52; Eb17; Ga79;
    Jb44
Höhler, Gertrud, Pb164
Holden, Anthony J., Ad8; Bb50(A);
    Kd73, 105; Wb37
Holland, Wilhelm Ludwig, Ac7; Ba5;
    Ea21; Pb66
Holley, Linda Tarte, Pk46(F)
Hollier, Denis, Eh5
Holmes, James S., Pa103
Holmes, Urban Tigner, Jr, Gb30; Je23;
    Kd47, 49; Qb45
Holmes, Urban T., III, Qb45
Holthausen, F., Gd.c2
Hölz, Karl, Fa165
Holzbacher, Ana-María, Gb146(C);
    Ha195; Sb51; Ub39; Uc35
Holzermayr, Katharina, Qa66; Wb33,
    36
Honda, Tadao, Kc42
Honemann, Volker, Pb360(T), 385
Horigome, Y., Sa71
Horigoshi, Kôichi, Qc33

Jesmok, Janet, Pd38
Jewers, Caroline A., Ha210; Pi32; Ue7
Jezewski, Mary Ann, Gb76
Jillings, Lewis, Pb250, 278
Jodogne, Omer, Md29
Johnson, Leslie Peter, Pb180, 209, 266;
  Qb62(A)
Johnson, Sidney M., Pb428
Johnston, Oliver M., Kd38; Na.d41
Johnston, R. C., Fc9; Wc6
Joly, Jehanne, Pk69; Xa20
Jonas, Pol, Kc40
Jónas Kristjánsson, Pf23(E)
Jonckbloet, W. J. A., Ac4
Jondorf, Gillian, Pa231
Jones, Bedwyr Lewis, Na.a21
Jones, Glyn E., Na.e38
Jones, Martin H., Pb360 (and H), 385,
  412, 467
Jones, Nerys Ann, Na.c114
Jones, Robert M., Na.b28; Na.e33, 50
Jones, Rosemarie, Db24(B)
Jones, W. Lewis, Ga9
Jongkees, A. G., Qb29
Jonin, Pierre, Gb68, 144; Gf22; Gg4
Jónsson, Finnur, Pf11
Jost, Jean E., Pd53
Joye, M., Pe9
Juárez Blanquer, Aurora, Nb41
Jung, Marc-René, Pi26

Kadler, Alfred, Kd31
Kaeuper, Richard, Ha209(G)
Kahane, Henry, Md28
Kahane, Renée, Md28
Kahn Blumstein, Andrée. *See*
  Blumstein, Andrée Kahn
Kaiser, Gert, Fa93; Gd.b30; Qa79; Qe3
Kakurai, Shukushi, Hg23; Pb132
Kalinke, Sister Jane A., Pf17
Kalinke, Marianne E., Pf22, 25–26, 29,
  31, 34, 42, 43, 44(B)
Kałłaur, Małgorzata, Gf27
Kamata, Tôji, Na.g16
Kamizawa, Eizô, Ea41; Ec4; Ef5;
  Fa100; Ge22; Ha74; He22; La43;
  Md32; Nb31; Pb318; Qd9; Sb29;
  Sc16

Karczewska, Kathryn, Fa180; Pa307
Karnein, Alfred, Pb290; Sa94–96, 107,
  109(C); Sc21
Kartschoke, Dieter, Pb468; Ra15
Kasper, Christine, Gd.c56
Kasten, Ingrid, Ha191; Md39; Pb 441,
  463(A); Sa140
Katô, Kyôko, Ea18; Ec7; Ed6; Ee3;
  Ef8; Eg13; Fb77; Gc6, 8; Gd24;
  Gd.a5, 12–13; Kd107, 119; Na.a40;
  Rb26; Sa130; Tb18
Katzenmeier, Ursula, Hc60
Kaufholz, Eliane, Ge23
Kawaguchi, Yuji, Kc83
Kay, Sarah, Dd14; Ha131, 181, 209(F);
  Hb37; Lc4; Md51; Rb33; Ud16;
  Uf3
Kazemier, G., Pe12–13
Keck, Anna, Sc38
Keen, Maurice H., Pa101; Qc46, 80;
  Sa103
Keimeul, Léon, Jd24
Kelle, Johann, Af16
Keller, Adelbert, Ac2
Keller, Hans-Erich, Pa146; Sa125;
  Wa29
Keller, Joseph, Db33
Keller, Thomas L., Pb239
Kellermann, Karina, Pb355
Kellogg, Judith L., Qa77; Qe23
Kellogg, Robert, Ha95
Kelly, Douglas, Cb9; Db24(D);
  Ea37(and A); Eh9; Fa94, 120, 124,
  141, 154, 172, 180–81; Fb54, 56,
  72–73; Ha123, 132, 169; Hb34;
  Hg95; La27, 45; Me41; Pa137, 147,
  322; Pe59(B); Qb54; Sa81
Kelly, Henry Ansgar, Sa66, 108, 115
Kelly, Susan, Na.c69
Kennedy, Angus J., Gb22, 65; Hc54
Kennedy, Edward Donald, Ga90;
  Pb416
Kennedy, Elspeth, Fa125; Ge52;
  Ha182; Lb5; Lc5; Pa104, 148–49,
  169–71, 279, 287
Kern, Peter, Pb291, 437(F)
Kernivineen, Maria, Na.c109
Kerr, Alexander, Qc47

Parkes, Malcolm, Qa34
Parshall, Linda B., Pb254
Pasero, Nicolò, Qd10
Pasini, W., Sa118
Pasternack, Carol Braun, Fa149
Pastoureau, Michel, Ba22(W); Ga38;
  Pa139, 182; Qa38; Qb33, 49, 51, 57
Pastré, Jean-Marc, Fa92; Gc30;
  Gd.b57; Ge61; Na.c105; Pb230–31,
  310, 319, 357, 360(S), 366–68, 399,
  419, 457; Pk72(I); Uc54
Patron-Godefroit, Annette, Pf32, 40
Patterson, Lee W., Gd.c21; Md38
Patterson, Shirley Gale, Pa48
Paupert, Anne, Ga87
Pavel, Maria, Fb93; Ge34; Ha177;
  Jf12; Kc65, 72, 77–78, 80–81
Paxson, Diana, Eb8
Payen, Jean-Charles, Db14, 22, 24(E);
  Eb15; Eh3; Fa83, 121; Gb57–58,
  61, 69; Gf19; Ha71, 76, 84; He48;
  Ja25; Nb24–25, 37; Qa55; Qf3; Qg3
  (*and* A, F); Sa109(D); Ta29
Payen, M., Qa8
Pearcy, Roy J., Pa250; Pd27
Pearsall, Derek, Gd.b7; Ha63
Pecoraro, Vincenzo, Mb13
Pedersen, John, Ja36
Peebles, Rose Jeffries, Me8
Peeters, J., Pb369
Pegg, Mark Gregory, Me30
Peil, Dietmar, Gd.c7; Pb370
Pellegrini, Silvio, Hb5
Pennar, Meirion, Pc9
Pensom, Roger M., Db50; Kd92
Pérennec, René, Hc50; Pb192, 241,
  292, 351, 360(O), 371, 400, 432,
  441
Peron, Gianfelice, Gd.c19; Ha151;
  Pa163, 239, 251; Wa37–38
Pérouse, Gabriel-André, Hf98
Perret, Michèle, Fa117; Ha203; Hg37
Perrot, Jean-Pierre, Eg18(L)
Perugi, Maurizio, Bb66; Pi28
Peters, Edward, Gb28
Peters, Ursula, Da11; Pb64; Qa128
Peterson, Linda A., Nb33
Petit, Aimé, Ba12; Fb83

Petzoldt, Leander, Hc75
Pfeffer, Wendy, Wa24
Pfeiffer, Ruth, Gd.b5
Pheifer, J. D., Pd68
Pichard, Louis, Eh7
Picherit, Jean-Louis, Hf103; Pa215
Pickens, Rupert T., Ac13; Ag4;
  Ea37(F); Fa102; Hc21; Hg33, 117;
  La47; Pa153, 201
Pickering, F. P., Gd.b3, 9; Pb196
Pickering, James D., Pd44
Pickford, Cedric Edward, Cb14; Gd.b8;
  Pa73, 77, 87, 105, 124; Qg4
Picoche, Jacqueline, Kd112
Picone, Michelangelo, Hb30; Ma34;
  Ph7, 14
Pierreville, Corinne, Ee8(B-C);
  Ef10(C, I); Eg17(E), 18(G);
  Pa299(B); Ue9
Piette, J. R. F., Na.b19
Pintarič, Mitra, Hc71
Pioletti, Antonio, Gb137, 147;
  Ha145(T); Hf35; Hg45, 50, 60;
  Mc51; Na.e37; Qe11
Piolle, J., Kf1
Pipaprez, Delphine, Jb57
Pirot, François, Pi12
Planche, Alice, Dc28; Ga20; Gc25;
  Gd.a4, 20; Uc27; Wb51
Plasman, Alain Marc, Eg17(S)
Pleij, H., Db34
Plouzeau, May, Wb31
Plummer, J. F., Hc20
Poag, James F., Ha149; Pb273
Pöckl, Wolfgang, Pg13
Poëssel, André-Edgard, Qg3(D)
Pohoryles, Bernard M., Kc32
Poirion, Daniel, Ac16 (*and* D-E), 19;
  Dc21; Fa137, 160; Gd.a6; Ha80,
  114, 117, 138, 146, 160; La29;
  Qb53; Qe12; Xa11
Pol, Roberto De, Pb372
Polak, Lucie, Ed5; Mc38
Polet, Jean-Claude, Eh8
Pollmann, Leo, Sc25
Ponchon, Thierry, Kc100
Pontecorvo, Aurelia, Pi2
Pontfarcy, Yolande de, Ga85; Na.a44

Sturges, Robert S., Db51; Lb4; Ub38;
  Uf2 (*and* A)
Sturm-Maddox, Sara, Db24(H); Fb58;
  Gd.a39; Ha174, 186–87; Hb48;
  Hc43; Hg46; Pa253, 327–28; Qa71;
  Qb64; Uc13; Wb35
Suard, François, Fa165; Ga80; Hc31,
  51; Pa280
Suárez, María Pilar, Hg90
Subrenat, Jean, Ga49; Gd.c10; Hf78;
  Pa299(C); Qa49
Sugizaki, Taiichirô, Qb81
Sullivan, Howard A., Cb20
Sullivan, Penny, Ga53; Hc45; Sa106
Susong, Gilles, Gb139; Nb39; Pa240,
  267; Qg3(E)
Sutcliffe, F. E., Pa82
Sutherland, D. R., Fa63; Sa49
Sutherland, Ross, Qf8
Suzuki, Tetsuya, Ee5; Gd.a33; Hg82;
  Md46
Svartvik, J., Ha90
Svenonius, Thure Leonard, Kc15
Sweeney, Del, Gb126
Sweeney, Michelle, Ha212
Sweetser, Frank, Pa120
Switten, Margaret, Qc55
Sylvester, Louise, Qa124
Szabics, Imre, Fa123; Hf37, 62, 101;
  Jb40; Kc68; Na.d57; Sb41, 50
Szabó, Thomas, Qb56(K)
Szarmach, Paul E., Me16
Szkilnik, Michelle, Eg20; Gd.b61
Szklenar, Hans, Xb2, 16
Szövérffy, Joseph, Pj1

Taiana, Franz, Sa80
Takamiya, Toshiyuki, Qb82
Takatô, Mako, Fb59, 63, 75; Ja34;
  Qc56
Tamura, Hajime, Qb55
Tanabe, Jûji, Qb28
Tanabe, Tamotsu, Na.a51
Tanaka, Hitohiko, Na.a45
Tarbé, Prosper, Ac3, 5; Ae9
Tarroux, Christiane, Hf102
Tattersall, Jill, Gd.b20
Tatum, James, Ma33

Tavera, Antoine, Nb32
Taylor, Archer, Kd50; Na.c51
Taylor, Beverly, Cb18
Taylor, Jane H. M., Pa202, 268, 301,
  311; Pe59(E)
Taylor, Karen J., Gb148
Taylor, Mark N., Sa147
Taylor, Robert A., Hb41
Tecchio, Donatella, Pi14
Tekaat, Manfred, Ba9
Tervooren, Helmut, Dd13
Tesich-Savage, Nadja, Pk14
Thedens, Robert, Pa44
Thelamon, Françoise, Qf4
Thelamopu, Françoise, Qa84
Thiébaux, M., Gc2
Thierry, Christophe, Pb387
Thiry, Claude, Pa296
Thiry-Stassin, Martine, Pa93
Thomas, A., Wa13
Thomas, Ann C., Nb15
Thomas, Heinz, Pb377; Wb43
Thomas, Neil, Na.e45–46; Pa281, 294,
  302; Pb258
Thomas, Patrick A., Sa122
Thomas, Peter Wynn, Na.a54 (*and* B)
Thomasset, Claude, Gd.b58;
  Gd.c42(A); Jb59
Thompson, Albert Wilder, Pa63
Thompson, David W., Fe8
Thompson, Raymond H., Pk29; Sb31
Thomson, Robert L., Na.a37(H);
  Na.d61; Na.e34; Pc7
Thoran, Barbara, Pb184
Thorpe, Lewis, Hf42; Pa119
Thumboo, Edwin, Ud4
Tiemann, Hermann, Ra9
Tigoulet, Marie-Claude, Pk40
Titchener, Frances H., Fe1
Tobin, Frank, Pb214; Sa58
Todd, Margaret W., Ge30
Togeby, Knud, Pa74; Pf23(C, F); Qb31
Toischer, Wendelin, Wb20
Toja, Gianluigi, Hg34
Tokui, Yoshiko, Qb37, 71, 77, 83
Toledo Neto, Sílvio de Almeida, Pg32
Tolhurst, Fiona, Ga99, 108
Tomasek, Tomas, Wb52

INDEX OF ROMANCES

The index covers items that deal exclusively or substantially with the romance named; for Chrétien's *chansons*, see Ac16(F), Ae5–12; Ah2, 6; Sc18; and V.

EREC ET ENIDE

Ac6, 12, 16(A), 17; Ag1; Ah1; Ba9, 11, 18, 20, 22(H-I), 33; Bb16, 46, 62, 68; Db24(H); Ea37(B); Eb3; Ec3–9; Eh5; Fa130 (chap. 5); Fb37, 43–44, 58, 70, 79, 82, 83(D), 94, 101; Fc4–5; Ga26, 32, 40, 53, 56, 63, 66, 79 (Hogetoorn), 92, 108(B); Gb38, 73, 157, 159; Gc19, 22; Gd3; Gd.c12, 14, 35, 37, 60; Ge20, 22; Gf 44; Ha92, 156 (chap. 3); Hb27, 31, 37, 39; Hc13, 20–80; Jb2, 23, 28, 35; Jc9; Je26; Jf10; Kc30–31, 33, 36–37, 42, 51; Kd51, 79, 97, 119; Ke11; La21; Ma24, 31, 33; Mb13; Md31, 49; Me27–29, 40; Na.d53, 58, 60; Na.e7, 21, 26, 45; Na.f23–24; Nb12(C), 51; Pa105, 277; Pb79, 86, 190–92, 231, 240, 301, 360(F), 364, 367, 373–74, 402, 411, 466; Pi7; Qa51, 56, 73, 130; Qb69; Qe15, 25; Sb32, 43; Ub34, 43(B); Uc23, 25, 34; Ud3, 10, 12; Ue6; Xa21; Xb19.

CLIGÉS

Ac16(B); Af17–18; Ah2; Ai1; Ba12–13, 22(G), 23; Bb25, 60, 73, 79; Db24(F); Ea21, 37(C); Ed3–7; Fa59, 130 (chap. 6); Fb41, 64, 80–81; Fc16; Fd6, 12; Ga29, 56, 77, 79 (Hogetoorn), 82; Gd.a30–31; Gd.b42(B); Gd.c6; Ge64; Gf39; Hd7–23; Jb31, 49, 53; Jc2, 7; Kb8; Kc41, 60; Kd87–88; Ma27; Mb14; Md7, 36, 47–48; Me31, 35; Pa191; Pb78, 141, 360(I); Pj4; Qa61, 100, 119, 129; Qb67; Qd13; Qe18; Qf8; Sc5, 9–10, 16, 19, 23, 26; Ub8; Uc39, 41, 45–46; Ud13.

LE CHEVALIER DE LA CHARRETTE (LANCELOT)

Ac3–4, 14, 16(D), 19; Ag2; Ah3; Ba4, 27, 32; Bb23, 26, 29, 31, 36, 45, 47, 51, 55–56, 59, 75; Db20, 35, 63, 69; Ea37(D, G); Ee2–8; Fa130 (chap. 6); Fb17, 26, 56, 71, 92, 96; Fd4; Ga22, 34–35, 37, 42, 46, 49, 79 (Brandsma), 108(C); Gb113–14, 148; Gc21; Gd.b36; Gd.c8–9, 12, 27, 31, 69; Ge31; Gf17; He15–77; Hf50; Jb5–6, 18, 33, 36–37, 43, 57, 59; Kc84; Kd42, 45, 50, 84, 101, 133; La22; Lb2; Ma28; Md8, 41; Mf8; Na.c56, 64; Nb12(G), 17, 29, 50; Pa54, 276, 285, 299(I–J); Pb360(J); Pg6; Qa76, 99; Qb25(II), 70; Qc60; Qd8, 11; Ra11, 13, 16, 20; Rb22, 27; Sb28, 34, 36, 42, 44, 53; Sc36; Ua22; Ub36, 41–42, 47; Ud2, 8 (chap. 2); Uf2; Xa23.

YVAIN (LE CHEVALIER AU LION)

Aa3(IV), 5; Ac2, 5, 7, 10, 16(C), 18; Ag3; Ah4; Ba8, 22(L); Bb18, 24, 44, 48, 52, 66, 70, 74; Db44(A), 49; Ea37(E); Ee4; Ef4–11; Fa123, 135; Fb37, 68, 72, 74, 83(A); Fc15; Fd1; Fe25; Ga27, 30, 39, 62, 67, 70, 79 (Hogetoorn), 80, 95, 108(D); Gb56, 64, 78, 97, 113, 125(E), 148, 150; Gc10, 16, 32; Gd.a27; Gd.b33, 35, 57(D); Gd.c7–8, 12, 31, 35–36; Ge34, 47; Gf29–30, 44; Hb27, 37; Hf18–107; Jb10, 19–22, 25, 29–30, 39, 47, 50–51, 60; Jf13, 16; Kc46, 56, 90–91, 98; Kd35, 53, 110, 122, 129, 135; Ke10, 15; Kf2; La28, 36, 42, 44; Mc35; Me20, 23, 25; Mf9–10, 12; Na.c30, 57, 102, 104; Na.d39–41, 59, 62; Na.e20, 27, 36, 43; Na.f26; Nb12(F), 16, 23, 43; Pa113, 234, 299(G), 313; Pb69–72, 82, 86, 92–93, 188, 205, 236, 241, 293, 318, 360(L), 437(F); Pc10–11, 15; Pd11, 63, 69, 83; Pe43; Pf10, 44(F-G), 53, 56; Pi23; Pk51; Qa45, 82, 102; Qc53–54; Qd6–8, 10, 12, 15, 17; Qe19–20, 25; Qg1; Ra11–13, 16, 20; Sb33, 35, 37, 43; Ub5, 22, 31; Uc9, 20, 27–28, 56; Ud8 (chap. 2), 14; Xa3, 12, 16–17; Xb10, 12, 14.

PERCEVAL (LE CONTE DU GRAAL)

Aa6; Ab5; Ac8–9, 11, 13, 15, 16(E); Af14–16; Ag4; Ah5; Ai2; Ba5–6, 14, 21, 22(E-F, N, P, Q, S), 25, 29–30; Bb17, 19, 34, 41, 49, 65; Cb28; Db24(G, K), 29; Ea21, 37(F); Eg4–23; Fa69(D-F); Fb30, 45, 55, 62, 90, 98, 100, 103, 105; Ga8, 12–13, 19, 45, 51, 76, 79(Zemel), 88–89, 94, 96, 105; Gb82, 93, 124, 125(F), 143–46, 156; Gc30; Gd.a6–7, 33, 38–40; Gd.b17, 57(C), 58, 60–61; Gd.c13; Ge51; Gf36, 40; Ha156 (chap. 4); Hg7, 9, 12, 16, 22–121; Jd13, 18–52; Je24–25; Jf7, 15; Kb9; Kc67, 105–06, 108–10; Kd82, 92; Ke3–4, 11, 13–14; Kf1, 4; La35, 45(D); Ma23, 30; Mb3; Mc30, 33, 39–40; Md45; Me13; Mf6–7; Na.c83, 105; Na.d42, 44, 46–50, 54–56, 63; Na.e24, 41; Na.g12; Nb9, 12(H); Nc3; Pa38, 56, 107, 183, 218, 270, 276; Pb28, 53, 68, 100, 103, 133, 168, 182, 208, 226, 229, 262, 300, 303, 328, 333, 354, 356, 360(O-S), 368, 377, 399, 419, 436, 456; Pc25; Pd13, 30; Pe1, 56; Pk88; Qa67, 70–71, 89, 94; Qb70: Qc6, 81; Qf3, 9; Qg2; Ra19; Rb32; Sb28, 38; Ta2–3, 6, 8, 10, 14, 38; Tb5–6, 15, 17–18, 22(C); Ub11, 13–14, 21, 25, 35, 40, 44, 48–49, 51; Uc10–11, 22, 24, 30, 35–36, 40, 42–43, 49–50, 52, 58; Ue4; Uf1; Xa1, 7–9, 18, 25.

PHILOMENA

Ac16(F); Ad6, 9; Hc39; Pa299(L); Wa13–39.

GUILLAUME D'ANGLETERRE

Ac16(F); Ad7–8; Kc29; Kd39; Pb360(T); Rb28; Wb20–54.

Other attributions: *LE CHEVALIER À L'ÉPÉE* and *LA MULE SANS FREIN*, Wc4–7 (see also Wc1–2); *LIÉTART*, Wc8; *PERCEVAL CONTINUATION*, Wc3.

11.	Aquila, A.J.	Alonso de Ercilla y Zúñiga: a basic bibliography, 1975
12.	Griffin, N.	Jesuit School Drama: a checklist of critical literature, 1976
		Supplement No 1, 1986
13.	Crosby, J.O.	Guía bibliográfica para el estudio crítico de Quevedo, 1976
14.	Smith, P.	Vicente Blasco Ibáñez: an annotated bibliography, 1976
15.	Duggan, J.J.	A Guide to Studies on the *Chanson de Roland*, 1976
16.	Bishop, M.	Pierre Reverdy: a bibliography, 1976
17.	Kelly, D.	Chrétien de Troyes: an analytic bibliography, 1976
18.	Rees, M.	French Authors on Spain 1800–1850: a checklist, 1977
19.	Snow, J.T.	The Poetry of Alfonso X: a critical bibliography, 1977
20.	Hitchcock, R.	The Kharjas: a critical bibliography, 1977
		Supplement No 1, 1996
21.	Burgess, G.S.	Marie de France: an analytical bibliography, 1977
		Supplement No 1, 1986
		Supplement No 2, 1997
22.	Bach, K.F., and G. Price	Romance Linguistics and the Romance Languages: a bibliography of bibliographies, 1977
23.	Eisenberg, D.	Castilian Romances of Chivalry in the Sixteenth Century: a bibliography, 1979
24.	Hare, G.	Alphonse Daudet: a critical bibliography. I. Primary material, 1978, II. Secondary material, 1979
25.	Geoghegan, C.	Louis Aragon: essai de bibliographie, I. Œuvres, Tome 1 (1918–1959), 1979, Tome 2 (1960–1977), 1979
26.	Lowe, D.K.	Benjamin Constant: an annotated bibliography of critical editions and studies (1946–1978), 1979

27.	Mason, B.	Michel Butor: a checklist, 1979
28.	Shirt, D.J.	The Old French Tristan poems: a bibliographical guide, 1980
29.	McGaha, M.D.	The Theatre in Madrid during the Second Republic: a checklist, 1979
30.	Stathatos, C.C.	A Gil Vicente bibliography (1940–1975), 1979
31.	Bleikasten, A.	Arp: bibliographie, I. Ecrits/Dichtung, 1981, II. Critique/Kritik, 1983
32.	Bergman, H.E., and S.E. Szmuk	A Catalogue of Comedias sueltas in the New York Public Library, Vol. I (A-H), 1980, Vol. II (I-Z), 1981
33.	Best, M.	Ramón Pérez de Ayala: an annotated bibliography of criticism, 1980
34.	Clive, H.P.	Marguerite de Navarre: an annotated bibliography, 1983
35.	Sargent-Baur, B.N., and R.F. Cook	*Aucassin et Nicolete*: a critical bibliography, 1981
36.	Nelson, B.	Emile Zola: a selective analytical bibliography, 1982
37.	Field, T.	Maurice Barrès: a selective critical bibliography (1948–1979), 1982
38.	Bell, S.M.	Nathalie Sarraute: a bibliography, 1982
39.	Kinder, A.G.	Spanish Protestants and Reformers in the Sixteenth Century: a bibliography, 1983 Supplement No 1, 1994
40.	Clive, H.P.	Clément Marot: an annotated bibliography, 1983
41.	Whinnom, K.	The Spanish Sentimental Romance (1440–1550): a critical bibliography, 1983
42.	Kennedy, A.J.	Christine de Pizan: a bibliographical guide, 1984 Supplement No 1, 1994
43.	Tremewan, P.	Prévost: an analytical bibliography of criticism to 1981, 1984
44.	Holloway, J.B.	Brunetto Latini: an analytic bibliography, 1986
45.	Craddock, J.R.	The Legislative Works of Alfonso X: el Sabio, 1986